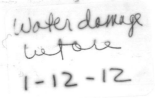

HAITI

By the same author

A History of Celibacy
A History of Mistresses
A History of Marriage
Sugar: A Bittersweet History

HAITI

A Shattered Nation

ELIZABETH ABBOTT

OVERLOOK DUCKWORTH
New York & London

To my sister Louise Abbott, with affection and gratitude

This edition first published in hardcover in the United States and the United
Kingdom in 2011 by Overlook Duckworth, Peter Mayer Publishers, Inc.

NEW YORK:
Overlook
141 Wooster Street
New York, NY 10012
www.overlookpress.com
For bulk and special sales, please contact sales@overlookny.com

LONDON:
Duckworth
90-93 Cowcross Street
London EC1M 6BF
www.ducknet.co.uk
info@duckworth-publishers.co.uk

Revised and updated from *Haiti: The Duvaliers and Their Legacy* by
Elizabeth Abbott, first published in 1988 by McGraw-Hill

Cataloguing-in-Publication Data is available from the Library of Congress
A catalogue record for this book is available from the British Library

Printed in the United States
1   3   5   7   9   10   8   6   4   2

ISBN 978 1 59020 141 1 (US)
ISBN 978 0 71564 080 7 (UK)

CONTENTS

INTRODUCTION

T HE DAY THE EARTH BENEATH IT CRACKED OPEN, HAITI staggered once more onto the world stage. Briefly, the world wept. Then, people rushed to rescue and repair, to feed and shelter, to restore to livability if not normalcy the battered victims of this battered nation.

And to donate, and to fundraise: individuals and governments pledged millions of dollars in relief money. As the author of *Haiti: The Duvaliers and their Legacy* (as the first edition of this book was called) and the magazine article, "Haiti: Where Rivers Run Brown,"[1] I was in sudden demand for media interviews and as a guest-speaker at Haiti fundraisers in Canada. The initial focus was simple: What had happened, and why? What could prevent its recurrence? How, besides check-writing, could concerned foreigners help?

Quickly, though, the criticizing began: Why was the relief effort so glacially slow? Where were Haiti's president and government? Where was all the pledged aid money? How could it be wealthy Haitians shopped in intact Pétionville shops that displayed Gucci handbags while, meters away, tens of thousands of their compatriots sweltered under flimsy tents and queued daily for biscuits and bottled water? Who (if anybody) was running the country: its (seemingly invisible) government? the (all-too-visible and vocal) Americans and other foreigners? Would the president-in-exile return home to minister to his once-adoring people? What in Haiti's history contributed to its leadership's paralysis?

Haiti's tormented past haunts and shapes its present and so publishers scrambled to acquire books about Haiti's history, mine among them. At first I was reluctant. I'd already said what I wanted to when I wrote *Haiti*.

But searing images from my life in Haiti and afterward reminded me of what still needs to be said. And the deadliness of the earthquake and the relentless horror of its aftermath were rooted in what I knew well: deforestation, with its concomitants of rural depopulation and urban overpopulation and overbuilding; inadequate resources and neglectful and dishonest officials, permitting shoddy construction standards; a culture of corruption and greed that rotted Haiti from within and—shamefully—permitted cynical foreigners to share the booty; an uncaring and inbred elite that shuns its civic responsibilities, and pursues instead immediate financial gains and social aggrandizement; foreign governments whose manipulative policies toward Haiti twist it like a marionette; and an international network of often-competing NGOs whose *raisons d'être* are catastrophes such as Haiti's earthquake.

First, here is how I came to write this book. In the 1980s I was the wife of Haitian hotelier Joseph Namphy, and the sister-in-law of Lieutenant General Henri Namphy, who headed Haiti's interim government after Jean-Claude Duvalier fled to France in February of 1986. Those relationships, and my job reporting for Reuters News Service, provided me with unique opportunities in researching my book, opening doors and allowing me glimpses into the private workings of Haitian government. The bulk of my research, however, consisted of interviewing hundreds of people and of ferreting out written materials, not so easy in Haiti's woefully undersupplied libraries and without the not-yet-invented Internet.

When I conceived this book, the Duvalier regime was tottering to an end, and Henri Namphy was a little-known military figurehead. Although he (briefly!) became a national hero in taking over from Duvalier, I assumed, as did most people, that his tenure would be short and transitional, and that a democratically elected president would soon succeed him. I never imagined that two years later his government would preside over Bloody Sunday, when Tonton Macoutes massacred thirty-four citizens trying to vote in elections then widely believed to be the last chance for democracy.

I wrote *Haiti* for non-Haitians, to try to convey through the perspectives of Haitians what Duvalierism was and what legacy it left in that suffering nation just seven hundred miles off the coast of Florida. My decades as a professional historian in Canada and two years as a journalist in Haiti shaped my work, not my relationship with a brother-in-law suddenly infamous as a brutal dictator. In the chapters dealing with him, I wrestled with the temptation to overstate the case and prove my impartiality by painting Namphy as a monster. In fact, the evidence points to an impulsive man overwhelmed by the Duvalier legacy and by the pressures of the Haitian presidency, who metamorphosed into the tyrant who was complicit in the Bloody Sunday massacre. The man who swore the oath of office on February 6, 1986, was not capable of saying, as he did two years later, "Haiti has only one voter. The army. Ha ha."

Henri Namphy was not always so cynical. Days after Duvalier's departure, when Reuters offered me the job of Haiti stringer, I discussed it with Henri. He reflected briefly and said, "Haiti needs a responsible free press. Take the job. I know you'll be objective and fair."

And, as the military government's policies increasingly alienated the people, I reported it. Once a very high-ranking Haitian official accused me of having caused the U.S. to postpone $3 million in military aid to Haiti because of a story I had written for *The New York Times*, about the army using live ammunition on demonstrators at Fort Dimanche. I was in the crowd and witnessed what I reported. I was told that Henri reproached the official brusquely. But by the time of Bloody Sunday, I doubt that he cared what I wrote, or who read it. Henri Namphy had become a desperate man I scarcely recognized.

At the same time, as military hostility escalated against Lavalas (the cleansing flood), the swelling popular movement that set in motion Duvalier's ouster, and against Haitian journalists who reported it, identification as Namphy's sister-in-law could have cost me my life. But no Haitian journalist exposed me; I was always treated with collegiality. Several went further, protecting me from bullets, tear gas and from panic-stricken crowds in the frantic stampedes from danger known in Haiti as *couris*.

These *couris*, still very much a part of Haitian life, are part of what led to this new edition of my book. The others? Here are some of the images that reveal so many truths about Haiti. Some are unambiguous. Others, riddle-like, will make sense in the context of later chapters.

One day when Jean-Claude Duvalier was still President-for-Life, I watched as two jeeploads of American Marines purposefully headed the wrong way up a one-way street, laughing as they drove. Another day, my kindly mother-in-law rebuked my son, Ivan, then eight years old, for having tossed pebbles down onto the roadside: "If you should hit a Macoute, they'll get out of the car and kill us all," she shouted. After police shot a burglar to death and left the body on the pathway for a day, Ivan grimaced as I helped him step around it on his way to school, but all he said was, "Mom, that's why Jean-Robert's family beats him for stealing." Jean-Robert was the little boy in a nearby shanty we used to hear sobbing as his mother berated him as a thief. His parents, my little boy explained to me, did not want Jean-Robert to end up with a bullet through his heart.

Then there was the evening just before the fall of Duvalier, when Joe's hotelier employer invited us to join him at a special event. As Port-au-Prince crackled with excitement at the prospect of deliverance from oppression, we joined scores of elegantly garbed men and women to sip the finest wines, munch crudités and devour a gourmet dinner, all provided by French winemakers in a marketing campaign targeted at Haiti's affluent elite. Yet, in the skewed world of Port-au-Prince, often when I left my house after my morning shower, I'd find a man bathing under the pipe that carried the soapy water from our bathroom out to the gutter.

Post-Duvalier, some things changed. From the roof of the Villa St. Louis, the hotel Joe managed, I watched the *déchoukaj*—uprooting, or destruction—of the large house next door, owned by Luc Désyr, the Chief of the Duvaliers' Secret Police. For months afterwards, I observed the daily lives of the squatters who camped in its ruins.

One fine morning, Claudette, my housekeeper, exclaimed: *"Kounye-a, pa gen larouze!"* These days, there is no dew. Claudette's epiphany followed days of discussion about an article I was researching on soil erosion and deforestation, and on Haiti's dearth of pollinating bees. Another time, on the patio of a bar, I listened to Department of Education inspectors lamenting the horrendous conditions of the schools they visited: dirt-floored, contaminated by flooding, lacking books, chairs, blackboards.

The violence, too, had resumed. On Friday June 17, 1988, after President Leslie Manigat had fired General Namphy, confined him to house arrest and cut his telephone wires, four gunmen scrambled over the high cement wall around my house in downtown Port-au-Prince and fired several heart-stopping shots. They fled only after Toussaint and Taffy, my shih-tzus, and Tommy, my elderly mongrel, barked and woke up our armed guard who shot at the attackers, driving them back over the wall. After we heard persistent rumors that they intended to return, I fled with my stepson to a friend's hotel, frantic about my dogs, whom no hotelier would accept.

In 1995, in a leafy neighborhood in the mountains above Port-au-Prince, a debonair Haitian introduced himself to me as "one of the Morally Repugnant Elite we've all read so much about" and later joked that "Aristide taught us how to appreciate Scotch." During the embargo following Aristide's 1991 ouster, he laughingly explained, fuel shortages often meant no ice cubes, forcing him and his friends to drink their single malts neat, at room temperature.

Hours before the earthquake struck in 2010, Switzerland's top court ruled that Swiss banks must return at least $4.6 million to exiled dictator Jean-Claude Duvalier, whom Transparency International estimates embezzled "the equivalent of 1.7 to 4.5 percent of Haitian GDP for every year he was in power"—somewhere between $300 to $800 million—catapulting him into the league of such major kleptocrats as the Philippines' Ferdinand Marcos and Nigeria's Sani Abacha.[2] (Shaken to their moral core by the earthquake, the Swiss quickly reversed this decision and froze the funds.)

Yet sometimes I am struck by hopefulness. It happened in June 2010, in Sertaozinho, Brazil, as I walked through the fields of a Sao Francisco organic sugarcane plantation and planter Leontino Balbo pointed excitedly at a churning stream and exclaimed, "That stream wasn't there two years ago! It was generated by the growth of the biodiversity of flora and fauna on the plantation!" If green miracles could happen in Brazil, why couldn't they also happen in Haiti?

Rereading my book was painful. Its publication had embittered my in-laws, who accused me of having "told the truth fifty years too soon." It had ended both my marriage and my life in Haiti, and deprived my son of his beloved stepfather.

We have rebuilt our lives. But most of the people featured in my book could have had no such lucky outcomes. *Haiti* remains a bitter reminder that most of them, like me, had once been hopeful that with the fall of the Duvaliers, Haiti would finally offer its long-suffering citizens a chance at lives of fulfillment, safety and pride. Instead, corrupt governments and international interference have ground the nation down so far that some people recall the Duvalier era as safer and more prosperous.

At the end of the road, the earthquake and its aftermath revealed all that was wrong with Haiti. The post-earthquake mantra—Building Back Better—can inspire Haiti's betterment only if the rot at the core of its social and governmental structures is targeted as an enemy as lethal as parched soil, bleached riverbeds, bare mountainsides and shattered cities.

Haiti is, in large part, a narrative told from the perspective of individual Haitians, and I have made only a few revisions, and added a few references to newer sources that clarify or in other ways elaborate on my text. The original version of the Epilogue ended in 1990, and so I have written a new one that summarizes what I believe are the key issues involved in understanding present-day Haiti.

Haiti is not a scholarly book, but many of the stories in it are the stuff of primary historical source material. As well, it is organized around themes that are central to Haiti's development and its current plight. Deforestation is at the forefront, and its sad progress is traced throughout the narrative.

Throughout *Haiti,* stories about relentless tree-cutting are interwoven into the narrative: linked with economic exploitation of colonial resources such as mahogany forests, the clearing and burning of land for sugarcane and other export crops, Papa Doc Duvalier's clear-cutting policies to counter the threat of armed incursions from the Dominican Republic, the roaring fires fueling the rural stills that produce rot-gut liquor known as *clairin,* and the ubiquitous charcoal in the coal pots that to this day cook most Haitians' daily fare.

Haiti also tells stories about eroding soil and shriveling crops, the economically forced relocation from hungry hamlets to the possibilities of bustling cities, the growing population jam-packed into shoddy housing in urban slums built without infrastructure, a burgeoning population condemned to a perpetual search for water, food, fuel, transportation, medical care, employment. These stories help explain the extraordinarily high number[3] of those killed, injured and made homeless in the catastrophic earthquake of 2010, which was made even deadlier by destroyed roads, impenetrable congestion, population density, leadership paralysis, foreign interventions *cum* aid that created blockages and confusion as well as salvage and succor.

The Duvaliers, of course, were masters of Foreign Aid–Attracting Rhetoric, their concern only that they benefited. They had no compunction about accepting aid even if it was destructive of Haiti, and lending agencies obliged by treating them as legitimate and credible leaders. The consequence was that the Duvaliers are responsible for about 40 percent of their struggling nation's debt load of $1.3 billion. (A month after the 2010 earthquake, when over four thousand souls Facebook-friended

Jean-Claude Duvalier, the Group of Seven countries announced the cancellation of Haiti's bilateral debts, about $1.2 billion.)

Foreign aid is seldom if ever a benign and/or unconditional gift of needed money, goods and/or services, and military or commercial interventions are often its inescapable concomitants. *Haiti* is rich in examples, notably sugar and rice, two traditionally (but no longer) essential crops, and pigs, traditionally (but no longer) the Haitian people's piggy bank.

First, sugar. I described how sugar smuggled from Miami and the Dominican Republic forced the Haytian American Sugar Company (HASCO), Haiti's second largest employer, to close its doors. I also reported that in the months following Jean-Claude Duvalier's flight, "extensive smuggling of basic goods like cooking oil, flour, rice, sugar and canned milk has lowered consumer prices but bankrupted several local manufacturers. Hundreds of thousands of Haitians have lost their jobs."[4] But back then I had no idea that this was part of an aggressive scheme designed to collapse Haitian agriculture and force Haitians into the factories (widely referred to as sweatshops) run by foreigners and by Haiti's elite.

Decades later, I see that my report presaged what was to come. I quoted the mill's explanation to the "30,000 to 40,000 small sugar-cane planters" whose livelihoods were being ruined that "unprecedented and ever-growing smuggling" was to blame and attributed the mill's failure "to an order by Mr. [Jean-Claude Duvalier] two years ago barring Hasco from refining sugar. . . . The Government then began importing refined sugar at world market prices and reselling it at a profit," a policy continued by the Namphy provisional Government that replaced Duvalier. "But now with all the smuggling," the mill spokesman said, "even the state can't compete with smuggled Dominican refined sugar."[5]

The story of the failure of Haitian rice-growing is similarly depressing. When I moved to Haiti in 1983, we used to drive to the Artibonite to buy our household rice from Joe's farmer friends.[6] A few years later, Artibonite rice had become difficult to find and the market was flooded by imported rice. Joe fretted about it and railed against the acquired taste for the refined white American rice that is so nutritionally inferior to the Artibonite's robust swamp variety.[7] At the same time, he was convinced that with improved cultivation techniques, Haitian rice production could be saved. But he was wrong, because decades later U.S. President Bill Clinton admitted that Haitian rice cultivation was the unsalvageable casualty of "a Devil's Bargain on rice." "Since 1981," Clinton confessed,

> the United States has followed a policy, until the last year or
> so when we started rethinking it, that we rich countries that
> produce a lot of food should sell it to poor countries and re-
> lieve them of the burden of producing their own food, so,
> thank goodness, they can leap directly into the industrial era.
> It has not worked. It may have been good for some of my
> farmers in Arkansas, but it has not worked. It was a mistake . . .
> I have to live every day with the consequences of the lost ca-
> pacity to produce a rice crop in Haiti to feed those people,
> because of what I did. Nobody else.[8]

But even this is not strictly true because Clinton did not act alone but rather took the rap for his many accomplices: U.S. lending institutions, corrupt (or myopic) Haitian officials, and the elite always ready for new coffer-stuffing ventures. It worked like this: In Haiti as throughout the colonized world, the IMF and the World Bank demanded a non-protectionist policy of open markets. The Jean-Claudist government, reliant on loans and assistance, did not resist;[9] the military junta's Finance Minister, American-educated, former World Bank economist Leslie Delatour, strongly supported these initiatives.[10]

Things were going according to plan (we learned from Clinton). A select group of Haitians worked with U.S. suppliers to flood Haiti with surplus rice and subsidized sugar, destroying Haitian agriculture. Then elite factory owners hired these same destitute men and women as they poured into Port-au-Prince from the ruined countryside. By the time Jean-Claude fled in 1986, Haiti was the world's ninth largest assembler of goods destined for U.S. consumption: clothes, electronics, teddy bears,[11] even fur coats. As the Duvaliers had always understood, well-managed poverty pays.

The story of PEPPADEP, which *Haiti* captured best of all, was the third in the trilogy of schemes that destroyed Haiti's agriculture. PEPPADEP was the campaign orchestrated by American, Canadian and French industrial pork producers to slaughter all of Haiti's Creole pigs after a small number were infected with African Swine Flu. As the story of PEPPADEP makes chillingly clear, if powerful foreign interests lobby to destroy a weaker country's agricultural sector, that sector is likely to be sacrificed. Thanks to PEPPADEP, millions of Haitian peasants lost one of their basic resources solely to safeguard North America's factory-farmed pig industry. And, as with sugar and rice, a few elite Haitians and their pig-raising North American partners profited from the introduction of special North American pig breeds.

Haiti includes a narrative about the elite. During the American Occupation (1915–1934), occupying forces favored the lighter-skinned, educated and urbane segment of society, solidifying their economic and political power. Afterward, an important part of Duvalier's (and later Aristide's) appeal was a ringing condemnation of the elite as irresponsible and self-seeking.

Yet the aftermath of the earthquake underscored how strongly entrenched this dynamic remains. There were media reports describing how, days after the earthquake, fine dining and gourmet living had resumed (if it was ever interrupted) mere yards away from homeless tent or even bedsheet dwellers. "For those with money, you can buy water from the Alps, smoked salmon from Scandinavia and cheese from Normandy," wrote a CBC reporter.[12]

Richard Coles, whose family businesses employ three thousand, and whose MultiTex produces and exports two million T-shirts a week to the U.S. and Canada, provides this stark analysis of his elite compatriots:

> We never respect the rule of law, we easily conspire to overthrow the government but never to rebuild the country, we use our access to the national palace to further our business interests but we never go to the national palace to say "do something for the people in [the grim slum of] Cité Soleil." We spend our money in the U.S. and not in Haiti. The country gave us everything and we gave nothing in return.[13]

Yet even in the reproving glare of media spotlights Coles and his peers maintain their power because their know-how, capital, access to power and international contacts make them so useful. They speak several languages, including Creole, French and English. They are closely connected or related or, at the very least, they know each other's families. Often enough, they intermarry.

In *Haiti,* some of my observations about the army and General Namphy need correction or clarification. In particular, Michel Laguerre's scholarly study, *The Military and Society in Haiti* (1993), has given new insights about military structure. For instance, though I knew that its often-unpaid members, whether serving as police or soldiers, were vulnerable to bribes, extortion and the temptation to moonlight, I did not know that systemic corruption in the Duvalierist military was an essential operational tool. In Laguerre's words:

> corruption is found in the process at all levels, from promotions to post assignments, and in the daily routine of military life. . . . Individuals who engage in small- or large-scale corruption and who are not caught are considered by the populace to be 'intelligent people'. If they are corrupt on a large scale, they are considered very smart. If it is small-scale corruption, they are simply helping themselves. . . . Army corruption . . . is an informal system without which the everyday functioning of the army could be impaired . . . it serves as a safety valve without which the officers would be forced to ask for annual raises in their salaries, in effect demanding money that is not available and thus creating tension between the government and the army.[14]

Laguerre's description of the Duvalierist military's *modus operandi*, and how profoundly it was rooted in the every-day life of millions of Haitians, is also a stunning exposé of the cynicism and calculation of those who designed it. Out in the countryside, for example, military officers could demand that local farmers plant their crops. Officers could conscript prisoners to perform personal services including farm work. They could use their connections to obtain the use of state land, and to avoid paying import duties on luxury goods.

The Epilogue, which brings Haiti's story up to date, returns again to this issue of a predatory army embedded in the fabric of society and considers these questions: How do you disband an army without jeopardizing the nation it served and was intricately connected with commercially, socially and economically? How do you integrate into civil society thousands of soldiers trained in firearms and little else, and mired in a culture of corruption? And—a question that President Aristide failed to answer—how do you survive politically after firing them?

So much has happened since I wrote this book. Since Henri Namphy's final ouster in 1988, a pack of presidents has ruled Haiti. Jean-

Bertrand Aristide, once so promising, had three truncated terms; his one-time protégé, René Préval, succeeded him twice, as the eleventh and finally the fourteenth president. In the turmoil of presidencies, military interventions, earthquake and cholera, the Duvaliers have become little more than murky memories. Michèle Bennett Duvalier has long disappeared from public view along with the two Duvalier children and a huge divorce settlement. Simone Duvalier, in shared exile with her son, died in 1997. [15] Jean-Claude, who until January 16, 2011 lived in a one-bedroom apartment in Paris, has developed a new *persona* as a low-liver rather than a lowlife. In his own estimation, he is a caring Haitian "broken by twenty years of exile" rather than a despot who terrified the *intelligentsia* into a vast diaspora.

Jean-Claude even has political aspirations and acknowledges that Duvalierism *may not have been* above reproach—"If, during my presidential mandate, the government caused any physical, moral or economic wrongs to others, I solemnly take the historical responsibility . . . to request forgiveness from the people and ask for the impartial judgment of history," he intoned during a radio broadcast into Haiti.[16] But in an email interview with Deborah Ball of the *Wall Street Journal,* he expressed astonishment that he was accused of "criminal behavior," and insisted that the fortune frozen by a Swiss bank represented his "family's savings" enriched by accrued interest. (He estimated that 20 percent was savings, 80 percent interest.)

Jean-Claude's faint hopes are encouraged by occasional expressions of nostalgia among desperate Haitians who recall the Duvalierist past as less terrible than the present. Jean-Claude, self-pitying and self-righteous, has the same perspective. "Look at what has been going on in Haiti since I departed," he reminded journalist Ball. "Why don't you ask the Haitian people if they had a better life during my presidency or if they have a better life now . . . and please let me know what you find out."[17]

Haiti asks—and answers—different questions about the Duvalier presidencies. What was Duvalierism and how did it operate? What was life like under Papa and Baby Doc? What was it in Haiti's history that allowed the Duvaliers to emerge and remain entrenched in power for almost twenty-nine years? These are crucial issues to consider because, over two decades later, the infrastructural chaos and domestic and international power dynamics of Duvalierism continue to dominate, a toxic legacy that must be understood if its consequences are to be eradicated.

PROLOGUE

THE TONTON MACOUTES MARCHED UP AVENUE JOHN Paul II in Port-au-Prince's pleasant residential district of Turgeau, their sweat-oiled faces livid with hatred. "No more hiding for Macoutes!" they shouted hoarsely. "We've laid low for two years, but now the army has freed us. Long live the army!" It was 7:20 a.m. on November 29, 1987, Election Sunday, the day Haitians hoped to break free after three decades of Duvalierist tyranny. They were to vote in the first open elections since 1957, when Dr. François "Papa Doc" Duvalier swept into power as President. Not quite two years earlier, the Macoutes' Supreme Commander Jean-Claude Duvalier had fled Haiti, and the Avenue Jean-Claude Duvalier had been hastily renamed after the man who had launched the first major attack against his dictatorship, Pope John Paul II.

The Macoutes were upward of fifty strong, the youth among them aged by anger lines and by the veins that stood out on their necks as they shrieked their refrain of defiance. Many had tied red or white kerchiefs over their mouths, bandit-style. Flashing against their dark fury as they stamped up the cracked asphalt road were their long, curved machetes known as *coulines,* and the machine guns held by a privileged few. Bringing up the rear was a black Honda Civic carrying four uniformed soldiers, the Macoutes' guides and protectors.

This enraged mob had already killed. Though almost everyone fled at the thundering rat-a-tat of their approach, one man, hampered by his children toddling beside him to Sunday mass, moved too slowly, and the Macoutes shot him dead on the sidewalk. Afterward they burst in on the mass the dead man had been hurrying to attend at the Church of the Sacred Heart, on Election Day a place to vote as well as to worship.

They stormed into the shaded chapel, howling Creole blasphemies and blood-curdling roars, slashing at worshipers who cowered under the long oak pews. Near the altar Macoutes attacked two women, battering them with the butts of their machetes, then turned and smashed the altar. Minutes later, intoxicated by destruction, the entire gang rushed out onto John Paul II, climbing the hill of Turgeau's boutique-lined main street, then turned left at the Rue Martin Luther King, the major thoroughfare that cuts through the heart of the Haitian capital.

A Swiss woman, shot in the back, managed to crawl into a courtyard where the residents then rushed her to a hospital for surgery that saved her life.

Soon they killed again, shooting a scrawny old man in ragged yellow pants and navy shirt, one of those the Haitians call *les malheureux,* the unfortunates. At the Rue Baussan they attacked the Church of St. Louis King of France, but halfheartedly, wasting bullets against its yellowstone walls and shattering the thin panes of its louvered windows with machetes held like dueling swords.

The Macoutes rampaged along Martin Luther King, over the craterous potholes near the multistoried Teleco building and past the incongruous, pale mauve-and-white Gothic arches of Cabinet Achille. Ranting and swearing, the band crossed Ruelle Rivière, where Papa Doc's longtime Finance Minister Clovis Désinor lived in his big, square, white house, and moved swiftly past Madame Lamothe's modern beauty parlor and the tiny, dark boutiques and old houses along the way.

Near the Cabane Creole nightclub the Macoutes slowed down and shot to death three more would-be voters, marked for death by the electoral slips each held. It was not yet 8 a.m. when they reached Avenue John Brown.

At the traffic light they turned left, marching down several blocks to the Ruelle Vaillant, a small tree-shaded street opening into a circle of unpretentious homes where usually children played and the bustle of Port-au-Prince seemed distant. At the mouth of the circle was the primary school Argentine Bellegarde, housed in a solid brick house with a plain, low-ceilinged cement shed added to cram in additional students. On November 29 that shed had become a polling station, and set up inside its dank interior were plain tables manned by voting officials working to process the hundred men and women clasping their electoral cards as they waited to vote in.

At about 8 a.m. the Macoutes poured into the schoolyard. "We're vigilantes here to protect you," one shouted, then suddenly sprayed the milling throng with machine-gun bullets. Scores of men and women fell, dead or dying. Macoutes without guns hacked at wounded victims who pleaded for their lives, severing hands still clutching precious electoral slips, cleaving limbs from torsos. Under the courtyard's almond tree a howling Macoute cut off a woman's head. Another, televised live on Swiss television, chased and caught a woman fleeing down a tiny alley and chopped her into pieces.

Other Macoutes pursued voters into classrooms, massacring them as they crouched huddled in corners, where they had tried to hide under tables, sewing machines, piles of school supplies, or behind the low walls. Later Claude Urraca, a reporter for France's *Le Point,* commented, "I've been covering Central America for years and I've never seen anything like that. It was savagery."

The gunfire and shrieking summoned journalists who raced to Argentine Bellegarde. As they stared in horror at the carnage, the Macoutes and their military protectors returned. "The Tonton Macoutes and the army were coming back to finish the job, to kill the journalists," recalled Peter F. Bentley, who, along with fellow *Time* magazine photographer Jean-Bernard Diederich, fled for his life. "He was shooting at me," Diederich said. "A soldier, his face hidden in the shadow of his helmet, raised an automatic rifle and fired. His bullets were hitting everywhere, and the fragments of glass and pavement were bouncing off my body."

Bentley and Diederich vaulted over dead and dying bodies in a race for the back door. As Bentley approached a ten-foot-high cinder-block wall, he saw a bullet strike British reporter Geoffrey Smith in the foot. Bentley scaled the wall, pulled himself over a second one edged with barbed wire, and escaped. Diederich headed for another wall, not caring that it was topped with broken glass to keep out intruders. Beside him someone fell but the attackers were gaining on him and Diederich climbed up and over the wall, ignoring the pain as shards gashed his right hand. Bleeding and shaken, the Creole-speaking photographer found refuge in a small house whose tenants bound his wounds and comforted him until a United States Information Service officer, Jeffrey Lite, arrived in an armored van and drove him to safety.

The Macoutes stampeded out of the Argentine Bellegarde school, spilling back onto John Brown, turning right onto Martin Luther King just blocks before the Rue Nazon, where their fellow bandits had earlier bombed and then shot at a polling station. They had slaughtered four voters and wounded several others, including a bullet-riddled eight-month-old baby brought by his mother to share the moment when, for the first time in her life, she would cast a vote for her troubled country's new President.

It was now almost 9 a.m. and the Macoutes' fury was temporarily sated. They returned back along Martin Luther King, still deserted except for the stiffening bodies they had left there earlier. The sun was high in the cloudless sky, and their long trek and the frenzy of massacre had fired them up. Splashes of scarlet decorated their clothes, and drying blood and flecks of human flesh now caked their long, curved machetes. "Liberty for Tonton Macoutes!" they bellowed as they swarmed along. "Two years in hiding are ended. The army has freed the Macoutes! Long live the army!"

The job was done. They and brother Macoute bands terrorizing other neighborhoods in Port-au-Prince had renamed Election Day "Bloody Sunday." They had successfully sabotaged Haiti's first free elections in thirty years and smashed the hopes of millions who longed for democracy, for a chance to choose an honest leader, for the first small step along the path to national dignity, liberty, and pride.

At 9 a.m. the few local radio stations still functioning—in the preceding week Macoutes had firebombed most major stations except for the government's Radio Nationale—interrupted bulletins of the mounting casualties to announce that the Provisional Electoral Council, impotent in the face of thirty-four confirmed deaths and at least seventy-five wounded in Port-au-Prince, had decided to annul the elections, postponing them to a future date.

That night, after hours of flashing teletype warning television viewers of an impending important announcement, Haiti's Provisional President and commander in chief of the armed forces, Lieutenant General Henri Namphy, appeared on the screen. Dressed in braided and decorated khaki, the stocky three-star general glowered at the cameras, his green eyes fatigued and angry behind horn-rimmed glasses. "There are things you don't know," Namphy declared, the hoarse voice gruffer than usual. But no revelations followed, just accusations against the nine provisional electoral councillors, by then all in hiding, blaming them for the failed elections and the violence, and firing them. Within seventy-two hours, Namphy added, nine new councillors would be chosen, and in January, new elections held. "On February 7, 1988, as I have always sworn, I will preside over the swearing in of a new, freely elected civilian President, and to him hand over the reins of office."

Americans, outraged at what was perceived as General Namphy's cynical betrayal of nearly two years and millions of dollars in a supposedly joint campaign toward Haitian democracy, vented their disgust and outrage. An eyewitness, Robert E. White, former U.S. ambassador to El Salvador, who observed the elections in the Port-au-Prince slum of Carrefour, said, "During the night, the military abandoned the streets to terrorists. During the day, the military collaborated with the terrorists." Twice shot at in full view of soldiers who merely looked on and did nothing to stop his assailants, White expressed his indignation that he was an American being terrorized by American bullets fired from American guns and characterized General Namphy's actions "a coup d'état."

A *New York Times* editorial stated, "When Sunday's election in Haiti was voided, it shattered hopes for democracy and denied Haitians their first chance in thirty years to elect a President. The culprits are General Henri Namphy's junta and the murderous Macoute thugs whose rampages gave the junta the pretext it needed to call off the vote."

Representative Dante Fascell, chairman of the House Foreign Affairs Committee, declared in a speech in Congress, "General Namphy, who might have been enshrined among the pantheon of this hemisphere's democratic heroes, instead has assured himself a prominent place in the gallery of those whom history will judge as enemies of their own people. . . . The time has come," Fascell asserted, "for the United States to join the Haitian people in saying no to the Tonton Macoutes and Duvalierism, with or without Duvalier."

Duvalierism without Duvalier was a system divested only of its namesake. Less than two years earlier, Jean-Claude Duvalier, smirking calmly, had boarded a United States C-141 cargo plane, and with his glamorous wife, Michèle Bennett, and a select group of friends and relatives, had flown off into gilded exile, champagne glass in hand. Beneath him millions of Haitians had cheered with joy. Duvalier has gone! Haiti is freed!

Duvalierism is Duvalier's legacy to Haiti: tiny pockets of prosperity amid nearly ten million illiterate and disease-ridden citizens scrabbling for existence on just under eleven thousand eroded square miles, with only their ancient African gods to comfort them. Duvalierism is a way of life, begun as a reign of terror, pillage, and debauchery by Dr. François Duvalier, popularly known as "Papa Doc." It continued under his son, Jean-Claude, contemptuously referred to as "Baby Doc," who then bequeathed Duvalierism to the men he named to succeed him, headed by Lieutenant General Henri Namphy as Haiti's Provisional President.

Just as the story of the Duvaliers and the infamous regime they created continues years after the last Duvalier left Haiti, it surely began long before 1957, the year Papa Doc became President. Its origins are to be found a century and a half earlier, in the incredibly complex and bloody world of slavery and revolution, and in human nature itself, lending to the Duvalier dictatorship its universal flavor, making it the stuff of literature and of international studies, and giving to a jaded world the Creole words *Tonton Macoute,* spoken in tones of horror and disgust.

Under the Duvaliers the Tonton Macoutes were one of the world's largest, best organized, and most lawless of goon squads, armed civilians with licenses to torture, steal, destroy, and kill.[18] But Papa Doc did not create them, he merely institutionalized them, acknowledging in law that lawless vein of cruelty and abuse inherent in Haitian society since its foundation.

After triumphant slaves listened to their new Declaration of Independence in 1804, an ex-slave, General Boisrond-Tonnère, cried out, "This doesn't say what we really feel. For our declaration of independence we should have the skin of a white man for parchment, his skull for inkwell, his blood for ink, and a bayonet for pen!" Wild cheers greeted his words, a forecast of the violent and bloody course Haiti would follow after independence.

The form that Duvalierism took was of course tempered by the first Duvalier, François, the country doctor, but the bloody path he traced across his country was already clearly mapped out. By the time he died he had hacked out a regime and stabilized it, on the one hand crushing all opposition, and on the other forcing supporters into total commitment to himself and to his system. When Jean-Claude assumed his father's position, the mechanism was firmly in place. It took fourteen years, shock waves of corruption, and unparalleled cynicism to dislodge the second Duvalier and a handful of his cronies. More than two years later the country remains tragically mired in the Duvalierist legacy.

How did it happen? What was it in their history and national character that propelled Haiti's millions to allow the Duvaliers to spring up and then to tolerate their regime for almost twenty-nine years? Why now that the last Duvalier has gone is Duvalierism so difficult to uproot? If it is true that people deserve the government they have, why is it that the Haitian people deserve Duvalierism, with or without Duvalier?

1 WRITTEN IN BLOOD

I N 1924 A TEENAGE BOY STOOD SHADED BY A STUNTED PINE
tree on the bank of a cold mountain stream. A few yards away a man
and three women held a struggling child while his mother scrubbed
mercilessly with lashed twigs at the running sores that covered his body.
His small, dark face, now distorted with pain, was not spared. Only
when the diseased flesh had been excoriated and blood flowed from the
wounds did the woman stop. As the motionless teenager watched, she
stayed the blood with crushed herbs and bandaged the wounds with
rags. The cruel treatment for the even crueler tropical disease of yaws
was finished. Snuffling quietly, the child took his mother's hand.

The incident made a deep impression on François Duvalier, the shy
teenager with the grave, myopic expression, who years later liked to recall how at that moment he had decided to become a doctor.

Duvalier succeeded in studying medicine and in fighting the yaws
that afflicted the vast majority of his people. But to do so he had to rely
on the help of foreigners, on the Americans who since 1915 had occupied Haiti, white men with loud voices and a contempt for his dark
people, Duvalier recalled bitterly, that he could see in their eyes.

At about the same time that François Duvalier decided to become
a doctor, the boy who would later become his general chief of staff was
also learning important lessons about his world. Eight-year-old Gérard
Constant was walking with his older sister Anna when suddenly, not far
from their house, a crowd began to gather. Standing apart, apparently
oblivious to the crowd, were five uniformed American Marines and a

single Haitian. The latter, an aging mason, clutched his shovel with one hand and gesticulated with the other. The hot dispute grew hotter, and the Marines shouted in fractured Creole, stabbing fingers at the mason and at an unfinished stone wall behind them.

As Gérard and scores of other Haitians watched, one Marine shoved the mason so that the smaller man staggered. The Haitians watched, silent and motionless. Little Gérard, sweaty fingers gripping Anna's, looked up at the black men all around him. "Why don't they do something? Why don't they stop those white men from hurting that man?" At the age of eight Gérard did not yet know the words for *humiliate* and *degrade,* but years later, in remembering the incident, he knew they were the words he had meant.

Suddenly the miracle happened. A man in the crowd could contain his fury no longer and leapt out at the Americans, tackling one. It was like a signal, and one man after another rushed to aid him. Gérard watched with joy as the five Marines fled at top speed from the Haitian men, who soon stopped the chase and turned back crowing with pride, their self-respect restored.

Gérard hated Americans. Everywhere in Haiti he saw them belittling his people, mocking their gentle manners and scorning their black skin. He dreamed of Americans, saw their ugly white faces in a recurring nightmare so intense, it woke him and dominated his thoughts. Night after night he would lie awake till dawn longing to kill them, wishing they would die, berating God for not sending them back to the far-off land they had come from.

Today for the first time Gérard understood that though he was just a silly little boy, his vision was shared by grown Haitian men. From that day on he hated less, and the great space where the hatred had been was filled with love for those Haitian men, whom he now knew could be as brave and fearless as he wanted to be. Years later, when the little boy had become a general and served President François Duvalier as chief of staff of the army, he had lost none of that love, but he had learned bitter lessons in how difficult it was for a Haitian to be brave and fearless, and to remain alive.

Both François Duvalier and Gérard Constant grew up in a conquered country whose citizens—impotent—could only cry out against their invaders and wait and hope for their withdrawal. They waited, while an entire generation grew up, for nineteen years. The American

conquerors had come to Haiti in 1915, and until 1934 they remained—
hated, hating, repressive, racist, and, sometimes, idealistic and generous
and kind.

Why did they come to this backward Caribbean island with its millions of illiterate black peasants? And, having come, why did they stay?

The answer begins in the past, when the slaves of the tiny colony, a
day away by boat from the Florida coast, revolted in a war so apocalyptic that its shock waves pounded Europe and also the fledgling American
Republic. Until it revolted, Haiti was one more French sugar and coffee
colony. Afterward, the blood and ashes of its Revolution fixed it forever
in the American psyche, and forged a bittersweet relationship so profound, it still touches the hearts of both nations.

Haiti, formerly called Saint Domingue, shares the western third of
the island of Hispaniola with the Spanish-speaking Dominican Republic. Christopher Columbus discovered it in 1492, and from the wreck of
his flagship, *Santa Maria,* founded La Navidad, the New World's first
Spanish settlement. French buccaneers first preyed on the floundering
Spanish colony in the early 1600s, stealing cattle and occupying out is-
lands. They were soon followed by settlers, who quickly killed off most
of the native Arawak Indian inhabitants by massacre, overwork, European epidemics, or despair. By the end of the century, when France defeated Spain in Europe, the Treaty of Ryswick acknowledged her claim
to that part of the island known as Saint Domingue.

Saint Domingue was a tropical paradise, with endless ranges of
spectacular mountains, neatly planted coffee trees, and rolling plains of
pale green sugarcane produced more cheaply there than on any other
Caribbean island. Fruit trees bore mangoes, bananas, and apricots and
mingled with bougainvillea, oleander, and a myriad of other trees and
flowers. Surrounding this Eden was the clear green-blue sea, its breezes
carrying salt-tinged solace from the steady heat of the tropical sun.

The colony became France's richest, the envy of every other European nation. With its fertile soil and its thousands of sugar, coffee, cotton, and indigo plantations, it furnished two-thirds of France's overseas
trade, employing one thousand ships and fifteen thousand French sailors. In addition, the colony supplied half of Europe's consumption of
tropical produce.

Saint Domingue was also one of the world's greatest markets for
the African slave trade because the slaves were driven so mercilessly that
half died within a few years of arrival and had to be replaced by fresh

African imports. Like the planters in the English Caribbean, French planters preferred to work their slaves to death and buy new ones rather than allow them to survive and reproduce themselves naturally.

One of the most important consequences of this policy was that even after centuries of slavery, the slaves of Saint Domingue, unlike their American cousins, were in large part raw African recruits who retained their languages, religions, tribal customs, and cultural values, including fierce pride and inconsolable anguish at the travesty their lives had become.

Because of its callous cost accounting and the breathtaking degeneracy of its "plantocracy," Saint Domingue quickly earned notoriety as home of the most brutal bondage known to mankind. With African life held so cheap while money to replenish supplies abounded, the French slave owners unhesitatingly indulged their crudest whims and excesses. Punishment by torture was routine, and few slaves escaped floggings with all manner of whips, including nail-studded wooden paddles and brine-soaked bulls' penises. They were also burned with boiling cane, chained, branded with hot irons, buried alive, manacled and smeared with molasses so ants would devour them, mutilated and crippled by amputation of arms, legs, and buttocks, raped, starved, and humiliated.

Working conditions were almost as punishing as punishment itself, as slaves toiled from dawn to sunset, naked under the boiling sun of midday or barely covered by rags. They were rewarded by miserable food in tiny quantities, and often forced to prepare it themselves after their field work was done. It was usually very late at night before they were free to return to their huts, where they fell onto mud floors for brief hours of respite.

For some women there was the additional burden of pregnancy, and a small percentage of slave women survived long enough to give birth, though miscarriages and stillbirths were more common. Slave children who survived infancy fared as badly as their parents, dying like the disease-infested flies that tormented them, knowing no childhood, little tenderness, and, for the few who persisted in living, a future so brutish that death was in every way preferable.

In one hundred years Haitian slavery killed nearly one million Africans, often after the briefest sojourn there. Thousands more escaped intolerable life by suicide, spiting their owners and guaranteeing a joyous return to Africa, where, they believed, their spirits would return.

Yet slavery did not disappear, and slaves developed ways of living, however briefly and reluctantly. Separated from family and tribesmen who spoke the same language, they soon and easily reached out to each other across the French-created Tower of Babel through Creole, the slave lingua franca, with its French-based vocabulary uttered in the familiar staccato rhythm of Africa and molded into African grammatical structures.

Through Creole they communicated more than daily exchanges. Remembering together, they also preserved their real world, for in the new world of horror the slaves endured slavery only through memories of past customs and ways of life. Their religions especially still lived and comforted them, and though the French outlawed every vestige of worship, including traditional drumming, dancing, and animal and vegetable sacrifice, they could not stamp out belief itself nor force Christianity onto a race whom Christians despised and slaughtered.

Africa had no one religion, and neither had African slaves. By reckless tribal mixing, however, the French attempt to sow discord and prevent revolt had a very different result—the union of slaves under the powerful Dahomeans, whose religion also prevailed over all others and in time converted most slaves to its rituals, especially its dances.

Over the centuries the vodoun of Dahomey evolved into the vodoun of Haiti, assimilating into its hierarchy Congolese gods, Arada spirits, even Catholic saints and rituals. All humans need spiritual explanations and relationships, and Haiti's vital, satisfying vodoun religion provided them.

Yet during slavery vodoun was still an evolving religion that was a crucial element in uniting its slave practitioners against the whites. Its complex theology developed only afterward, when its newly freed people turned inward, and as they built their own nation, created their own national soul. Until then vodoun was as simple as its most familiar song, chanted around late-night campfires as weary slaves cooked their meager provisions and waited to eat:

"Eh! Eh! Bomba! Heu! Heu!
Canga, bafio té!
Canga, mouné de lé!
Canga, do ki la!
Canga, li!"

("We swear to destroy the whites and all that they possess; let us die rather than fail to keep this vow.")

French slavery in Haiti began with two elements—the white Frenchmen and the black Africans they enslaved. Soon, however, another profoundly important element was added. This was the mixed-blood, whose existence complicated slavery, refined racism, and created in Haitian society relationships and loyalties that divide it to this day.

The first mixed-bloods were children borne by African mothers and French fathers. These exotic beings, conceived in lust and by chance, coupled the beauty of dark Africa with pale Europe, and so often did they conquer paternal hearts, with their familiar features etched into darker skin and framed by curlier hair, that new rules were made for them and they were considered to constitute a new breed of humanity. They were called mulattoes, a name afterward given to all light-skinned Haitians, whether their color stems from a union of black and white or mulatto with mulatto.

Years passed, and the number of mulattoes multiplied. Originally the product of sexual desire, they quickly became even more its object. Mulatto women especially won white men's hearts, accumulating wealth and even whiter children, and the undying jealousy and hatred of colonial white women. Yet no matter how many individual whites loved individual mulattoes, affection did not transcend rigid notions of class and caste, and by the eighteenth century the mulattoes were persecuted in every aspect of life. Legislation governing them was restrictive and vindictive. They were forced to police desperate slave rebels, forbidden to wear European fashions, excluded from most professions and public offices, and deprived of civil liberties, including the right to defend their women against sexual attack by any white man.

The mulattoes quietly acquired property, slaves, and education, and created within their own class men and women who soon equaled and often surpassed their degenerate white overlords in wealth and erudition. They also assimilated the values, manners, and culture of France, disassociated themselves from enslaved blacks, and cultivated a profound contempt for the slaves' color, manners, values, and religion. The physical product of both white and black, the mulattoes evolved as a class separated from both, a buffer between them, neither one nor the other.

By 1791, everything had changed. The slaves had been plotting for months, using their drums to telegraph their plans for revolt just as they had always shared their news and grievances from plantation to plantation. Three decades earlier, under their African-born leader Mackandal, they had attempted to free themselves by poisoning thousands of their white oppressors, serving up death in broth and tea and juices, ladling it into wells, mixing it into medicine. This time, they vowed, they would not fail.

On the night of August 22, they reached the point of no return. Boukman was a giant of a man, foreman on a plantation near Cap Fran-çois, now called Cap Haitien. He was also a *houngan,* priest of the vodoun rites which both tribal African and Haitian-born Creole slaves clung to in Christian-blessed bondage. When several hundred slaves had assembled, Boukman issued his final instructions. Then the rebel pact was sealed in a vodoun ritual during which the worshipers drank frothing warm blood from a newly sacrificed black pig. Afterward, Boukman prayed aloud.

"The god who created the sun which gives us light, who rouses the waves and rules the storm, is hidden in the clouds, but still he watches us. He sees all that the white man does. The god of the white man inspires him with crime, but our god calls upon us to do good works. Our god, who is good to us, orders us to revenge our wrongs. He will direct our arms and aid us. The god of the whites has so often caused us to weep. Listen!" Boukman thundered at the end of his prayer. "Listen to the voice of liberty, which speaks in the hearts of all of us!"

The slaves listened, and began their Revolution. It lasted thirteen years, a war made endurable because slavery was not. Scorching the earth, burning every habitation, and destroying every vestige of the plantations, the rebels slaughtered beast and man, raped women before killing them and their children, tortured prisoners of war with the obscene refinements they had learned as victims. Made superhuman by belief in their gods' invincibility, they hurled themselves at European battalions shrieking "Bullets are as dust" and won battle after battle.

Then from the ranks of the humblest black soldiers, ragged in pillaged silks and satins or entirely naked, armed with a few captured firearms, rusty swords, picks and hoes, emerged Toussaint Louverture, the leader who would change the course of the war and force history to acknowledge him as one of the great geniuses of revolution.

Ascetic, enduring, courageous, and untiring, the small, ugly, and middle-aged Toussaint rose to command and lead his people through years of battle, intrigue, and diplomacy to spectacular victories, defeating Spain in 1794, England in 1795, and Napoleonic France in 1803. He created a stable agricultural economy and in large measure succeeded in conciliating blacks and whites and mulattoes. Toussaint also recognized genius in others and, unafraid, appointed a white man as his chief of staff and assigned mulattoes and blacks as generals.

The two greatest of these generals were Jean-Jacques Dessalines and Henri Christophe, both illiterate blacks, Dessalines the ex-slave of a black man, Christophe the Anglophile ex-slave waiter from Grenada. Christophe learned his military trade as part of the Volunteer Colored Fighters that Haiti had sent to reinforce American troops under Major General Benjamin Lincoln at the Battle of Savannah during the American Revolution.

Toussaint himself did not live to see Haitian independence, but because he identified and rewarded genius in others, even illiterate ex-slaves, he lives on in memory as "the Great Liberator" whose dream for his people inspired their generals long after he was in his grave.

Begun by slaves sworn to liberty or death, inspired by vodoun beliefs and leaders, ultimately the war changed not only the little Caribbean nation but affected France and England as well and caused radical transformations in the great revolutionary neighbor to the north, the Republic of the United States.

A mere decade after she had conceded her former colonies' independence, England watched closely as France, already devastated by her own revolution, coped with Saint Domingue's. In 1793, when England and France ended their uneasy peace and openly declared war, England intrigued with Haiti's anti-revolutionary French planters. In return for helping the English officers win the military victory they confidently predicted, the planters would be guaranteed that Haiti would be restored to a prerevolutionary state. Blacks would once more be enslaved, and mulattoes would lose their newly acquired civil rights. When the planters agreed, England sent an army to capture the Caribbean's richest sugar island, partly as compensation for losing her thirteen colonies and partly as revenge for the help France had given the rebellious American colonists.

Anticipation and reality were far different. Through a host of international political and military convolutions, Saint Domingue had already smashed its own rebels and then contingents of Spanish soldiers. When Britain sailed into the tumultuous island, she too had to contend with Toussaint Louverture, now a general of revolutionary, abolitionist France. At his hands England lost vast numbers of soldiers, and in 1798, after signing a convention with General Toussaint, the English commander in chief evacuated the scene of English shame.

Four years later newly Napoleonic France repaid Toussaint by betraying and kidnapping him, then shipped him off to fatal imprisonment high in the French Alps. Toussaint died, but the dream he had instilled in his people continued to fire them by day as by night. "In overthrowing me you have cut down in Saint Domingue only the trunk of the tree of liberty. It will spring up again from the roots, for they are many and they are deep," Toussaint proclaimed defiantly on the eve of his own death by betrayal.

Toussaint's faith in the Haitian people's determination was justified when Napoleon sent his brother-in-law, General Leclerc, to fight "a war of extermination" against the Haitians. "Follow your instructions exactly, and . . . rid yourself of Toussaint, Christophe, Dessalines, and the principal brigands," Napoleon instructed. "Rid us of these gilded Africans, and we have nothing more to wish." Against Toussaint's generals, including Dessalines and Christophe, Leclerc fought a hopeless campaign that lasted until November 18, 1803, and cost the French fifty thousand soldiers' lives, with countless more wounded. "We have," concluded Leclerc glumly, "a false idea of the Negro."

On January 1, 1804, Saint Domingue proclaimed its independence from perfidious France, adopted the ancient Arawak Indian name of Haiti, and adopted as its flag the revolutionary tricolor with the white of the white man struck out of it. Boukman's Revolution had been born and baptized. A few months later General Jean-Jacques Dessalines had himself declared Emperor, just as Napoleon had, and the history of Haiti, the world's first Black Republic, began to unfold.

That history did not include friendly relations with the United States. Despite Savannah, where Haitians inspired by American revolutionary principles of freedom had so proudly fought, the first republic in the New World showed only contempt for the world's first Black Republic, even denying a Haitian Savannah veteran the right to land in Charleston because he was black. Even more startling was Thomas Jefferson's plan, a foreshadowing of Cuba's Mariel boatlift, to rid the States of slave criminals by exiling them to Haiti.

During the long War of Independence the Americans had made one notable exception, when President John Adams defied Southern horror at slave liberation anywhere and in 1800 sent warships to Toussaint to assist him in his deadly struggle with the mulatto General Rigaud.

After months of terrible hostilities and thousands of deaths, Rigaud and his mulatto forces were smashed. Adams's gesture toward Toussaint was sternly moral, putting America's guns where its obligations were, but it remained a singular one. From 1800 on, when the United States reconciled with France, the Haitians could expect no more help from the Americans.

French pressure to embargo Haiti was only one reason for cold Haitian-American relations. The overriding reason lay in America itself, in slavery. The freedom-loving American republic held slaves, while the freedom-loving Black Republic was dedicated to smashing slavery everywhere. Worse, Haiti provided the moral support those still in bondage required to motivate them. Gabriel Prosser's Virginia 1800 uprising was Haitian-inspired, for example. So was Denmark Vesey's in 1822, which inspired John Brown and was described as "the most elaborate insurrectionary project ever formed by American slaves. . . . In boldness of conception and thoroughness of origination there is nothing to compare with it."

Both slavery's defenders and abolitionists had to agree with a congressman who said in 1804, "We have only to look at St. Domingue. There the Negroes felt their wrongs, and have avenged them: they have learned the rights of man, and asserted them; they have wrested the power from their oppressors, and have become masters of the island."

To the Americans, Haiti's shadow menaced rather than inspired, and they began to see all free blacks and mulattoes as potential revolutionaries. State after state wrote legislation persecuting them, the blood and ashes of Saint Domingue providing the ink and dictating the script.

In the same vein the tiny, complex, tormented, and magnificent Toussaint Louverture captured the reluctant attention of mostly racist America. "The life of Toussaint L'Ouverture has not been recorded as often as that of Napoleon," wrote historian Henry Adams. "Nevertheless, no man exerted such influence upon the history of the United States than did Toussaint L'Ouverture. His influence upon our destiny has been more profound than that of any European head of state."

A modern historian of Afro-America goes further, showing how Haiti's bitter and successful Revolution changed the nature of all subsequent slave revolts. Until 1804, explains Eugene Genovese in *From Rebellion to Revolution: Afro-American Slave Revolts in the Making of the New World,* revolting slaves hoped mainly to restore their African ways of life in their new homeland, but Toussaint and afterward Dessalines and Christophe were no mere dealers in dreams of an African paradise lost. Visionary and firmly anchored in their modern world, they sought to create in Haiti a modern black state, with an economy geared to the vital export sector and therefore to the world market.

"Toussaint's revolution," Genovese observes, "did not seek to turn the blacks of Saint-Domingue into Europeans but to lead them toward a recognition that European technology had revolutionized the world and forced all people to participate in the creation of a world culture at once nationally varied and increasingly uniform. From that moment, the slaves of the New World had before them the possibility of a struggle for freedom that pointed towards participation in the mainstream of world history rather than away from it."

Haiti, however, found herself barred from participation in world commerce, the all-important prerequisite for entry into world history, and it was the United States more than any other nation that blocked her. By her audacity in freeing her own slaves, and in defying every notion of black inferiority by defeating three European giants, Haiti had committed the unpardonable sin. As Senator Thomas Hart Benton remarked in 1826, "We receive no mulatto consuls or black ambassadors from [Haiti]. And why? The peace of eleven states will not permit the fruits of a successful Negro insurrection to be exhibited among them."

In addition to this were the complications of international alliances, with English, French, and American diplomatic scrimmages leaving Haiti the perpetual loser. Beginning with a trade embargo in 1806, the United States began a century of commercial ostracism that sabotaged Toussaint's vision of an international commercial orientation and forced Haiti's neck into an economic noose that strangled bright hopes and pushed her further down the road to economic and social catastrophe.

With reasonable American or international support, Haiti's leaders might have salvaged her, creating the modern nation Toussaint envisioned. Without it, isolated and abandoned, the never-ending battle to conquer the legacies of slavery was doomed to failure.

Haiti deteriorated more and more, and as the great dreams clouded, its citizens looked back rather than forward, invoking the nation's glorious history and the legends that had grown up around it. As decade succeeded decade, this history and its legends dominated the present like a specter, crushing it, as leader after leader identified himself with Toussaint, Dessalines, and Christophe and demanded as his due absolute power, unquestioning obedience, and slavish devotion.

Slavery too was a murdered evil whose tentacles reached out even from the grave. Its death had freed the slaves in law but had not unfettered their shackles of illiteracy, mistrust, indiscriminate violence, and, above all, bitter disunion stemming from their own brand of racism— the contempt, resentment, and hatred between Haitian blacks and mulattoes.

The long, savage war had also ravaged the land. Plantations and agriculture had been destroyed. Twelve years of war had decimated a generation of soldiers, and women outnumbered men three to one. Despite independence, fear of renewed French attacks destabilized and demoralized Haiti's citizens. With these critical conditions to work with, the second great leader began the process of reconstruction.

Like Toussaint Louverture before him, Jean-Jacques Dessalines took drastic measures to reconstruct the ruined economy. Basically, he established a state serfdom, where all men except a tiny group of administrators were either soldiers or laborers "attached to a plantation," as were all women. Because these farmers were now freedmen, slavery's whip was abolished and the working day was shortened.

For most freedmen life in the new peasant society was a far cry from what they had expected when, on Independence Day, Dessalines had shouted in furious triumph, "Swear now, with clasped hands, to live free and independent and to accept death in preference to the yoke." Defining his own kind of freedom, he drove his people much like the despised French "slaveocracy," crying defiantly that "the laborers can be controlled only by fear of punishment and even death; I shall lead them only by these means; my 'morale' shall be the bayonet."

Dessalines's bayonet was a stark reality, and it was wielded by a huge army. Urgent defense needs also demanded the construction of dozens of protective fortresses, which to this day dot the countryside in various degrees of decay. This overmilitarization plagued Haiti and contributed to resurgent racial tensions, as illiterate blacks escaping the drudgery of the soil sought positions in the army that they could not find in the mulatto-dominated civil service, for even Dessalines could not design a bureaucracy manned by illiterates like himself.

Dessalines was also an unrepentant racist who contributed to this black-mulatto conflict and to violence, for he was a violent man who lived and died by the sword. Then, as Emperor, this most virulent of racists suddenly announced his intention to outlaw all distinctions of color.

This he planned to achieve—anticipating Trujillo in the Dominican Republic—by forced intermarriage of blacks and mulattoes, "bronzing" future generations of Haitians to a fine uniform hue and ending forever the distinctions of color he had belatedly realized were destroying his people.

To begin the "bronzification," Dessalines proposed that mulatto General Alexandre Pétion marry Dessalines's daughter Célimène, black, beautiful, and, unbeknown to her father, already pregnant by a lover whose life he was to take when he eventually learned the truth. Pétion tactfully declined, and soon afterward Dessalines was murdered. Ambushed and shot by unidentified mulattoes, the mystery of Dessalines's death still burdens the Haitian people.

The fact that he died at all adds to the problem, for everyone believed Dessalines had the mystical power of "doubling," being in two places at the same time. They said his wife, Claire-Heureuse, had sabotaged him, entering the forbidden room where he kept his magical artifacts. She found him there, and was said to have exclaimed, "But, Jean-Jacques, I thought you had already left for Port-au-Prince! I heard your horse galloping, and that's why I came in here, to see why you've never let me enter." At that very moment, people said, Dessalines needed every ounce of concentration, for his doubled self riding hard toward the capital had just been attacked. Claire-Heureuse's clumsy interference distracted him, and the bullets pierced his heart, killing both of his manifestations.

The identity of his killers was—and remains—a troubling consideration. Was he murdered by mulatto General Guérin and rebellious, unpaid soldiers, as the standard history books claim, or was the real culprit the mulatto General Pétion, who did away with Dessalines to avoid marrying Célimène? The truth is unknown, but the interest with which Haitians still debate it is living proof of the albatross their history has become.

Dessalines was succeeded by Pétion, and also by black General Henri Christophe. In open schism, the mulatto South elected the highly educated and refined Pétion, while the black North supported the self-taught and polished Christophe. Divided, each ruled over a decade, their entirely contradictory policies adding to the chaos of Haiti's chaotic history.

For the first years of his thirteen-year reign—for he too declared himself King—Christophe was benign where Dessalines had been savage, while still remaining faithful to Toussaint's economic vision. He exacted long hours on the plantations with forced labor in prison the price of shirking, but he rewarded diligence with modest prosperity and relative security. Strict and paternal, he demanded his people wear neat, clean clothes in public places, and he virtually stamped out theft by planting valuables as snares and punishing those who failed to return them to the authorities.

A privileged group of nobles enjoyed a very different and pampered court life in splendid French-style palaces. One of them, Sans Souci Palace, was a two-storied wonder encircled by galleries through which glass casements looked down into the courtyard. Spacious and elegant, fitted with Haitian mahogany and princely furnishings, Sans Souci was cooled by a network of subterranean streams, Christophe's own idea—as were the spy holes in the kitchen walls, to protect the royal family from poisonous cooks.

Annexed to the palace were the administration buildings, ministries, mint, library, chapel, garrisons, hospital, even the prison. This and his other architectural monuments satisfied the Emperor's need for luxury and also impressed and instilled great pride in his subjects. Most important of all, the very complexity of the royal lifestyle bound the entire nobility to Christophe personally, and therefore to the state he embodied.

Christophe's most magnificent monument was the mighty Citadelle La Ferrière, today rated by UNESCO as one of the wonders of the new world. Built on a mountain peak at an altitude of nine hundred meters, La Ferrière took fifteen years to construct, straddles an area of one hectare, and was invulnerable to attack by nineteenth-century weaponry. In emergencies it could house five thousand men, and an elaborate system of basins and pipes collected rainwater to supply them for the longest siege. The work of thousands of Haitian workmen under the supervision of a Haitian military engineer, only Haitians could visit it and from its vast battlements gaze down onto the bay where Christopher Columbus's *Santa Maria* weighed anchor on Christmas Eve 1492, and to where Columbus had built La Navidad, the first Spanish settlement on the new continent.

Despite these and other precautions against potentially dangerous foreigners, Christophe was free of Dessalines's bitter hatred of whites. During some of Dessalines's worst excesses Christophe had managed to save several Americans and Englishmen, and in fact his fondness for England made him an outright Anglophile. Of Europeans he hated only the French, and he declared publicly that "his constant aim should be to increase and perpetuate the rage which a sense of their wrongs had long ago enkindled; nor should the name of France, associated as it was with the recollection of so many injuries, be ever uttered among them but with execrations."

Like most black Haitians, Christophe had suffered personal tragedy at French hands. During a short-lived peace with France, he had entrusted his nine-year-old son and a considerable sum of money to French General Boudet to supervise the child's education in France, where he would receive the fine education his illiterate father had never had. Instead, Boudet abandoned the boy, who soon died of hunger, cold, and misery in the Orphan Asylum in Paris.

In 1811 trouble over funds deposited in a Baltimore bank prompted Christophe to seize American cargoes to the value of $132,000, and afterward he refused to receive American ships or agents. On the other hand, when Haitians cheated an American coffee exporter, Christophe punished them by pouring water on their heads and inquiring, "Are your heads cool yet?" Later he condemned them to forced labor on the Citadelle.

For mulattoes, however, Christophe shared Dessalines's loathing, and though in wartime he had often saved white lives, he had not shown the same solicitude for mulattoes. At the beginning of his reign he promoted and rewarded light-skinned individuals impartially. But the rival mulatto-run South was a source of never-ending bitterness, and in 1811 Christophe renewed his war against Pétion. Pétion's victory provoked in the "Black King" a hatred of mulattoes "so deep and fiendlike, that nothing would satisfy the direness of his vengeance but the utter extermination of that race," wrote one of his contemporaries.

From then on Christophe hounded his mulatto generals and murdered a few, tortured hundreds of mulatto prisoners of war, and ordered a mulatto woman from Gonaives executed because she had prayed for Pétion's victory. Even more brutal was his execution of a group of Cap Haitien mulatto women whose priest heard their prayers and then betrayed them. Wretched at losing their prerevolutionary privileges over the despised blacks, the women urged the Virgin Mary to kill the Black King "by some dreadful death—for that none could be too dreadful for him to suffer." Christophe listened to the priest, ranted with fury, and ordered the women killed.

In a nation whose history is written in blood, illiterate Christophe too added his scarlet flourishes. Increasingly his cruel streak dominated, and blacks as well as mulattoes were cut down. The people grew weary of the bloodshed and compared his severe regime with Pétion's slack one. The army divided and mutinied, and finally he faced general rebellion. By then crippled by a stroke, his authority eroded, Christophe chose his own exit, shooting himself through the head with one of the pistols he always carried, one that legend tells us was loaded with a silver bullet, the only kind that could fell him.

Pétion's regime in the South paralleled Christophe's chronologically only, for he died in 1818 and Christophe in 1820. Pétion, however, reversed entirely the Toussaint-Dessalines-Christophe policies that made the North thrive. He parceled out land so that farm laborers became peasant owners, and thereby destroyed the plantation basis of Haiti's former economic prosperity. To please his fellow mulatto aristocrats, he restored to them the lands Dessalines had confiscated, even compensating them for crops lost during Dessalines's reign.

The immediate result of Pétion's land legislation was that most Haitians became landowners, and a significant minority sharecroppers. The long-term result was that Christophe's laws against subdividing land were abolished, Haitian agriculture became unworkable, and today most peasants barely subsist on ludicrously small plots they own while sharecroppers live in the direst misery.

In terms of Haiti's bitter racial problems, Pétion was a moderate who during the war saved many white lives and in power never overtly favored the mulattoes. Even so his regime legitimized their supremacy in political power, land ownership, and educational attainment. By feuding with Christophe, and encouraging hard-driven laborers from the prosperous North to flee to his easygoing though increasingly impoverished South, Pétion effectively sabotaged all that Christophe was doing, including granting equality to black freemen.

In ideology alone was Pétion faithful to the ideal of liberation. He expressed it most eloquently when he gave money and arms to a desperate Simón Bolívar on condition that he abolish slavery wherever he could. Pétion's gesture was made all the more poignant by his fear of reprisals against Haiti by furious slaveholding nations, and so his offerings were made in secret and he refused any public acknowledgment.

Less dramatic but more practical had been Dessalines's and Christophe's persistent attempts to buy slaves whom they would liberate. Dessalines had had a standing offer to American sea captains of $40 for each black or mulatto they brought into Haiti. He had also made a similar offer to the British West Indian slave traders for male Africans whom he wanted for military service. Continuing Dessalines's policy, Christophe bought slaves offered him by traders, then freed them and put them to work on his projects. Pétion never took such direct action, but instead put his hopes in Bolívar, who in 1816 redeemed his promise to Pétion by freeing the slaves of Venezuela.

When a debilitating tropical fever killed Pétion in 1818 and ended his kind and uncommitted regime, the South he had ruled over stood in stark contrast to the rich prosperity of Christophe's North, for under Pétion the South had become poor. Sugar culture, requiring large land-holdings, capital investment, and disciplined labor, was impossible, and even less regulated coffee cultivation faltered. Personal discipline crumbled as Southerners became their own bosses. The Southern treasury was empty, the coinage debased. The people were free but poor, while Christophe's were prosperous but rigidly controlled.

Pétion's mulatto councillor and disciple Jean-Pierre Boyer succeeded him, and when Christophe died two years later, Boyer conquered the North. Ironically, Boyer also conquered Hispaniola's other two-thirds and liberated its slaves, succeeding where Christophe had failed. Then for twenty-five years he pursued Pétion's policies and oversaw the destruction of the revolutionary dream. Though virtual national bankruptcy drove him to draft Christophe-type labor legislation, the measure had major flaws and in any case came too late. Boyer's decision to pay France a huge indemnity in return for formal recognition of Haitian independence further drained the treasury and mortgaged the country's future.

Haitians died poorer than they had been born, and their children, inheriting fractions of the family plot, became even poorer. The quarter century of indolent decline ended in January 1843 when dissident blacks revolted and Boyer became the first in a long series of presidents to flee into exile. From then until the American occupation of 1915–34, only one of Haiti's twenty-two presidents served out his term of office, while three died natural deaths. Three died by violence, and fourteen more, like Boyer, were driven from Haiti by revolts, the fourteenth providing the Americans the excuse they had been seeking to intervene and begin their long occupation.

The 1843 revolt signaled the end of mulatto presidencies, and for fifteen years black generals ruled. None of them, however, was a leader of greatness, and the Haitian tragedy continued unchecked. The first of these black presidents, illiterate, usually inebriated, octogenarian General Philippe Guerrier, lasted one year, till he died of old age and was followed by another octogenarian, Louis Pierrot, Christophe's brother-in-law. Pierrot's terror of assassination, coupled with senility and bad temper, hastened his downfall, and another aged general, one-eyed Jean-Baptiste Riché, was installed. Riché died in 1847 of an overdose of drugs taken to increase his strength, and a fourth illiterate black general, Faustin Soulouque, succeeded him.

Soulouque's regime differed from the others in longevity and degree. Two years into his reign the event occurred that transformed Soulouque from a minor and incompetent President into the personage known as "Soulouque the Ignorant." Despite his diligence in vodoun, he was not adverse to heeding Catholic wisdom when that was expedient. So in 1849, when the Virgin Mary appeared in downtown Port-au-Prince and relayed God's desire that he become Emperor, Soulouque was more than willing. Though he later acquired trunks full of bejeweled valuables, he rushed happily to his coronation with a crown of gilded cardboard and stuck it on his head to become Faustin I.

As Faustin I he and his Queen, Adelina, and an extensive court of instantly created nobles, ruled for a decade, overthrown only in 1859 after destroying Haiti with corruption, debt, debased currency, and a series of military defeats after repeated attempts to recapture the Dominican Republic. Soulouque's legacy to his successor was a country in even worse condition than when he had inherited it, with its fundamental problems still unresolved, including its ruinous class/caste structure, whereby blacks dominated the powerful army and mulattoes ran the country, owned the land, and controlled the economy.

Soulouque also left Haiti fervently and overtly vodounesque. An ardent believer and practitioner, he promoted vodoun, which by mid-century reached full maturity as the religion of all the Haitian people. Embryonic vodoun had fired the Revolution, but afterward Toussaint, Dessalines, and Christophe suppressed it, fearing its powers of inspiring insurrection. Their less illustrious successors had ignored, tolerated, or halfheartedly discouraged it, and as a result it had time to develop and ferment until its gods had multiplied into satisfying legions and its rituals were so complex that a truly learned *houngan* could devote a lifetime to studying them.

As a mature belief system, vodoun synthesizes African beliefs and practices and embellishes them with rituals and trappings borrowed from Catholicism. Unlike Catholicism, however, vodoun has no hierarchy, no formal theology, no seminaries, and no bible. It is not concerned with sin and moral law, considered the province of social custom and Christianity. It does not see life as a perpetual struggle between good and evil but as a mixture of good and evil, in proportions varying from person to person and from spirit to spirit.

If a vodoun creed existed, sociologist James Leyburn suggests in *The Haitian People* that the creed might go:

> I believe in scores of gods and spirits, guardians of earth and sky, and of all things visible and invisible;
>
> I believe that all these . . . *loa* or "mysteries" are potent, although less majestic than the good God of the Christians; that some of them came with our ancestors from our former home in Africa, while others we have learned about in our Haitian fatherland; that these *loa,* like us, are capable of good and evil, gentleness and anger, mercy and respect;
>
> I believe in the efficacy of sacrifice; in the pleasures of living; in respect due to twins; in the careful cult of the dead, who may return to our abodes; in the spiritual causation of diseases and misfortune; in the dance through which we may be "mounted" by our *loa;* in the possibility of interfering with the normal flow of events by means of magic; in the efficacy of charms and spells; and in the Holy Catholic Church.

The universe was created when the Great Serpent moved under the earth he was holding aloft from the sea, undulating his seven thousand coils to form the heavens and the stars and the mountains and valleys beneath. From that time on humans have cohabited with their gods, or *loas,* and the spirits of many humans eventually become *loas.* And just as Catholics have their special saints to intercede for them, vodounists have their special *loas.*

Vodoun is practiced through the very process of living, by belief, by daily rituals, by incantations. But on certain occasions *cérémonies* are held to commemorate special events such as Mardi Gras or November, which is the month of Baron Samedi, the cantankerous god who guards the crossroads and the cemeteries. *Cérémonies* are also necessary to deal with such human needs as sickness, death, and serious problems.

The *cérémonie* is held in a peristyle. In the middle is a pole, or *poteau-mitan,* often painted in serpentine spirals. The *houngan* or his female equivalent, the *mambo,* calls on the gods, who enter by riding down the *poteau-mitan* and then leap out to "possess" a worshiper, pre-empting his spirit and controlling his body.

The gods are summoned by prayer and incantation, by sacred and intricate cornmeal drawings, or *vèvès,* and by the drums, which beat a tattoo so rhythmic and insistent the gods almost always respond. So do the worshipers, swaying in trances or dancing with total abandon.

Vodoun dances are always circular, in recognition of life's eternal circle. Dancing is individual, though dancers trace the same traditional steps. Dances from different vodoun rites emphasize different parts of the body.

Cérémonies also take place in the chapel, or *houmfor,* where the *houngan* keeps his sacred objects: the drums, the sequined flags, the jars and the dolls, the magical rocks and bones, the images of the saints and other paraphernalia. Sacrifice also plays an important role in both public and private *cérémonies,* for the gods are demanding and must be honored and cajoled with food and liquor, chickens, goats, pigs, and cows.

Over and above these important rituals and *cérémonies, houngans* spend the greatest part of their time healing. They are the only doctors most Haitians have access to and they employ combinations of herbal medicine, folklore, and magic to cure trusting patients. They also prepare amulets or charms to ward off evil. Infrequently they engage in black magic, and through *ounga* and bad-luck charms attack and destroy enemies.

Christianity coexisted with vodoun, but in all but the most sophisticated it failed to supplant it as the primary belief system. Disgraced by degenerate priests who drank, fornicated, and sold blessings like vodoun charms, Catholicism actually contributed more to developing vodoun than to founding a strong Catholic faith in the profoundly religious Haitian people. Officially disowned by the Vatican since Dessalines's Constitution of 1805, Haitian presidents, including Dessalines, Christophe, and Pétion, had all attempted reconciliation, but the Holy See adamantly refused all their overtures. Only in 1860, when Protestant missionaries were boasting of large-scale conversions and the hated Freemasons were alarmingly active, did Rome relent. In the Concordat of 1860 it belatedly recognized Haiti and began the serious business of creating the infrastructure of an official church. It also began a campaign to stamp out vodoun.

Caught in the midst of this were millions of vodounist Haitian peasants, who responded to all attacks on vodoun with surprised resignation and never faltered in their profound commitment to its beliefs and practices. Seldom married, they lived in stable, often polygamous unions and raised large families, deeply attached to one another and to the rites of their ancestors. By mid-century vodoun was ineradicably impregnated in the Haitian psyche. The consequences this would have in the future were far-ranging, and after another century had elapsed the great Machiavellian François Duvalier would study vodoun with as much devotion as an *houngan,* and then twist and use it to keep an entire population at his pitiless mercy.

In a mid-century interlude a President unlike most of his mediocre predecessors ascended to power. General Lysius Salomon was not a great leader, but intelligent and capable, and his presidency represented Haiti's last chance to derail from the historical train of racism, wanton violence and bloodshed, corruption, and pitiless suppression of its millions of increasingly impoverished peasants.

Salomon failed, sabotaged by armed revolts and invasions, and the inexorable force of Haiti's sad history. Those who succeeded him merely rushed their country along the rails to ruin until the Americans invaded and, for nineteen years, braked the onslaught of history, which was refueled again in 1934 and reached full speed in mid-twentieth century under President-for-Life François Duvalier.

2 THE AMERICAN OCCUPATION

IN LATE OCTOBER 1887 THREE MEN SAT IN KAI TI-TOINE, A small rum shop on the banks of Grande-Rivière-du-Nord's swollen Vagabond River. As they drank they slapped down dominoes onto the rough table in front of them. Tiresias Antoine Augustin Simon Sam, tall, black, full-featured, with sensitive eyes, bore little family resemblance to his cousin Vilbrun Guillaume Sam, with his close-set eyes and the short-cropped hair that did not disguise his prominent ears. In politics, however, the Sams were as alike as twins, both antigovernment guerrilla, or *caco,* officers, forever engaged in sporadic warfare against the despised Port-au-Prince government in the South. Even now they were up in arms against President Salomon, though he was Tiresias's uncle by marriage, because of Salomon's recent reversal of a clause in the Constitution forbidding him to hold office for a second term.

Their companion this evening was close friend Alex Sonthonax, a successful jeweler. After a few shots of rum and a long game of dominoes, which Sonthonax won, the three men prepared to leave. They were going to a vodoun *cérémonie* at the temple, or peristyle, of a powerful *houngan* called Brave-Mich, and already they could hear the familiar staccato thrumming of ritual drums. When they arrived at the forest clearing near Brave-Mich's peristyle, the *cérémonie* was well under way, with the cornmeal ground drawings or *vèvès* smudged beyond recognition and several dancers already possessed by the spirits. In the center was Brave-Mich, surrounded by white-garmented assistants, or *hounsi,* and he paid no attention as the Sams and their friend joined them, dancing, chanting, and flailing their arms unselfconsciously as they surrendered themselves to the world of their gods.

Suddenly one of the *hounsi,* swaying and moaning gently, reached out and tugged at Tiresias's hand, bidding him halt, bidding him listen to the words the goddess Erzulie spoke through her.

"You are going to become very powerful," she told him, holding tight to his hand and staring at him with the glazed eyes of those the spirits possessed. "President, that's what it is. You are going to be President."

So saying she released him and turned toward Guillaume. She squeezed his hand for a minute, then spoke again. "You too will be President," she intoned in her monotonous whine, and Sonthonax saw Guillaume's startled expression. "But don't be in too much of a hurry," the *hounsi* warned, "for it won't last very long, and it won't be very good."

Hours later, drenched with sweat and grimy with the dust raised by scores of tireless dancers, Sonthonax and the Sams returned home. Dawn was breaking, and through the dappled shadows of the forest it was easy to find their way.

On the thirty-first of March 1896, Tiresias Antoine Augustin Simon Sam, by then a popular general in Haiti's confused and overstaffed army, became President, one week after his predecessor, Florvil Hippolyte, had suffered a fatal stroke while en route to stamp out a revolt in the Southwest. Nicknamed "The Incompetent," Sam ushered in the twentieth century at the head of a cynically corrupt and increasingly unpopular administration.

The worst offender was his Finance Minister and cousin Guillaume Sam, who enriched himself through a spectacular system of ordering nonexistent goods for which he received payment. President Sam himself, later convicted of fraud *in absentia,* showed his strong family feelings by allowing scores more of his relatives, including forty-eight who were deputies in the National Assembly, to plunder the national treasury.

As a result of this massive public peculation, debt piled upon debt, civil service salaries were cut by 20 percent, and public works stagnated while contractors remained unpaid. A few public works were undertaken, a new civil tribunal and a tramway system in Port-au-Prince, and the beginnings of a railway system including a railroad track Sam had run from his hometown of Grande-Rivière-du-Nord to Cap Haitien.

In 1902, his term of office ended, and in fear of his life, Sam resigned. On the thirteenth of May, dishonored and in national disgrace, he escaped murderous mobs as diplomats physically escorted him to the docks, where he set sail for Jamaica and thence for Europe.

Haiti's rush toward disaster now gained momentum, hurtling it along to the inevitable conclusion. After much confusion, Tiresias Sam was succeeded by Nord Alexis, an ancient black man from the North. On December 2, 1908, after a revolt by General Antoine Simon, the ninety-two-year-old Alexis fled for his life to Jamaica.

General Simon, a black man from the South, became Haiti's new President. On August 2, 1911, after a ferocious *caco* revolt led by black Cincinnatus Leconte, a descendant of the Emperor Dessalines, Simon too sailed for Jamaica.

President Leconte survived one year, coming to a terrible end when unknown assailants murdered him and hid his body. To cover their crime the conspirators placed explosives in the Presidential Palace, built by President Salomon, and at 3:30 a.m. on August 8, 1912, Haiti had neither President nor palace.

The new President, a Northern mulatto named Tancrede Auguste, died on May 2, 1913, a victim of severe anemia caused by advanced untreated syphilis, though most Haitians believed he was a victim of poison.

Four black presidents then ruled in rapid succession, each ousting his predecessor: Michel Oreste, Oreste Zamor, Davilmar Théodore, and Vilbrun Guillaume Sam, the eighth president since Tiresias had fled Haiti in 1902.

One American observer saw Haiti's ongoing tragedy as a game. His description also explains what many Americans thought about Haiti and why they had no qualms about invading and occupying it.

"These Haitian revolutions proceed habitually by fixed rules, somewhat like a game of checkers," wrote William Seabrook in *The Magic Island.*

The Protector of the Liberties of the People, with an increasingly augmented ragtag and bobtail army, marches southward, liberating various villages, and camping presently before the important commercial city of Gonaives, generally defended by a government army. The German and Syrian merchants of the town come out and beg the besiegers not to burn it. Once or twice, purely through mutual misunderstanding, a part of the city has been burned, but usually the matter is arranged without arson or bloodshed in a manner profitable to the new Protector of Liberties, and his troops receive their first pay.

Thence they march upon Saint Marc, which is connected with Port-au-Prince, the capital, by a railroad line. As they approach the Saint Marc railroad head, predictable events are also happening in Port-au-Prince. The minister of war calls on the president and says, "Excellency, this is awful."

"How awful?" asks His Excellency. "Well, perhaps with one hundred thousand dollars . . ." replies the minister of war. The minister of finance is called in. When they learn from him what government funds they can grab in a hurry, they vote it in a lump "to maintain the government." It may be as much as two hundred thousand dollars. Most of it they put aside privately for emergencies. A little of it is given to the army, which entrains northward. The generals of this defensive army, having received their pay in advance, put up a harmless demonstration, and retire to Port-au-Prince, announcing that all is lost.

At this point, as the liberators are clambering aboard trains at Saint Marc, it is customary for the president, the minister of war, and the minister of finance, taking with them the emergency funds, to sail for Jamaica.

When the Liberator of the people arrives, therefore, in Port-au-Prince, there is no argument. He finds the palace empty, swept, ready and waiting for his occupancy, and a few days later he is elected president. It is an almost iron-clad rule of the game that he mustn't loot or burn in Port-au-Prince. That wouldn't do at all.

And this, more or less, is the manner in which Guillaume Sam made himself president in March, 1915.

Sam was to be the last of the incompetent, ignorant, would-be autocrats. In fact, he was already notorious throughout Haiti for ordering the massacre of civilians in the mulatto-dominated town of Jacmel while commandant there. Had senile old President Nord Alexis not reprieved him, Sam would have died in prison at the perpetual hard labor a court-martial had sentenced him to.

A French diplomat elaborated further, describing Sam as "authoritarian, vindictive, pitiless towards foes, cruel to those whose existence, rightly or wrongly, he considered a menace to his own authority." And, like so many black presidents before him, Sam looked for enemies within the ranks of the mulatto elite. One of his first presidential acts was to charge scores of mulattoes with political dissidence and imprison them, garbed in humiliating striped sleeveless pajamas, in the miserable National Penitentiary not far from the palace. Then he summoned *caco* soldiers into the capital where they set up camp mere meters away.

As for the country, it too was in continual turmoil. It was hopelessly in debt, for foreign governments lent indiscriminately, enslaving Haiti with foolish debt, then mercilessly demanding repayment, which the impoverished and horribly mismanaged country could raise only by borrowing again. Cynical Germany made massive and usurious loans to revolutionaries who used the money to overthrow the incumbent President and install themselves in power. When the German loans fell due, the new President obligingly borrowed from France to repay them, and later American money repaid France.

American railway interests also claimed exorbitant sums for providing Haiti with a rudimentary and poorly built railroad system. Haiti's Banque Nationale, formed by its French, German, and American creditors to act as watchdog over their interests, was on the verge of failure. German and French gunboats, diverted from the war now being pursued in Europe, as yet without American involvement, had orders to function as muscled debt collectors.

But the magnet that really drew these European imperial powers toward small, struggling Haiti was not its debts, but its strategic position. The United States had already occupied Cuba in 1898 and in the same year acquired Puerto Rico, had taken Panama in 1903, had established a customs receivership in the Dominican Republic in 1905, had occupied Nicaragua in 1909, and planned the occupation of Haiti for purely strategic reasons at least a year before the actual intervention.

A November 1914 Navy Department "Plan for Landing and Occupying the City of Port-au-Prince," predicting the inevitable scenario, read:

Situation: The government has been overthrown; all semblance of law and order has ceased; the local authorities admit their inability to protect foreign interests, the city being overrun and in the hands of about 5,000 soldiers and civilian mobs.

For years before that, "in the name of humanity, morality, and civilization," Secretary of State Elihu Root had been monitoring Haiti and hoping the "psychological moment" would arise so the United States could establish "the right sort of relations."

Under the doomed Guillaume Sam, the psychological moment came all too soon. When it did, the right sort of relations were immediately established.

One mild spring afternoon, three brothers of a wealthy mulatto family stood chatting in front of their house on the Rue Lamarre. A group of horsemen drew up beside them, and with dismayed surprise the Polynice brothers recognized President Sam's chief of staff, General Charles Oscar Etienne, popularly known as Charles Oscar.

"You are plotting against the President," the general screeched, "assembling in public for the purpose of plotting destruction and havoc."

"You are sadly mistaken," one brother began, but drew himself up short as the soldiers waved menacing rifles in his direction.

"If I hear a shot anywhere," Charles Oscar finished his harangue, "a shot in the North, in the South, in the Artibonite, any shot at all, then you can be sure, you scum and you scoundrels, that the first thing I'll do will be to arrest you!"

Three days later, in the North, a determined pack of ragged *cacos* led by would-be President Dr. Rosalvo Bobo attacked and occupied Cap Haitien. When news arrived of this incident, merely one in scores, General Charles Oscar ordered the arrest of the Polynice brothers. In the National Penitentiary in downtown Port-au-Prince they joined 164 other political prisoners, including former president Zamor, who had returned home from unhappy exile, and many Northern rebels who in time-honored Haitian tradition had been forced to walk the 170 miles to the penitentiary.

On July 26 a reckless band of Dr. Bobo's insurgents attacked the palace itself. With difficulty the army repulsed them, and afterward an infuriated Sam ordered his general to "do the necessary." Charles Oscar decided this meant to execute all political prisoners, and he rode over to the National Penitentiary and gave the order. To the wails and cries of men being slaughtered, Charles Oscar stood and watched the shooting, stabbing, disembowelment, and dismemberment of 167 helpless men.

Meanwhile the Port-au-Prince masses decided to liberate the prisoners. Led by Bobo's men, they stormed the penitentiary, only to discover that it had become a charnel house. Then, as they stood nauseated and gagging, two men inched and wriggled their way from under the heap of bloody and unmoving bodies and gasped out their story. The crowd saw and heard, then in collective fury marched through the city after their President.

As they attacked the palace, President Sam scraped a hole in the plaster wall separating it from the French Legation. He pushed his pregnant wife, Lucie Parisien, through, and their five children, then threw them all on the mercy and diplomatic immunity of the French, who separated Sam from his family and hid him in a bathroom. During the attack on the palace he had taken a piece of mortar in the buttock, and in his bathroom hideout he cleaned and dressed the wound with chloroform and gauze.

Morning came, and with it a mob howling for Sam's head. A delegation of four bourgeois gentlemen knocked and according to Seabrook held the following dialogue with the ambassador:

> "He is no longer here," lied the ambassador transparently.
>
> "Sir, we believe you; your word is enough for us, but unfortunately it will not suffice for the populace. It is better that we should enter discreetly and verify the fact than they should enter to search," the mulattoes replied gravely.
>
> "I must warn you," said the ambassador, "that either course would be equally a violation, which I am compelled by law and duty to forbid."
>
> "We regret it," said the gentlemen.
>
> "Unfortunately," said the ambassador, betraying Sam, "I have not the armed force at my command to prevent you."

Inside the legation they nearly missed him. They did not see the door; the bedstead had been cunningly placed against it. But one of the men, and then more than one, could smell the strong odor of disinfectant. They sniffed, then followed their noses and discovered the door.

A minute later their livid President stood before them, arms crossed imperiously across his chest, and shouted at them in the shrill tones of terror, "What do you want?"

As they led him down the staircase to the waiting crowd, Sam suddenly gripped the wooden railing. After a minute one of his captors bludgeoned his wrists with his gold-headed walking cane, breaking both of Sam's arms. Outside they quickly disposed of their prisoner, lifting him up and hurling him over the gate so they would not see what happened next. It was slow murder, as the avenging Haitian mob seized their President and hacked him to death with knives and sharpened sticks and savage bare hands, dismembering him. Only then did they leave the legation, scattering his pieces far and wide over the city. His head was paraded on a spike for the edification of passersby.

Over at the Dominican Legation, General Charles Oscar was also dying. Edmond Polynice, whose three sons had died the day before, did for Sam's general what the crowd was doing for Sam. Dressed formally in long-tailed suit and lemon-yellow silk gloves, the elegant little man pinned on his red Legion of Honor ribbon, slipped a revolver into his pocket, knocked at the door of the Dominican Legation, and sent in his calling card to Charles Oscar. The general, cruel but courageous, met him in the drawing room. Polynice shot him three times through the heart, once for each of his murdered sons.

Charles Oscar was dead, and so was the President whose demise he had helped precipitate. But Sam had been warned. "Don't be in too much of a hurry," the possessed *hounsi* had told him, "for it won't last very long, and it won't be very good." Sam's presidency had lasted only four months.

The President was dead. The men who had butchered him now raised bloody fists in support of Dr. Rosalvo Bobo, the brilliant but unbalanced doctor from the North. Bobo acknowledged their cheers and proceeded to subdue those few in the capital who had not hailed him as their next President. The filthy, reeking streets swarmed with *caco* soldiers, distinguishable from the mass of other ragged barefoot Haitians only by the red patch sewn on to whatever they wore. And in Port-au-Prince Harbor, Rear Admiral William Caperton of the United States Navy ordered five companies of Marines and sailors into the capital. The American occupation of Haiti had begun.

It solved none of the terrible problems that had brought Haiti to such a humiliating impasse. The occupying Americans unwittingly redefined and honed the racism at the core of the Haitian psyche. But in Haiti the permanent quarrel was between black and mulatto, for whites were mere transients. And when they left the mulattoes were once again in firm control. *Noiristes* nursed on the breast of American racism, but in full maturity they turned instead against the mulattoes, whose class again dominated their world.

The first 350 Americans to land were white, and so were all those thousands who followed. Many were Southerners, and extrapolated from Jim Crow experiences at home to new encounters with Haiti's dark people. "Never trust a nigger with a gun," was one cardinal tenet, and the Marines spent their first nights in sleepless watch for *cacos*, ready at a second's notice to fire.

They dreaded the nights broken by the throb of vodoun drums and the thin eerie wails of conch shells blown like nature's shrill trumpets. The Marines began a campaign to eradicate from the countryside every vestige of the traditional religion of this profoundly religious people, and to punish and imprison those who practiced it.

"It hurt, It stunk, Fairyland had turned into a pigstye," wrote one young Marine of the Haitian version of tropical paradise. "More than that, we were not welcome. We could feel it as distinctly as we could smell the rot along the gutters. . . . In the street were piles of evil-smelling offal. The stench hung over everything. Piles of mango seeds were heaped in the middle of the highway, sour-smelling. It was not merely that these, mingled with banana peels and other garbage, were rotting—the whole prospect was filthy."

So to the Marines were the people who inhabited latrine-scented Port-au-Prince and the provinces. In reams of unabashedly racist letters and reports they described Haitians as "coons," "niggers," and "apes." Physically the small, hungry Haitians compared favorably with the "corpulent mammies" and "strapping bucks" of the United States, except for their very dark skin, which provoked constant comment. They were "so black that the darkest resident of Harlem's black belt would be suspected there of being a white man," reminisced a Marine captain in *National Geographic*. His own "Number One Boy," Destiné, "my first venture in black ivory" and "the sort of tropical servant . . . who make the White Man's Burden bearable," was "short, slim, jet-black, with a nose like a squashed tomato and lips so thick they gave him the appearance of having a bill like a duck."

Colonel Littleton T. Waller voiced another important concern: "What the people of Norfolk and Portsmouth would say if they saw me bowing and scraping to these coons—I do not know—" he confessed to a friend. A leading American civilian official, picking at his meal during a formal luncheon because he was mesmerized by the stout Haitian Agriculture Minister, had similar thoughts. "I couldn't help saying to myself that that man would have brought $1,500 at auction in New Orleans in 1860 for stud purposes," he later recounted to a highly amused Franklin Delano Roosevelt, who preserved the story for posterity by repeating it.

"The Americans have taught us many things," *Le Nouvelliste* newspaper owner Ernest Chauvet told author Seabrook. "Among other things they have taught us that we are niggers. You see, we really didn't know that before. We thought we were negroes."

When all-white wives arrived to join their Marine Corps husbands in 1916, tensions increased. Now squeamish white women shrank away from gallant Haitian embraces, refused polite invitations to dance, and, in general, snubbed, wounded, and humiliated the Haitians they met. "Let me tell you a real joke," said Ernest Chauvet to Seabrook. "On this entire island there are perhaps eight or a dozen American women who meet our Haitian elite without contempt or patronage, and these same eight or a dozen are perhaps the only American women on the island who, when they return to their native America, are at home in their own high society, Newport, Bar Harbor, Park Avenue, yachts in the Sound, boxes at the opera, snapshots in the rotogravure sections, and prize pups at the Madison Square Garden."

Elite Haitians grew increasingly repelled as the incidents of vulgarity multiplied. Drunken Americans were a common spectacle in alcohol-restrained Haiti. Whoring, traditionally confined to seduction of hapless black servants, now went public in 147 new dancing halls and saloons mainly staffed by the light-skinned Dominican girls the Americans preferred. Jim Crow hotels sprang up, segregated Catholic masses, residential white ghettoes.

Politically this was also true, and though the Americans insisted on the semblance of democracy, they refused even the slightest democratic substance. Nowhere was this more obvious than in the American-sponsored Haitian presidential "elections." The State Department approved the first occupation President Philippe Sudre Dartiguenave after he agreed to surrender financial control and receivership of the customs, Haiti's sole source of revenue, asking in return only for Marine protection against assassins. He was the sole candidate; his rival, Dr. Rosalvo Bobo, had earlier disqualified himself with fits of irascibility.

On August 12, 1915, under Marine protection, Dartiguenave was elected by cowed members of the National Assembly. "The things we were forced to do in Haiti was a bitter pill for me," Daniels later admitted, "for I have always hated any foreign policy that even hinted of imperialistic control." For the nineteen years of the occupation,

Dartiguenave's "election" was typical of American-imposed "democracy."

Dartiguenave's lackey government faltered so badly that only the immediate imposition of martial law and press censorship salvaged it. After Colonel Waller succeeded Admiral Caperton in 1916, little changed. With his colleague Major Smedley D. Butler, whose name in Nicaragua had become synonymous with the bogeyman, Waller carved American occupation policy into Haiti by brute force.

The recalcitrant deputies in the National Assembly were ruthlessly disposed of. After they had drafted an anti-American Constitution, the Americans simply dissolved the Assembly. Afterward, quickly, they imposed their own Constitution, about which Roosevelt later boasted, "The facts are that I wrote Haiti's Constitution myself, and if I do say so, I think it's a pretty good Constitution." In a June 1918 plebiscite, when François Duvalier was eleven years old, intimidated Haitian electors approved this imported Constitution by 98,225 to 768, with 67 out of 96 polling places reporting only yes votes.

This cynical move to completely dominate Haiti's government was coupled with an all-out campaign against vodoun, known to inspire Haitians to revolt. The Americans also disliked vodoun's trappings of ritual drumming and melancholy blasts of the conch shell, and they repeated and believed terrifying tales of human sacrifice, ritual murder of children, and blood drunk from human skulls. Orders were issued, and throughout Haiti troops guided by the telltale drumming rushed to *cérémonies,* where they smashed or confiscated sacred drums and other objects, drove away the worshipers, and arrested and imprisoned *houngans,* priestesses or *mambos,* and their acolytes.

Despite the persecution, vodoun was not eradicated, merely driven underground. Drums were muffled, guards posted, traditional teachings kept alive clandestinely.

Haitians reacted with outright violence when Waller decided to fight endless guerrilla warfare and military transportation problems by building roads in the virtually roadless—and carless—nation. To this end he revitalized an old forced-labor law called the *corvée* and applied it mercilessly.

The *corvée* provoked more unrest than any other single incident under the occupation. Roped together like slaves, underfed and brutally overworked, the *corvée* laborers worked under overseers who gunned down any man who attempted escape. Ultimately the *corvée* sparked revolts leading to all-out war, and in the Cacos Wars of 1918–22, occupation forces killed thousands of Haitians who resisted with more bravado than skill. The wars also created a martyr out of *caco* rebel leader Charlemagne Péralte, murdered when two Marines blackened their faces, infiltrated his camp and shot him, then paraded him victoriously on a crucifix-like structure exactly like a slain Haitian Christ.

Charlemagne Péralte was dead, but world-famous painter Philomène Obin immortalized him in *The Funeral of Charlemagne Péralte*, in which no fewer than 750 mourners are depicted. Bit by bit there rose up a legion of words and ideas—and images—which motivated and mobilized far more Haitians than Péralte or any single *houngan* ever could. Black intellectuals, galvanized into expression, articulated new notions of Haitian national identity in which Africa, not Europe, was paramount.

"All people instinctively go back to the past in order to search in their history for lessons of collective patriotism, for new rules of conduct, whether it be for the purpose of being able better to defend their threatened existence, or for recovering more rapidly from their fall," wrote one. Suddenly the Creole language, the vodoun religion, Haitian customs and traditions, even their dark skin, assumed new significance. Ethnology won scores of fanatic converts, and the search for understanding Haiti's roots had begun.

In the 1930s and 1940s blacks discovered unexpected allies in the many mulatto intellectuals who, shattered by their personal encounters with crude white racism, also sought meaning in their diluted African ancestry. At the same time a passionate national debate began about the role and shameful track record of the elite that had allowed this occupation to happen—and even welcomed it. Dr. Jean Price-Mars led the debate, and in his condemnation of the irresponsible selfish elite, he converted some thoughtful mulattoes as well as blacks, from whose ranks he had sprung.

In belittling Africa and aping Europe, the elite had betrayed Haiti's millions. No more! declared the new nationalists. Internal racism must die, and favored Haitians must work with and on behalf of the suffering masses. But the first task was to rid Haiti of the invader. "Man, you are a stranger and you tread the soil that my father trod," wrote fiery mulatto writer Jacques Roumain.

Roumain and dozens of other nationalist writers were arrested time and time again, condemned by American courts-martial and sentenced to fines, imprisonment, and even hard labor. The result was a politicization of intellectuals, driven by persecution from poetry to pragmatic action. Roumain founded the Haitian Communist Party. Price-Mars and future nationalist President Sténio Vincent formed the Patriotic Union, attracting a membership of sixteen thousand that organized resistance to the occupation.

The shame of the occupation penetrated to the core of Haiti's proud elite. Lamented a well-traveled mulatto cited by Emily Balch in *Occupied Haiti*:

> Although foreign domination is never a good thing, medicine teaches us that painful operations sometimes effect a cure. The American invasion might have been a good thing if, although unjust and even infringing for a time upon our independence, it had been temporary and had led ultimately to the reign of justice and liberty. But such is not the case. The Americans have not even this excuse. They have made themselves the allies of the evil past of oppression and tyranny; they have abolished liberty, justice, independence; they are bad administrators of public funds; they offer a peace of degradation and subjection, shame and dishonor. They push forward like the rising tide; they attack our traditions, our soul. Is it not claimed that they want to change our culture, our religion?
>
> Even the good that they do turns to our hurt, for instead of teaching us, they do it to prove that we are incapable. They are exploiters. How can they teach us when they have so much to learn themselves?

One old black peasant told Seabrook that he saw the occupation very differently.

> Ten years ago this country was full of *cacos* (bandits) and there were no roads. The *cacos* often robbed and murdered us. Our own government tax-gatherers often robbed and starved us, then gave us nothing in return. It was hardly worth while to plant. It took four days on a donkey to go down to the city. And if we weren't killed by *cacos* or drowned fording streams, when we did reach the city we were con-

scripted to fight for the government, or on one side or the other of some new revolution which was going to make things better and never did. Now the bandits are all gone, there is no more revolution, I live in peace, I plant all I can, I pay a reasonable tax, I go to the city in the motor bus in four hours, and I am not conscripted, and while I am away, my wife, my children, my ears of corn, and my little goats are safe as if they were all in the arms of Jesus. . . .

And to young medical student François Duvalier, the occupation and the white man's treatment of his black compatriots had yet other connotations:

I then recalled the route traversed by my ancestors of far-off Africa—

The sons of the jungle
Whose bones during "the centuries of starry silence"
Have helped to create the pyramids.
And I continued on my way, this time with heavy heart,
In the night.
I walked on and on and on
Straight ahead.
And the black of my ebony skin was lost
In the shadows of the night.

By 1922 widespread hostility to puppet President Dartiguenave forced the Americans to change the government's face though not its orientation. In another show of "democracy" the National Assembly elected mulatto Louis Borno, unabashedly pro-American and convinced that the occupation would modernize Haiti. Borno was at least as unpopular as Dartiguenave, and another decade of Haitians grew up in hatred. "We were children when the Americans arrived in Haiti," wrote one nationalist friend of François Duvalier, "and we grew up enraged in the presence of a flag that symbolized a military occupation."

Toward the end of Borno's presidency another group of young intellectuals formed. Known at first as the "Three D's," François Duvalier and Lorimer Denis soon lost Louis Diaquoi to premature death. Denis was a lawyer and journalist. His best friend, Duvalier, was a medical student with a passion for ethnology. By 1932, mature and confident, Denis and Duvalier assumed the name *Griots,* African magicians and storytellers, and in a series of forceful essays analyzing a broad range of Haitian realities and history won a wide and often fanatical following.

Haitian intellectual giant Jean Price-Mars was the *Griots'* idol, and from his writings they extrapolated their own revolutionary theory. Black-oriented almost to the point of obsession, they hailed African values, Pan-Africanism, and embraced *noirisme,* including its claims of special black sensitivity and artistic temperament inherited from African forefathers. They eulogized vodoun and condemned Christianity and its racist Catholic priests as agents of imperialism. They also bitterly censured the irresponsible, self-seeking elite and called for a revolutionary transfer of power to authentic spokesmen for the black masses. Before the Americans left his country, and two decades before he began his own occupation, the blueprint for Duvalier's political ideology had already been neatly articulated.

Duvalier's distant cousin Clovis Désinor was a *noiriste* convert from his earliest teens. So poor that he lived entirely on the goodwill of his classmates at the Lycée Pétion, Duvalier's alma mater, Clovis read voraciously whatever books he could borrow. When he was only fourteen, and ridiculous in his outgrown trousers and shirts, the older Duvalier honored Clovis by permitting him to join his small circle of intellectuals, who spent hours discussing politics, history, and ethnology and in their spare time wrote for *Les Griots.* Clovis was especially flattered because Duvalier was in medical school, and with his tailored suits and old-fashioned manners, seemed utterly worldly and brilliant.

Not everyone saw Duvalier from Clovis's awed perspective. A pretty mulatto, Marcelle Hakime, met François Duvalier when she entered the medical school as its sole—and first—woman student. Duvalier was already in the third year. The friendship that sprang up between them was casual and proper. Marcelle was aware of François' *noiriste* views, but she ignored them as he too appeared to do in his personal relationships, which included several close mulatto friends.

Marcelle liked Duvalier well enough but pitied him even more. Though he had a reputation for great intelligence, he was a mediocre student, so absorbed by his other interests that he studied only enough to pass. He also came from a very different background than most in the predominantly mulatto faculty, and Marcelle guessed that he suffered serious financial pressures.

For his part Duvalier never mentioned the relentless insecurity. His father, Duval, earned a pittance as a justice of the peace, and François had been raised in the classic struggle of the black middle class to maintain genteel poverty and not slide into the savage squalor that surrounded them. Duval had managed to send François to the excellent Lycée Pétion, and now thanks to the American occupation, with its generous program for medical students, François was able to realize his childhood dream of becoming a doctor.

For Marcelle, who was to become Haiti's first woman dentist, school was a haven. But for the impecunious and preoccupied François Duvalier, she suspected, the medical school and its lifestyle had a very different meaning.

Duvalier's career in medical school paralleled the grand finale of the occupation, and climaxed in his graduation, and Haiti's liberation. In his second year he had joined the nationwide student strike against educational policies. The Americans had responded harshly, reimposing a curfew and martial law.

Then on December 6, 1929, the situation turned critical. To cow the population of the town of Cayes, the Marines dropped bombs in the harbor. Instead, the explosion triggered fury and hatred, and sent mobs of stone-hurling peasants to attack the Marines. Massacre ensued, with at least two dozen Haitians killed and scores wounded when the Marines fired on them.

As Haitians united in national mourning, the Americans exonerated the Marines, even decorating their detachment commandant for his "commendable courage and forbearance." Stateside, however, the massacre and the student-turned-general strikes of 1929 precipitated plans for withdrawal from Haiti. The Hoover administration also decided to dump Borno, kept in power only by Marine guns. Accordingly, a fair election was permitted in the National Assembly, and in November 1930 the deputies voted for nationalist Sténio Vincent against the pro-American, pro-Borno, and moderate candidates.

Soon afterward martial law ended. The Hoover administration, its political conscience salved, next attacked the thorny financial questions that remained the sole obstacle to physical withdrawal of the Marines. Vincent, frantic to be rid of them, cooperated fully and signed an agreement allowing American supervision of Haiti's fiscal operations until 1952. On August 21, 1934, a month after Dr. François Duvalier received his medical diploma, the Stars and Stripes were lowered all over Haiti, President Vincent referred to himself as "Haiti's Second Liberator," and the Marines sailed away. After nineteen humiliating years, the American occupation of Haiti had ended.

The occupation had many important effects on Haiti, some of them more lasting than others. Tourists began to arrive. The Americans built one thousand miles of roads for the three thousand vehicles that had arrived under their administration and linked the country through provincial airfields. Port-au-Prince and Cap Haitien enjoyed automated telephone exchanges, and in 1927 the country's first radio station opened. Medical facilities mushroomed, with 147 clinics and fifteen hospitals being built. The most famous of these was the Maternity Hospital for Marine Wives, located in the private home of President Sam's relatives and later transformed into the Hotel Oloffson. And the *gourde*, Haiti's monetary unit pegged at twenty cents to the U.S. dollar, enjoyed a stability unusual in Latin America.

Unfortunately, few of these concrete achievements survived the American withdrawal. The problem was that they were superimposed on Haiti, whose infrastructure remained virtually unchanged and unable to cope once the Americans were gone.

A significant and more permanent change was made in the army. Before 1915, swollen, over-officered (with more than three hundred generals and fifty colonels), and dangerously political, the new military or Garde D'Haiti was stripped down, highly trained, and efficient. It was also a political instrument that would in future make and break presidents until Duvalier found a way to subordinate it to his will.

Another change was that the mulatto elite was once again firmly entrenched in power. At the same time, however, the occupation had also promoted the development of *noirisme*, the black-oriented political thought and scholarship that formed an entire generation of intellectuals. In 1934, as the roar of celebration penetrated even the spartan wards of Port-au-Prince's St. François de Sales Hospital, where he was a resident, the occupation forces left Haiti, and the Black Republic once again resumed her own way of life.

3 PAPA DOC COMES TO POWER

THE AMERICAN OCCUPATION HAD DESTROYED HAITI'S ferocious national pride in its military prowess. Even rebel *caco* leader Dr. Rosalvo Bobo had eagerly welcomed the Marines—until he realized they were not going to make him President Sam's successor.

The American occupation, in a word, challenged Haitian history. The Haitians, defeated and humble, created new legends of men like Charlemagne Péralte. Ephemeral though his real influence was, Péralte became a symbol, his name evoked as a rallying point for anti-American defiance.

The Americans left on July 28, 1934, and in wild nationalistic over-reaction, Haitians celebrated both Sténio Vincent's election and the American withdrawal that followed it as proof that they again controlled their collective destiny. But three years later an event occurred that shocked the outside world and laid to rest forever the myth of Haiti's national force. This was the Dominican Vespers, a massacre and shame of such stupendous dimension that it has still not been assimilated into the national psyche.

For rural Haitians, the vast majority, the American occupation had had little relevance. They appreciated the scattering of clinics and the abatement of *caco* banditry, but little else had changed for them, and hundreds of thousands chose to migrate to the richer worlds of their Caribbean neighbors. There, under the broiling sun of the unshaded cane fields, they wielded their machetes and cut cane.

In 1937 Cuban dictator Fulgencio Batista abruptly expelled the Haitian cane cutters. Desperate, they invaded the cane fields, or *bateys,* of the Dominican Republic. But upward of 100,000 Haitians had already settled there, and to the Dominican dictator Rafael Leonidas Trujillo, this latest onslaught was intolerable.

Despite, or perhaps because of, his black Haitian grandmother, Trujillo hated the "despised Negro aliens whose vodoun, cattle rustling, and presence on Dominican soil was the ruin of a good life for Dominicans." Trujillo's antidote was to begin bloodletting, and the rivers of blood that flowed were Haitian.

In a massacre unparalleled in the Caribbean or North America, the Dominican National Police and Army rounded up Haitian men, women, and children and systematically slaughtered them. The Dominican Vespers began on October 2 and lasted three days. Few bullets were used. Instead, twenty to thirty thousand Haitians were bludgeoned and bayoneted, then herded into the sea, where sharks finished what Trujillo had begun. Thousands more, fleeing across the ironically named Massacre River, were cut down in midstream by pursuing Dominicans. A few thousand escaped to die or recover on the mud floors of huts and improvised aid stations at Ouanaminthe on the Haitian side of the Massacre. Four hundred made it to a Cap Haitien hospital where American journalist Quentin Reynolds interviewed them, preserving the horror for history.

The Dominican Vespers confirmed that without the Americans, Haiti was at the mercy of her neighbors, even the little neighboring republic. From then on, Haitian sword rattling could never be more than an internal affair. In foreign relations, other strategies had to be devised.

The Vespers also rammed home another lesson. As Dr. Jean Price-Mars had already showed, the Haitian elite cared nothing for the masses. In the Dominican Vespers Haiti's pitiless leaders saw not a tragedy but a commodity they could sell: 30,000 murdered Haitians. Decades later President François Duvalier would refine this concept, and his son perfect it, selling not the nation's dead but its poor. Under Jean-Claude Duvalier, people's wretchedness was his government's most enduring and salable commodity, and one that, like well-mulched crops, yearly produced the foreign aid he routinely plundered.

Were the Vespers merely a deadly racist plot by light-skinned Dominicans and Haitians to dispose of unwanted blacks? Or were Trujillo and his henchmen avenging their own ancestors, cut down by Henri Christophe's men in Santo Domingo on February 25, 1805?

Whether or not 1937 was Trujillo's answer to Christophe, it was an indulgence that cost him very little—$525,000 in cash. The settling of the account was swift and breathtakingly cynical. It also indicates that Price-Mars's Haitian-Dominican conspiracy theory was well founded. At first, news of the Vespers was concealed. Then, after a horrified world press certified and described them, Sténio Vincent officially exonerated his cousin Trujillo of any complicity, denounced the newspaper reports, and congratulated Trujillo on his "searching investigation" into the matter. Finally, the blameless Dominicans agreed to pay $750,000 in compensation for the dead Haitians, haggled down to $525,000 in American small bills. This was immediately grabbed by Haitian officials, and nothing was left for the heirs of the wretched victims.

Consistent with Price-Mars's analysis of their irresponsibility, the elite failed to denounce the transaction. A British ambassador blamed their apathy on "the contempt in which the educated Haytian holds the peasant, whom he regards as belonging to a race apart, and with whom he has little real sympathy." Millions of blacks did not share their elite's complacency about the murders. In villages everywhere *rescapés*—those who escaped—told their terrible tales. Recently and magnificently, so did Haitian novelist Edwidge Danticat in *The Farming of Bones*. But the *rescapés* were as powerless as their audiences, and the Dominican Vespers, unavenged, went into Haiti's history as a shame too great to dwell on.

On December 24, 1939, hundreds of miles and two years away from the massacre of downtrodden blacks, young Dr. François Duvalier married Simone Ovide. Duvalier, now thirty-two, was barely surviving professionally. He was shy, pedantic, poor, and black. He still devoted more time to writing for the *Griots* weekly journal than to medicine. He had been refused as an army doctor because of his poor eyesight, and he scraped by on a small salary as medical consultant at the Emilie Séguineau Clinic, an old-age home.

Duvalier had been in no rush to marry, and not merely because of his poverty. The private sorrows of his own family life were restraint enough. Though he seldom spoke of it, Duvalier had been raised by his aunt, Madame Florestal, rather than his mother, Uritia Abraham, and despite the love lavished on him by his father, Duval, he had been deeply resentful and ashamed that his mother was a madwoman, locked away from prying eyes until she died when he was fourteen, and that even as a small boy he had not been allowed to mention her.

Simone Ovide, his wife-to-be, was as rational as his mother was not, and Duvalier's fears melted away. Simone too came from humble stock, the unwanted, unexpected consequence of mulatto businessman Louis Fame's sexual tryst with Clélie Ovide, a pretty, illiterate domestic servant. As a child Simone had been buried in a special kind of orphanage, raised and educated in a manner that acknowledged her light skin as much as her illegitimacy. But with her adoring mother she was plunged into the world of her people, especially into vodoun, for Clélie was a fanatic believer, and despite Simone's veneer of bourgeois sophistication, she too was devoted to the ways of her gods.

When Duvalier met her, Simone was a painfully thin, exotically pretty nurse, with high, sculptured cheekbones, a shy demeanor, and such a look of fragility that she seemed tiny even next to the shorter Duvalier. He was also attracted to the depth of her beliefs, the ethnologist enamored of his subject. What Duvalier analyzed, Simone believed. They were in all ways the perfect couple, and so, in Pétionville's elegant Church of St. Peter, the poor doctor married the even poorer nurse and began the Duvalier dynasty.

In 1941 Sténio Vincent announced that "ill health" prevented him from seeking reelection. Seven years after celebrating the end of the American occupation, disillusioned Haitians now cheered the departure of Vincent, the "Second Liberator" turned dictator. Vincent routinely jailed opposition journalists and politicians and established a secret police to monitor his people and their mail. He accepted money from Trujillo and he and his officials siphoned money from government funds. It was time for a change.

On May 15, 1941, the Haitian legislature elected Elie Lescot to succeed Vincent. He was Trujillo's personal choice, and also the Americans'. American ambassador John Campbell White wryly described the proceedings: "The voting was done on little scraps of paper which were put into two urns, one of the urns being emptied into the other. One Senator and one Deputy read them out and then the ballots were passed around for scrutiny by a sort of Committee of Control. One ballot was reported blank and another contained a vote for President Vincent. All the remaining 56 were for Lescot, his name being inscribed in various forms—sometimes the bare name, and sometimes there were appropriate sentiments, in one case, I believe, a short poem."

As President, Lescot's first act was to accompany Vincent to the gangplank of the ship that carried him off into two years of prudent exile, so hated had he become. His next step was to name himself "Commander in Chief of the Armed Forces" and personally assume command of the Presidential Guard and the Port-au-Prince police. By December 1941, Lescot was firmly in control of the crucial military and made the immensely politic move of declaring war on Japan, Germany, and the Axis, five hours before the U.S. did.

In Germany, Hitler was furious. "Where is it, this Haiti?" he reportedly demanded. When finally an officer located it on a map, Hitler peered, then snarled, "Haiti? When the war is over, I swear I'll turn Haiti into my stables."

The effect on the United States was more positive, and harking back to Savannah, Lescot offered his American "allies" twenty thousand Haitian troops and fifty thousand farm laborers. The U.S. declined the offer, but because Haiti remained in a state of war, however theoretically, he ordered the Constitution suspended for the duration and then set off for Washington to indulge in war talks.

A German U-boat sank his luggage on the return voyage, but otherwise Lescot's mission was wildly successful. The U.S. agreed to buy all Haiti's cotton and sisal, even though the latter supplanted primary food production, and the *gourde* was strengthened. Militarily the news was even better, with five U.S. Coast Guard antisubmarine patrol boats, field artillery, and six Douglas O-38s sent to Haiti.

Secure in power, Lescot next turned to consolidating his position. He jailed Haiti's wealthy German and Italian merchants and confiscated their assets, including their businesses. Since the Germans dominated the lucrative coffee and cotton export trades, the spoils were enormous, and the political friends to whom Lescot distributed them were duly grateful.

An anti-populist mulatto, he lent his support to the Catholic Church's ongoing anti-vodoun campaign, begun even before his presidency. The fanatically anti-vodoun Bishop of Gonaives, Monsignor Påul Robert, spearheaded the project. On Sundays he preached bitter sermons against vodoun, equating it with Satanism. On weekdays he and fervent disciples invaded peristyles, smashing the sacred rattles or *assons*, which summon the gods, and destroying drums, drinking vessels, pots where spirits lived, and any other artifacts of worship.

Despite extravagant claims of success, the Catholic Church failed miserably to obliterate Haiti's traditional beliefs, just as they failed to stamp out encroaching Protestantism, by then claiming 5 percent of the population and daily converting more. Millions of black Catholics reacted bitterly to white European priests demanding they renounce all they held dear, sacred, and self-evident. Hundreds of thousands more, prosperous mulattoes and blacks, heard with resentment these same white men accuse them of secretly practicing vodoun—even though most of them did.

The defeat of the anti-vodoun vendetta came on February 22, 1942, when unknown assailants riddled a Catholic church with gunfire as its priest celebrated an anti-vodoun mass. The message was typically Haitian, and the Church-Lescot alliance conceded defeat. Haiti, land of vodoun, would remain vodounesque.

During this frenetic anti-vodoun campaign, *noiriste* Dr. François Duvalier immersed himself in the traditional beliefs. "Vodoun," he wrote, "elaborated on the soil of Africa whose anguished mystery it reflects, also expresses overwhelmingly the conscience of a race as it confronts the enigmas of this world."

In the present it perpetuated the African past. In the past it had inspired the slaves to such an indomitable pitch that it effectively caused Haiti's independence. From this it was only a short step for Duvalier to extrapolate to the future, and to what vodoun could do for him.

In 1943 Duvalier's life changed. The Inter-American Affairs Commission sent Dr. James Dwindle to Haiti to direct a massive medical campaign against yaws, the crippling tropical disease affecting three-quarters of all Haitians. Highly contagious, yaws enters the body in the form of a spirochete through the bare soles. Left untreated, it eats away at its victims. Their limbs wither and deform, they suffer great purulent ulcerations all over their bodies, and they lose their noses and lips just as lepers do. Also like lepers, they were often driven off with stones by un-afflicted neighbors.

Dr. Dwindle arrived and began interviewing Haitian medical personnel. François Duvalier spoke heavily accented but understandable English, and largely on that basis Dwindle hired him to direct the Rural Clinic of Gressier, fifteen miles southwest of Port-au-Prince, the most yaws-ridden area of Haiti. Duvalier was temporarily diverted from his obsession with vodoun into an obsession with the wondrous properties of penicillin. He put aside ethnology for medicine, and various international medical journals published the results of his research.

The anti-yaws campaign orchestrated through the Gressier clinic finally succeeded in ridding Haiti of the dread disease, and in transforming the shy scholarly myopic little Duvalier into the great country doctor. By June more than one thousand daily rode their mules down mountain tracks or hobbled on decaying feet along dusty village paths to the clinic where they were finally cured. A second clinic in Cayes-Jacmel was also overrun. The commission decided to establish nationwide mobile clinics, and in preparation sent twenty doctors for two semesters of training in public health medicine at the University of Michigan. Duvalier was among them, and at war's end he spent an academic year in Michigan. His shaky English sabotaged him and he failed his courses.

Duvalier returned to Haiti and its yaws. To the Americans he was reserved and unimposing. To hundreds of thousands of his Haitian patients he was Papa Doc, the bookish young doctor who lived and moved freely among his people, sharing and saving their lives.

While Duvalier cured in the hinterland, in Port-au-Prince politics President Elie Lescot had overstepped the outer limits of corrupt autocratic government. An unbeatable coalition formed against him—Trujillo, the U.S., and a majority of Haitians. In a pamphlet he distributed to the signing members of the United Nations, Trujillo outlined his correspondence with the Haitian dictator, revealing corruption and compromise on scales amounting to treason. The U.S. leaked word that it would support a military coup against Lescot. And by the hundreds of thousands Haitians both rich and poor expressed outrage and joined in a national strike against him.

Lescot responded furiously. "The most drastic measures will be taken to reestablish order," he thundered on Haiti-wide radio. To no avail, and days later Lescot was deposed, a three-man military junta replacing him until his successor could be elected.

Lescot's successor was Dumarsais Estimé, a *noiriste* whose slogan was the catchy *"Un noir au pouvoir"* ("A black man in power"). After decades of white then mulatto domination, Haitians responded wholeheartedly to his real efforts to improve their lot. He increased the daily minimum wage from thirty to seventy cents, and more workers earned this munificent salary because Estimé also succeeded in encouraging local businesses to expand and foreign investors to come. Men found work clearing sixty acres of hideous Port-au-Prince slum, then building Estimé's International Fair on the site, and the boat- and planeloads of curious tourists who visited it spent easy money and provided yet more jobs.

Apart from a few well-qualified mulattoes—very few, for he despised them—Estimé relied on blacks such as his Under Secretary for Labor, Dr. François "Papa Doc" Duvalier, later Public Health and Labor Minister. But it didn't last. Blacks in power were no less corrupt and greedy than mulattoes. The old hatreds between blacks and mulattoes resurfaced stronger than ever, and the mulattoes found an ally in black Colonel Paul Magloire, who saw in their power and money the means to grab power away from Estimé. He masterminded an army coup, retired from the army, and on October 8, 1950, ran and won the general presidential elections.

Estimé's ouster was a turning point in François Duvalier's life and politicized him as nothing else had done. It also created in the phlegmatic doctor an undying mistrust and hatred of the army as he watched the military plot and, in short measure, put an end to Estimé, *noirisme*, and Duvalier's modest new career.

Duvalier refused office under Magloire. Instead he returned to the American medical mission, brooding and bitter. One memory haunted him above all—his mentor Estimé forced to walk between two rows of soldiers as he left his homeland for penurious exile to die, brokenhearted, after only three years.

"Do you see those men in uniform?" Duvalier would ask his friends bitterly. "They're not to be trusted. Do you remember what they did to Dumarsais? But the same thing will never happen to me."

Estimé's influence on him was profound. After years of purely scholarly and scientific research and writing, Duvalier and his *Griot* friend Lorimer Denis wrote *The Problem of Classes Throughout Haiti's History*, a political treatise in which Duvalier the politician emerges for the first time. The new Duvalier was incisive and feisty, prepared to distort history to serve his own ends. And those ends—*noiriste* entirely—were to rectify the age-old wrongs practiced on the oppressed black masses, first by white men, then by their mulatto successors.

His conclusions were that the bloody conflict between black and mulatto had to be reopened, because Haiti's entire class structure was predicated on it. The ruling class, born of French colonial racism, had for over a century refused its mission to lead its people. Instead, said Duvalier, they devoted themselves entirely to "A Snobbish Attitude, Distinguished Manner, Impeccable Clothing, Good Birth, Money, Risk and Intrigue." Only Estimé and his 1946 "Revolution" had managed to restrain them, and this "Revolution" was the culmination of generations of struggle.

The Problem of Classes was hardly original. Years before, Dr. Price-Mars had analyzed the elite and judged them irresponsible. But Duvalier went much further, fueled by the heady *noirisme* of Estimé and by his plunge into Haiti's real-life politics. Estimé disliked white people and hated mulattoes with all the bitterness of the disadvantaged black. Yet at the same time he had such a weakness for mulatto women that the tan Oldsmobile he seduced them in was known as "The Tomb of Virgins." His love affair with Katherine Dunham, black in America, mulatto in Haiti, was riddled with inconsistencies. He refused to greet her mulatto friends, but at the dances he escorted her to, he—and most of the other *noiristes*—left black women to sit watching as black men danced the night long with the mulattoes they both despised and adored.

Only toward whites did Duvalier and Estimé differ, though only in degree. Estimé disliked them, while Duvalier was neutral. Both had had humiliating experiences with them, but Estimé's had been incomparably worse. He had been invited to Washington for an international conference, greeted by a twenty-one-gun salute, then refused accommodation with the other heads of state because the host hotel had just discovered he was black. He finally found lodging in a Negro hotel and left the States humiliated and confirmed in every anti-white prejudice he had ever had.

Duvalier sympathized, but he was a much less passionate man than Estimé, and the discrimination he had been victim of during his two semesters at the University of Michigan left him mistrustful. Though he hated Americans as occupiers, he was a wholehearted admirer of their medical contributions to Haiti. In particular he credited them with "magnificent results" in the campaign against yaws, which the Haitian medical establishment had simply ignored. He felt it was impossible to overstate the impact of yaws, for it sapped the strength from the people, causing untold social and economic hardship, and it even had racial connotations, for the vast majority of rural blacks had it, keeping them permanently enfeebled.

White Americans had not merely employed Duvalier to fight his people's disease, but had conferred responsibility and prestige. The hatred of whites that his speeches sometimes expressed was more a theoretical stance than a deep prejudice. More than anything else it was a polemical tool he used in propaganda—and most of his speeches were sheer propaganda—so he could paint pathetic pictures of blacks and evoke savage images of their white oppressors.

Meanwhile, Magloire swam into power on waves of support. The Church much preferred him to the vodoun-tolerant Estimé, the army was his, and the elite knew in advance they could use him. The Americans too were friendly, and even Trujillo had nothing against him. Only the huge and silent black majority wondered why Estimé was no longer their President.

Magloire ended Estimé's populist programs, and though the economy continued to be mildly prosperous, only the elite and Magloirists benefited substantially. Public works proceeded, including the giant Péligre Dam project designed to irrigate eighty thousand acres of fertile but parched farmland in the Artibonite Valley. Roads, schools, medical clinics, and irrigation projects were constructed, though at suspiciously escalating costs.

Tourism boomed, as the international theater and literary world discovered Haiti, with Noel Coward, Paulette Goddard, Truman Capote, and Irving Berlin rubbing shoulders with Katherine Dunham, Harold Courlander, and other Haiti habitués. Graham Greene also began to visit Haiti, traveling to Cap Haitien and Jérémie, attending vodoun *cérémonies,* and immersing himself in the country whose tragedy he was to offer to the world a decade later as *The Comedians.*

On January 1, 1954, in Gonaives, Magloire presided over his finest moment, the one hundred and fiftieth anniversary of Haitian independence. In the dusty, arid City of Independence, he built a modern cathedral directly across from the public square, with its huge statue of Dessalines on a rearing horse. The show-stopping moment was the dramatic reenactment of the last battle between Haitian ex-slave revolutionaries and Napoleon's soldiers. To roars of applause from the audience, Haitians rich and poor, foreign residents and visitors—but not Duvalier, who despised Magloire—the bloody battle was restaged, with the French generals played by the lightest-skinned cadets from the Military Academy. Magloire personally assigned the role of young General Leclerc to cadet Henri Christophe Namphy, known as "Ti-Blanc" or "Little White," because of his green eyes and light skin.

But like all Haitian honeymoons, Magloire's too soon palled, as graft, corruption, and mulatto domination grew out of all proportion and a disillusioned people began to complain. Magloire responded in typical presidential fashion. Arrests began, and the hounding of opponents real, suspected, and potential. Magloire jailed the people's darling, Port-au-Prince Deputy Daniel Fignolé, who in one half hour could mold a listening crowd of thousands into a quivering mass of obedience. He rounded up unfriendly journalists and sought out and jailed all other opponents.

Thousands, forewarned, went underground, subsisting on charity while friends and relatives supported their families. One of these was Marcelle Hakime's husband, journalist Pierre-Edouard Bellande, the tall and striking mulatto whom Magloire persecuted for his critical newspaper editorials in *L'Ordre*. Bellande spent most of the Magloire years in the arid village of Font Parisien, near the Dominican border, surviving on his meager earnings as a peasant woodcutter. On her own in Port-au-Prince, Marcelle raised their three children and supported them through her income as a dentist.

Marcelle's casual friend François Duvalier was another Magloire victim. After Magloire informed the Americans that Duvalier was involved in on-the-job political activism, they fired him. Duvalier promptly dropped out of sight in the hidden world of Haiti's political opposition. His family life was disrupted, but internal exile did not seriously hurt him, though his seventy-year-old father, Duval, was briefly arrested when he refused to reveal his son's whereabouts. Duvalier had only the revenue from a single *tap-tap* to feed his family, which now included toddler Jean-Claude. To help out, his old colleague Clément Jumelle and his brother Ducasse, both now serving in Magloire's government, donated $30 weekly to Simone.

His family thus provided for, Duvalier lived in comfortable hiding. For a while he lived right next door to their old gingerbread house on the Ruelle Roy. Then in 1955, disguised as a myopic and moon-faced woman, he moved across the street to camp out with the Canadian-educated Haitian Father Jean-Baptiste Georges.

During these years of concealment the abstemious Duvalier read and wrote. It was like being back at school, and as he had done as a student, Duvalier studied obsessively, guzzled soda drinks and gathered around him a group of devoted friends and political believers. One was Luckner Cambronne, later to become his bagman and Simone's lover. Another was Port-au-Prince Police Chief Colonel Marcaisse Prosper, who guaranteed that the police would not arrest him. Last and most important was Clément Barbot, fired when Estimé fell, whom Duvalier had managed to find another job.

What Duvalier became during his years of dodging detection in Port-au-Prince was far more striking than what he did—he shed his past as a dedicated country doctor and engagé scholar to become a politician. Former friends, and they were legion, claimed he studied a copy of Machiavelli's *The Prince* to tatters. Certainly during this period he nursed qualities without which his unique dictatorship could not have evolved— total lack of personal loyalty, universal mistrust of individuals, an ability to lie and break promises with stone-faced regularity, and a penetrating ability to identify an individual's Achilles' heel.

Duvalier also learned other lessons—for example how crucial the financial means were that had always eluded him. The subterfuge he had to employ in saving his own skin developed into a lifelong addiction. And reminiscent of Estimé, who was reluctant to strip off his revolver even to make love, Duvalier took to caching guns everywhere. Lastly, separated from his home and family, Duvalier turned more and more for spiritual comfort to the gods and the rituals he knew so well. In fact, his acquaintance Katherine Dunham, despite her own personal fascination with vodoun rites, felt that he plunged into them with an intensity that bordered and perhaps trespassed on the pathological.

By 1956 Magloire was finished, though he fought ferociously to remain in power. By May four candidates had already declared to replace him. They were his own favorite, Clément Jumelle; the urban proletariat's favorite, Daniel Fignolé; the elite's son, Louis Déjoie; and the country doctor-in-hiding, François "Papa Doc" Duvalier.

Even with his successors lining up for position, Magloire refused to step down. In May students struck to demand his resignation. Tracts attacking him littered the streets. On May 21 Congress declared a state of siege. By November random bombings kept the capital panic-stricken. Still Magloire clung to power, and finally the American ambassador and the papal nuncio united to urge him to resign.

Magloire began a last-ditch effort to keep power by the brute force of the army that had first thrust him into it. He packed his prisons with opponents. He arrested Colonel Léon Cantave, the only senior officer courageous enough to admit that the army had turned against him. He had already imprisoned candidates Fignolé and Déjoie, was searching for Jumelle and Duvalier, and now he herded forty more serious political activists behind bars.

Port-au-Prince froze. Merchants signed pledges to open their shops, then shuttered them and stayed home. Schools closed. Workers idled. On December 12 Magloire conceded defeat. Supreme Court Chief Justice

Nemours Pierre-Louis became Provisional President. On December 13 ex-President Paul Magloire and his family flew off to Jamaica.

Port-au-Prince had rid Haiti of Magloire, but the provinces too had suffered his repressions. As soon as he was gone they also burst into feverish celebration, and then buckled down to serious electioneering. What happened in the provinces was all-important, for in Haiti's second-only popular election, provincial votes would outweigh Port-au-Prince's by more than four to one.

In the charming old French colonial city of Jérémie there were two main camps, with the black majority Duvalierist and the mulatto elite Déjoieist almost to a man. Jérémie was a microcosm of Haitian society, and seven years after Duvalier's election was destined to be the site of a massacre, or vespers, that to this day touches the quick of the Haitian soul.

Famed as the birthplace of France's mulatto General Alexandre Dumas, whose son and grandson gave the world *The Three Musketeers* and *The Lady of the Camelias,* Jérémie was also Haiti's most color-obsessed city, with a social structure akin to apartheid and every aspect of life defined by color/class lines. Intermarriage between black and mulatto was acceptable only if the black was a successful male and the mulatto a woman, for no mulatto man dared disgrace his family's name by darkening its blood with a black wife. Even casual social intermingling was limited, and mulattoes partied at the exclusive Excelsior Club, while aspiring blacks had to be content with the Essor Club, recently founded by Saint-Ange Bontemps and several of his bitter *noiriste* friends.

Politics especially was skin-colored, with Jérémie's mulatto elite ruling the city ever since Haitian independence. When Magloire appointed Jérémie mulatto Joseph Lataillade as Under Secretary of the Interior, the political opposition in Jérémie went to ground in earnest, and repression, arrests, and incarcerations followed swiftly. Young *noiriste* leaders Bontemps and Rodrigue Numa, ambitious and aggressively anti-Magloire, were frequently arrested. Numa, accused of distributing anti-Magloire tracts, was hanged from a beam and, as his naked body swung helplessly, was whipped until his flesh ran with blood and he was senseless.

Later on, young *noiriste* teacher, lawyer, and journalist Antoine Jean-Charles joined Bontemps and Numa in prison after his conviction for inciting the people to rise up and torch the houses of the hated mulatto bourgeoisie. Jean-Charles and Bontemps were found guilty and sentenced to die. Reprieved after weeks of clocking death in a slimy common cell, they emerged resolved to dedicate their lives, even to sacrifice them, to the cause of rescuing black people from the tragedy of their wasted lives in the Black Republic. Thankfully they turned their attention to the man they considered Estimé's successor, the respected *noiriste* scholar Dr. François Duvalier.

The 1957 election campaign was long. Duvalier campaigned tirelessly, and in hacking his path to the presidency he revealed, emphasized, and surrendered to aspects of his character his former simple life had not demanded. He remained enigmatic to his contemporaries, a complex personality whose essence was chameleon-like changeability.

From this period of the campaign a debate about Duvalier's intelligence emerged. Daniel Fignolé, charismatic and passionate defender of the urban masses, publicly scorned Duvalier as "a profoundly stupid little man." The remark was nothing more than rhetoric, calculated to discredit the country doctor who was quietly eroding Fignolé's political base by the strategy of identifying himself as legitimate successor to Estimé and the Revolution of 1946. This was a shrewd move, and since Estimé had died in 1953 he could never return to haunt his usurper. Madame Estimé supported Duvalier so wholeheartedly that she appeared beside him like an approving shadow on his entire campaign trail.

Another astute move was to endorse women's votes and to establish the Faisceau Féminin, or Feminine Torch, a women's group devoted to electing Duvalier. In Port-au-Prince a young woman from Mirabalais was one of his most ardent Feminine Torch workers. Her name was Rosalie Bosquet, and soaring upward with her protector Duvalier, she would quickly gain notoriety as Madame Max Adolphe, Commandant of the Tonton Macoutes. From the very beginning Duvalier knew how to attract and keep the kind of supporters who would help push him into power.

Duvalier also knew what to say, his organizers did their homework, and each speech reflected the specific concerns of its audience. He conveyed absolute integrity and sincerity, no trace of arrogance, and the common touch that endeared him to hundreds of thousands of those whose buttocks he had once stabbed with yaws-killing penicillin. Papa Doc was no Fignolé, but then Fignolé was no Papa Doc.

In Estimé's hometown of St. Marc, Duvalier went to the heart of the matter, telling the people what they wanted to hear. "Whether one wishes it or not, Estimé the Great, ousted from power by the grossest military coup d'état, despite outpourings of popular support a mere two days earlier, remains the symbol of the Haitian who still lives the life of a pariah in the Caribbean basin. With the dictator Paul E. Magloire, that instrument of reaction, our country has just come out of a six-year democratic relapse."

In a radio address to the all-power army, which he would soon smash, Duvalier was more diplomatic—he flattered, he misled, he lied. He thanked the officers, so many of whom he would later kill, for having "helped the Haitian people liberate themselves from the slavery installed six years ago by Paul Eugène Magloire."

Duvalier the presidential candidate was fifty years old, impeccably neat, and primly dressed in dark suits in winter and white suits in summer. He appeared everywhere with his wife, Simone, at his side, her frail innocence and schoolmarm dresses as disarming as his own grave respectability. He had two other constant companions, his short, dark, proper father, Duval, and the familiar, reassuring Madame Dumarsais Estimé. Beside them, and sometimes beside his own young children, Duvalier exuded political naiveté, personal goodness, and calm purpose.

Jumelle and Déjoie also had their followers, but it soon became clear that the real contest was between Duvalier and Fignolé. Yet on September 22, 1957, Duvalier had to face only Déjoie because by then both Jumelle and Fignolé had been eliminated from the running. The story of their elimination, murky and complex, is one of the first indications of Duvalier's stunning ability to diagnose his country's politics and to jab the right remedy in the right place.

But September 22 was still far off, and bombs and serious public unrest were the order of the day. Chief of Staff General Léon Cantave suspected Provisional President Franck Sylvain. To neutralize his power and prevent further trouble, Cantave forced a new government representing the major candidates. This idealistic but unwieldy coalition soon collapsed, and Duvalier and Jumelle resigned. Duvalier hoped by resigning to provoke Cantave to establish a military junta, for he was now convinced he would win in his version of a fair election, which only the army had the power to ensure. Duvalier even used to fantasize to close friends—wistfully and wryly—that Colonel Roger Villedrouin would assume power and eliminate all electoral fraud. Villedrouin was a Jérémie mulatto, and to his dying day would never support Duvalier, yet in this man unlike other senior officers Duvalier saw strictest impartiality and, in that, his own success.

But no military junta materialized, and instead the Fignolé-Déjoie government remained in power. When presidential elections were set for June, Duvalier and Jumelle, certain of losing, conspired to sabotage them. On Flag Day celebrations on May 18, riots erupted. Two men died and there were many wounded. The Fignolé-Déjoie government fired Cantave and simultaneously Cantave dissolved their government. In the midst of crisis the impasse was resolved by a Duvalier supporter, Clément Joseph Charles, who donated $46,000 to Cantave—in Duvalier's name—to pay the soldiers. The scenario was reminiscent of preoccupation days. The army divided, and on May 25, Haiti was rocked by a mini-civil war, to the delight of Port-au-Prince's mobs, who rushed to the battle ground as to Carnival.

While gunfire killed seventeen and shattered scores more, Fignolé deserted Déjoie and met with Duvalier and Jumelle. A deal was struck between the three, and the next morning astonished Haitians learned that their new Provisional President was Daniel Fignolé, and that Fignolé's chief of staff was General Antonio Kébreau. But Fignolé had made a stupid move—as always, he had underestimated François Duvalier.

Fignolé was uneasy in the power he had won too easily. "Even if you see my head on a bayonet, remain calm and don't leave your homes," he warned the people in the teeming stinking slum of Bel-Air, his Port-au-Prince stronghold. But for nineteen days Fignolé was Haiti's President, and one of those destined for foreign exile, not death.

On the nineteenth day General Kébreau betrayed Fignolé, sending Captain John Beauvoir and several officers to storm a cabinet meeting where they arrested Fignolé. "The meeting is adjourned," Beauvoir announced. For two days nothing happened. Then, set off by rumors that Fignolé was jailed in Fort Dimanche, all hell broke loose. This was Déjoie's play—his supporters, trying to destabilize Kébreau, whom they now realized was pro-Duvalier, started the rumor. Slum dwellers from Bel-Air and La Saline streamed by the thousands toward the American-built Fort Dimanche to free their President and their hero.

The march to free Fignolé began and ended in violence. The crowd was angry, and as they tramped out of the city they crushed cars with catapults improvised from inner tubes so powerful that four men had to operate them. They shot out streetlamps, darkening the city, set fires, and then cut the fire hoses of trucks sent to extinguish them. Numbering in the thousands, the poor people of Port-au-Prince stormed Fort Dimanche to carry Fignolé back home with them, but Fignolé was already in a Haitian coastguard cutter bound for Miami, and as they hurled their sticks and stones and curses, the police trained their guns at them and began to fire. Then as the living fled for their lives, the police followed them, guns blazing, until corpses blocked streets all over the city, and terrified pedestrians, running for cover, discovered they were running in human blood.

Albert Salas worked all night saving lives. Salas was a medical technician, and as people all over Bel-Air begged him to treat their wounded, he dashed from house to house extracting bullets, stanching gaping wounds, and sometimes, frustrated and angry, watching a mortally wounded patient die.

In the morning army trucks arrived and removed the bodies. Salas, exhausted and bitter, watched them as silently as he had death. Creaking engines of the fire department followed and flooded clean the grisly streets. Out of sight, across the city in a place called Cité Bouteille, the corpses were tossed into a common grave and buried.

Nobody replaced Fignolé, but Kébreau worried because the United States refused to recognize his new provisional military government. "They won't, until you announce general elections," remarked a foreign journalist to whom Kébreau confided his anxiety in an interview.

"Will that do it?" said Kébreau. "All right then, I'll do it. I'll call general elections for September 22."

Kébreau had been well advised, and the next day the State Department officially recognized his government, and an interested world press circled September 22 on their calendars.

September 22 was a Sunday. On Friday, Jumelle also recognized his own hopeless position and belatedly withdrew his candidacy. The contest between survivors Duvalier and Déjoie was about to reach its inevitable conclusion. At 6 a.m. the polls opened.

In far-off Jérémie, almost a day's roughshod drive from the capital, young Antoine Jean-Charles arrived early at the polling station. This Sunday morning, depositing the ballot with Duvalier's name into the box, he smiled serenely at the monitors, then walked away with a light step. In more prosperous areas of town, he knew, the mulattoes would be voting for Louis Déjoie, but he was not worried. General Kébreau had saved the situation after the May 25 civil war. Electoral cheating was minimal, and Duvalier would win.

Antoine Jean-Charles had worked for Duvalier, organized rallies not only in Jérémie but also in the outlying districts. He had driven there in his uncertain car, gassing it up out of his meager $40 monthly teacher's salary. He had provided paper and stencils for the campaign literature he drafted and distributed, paid phone bills—in short, he paid for anything he needed to ensure that Papa Doc would be victorious.

Jean-Charles had even put his own life at Duvalier's disposal. He had been speaking at a backwoods rally, testifying to the people about Duvalier's merits. A Magloire man had aimed a pistol at him. The assassin fired, and beside Jean-Charles a man slumped down dead. The crowd gasped, the killer fled. "You're just like Henri Christophe! Only silver bullets can kill you," a man cried out. Jean-Charles was too shaken by near death to say a word. Afterward he grew to enjoy his new bulletproof reputation, though he knew only too well it was undeserved. The great Henri Christophe had indeed been charmed, and some said Duvalier was too, but as for himself, he had merely faced an incompetent killer.

Long, exhausting months later, September 22 repaid all efforts and risks. François Duvalier was elected President, and once again the Estimé "Revolution" would right Haiti's wrongs.

In Cayes eighteen-year-old Jean Joseph Charles voted for Louis Déjoie. Cayes was Déjoie territory, and so rabid were the partisans of the handsome gentleman farmer that only military intervention had allowed Duvalier to enter the town to campaign.

Though he was only eighteen, Charles had actively campaigned for Déjoie, and one of his proudest moments had been during a round of thundering applause in his hometown of nearby Camp Perrin after he had delivered a rousing speech. People listened because he was articulate and commanded his beloved French language with style. They also listened because he was the nephew of Senator Antoine Télémaque, had attended a fine private school in Cayes, and was one of Camp Perrin's sharpest-dressed young men. Charles was, in short, the epitome of a rising young black who, having overcome his illegitimate birth, was out to change the world and make it a better place for everyone, including himself.

On September 22 the voting was heavy. When the results were announced, Cayes had voted heavily in favor of Louis Déjoie.

On September 22, in the picture-pretty colonial town of Jacmel, Lucien Charles cast a defiant vote for his favorite candidate, Dr. François Duvalier. Jacmel was Déjoie territory, but the back country was Duvalierist, and so was Charles, a young black *houngan* from Cayes-Jacmel. He had first seen Duvalier almost by accident. When Duvalier had come to Jacmel to campaign, militant Déjoieists had gone to Army General Headquarters and demanded that Duvalier be barred. The local commandant, *noiriste* Captain Gérard Constant, refused angrily.

A Déjoieist gang, undeterred, had met Duvalier's campaign troupe at the gates of the city, but before they could take threatened action, Constant arrested them and Duvalier continued into Jacmel. Some of his entourage, intimidated, had fled back to Port-au-Prince, but Duvalier, calm and imperturbable, showed no emotion at all. Neither did his wife, Simone.

The Duvaliers stopped and held court at the Pension Craft, Jacmel's renowned Victorian-style inn, but few arrived except curious students. It soon became obvious the public rally planned for the next day on the square overlooking the sea would be a humiliating failure. Reinforcements would have to be brought in. Trucks, borrowed from rare Duvalier partisans, went out into the back country to round up rural blacks longing to see the man who had once cured their yaws and now promised to cure their world.

Houngan Lucien Charles was among those willing conscripts. At thirty-one he was already respected for his mastery of the vodoun mysteries, his wealth, and his large landholdings, which supported his common-law wife, the *hounsi* who were also his concubines, and the troop of children he had fathered. All in all he was a man of consequence, and when he voted he wanted to vote for the right candidate.

Charles listened to Duvalier, who spoke gravely and with a sincerity that impressed him. He knew he had the magical power to cure people and to converse with spirits, but Duvalier had both Western and mystical powers, and Charles recognized the other man's superior strength.

On September 22 the short, stocky Charles arrived early at the polling station. Then, despite the hostility of soldiers, and the certainty that he was voting for the losing candidate, he pushed a ballot marked with Duvalier's name into the box, then walked outside and waited until the band of friends he had come with had also voted.

On September 22, 1957, Déjoie supporter Marcelle Hakime Bellande voted for François Duvalier. She did so because at nine in the morning armed Duvalierists broke into her house and forced her to accompany them to the polls. With guns pointed at her, Marcelle went off with them, but despite their threats refused to bring her underage children along, even Michèle, whom her old pal and Ruelle Roy neighbor Dr. François Duvalier himself had brought into the world.

This Election Day kidnapping angered Marcelle as much as it frightened her. Early on in the campaign Duvalier had urged her to campaign for him. Marcelle had refused diplomatically. "I don't want any trouble with my husband," she replied, knowing that Duvalier was well aware of Pierre-Edouard's commitment to Déjoie. Still, she had felt enough personal loyalty to Duvalier to expose a Déjoieist plot to ambush and kill him, sending him word by a fellow doctor to warn him of the danger.

Marcelle had feared for her country's future ever since the one-day civil war in May. She had been downtown near Dessalines Barracks, where Duvalier and the others had conferred and from which Fignolé had emerged the brief winner—and long-term loser. On that day she had seen the people of Port-au-Prince swarm through the streets shouting "Down with the government," "Long live Fignolé," "Down with the army," and as they ran they smashed radio stations and shops until finally Fignolé took to the air. "I am your President," he had reassured his rampaging people, "go home without saying a word."

Marcelle had been stunned at the hypnotizing effect of Fignolé's message, blasted out on the stations still operating. Instantly calmed and quiet, they turned away and by the thousands walked off in utter silence because Daniel had told them to.

Marcelle had neither liked nor supported Fignolé, but after his ouster she had had premonitions of impending tragedy. On September 21, the day before the elections, hearing that many of her Déjoieist friends had been arrested, she began to glimpse the form the tragedy would take. On September 22, after she had voted, the thugs released her and she returned home alone. As she drove, taking a roundabout route to see what was happening, she saw the army had already closed several voting stations. The polls had opened at 6 a.m., and the official closing was at 6 p.m. Marcelle glanced at her watch—it was not yet 10 a.m., eight hours early. Duvalierists everywhere had flocked to the polls at the crack of dawn, and now they were closing them to prevent Déjoieists from voting.

On September 22, 1957, eighteen-year-old Albert Salas had no one to vote for. His candidate, Daniel Fignolé, had been trussed up like a goat, thrust into a sack, and set out on a small gas-powered fishing boat to be drowned. Only the curiosity of the boat's white owners had saved him. They had heard strange strangling sounds, ripped open the sacks, and rescued Daniel. Salas had never swallowed the official story that his idol had been exiled in the relative comfort of a coast guard cutter. He believed what everyone in Bel-Air believed, and until Daniel himself told him otherwise, Salas would continue to believe that only a miracle had saved Daniel.

Salas was an ardent member of MOP, the workers/peasants movement that was the basis of Fignolé's support. He had known Duvalier personally, for when the little doctor was MOP's secretary general he had often sent Salas out to buy cigarettes to distribute to MOP workers and members. Duvalier had long since quit MOP. He'd also stopped visiting Fignolé territory.

Fignolé hated Duvalier, telling a wide-eyed young Salas and his friends that the doctor was a monster a thousand times more dangerous than Déjoie. Duvalier had raped his eldest daughter, Marie-Denise, Fignolé told them, and was so steeped in mysticism that months before the elections he had spent three days in his house, entirely naked, sitting on a rock working magic.

On September 22, remembering how Fignolé had repeated over and over, "Between Déjoie and Duvalier I'd a thousand times prefer Déjoie," Salas braved the hostile monitors and cast his vote for the man he despised as an arrogant, empty-headed mulatto industrialist.

On September 22 twelve-year-old Ulrick Masson lay feverish on a narrow cot in Port-au-Prince's General Hospital. Ulrick came from the distant town of Mirabalais, but the doctor who visited the clinic there had been unable to cure him, and his parents had scraped together the money for bus or *tap-tap* fare to transport their deliriously ill son to the capital.

Ulrick knew little about politics. All his energies went into trying to conquer the difficult French language in which they taught him at school when Creole was all anyone in his family and neighborhood ever spoke.

On Sunday morning September 22, Ulrick opened his eyes to see a doctor enter the crowded ward, Doc Raoul, followed by several civilians. They threaded their way up the aisle, stopping briefly beside each sick man's bed. Ignoring the isolated protest or exclamation, they worked quickly, pressing each patient's thumbprint onto their control sheets, then giving him a Duvalier ballot to cast. When they reached Ulrick he was astonished to find he too had to vote. Lying helplessly, he allowed Doc Raoul to ink his identifying thumbprint. Seconds later twelve-year-old Ulrick had cast his illegal vote for François Duvalier.

When everyone had voted Doc Raoul nodded with satisfaction. Then, without a word to the patients, he turned and left the ward.

On September 22 Voltaire Jean rose early in his new cabin in Port-au-Prince's wooded rural suburb of Canapé Vert. Today he was going to vote for his friend Dr. François Duvalier, and he knew that once Papa Doc became President, he would never again lack for work and his future would be assured.

Boss Voltaire was forty-two years old and a mason-foreman skilled enough to have almost steady work. He also had had working with him a construction foreman who was a personal friend of Duvalier's, and because of him, he too had come to know the man who was going to save Haiti.

Every weekend Boss Voltaire Jean would take a *tap-tap* or sometimes even walk the long distance from Canapé Vert to the Ruelle Roy, where in the courtyard outside the Duvalier's house he would spend hours playing dominoes with other men who congregated there. They were simple people, and Duvalier did not invite them inside the house. Nor did he ever join them in the game. However, he spent hours watching them play, ordering soft drinks and cigarettes for them, studying their moves, and, afterward, talking.

Boss Voltaire loved to listen. Duvalier was such a dignified man, always dressed in a suit despite the heat, always looking as if he was about to go out. It never ceased to be a pleasure to hear him telling them how wonderful Haiti would be when he became its President.

"I'll raise the daily minimum wage from three *gourdes* to ten," Duvalier promised, and just thinking about what he would do with that ten *gourdes* or $2.00 every day flooded Boss Voltaire with pride. Duvalier was also going to give them clinics, and build brand-new schools. Boss Voltaire was doubly pleased. Not only would his six children have clinics and schools to attend, but he would undoubtedly be one of the foremen Duvalier's Public Works Minister would hire to construct them.

On September 22 Voltaire Jean walked up to his neighborhood polling booth, greeted the monitors calmly, and from his pocket took out his ballot with Duvalier's name on it.

In the Artibonite Valley town of Lestère, thirty-six-year-old Orestil Louissaint voted for Dr. François Duvalier, the candidate whose campaign he had nearly bankrupted himself supporting. A Jacmel native who had moved to Lestère in 1952, Louissaint had established his little store and gas station on the edge of a wooded rural area that few ventured to enter. In those days the woods had been the haunt of local bandits who preyed on travelers and hung their victims' corpses up in trees in ghoulish warning against trespassing. But Louissaint had known he could prosper there, and with his wife and those of his fourteen children already born he settled in and began to work.

During the 1957 electoral campaign Louissaint had been approached by both Fignolé and Déjoie organizers, but politics did not interest him. Then one day the district prefect brought his good friend Duvalier to Louissaint's house to meet him, and the storekeeper reluctantly agreed to support him. Duvalier was elated and returned with three local men to form an organizing committee. Louissaint pitied the little doctor, so hopelessly poor that his old car had had three flats before it reached Lestère from Port-au-Prince.

Duvalier's lack of campaign funds was notorious. "I have no money," he told Louissaint forthrightly. "I can't pay, but will you allow me to buy my gas on credit?"

Louissaint agreed, and during the first stage of the campaign, before the May civil war, Duvalier sent his workers from all over the Artibonite and Gonaives to Louissaint, until his tab totaled $11,000, at $.50 a gallon.

Duvalier's mounting debt was by then a serious liability, and Louissaint was having trouble paying the mortgage on a house he was buying in Port-au-Prince. However, his personal political calculations, and also a recurrent dream, confirmed that Duvalier would win in September, and so he smiled and authorized Haiti's next President to continue to charge his gas at his own single pump.

By September 22 Duvalier and his men had run up a total bill of $12,600, and when Orestil Louissaint cast his ballot for Duvalier, he was voting for his own personal financial survival as much as for Haiti's salvation.

On September 22 Ganthier Magistrate Jean Julmé smiled with satisfaction as he voted the Duvalier ballot his opponents had almost prevented him from delivering. Julmé was not merely a Duvalier fanatic. He was also standing election himself as deputy for the Ganthier constituency, which included the town of Croix des Bouquets and five rural sections. Julmé was a surveyor and owned large tracts of land, so that though he was only in his mid-thirties, he was one of Ganthier's squires in the backward rural area. He was a fiercely ambitious man who spent every waking hour campaigning for his own election as well as Duvalier's and peppered his conversation with references to the Virgin Mary.

On the night of September 21 Julmé drove up from the capital with a carload of Duvalier-Julmé ballots for the next day's elections. At the town of Croix des Bouquets he stopped to deliver a few hundred of them to a local organizer. In that brief time a rival political organizer had driven nails through all his tires, ruining them. In this town at this time of night, Julmé realized, it was impossible to have his tires repaired to reach Ganthier with the Duvalier ballots. Coldly furious, he walked to a partisan's home and, using the old crank phone system, placed a call to his nephew Athanase in Ganthier. "Don't worry," the young man reassured his uncle. "Ganthier will vote for Duvalier tomorrow no matter what."

Athanase prepared for a long night. First he contacted the local priest and borrowed his portable typewriter. Then he set to work, and by the next morning he had typed hundreds of the unofficial Duvalier-Julmé ballots that on September 22 the inhabitants of Ganthier stuffed into the ballot boxes.

It was late on September 22 when Julmé, in a borrowed car, reached Ganthier. It didn't matter. By the time he cast his Duvalier-Julmé vote it was merely a drop in the deluge that was to sweep both of them into office.

By 6 p.m. on September 22 almost a million Haitians had voted. Dr. François Duvalier swept the polls with 679,884 votes to Déjoie's 266,992. Clément Jumelle also drew 9,980 votes, though he was no longer a candidate. Duvalier won the North and most of the rural areas, losing to Déjoie in Cayes, Jacmel, Port-de-Paix, and the entire city of Port-au-Prince and its breezy suburb of Pétionville. Papa Doc had finally become President-elect of Haiti, and the men who supported his ticket also swept the Senate and Legislature.

Both Duvalier's and Déjoie's partisans had cheated as much as possible, and the voting system facilitated this. Because Haiti was primarily illiterate, with 90 percent of its men and women unable to sign their own names, ballots were individually printed and distributed by each candidate, so a voter had only to present his ballot. This system made secrecy virtually impossible. It also made intimidation easy, because a voter could be identified by whatever ballot he carried.

Voter registration did not exist, and multiple voting was very common, with only inked thumbs to identify who had voted. In theory each polling station had monitors from all political parties, but in practice boxes were stuffed, stolen, and miscounted. In Déjoie strongholds such as Port-au-Prince, soldiers under Kébreau's orders closed polling stations early, trying to prevent a Déjoie landslide—they had urged Duvalierists to get up early and vote right away.

Yet, despite all the cheating, the results represented Haitian majority opinion. Had Fignolé still been in the contest, Duvalier's victory might have been Fignolé's, or at any rate much reduced. As it was, Duvalier swept the polls with a vote that almost certainly reflected Haitian opinion, with Déjoie smashing his opponent only in his known strongholds.

The most tragic feature of the elections was not the widespread cheating by both candidates but the fact that the clear Duvalier majority was not accepted by the approximately one-third of Haiti's population who had voted against him. One of democracy's cardinal tenets is that the majority decision prevails, and that dissenters must live with it for the stated duration of the government, freely criticizing whatever measures they object to with the understanding that their opposition is constructive, healthy, and loyal.

Duvalier's September 22, 1957, victory served as a signal for anti-Duvalier forces to attack and unbalance the President-elect so that by the time he was installed on October 22 he would preside over a government whose very existence was imperiled by those it had defeated at the polls. Much of this opposition was muted and sincere, the disgruntled discontent of citizens whose experience of democracy was entirely vicarious. But there was also cynical and calculated opposition, and before he had even recovered from the euphoria of his electoral victory, François Duvalier had become its victim.

Louis Déjoie immediately challenged Duvalier's victory—the elections were rigged, he declared, except of course in Port-au-Prince and other areas where he had won. In Haitian political tradition, Clément Jumelle and two of his brothers went underground and began plotting. And in the capital Fignolé's working-class supporters, and Déjoie's business and professional partisans, refused to acknowledge Duvalier's victory.

Four days after the elections Déjoieists called a general protest strike. Though Duvalier was only President-elect and Kébreau still headed the government, armed Duvalierists helped the police break the strike by threats, force, and supervised looting. Kébreau passed a law never repealed even after Duvalier was installed: businesses closed by unjustified strikes could be reopened by state employees. And in the few instances in which defiant storeowners shut their doors, armed goons immediately stripped their shops of all merchandise.

The worst post-election violence came when Déjoie partisans attacked a police post in the cool, pine-studded mountains of Kenscoff, nine miles above Port-au-Prince. They gained entry by asking for a curfew pass for a woman in labor, then shot and killed the sentry and four soldiers sleeping on the simple barracks cots. Opposition politics, Haitian style, had begun before the Duvalier regime was even installed.

Kébreau responded with martial law and orders to arrest or kill. Hours after the Kenscoff killings, Déjoie partisan Shibley Talamas paid for them with his life. Talamas was a U.S. citizen, born in Haiti of Syrian descent. Ignoring the 10 p.m. curfew, Talamas drove to Pétionville to bring his wife's obstetrician to Canapé Vert Hospital, where he had first taken her when her labor pains began. Police arrested and held him for curfew violation, and by the time they released him, his daughter was already born. Talamas went first to the hospital, then to see American ambassador Gerald Drew after friends warned him the police had searched his house and were looking for him. American consular officials, reassured by a Haitian policeman, insisted that Talamas surrender himself and personally escorted him to a police station.

On the day his daughter was born, Talamas died. The police transferred him out to Fort Dimanche, where interrogators trying to elicit information about the Kenscoff killings beat him to death. Talamas was delivered to the National Penitentiary, where a duty officer refused to accept a corpse.

The United States formally protested his death, and in response the Haitian army released an autopsy report stating that the three-hundred-pound Talamas had died of heart failure. The Americans were livid and suspended three technical aid programs. All this happened before Duvalier was installed in power, and the Talamas murder was one of the Kébreau government's legacies to his new regime.

Slim and neat in his cutaway and white gloves, in better health than he would ever be again, a serene-faced Duvalier entered the National Palace, which would be his home until he died. In the Room of the Busts, facing the bronze statues of those Haitian presidents who had gone before, and flanked by his officials, including former President Dumarsais Estimé's cousin Rameau and Chief of Staff General Antonio Kébreau, François Duvalier swore the oath of office. It was October 22, 1957.

4 PAPA DOC, PRESIDENT

F ROM HIS FIRST DAYS IN THE CURSED PRESIDENTIAL chair, Duvalier tirelessly eliminated his opponents. Before he could begin to implement policy, he explained to his intimates, he had to ensure his own power. With vicious Clément Barbot in charge of his secret police, and hooded men called *cagoulards* as his armed goons, Duvalier instituted the sneak arrests and brutal interrogations often followed by death or permanent disappearance that were to mark his regime.

He began on November 2, a fortnight after he had entered the palace, ordering the arrests of hundreds who publicly contested his election. Among them was Marcelle Hakime's husband, Pierre-Edouard Bellande, who with his wife had sinned by refusing to campaign for Duvalier, and who further infuriated him by refusing a diplomatic post that would have paid $2,000 monthly and whisked him safely away from Haitian politics.

In a huge common cell in the National Penitentiary on the Rue du Centre, Bellande and fifty other political prisoners spent their days debating a plan of action. Once they were in agreement, they smuggled news of their activities to those journalists still at liberty and began an eight-day hunger strike that became instant news and a press scandal. The raw Duvalier was still sensitive to publicity and released journalist Bellande, but the persecution intensified. Detectives watched Bellande's new house on the Rue de la Reunion, and Marcelle and their four children lived in permanent fear. Then Duvalier attacked on another flank, and the lives of an entire family changed forever.

* * *

Yvonne Hakime-Rimpel was Marcelle's beautiful older sister, a feminist leader whose magazine *L'Escale* had fought for women's rights long before Duvalier's election. She also spoke out on political matters, and after Duvalier hinted that Haiti's national flag should be changed from red-and-blue to black-and-red, she criticized him. On the night of January 5, 1958, armed, hooded *cagoulards* smashed down her door and stormed upstairs to where Yvonne, her husband, and eight children lay sleeping. Without a word they grabbed two daughters sleeping in the same room, savagely beat them, then dragged them downstairs and pitched them outside onto the sidewalk. Yvonne, in slippers and night-gown, was pushed into a car and driven away.

In the rural suburb of Delmas, Yvonne's abductors stopped at a deserted field. Despite her great fear, she counted nine men. One was Haiti's President, François Duvalier, in the khaki uniform of the military he despised. Another, in civilian garb, was Elois Maitre, the baker to whom her brother sold flour. The *cagoulards* stripped her and began one by one to rape her. When the last *cagoulard* had withdrawn from her, they began to beat her. The beating was so brutal, Yvonne faded in and out of consciousness, but before she could die they kicked her naked body into a trench. "Now finish her off," said Duvalier in his unmistakable nasal voice, and Yvonne closed her eyes to die.

"Let me," another man said, and she recognized Maitre's voice. "No, let me!" Maitre repeated more loudly. Then bullets shattered the air and she felt them whiz beside her and tunnel harmlessly into the soft earth.

After a brief silence Maitre spoke again. "She's as dead as she'll ever be," he announced. "Come on, men. Let's get out of here."

In the hole Yvonne lay silently until long after she heard the sound of their cars in the distance. Then she pulled herself up and crawled slowly along the ground until she found her torn nightgown and one slipper. Bloody and filthy, she limped through the blackness until she came to a small house. A peasant woman opened the door to her feeble knocking, but to her plea for refuge screamed, "Zombie! Zombie!" and slammed the door in Yvonne's face. The owner of the second house she reached also turned her away.

A casual acquaintance found her lying on the sidewalk and drove her home. But they could not stop because policemen surrounded Yvonne's house, so they sped away to one of her relatives. The latter kept her until dawn, then drove her to the L'Asile Français Hospital, where she was registered under a false name and, for the three months she was hospitalized, guarded night and day by her family.

Her brother-in-law Antonio Rimpel, Duvalier's Finance Minister, refused to help. "There's nothing I can do," he told his relatives when they arrived at his house at 1 a.m. on the morning their mother was being tortured. Rimpel counseled silence, and in the terror of Duvalier's new Haiti, the Hakime-Rimpel family maintained it.

Bel-Air is Port-au-Prince's oldest neighborhood, and one of its poorest and most crowded. It was also Fignolé territory and, after Duvalier became President, a hotbed of opposition.

Duvalier chose as the site of his operation the plain old cross at the corner of the Rue du Peuple and the Rue des Ramparts, where every week thousands worshiped at the foot of a cross and the bronze statue of a fighting cock. In March, fewer than five months in office, Duvalier sent a man to hack the cock away from its base. "Why?" demanded the curious crowd that immediately gathered. The man ignored them, put the cock under his arm, and drove off.

That night nine policemen arrived in Bel-Air and stood sentinel, keeping the people away from the old shrine. Nobody could pass, and the people of Bel-Air, scarred by memories of last year's slaughter, retreated to their homes. By ten o'clock truckloads of soldiers reinforced the police, and the news spread instantly throughout the slum: venture outside and the men in olive green have orders to shoot to kill.

Albert Salas was inside, crouched with his friends René Sanon and Carlo Nan, on the gallery of Sanon's house just off the Rue du Peuple. Motionless, the three young men watched.

Through the darkness two trucks lumbered up the hill, and Salas could see clearly the cargoes: men, women, and children, and several uniformed policemen, gagged with rags, their bodies immobilized with ropes. A few worked off the gags and cried out, terrifying shrieks that were quickly stifled. The trucks backed up against the still-drying cement pit. Men in civilian clothes jumped up and pushed the victims into it.

Another truck arrived, and its passengers too were pushed inside the pit. As a civilian official paced up and down issuing instructions, workmen arrived and began to shovel the piles of earth back down into the hole, until the pit was filled. Then they mixed and poured cement, rolled and leveled it, and soon all that was left of the massacre was a pristine cement floor. Before the last worker left the official walked up to the handiwork he had supervised, raised his arms as if to strike a mortal blow, and plunged something into the wet cement. Then he too left, and only soldiers remained guarding the tomb.

Salas woke before dawn and rushed back out to the gallery. Two soldiers remained as sentinels, and a crowd already stood staring uncomprehendingly at the old wooden cross that their President had had embedded in a platform of cement. The people never again worshiped there.

In vodounesque Haiti, Duvalier knew he had to do more than propitiate some spirits. If he were to succeed in gaining complete mastery over his people, he needed Haiti's most powerful spirits always at his side.

The road out of Port-au-Prince toward Haiti's great Artibonite Valley stretches open and dusty between the serene turquoise-tinged Caribbean on the left and ancient rolling mountains on the right. The mountains, once covered with mahogany and oak and choked with vegetation, were by the 1950s rapidly balding, their flaky limestone surfaces gleaming naked where life had been. Every day woodcutters arrived with axes to hack away more of even the scrubbiest trees to roast into charcoal, the urban Haitians' cooking fuel.

Near the top of one such bald mountain is a vast cave called Trou Foban. Trou Foban is but one of many caves, but unlike the others it has been known since slavery as the home of evil spirits who roamed throughout Haiti until they gathered there and settled. In Haiti spirits prefer natural dwellings just as they did in Africa, especially under waterfalls and in trees and under rocks. The great cave Trou Foban was also greatly feared for the supernatural might of its spirits. Only especially powerful *houngans* held *cérémonies* there, for the denizens of the other world are not to be trifled with.

In early March 1958, Haitians believe, François Duvalier and a *houngan* with his acolytes began the long trek up to Trou Foban. It was afternoon when they set out up the long difficult climb and dusk when they arrived. After elaborate secret preparations the mystics called upon the spirits, inviting them to leave their home and follow Duvalier into Port-au-Prince, where he offered them a new shelter. The incantations were successful, and the spirits accepted his invitation.

Late that night, as he tramped back down the mountain to the roadside so far below, François Duvalier was followed by a host of spirits who went to live in his mystic room in the National Palace. They remained with him until he died, and because of them, the story goes, no living human could overthrow him.

On July 28 Duvalier faced the most serious crisis of his nine-month presidency. It came in the form of an invasion that nearly toppled his fledgling regime. Duvalier emerged unscathed and obsessed by the vision of a legion of civilians armed, trained, and loyal solely to himself. Papa successfully aborted the Pasquet invasion, but months later that invasion gave birth to the Volunteers of National Security, known throughout Haiti and the world as the notorious Tonton Macoutes.

Leading the invasion was ex-Captain Alix "Sonson" Pasquet, a former commandant of Dessalines Barracks, now exiled in the U.S. Pasquet's plan was breathtakingly simple. With his force of seven, including five Americans, he would sail into the coastal village of Montrouis on a yacht, then proceed by land to Port-au-Prince. There he would overpower the barracks he knew so well, capture the ammunition depot, and then ask for reinforcements from the population he was certain was waiting for liberation.

Trouble began after they had anchored the *Molly C.* A suspicious Montrouis peasant reported them to the authorities. Cornered and unable to explain why they were dressed in Haitian military uniform, the invaders shot the three soldiers sent to investigate, stole their jeep, loaded it with weapons, and set out for Port-au-Prince, eighty kilometers distant. When the jeep broke down they hired a *tap-tap* named "In Spite of All, God is the Only Master" and drove it directly to the barracks, mere blocks from the palace. At the barracks' gate, the impressive Pasquet announced that he was delivering prisoners, and the gullible sentry opened the gates and admitted the garishly painted bus. Without hesitation Pasquet led his men into the administration building, surprising and killing two men, wounding a third, and holding the entire dormitory under armed guard.

With Haiti's main barracks at his mercy, Pasquet sat down at the telephone and began to talk. It was a fatal error, and others compounded it. With virtually nothing but surprise on his side, Pasquet should have stormed the palace where Duvalier lived and kept the army's ammunition supplies, leaving only a small quantity in the barracks. Failing that,

Pasquet should have ensured perfect secrecy as to his strength, fostering the impression that he commanded hundreds. Lastly, and crucially, he should have realized that the people of Port-au-Prince were not going to rise up against Papa Doc to follow three mulattoes and their foreign white companions. That the invasion should end in tragedy for the invaders was a foregone conclusion.

Nonetheless, the invasion tested Haiti's popular political waters, rallied support for the President, and gave him justification for ever-widening and deadlier repression.

It was midnight when Pasquet began to telephone, urging officers to revolt, calling friends. He even phoned Duvalier. "The little maniac dared to order the chief of state to lay down his arms and present himself at the Dessalines Barracks with a white flag," a furious Duvalier reported afterward.

Meanwhile, from another room, the wounded officer managed to get to a phone. National Penitentiary commandant Major Gérard Constant had already dialed and failed to contact both barracks and palace. Only the commandant at General Headquarters was at his phone, and like Constant he had heard the shooting but knew nothing about its origin. Suddenly the phone under Constant's thick fingers rang, startling him. He snatched up the receiver. "Please help me, I'm wounded," he heard a feeble voice whisper. The man then identified himself. The line went dead.

Constant phoned the General Hospital, demanded an ambulance, and arranged for a military escort.

The phone sounded once more. "Gérard, it's Sonson. Sonson Pasquet," Constant heard with astonishment. Sonson Pasquet had been in his class in military college.

"Sonson? Where are you?"

"At Dessalines Barracks. I've taken it, why don't you come and see? The password," Pasquet added, "is Mollie C."

"Where is Chief of Staff General Flambert?" Constant asked.

Pasquet's laugh was brittle. "We're in charge here, Gérard. And we're going to get the President. I want you to release three officers you're holding as political prisoners in the penitentiary." He named three men, of whom only Raymond Chassagne was in custody.

Constant said he would consider the request, hung up, and immediately dialed the palace. This time Lieutenant Colonel Pierre Merceron replied, spoke briefly, then passed Constant to Duvalier.

Quickly Constant repeated his conversation with Pasquet, then inquired solicitously, "How do you feel, President?"

Duvalier's voice was strained but unemotional. "I am firm and unyielding, just as I was on May 25." At this reference to Haiti's one-day civil war in 1957, Constant nodded. "We've got everything under control," Duvalier continued. "Stay at your post, Constant. We'll be in touch with you."

The phone rang again. The invaders had at first denied entrance to the General Hospital's ambulance. It returned again and was admitted, but too late, for the wounded officer was already dead. And, reported the officer who had escorted the ambulance, there were only eight invaders, and one of them was also wounded. Seconds later Constant was again on the line to the palace.

Constant's call only confirmed what Duvalier and the palace already knew. Euphoric with their first successes, the invaders had forgotten elementary principles of war, and when Henri Perpignan was seized by a craving for his old Haitian-blend cigarettes, he simply sent one of the prisoners to buy him some. As soon as the man was out of the barracks, he began to talk, eagerly answering every question while a Duvalier official smoked the cigarettes.

Another eyewitness arrived with an identical story. This was Colonel Louis Roumain, imprisoned in the barracks, who tipped his chair through an open window in the barracks, fell down onto the street, picked himself up and hurried over to the palace. The stupefying truth was, the palace concluded, that an entire army barracks had been captured by three mulattoes and five white men, one of the latter bleeding profusely from a leg wound.

In his crowded palace office, the exhausted Duvalier, in khaki uniform and helmet, smiled and nodded. Around him the officers laughed. Eight invaders! It was almost over.

Except that Dessalines Barracks was still under Pasquet's control, so at dawn Duvalier ordered official radio broadcasts charging that Magloire partisans and Dominicans had launched an invasion. "Go to the palace and help your President!" the announcer urged his listeners. "Despised Magloirists have taken the barracks. On top of that, they have foreigners with them."

Duvalier partisans responded to the call, and palace officials armed each one of them, including young Clovis Désinor. By daybreak these civilians, reinforced by *cagoulards* and soldiers, attacked the barracks.

General Flambert, whose midnight stroll out of the barracks had earlier saved him from capture, directed operations and attacked with grenades.

Alix Pasquet's head was blasted open. A former Haitian lieutenant lay riddled with bullets. Florida Sheriff Dany Jones and *Mollie C's* skipper, Joe D. Walker, lay dead of bullets to the head. Florida Sheriff Arthur Payne, his earlier wound weakening him, was shot as he lay begging for his life. "I'm a journalist, I'm a journalist!" he pleaded as he died. Duvalierists had recaptured the barracks, and the bizarre, impossible Pasquet invasion was over. There remained only the accounting, and the revenge.

Gérard Constant went immediately to the palace. Duvalier, looking tiny in his military garb, was surrounded by civilians who had rushed out to help him.

"Excellence, if this were President Hippolyte, the town would be on fire now," someone declared, urging Duvalier to order a new wave of arrests of suspected anti-Duvalierists.

Duvalier smiled faintly. *"Eh bien, mon cher,"* he said mildly. "Other times, other customs."

The Pasquet invasion taught Duvalier a lesson he never forgot. It was that military men intrigued, plotted, and rebelled, but plain ordinary citizens responded loyally to their President, and it was they who would ensure that the military would not succeed in ousting Duvalier as they had ousted Estimé in 1950, arresting him and marching him off to ignominious exile. Duvalier never forgot the sight of that other President, forced to walk between two rows of hard-faced soldiers, helpless despite his people's support. "That will never happen to me," he had vowed then. Now, after the Pasquet fiasco, he crystallized his plans to guarantee that it never did.

Invasion hysteria gave him the opportunity to invoke nightly curfews, government by decree, execution of plotters, and imprisonment of those daring to speak out against the government. Playing on American sensibilities, he accused the U.S. of encouraging the invasion by five of its own citizens, then accepted increased aid and, as a Christmastime offering, allowed a Marine mission to train Haiti's army, now equipped with Italian weapons.

Arrests proliferated, and so did summary executions, including the shooting of two of Clément Jumelle's brothers. As Haiti reeled under the shock of these savage new measures, Duvalier moved swiftly and emasculated the army, firing Flambert and another general, ten colonels and forty lieutenant-colonels, and most officers trained under the Marine occupation. He replaced them with younger men and, by a decree of 9 January 1959, unified the services under his personal direction and authority as Supreme Commander of the Armed Forces, and restructured the army to make it extremely difficult and dangerous for decentralized and competing officers to orchestrate a coup d'état.

Duvalier also created a new Presidential Guard, an elite corps who lived in the palace. In a final crescendo of domination, Duvalier also restructured the *cagoulards* into an armed civilian militia patriotically named Volunteers of National Security, but known almost exclusively as the Tonton Macoutes. These were bogeymen of Haitian folk belief who prowled at night in search of bad little boys and girls whom they thrust into their *macoutes,* the straw satchels peasants carry. Duvalier's Tonton Macoutes carried guns instead of satchels but they also prowled at night, and their victims were seldom seen again.

At first Macoute costume was limited to sunglasses, hip-riding pistols, and arrogance, but later they wore the dark blue denim of the agricultural laborer and the *caco* guerrilla, with wide-brimmed felt cowboy hats and rebel-red scarves, which had often been the *cacos'* only badge. Black and from impoverished backgrounds, Macoutes were recruited from every corner of the country, tantalized by this chance at power, prestige, the joys of serving their President, and protection from other Macoutes. They joined by the thousands, whole families often chipping in for the purchase of the envied VSN identification card that permitted men to hack their way up through the hunger of Haitian life.

In the early stages Macoutes were commanded by army officers, but such a profound enmity soon sprang up between army and VSN that a delighted Duvalier decided the time had come to separate them. He appointed his ruthless friend Clément Barbot to lead the Macoutes and elevated them over all soldiers so that Macoutes had the right of life and death over any member of society, and could with impunity punish or kill even the men in olive green, the soldiers Duvalier feared so pathologically.

Duvalier did not introduce the goon squad or secret police to Haiti. Since slavery and the slave patrols they had been a part of society. Duvalier's genius lay in how he designed their hierarchical structure as a giant-bottomed pyramid with most Macoutes at the bottom and a few Duvalier fanatics as commanders. At the pinnacle, in absolute control, was Duvalier himself. Socially, the Macoutes came from the most disadvantaged classes and regarded the VSN as their sole escape from the relentless misery and hard work that inevitably awaited them. Virtually all-black, the Macoutes were suddenly elevated into positions of power over even the richest, lightest-skinned merchant, whom they could and did terrorize, extort money from, and just plain rob. But Macoutes were more than milling mobs of thugs. They were also important men—*chefs de section*—rural section chiefs who ruled their huge populations with iron control, and personally came to the palace to report to Duvalier any possible breath of subversive activity or even thought.

They were also *houngans,* for few knew better than Duvalier how crucial are vodoun priests to the Haitian people. With the double protection of the gods in the heavens and Duvalier in the palace, legions of *houngans* also enlisted as Macoutes and gave Duvalier not merely loyal service but also prayed mightily for his continued success as President.

Duvalier also tapped another important source for recruits—the oppressed and overburdened half of the population who were female, and thousands of poor black women joined the Fillettes Laleau, the VSN's female counterpart. These Fillettes were armed, mean, and often more dangerous than Macoutes, for far fewer girls and women joined than men, but those who did were usually tougher and more dedicated to service than many more opportunistic Macoutes.

With advance-guard feminism, Duvalier even appointed women as Macoute commandants. In Jérémie a convicted thief, Sanette Balmir, rose to command the local Macoutes. She proved by her every action that in her short homely person Duvalier had correctly identified a bitter, brutal, and vengeful woman who until her death would remain fanatically loyal to his leadership.

Duvalier's personal militia now infiltrated every layer and niche of society. Obsessed by the fear of revolt, unable to put the Pasquet invasion into any sort of perspective, Duvalier lost sight of all objectives but one: retain power, monopolize power, aggrandize power. By the late 1950s, Papa Doc, who once labored to heal his people, had become a maniacally single-minded autocrat.

Duvalier's political motto was "Gratitude is cowardice," and he determined to show neither. The merest glimmer of disaffection, a whispered warning, even mere whim, destroyed careers and sometimes lives. The flight of the intellectual and professional class out of Haiti escalated, and the poorest country in the Western Hemisphere had the dubious honor of staffing hospitals and schools all over Africa and North America.

Clément Jumelle was the only 1957 presidential candidate still in Haiti. Hiding in peasant huts, moving constantly, Jumelle and his wife escaped death only by continual flight. After Duvalier murdered his brothers Ducasse and Charles, and imprisoned Gaston and two of his sisters, Jumelle never again smiled. His health deteriorated, and slowly he lost hope of anything but daily survival.

Yvonne Hakime-Rimpel left the hospital a changed personality. Once robust and outgoing, she became a fearful woman devoted entirely to her children. Her marriage to Rimpel faltered. For the rest of her life she was plagued with bad health.

Yvonne's sister Marcelle fared little better. Her husband, Pierre-Edouard, had gone into hiding. Patients anxious about her political problems ceased to arrive at her clinic. Her four children continued at school only through the charity of the nuns because they could no longer pay their tuition fees. And for these four children, childhood was becoming a nightmare in which Tonton Macoutes patrolled outside the house, voices were hushed, and adults suddenly lost the power to protect and nurture.

Out in far-off Jérémie, Duvalierist Antoine Jean-Charles fared much better. His candidate had won, and within a short time Duvalier rewarded him by appointing him regional attorney general. Jean-Charles also applauded when he heard that Duvalier had imprisoned Antonio Rimpel, his mulatto Finance Minister. "Rimpel's a thief, and Papa Doc wants to show the world he won't tolerate stealing the way other presidents did," Jean-Charles boasted loudly and often to anyone who cared to listen. He rejoiced at the turn of events. The struggle had been long and hard, but at last he had solid proof that he and other Haitians had been right when they chose Duvalier.

In Lestère the gas station owner, Orestil Louissaint, regretted the day he had first laid eyes on Duvalier. The President now owed him $12,600 for the gas he had bought on credit for his 1957 electoral campaign, and the debt was destroying Louissaint. The last time Duvalier had come to his house Louissaint had broached the matter. As chubby six-year-old Jean-Claude ate thick, spiced ham sandwiches, his father pulled out his checkbook, scribbled in his enormous script, then handed Louissaint a check for $300. Louissaint glanced at it in disbelief, then shook his head.

"I've got a mortgaged house in Port-au-Prince," he exclaimed. "I'm going to lose it if you don't pay me."

Duvalier put the rejected check back into his pocket and nodded. "*Eh bien.* Go and see the Finance Minister," he said calmly. He picked up his glass of 7-Up and sipped. "He'll settle your account for you."

Louissaint did as instructed, but at the Finance Ministry he was told no allocation had been made for paying him. He went immediately to the palace, where after several hours Duvalier received him. He heard Louissaint's tale impassively. "*Eh bien.* Go to the Interior Minister," he said finally. "He'll pay you."

The Interior Minister was Dr. Aurèle Joseph, Duvalier's inseparable companion during the anti-yaws campaign. "Certainly I can pay you," Joseph said, tapping his fingers on his desk. "All you have to do to receive payment is to join the VSN."

Louissaint couldn't believe his ears. Become a Macoute, Orestil Louissaint, Lestère's most prosperous merchant and an officer in the Masonic Lodge!

Three months later Duvalier summoned Louissaint and five other leading Duvalierists to the palace. They were his special commission, Duvalier informed them, and every eight days they were to come to Port-au-Prince to report on what was happening in their area. The others agreed enthusiastically, and at every palace meeting spewed information, inventing it when there was none and flattering the President in the most extravagant terms. All except Louissaint, who sat silently through the performance.

At one meeting Duvalier called him in before the others. "Now then, Louissaint," he said cajolingly. "How is it that you, one of the first of my Duvalierist children, never have anything to tell me?"

"Excellence, I work so hard I have no time at all to inform myself about my neighbors' doings," Louissaint replied.

Duvalier said nothing, but immediately afterward he gave the other five commission members revolvers, leaving Louissaint unarmed.

"But, Excellence! I've already received several threats from Déjoie-ists who say they're going to burn my gas tanks."

Duvalier regarded him coldly. "I have no more guns," he said.

Never again did Duvalier receive him in the palace, and a year later debt-crippled Louissaint lost his house in Port-au-Prince. . For him, and his fourteen children, the Duvalierist dream had become a nightmare.

Duvalier's 1959 New Year's present was ominous. On that night Cuba's dictator—and Duvalier's friend—Fulgencio Batista fled for his life, and young Communist guerrilla Fidel Castro installed himself as Cuba's new President. Duvalier panicked, immediately foreseeing hotbeds of Haitian resistance springing up under Castro's protection. To forestall it he wooed Castro like a desperate lover. He recognized Cuba, sent gifts of medicine, and pardoned several important political prisoners, including two of Clément Jumelle's sisters and their brother Gaston, softening his grim regime.

To no avail, for from the very beginning Castro welcomed anti-Duvalierists with open arms. Louis Déjoie, unmoved by Duvalier's remission of his *in absentia* death sentence, landed in Cuba three days after Castro took over. There, allied with Fignolé and Jumelle partisans, he formed United Opposition, which blasted Creole programs to Haiti, trained an invasion force, and worked unceasingly to uproot Duvalier.

The would-be invaders had access to impressive supplies of firearms, ships, bazookas, tanks, planes and machine guns, for Castro was willing to place at their disposition whatever they needed from his own as yet uninventoried booty from the deposed Batista's arsenal. Professional American arms dealers also approached the Haitians and offered to underwrite their invasions. However, despite its common goals, the misnamed United Opposition was riddled with dissension. Yet Castro insisted on unity and a common political program. "Revolution, yes; occupation, no," he repeated over and over. Within months the fragmented United Opposition left Cuba. They remained so mistrustful of each other that at the year's end, when they gathered in New York City, they failed to draft a New Year's message to the Haitian people—they could not agree on its wording.

"Exile," concluded a disgusted Paquin, "instead of uniting the politicians, divided them. What was really keeping Duvalier alive and well was the divisiveness of the opposition in New York . . . instead of fighting Duvalier, [they] were building a list of their enemies in exile to prevent them from returning to Haiti when the new regime assumed power. . . . It was a world of make-believe, a carnival of words and circumstances, an intellectual fantasy."

The fortunate Duvalier had other friends in addition to his incompetent enemies. The United States decided to stand by their anti-Communist ally. So did Trujillo, no fonder of Castro than Duvalier was. Aid money increased, and military assistance to ward off Cuban-based invasionary forces was given. Once he got over his initial shock, Duvalier used the new Cuban Communist threat as a weapon to maneuver in the outside world as effectively as he had inside Haiti.

The one former political rival not actively plotting against Duvalier was Clément Jumelle. By April 1959, Jumelle's only struggle was to continue living. Deathly ill with uremia, with his wife he found refuge on Cuban soil, in this case the residence of the Cuban ambassador in Port-au-Prince.

Ambassador Antonio Rodriguez y Echezabal found the dying man on his patio. For five days he spared no effort or expense to save him, even sending for Cuban specialists, but on April 11 Jumelle died.

Jumelle's death did not end his persecution. Rodriguez heard that Duvalier wanted the corpse, either for vodoun rituals or to prevent a huge public funeral with Jumelle supporters mourning for their leader. There are several versions of how the Cuban outwitted the president. Jumelle's cousin Lyonel Paquin's seems the most authentic.

> As soon as Clement Jumelle died, the ambassador notified the government; he also called Celcis Funeral Parlor and asked them to pick up the body. The details of the funeral arrangements were thus well known to all. This is precisely what the Cuban ambassador and Jumelle's friends had wanted.
>
> A blue Ford belonging to one of the doctors treating the late Clement Jumelle was parked in the back-door entrance of the house. The back of the car was stripped of its seats. In that space the body of Jumelle was stuck, wrapped in white linen and well camouflaged.
>
> The funeral-parlor hearse drove in and orderlies handling a straw stretcher went in—and out with a rather light cargo. The Duvalier people did not lose time to make sure that Jumelle's body was in there. They found the stretcher empty. They felt rightly cheated but had to restrain their thirst for vengeance because they were on Embassy ground. How would Duvalier take that mystification? Who among them

would pay for that? Pandemonium reigned in their camp. The empty hearse left.

Behind it, the blue Ford followed surreptitiously and sailed smoothly to the medical clinic of Clement's brother Gaston, located on rue Magny. There, a team of medical doctors removed Clement's vital organs, which were interred in a safe place.

Thus assured that Duvalier could not eviscerate Jumelle's cadaver for bizarre vodoun rites, the family prepared for the funeral immortalized in Graham Greene's *The Comedians*. At an intersection a black police van screeched to a halt beside them. Police and Macoutes carrying tommy guns raced over and hauled the coffin out of the hearse and furiously slammed it into their van. Jumelle's cousin Maurice Lédy stood, shocked into silence. The widow flung herself onto a Macoute, cursing him as he stole her husband's body. Duvalier's henchman Luc Désyr was there, Lédy noted, his body braced as he watched the agitated crowd, smiling a little and murmuring to himself. Within a few minutes the operation was over, and the coffin snatchers sped away.

With pandemonium behind him, Lédy and several other men managed to flag down cars and followed the coffin, slowing down only as they neared the palace. Then they watched helplessly as the police van drove through the palace gates and disappeared. "Duvalier's going to capture his *loa*," someone whispered. "Duvalier's going to use the body for magic."

Lédy jumped out of the car and ran without stopping to the Grande Rue. There he caught a *tap-tap* for his hometown of Léogane, where his father was a foreman in the Public Works Department. For months he would stay inside the house, too frightened to face Duvalier's world.

Inside the palace, Lédy heard later, Duvalier received the portly, swollen cadaver with grave relish. As a host of Macoutes stood around watching in awed fear, their President mounted the body and called upon its spirit. He was too late. Jumelle's spirit had already flown, and in his disappointment Duvalier blamed the family, who had cheated him of his prize.

Hours later a vanload of Macoutes delivered Jumelle's closed coffin to his family in their hometown of St. Marc, ordering them to inter it immediately. When the family insisted on opening the coffin so that mourners could view it, the Macoutes angrily removed it again, drove to the local cemetery, and paid gravediggers to bury it then and there.

Deprived of a Church blessing, and riddled with doubt because of persistent rumors that Duvalier still had the body, the family dug up the shallow grave and opened the coffin only to find a thin stranger rather than their corpulent brother. The next Sunday morning the French curé Father Joseph Marrec preached against Duvalier, and thereafter omitted the traditional prayers for the nation's President.

A week later two of Jumelle's sisters, heedless of consequence, drove up to the palace gates and, until soldiers grabbed and silenced them, stood clinging to the fence and hurling insults at the top of their lungs. "We hid you in St. Marc when Magloire was hounding you," they shrieked. Duvalier, inside the palace, gave a curt command. The sisters were arrested, imprisoned in the National Penitentiary, and beaten. He released them and their brother Gaston months later, as a public relations gesture for the outside world.

In October 1957, François Duvalier had entered the palace in the best health he would ever again enjoy in his life. He was a slight man whose weight hovered at one hundred fifty pounds. He had been diabetic since early adulthood, and also suffered chronic heart disease, with phlebitis and a limp so pronounced that he seemed unable to walk a straight line. Degenerative arthritis attacked his hands and wrists. Writing was a painful chore, and lifting the telephone often caused him such anguish that he relied on those around him to convey it to his ear.

Duvalier was frugal in his social relations, and was known as a withdrawn and undemonstrative man. Lyonel Paquin, after observing him during an interview, car ride, and social visit, described him as "owlish looking . . . motionless, serene like a Buddha. . . . [I] noticed his likeness to a sad frog with a heavy lower lip and a sad, almost painful wryness in his countenance."

His personal physician was Dr. Jacques Fourcand, a Jérémie-born neurosurgeon who had studied in the States and worked in various American hospitals, including New York City's famed Bellevue. On May 24, 1959, Duvalier had a heart attack so massive, it almost ended his short presidency before it could become anything but a brief and bitter memory. Exactly what happened remains a matter of controversy. Dr. Fourcand insists that Duvalier also went into a diabetic coma, and that he was correct when he administered insulin. But the fact was that Duvalier did not revive but remained comatose, and it was only the frantic intervention of his loyal Tonton Macoute chief Clément Barbot that saved him.

Another young doctor told nurse Simone Duvalier he thought Fourcand was trying to kill Duvalier and suggested that glucose might reverse the effects of what he conjectured was an insulin overdose. Simone discussed this possibility with Barbot, who strode out of the palace and returned almost immediately with glucose. With glucose pumping through his body, Duvalier stirred. Barbot notified the American ambassador Gérard Drew, and with his approval the American Naval Mission rushed cardiologists from the U.S. Guantanamo Naval Base to save the dictator's life.

For a month they cared for him, reinforced by two New York doctors flown in as special consultants. Slowly and painfully, life returned. But what proved much more significant than the deteriorated state of his body was the uncertain state of his mind. Fourcand and other close Duvalier associates believed that oxygen deprivation during the nine hours Duvalier had been comatose and incorrectly medicated had caused irreversible neurological damage. Since the heart attack, Barbot said, the President "had never been the same man."

Independently and on several occasions, Barbot and Dr. Loughlin notified U.S. officials about Duvalier's mental condition, but the Americans dismissed the information and declared that Duvalier's government was constitutional and they would support it.

For another twelve years the Haitian tragedy was compounded by the dictatorial leadership of François Duvalier, mad son of a mad mother.

Duvalier convalesced in a Haiti of bombings, arson, and armed attacks. In addition to invasion from without and destabilization and terror from within, his enemies even resorted to the vodoun all Haiti knew Duvalier himself practiced. One evening they stole his father's corpse, digging it up from the coffin Duvalier had followed to the cemetery only a month before the election. The vandals cut out the heart, then fouled Duval's moldly corpse and tombstone with human feces. That was why in 1971 the Duvalier family buried Papa Doc's body secretly, forever safe from sacrilege, leaving the family vault empty.

Duvalier was to spend the rest of his life in subduing the people he had won over in the 1957 election. He had campaigned hard and cunningly to win, using the magic of Estimé and the reassuring presence of Madame Estimé. He had said all the right things and enlisted all the right people—loyal, devoted *noiristes,* disgusted with the savage injustices inherent in Haitian society, and *houngans,* the people's priests, who healed, settled disputes, and made sense out of a complex world. But with victory came not the recognition owed to an elected leader but opposition so immediate, deadly, and unending that merely to survive each assault was a full-time occupation.

The attack on the Kenscoff military post, the constant bombings and threats, the utter refusal to accept Duvalier's electoral victory—all these killed any chance that he would ever be the great President he longed to be or implement promised social changes so fundamental that he referred to them as revolutionary. In the first days of his presidency he forgave Déjoie and Jumelle, begging them for cooperation, even offering them official posts in his government. They refused, preferring to go underground, each convinced that within six months he could prise the little doctor out of power.

By 1959 power in all its dimensions was Duvalier's obsession. The good intentions that had once inspired him dried up as he devoted his life to maneuvering and manipulating to keep control. Duvalier the proud intellectual suddenly shied away from all those who knew and could articulate what he was becoming. Instead he surrounded himself with illiterate Macoutes who did not reproach him and who guaranteed his political survival. He abandoned the principles that had endeared him to his people, and with breathtaking cynicism he breached all natural laws of decency and honor. And though he never forgot that he was a doctor, he personally served up tortures and murders, each one a negation of the Hippocratic Oath.

In 1959 Pierre-Edouard Bellande was still in Haiti, and safe in the Venezuelan Embassy. He was not alone; he shared his sanctuary with eighteen others, including a young woman with a two-month-old baby. On the outside, his own family and friends were not safe. Ever since his flight, Macoutes had returned time and again to search his house, destroy the family archives, even the children's report cards, and they had carted away the vast library with its five thousand law books in a country that was now lawless.

Macoutes had also machine-gunned his cousins' house after Duvalier discovered they had once sheltered him. Nobody was killed because a young government radio operator had overheard the order and warned them. But their lives were ruined. It was all because of him, and Bellande realized he had to leave his homeland.

Duvalier was furious that Bellande had escaped him. He refused him a safe-conduct to Venezuela and sent a stream of cajoling messages urging him to leave the ambassador's residence, assuring him that nothing would happen. Outside the house, Macoutes kept up a constant harassment, circling it and firing in the air. Venezuelan ambassador Enrico Miliani was a feisty man, and when he heard too many shots he would get out his pistol and shoot too. In addition, he armed all his guests.

Finally the fugitives left, among them assorted journalists, politicians, former ministers, and a tailor. Twelve members of the diplomatic corps escorted them to the airport by arriving at the embassy where the Haitians sneaked into the cars and ducked down while the national flags of Mexico, Brazil, Peru, Venezuela, Chile, and several other countries were draped over each car, covering them.

At the airport the diplomats circled the travelers, and though Macoutes swarmed around and shouted threats, diplomatic immunity prevailed over goonism, and Bellande and seventeen others arrived safely in Venezuela, where he began to beam shortwave anti-Duvalier Creole programs into Haiti every day at lunchtime.

Back in Haiti, Duvalier declared Ambassador Miliani *persona non grata*. When Venezuela replaced him with one then yet another ambassador who also harbored fugitives, Duvalier expelled them too and finally the two countries cut relations and did not resume them for eleven years.

Duvalier had cowed much of the civilian population and driven out or underground all political opponents. Though Castro's Cuban triumph had initially caught him off balance, he had recovered to turn it into his own strongest selling point in his relations with the Americans. Whatever else he might be, Duvalier was no Communist, and jittery as Castro had made them, the Americans were prepared to overlook torture, murder, and disappearances and listen with eager ears to reassuring speeches about democracy, human rights, and unmitigated anticommunism.

But Duvalier's power was still not secure. There remained within Haiti two important elements that offered stubborn moral resistance to Duvalierism, the Church and the students. By 1959 he was ready to move to crush the most powerful of them, the Church, and he struck out against it by expelling its foreign priests, challenging the Vatican itself, and forcing clerical "Haitianization" so that he could control through pliant local priests the one institution that refused to bow to him.

The first two priests expelled were Father Etienne Grienenberger, superior of the Holy Ghost Fathers, and St. Marc's long-time parish priest, Father Joseph Marrec. Grienenberger was a friend of Magloire's and an outspoken anti-Duvalierist who had personally reported the Bel-Air massacre to Pope Pius XII and refused to sing mass in the church next to a Satanic site. Father Marrec had meddled in the scandal of Clément Jumelle's burial and for weeks afterward had preached against Duvalier in his parish church. The official reasons for the expulsions stressed the priests' uncooperative attitudes and charged them with working toward "social disintegration."

As a thousand Catholics knelt in prayer for the expelled priests, Clément Barbot and a contingent of Tonton Macoutes armed with *cocomacacs*, or nightsticks, invaded the Port-au-Prince Cathedral, smashed heads and sacred objects, then arrested sixty worshipers. The official justification for this outrage? "Even Christ went into the temple and chased out evildoers." The incident was a warning. Duvalier was on the warpath, and nothing would stop him except total victory over the Church.

One morning during this new phase of post–heart attack Duvalierism, Duvalier and a cavalcade of Tonton Macoutes left the palace for the vodoun-impregnated district of Croix-des-Bouquets, nineteen miles out of Port-au-Prince. At the large public square in front of the Catholic church they disembarked, and Duvalier strolled peacefully about, shaking hands, chatting with the people, biding his time.

By noon hundreds of men and women crowded in from the surrounding countryside, at least half *houngans* and *mambos*. The Macoutes had been thorough, driving through the back roads and stopping at every peristyle they saw to spread the word: "The President has come to talk to you, he's waiting for you in the town square."

In his prim white suit Duvalier met his people, standing on a pedestal improvised from vegetable tables at the nearby market. As the people assembled and stood waiting, he began to talk, switching from the French they could not understand to the Creole they could, telling them about the greatness of his revolutionary principles and urging them to devote themselves to helping him succeed against his enemies.

He finished with a statement that was both simple and chilling. "Never forget that I am the supreme authority of the State," he warned them. "Henceforth, I, I alone, I am your only master." The *houngans* and *mambos* understood exactly what he meant. He was one of them, and for the good of every single Haitian they would have to pray for him, and never forget to make the proper sacrifices to the spirits who alone could protect him.

By April 1961 relations with the United States were well if not totally under control, and Duvalier made a political move that made a mockery out of democracy, a travesty of justice, and a full-fledged dictator out of the country doctor who had once wanted to serve his people. Duvalier suddenly dissolved the Legislature and ordered elections to be held three weeks later. At first it was not clear who was running. Certainly the candidates were all Duvalierists, but was Duvalier himself again running for President? The Constitution expressly forbade it—a president could not succeed himself. The ballot circumvented the issue, carrying Duvalier's name but not specifying if he was a candidate or merely mentioned as incumbent President of the Republic.

Election Day did nothing to demystify the question, and so voters merely selected from among the candidates for deputy. Many voted voluntarily. Others were conscripted, including Americans, Canadians, and other foreigners, herded by a Cap Haitien Duvalierist fanatic to the polls. Most stayed home, but despite what observers considered a skimpy turnout, the ballots took over a week to count. The results, for Duvalier, were worth the wait: 1,320,748 to 0 in favor of his candidates and, to the surprise of all but the politically savvy and cynical, in favor of a second six-year term for Duvalier.

Duvalier accepted the results of Haiti's estimated one million eligible voters with a show of resignation and humility. "I accept the people's will," he said upon hearing of his impossibly stunning victory. "As a revolutionary, I have no right to disregard the will of the people." An editorial in *The New York Times* was more caustic. "Latin America has witnessed many fraudulent elections throughout its history but none has been more outrageous than the one which has just taken place in Haiti."

Post-election euphoria lasted only a month. The May 30 assassination of fellow dictator Rafael Trujillo pierced Duvalier like a dart. Terrible enough if Trujillo's security system had failed. Worse, much worse, that loyal acolytes had turned on their leader and gunned him down as he sped off for an evening with a courtesan. Duvalier, awed by the implications, devoured newspaper accounts of the killing and sent his own Dominican-based agents to furnish him with every detail they could glean.

The recent treachery of Clément Barbot underscored the lesson to be learned from Trujillo's death. A friend so intimate that his wife and Simone Duvalier were like sisters, their children inseparable, Barbot had literally saved Duvalier's life in 1959. Then he had run the country while Duvalier convalesced, afterward handing back the reins of power without the least reluctance. He also headed the Tonton Macoutes, who kept Duvalier in power, and did so efficiently and loyally. Barbot's first disloyalty was mere greed—not sharing with Duvalier money extorted from businessmen. More seriously, after the heart attack, he questioned the President's sanity. Prodded by advisers and sycophants jealous of Barbot's virtually limitless powers, and suddenly jealous himself, Duvalier struck.

Barbot was captured after a French Embassy party and imprisoned in Fort Dimanche, already notorious as the death site of thousands of Haitians. Following in the footsteps of his own victims, he endured interrogation by torture, followed by eighteen months' imprisonment, during which he prepared for certain death. It never came. Lulled by reports that Barbot had experienced religious rebirth in prison, Duvalier suddenly released him, gave him a new British car, and kept him under constant surveillance. Barbot crept out only to attend prayer meetings, often at the Canadian-run Villa Manrèse Jesuit seminary, and showed no sign that he was anything but the burned-out case he seemed.

Duvalier's pre–heart attack lapses into brutal repression now became policy. The man who had thrust a helmet on his head and supervised the rape and failed execution of Yvonne Hakime-Rimpel now orchestrated so many such scenes, he had to delegate to others the grim duties of torturer and murderer. Sometimes he participated himself, vicariously, through peepholes cut into the walls of palace "interrogation" rooms. Yvonne Hakime-Rimpel herself witnessed this when, years later, Macoutes suddenly appeared and took her to the palace. During hours of interrogation, persistent but without physical abuse, they asked her, "Who was responsible for beating you that night? Was it the government? Do you think it was *Duvalier?*"

Yvonne, seeing the flash of a spectacled eye peering through the wall, gave the only answer she could. She did not know who had beaten her, but it was not soldiers or the government who had done it. Above all, it had certainly not been Duvalier.

During the 1960s the tortures, murders, and "disappearances" skyrocketed. A famous case was that of Eric Brièrre, a young mulatto who tried to assassinate Duvalier and paid with his life, tortured to death in Fort Dimanche while his father had to listen from another cell. Eric died after torture so gruesome that one witness, Major Roger St. Albin, vomited at the sight of his corpse.

All Haitians were touched one way or another. Curfews were common, and roadblocks manned by Macoutes or soldiers who demanded money, often as little as a dime, to allow travelers to continue. Haitians in every city, town, village, and even remote hamlets suffered the terror of midnight searches, the blood-chilling and perfunctory knock before Macoutes broke down the door, the indiscriminate beatings, the destruction of precious family documents, meaningless interrogations, and the tragedy of family members handcuffed and thrust into Macoutes' cars, never again to be seen. Even foreigners enjoyed little immunity. An old Jamaican, storekeeper Cromwell James, who had come to Haiti during the American occupation to better his fortunes, spoke out fearlessly against the terror and was immediately subjected to it. After three weeks in jail he was released so wounded that within a week he died of gangrene.

Even more astonishing in diplomatic bravado was the arrest of the twelve-year-old son of Colonel Robert Heinl, the Marine officer in charge of training Duvalier's troops. As Michael traveled to school in a *tap-tap,* he looked out at the country Duvalier himself described as "rotting in misery, hunger, nudity, sickness, and illiteracy." To a friend beside him Michael commented, "How poor those people are," and for his sensitivity was arrested by the *tap-tap*'s Macoute driver and taken directly to the palace.

Before worse could happen young Jean-Claude Duvalier saw Michael, his classmate at Collège Bird. "Release him! He's Michael Heinl!" Jean-Claude protested, and at his insistence Michael was freed unharmed, though the incident caused permanent strain in Haitian-Marine relations and permanently poisoned Colonel Heinl against Duvalier. A decade later Heinl and his wife, Nancy, published a voluminous history of Haiti entitled *Written in Blood.*

Duvalier also continued to pursue the Church and intellectuals, expelling priests and cowing, imprisoning, and killing teachers and their students. The priests were mainly foreign, the students mainly anti-Duvalierist elite. On November 24, 1960, Duvalier again struck out at the Church through Monsignor Poirier. Macoutes marched the old man onto a plane for Miami wearing underpants and a cassock with one dollar in his pocket, his false teeth still soaking in a glass back at his residence in Port-au-Prince. The Pope, "pained by the violation of the church's sacrosanct rights and by the unjust and inconsiderate treatment" of Poirier, excommunicated all those responsible for his expulsion. In November 1960, therefore, Haiti's President François Duvalier ceased to be a son of the Holy Roman Catholic Church.

This Roman censure weighed lightly on Duvalier, who fostered his image as a great mystic and declared his government a crusade and a sacrosanct mission. Excommunicated or not, he remained bent on ridding Haiti of independent-minded foreigners he could not dominate, and he continued the expulsions. A trickle then a flood of religious expulsions followed Poirier's, and Episcopalians and Protestants were swooped up in the same net. Duvalier relaxed the pressure, but only temporarily, after he expelled Gonaives Bishop Jean Robert, famed for his relentless persecution of vodoun practitioners. In sermon after sermon Robert denounced as demons all those who believed in vodoun and refused to accept in the local seminary any young men whose relatives were known to practice it. He also liked to make lightning attacks on local peristyles, where his band of fanatics smashed the sacred objects of worship.

For decades Robert ruled sternly over Gonaives, but his predominance came to an abrupt end when Gonaives *houngan* Zacharie Delva, an effeminate homosexual revered by Duvalier for his mystical powers, became a palace favorite and, after Clément Barbot was fired, the second most powerful man in Haiti. Duvalier rescued him from his humble roadside snack cart, called him "Le Leader," and made him his special assistant, above Macoute or military authority, responsible only to Duvalier, utterly powerful and absolutely terrifying. One of Delva's first acts of power was to destroy Robert, the man who had destroyed so many of his own vodoun colleagues.

Former ethnologist Duvalier, who especially hated Robert, gave Delva full rein, then justified the expulsion on three grounds. Robert tolerated the pillaging and destruction of archaeological and folkloric treasures, he injured Catholics by wantonly refusing to baptize, marry, or give them Communion, and in 1957 he had spoken out against candidate Duvalier. *Houngan* Delva underlined his victory over Robert by holding a vodoun *cérémonie* on the steps of the cathedral. To the rhythmic thrum of the traditional drums and the anguished squeals of sacrificial black pigs, Delva chanted, swooned, and, as the faithful watched, swallowed warm pig's blood from a silver chalice.

In the hills outside Jérémie, Antoine Jean-Charles's oldest brother, Abner, joined the Tonton Macoutes. Mentally retarded and illiterate, Abner regarded the VSN card he could not read as the most precious document in the world, and when he shucked his farmer's rags for his Macoute blues, he held his head high, swaggered a bit, and for the only time in his life felt himself to be a man.

5 THE HEIGHT OF THE TERROR

GENERAL GÉRARD CONSTANT CONTINUED THE DEBATE with himself that had begun after Duvalier named him chief of staff. The issue was simple yet impossible: as general chief of staff, should he or should he not oust the President?

It was early April 1963. Nine months earlier, the evening Constant was named chief of staff, U.S. Marine Colonel Heinl and the embassy's CIA chief had offered to help him stage a coup d'état against Duvalier, whom John F. Kennedy had sworn to destroy. Constant had only to ask and, in 1962 as in 1915, the Marines would land in Port-au-Prince Harbor. "I'd rather have my arm chopped off," Constant had replied. Now another serious plot was being prepared, and several Haitian colonels had approached him, urging him to join them in it. Like Constant, they had all begun as enthusiastic pro-Duvalierists. Now, six years later, they risked their lives plotting against the President.

They planned to act in the small hours of April 11, armed with weapons from the American Embassy. Constant listened to them and with leaden heart declined to join them. He could not bring himself to commit treason, no matter how just the cause. And he had once loved François, loved his unassuming manners and his dedication to restoring to black Haitians the dignity of a decent life.

Constant also had another reason. He was convinced that François was dying, limping through the palace in crooked lines, his dark skin gray-tinged, his limbs swollen, his heart a bigger enemy than all Haiti's colonels combined.

*   *   *

On April 10 the rebel officers learned they had been wrong about American arms. Undeterred, they asked an officer in the Dessalines Barracks to give them the key to the armory. Within hours the officer's loyal Duvalierist brother had informed Duvalier. That evening Duvalier summoned all his colonels to the palace. Four of the ringleaders fled to the Brazilian Embassy instead. Those not implicated went, trembling, to the palace. Only Colonel Charles Turnier, pro-American and popular, opted to play for time, protesting his innocence now so that he could oust Duvalier later on.

Duvalier, unmoved, had him arrested and interrogated about his fellow conspirators. Turnier uttered not a single name, and when his captors had beaten him almost to death, they shot him. For days afterward his pulped body lay on the barracks parade ground in grim warning to other would-be plotters.

Duvalier was far from satisfied that he had purged the army of all dissident officers and dismissed seventy-two more. Then, because former officers outnumbered their working brothers, Duvalier prepared one of his famous lists, ex-officers designated as new victims for the death cells of Fort Dimanche.

Exiled anti-Duvalierists responded by bombing Port-au-Prince with leaflets urging the army to rise up against "the gorilla Duvalier, the tyrant vodounist." Frightened Haitians risked brief glances at the leaflets and silently cheered. The next time the plane took off from the Dominican Republic, they knew, it would contain real bombs and not propaganda.

Duvalier made his next move. From April 22 to May 22, he announced, Haiti would celebrate a "Month of Gratitude." All officials had to stand up at public rallies and praise him, and for those who could not find the words, the palace provided ready-made speeches. Duvalier's motive was age-old and universal. Just as the Mafia and Hell's Angels and terrorist groups require initiates to commit themselves forever by an unforgivable crime, so Duvalier forced as many public figures as he could to go on permanent public record as his partisan if not fanatic ally.

His plan worked. One after another men stood up and committed themselves, some heartsick at the hypocrisy, others, like Dr. Jacques Fourcand, rising to Himalayan heights of oratory. As Duvalier listened delightedly, Fourcand labeled the U.S. a "nation of sluts" who raped black girls in Alabama and loosed police dogs on them. If Haitians joined

Americans to plot against Duvalier, Fourcand warned, "blood will flow in Haiti as never before. The land will burn from north to south, from east to west. There will be no sunrise or sunset—just one big flame licking the sky. The dead will be buried under a mountain of ashes because of serving the foreigner."

Clément Barbot had been biding his time. By April 1963 he was ready. On the morning of April 26, adding a new dimension to Haitian savagery, Barbot struck at Duvalier's eleven-year-old son Jean-Claude and fourteen-year-old daughter Simone as they entered College Bird, mere blocks from the palace. Their chauffeur fell dead along with three bodyguards. Jean-Claude and Simone scrambled terrified but unharmed into the school yard and the protective embrace of a Methodist teacher, but Barbot had struck Duvalier an intolerable blow.

Duvalier reacted with unprecedented ferocity. From then on no child was safe in Haiti, no mother or grandmother, for at any moment Duvalier might take them as hostages to punish those he suspected of plotting against him. Waves of killings began that afternoon. Tonton Macoutes shot as many former or retired army officers as they could find, on the grounds that most possessed arms and therefore could have shot at the children. For good measure they also gunned down anyone driving a car like the assassin's.

Meanwhile Duvalier, fixated on revenge, dreamed up a new culprit. Rejecting all suggestions that Barbot might be the mastermind, he suddenly concluded that ex-Lieutenant François Benoit must have been the assassin—because he was a sharpshooting champion. Macoutes stormed the innocent Benoit's house and machine-gunned his parents, infant son, visitors, servants, even the family dogs. Then out of frustration that Benoit and his schoolteacher wife had escaped them by happening not to be home, the Macoutes also murdered a passing pedestrian named Benoit Armand, simply because his first name was Benoit.

The U.S. reacted to this and other murders with five different official protests. When these went unanswered Kennedy rushed warships to Haiti. On the Dominican border new President Juan Bosch threatened to do the same. Privately, however, Bosch suggested that sending a psychiatrist for Duvalier would be more helpful. And the OAS responded to the international outcry by voting to investigate internal repressions in Haiti.

Duvalier replied with snarling contempt. "Bullets and machine guns capable of daunting Duvalier do not exist. They cannot touch me. . . . I am already an immaterial being," he declared publicly, leaguing himself with the giants Henri Christophe and Jean-Jacques Dessalines, whom only silver bullets could harm. "No foreigner is going to tell me what to do!" he vowed.

Now came cat-and-mouse diplomatic moves. On April 30 an OAS investigative committee arrived. Duvalier sent trucks to bring peasants into the city, plied them with rum, and then relied on the improvised carnival to impress the foreigners. He also spoke to them only in Creole, which none understood, cursing them and not caring if they suspected it.

Duvalier was equally reckless in the face of American pressure. He imposed martial law and a nightly curfew. "The Tonton Macoutes searched everywhere," said an American who left the country. "Everywhere you see people with their arms in the air, being patted under the shoulders as police frisk them for guns." On May 7 the U.S. ordered its functionaries evacuated. In American eyes Duvalier's government was falling apart. "The United States has for some time hoped for the fall of the Duvalier dictatorship in Haiti and it could be that the opportunity will present itself this weekend," wrote *The New York Times*. The New York *Herald Tribune* was more explicit: "Duvalier's black magic . . . which metamorphoses so easily into [Cuban] red magic, can no longer be accepted by us as a purely internal affair. And that is why we must take the bull by the horns and envision intervening 'now,' when it can serve our interests. . . ."

In New York the Haitian Consulate booked flights to Paris for the entire Duvalier family. The rumor mills boiled. The situation had finally become impossible, and Papa Doc was fleeing as well. On the fifteenth Duvalier announced a press conference, and international reporters spent the morning at the Hotel Oloffson hotly debating whether they were about to hear the dictator resign, as Voice of America had announced. Instead, Duvalier suddenly halted the killings, the incendiary speeches on the radio, and the roadblocks that pocked Port-au-Prince.

At the press conference the reporters waited tensely. Duvalier arrived late as always, denied all charges of repression, and accused the U.S. of fomenting Haitian unrest. Before he shuffled off he smiled and said, "I would like to stay longer with you but I'm very busy today." The hoax of Duvalier's abdication was over.

That evening the Paris tickets were canceled, and a Macoute parade honoring Duvalier paraded through the capital. The false departure bought Duvalier time he wanted and tickled his cynical humor as well.

As he had shrieked to his people during their Month of Gratitude, "God and the people are the source of all power. I have twice been given the power. I have taken it, and damn it, I will keep it forever."

Duvalier's final triumph against President Kennedy and the U.S. came when he demanded withdrawal of once tough-talking Ambassador Thurston. Washington agreed, considering compliance with the request a crucial prerequisite to positive new American-Haitian relations. While some Haitians crowed and the diplomatic corps rallied in support of him, Ambassador Thurston left Haiti and, on Duvalier's orders, could not even return to fetch his personal belongings.

Meanwhile, Clément Barbot's family escaped to the Argentine Embassy. Barbot, whose attack on the Duvalier children had precipitated the crisis, then went into lightning action. "Duvalier is a madman," he said in an interview with an American journalist, and he repeated how the President frequently cited three hundred as the number of people he wanted to kill every year. Barbot's terrorist attacks lasted until July 14, when a peasant informed on him and his brother Harry, a pediatrician. Duvalier sent forces to the sugarcane field they hid in, set it afire, then shot the brothers down as they stumbled out. In remembrance, Duvalier had photos of the dead man plastered on police station walls.

In the late summer of 1963 Graham Greene was inspired by an article about Papa Doc's Haiti to make his third and last trip there. Much of what Greene experienced later appeared in his novel *The Comedians*. "It was the most critical year of Papa Doc's rule and perhaps the cruelest. . . . It was a dark city in which I arrived that summer, and though the curfew had been raised no one ventured abroad after dark." When Greene did, however, he saw a city alive only to fear. "In the public park the musical fountain stood black, waterless, unplaying. Electric globes winked out the nocturnal message, 'I am the Haitian flag, united and indivisible. François Duvalier.' No wonder that for years afterwards Port-au-Prince featured in my dreams. I would be back there incognito, afraid to be spotted."

Even in daylight the capital was frightening. "No pedestrians passed the palace—it was thought dangerous to walk under those blank windows through which Baron Samedi, the haunter of graveyards, might be peering down: even taxi drivers would avoid that side of the square." In retrospect, what most astonished Greene was that Duvalier survived

Duvalierism. "I little thought that Papa Doc would survive to die a natural death years later."

Aubelin Jolicoeur was one real-life character who appeared as Petit Pierre in *The Comedians*. A local journalist and Tourist Bureau official who greeted tourists and reported on their activities, Jolicoeur was still courageous enough to publish passages that to Greene showed "an odd satirical courage—perhaps he depended on the police not to read between the lines. . . . He was a tiny figure of a man. He was just as I had remembered him, hilarious. Even the time of day was humorous to him. He had the quick movements of a monkey, and he seemed to swing from wall to wall on ropes of laughter. I had always thought that, when the time came, and surely it must one day come in his precarious defiant livelihood, he would laugh at his executioner." Yet Jolicoeur also survived, sometimes in favor and sometimes in disgrace, protected by his powerful mentor Tonton Macoute Commandant Madame Max Adolphe.

Greene stayed for months, until he had penetrated the Haitian reality as much as its great fear penetrated him. In the nearly empty Hotel Oloffson he and host Al Seitz amused themselves by co-authoring an article later published in a London newspaper: "The Mechanics of Running an Empty Hotel." Papa Doc had passed legislation forbidding bankruptcy or closing of businesses, and so daily the big American, a former University of Georgia football player, spent his days on the veranda overlooking the murderous city playing backgammon with Jolicoeur, Antoine Hérard, the Duvalierist mayor of Port-au-Prince, and Syrian-Haitian art dealer and secret anti-Duvalierist Issa El Saieh. Their drinks were served by César, who appeared as Joseph in *The Comedians,* limping as César did after a beating by Macoutes.

"Poor Haiti and the character of Doctor Duvalier's rule are not invented, the latter not even blackened for dramatic effect," Greene said in introducing his novel. "Impossible to deepen that night."

When his enemy John F. Kennedy was assassinated on November 22, Duvalier reveled in his death. That night, only the palace was lit up with electricity rationed for everyone else as Duvalier and his intimates celebrated Kennedy's demise. Privately, Duvalier claimed credit for it. Many and powerful were the *cérémonies* of blackest magic he had offered up to the pantheon's dark gods, and Kennedy's death seemed proof that he had succeeded. Duvalier was especially convinced by the date, for since his first—and dodgily genuine—electoral victory on September 22, 1957, he had regarded twenty-two as his special number.

In 1962 Kennedy had virtually cut off American aid. Now he was dead. Early in 1964, report Nancy and Robert Heinl, Duvalier sent an envoy to Arlington Cemetery to bring back a vial of graveside air, a morsel of earth, and shreds of funeral flowers for new rituals. But Kennedy's *loa*, like Clément Jumelle's, had already departed, and it took two more years of intricate diplomacy before Duvalier's new "friend," President Lyndon Johnson, restored the flow of funds to his starved nation.

On January 9 Jérémie Attorney General Antoine Jean-Charles stared, horrified, at the telegram his Macoute clerk Antonio Benjamin had just handed him. "Urgent you come to Port-au-Prince immediately. Stop. Signed Luc François, Minister of the Interior."

Benjamin coughed awkwardly beside him. "Maybe it'll be nothing. Maybe they just want you to report on something."

Jean-Charles pushed his glasses back firmly onto the bridge of his small pug nose. "I'm not worried," he replied stoutly in his habitually cracking voice. But he was lying, because everyone knew that a summons to Port-au-Prince almost always meant death.

Two days later Jean-Charles sat next to his wife in the bedroom they shared with their two children. A small suitcase lay at his feet. Claudie's face was contorted with pain, and her small hand gripped his so hard it hurt him. Later he drove slowly down the white-pebbled road overlooking the lush greenery and the red tin roofs to the airport.

In Port-au-Prince the Interior Minister accused Jean-Charles of plotting with Duvalier's brother-in-law Lucien Daumec to overthrow the President.

"I refuse to answer except to Dr. Duvalier," he said hoarsely.

The next day the Interior Minister accompanied Jean-Charles to his interview with President Duvalier. Duvalier kept them waiting two hours, but Duvalier kept everyone waiting. At 1:15 he received them in his office, as impeccably dressed as Jean-Charles remembered. His security chief Luc Désyr was with him, white-suited and simpering, peering out at them through thick spectacles. The men exchanged brief pleasantries. Then Duvalier stood up, snatched the revolver from his desktop, and began to shout. "I sent for my wife, but instead of coming, she sends word she's sitting down to dinner," he ranted. "This won't do, I tell you. I'm going to go back there and order her to come here at once."

He lumbered out, revolver in hand, leaving the others to wait in shocked silence. Minutes later Haiti's tall, emaciated First Lady entered the room behind her husband. Simone Duvalier greeted the men with a strained smile and sat down next to Duvalier.

Duvalier turned toward her. "It's important for you to be here," he said solemnly. "I want you to hear what these men have to say about that . . . white bird's beak of a brother-in-law of yours."

Simone, silent, stared straight ahead. Her sister's husband, for so long Duvalier's personal aide and speech writer despite his Communist past, had suddenly met the fate of so many other Duvalier intimates—stripped of power and imprisoned. He had also been forcibly divorced from his wife.

Carefully Duvalier placed his .45 revolver on his desk, then nodded to Désyr. The notorious security chief opened the interrogation. His questions, belying his benign expression, were blunt, difficult, and accusative. But Jean-Charles was innocent, and he had a wife and two babies to live for.

"The only contact I ever had with Lucien Daumec was when he wrote asking for my advice about restructuring Jérémie's electoral constituencies," he replied. "I considered his request incorrect because he didn't go through proper channels, contacting me through the Justice Minister, whom I report to. He didn't do it that way, and so I burned his letter."

Much later during the three-hour grilling Jean-Charles turned and spoke directly to Duvalier. "You've never done anything for me, Excellency," he said forthrightly. "I'm the one who's always done things for you. In '57 I campaigned for you night and day, and when we needed gas to go out into the countryside, I paid for it out of my teacher's salary. I never plotted against you, Excellency. Why would I? The truth is, I've always been your loyal follower and you have nothing to reproach me with."

Behind his thick glasses Duvalier blinked and a smile quivered on his heavy lips. He signaled to Désyr, and the interrogation ended. Jean-Charles walked over to shake the President's hand, but Duvalier rose, put one arm around him, and led him away from the others. "You've convinced me that you're innocent," he said. "Now then, are you married, Jean-Charles? Any children?"

"Two, Excellency," Jean-Charles replied, then took the envelope Duvalier handed him and slipped it into his jacket pocket.

"I want you to send your reports directly to me, Jean-Charles," Duvalier said. His hand tightened and squeezed Jean-Charles's shoulder. "Once a month at least, I'll be expecting to hear from you."

In the euphoria of his reprieve, Jean-Charles nodded, but he understood that Duvalier wanted him to become a member of the SD, the Service d'Information, his secret police. He also knew he would never write a single such report.

Duvalier's Big Brother preoccupations extended far beyond the astonishingly intimate details of his citizens' private lives. It also included the Catholic Church, kept at bay for years. By 1964 Duvalier was ready for full-scale battle, when he accused two Canadian Jesuits of importing subversive literature and drafting plans in which the Society of Jesus intended to overthrow his government. Declaring himself shocked and deceived, Duvalier expelled the whole order. Before that he imprisoned several priests, some in their seminaries, one in Fort Dimanche. On February 10 he closed down the Jesuits' wonderful mountaintop Villa Manrèse. He also shut down its school and imprisoned its three maids. "Public opinion is already aware of the vast plot against the internal and external security of the nation, devised by the Jesuit Fathers of the Villa Manrèse," declared the communiqué justifying the action.

To expel the Jesuits, the most powerful and non-Haitianized of all the orders, was Duvalier's ultimate defiance. Nor could he refrain from gloating. "They had been expelled from a great number of countries," he recalled, "for mixing into the internal policies of governments of sovereign States. But I cherish the hope that they will give an adequate formation to future members of the indigenous clergy and that they will understand the meaning of my nationalist revolution."

The Jesuits were expelled wholesale, followed later by the Fathers of the Holy Ghost and the Fathers of the Sacred Heart. But other orders and congregations merely lost their leaders and most assertive preachers, whom Duvalier replaced, just as he had striking students, with Macoutes who fancied they felt the religious vocation. During the height of the Duvalierist terror, Catholics could celebrate mass sung by Haitian priests who wore guns and who reported instantly any confessions they considered politically interesting or suspect. The Jesuits had not been so cooperative, and prior to their expulsion declined to divulge details of confessions made by Clément Barbot when, pretending religious obsession, he had spent most of his time in church.

The same process of Macoutization infested even more deeply the proliferating Protestant churches, and hundreds of Haitian pastors had a Bible in one pocket and a VSN card in the other. Vodoun's *houngans* and *mambos* were even more thoroughly infiltrated, and so by 1964 Duvalier had cowed the entire religious establishment of his deeply religious nation.

As fast as he quashed one trouble spot, another rose up. In the summer of 1964 Duvalier faced two new invasions. Attacking then retreating, the guerrillas inflicted serious damage on Haiti's tiny five-thousand-man army. Each group operated independently, but had as common denominators American-based exile leaders, including Catholic priests Jean-Baptiste Georges, who once hid Duvalier, and Gérard Bissainthe, so fanatically anti-Duvalierist that they both risked American jail sentences by buying arms. Their groups also shared tolerance if not outright enthusiasm from the U.S. and Dominican authorities, and a pattern of incessant suspicion, internecine squabbling, and betrayal.

In the first invasion Haitian rebels known as *Camoquins* invaded from the Dominican Republic, where Juan Bosch encouraged them to operate. Their invasion came as no surprise to Duvalier; it was difficult to surprise a man so well informed by his vast international network of spies. Before it happened Duvalier even protested to the United Nations Security Council, but the council failed to chastise the Dominicans, and the invaders, stunningly incompetent, went ahead as planned.

The *Camoquin* invasion irritated Duvalier but cast not even a shadow on the historic event he had set for June 14. This was a nationwide referendum to authorize his becoming President-for-Life, an idea first suggested to him the year before during the gimcrack carnival he had staged for the OAS team investigating charges that he repressed his people. "The fanatic crowd," Duvalier later revealed in his *Memoirs of a Third World Leader,* "raised up for the first time cries of 'Duvalier, President for life. Duvalier, President forever.' Yes, I replied then, 'that is your desire, that is your will, that I be the eighth President for life in our history. I am ready to reply to the wish of the nation.' "

By mid-1964 Duvalier judged the time propitious to formalize the people's desire. Soon the newspapers competed with articles eulogizing the President. Street bands sang carnival songs extolling "Papa Doc for Life." Uniformed Macoutes paraded to salute him.

On April Fool's Day the corpulent Constant stood at the head of his men and in his elegant French pronounced the ridiculous words

"Thanks to you, Excellency, and under your prestigious command, the Armed Forces of Haiti have many times fulfilled with honor and competence the sacrosanct mission of maintaining territorial integrity, victoriously holding battle against secret forces which organized in order to compromise national sovereignty and independence."

Duvalier listened gravely and responded just as handsomely. "General Constant, Duvalier, the President of the Republic, who is prouder of his title of revolutionary chief than of that of chief of state, accepts and appreciates your gesture. I understand you, for I remember you were a lieutenant in 1957 when you risked your position in greeting me in Jacmel. . . . Now you are a general."

Constant stared distantly as he listened, his face stern and his eyes hidden behind dark glasses. How utterly deceived he had been, he reflected, remembering his enthusiasm when he first listened to the presidential candidate François Duvalier as he campaigned in Jacmel.

At the OAS the Costa Rican delegate openly voiced his disapproval after the Haitian Assembly abolished the Constitution and prepared to draft a new one providing for a President-for-Life. Ganthier Deputy Jean Julmé, by 1964 president of the Assembly, rushed to his chief's defense and on his behalf rattled Haiti's trusty sword, its OAS voting muscle. "We hope OAS members will not fail to make Mr. Facio understand how and why he must act to avoid Haiti withdrawing its representative," he declared, repeating the words he had drafted at home in his daughter Nadia's school notebook. Julmé gazed around at his fellow deputies and his voice rang out again, made steely with his personal indignation that foreigners were trying to interfere in such a sacred matter as Duvalier's presidency-for-life.

Julmé's yes vote on June 14 was only one of the 2.8 million that drowned out 3,234 brave dissenters. Duvalier graciously accepted the verdict, coming as he said it did from "a vast movement, the entire nation, the university youth along with phalanges of invincible peasantry, syndicates and the Armed Forces, the Tonton Macoutes and businessmen and industrialists, all the vital forces of the country." But even as Port-au-Prince feted, the *Camoquins* moved, scarcely allowing the new President-for-Life a moment's respite from the debilitating festivities. The last drops of rot-gut liquor, or *clairin*, were still intoxicating bemused peasants when the *Camoquins* left the sanctuary of the Dominican Republic and landed in Saltrou in Haiti's Southeast.

Duvalier's reaction was characteristically ferocious and devious.

He ordered his protégée Madame Max Adolphe, warden of Fort Diman-che, to select twenty-one political prisoners for an unspecified purpose. Rosalie Adolphe was caught off guard and decided Duvalier was planning an amnesty to commemorate his presidency-for-life. Leaping at the chance, she listed many of her own imprisoned friends, imagining she was reprieving them. Instead, they were executed.

The next day Duvalier leaked the news to the American Embassy. The men had been killed, the horrified Americans were told, to warn them—the Americans—against their policy of aiding anti-Duvalierist rebels.

Duvalier arrested and killed hundreds of others, most related to exiles who, being safely abroad, might also be anti-Duvalierist. And as was now his custom, Duvalier no longer exempted women and children from his death lists. Most murders he delegated to willing henchmen, but not all. When rage overpowered him, he would shuffle down into the palace basement and, bracing his aching right hand with his left, personally dispose of his enemies with his own revolver.

Duvalier had had reasons other than blind ambition to force his presidency-for-life on a reluctant nation. Notwithstanding the 2.8 million yes votes delivered by considerably less than 2 million eligible voters, even Duvalier's closest councillors opposed the move as they opposed nothing else. Murder they overlooked or rationalized as "execution." Torture they either participated in or accepted as an evil necessary in interrogations, and some of them convinced themselves it was not widespread. Duvalier could be so reassuring, so proper in his beautifully tailored suits, so baroquely gallant with women, so dry in manner—far easier to believe his disclaimers than to agonize about what was happening. Then too, it is always easier to believe something when your life depends upon believing it.

Duvalier had become the antithesis of the progressive black populism of Duvalierism and had set in motion a machine of terror that was unstoppable. He and his regime were beyond forgiveness, and no one understood it better than himself. Because of that he had concluded that he had only one choice, a redefined status so omnipotent that it would protect not merely his dying carcass but also his wife and four children and those few intimates he also called his children.

His presidency-for-life removed any possibility that Duvalierism might die an electoral death—now nature, not elections, was the only hope. The terror continued, and only in bizarre symbols did Duvalier ever attempt to give his people anything of the program he had ridden to power. The most crucial symbol was the Haitian flag, the blue-and-red tricolor that the great historic leaders had won over a century earlier. Duvalier changed it, and on June 21 soldiers hoisted Haiti's new black-and-red flag up the palace flagpole.

The Vespers of Jérémie began when a baker's dozen of young Jérémie expatriates sailed from Miami, landing at the remote village of Dame Marie on the tip of the peninsula, miles away from their original destination of Jérémie, where they intended to seize the army barracks and use it as a base to overthrow Duvalier. The President-for-Life responded to this latest attack with savagery the more appalling because it was measured, meted out in bloody morsels of murder. By 1964 Duvalier had already killed thousands of Haitians, but the Vespers of Jérémie struck the soul of an anguished nation, and the reverberations still resound today in Haiti.

The invaders were members of Young Haiti, a U.S.-based resistance group. They were also Duvalier's nightmare, the incarnation of everything he despised and longed to annihilate. Twelve were mulatto. The thirteenth was a black, Marcel Numa, a little-educated motorboat mechanic politicized in New York. What incensed Duvalier even more was that his former Education Minister, Jean-Baptiste Georges, was their counselor and fund-raiser, and even supplied them arms.

Jeune Haiti invaded in August. They came as soldiers, and from the beginning their progress was traced in blood. By August 9 the army had beaten them back from the Jérémie area they hoped would rise to join them, and although they captured Lieutenant Léon Achille, they lost Yvan Laracque, the first of their number killed in action.

"Bring me his body," Duvalier ordered, and the bullet-riddled Laracque was flown to Port-au-Prince, but not for burial. Instead, dressed in underpants and a torn army shirt, the stinking, bloated, and fly-infested corpse was propped into a garden chair at a major downtown intersection. There, under a giant Coca-Cola sign saying "Welcome to Haiti!" Tonton Macoutes guarded it for ten days. Duvalier relented and permitted the Laracque family to bury it only after the Liberian ambassador protested that the ghastly exhibit was a disgrace to men of African descent. Also released for the funeral was Laracque's ten-year-old son, held in Fort Dimanche and so traumatized that he lost the power of speech.

Duvalier, now calling himself Supreme Commander of the Armed Forces, also supervised the military aspect of defeating *Jeune Haiti*. To help him he named three majors to a Commission of Inquiry, and also young Lieutenant Jose "Sonny" Borges, abruptly plucked from the other side of Haiti where he had been fighting *Camoquins* and flown to Jérémie to fight mulattoes.

The Jérémie assignment was an acknowledgment of Borges's legendary brutality, earlier refined by his friend Clément Barbot. That friendship had once cost him his commission, but recently Duvalier had reinstated him, and in gratitude Borges dedicated himself to justifying his professional reprieve by savagery and personal cruelties. Borges was, in a word, the perfect man to implement one part of Duvalier's scheme to subdue the rebels—terrorize their families and so dissuade others from rising up and joining the insurrection.

"We mustn't forget that Castro began with little forays too," Duvalier said over and over. "These things start small and end up out of control. Above all we must always guard against groups like these getting new recruits among the people." At the same time he realized that in the mountainous terrain the rebels had withdrawn to, the government troops could not expect instant success. He was not unduly worried, certain the peasants would never support the mulattoes. Still, guerrilla movements had to be stamped out quickly, and Duvalier hated *Jeune Haiti* with a special vengeance because it was led by university-educated, U.S.-based Jérémie mulattoes, a combination of everything he loathed and feared.

Borges arrived to find the "political aspects" of the campaign already blueprinted in the form of a list of victims. Local Tonton Macoute Commandant Sanette Balmir and her sometime friend and Maccute colleague Saint-Ange Bontemps had prepared it, and all but one of their victims were mulattoes, though only a few were directly related to *Jeune Haiti* invaders. One common link was that most had figured on the list submitted in 1959 to Attorney General Antoine Jean-Charles. The other was that either Sanette or Bontemps had personal scores to settle with them.

Sanette had been one of Duvalier's earliest supporters, and Duvalier had rewarded her loyalty by appointing her commandant of Jérémie's Macoutes. A convicted thief and prostitute who had served time in the Jérémie Penitentiary, Sanette by 1964 was a fat, aging diabetic who lived with her woman lover and a child and used her powers as Macoute chieftain to lord it over the townspeople who had once mocked her as she did forced convict labor on the streets of Jérémie. She particularly hated mulattoes and regarded it as her personal mission to avenge every slight and humiliation she and her black people had ever suffered at their hands.

Bontemps hated mulattoes as much as Sanette, and willingly joined her in persecuting them. Even in manhood Bontemps writhed at the memory of schoolboy humiliations, when white and mulatto priests had favored mulatto children, even cuddling them in class and treating the stupidest as if he were a genius. But Bontemps was also a dangerous drunkard who had already murdered with impunity, and who in 1960 had stabbed a young Cuban invader to death then licked his blood from the knife. Even Sanette feared him, and when Borges arrived to join them, Sanette was glad of his presence.

Borges, always a dynamo of energy, threw himself into the job on the very day he arrived. With Bontemps beside him, he arrested three men and threw them into a single cell at the local barracks and the next day added six more, including wealthy philanthropist Pierre Sansaricq.

It was the same day news arrived that Young Haiti had won its first victory; Lieutenant Léon Achille was now officially listed as a prisoner of war. A contingent of local Macoutes stormed over to the barracks. There, in a sea of human excrement, urine, and blood, they pistol-whipped the men, kicked them, and beat them with sticks. In very little time the lone black, Michel Mézile, suffered a fractured skull, Guy and Victor Villedrouin broken bones, and Louis Drouin a cranium so severely smashed he never regained consciousness. Afterward the Macoutes pushed the wounded men back into a single cell to await execution. Three were spared and lived to describe their sufferings, and six died. The Vespers of Jérémie had begun.

Back in Port-au-Prince, Duvalier was as always suspicious of even his most enthusiastic henchmen and sent another agent to report on them. This was black Jérémie-born Dr. Jacques Fourcand, his personal physician. But Fourcand balked at killing his own townsmen and, instead of joining the others, drove directly to St. Antoine Hospital, claimed he had injured his foot, checked himself in, and climbed into bed.

"Where is Dr. Jacques Fourcand in Jérémie?" wired Duvalier to Barracks Commandant Lieutenant Abel Jérome. The commandant, astonished, began to inquire and reported Fourcand's hospitalization, and until the end of the vespers, Duvalier's doctor remained incommunicado and saw no one but his promiscuous former lover, Nicole Stoodley, the despair of the well-behaved mulatto community.

Abel Jérome envied Fourcand. He too would have liked to climb into bed and sleep through the mounting horror. Like most army men, he resented the Macoutes, and since his posting to Jérémie he had already had a serious run-in with Sanette. She and a jeepload of her Macoutes had been heading out to the nearby village of Marfranc when Jérome stopped them. He knew why they were going. Sanette had boasted all over town that she was going to gun down "that big white fish" Robert Rocourt, a Protestant pastor who was not merely a mulatto but who had even had the gall to marry a white American nurse.

Jérome had leaned his elbow against her jeep and spoken harshly. "If you go, Sanette, you'll do it without my permission and against my advice. What's more, I can guarantee that Duvalier himself will be furious if you touch a hair of that man's head."

Sanette had argued and cursed him, but she knew he was right. When Duvalier was still a country doctor fighting yaws, he had visited Robert and Esther Rocourt's missionary clinic and had afterward felt a tender spot for them. It was unfair, Sanette was furious, but finally, in a rain of dusty pebbles, she drove away, her mission of vengeance deterred.

Now, in 1964, with mulatto rebels attacking the government, Sanette knew the time had come to unleash her implacable hatred. Secure and confident, she phoned Duvalier and reported Jérome's failure to cooperate in the process of liquidation he had ordered.

Meanwhile other Macoutes began to have second thoughts. At a public meeting on Sanette's broad upper veranda one of them protested openly, "You're going too far. Let's remember that we're all from the same town. We can't let so much blood flow in Jérémie. We have to see things clearly."

But Sanette had seen things clearly from the days she had swept the town's streets wearing white-and-black-striped prison garb, the butt of ridicule for all who passed and cursed her. She had known what she had to do ever since the soldiers ran her to ground like an animal, stripped the clothes off her back, and held her down while they spread her buttocks and probed with ungentle fingers in her rectum and vagina until they found the money she had stolen and hidden there. In August 1964 no words could move her. Her chief and protector Duvalier had ordered her to take action, and action she took. The Vespers would not be stopped.

On August 11, late at night, ten more mulattoes were arrested. The Macoutes found Gérard Guilbaud and his wife, Alice, sister of rebel leader Louis "Milou" Drouin, already in bed. Gérard, in pajamas, opened the door.

"We've come to arrest your wife."

"Arrest my wife?" Gérard replied. "Then I'll go with you."

"Good, let's go."

At the barracks the Macoutes interrogated them about Young Haiti, but they knew nothing, had had no inkling Milou was planning an undertaking even more dangerous for his family than himself. Helpless, knowing nothing, they could only shake their heads.

Quickly bored, the Macoutes pushed the Guilbauds into an office where eight others, including Alice's sister Roseline, waited with resignation and terror. The Macoutes leered at them.

"Take off all your clothes," one of them ordered. As Alice Guilbaud's eyes widened in shock, he bawled, "Didn't you understand?"

Gérard turned to his wife. "Alice, get undressed. You can see we're finished anyway."

The Macoutes gawked at Alice's body. Some gyrated their pelvises obscenely. When Roseline Drouin Villedrouin too stood naked before them, they laughed mockingly at her shaved pubus and the thick welts from recent surgery still flaming red against her beige skin.

Not everyone enjoyed the spectacle. "I didn't come here for that, gentlemen," protested respectable old Duvalierist André Jabouin, forced to witness the interrogation. "Don't treat these women so disrespectfully."

When Barracks Commandant Abel Jérome arrived later, he found all the prisoners still naked. "Sanette sent the order," a soldier answered his furious inquiry.

"Have them dress immediately," Jérome snapped, and still laughing, the Macoutes tossed their victims their nightclothes and pushed them into a common cell to await execution. There Alice and Roseline stumbled against their father's unconscious body.

"Papa!" they cried, cradling his broken head on their laps. But Louis Drouin would never speak again, and soon afterward his daughters were taken away without him. Later, as an abattoir truck carted his daughters and their husbands to their death, Drouin's cadaver was dumped into a ditch in the local cemetery.

The death van quickly traveled the five miles along the white limestone road leading to Numéro Deux, the wooded plain behind Jérémie's tiny airport. A Macoute firing squad stood waiting, and nearby was a shallow and freshly dug pit. Alice and Gérard Guilbaud were placed in front of the jeering Macoutes. The Macoutes fired, and a religious medal around Gérard's neck deflected one of the bullets. Momentarily shocked, the superstitious Macoutes crossed themselves fearfully before firing again.

The next volley felled Alice, already crouched beside her husband's body. To finish her off, a Macoute leaned over and plunged a knife into her heart.

That night, and for many nights afterward, the townsmen of Jérémie trembled. Curfew at 6 p.m., strictly enforced, continued for all but Macoutes and policemen. Shots and sirens pierced the still, dark nights, and though few dared to speak openly, soon everyone knew what the Macoutes were doing to the town's mulattoes out of Numéro Deux.

On September 8 Young Haiti forayed out of Macaya Mountain and at the little town of Dallest battled with Haitian troops and three rebels died. A few days later two more died.

The army also rescued Lieutenant Achille. Near death from five infected gunshot wounds and the gash from a machete the rebels had sliced across his neck because he would not reveal army strategy, one leg and one arm broken, Achille used the confusion of a gun battle to escape. As his captors fought his comrades, he dragged himself to a stream and hid, delirious and weakened from the bleeding. Downstream a peasant woman noticed with wonder then horror then sudden comprehension that the clear water she was laundering in was reddening. She leapt up, traced her way to Achille, then ran and alerted the soldiers thrashing through the woods in futile search for him.

An army helicopter landed and transported Achille to the airport at Les Caves, where newly appointed Commandant Lieutenant Henri Namphy met him. Namphy heard the army doctor's diagnosis in silence. He barked out a few orders, then held Achille's head and poured so much *clairin* down his throat that the sick man passed out. Namphy and another officer secured Achille's arms and legs, and the doctor extracted five bullets.

Afterward, Achille was airlifted to the Military Hospital in Port-au-Prince. Duvalier visited him and stood at his bedside taking silent stock of his injuries. Nobody knew what passed through the President's mind, but soon everyone in Jérémie knew about the savage reprisals he authorized as he opened another chapter of the Vespers.

Sanette Balmir, catapulted into power, was revitalized. She looked suddenly younger than her nearly sixty years and, despite obesity, had boundless energy. With Macoute-blue denim trousers and scarlet neck scarves and a black wig to cover her short, graying hair, Sanette stormed through town with jeeploads of her Macoutes, and no one could stop her.

Abel Jérome no longer dared try. At the beginning of September he had received a letter from Duvalier dated August 30. "I am asking you to collaborate closely with Madame Sanette Balmir, the great national heroine of Jérémie," Duvalier said pointedly. "She will be able to give you further particulars. This is a formal order." It was signed Dr. François Duvalier, Supreme and Managing Chief of the Armed Forces of Haiti.

Sanette's ferocity had won out over more moderate counsel, and in a period of popular terror and hysteria, Duvalier had placed her in command. When she and Saint-Ange Bontemps suggested more names, he obligingly authorized more liquidations.

On September 19 Macoutes roamed the darkened streets with sirens wailing, announcing the new round of arrests. Duvalier, suspicious of Jérome's reliability, wired a faithful aide instead, "Take rigorous action against the Sansaricq family. Stop. Duvalier." The second phase of the Vespers of Jérémie had been ordained.

Commandant Jérome picked up the phone and heard the order to reimpose the 6 p.m. curfew. He cursed silently. The killing was on again, and he was in the middle of it. Chain-smoking, his usual smile frozen out by bitter resentment, Jérome went out to patrol the streets of Jérémie, driving a commandeered ambulance because Macoutes had driven off in the barracks jeep.

At 1 a.m. an oncoming jeep stopped and fellow soldier Sonny Borges and Macoute Saint-Ange Bontemps, in the front seat, leaned out to greet him. Jérome peered inside and realized the thirteen civilians crammed inside were going to their deaths. He knew them, all members of Pierre Sansaricq's family, including his crippled sister and two-year-old granddaughter Régine. Suddenly Jérome pointed to a pretty young woman among the doomed prisoners. "Give her to me," he said harshly. "Settle your own affairs with Jérémie people, but not her. She's from Port-au-Prince."

Saint-Ange shrugged and allowed Jérome to pull Sansaricq's

daughter-in-law from the jeep. Then, accelerating, he and Borges drove off to deliver the rest of the Sansaricqs to the barracks. Then they rounded up three more victims, teenagers Lisa and Frantz Villedrouin and their mother, Adeline.

On the rolling wooded plain of Numéro Deux the mulattoes stepped out into moonlight so clear it illuminated every part of their final drama. Only the shallow grave that convicts had dug that afternoon was hidden from view.

The two families, children clinging to their mothers, turned to face their executioners. André Jabouin, again forced to attend as a civilian witness, made a final compassionate attempt to intervene. "Give me that little girl," he pleaded, holding out his arms to two-year-old Régine Sansaricq. "I'll say I adopted her."

"Listen, Jabouin, to be a Duvalierist you have to be bloodthirsty. Where is your manly courage?" retorted a young Macoute and drove a knife into Régine's heart.

"Shit on all of you, you pack of dogs!" shrieked the child's mother. "You'll pay for your crimes one day. Pigs, cowards, filth—"

Lieutenant Sonny Borges struck her as she fell dead, riddled with bullets, then pushed her headfirst into the pit.

Her four-year-old son, holding on to his six-year-old brother, saw his mother die. "I have to go pee-pee," he sobbed.

"Don't cry, I'll dry your eyes for you," crooned Borges, taking him gently by the hand. Then, smiling beatifically, Borges pushed a lighted cigarette into the boy's eyes while a Macoute known as "Cowboy" snatched the child by one arm, tossed him into the air, and stuck his belly with a knife. The boy shrieked, sighed, died.

"That child wriggled just like a worm!" Borges exclaimed.

When it was eighteen-year-old Lisa Villedrouin's turn to die, Cowboy tried to rape her. Then before her body was tossed into the pit, he stuck his hand into her vagina. "You guys!" he shouted to the others. "She was a virgin!"

Back at the barracks Abel Jérome read with disbelief a telegram he had just received from Port-au-Prince. "Do not execute the Sansaricq family. Stop. Duvalier."

Duvalier must have done this on purpose! flashed through Jérome's mind. Aloud, to his men, he shouted, "I can't work miracles! I can't bring people back to life. What do they want me to do? What do they want, these people in Port-au-Prince? They're driving me crazy!"

*   *   *

In his Port-au-Prince palace, Duvalier heard about the executions and waited for Young Haiti's next move. It came soon. Hungry, demoralized, and entirely unaware of what was happening in Jérémie, Young Haiti's reduced force of seven realized that they could not stay any longer in the mountains because they had nothing left to eat. They chose Marcel Numa, their sole black member, to disguise himself as a peasant and try to buy food, for in Haiti a mulatto peasant would be an anomaly sure to provoke instant curiosity and suspicion. Numa strolled nervously into the market at the coastal village of Coteaux. Peasants identified him almost immediately from photographs the authorities had circulated and notified the police. He was arrested and shipped to the barracks in Jérémie.

Numa had no visitors. The night before, Friday, September 26, his father, Louis, and brother Liénard had been been thrown into the penitentiary. Marcel's oldest brother, Rodrigue, was Haiti's ambassador to the Ivory Coast. A *noiriste,* Rodrigue had been imprisoned and so brutally treated by Magloire's government that Duvalier later cried out in public, "Who has known such suffering for our cause as Rodrigue Numa?"

Liénard and Louis Numa, up to that moment convinced Duvalierists, sat in their dark cell and brooded. Beside them was Pierre Sansaricq, who everyone thought was already dead. Sansaricq knew his family had been destroyed, and his bitterness exceeded their own. "Why?" he asked them over and over. "Why?" But the Numas, expecting to be shot at any moment, had no answer for him. They could think only of Marcel, who had gone to New York and never again communicated with them. Now, because of him, the family was ruined. "What is a black Numa doing with that arrogant mulatto lot?" old Louis demanded over and over, but no one, neither his black son Liénard nor mulatto Pierre Sansaricq could answer him.

In the outside world the Numas had a powerful defender in their close friend Abel Jérome, who went to Port-au-Prince and persuaded Duvalier that the Numas did not deserve execution. Duvalier scribbled out a release order on a calling card, but the reprieve did not extend to Pierre Sansaricq, who was soon afterward executed.

In the mountains Young Haiti's rebels were doing little better than their Jérémie connections, and on September 29 two more were killed. On October 19 the army captured their leader, Louis Drouin, already wounded, and sent him into Port-au-Prince to join Marcel Numa in Fort Dimanche.

That night, and the following night, the properties, stores, and goods of the slaughtered mulattoes were delivered over to the masses. "Pillage their properties and goods," Duvalier had instructed, and Bontemps and Sanette Balmir, whose fortune was built on money extorted from local officials and military officers, gladly complied. Stealthily they went from house to house, stripping them. Then Bontemps, Macoute deputy of the people, went into the Church of Ste. Hélène, the community of shacks built like human roosts on the bare hill overlooking the green sea, and invited Jérémie's poorest parishioners to share the long-coveted wealth of the mulattoes. His promise was hollow, because when the avaricious mobs arrived to pillage and steal, they found only trifles and junk, slim pickings indeed.

On October 20, with Young Haiti nearly exterminated, one last hostage was executed. The victim was a mentally retarded woman whom Abel Jérome attempted to reprieve, but her cousin Nicole Stoodley, herself safe because she was Sanette Balmir's friend and Jacques Fourcand's lover, wanted the execution carried out. Nicole and her mother were the handicapped woman's only surviving relatives, and if she lived, they would have to look after her.

Abel Jérome, repelled by Nicole's attitude, phoned Duvalier, but the President cut him short, and that night the helpless woman was shot.

The Vespers of Jérémie were over. One week later the three remaining guerrillas were killed. They had refused to surrender when their ammunition ran out and had hurled stones at the oncoming soldiers until bullets felled all three.

Duvalier was elated at the news but, ever suspicious, ordered their severed heads brought to the palace for his personal inspection. Afterward the Foreign Affairs Ministry announced "total victory" over Young Haiti and, as gruesome proof, published a photograph of the heads of the last three to die.

Duvalier had taken the mulattoes' lives. Next he took their worldly possessions, officially declaring them traitors and nationalizing their properties.

The Young Haiti story ended as Marcel Numa and Louis Drouin, tried, convicted, and condemned to death by a military court, awaited execution in Fort Dimanche. They intrigued Duvalier, and he brought them to the palace for personal interviews. Duvalier also sent for Marcel's father, Louis, perhaps to test his loyalty, perhaps to provoke last-hour repentance in his son. Yet, even seeing his father face-to-face, Marcel stubbornly refused to renounce his allegiance to Young Haiti. Finally, instead of pleading for his son's life, Louis Numa turned to Duvalier and said disgustedly, "President, I give him to you. Do with him whatever you want."

Duvalier found Louis Drouin much more interesting and spent hours debating political theory with him. A Duvalier aide who was present described their conversation as an intellectual exchange of ideas, courteous and mutually challenging. Duvalier queried Drouin about his socialist views, and then Drouin listened gravely as Duvalier justified his own principles and methods. In fact, their talk seemed so positive that Drouin returned to Fort Dimanche convinced that Duvalier would reprieve him, and Numa with him.

When soldiers opened their cell door early on November 12 and led them to the prison barber shop, Drouin and Numa exchanged jubilant grins as they were bathed, shaved, trimmed, and outfitted with clean clothes. But it was death they were being groomed for, and as the truck stopped at the Port-au-Prince cemetery's south wall, they understood their error. Faced with television and radio crews, and a crowd of thousands, their initial stares of stupefaction gave way to smiles, proud and resigned.

Thousands watched them, including schoolchildren and army officers forced to attend, and truckloads of peasants roused from their beds in the mountains and driven down to witness the spectacle. The friends were tied to stakes a body length apart. They refused the last rites from a French priest, and within hearing range of each other and microphones that picked up even their death rattles, they cursed Duvalier with their last breaths.

Afterward the few literate spectators in the cemetery began to read from ghoulish "programs" distributed to the crowd. "Dr. François Duvalier will fulfil his sacrosanct mission. He has crushed and will always crush all anti-patriotic efforts. . . . The Duvalier revolution will triumph. It will trample the bodies of traitors and renegades and those who sell out. . . ."

For weeks afterward on television, Drouin and Numa died again and again, unrepentant.

In Abidjan, Haitian ambassador and fanatic Duvalierist Rodrigue

Numa stared unbelievingly at the cable just received from Port-au-Prince. That afternoon a stony-faced Numa signed a letter resigning the post he had held with such joy, for how can a man represent a government that has just executed his little brother?

For Haiti's new President-for-Life, the loss of his loyal Ivory Coast ambassador was nothing compared to his resounding triumph over the thirteen rebels of Young Haiti. "We have entered into the temple, and we have thrashed and chased out the merchants in order to open your eyes," he declared in a speech that he later published in his *Memoirs of a Third World Leader.*

From this premise it was an easy step for a Christ-likened Duvalier to authorize the State Printing Press to issue the *Catechism of a Revolution.*

"Who are Dessalines, Toussaint, Christophe, Pétion and Estimé?" went the new catechism.

"Dessalines, Toussaint, Christophe, Pétion and Estimé are five founders of the nation who are found within François Duvalier."

"Is Dessalines for life?"

"Yes, Dessalines is for life in François Duvalier."

The booklet closed with the new Duvalierist rendition of the Lord's Prayer: "Our Doc, who are in the National Palace, hallowed be Thy name in the present and future generations. Thy will be done at Port-au-Prince and in the provinces. Give us this day our new Haiti and never forgive the trespasses of the anti-patriots who spit every day on our country. Let them succumb to temptation, and under the weight of their venom, deliver them not from any evil."

6 PAPA DOC'S FINAL YEARS

HAITI HAD BECOME PAPA DOC'S PRISON. EVEN HIS splendid palace had a torture room, its walls painted rusty-brown to camouflage blood splattered from its victims. Duvalier took such a personal interest in the actual torture session that he had peepholes drilled, enabling him to sit in discreet comfort in another room and monitor the proceedings. Standard procedure was to immobilize prisoners into the "jack" position, a technique inherited from French slave owners. They were bent over, feet and hands bound with a stick passed behind their knees and at the top of their forearms. Then they were flayed with batons and rifle butts. For variety and special cases, the palace also offered the coffin-shaped iron maiden, reminiscent of instruments the medieval Church used.

The palace was only one branch of the national penal system. An even more important one was Fort Dimanche, the military post built by the Americans during their occupation, which Duvalier transformed into a political prison so horrendous, its very name was synonymous with death.

Located on the dusty outskirts of the once-pretty French colonial city of Port-au-Prince, the exterior of Fort Dimanche was no more forbidding than any other military installation. Inside, however, with its cells crammed so full of starved men that they had to sleep in shifts, the sounds of torture resounded as regularly as a cock's crow. Gruel was slopped twice daily onto the floor, and in one-minute daily showers men drank all the water they would have until the next day. Sanitary facilities consisted of a foul, overflowing bucket. Men and women weakened quickly, disintegrating as malnutrition destroyed their bones and tissues, decayed their teeth, and puffed their bodies into a grim travesty of life before death.

The prisoners passed these final days of their lives in discussion and prayer. Some, hopeful to the end, tried to cure their diarrhea by scraping lime from the walls and mixing it with food. Flesh, beaten and sore, was bathed with lime and urine, soothing it, preventing infectious eruptions that would kill.

Few left Fort Dimanche alive, and its grounds swallowed thousands yearly. Once an officer posted there arrived at General Gérard Constant's office at Army Headquarters and broke down in tears describing the horrors he saw daily. "Do something, General," the man had begged, but Duvalier kept the army impotent, and Chief of Staff Constant did the only thing he dared—he kept silent.

When Fort Dimanche became a VSN post, Papa Doc installed as its commandant his protégée Madame Max Adolphe. Striding about the death house, Madame Max indulged in real life the pornographic fantasies she loved to read about, torturing the genitals of naked prisoners.

Fort Dimanche was the most notorious of Duvalier's prisons, but only one of hundreds. Some prisons were more informal. In a new twist, many powerful Macoutes had private cells in their own homes, and into these men and women disappeared without trace. Law was defined by the pistols strapped cowboy fashion onto the hips of Macoutes. With powers of arrest over every other citizen, exempt from ordinary human law, these loyalists had only Duvalier himself to account to, and toward them and toward nobody else was Duvalier a forgiving father.

Duvalier forgave Luc Désyr, Elois Maitre, Lionel Woolley, and Major Jean Tassy. On August 4, 1965, they arrested Jean-Jacques Dessalines Ambroise, his pregnant wife, Lucette Lafontant, and their cousin Alix Ambroise, and took them to the palace, where Luc Désyr greeted them mockingly, "Your hole is already dug. You won't leave here alive this afternoon."

Alix was beaten then released, but Jean-Jacques, a founding member of the Communist Popular Party of National Liberation, was tortured until nearly dead, his bones broken and his internal organs irreparably damaged. Then Désyr condemned him to a *cachot,* a tiny coffin-like cell without room to move where prisoners slated for especially lingering deaths were confined and given no food or water until they died of their injuries, infections, dehydration, starvation, and the absence of all hope.

Lucette, pregnant and so terrified that she lost the power of speech, was tortured until she too died. Before she did Désyr ordered one swollen breast sliced off, a procedure Duvalier enjoyed observing. Afterward, her bulging, ruined body clasped in the embrace of a woman cell mate, Lucette too died.

By 1965 Macoutism permeated Haiti. Even in the councils of state the Macoute-oriented mentality prevailed, and the intelligent, responsible Duvalier *noiristes* who had once formed the core of Duvalierism found themselves shunted aside or out. Increasingly the ideals of Estimé's 1946 "Revolution" and the 1957 Duvalier "Revolution" became mere words in speeches.

Clovis Désinor lived with a sense of constant betrayal. The more he heard about how Duvalier's bagman Luckner Cambronne bullied and extorted money from businessmen—or any Haitian with any cash—the more disgusted he became. Several times, presuming on his childhood friendship with Duvalier, he complained about Cambronne. "You're letting him betray everything Duvalierism stands for," Désinor declared. "What he calls fund-raising is nothing more than theft."

Unfailingly, Duvalier defended his bagman. "The country is dry," he replied. "He's forced to be aggressive to find money."

In 1965, as Désinor drafted the speech Duvalier would give at the ceremony inaugurating the new international airport, he felt entirely vindicated. Ever since 1962, when the Americans had canceled a $3.6 million airport loan at the last minute, he had resolved to find the means to salvage Haiti from among its own population. "Together we can do it," he vowed, harking back to his own bookless days at Lycée Pétion when generous classmates' books had saved him.

From 1962 until 1965 Désinor had begun every morning with a close scrutiny of the accounting figures that traced the progress of the airport. Inch by inch it went up, financed penny by penny, its engineer, Alix Cinéas, as committed as Désinor to succeeding in the construction. And on the day it was ready to be opened the total cost was less than half of the 1962 estimate of $3.6 million. For the large and impressive terminal building Désinor had spent $200,000, and for the native-concrete runway so solidly constructed it would not need repairs for over a decade, $819,000.

"This airport is for all Haitians," Duvalier read later in his light voice. Behind him Désinor beamed with pride. Like the shameful Cambronne-sponsored monstrosity called Duvalierville, Haiti's new airport also bore François Duvalier's name. Unlike Duvalierville, however, François Duvalier International Airport was a source of Haitian pride and a proof of Haitian ability.

Once Duvalier had been an honest man. As a follower of Estimé, hunted down by Magloire, an exile in his own country, he had drafted a constitution so idealistic that it called for the death penalty for the crime of embezzling public funds. Only after less starry-eyed friends had insisted did Duvalier modify this particular clause.

Once Duvalier had been satisfied with his modest lifestyle. By the mid 1960s he too had become a thief, and on a spectacular scale. Swiss bank accounts, important real estate transactions, jewelry, and a lavish jet-set existence became the Duvalier family's norm. While the President toiled in the palace and never traveled farther than the provinces, Simone and the four children saw the world, dressed *haute couture,* and developed tastes for the high life.

Once seduced, the formerly puritanical Duvalier became thoroughly corrupt. No deal was too petty to interest him. After the Vespers of Jérémie, local spies told him about the gold supposedly buried in Charles Guilbaud's yard. Duvalier immediately sent trusted Macoutes to search for the coins Saint-Ange Bontemps had already dug up and stolen. For more than two weeks the men worked, meticulously combing house and yard, frightened to tell the President they could not find the treasure. When they finally reported their failure, Duvalier, for once outwitted, was coldly furious.

The big money, of course, was harder to come by, but whenever he could Duvalier grabbed at it. On November 14, 1966, he finalized a deal that betrayed his people as crassly as his murderous government. Though he never ceased to attack the Dominicans for actively supporting Haitian rebels, greed swallowed pride and he contracted, for a fee per head, to provide Haitian sugarcane cutters for the Dominican *bateys* where they would work in conditions tantamount to slavery. Hiring was done in Haiti, the cutters afterward transported over the border. Duvalier received close to $1 million yearly, payable in American funds. The agreement spelled out conditions of work and salary, all of which were always ignored. This included the one dollar out of every fifteen earned, withheld until the Haitians returned home, where they would receive it in American funds. The dollar was withheld, but the cutters never saw it. The Haitian authorities pocketed every dollar.

The government's accounts were not all reported, so it was easy for him to drain them. The Régie du Tabac in particular, a tobacco monopoly later transformed into a bizarre non-fiscalized tax agency into which money poured from consumer taxes on milk, herring, codfish, soap, detergents, and matches, provided Duvalier with an estimated $10 million annually. Not all went into his foreign accounts or living expenses. Millions went to support his extended family, the thousands of important Tonton Macoutes and corrupt Duvalierists whose loyalty required constant stoking.

Haitians grew poorer so rapidly that a United Nations report listed Haiti almost alone among world nations whose economy shrank rather than grew. The GNP slumped in an average year by 2.3 percent, while the cost of living shot up. Soil erosion and natural disasters caused a 13 percent drop in agricultural production, and that in a nation primarily agricultural. Haitians also had a life expectancy of forty years, the highest infant mortality rate in the Western world, the lowest literacy, the lowest percentage of children in school, and the lowest intake of calories and protein. The country's foreign debt skyrocketed from a modest $4 million under Estimé to $52 million under Duvalier. Much of the money lent lined individual pockets while the projects it was earmarked for remained mere pipe dreams to lure bankers. All the capital plus interest became the obligation of the Haitian state, and even starving peasants were forced to contribute to its repayment.[19]

The year 1966 was one of Duvalier's happiest. Firmly in power, hardened veteran of scores of uprisings, plots, and invasions, master of his society and of the representatives of foreign governments, Duvalier enjoyed a series of successes he considered all-important.

The first, a whistle-stop visit by Ethiopia's Haile Selassie, was purely symbolic. Selassie stayed only one day, but Duvalier packed it with enough ceremonies, speeches, and mutual eulogizing to make it a great national event. In fact, Selassie was the only foreign chief of state to visit during the entire regime, and Duvalier's gratitude seemed unbounded. Selassie left Haiti weighted down with the navel-long Necklace of the Order of Jean-

Jacques Dessalines the Great, while Duvalier saw him off wearing the even longer Great Necklace of the Order of the Queen of Saba.

Selassie's visit was a personal triumph for Duvalier, and it made for good publicity. But what obsessed Duvalier and took up much of his time were his difficult negotiations with the Catholic Church, whose mighty Society of Jesus he had just two years earlier expelled from Haitian soil.

As zealous missionaries converted thousands of former Catholic-vodounists to a plethora of Protestant cults, the Catholic Church meandered along under uncertain leadership, "a flock without a shepherd" in Duvalier's words. A concerned Pope Paul VI invited Haiti to discuss the situation, and Duvalier agreed willingly. From January until August he hammered out the details of a new agreement, or concordat, to replace the one President Fabre Nicolas Geffrard had signed in 1860. Duvalier knew exactly what he wanted: a native hierarchy, the right to appoint its members himself, and annulment of his own excommunication. In return he offered a profoundly religious population of several million, the vast majority Catholic, and the challenge of a host of proselytizing Protestant missionaries who were pouring into Haiti, feeding the starving and converting them by the chapelful.

Rome in its turn also had considerable negotiating leverage: its enormous prestige, its place as Haiti's traditional religion, and the immense wealth of its various orders. From Duvalier it wanted guarantees of safety, redress for Bishops Robert and Poirier, other priests, and also the entire orders he had expelled. Other problem areas were the closure of the Catholic newspaper *La Phalange,* Zacharie Delva's vodoun *cérémonie* on the steps of the Gonaive cathedral, Macoute invasions of churches, and the delicate issue of vodoun, virtually acknowledged as Duvalier's state religion, with *houngan* Delva second only to Duvalier in the nation's power structure.

The Vatican found Duvalier a formidable negotiator. No point was small enough for him to concede, no pressure so great he could not withstand it. When only two of his four nominations for bishops were accepted, he maintained a cold silence for nearly three weeks. Finally his agitated delegate, Fritz Jean-Baptiste, wired him an urgent reminder. Duvalier replied that he regretted that his demands had not satisfied the Vatican, and said that he would soon propose new names. He waited a whole week after that, then wrote the Pope directly, his tone polite but firm, and reiterated the demands he had already made.

Paul VI was slow to respond, but in July he sent a special papal delegation to Haiti. The three men arrived on August 11 and immediately entered into intensive negotiations. On August 15 they signed an official protocol, undoubtedly the most masterful diplomatic coup Duvalier ever made.

The protocol reiterated the right accorded the Haitian President by the 1860 concordat to name all vacant bishoprics, subject to papal approval. In 1966, with Pope Paul VI's approval, Duvalier named François Wolff Ligondé as Archbishop of Port-au-Prince, Claudius Angenor, Bishop of Cayes, and General Gérard Constant's younger brother Emmanuel Constant as Bishop of Gonaives. His other nominations, Jean-Baptiste Decoste as Assistant Archbishop of Port-au-Prince and Carl-Edward Peters Assistant Bishop of Cayes, were duly listed, as were the wide range of topics discussed, from the preparation of Haitian priests to the Church's social work. In a separate agreement Duvalier did not rescind the expulsion orders against the bishops but he did provide them miserly monthly pensions of $100 each. The Jesuit expulsion also remained in force, but without any softening pensions or even words, and no other sensitive issue was even broached. In conclusion, Haiti reaffirmed the special place of the Catholic Church in Haiti and agreed to grant it special protection on the understanding that it did not attempt to interfere in politics. An amazing document, all in all, and Duvalier was justly proud of it, though it must have given Paul VI some restless nights.

One dark spot marred 1966, Duvalier's most productive year ever—the publication of Graham Greene's *The Comedians,* the powerful novel that told millions the truth about Papa Doc's Haiti. Greene drew many incidents from real life, including the stealing of Clément Jumelle's corpse—"in a dictatorship one owns nothing, not even a dead husband."

Papa Doc hated *The Comedians,* and in an interview with the Port-au-Prince daily *Le Matin* he declared, "The book is not well written. As the work of a writer and a journalist, the book has no value."

Greene, who never returned to Haiti, was pleased. "*The Comedians,* I am glad to say, touched him on the raw. . . . Was it possible that I disturbed his dreams as he had disturbed mine? . . . A writer is not so powerless as he usually feels, and a pen, as well as a silver bullet, can draw blood."

*   *   *

The year 1967, year ten of the Duvalierist "Revolution," was anticlimactic. Duvalier celebrated it in scores of memorial speeches, but the apex of his rule had come the year before, when he had forced from reluctant Rome a Haitianized Catholic Church, embraced Haile Selassie, survived the American freeze on almost all aid funds (and now saw it thawing), and resumed diplomatic and consular relations with the Dominican Republic after Joaquin Balaguer was elected President on June 1, 1966.

To mark year ten of the presidency Duvalier published his *Breviary of a Revolution,* copying Chairman Mao's "Little Red Book" in the small dimensions a fanatic could tote in his pocket.

In year ten Duvalier was also honored by the State of Israel. In 1947 Haiti cast the crucial U.N. vote on the partition of Palestine, a vote without which the State of Israel would not have been created. Israeli gratitude has never cooled, and when the U.S. ostracized Papa Doc, Israel sold him Uzis for his Tonton Macoutes and thrilled the dictator by translating into Hebrew his most important political treatise, *The Class Problem Throughout the History of Haiti.*

The class problem—or really Haiti's mulatto-black problem—analyzed in the book was still a Duvalier obsession. "Any foreigner or any Haitian who will have it that the class issue does not exist lacks intellectual honesty," he declared.

In year-ten celebration speeches, however, Duvalier did not mention Haiti's class problem, though after a decade in power he had pushed blacks forward more than any previous President since Henri Christophe. Perhaps he realized he had also killed too many to boast about his peculiar brand of *noirisme.* Instead he focused on Haiti's economic crisis, blaming it on American and other international lending institutions who had cut off his aid.

Duvalier's second preoccupation was with internal stability. "The policy of my administration at home is pursuing the strengthening of political stability, social peace and public order. Such a policy has kept the government safe from the danger of armed surprise attacks. . . . It is the safeguard of the integrity of the national territory." Tacitly admitting his iron dictatorial rule, he justified it with an odd historical reminder: "Monarchy was absolute prior to becoming parliamentary and the world adapted itself to it for centuries."

He also admitted his people's poverty. "The peasant, the worker, the urban proletariat earn a paltry income; the mass of consumers has only a reduced purchasing power at its command." A series of natural catastrophes had struck Haiti, and Duvalier blamed them for some of the economic slowdown.

In the face of this economic disaster, foreign persecution, and faltering domestic harmony, Duvalier expressed "fears that all the sons of this Haitian Homeland fail to be aware that they shall have to be watchful in order to deter any return to slavery, to subjection!" He concluded his analysis of his ten years in power with the stirring reflection that "Haiti and the Haitian were born to glory, to greatness, to life, to immortality."

The Swiss-based International Commission of Jurists gave Duvalier's Haiti a different year-ten evaluation:

> It is difficult to describe the present state of affairs with any accuracy. The systematic violation of every single article and paragraph of the Universal Declaration of Human Rights seems to be the only policy which is respected and assiduously pursued in the Caribbean Republic. The rule of law was long ago displaced by a reign of terror and the personal will of its dictator, who has awarded himself the title of Life President of the Republic, and appears to be more concerned with the suppression of real or imaginary attempts against his life than with governing the country. He is leading his nation not in the direction of prosperity but towards the final disaster that can be seen in its political, social, and economic collapse.

Duvalier was not merely an obsessed president. He was also a father whose favorite children were his oldest daughter, Marie-Denise, and his youngest child and only son, Jean-Claude. Marie-Denise was a beautiful, headstrong woman. Her huge, mocking, dark eyes and her voluptuous figure did not belie her willful nature. Despite her father's vigilance, and though she continued to live in the palace, when Marie-Denise finally met the man she wanted to marry, she was already notorious for her sexual appetite and for the train of lovers she had taken.

The man to whom she gave her heart as well as her body was handsome, strapping, six-foot, seven-inch Max Dominique, a thirty-four-year captain in her father's Palace Guard. His wife and children Marie-Denise regarded as mere inconveniences, and soon convinced

Dominique to divorce and marry her. Duvalier was not pleased with his daughter's choice of husband, but Marie-Denise was determined, and very soon she was Madame Max Dominique. Duvalier, powerless before this daughter he adored, reluctantly accepted the marriage and promoted Dominique to colonel, then placed him in command of the Port-au-Prince military district.

Shortly after, Marie-Denise's younger sister Nicole also married, before she eschewed men altogether to live openly as a lesbian. Duvalier preferred her husband, a green-eyed mulatto, Luc Albert Foucard, brother of his private secretary, Madame Francesca Foucard Saint-Victor. Saint-Victor was also Duvalier's mistress, and told her family she alone excited the impotent and sick old man. Rivalry between the two new brothers-in-law began, with palace intimates siding with either Nicole or Marie-Denise and seeking every opportunity to plant poisonous information about the other in Duvalier's ever-suspicious ears. Simone Duvalier, jealous of Saint-Victor, took Marie-Denise's side, while Saint-Victor naturally rallied around her brother and the homely new sister-in-law.

Slander and vilification continued until Papa Doc's sixtieth birthday celebrations in April of year ten. Then—literally—the feud turned explosive. The first bombs went off during the public birthday celebrations and killed an ice-cream vendor. Duvalier suspected Dominique was responsible and that he was trying to sabotage Foucard, Duvalier's new Minister of Tourism, and ruin the public festivities Foucard had planned.

The next bomb was thought to be Foucard's revenge, and although Communists claimed they and not the brothers-in-law were the saboteurs, Duvalier dismissed this as nonsense and determined to get rid of Dominique.

Duvalier had always been suspicious of his army officers, and now he found it easy to believe the majestic and popular black Dominique was plotting a military coup. Working closely with Foucard, Duvalier transferred many of his young Palace Guard officers to the provinces and two weeks later demoted them. Three weeks after that he ordered them back to Port-au-Prince. Assuming that their punishment for imaginary crimes was finished, and hopeful of returning to their former positions, none of the nineteen escaped. A grave error, for in Port-au-Prince they were at once disarmed, arrested, and thrown into Fort Dimanche.

Duvalier also purged Cap Haitien, Dominique's hometown, firing Tonton Macoutes, arresting those who did not manage to escape, and authorizing the public to pillage their properties. Later, for good measure, he also eliminated several Tonton Macoute leaders in the capital. Terrified, 108 prominent Macoutes and Duvalierists fled to Latin American embassies. Duvalier also arrested two of his Macoute ministers, Interior Minister Jean Julmé and Justice Minister Rameau Estimé, sentenced them to three months' imprisonment for criticizing him, and threw them into Fort Dimanche.

On June 8 Duvalier abruptly summoned his general staff to the palace. General Gérard Constant was there, and Duvalier's son-in-law Colonel Max Dominique with his wife, Marie-Denise Duvalier. For two hours the President kept them waiting. He finally arrived in military costume and ordered the men to follow him into waiting cars. In her Thunderbird a grim-faced Marie-Denise followed. The cavalcade of terrified officers soon turned down the heavily guarded gravel road leading to Fort Dimanche. Marie-Denise braked and stopped, then sat waiting. If she did not see her beloved husband return alive, she had vowed to blow her father to smithereens with the machine gun she had slipped under the front seat.

It was now noon, and in the bright sunlight the officers followed Duvalier as he limped slowly down to the end of the rifle range. There, bound to nineteen stakes, were the nineteen officers. One of them was Major Sonny Borges, the scourge of the Jérémie mulattoes. Another was Duvalier's wife's military aide-de-camp, Lieutenant Joseph Laroche. Another was Captain Harry Tassy, condemned because after Duvalier's tubby, doe-eyed youngest daughter, Simone, fell in love with him, he had refused to marry her. Another victim was a young lieutenant who had taken young Jean-Claude Duvalier into a private home and abused him.

Duvalier's staff officers, including Max Dominique, were each handed a rifle and directed to stand opposite one of the men they had known so well, all of them loyal Duvalierists and most also intimate friends of Max Dominique. Behind each man stood a Macoute, gun cocked and ready to blast at the least sign of disobedience or even hesitation. "Fire!" shouted Duvalier, and in a blast that reverberated throughout the prison, nineteen officers shot nineteen officers.

Duvalier was still not satisfied. Two weeks later, commandeering trucks as he always did for such occasions, he sent out into the countryside for a captive audience of peasants. As they watched obediently in front of the palace, Duvalier appeared.

He began to call out names. "Major Harry Tassy, where are you? Come to your benefactor." After a theatrical silence he remarked, "Absent." Eighteen names later he reached a crescendo: "All of them have been shot," he announced, and as the crowd stirred with collective shock, he began another roll call of those who had fled to Latin American embassies. "They have run away after having received Caesar's favors," Duvalier said. "They are no longer Haitians. Beginning tomorrow the general court-martial will receive orders to work on their trial. They will be tried according to the law, for we are civilized."

The final scene was almost as dramatic as the execution of the nineteen officers. "I am an arm of steel, hitting inexorably . . . hitting inexorably . . . hitting inexorably . . . I have shot these . . . officers in order to promote the Revolution . . . I align myself with the great leaders Kemal Ataturk, Lenin, Kwame Nkrumah, Patrice Lumumba, Azikwe, Mao Tse-tung." The next day, now regretting that he had spared Max Dominique's life, Duvalier decided to kill him after all. But after Marie-Denise and her mother went down on their knees and begged for the young man's life, Duvalier relented and exiled him instead. Then Marie-Denise left Haiti with Dominique and took with her Simone, her youngest sister. As their plane took off Duvalier gave a signal, and Macoutes shot and killed Dominique's chauffeur and two bodyguards. Later his father was arrested and thrown into Fort Dimanche, where he died from ill treatment.

Back in the palace Duvalier shuffled into his office and sat at his glass-topped desk, gazing at photographs of his family. Soon he broke down in tears. Still weeping, he began to phone close associates, telling them how wretched he was at losing two of his daughters. Then his grief transformed into anger that his wife had stopped him from shooting Dominique so that he could keep his children at home with him.

On August 1 Duvalier formally charged Dominique with treason, fired him, and ordered him back to Haiti to stand trial. Naturally, Dominique refused. Duvalier was stunned. Though he was absolute master of his country, his own family defied and defeated him. He blamed his wife and was so nasty that she threatened to join the Dominiques in Spain. The little doctor, enraged, struck out and flailed at her with all his might. Huge, fifteen-year-old Jean-Claude intervened. He pushed his father into another room, locked the door, and left him there.

After three hours the furious President pulled an emergency alarm. Guards came running, and Tonton Macoutes. Duvalier announced a curfew, and then astounded the soldiers and Macoutes with a vituperative monologue against his wife, Simone, denouncing her role in saving

Dominique's life and accusing her of failing to help him as Argentinian dictator Juan Perón's Evita had helped her husband.

Toward the end of year ten, Duvalier released Jean Julmé and Rameau Estimé, his former Interior and Justice ministers, from Fort Dimanche. Julmé had attempted suicide, trying to pierce his brain by forcing a stick into his ear. Both men were starved, their weakened bodies ballooned out with symptoms of protein deprivation. Restored to their families, the once-powerful ministers had to be nursed and fed like helpless babies.

Not long afterward Duvalier once again contacted the two men. Acting as if he had never jailed them and ordered them subjected to months of brutal humiliation and deprivation, he invited both to resume their former positions. "My shaky health prevents me," Julmé replied, and refused the job. Estimé's physical condition was no better, but he thought it prudent to accept the offer, and soon after swore the oath of office again. Haiti now had a Justice Minister with personal experience of the treatment to which Duvalier's justice condemned so many.

Duvalier did not appear annoyed at Julmé's refusal. One day a palace messenger arrived at the big white house in breezy Pacot and delivered Julmé a gift from the President. It was a slender pamphlet Duvalier had written about Haiti's foreign relations, and when Julmé turned the first page he saw with a sort of wonder the dedication in Duvalier's enormous handwriting: "To my old comrade Jean M. Julmé, in remembrance of the battles which ended in 22 September 1957. Affectionately, Dr. François Duvalier."

In Jérémie, on the night of March 18, 1968, a loud knocking sounded at the door of former Attorney General Antoine Jean-Charles, now demoted to Judge of Instruction. Still in his bathrobe, Jean-Charles went outside and found his yard surrounded by soldiers. "Where is your brother Abner?" an officer demanded. "We know he's a Communist, and we've been told you're hiding him here."

Jean-Charles braced himself. His oldest brother, Abner, slightly retarded, did not understand what communism was, and had even failed to earn a living after he joined the Tonton Macoutes. He had gone to the Bahamas on a small fishing boat, but Bahamian policemen beat him, arrested him, and returned him to Haiti, where he finally found work in a *guldive*, or native distillery, where cheap liquor was manufactured.

To protect his family's lives Jean-Charles revealed Abner's where-abouts. Soon afterward Abner was arrested, accused of communism, and sent to Fort Dimanche. Sixteen others from his village of Basse-Guinaudée shared his fate, including a seventy-year-old peasant. All seventeen dis-appeared into the bowels of Fort Dimanche; none was ever heard from again.

All Haitians had to be cautious, but those at gravest risk were Communists, suspected or real. For an entire decade Duvalier hammered them, reassuring the Communist-shy Americans that whatever else he might be, Communist he was not. At the same time he enjoyed American discomfort at the aggressively anti-American tone of confiscated Haitian Communist literature, which could only help his own cause.

In fact, Duvalier was an intellectual long exposed to leftist doc-trines of all camps and neither shared, admired, nor feared them. He did, however, fear Castro's Cuba, and from the first days of the Communist takeover understood the role Cuba would play in attacking him.

Haitian Communists, so disunited that Haiti had two Communist parties whose adherents battled each other in vicious articles they pub-lished in bourgeois newspapers, presented minor security threats. As propaganda vehicles, however, they were important, for Duvalier could use them as evidence of the dangers to which his country, like Cuba, was exposed.

Communism also helped Duvalier identify his enemies. The impos-sibility of Communist sympathizers to sympathize with his own revolu-tion made them enemies, and they had to be eliminated. Indeed, what easier way to rid himself of any enemy, suspected, real, or potential, than by labeling him a Communist?

The 1965 murder of Jean-Jacques Dessalines Ambroise, the Com-munist leader of the Popular Party of National Liberation (PPLN), had one consequence Duvalier certainly could not have foreseen. It killed off a dangerous enemy, but it also provoked the union of both Ambroise's party and the rival Party of Popular Accord (PEP). In December 1968 PPLN and PEP merged to form the United Party of Haitian Communists (PUCH), committed "to overthrow the Duvalierist Dictatorship and to take power in the name of the united front of all the anti-feudal and anti-imperialist forces led by the working class, to destroy the present eco-nomic and social regime and bring about the essential transformation of the revolution of national liberation on the social, economic, political, and cultural fields." What alarmed Duvalier most were PUCH's tactics: armed struggle, bombs, guerrilla attacks. With the advent of PUCH, Duvalier's war against communism entered a new and much more terrible phase.

Who were Communists? Where were they? What fields nourished them? Duvalier thought he knew. Schools were among the worst offenders, he believed, along with colleges, universities, workers' associations, and churches. He also suspected Haitians returning from foreign countries because of the left-wing contacts they might have established there.

He had defined the enemy, and the enemy was everywhere. The war was on, and Duvalier waged his battles on as many fronts as possible.

For all the frenetic witch-hunting, there were real Communists, the members of PUCH, Haiti's United Communist Party. On March 26, in a unique little village thirty-six kilometers north of Port-au-Prince, PUCH members began a guerrilla operation. The village they chose was Cazale, home of the descendants of Polish soldiers sent by Napoleon to fight the Haitians but who so admired their enemy that they changed sides and joined them. Respected throughout Haiti, the Cazale villagers are a mix of Polish and Haitian bloodlines, many blond with Slavic cheekbones sharp under tawny skin. Primarily Protestant, steeped in notions of fundamental freedoms from their exotic heritage, and residents of the only village in Haiti without a single *houngan* or *mambo,* the people of Cazale became PUCH's testing ground.

On March 26 the young Communists defiantly declared themselves, took down Duvalier's black-and-red flag and ran up the old blue-and-red in its place, then waited for Duvalier to act. They did not have to wait long. Soon contingents of Macoutes and soldiers stormed Cazale, and terrible battles followed, which few Communists survived. Those who did fled to the mountains, and from there slowly crept into safe houses where they hid and considered their defeat.

In Cazale the villagers paid a heavier price. The Macoutes made examples of them, holding them up to all other Haitians who might even consider sedition. Hundreds were beaten. A dozen were tied with ropes and dragged behind cars and trucks until they died. Some were hanged, and a few were shot. The total death toll stood at twenty-three, but hundreds more disappeared forever, and Cazale mourned them as dead.

Some of the victims were chosen at random, but most were suspected of having Communist ties. The Macoutes regarded Alix Lamauthe as a likely candidate, simply because he was young and had recently returned home from Europe. They decapitated him and sent his head to Duvalier as a trophy, gory testimonial to his latest victory over communism.

"The time has come for all Haitians to rise, help the revolutionaries, and continue the operation that has begun in Cazale," the Communists proclaimed over shortwave radio. But communism could not win over Duvalierism. Betrayed and infiltrated from within, PUCH members were soon fighting not for Haitian liberation but for their own lives. One after another their safe houses were attacked, their inhabitants killed.

PUCH defended itself and moved aggressively throughout the country, killing soldiers and Macoutes. When their funds were low one PUCH group went out and held up a bank, Haiti's first-ever bank robbery. They got safely away, and PUCH activities were afterward financed by the stolen money.

These were mere holding operations, and Duvalier's ultimate victory came on June 2, 1969, in Port-au-Prince. Soldiers opened fire on a house on Martin Luther King Street, and soon twenty-two Communists were dead, including important PUCH central committee members. The final Communist tally was said to be 204 killed.

In June 1969 expatriate university student and artist Jean Joseph Charles was so homesick for Haiti that he brushed aside all his friends' pleas and boarded an Air Canada flight to Port-au-Prince. Hours later, tears of joy mingling with inexplicable sadness, he trudged across the tarmac toward the modern new terminal building. Three people were there to meet him—Tonton Macoutes in civilian clothes, their hallmark dark glasses as ominous as he had remembered. An hour later Charles was standing naked in the Criminal Investigation Building warding off blows as a Macoute asked him mechanically over and over, "Why did you come back here to spread your Communist filth? Did your Communist comrades in Canada tell you to come here to poison Haitians against the government?"

A few days later they transferred him to Dessalines Barracks, where he learned how to be a prisoner. His torturers were called correctors, the beatings corrections. Charles learned to assume a humble mien and accepted even murderous blows without trying to defend himself. He witnessed murder and swore he had not noticed. One morning they beat a man to death before Charles's eyes, "correcting" him to stiff perfection.

Later on they transferred Charles to Fort Dimanche, where he shared a fetid cell with more than forty others, snatching sleep each night in two-hour relays. He drank his own urine, slaking thirst. He sat unmoving as sleek brown rats crawled over his body. He endured the torment of mosquitoes and bugs that infested the fort. He warded off the guards' blows as he shuffled daily toward the life-saving drops of water in the shower. He knew he was going to die there, and he often wished they would shoot him. When he remembered God, he prayed.

In his own prison of pain, Duvalier was coming to the end of his term. On May 20, 1969, doctors at St. François de Sales Hospital operated on his prostate gland, and rumors of his deteriorating condition spread throughout Haiti and to Haitians abroad.

On June 4, in response to the news, exiled Colonel René Léon tried to precipitate a heart attack as well. Buzzing the palace in a four-engine Lockheed Constellation, Léon and his Canadian and American mercenaries dropped six incendiary bombs, five of which failed to ignite. In the panic-stricken capital antiaircraft gunners responded with furious firing that also missed its target. Finally, out of bombs, Léon retreated to the Bahamas, and Duvalier, whose heart did not fail, informed the United States that Cuba was now dropping bombs on him.

Papa Doc but not Port-au-Prince escaped unscathed. Panicked pedestrians ran through the packed streets, trampling those who stumbled. Cars and trucks smashed into one another. Students and teachers at the Medical Faculty jumped out of windows, twisting and spraining ankles and wrists. Punctuating it all were the shrill cries of sidewalk vendors whose carts and trays were upset by the fleeing mobs.

On July 1 New York Governor Nelson Rockefeller arrived on the Haitian leg of a Latin-American fact-finding mission. Duvalier hauled himself out of bed, put on one of his immaculate suits, and welcomed the American with great fanfare. Rockefeller was agreeably surprised. Until Haiti his tour had been disastrous, pocked with anti-American demonstrations and unpleasant incidents. In Duvalier's airy palace, with 30,000 cheering and banner-waving Haitians outside, Rockefeller felt right at home. On the balcony he cradled the feeble Duvalier with one hand and waved back at the crowds with the other.

For Papa Doc it was wonderful propaganda—a Haitian and an American standing in a near embrace while beneath them the happy and contented Haitian people roared in pride and approval. Rockefeller later justified himself to a critical congressional subcommittee: "There were thirty thousand people out front. If you're a politician, your natural instinct is to respond."

Soon the United States sent Haiti a new ambassador, Dr. Clinton E. Knox, a black who responded enthusiastically to Duvalier's diatribes against American racism and often reminded journalists of how much Duvalier had achieved for black Haitians while wresting power and privilege from the domineering mulattoes. Partly on Knox's recommendation, the Americans resumed aid to the devastated country, and Duvalier congratulated himself on his success in repairing the rupture between the two republics.

The President also patched up his own quarreling family, and less than two years after exiling her husband and killing her father-in-law, Duvalier sought a reconciliation with his beloved Marie-Denise. She returned alone and spent Christmas with her parents. Before Marie-Denise sent for her husband, now pardoned, and her baby, named Alexandre after his murdered paternal grandfather, she took charge of and reorganized her father's life. Her doting mother approved her every move, especially when she fired Francesca Saint-Victor and installed herself as her father's secretary.

Marie-Denise also dismissed many of the Tonton Macoutes whom Duvalier liked to have clustered around him in the palace. She then disposed of her sister's husband, Luc Fouchard. In divorce Duvalier style, she simply had him shipped out of the country, barred from ever returning. Nicole also left Haiti and moved to Miami, where she lived monogamously with her woman lover. Her daughter Natasha remained in Haiti to be raised by her grandmother, Simone Duvalier.

Now the palace felt like home, and so Marie-Denise moved her once-disgraced husband, Max Dominique, and baby son back into it. Forceful, intelligent, and fearless, Marie-Denise was also one of the few human beings Duvalier trusted as well as loved. As his health declined and medical crises followed one after another, he welcomed her taking over from him, bearing the load he no longer could. Marie-Denise was both generous and tough, the antithesis of her mother.

It is in the nature of dictatorship that the question of succession assumes proportions unimaginable in nations whose systems of government are responsible, delegated, and grounded in the security of permanent civil services. Haiti's case was altogether different, and each time Duvalier's brown skin looked a little grayer, each time the effort of crossing a room seemed beyond him, each time whole days went by before he was strong enough to change out of bathrobe and slippers, anxious Duvalierists and eager opponents discussed obsessively the question: Who would succeed Duvalier?

Many Duvalierists thought that Finance Minister Clovis Désinor was the logical successor, but even though Duvalier had hinted that he favored Désinor, he was in fact looking to his own children for a solution. Marie-Denise arrived just in time to provide it. It was true that Duvalier had a son, but Jean-Claude was a teenager, and in all respects inferior to his dynamic older sister. Marie-Denise had also reunited her family, reconciling her parents and helping her little brother escape from his cloistered life by arranging for him to travel in Europe. Her only drawback was her sex, but even in male-dominant Haiti her father had appointed women to command his Tonton Macoutes, and in many ways appeared to trust them more than men. Who would succeed Duvalier? In 1970 more and more Haitians speculated that the answer was Marie-Denise Duvalier Dominique.

By April 1970 Duvalier was declining fast. He could no longer chew properly, and each meal had become a torturous affair. Every five minutes he had to swallow one or two pills from the huge pillbox: digitalis, painkillers, uretics. He urinated frequently, and the trip to the toilet strained his phlebitic legs, exhausting him. In this precarious condition François Duvalier faced the most serious insurrection of his entire presidency.

Colonel Octave Cayard was the *noiriste* commander of Haiti's three-vessel coast guard, and a great Duvalier favorite. The President had lavished gifts on Cayard, including vast land tracts where he raised poultry and cattle. A less likely candidate to lead a rebellion could not be imagined.

In Duvalier's Haiti, however, nothing was impossible, nothing unthinkable. "A good Duvalierist is ready to kill his children, and children their parents," said Luckner Cambronne, and by the same token a Duvalierist had no loyalty, no commitment. When fear and brutality annihilate the human factor, loyalty becomes a commodity that like any other must be purchased again every Monday morning.

Colonel Cayard was loyal after this fashion, and when Duvalier ordered him to the palace along with men suspected of plotting a coup d'état, Cayard knew he could not go. He was well aware that the army simmered with discontent, and he was close enough to serious dissidents to know that under torture they might call out his name, guaranteeing his death.

Without the slightest preparation, motivated entirely by panic, Cayard enlisted 118 out of 325 coast guard members, commandeered all three of Haiti's ships, and sailed out into the bay of Port-au-Prince, where he radioed Duvalier to surrender.

The President, surrounded by his family and general staff, furiously ordered all radio communications cut. "Yesterday he was on his knees at Duvalier's feet. Today he gives him an ultimatum," Simone Duvalier commented acidly.

Cayard, rebuffed, ordered his men to fire. Just before noon they began to shell Port-au-Prince and the palace. The palace took an indirect hit on the west wing, with one soldier injured and little damage. Haiti's air force, as inadequate as its mutinous navy, attacked the ships, as did a shore battery, but without result. Again, Port-au-Prince was not as lucky as the palace. As bullets whistled over the American Embassy, Ambassador Clinton Knox trembled within. At the Hotel Oloffson, Al Seitz pushed his wife and their two babies into the wine cellar.

The rebellion ended when Cayard ran out of fuel. An appeal broadcast to the free world produced only silence, and finally his three mutinous ships sailed off to the American naval base at Guantanamo Bay. There the Americans disarmed the rebels and sent them on to Puerto Rico. All but the wealthy mulatto, Fritz Tippenhauer, sought political asylum. The Americans repaired the ships, so unseaworthy that two had had to be towed in, and returned them to Haiti, where they became part of a revamped navy. The Cayard rebellion was over, and François Duvalier was still in the palace.

For days afterward Port-au-Prince boiled with excitement. From abroad messages poured in from Haitian diplomats supporting Duvalier. Inside the country, workers' syndicates and organizations vied in composing expressions of sympathy and eternal loyalty. Ministers and deputies, except Cayard's brother Volvick and six others who were arrested, joined the chorus.

The American ambassador gave an interview to UPI and said, "President Duvalier's position seems solid to me. The Armed Forces and the people seemed absolutely loyal to the Government." Despite the reality of the rebellion, Knox dismissed rumors of trouble. "I haven't been here six months yet, but I'm used to hearing five to ten rumors a week."

Duvalier made public appearances and addressed the nation in a triumphant message. "It is the fate of governments which have been charged with the mission of changing the lot of the 'Great Deprived Masses' to face conspiracies from those eternally unsatisfied and always thirsty for recognition and power," Duvalier lamented. "Always follow the star of the Leader of the Revolution and have full confidence in his Destiny because he has been chosen by the gods to fulfill a great mission. His arm of bronze will never flinch."

On November 12 Duvalier suffered a mild stroke. Everyone who saw him diagnosed his case as terminal. Certainly he could not last much longer. Who would succeed him? Who could hold the nation together and prevent a wholesale slaughter of the First Family and all those thousands of its hangers-on who had kept it in power?

But Duvalier was not quite dead, and the decision was still his. The choice he made had to be acceptable to the country after his death, for his top priority in choosing his successor was to ensure the safety of his family and intimates, most so compromised that their fall from power could not be permitted. Many regarded the army, Haiti's traditional king-maker and king-breaker, as the only guarantee of stability during the transitional period, and Simone Duvalier pleaded with her dying husband for a military junta or strongman, arguing that otherwise she and her family would be forced into exile.

But Duvalier still mistrusted the Haitian military, the source of the recent Cayard Rebellion and hatchery of malcontents. Furthermore, the army was a feeble force, with Tonton Macoutes outweighing it at least twenty to one, and so emasculated that its general chief of staff lacked even the power to transfer sub-officers. The army, Duvalier concluded, was not the vehicle to ensure that Duvalierism survived intact.

The choice was therefore narrowed down to two—Marie-Denise or Jean-Claude—but those close to Duvalier warned him that many Haitians would not tolerate a young woman as President. His choice—by default—was Jean-Claude.

Duvalier's decision was made with anguish. Had he been a monarch, the succession of his son would have been unquestioned, but he was a President, albeit for life, and he had always maintained the myth that his was a popularly elected regime. What claim then had his son to succeed him? Furthermore, Jean-Claude was a nineteen-year-old without the least interest in affairs of state, whereas his father had survived only by sacrificing every waking hour of his life to government, neglecting nothing, manipulating Haiti like a nation of marionettes. Nor was Jean-Claude a young man who inspired confidence in his acquaintances, from his classmates, who snickered about his failing grades, to foreign newsmen, who snickered about his obesity and a gait so awkward that it defied description but not mocking imitation.

But other factors counted too, and the dying President added them up. Jean-Claude was a Duvalier, and the only Duvalier son. He had been brought up to palace life, and though the details and intricacies of politics bored him, life with his Papa Doc had steeped him in Duvalierist maxims and attitudes. He would inherit the well-functioning machine of state his father had taken thirteen years to structure. If the transition was orchestrated correctly, he would step into his father's place without losing a beat of the Duvalier momentum. Papa Doc made his decision.

The new President-for-Life must be surrounded by pliant sycophants and loyal strongmen. Those who balk at a monarchical succession must be eliminated. Clovis Désinor, for instance, a loyal Duvalier *noiriste* since the 1930s and a trusted minister, was also an intimate who had long spoken out against the succession of Jean-Claude. One day François and Simone spent a pleasant evening in the Désinors' airy house in Canapé Vert. The next day Désinor learned from an official communiqué that Duvalier had fired him. No reason was given, but everyone knew it was because Désinor, filled with his own presidential ambitions, could not be expected to support Jean-Claude.

On November 18, Armed Forces Day, Duvalier also eliminated other top-ranked officials. Duvalier chose that day's massive public ceremonies to present his son as his successor. First Jean-Claude stood beside his father on the east balcony of the palace, watching the parades. Afterward, his puny resources sapped, the President retired to his office to rest.

The ceremonies were not finished, however, for he had decided to lavish decorations on his most trusted soldiers and Tonton Macoutes, including Aderbal Lhérisson and Madame Max Adolphe. Gérard Constant accepted his diploma of honor from Jean-Claude, then shook the impassive schoolboy's hand. As he left the room someone said, "You didn't give him a military salute."

"Why should I?" Constant retorted.

By that evening Duvalier knew all about Constant's defiance, and on December 8 the new member of the Toussaint Louverture Order of Civil Merit was summoned to the palace for the last interview he would ever have with Duvalier. When he left shortly afterward Constant was retired, and Claude Raymond, a tough young colonel who was also Duvalier's godson, became Haiti's new chief of staff.

Constant was shocked and deeply troubled, but a few days earlier he had guessed what might happen to him. That was the day he picked up the newpaper *Le Nouveau Monde* and read that Duvalier had chosen Jean-Claude to succeed him, and not, as Constant had always assumed, the army with himself as Provisional President.

"We all know that Caesar Augustus was nineteen when he took Rome's destinies into his hands," Duvalier reminded his people, "and his reign remains 'the Century of Augustus.'" The fifty-year-old general was out, and the teenaged civilian, so young and raw he was not even old enough to vote for himself, was in.

Papa Doc simply swept away the latest Constitution, legislating his own will into the national law. His agent in this endeavor was Luckner Cambronne, especially honored in November for his dynamic Duvalierism. On January 13 Cambronne asked his fellow congressmen to amend the Constitution so that Jean-Claude could be named President-for-Life. By January 22 the amendments had been made and published, and now Haitian presidents no longer needed to be forty.

Jean-Claude dutifully accepted his nomination. "I believe I understand that you want the nation to avoid internecine battles, deadly for the country's future. . . . I believe too that I understand you want to assure the continuity of the Revolution, giving it time—such a precious factor—to entrench itself in the national conscience," he recited woodenly.

The next day a national referendum elicited the people's feelings about the succession by explaining that Jean-Claude was his father's chosen successor and finishing, "Does this choice respond to your aspirations? Do you ratify it? Answer: Yes." With such a ballot it was difficult to disagree, and not a single Haitian did. The official tally, solemnly reported, was 2,391,916 unanimous yes votes. Everywhere walls and billboards were covered with posters of the enormous President-designate sitting impassively in front of his elderly Papa Doc, who stood with one frail hand on his son's meaty shoulder. "I have chosen him" was the moving caption.

On April 14 Papa Doc celebrated his sixty-fourth birthday in bed. Though Jean-Claude was his official successor, Marie-Denise had once again taken over from her father and, with Duvalier favorite Luckner Cambronne, was playing regent for the schoolboy figurehead.

Days later Duvalier called in three of his top military men, carefully vetted and promoted to ensure the peaceful transition of power. To them the dying man admitted what the world had long since known: "My government has not been what I wanted it to be," Duvalier faltered. "I've had to do things, things that weren't what I set out to do." Then, as the officers mumbled disclaimers, he continued, with tears streaming down his shrunken, gray cheeks, "My mission is at an end. I'm about to die. I know that choosing Jean-Claude was not the best option, but I did it because I wanted to guarantee the security of those who have taken such heavy responsibilities on my behalf." At the very end, Gratitude was no longer Cowardice.

On April 21, the President-for-Life sat up in his sickbed. Then, as he tried to eat his supper, his treacherous heart betrayed its last victim. The Duvalier family were with him, and as they bent forward to decipher his last words, François Duvalier died.

7 THE REVOLUTION CONTINUES

THE SICK LITTLE DOCTOR WAS DEAD, AND HIS HEIR WAS a phlegmatic, overweight nineteen-year-old who relied mainly on his older sister and mother to help him. His legacy was vast and complex, the eroded, western end of a tropical island teeming with millions of illiterate peasants on the edge of starvation and desperation. Rebellion was a constant menace, for though Papa Doc had obsessively hunted down opponents, to his last minutes he had confronted new ones, armed and deadly. Foreign observers noted the advent of the child dictator and unanimously predicted a bloody rule that could not last out the year.

Yet for almost fifteen years Jean-Claude governed as President-for-Life. How did it happen? Why was he not overthrown, exiled, assassinated? When his fortunes did change, why was he permitted to leave at the head of a cavalcade of limousines filled with family, friends, and servants and flown first-class into opulent exile?

"Whenever an old man dies, a library has burned down," goes the African saying. On April 21, 1971, Duvalier's great store of knowledge, experience, and cunning burned down, but the way of life he had scripted for his people lived on. In that way of life is to be found the solution to the puzzle: Why were the observers wrong? What miracle had Papa Doc worked so that for fifteen years after the incineration of his library, the wisdom it contained still dominated the land?

The answer is that Papa Doc had studied, learned, and understood his country. He was expert in its internal racism, its obsession with the glories of its history. He manipulated the sensibilities of its impressionable people and toyed with foreign powers who intervened, slapping them down like dominoes in a winning game. He knew the power of terror, and through his Tonton Macoutes institutionalized it. He nurtured his people's reverence for the cult of personality, then filled it with his own.

In Haiti the other world of spirits and the real world of harsh sunlight have always coexisted, and Duvalier was master of both. His magical powers were legendary, and people believed he shared with Dessalines the ability to double himself. "Even if you kill me, I'll still be in the palace," he used to say, and Haitians understood the futility of attacking a man possessed of such pure energy that he could be in two places at once.

Through legions of his *houngans* and *mambos* he controlled his people's wills, and discovered their secrets when their priests betrayed them to him. His vodoun practices convinced believers of his great powers and lent his authority an aura of inevitability no logic could dispel. The flock of evil spirits from the Trou Foban housed in his palace was an additional guarantee of his invincibility. Each time Duvalier ordered an enemy's head severed, his people understood that their President would commune with the dead man's spirit. Sometimes he would even swallow it, thereby fortifying himself with the soul and wisdom of yet another mortal.

As profoundly important as his mastery of Haiti's spiritual world was, Duvalier never neglected brute physical force. The eunuch army, emasculated to docility, boiled with intrigue but remained impotent even under its loyal new General Claude Raymond. Haiti's real power, the Tonton Macoutes, were loosely structured and organized so that at the commanding end of each link was Duvalier the Supreme Commander. Mutiny was virtually impossible, and in any case Duvalier's largesse made it unthinkable. By the time of François's death tens of thousands of Tonton Macoutes controlled his people, a brutal force of armed civilians drawn mainly from poverty or from the spiritually powerful vodoun priests, Protestant pastors, and, more rarely, Catholic priests.

Duvalier had risen to power by promising to eliminate the crashing inequities between black and mulatto. Instead he used that terrible schism to maintain his own power, pitting blacks against mulattoes, persecuting some mulattoes while favoring others, including those who married into his family. With infinite cunning he raised up black men, but for every decent meritorious Clovis Désinor there was a Zacharie Delva, for every Gérard Constant, a Luc Désyr, for every Antoine Jean-Charles, an Edouard C. Paul. Duvalier used the noble side of *noirisme* to lure the conscientious and the bitter, and used his country's blackness to reproach a disapproving world.

As Haiti sank further into agricultural and economic ruin, as exports and tourism dwindled, Duvalier offered up his people's terrible poverty to prise money from the outside world. Suffering was Haiti's vast new crop, and François Duvalier its enthusiastic salesman.

The Americans' terror of communism was Duvalier's other diplomatic weapon, and with utter cynicism he waved it Damocles-like over their heads. He fostered anti-American resentments born during the occupation and contemptuously dallied with diplomats until he found men who responded to his earnest, twisted explanations.

Even François Duvalier's complex personal relationships usually had political dimensions. Only for his children, father, and wife did he seem to feel uncompromised love, and his affection and concern for his friends could at any second evaporate into furies of mindless vengeance. He had loved Octave Cayard, and wept uncontrollably at the news of his treachery. He had not loved Macoutes like Jean Julmé, and struck them down with sudden savagery. In human relations he was a master, cunning and subtle, cultivating devotion among good and bad men, deceiving, twisting, destroying. And exiling. For one of Duvalier's greatest weapons was exile, ridding Haiti of malcontents and its finest minds and talents, men and women most equipped to overthrow the regime he had established. While Haiti wallowed in mediocrity, Zaire, Canada, the United States, France, Senegal, Benin, Togo, and many other countries received hundreds of thousands of Haitians who contributed to their societies.

When Papa Doc died on April 21, 1971, he left behind millions of Haitians hopelessly divided. Tens of thousands were Macoutes, utterly committed to the regime. His people shed real tears when Duvalier died, in genuine mourning, in relief, in fear, in disbelief. Jean-Claude, who shed no tears, had lost a father but gained a country and a people. "After Duvalier, Duvalier!" cried loyalists vying to stabilize a rocking boat. The nineteen-year-old President-for-Life had inherited a terrible legacy.

Jean-Claude was installed as President-for-Life on April 22, his father's lucky number. On April 23 Papa Doc received his last visitors, thousands of citizens who filed past the refrigerated glass display box he lay in and gazed with awe at their dead President-for-Life. He wore glasses, and his most cherished book, *Memoirs of a Third World Leader,* lay on his pillow facing a gold cross. Twenty-two soldiers and twenty-two Tonton Macoutes formed his guard of honor, monitoring the streams of mourners who stared and wept and prayed over the corpse. If any rejoiced, they dared not show it.

On April 24 Papa Doc left the palace for the last time. The funeral service lasted six hours and was broadcast outside to the hushed crowd. Outside, the bronze casket passed dense crowds. The black Cadillac hearse inched along, preceded by officers carrying Duvalier's vast collection of decorations, each nestled in a scarlet cushion.

Then on the way to the cemetery Papa Doc performed his final miracle. A wind suddenly gusted out of the palace, and like a mystical cyclone whipped along the funeral route, raised dusty whorls, and obliterated the sunlight.

"Master Sarazin is leading his spirits out to follow Duvalier," shouted horrified spectators. "The evil ones from the Trou Foban are following their master!"

Panic ensued. Drummers dropped their sticks and fled; Tonton Macoutes fired Mausers aimlessly and ran; mourners panicked and with shrieks of terror tried to escape the onslaught.

For two hours the phenomenon whipped through downtown Port-au-Prince, until it reached the cemetery. There others understood it differently. "Duvalier has burst his grave," people shouted. They, and soon all but the most sophisticated Haitians, believed that Papa Doc's spirit had returned to Jean-Claude, who for security and psychological reasons—and because the closed coffin now contained a stranger's body—had not left the palace for the burial.

The obese new President-for-Life was no longer a mere orphaned child. He was now succored by his father's spirit. "After Duvalier, Duvalier!" The history of the second half of the regime had begun.

The junior Duvalier inherited a mature and established system, but as the new dictator his own predilections and personality would stamp the regime with his unique style. Jean-Claude began his presidency in a state of shock. He had not gone to his father's funeral because the palace doctors had pumped him so full of Valium, he could scarcely walk. Despite the months devoted to arranging his own accession to power, Jean-

Claude had never fully grasped that his father would actually die. Furthermore, he had hated being President-select and from the beginning had rebelled against François's reluctant decision to appoint him.

"What about Marie-Denise?" he had protested over and over. But Marie-Denise was a woman, whereas he and only he could carry on the family name.

So for months after his inauguration in April, Haiti's new President-for-Life stumbled through each day on massive doses of numbing tranquilizers, until he began tentatively to cope with his situation. Then his overriding concern was to maintain his indolent lifestyle, to continue into precipitate adulthood the habits of his childhood. "I'm never going to kill myself working the way my father did," he used to tell his friends.

The founder of Duvalierism had been an obsessive workaholic, and his dedication to detail was an important feature of his regime. "No one shares Duvalier's power or helps him to exercise it in anything other than a menial way," wrote Robert Rotberg in *Haiti: The Politics of Squalor*. "He alone decides whether the capital will be provided with new storm sewers, whether generators will be transported to the Peligre dam via Port-au-Prince or St. Marc, whether foreigners will receive economic concessions, local businessmen special favour, and ordinary Haitians exile permits. He personally examines and decides whether or not to authorize minor research projects, grants university degrees, selects the kind of material to be used for a new highway, and determines the orthography to be employed for literacy training in Creole."

Not so Jean-Claude, brought up in the palace watching his father deprive himself of all the human pleasures his son loved—sports, partying, watching movies, playing his viola, and listening to music. More important, Papa Doc had also deprived his son of a father, and Jean-Claude felt inadequate to take over from a man who had not bothered to prepare him.

"The son of a bitch never told me anything," the teenaged President complained. "He never had time for me." Jean-Claude's main personal contacts with his father had occurred when he played his radio or records too loudly. Papa Doc, always working in his office, would then stomp into his son's bedroom, fling open the door, and in wordless fury yank the radio or stereo cord out of the wall. Only after he had slammed the door behind him did Jean-Claude dare to resume his music, decibels lower.

Now, fatherless, Jean-Claude mourned as much for his lost boyhood as for his remote and forbidding father. But it was not his lonely palace life he remembered, the long afternoons spent alone on his tricycle, pumping up and down the heavily guarded palace lawn, scattering the sentry geese in protesting cackles as he rode. What he missed above all else was his unpressured adolescence at Collège St. Louis de Gonzague, the prestigious school that had resolved the problem of his mediocre schoolwork by giving him failing grades but promoting him anyway. Only once had Jean-Claude excelled, when the Education Ministry had provided advance copies of the state-administered high school graduation exams that various cabinet ministers prepared and coached the President-select into memorizing. Unembarrassed about his academic failure and indifferent about his immense size and knock-kneed gait, the world's youngest President remembered St. Louis as a paradise on earth, which he longed to recreate, minus the schoolwork, by surrounding himself with other young men.

His intimate circle came from wealthy, privileged Haitian families, all but two mulatto. Jean-Claude was a dictator surrounded by Macoutes and ministers, and friendship with him could build fortunes or save lives. But his friends were suavely confident young men, and privately, among themselves, they mocked Jean-Claude's fat body, his vacuous semi-smirk and thick, boot-shaped sideburns, his total lack of sophistication.

Yet Jean-Claude only looked ridiculous, and over the years his friends forgot his appearance and grew genuinely fond of him. He was polite and well-mannered, affectionate and caring with his mother and sisters, and good-humoured and comfortable with his friends. However, he was irritatingly immature, a spoiled, grown-up baby who thrived on one-upmanship—if one of his friends arrived at the palace with something new, Jean-Claude would invariably and with languid triumph produce a finer one, be it a car, a watch, a suit, or a stylish pair of shoes.

True to his vow not to kill himself with overwork like his father, Jean-Claude took almost no interest in politics or administration, leaving both to his domineering mother, Simone. For years she was unofficially known as "Mama Doc" and shared her power with her longtime lover Luckner Cambronne, as greedy and ambitious as she was, and now that Papa Doc was dead, openly acknowledged as Simone's partner. At first Jean-Claude's cherished sister Marie-Denise acted as his secretary, just as she had done for Papa Doc. Then in August, Cambronne ordered the arrest of a cousin of her husband, Max Dominique, and neither Simone nor Jean-Claude intervened. Furious at their betrayal, Marie-Denise left Haiti for the second time to join Dominique in exile, where a vengeful Cambronne stripped her husband of his diplomatic post. Unperturbed by his sister's personal crisis, Jean-Claude simply replaced her with his closest friend and allowed Mama Doc Simone and Cambonne to continue running the country.

Jean-Claude's new secretary was Auguste "Ti-Pouche" Douyon, and of all his friends Ti-Pouche was the most loyal, even after the Duvaliers were exiled to France. "When we were students at St. Louis de Gonzague, we dreamed together of a Haiti become much more beautiful, and rid of hunger, sickness, and ignorance," Jean-Claude enthused as he announced Ti-Pouche's appointment. Outside of St. Louis, however, and let loose in the palace, the dreamers quickly forgot these noble sentiments, if ever they had had them.

Ti-Pouche was a high-spirited, clever, and opportunistic young man, small and engaging. He was also an astute connoisseur of Haitian art, and over the years built up a personal fortune as a dealer. With the rest of the palace gang, Ti-Pouche immersed himself in Jean-Claude's unceasing rounds of partying and womanizing, hunting and sports, the only things the President was genuinely interested in.

But outward appearances had to be preserved, and though he complained of boredom, Jean-Claude had to attend purely ceremonial functions. He balked only at rehearsing the speeches written for him. "Just give it to me," he would say impatiently as a minister obsequiously handed him a sheaf of papers for approval. "I'm sure it's fine." He would thrust the speech aside and the first and only time he would read it would be in public, his delivery monotonous and uninflected as he plowed through the script he too was hearing for the first time.

One of his first speeches was to the American students of Goshen College, which has a Port-au-Prince campus. "My dear friends," Jean-Claude read with wooden solemnity, "I am happy to receive you this morning and to thank you for your congratulations to me on being the youngest president in the world. I found in your remarks that aura of sincerity and spontaneity that characterize the American youth and people. The University of Goshen is very dear to my young president's heart, consumed as I am by the same ideals and worries that have always characterized university youth."

But Jean-Claude had no consuming ideals, only passions. One was driving fast cars, which he did expertly. Another was racing motorcycles.

Day after day Haitians passing the palace would stop to lean against the wrought-iron fencing around the lawn and watch Jean-Claude mount his Harley-Davidson. Oblivious to spectators, unconcerned about security, he would heave his bulk onto the seat, his gut hanging down against the handlebars. Then he would lunge at the starter and rev up in a cyclone of exhaust fumes and noise. Despite his great size he rode well, and was so engrossed in the sport that he even studied and understood the bike's mechanics. He also patronized motorcycle racing as the Great Protector of Sport, offering not merely trophies but his own personal participation.

Jean-Claude also loved hunting, and he and his friends spent hundreds of weekends in the Artibonite Valley or the Central Plateau hunting ducks, doves, guinea hens, and even homing pigeons, extinct everywhere in the world except Haiti, and nearly so there. The gang would meet at the palace at 3 a.m. and transfer to a convoy of jeeps. Before sunrise the hunt would begin, and Jean-Claude was exceptionally good at it. Not only was he a magnificent shot, he was also lucky. It was unnerving, the friends used to grumble, how they had to tramp about looking for game while Jean-Claude would just stand somewhere and suddenly all the doves or other birds would fly directly above him, easy targets for his expert gun.

Afterward, at the Duvalier ranch at Croix des Bouquets, they would clean the birds and relax, gossiping, telling jokes, discussing girls. None were heavy drinkers, and Ti-Pouche alone got drunk. Though Jean-Claude ate huge quantities of food, he drank sparingly, over the course of an afternoon or evening sipping one or two scotches with 7-Up or soda. He was never drunk, and until years later, when he met Michèle, was never stoned, for drugs were not part of the group's amusements.

Girls were, though, and Jean-Claude pursued them with as much devotion as he did racing, though without the passion. He seldom fell in love, but instead flirted and indulged himself in casual sexual interludes. Long hair was Jean-Claude's weakness, and for years his friends invited a succession of long-maned girls to his parties. He had no trouble seducing them, for a favorite girl could expect not only jewelry and money but even a car in appreciation of her prowess in Jean-Claude's bed.

Jean-Claude's lovers, mainly though not exclusively female, required stamina as well as greed and ambition, for in bed as in other sports the President had exceptional, even phenomenal, staying power. He was a clumsy lover whose idea of sophisticated foreplay was to pay a girl to lie naked on a chaise longue while he doused her with champagne, then writhe in real or feigned pleasure as he licked it from every crevice of her body.

But that required only a thespian flare. The stamina was required during the sexual act itself for, unlike his impotent father, Jean-Claude could sustain erections for hours, and though not sadistic, he was a large and awkward young man.

The partying and self-indulgence were the President's main priorities, but he was nonetheless the focal point of the regime, and his essential shallowness had to be concealed. Simone Duvalier did this by registering her son in the University of Haiti's law school. Professional school was certainly appropriate to Jean-Claude's age and social status, though not his appalling academic record. Predictably, the charade of Jean-Claude-as-student was conducted with Haitian-style insouciance.

In October, the traditional month for Haitian school opening, the First Lady summoned to the palace Grégoire Eugène, a constitutional law professor whom her dead husband had twice barred from leaving Haiti for teaching posts in Africa and in Montréal. In her office Simone informed Eugène he was going to have a special student, her son, the President-for-Life.

"Dr. Duvalier specified in his will that Jean-Claude must study law," Simone explained in her soft voice. "So I've called you here to arrange private lessons for him."

Mondays were Eugène's assigned days. On Tuesdays Professor Hubert De Ronceray would teach Jean-Claude sociology, and on Thursdays Professor Gérard Gourgue would lecture on penal law. Jean-Claude's behavior at the university prepared Eugène for the tutorials, for though the young President appeared to sit dutifully among the two hundred other law students in the crammed hall, he always dozed off and slept soundly through the whole lecture. Nonetheless, every Monday at 4 p.m. sharp Eugène would present himself at the palace, formally dressed in suit and tie, briefcase in hand, humor leavening impatience. An officer would greet and escort him to the President, who was either playing records, his viola, or else crawling around the floor of his playroom whizzing toy cars about the carpet.

By 5:30 the two would finally be installed in Jean-Claude's office. A secretary sat beside them to take notes, and an older woman peered at bookshelves or else poked in drawers as if trying to locate something. She was, Eugène knew, a spy Simone had planted to report on any conversation he and the President might have.

By 5:45, fifteen minutes after the lesson had begun, Jean-Claude would be asleep. Sometimes, to keep him awake, Eugène would discuss subjects other than law. Often he simply pretended not to notice that Jean-Claude was asleep and lectured to his impervious figure while the secretary diligently recorded his words and the old lady memorized them.

Despite his emptiness, despite his bone-lazy refusal to exert himself on their behalf, Jean-Claude Duvalier was for years his people's best-loved president. Everywhere he went they cheered him, reached out to touch his fleshy hand, even tried to carry him. After hunting, or on his regular grandstanding provincial tours, or *tournées,* he would sit down and talk with the people, play dominoes with them, hand them easy money when they stammered out their terrible problems.

After thirteen brutal years under the father, long-suffering Haitians rejoiced to discover in the son an affable, mild-mannered playboy. This much-vaunted popularity also owed much to palace strategy, masterminded by Mama Doc, who had learned all about Haitian politics from a lifetime with Papa Doc.

From the earliest months of her son's regime, Simone Duvalier accompanied him on *tournées* into the remotest reaches of the countryside, with parades, receptions, and speeches marking their passage. And on New Year's Day the Duvaliers continued the tradition of throwing largesse to the masses, speeding through Port-au-Prince in a convoy of gleaming limousines from which they tossed money into the cheering throngs who swarmed the streets, hoping to catch a *gourde* or two.

After initial predictions that Jean-Claude's would be a short-lived regime, the outside world too responded warmly to the young man. Tourists, mainly Americans, poured back into the country, eighty-three thousand strong in 1971, and in mounting droves each year afterward.

Thousands of Haitians ventured home after years of exile. Black Americans also gravitated toward the black republic, a newly respectable destination. Among them were Dick Gregory, honeymooning Wimbledon champion Arthur Ashe, and Cassius Clay, before his metamorphosis into Muhammed Ali.

Nicaraguan dictator Anastasio Somoza Debayle also came, accompanied by his wife, Hope Porocarrero. The appreciative Haitian government gave them full honors, including renaming a part of Delmas Road, Avenue Somoza.

National and international acceptance brought more than media plaudits and increased tourism. It also won for Haiti considerably more American aid money than Papa Doc had managed to attract, a major triumph for the nonproductive parasite regime of Jean-Claude Duvalier. In the first year of his rule the United States raised its assistance to $4.3 million from $3.8 million. In every year after the figure rose until 1975, when a new element was added in the person of Haitian lobbyist Lucien Rigaud, and aid money skyrocketed to become Haiti's major source of revenue.

In proportion to the amounts given, little was accomplished, with a few cosmetic public works projects, most in Port-au-Prince, bolstering the illusion that the new Haiti was, if not exactly new, at least under renovation. In the private sector existing hotels were encouraged to expand, new ones to open. In each case the Haitian government pledged to finance up to 40 percent of the cost. And to help fill them, a 1972 law reform inaugurated the Haitian "quickie divorce," enabling foreigners to divest themselves of their spouses in a mere twenty-four hours. By the early 1970s business confidence improved, foreign and local investment increased, construction was up, and the poorest country in the Western world seemed less poor.

In fact, Haiti's antiquated and incomplete system of accounting, the right hand of its endemic corruption, guaranteed that little trace of aid money, and of the nation's internal revenues, would be left. The Régie du Tabac provides a good example. The oddly named Régie, an unfiscalized tax agency, collected about 10 percent of the total public-sector revenue but was not responsible to any centralized agency. As a result Régie director and Duvalier bagman Henri Siclait dipped deep into his department's coffers to enrich the Duvaliers' Swiss bank accounts and also to increase his own personal real estate holdings to 365 houses, an annual rental income for each day of the year.

Departmental accounting was equally fuzzy. Typical is the Health Ministry's disbursement process, described by economic analyst Dr. Jean-Claude Garcia Zamor. "An analysis found that thirty-one separate steps involving a host of actors both within and outside the ministry were required in order to disburse funds. Even the initial determination of the availability of money was clouded. It appeared that the chief of accounting made such a determination according to criteria that were largely undocumented and unknown to others."

In other words it was business as usual in Haiti, with Former Duvalierist terror had been replaced by a surface tolerance that merely masked an unchanged infrastructure. Papa Doc had devoted thirteen years to crushing opposition, and his widow and other political heirs took advantage of their legacy and Haiti's built-in corruptibility to enrich themselves as quickly and amply as possible. But to do this they had to camouflage the true face of their wretched country.

A key part of their policy was Jean-Claude's image as Haiti's darling. Hence the *tournées* on which he dutifully accompanied his mother, the saplings he planted in apparently commendable campaigns to end Haiti's disastrous deforestation, the droning public speeches. To forestall opposition from teachers, a potential trouble spot in any dictatorship, he announced a $30 increase in their meager monthly salaries. To avoid losing the gratitude of public officials, his government continued to tolerate wholesale embezzlement and the system whereby one man could hold a plethora of posts so he could draw—though not earn—enough income to live in bourgeois comfort at the expense of the nation.

Most callous was Cambronne's blood-plasma business, which earned him the nickname "Vampire of the Caribbean." Through his company, Hemocaribian, he shipped five tons of plasma a month to American laboratories directed by Armour Pharmaceutical, Cutter Laboratories, Dow Chemical, and others. Haitian blood is extremely rich in antibodies, for survivors of the country's high disease and infant mortality rates develop richer supplies of antibodies than necessary in less unhealthy societies. Haitian blood was therefore in great demand, and Cambronne did all he could to satisfy it. He organized clinics that paid donors, indiscriminately chosen, $5.00 a pint for their blood, then resold it at $35 a pint to the United States.

Cambronne also dealt in cadavers, in almost as much demand. To save the living, medical students must dissect the dead, and obtaining corpses in sufficient quantity is the perennial problem of medical schools. Haitian cadavers, readily available once Cambronne entered the business, had the distinct advantage of being thin, so the student had not layers of fat to slice through before reaching the object of the lesson.

Cambronne, using the refrigerated container service recently introduced into Haiti, supplied these corpses on demand. When the General

Hospital failed to provide him with enough despite the $3.00 he paid for each body, he simply stole them from various funeral parlors. More than one mourning Haitian family opened a coffin for a final viewing to discover it was empty.

Rumors even circulated that Cambronne resorted to killing the poor urban homeless when he was having trouble filling his quota, and an apocryphal tale about the cadaver trade is still widely repeated. Cambronne, the story goes, was criticized for the moldy condition in which his corpses often arrived in the States. Determined not to lose the business, he instructed his secretary, "All right, then. Phone and say I'll start shipping the bodies up alive. Then when they need them, they can just kill them."

Blood and bodies were macabre businesses, but for pure cynicism even they could not rival the railway scheme he had carried out years earlier under Papa Doc. In the pathetically underdeveloped nation struggling to combat every developmental problem known to man, Luckner Cambronne sold approximately 150 kilometers of railroad to his African cousins and pocketed the money for himself, for his insatiable gambling and for the mulatto mistresses he kept behind Simone's back. For days Haitians watched in wonder as workmen pulled up and carefully stored the entire rail system linking Port-au-Prince to Verrettes via St. Marc, originally installed to transport passengers and freight. Down to the harbor it went, and on to Africa. Cambronne was much richer, and Haiti poorer.

Then in late 1972 Cambronne too had to flee. Simone was away in Miami with her daughter Nicole. Cambronne made a routine phone call to Jean-Claude. "The President is not available," he was told. Alarmed, he rushed downtown to the palace, where soldiers crossed their rifles to bar his entry. Terrified, Cambronne ran down the driveway, leapt into his car, and sped to the Colombian Embassy, where he claimed and was granted political asylum. Days later, safe and sound, he arrived in Colombia.

Cambronne's ouster had been engineered by his successor, Dr. Roger Lafontant, whom Simone had exiled after Papa Doc's death but whose obsession with power drove him to return over and over. "A dog who bites once will bite again," Papa Doc had often said of the clever young Lafontant after he had betrayed his fellow medical students to Duvalier in the 1960 students' strike. In 1972 Lafontant bit again. Using a ploy he was often to repeat, he claimed to have uncovered a coup d'état plot headed by Cambronne. He then "loyally" saved Jean-Claude from his mother's lover and installed himself as Interior Minister in his stead.

Lafontant lasted only a few months. Simone returned to find Cambronne disgraced and her old enemy Lafontant ingratiating himself with a gullible Jean-Claude. She ousted Lafontant, but she could not govern alone, and Jean-Claude did not even try to help her. Haiti's upper-level power structure had a gaping vacuum, variously filled by a juggled mix of feuding ministers, until 1976, when a clear winner emerged in the person of Henri "Ricot" Bayard, Commerce Minister and personal family friend. Jean-Claude especially liked Bayard, who treated him kindly, like a father. The President was equally charmed by Madame Edith Bayard and daughter Michelle, with whom he was close friends, and for years considered the Bayard house as his home away from the palace.

On the surface, new-style Duvalierism was much more palatable than its Cambronne or Lafontant versions. Reassuringly, it emphasized economic development and public relations, with modest gains such as the 4.8 percent annual rise in the GNP between 1972 and 1974 touted, while the 8 percent annual increase in imports was blamed on uncontrollable external factors. Trickles from the massive injections of foreign aid paved some roads and constructed clinics, schools, and dispensaries, buttressing the myth of progress and economic development and encouraging ever-escalating donations.[20]

Politically, liberalization was the watchword. Jean-Claude's regime had begun well, with his first presidential address offering amnesty to all political exiles. Then the Tonton Macoutes had been tamed but also honored, some leaders fired, most rank-and-file disarmed, and the whole organization recognized by a national holiday, July 29, when even the President donned the blue to salute the Macoutes in formal ceremonies. And why not, since the new official line was that they were now pillars of society and security? "The VSN participate alongside the armed forces in ensuring the security of the country," Jean-Claude explained to American journalist Hope Applebaum. "They also organize the peasant masses and help them, and help rural literacy workers in their program."

Tamed indeed, and that was before Macoute chief Madame Max enrolled them in reforestation programs. Weekend after weekend, truckloads of Macoutes drove out to desolate rural areas to plant millions of saplings in the arid soil, most of which would wither and die of neglect or else survive to treehood only to be chopped down by peasants desperate for survival and unable to weigh the consequences for tomorrow of burning charcoal.

Yet, despite its economic boomlet and the facade of liberalization, Haiti remained imprisoned in Duvalierism, with its primary objectives still to enrich the Duvaliers and their loyalists and to keep them in power. By the 1970s the nation's five million crushed citizens were merely props in the charade, visible objects of misery that the Duvalier government peddled to the world in return for the gigantic handouts that could then be stolen.

Even politically ingenuous Jean-Claude, and certainly all those around him, understood the crucial importance of cajoling the Americans, satisfying their demands for liberalization, proving with yearly statistical studies and analyses that, surely though slowly, Haiti's rulers were leaving nasty old ways behind.

First of course there was always a brisk spring cleaning. Emaciated political prisoners were trucked away and hidden in army barracks, while criminals and soldiers took their places in the cells, a mere dozen lounging where normally hundreds lived and died. Hardened excrement was scraped off cell walls and floors, which after a severe hosing down were quickly repainted. Offal buckets were emptied and rinsed, beds and mattresses and sheeting were hauled in, vats of tempting food were cooked, and nary an agonized shriek or howl was to be heard.

The Americans and other human-rights advocates, reporting what they had seen, seldom suspected how thoroughly they had been duped. "The improvement in the political atmosphere here has enabled numerous United States and international assistance organizations to resume or step up their activities here," declared *The New York Times* and cited a foreign economist as saying, "We now think our help has a chance of getting to the right people."

Even inside Haiti few realized what horrors were still perpetrated in the barracks and prisons they passed by every day. And those who did know often exonerated Jean-Claude of guilt, simply because they believed—or hoped—that he could not have known, for he would certainly never have tolerated such abominations.

At first Jean-Claude did not know. The great spoiled child knew little of life outside the confines of his own gilded existence. "I don't want blood on my hands because once you start tasting blood, you can't stop," Jean-Claude once confided to his friends during an unusually somber Saturday-night discussion.

*   *   *

It was during this brief period of innocence that Jean-Claude learned that Senator Barry Goldwater was in Haiti, a guest at the Oloffson. He found Goldwater lunching in a Pétionville restaurant and presented him with special VIP bodyguards, a contingent of Léopards, the newly formed anti-insurgency unit trained and financed by the U.S. Wherever Goldwater went "Barry's Boys" followed, right to the entrance to the Sir John Gielgud Suite at the Hotel Oloffson, and to the Lillian Hellman suite, where Goldwater's traveling companions, General and Mrs. Quinn, were staying. Guarded night and day, the Goldwaters and Quinns had to adjust to Léopards waiting with feline readiness outside their bedroom doors and watching, ill concealed, in poolside shrubbery and even on the hotel's broad veranda.

Ever solicitous, Jean-Claude insisted on providing his own military helicopter to transport the American senator and general to visit Goldwater's old friend Larry Mellon, founder of the Albert Schweitzer Hospital in the provincial town of Deschapelles. Goldwater and Quinn accepted the offer and the helicopter whisked them off. Unfortunately, when they landed, it was not at Deschapelles, and for frightening minutes the Americans wondered if they had been kidnapped. But no, the pilot had merely become lost. After effusive embarrassed apologies and new calculations, the helicopter once again lifted up and soon the Americans were safely deposited at Mellon's hospital.

Haitian reforms, real, attempted, and fake, were all part of the new government's strategy to extract money from foreign donors, especially the United States. In 1974 the most ambitious scheme to date was put into effect, and as a result American aid skyrocketed, quadrupling between 1975 and 1976. Chief player in this scheme was Lucien Rigaud, an aggressive, prosperous Swiss-trained businessman whom Jean-Claude personally put to work to tap the American millions.

Rigaud, his Swiss wife, Claire-Lise, and the first of their three children had returned to Haiti from Switzerland in 1970. One of the privileged mulatto elite, Rigaud enjoyed his family's birthright of a ranch, beach house, and his own home in the cool mountains above Pétionville. He also carried firearms, a consequence of his friendly relationship with Jean-Claude's father, François.

Rigaud had met Papa Doc when he and his brother decided to open Haiti's first container business, Haitian Trailerships, Ltd., an agency of Sea-Land Service, Inc., then the largest carrier of container-ized freight in the U.S. But the concept of sealed containers was beyond the ken of the Macoutes who patrolled the harbor; obviously, they con-cluded, Rigaud must be running guns. Papa Doc, quickly informed, summoned Rigaud to the palace. Rigaud explained the concept of con-tainerization, showing how it reduced insurance costs. He also pointed out that without cheap and safe transportation, the fledgling electronic assembly industries would never come to Haiti. "Without containeriza-tion, you might as well close down Port-au-Prince Harbor," he con-cluded.

The dying President listened carefully. Then he leaned forward across his desk. "Will you be personally responsible for what's in the containers?" he asked.

Rigaud nodded. "Of course I will."

Duvalier stared at him. "I trust you. But if there's anything in those boxes but goods, I'll shoot you."

By late 1973 Sea-Land was so successful, it effectively controlled Port-au-Prince Harbor. Rigaud became increasingly influential with Americans doing business with Haiti. Soon his reputation spread to Washington, and in the fall of 1973 Stephen B. Elko, administrative as-sistant to Pennsylvania Congressman Daniel J. Flood, appeared in Rigaud's office. Flood, the powerful chairman of the huge Appropria-tions Subcommittee on Labor, Health, Education and Welfare, wanted Rigaud to introduce him to Jean-Claude Duvalier. Rigaud obliged, and alone with Jean-Claude, Elko urged the President to send Rigaud to Washington to negotiate for vastly increased foreign-aid funds.

Jean-Claude was easily convinced and sent for Rigaud. "I'd like you to become our ambassador in Washington," he said. "You're the man the Americans trust, and you can get us the money we need here. Haiti is poor. The Americans squashed my father. But you, you can re-verse all that."

Rigaud refused outright. He would serve as best he could as a citi-zen, he replied firmly, but never would he accept an ambassadorship.

A week later Jean-Claude sent him a diplomatic passport, airline ticket, and a bag of American money; Rigaud returned them all and pro-ceeded to Washington at his own expense. However, he did not go alone, for with time-honored Duvalierist caution, Jean-Claude sent an air force major, Roger Cazeau, to accompany and spy on him.

In Washington, Rigaud discovered he could be effective only with

Jean Claude's power of attorney, which he demanded and obtained. In the capital he and Cazeau, Madame Max Adolphe's brother-in-law, shared Elko's apartment in the Congressional Hotel, where Flood also stayed, and they worked out of Flood's office. Flood introduced Rigaud to other prominent congressmen, and they often partied late into the night.

Jean-Claude's faith in Rigaud was entirely justified, and in 1975 Washington upped its aid money to $35.5 million from $9.3 million in 1974. The money was for Haitian development projects, because Rigaud was utterly convincing as he described what was necessary to haul Haiti into the twentieth century. But the money was also to line American and Haitian pockets, and as the appropriations were voted Rigaud discovered just what was expected of him.

"Here, put my share right in here," Congressman Flood told him one day, pointing to a drawer in his office desk.

The money that actually reached Haiti was to finance projects that never materialized: roads, piers, drinking water, and sanitation. One project dear to Rigaud's heart would have provided five hundred public latrines for Port-au-Prince, which had none. Rigaud estimated that without latrines, slum dwellers deposited the equivalent of 1,750 truckloads of fecal matter in courtyards and gutters every day. "When you breathe in that funky scented Port-au-Prince air," he declared, "do you realize what it is you're inhaling?" But like so many projects, that one evaporated into the realm of financial scam, and while Americans and their Haitian cronies enriched themselves, millions of Haitians still lived without benefit of a single latrine.

Everyone wanted his share of the booty, most of all Jean-Claude Duvalier. Rigaud refused to cooperate, and was quickly made to understand the wrongness of his attitude.

"My friend," said Major Cazeau, "you don't understand. You are going to die. The Duvaliers are crooks, and if you don't bring them something, you're contemptible to them, and dispensable."

Rigaud replied impatiently, "General Rigaud was my ancestor. I have a name to uphold. Certain things are out of the question." On this Rigaud stood firm, and rather than compromise left Washington for good, devoting himself entirely to his business and his young family.

Despite Rigaud's defection from Washington, American aid to Haiti continued at or above the same levels he had pumped it up to, and Flood continued to find his desk drawer filled with greenbacks by cooperative Americans for whom he had secured lucrative contracts. Contractors and officials both American and Haitian grabbed as much of it as they could, and some of the money even trickled down to the millions whose suffering it had been pledged to alleviate. But the overall impact of the aid money was negligible, and *la misère,* a pitiful struggle for existence, was the lot of most Haitians.

Escape was difficult, with the Dominican Republic and the Bahamas already saturated with unwanted Haitians and other countries also barring their doors. Boats sailing in the dead of night for Miami always left packed to the hulls with passengers, but not all Haitians dared or cared to leave their native soil. So out in the desolate countryside, peasants by the thousands packed up their belongings and made their way into the cities.

Port-au-Prince was the main destination, and the city designed for fifty thousand soon was home to over a million, two hundred thousand of them living homeless on the dirty streets, more subsisting in wretched huts furnished only with disease and despair.

One new arrival, from the North, was twenty-year-old Dieudonné Lamothe, his mother Anne-Marie's only child but one of eleven of his father's. He was a timid, quiet child whose greatest pleasure was sports. He swam in the muddy river, played soccer and hide-and-seek, or *lago,* and went running, effortlessly, swiftly, purposelessly, for the sheer joy of it. Dieudonné played and ran so much, Anne-Marie had to hide his pants to keep him at home.

When he was older Anne-Marie sent him to relatives in Gonaives, where he could attend school, but at mealtimes, just as at home, he never got enough to eat. At school he excelled in football and math and sometimes dared to dream of becoming an engineer. Then he failed tenth grade. Anne-Marie refused to be discouraged and found another cousin in the Port-au-Prince slum of Bel-Air her son could live with. This time he passed the tenth grade, though he had few friends and the Bel-Air gang ignored him because he was a hillbilly from the provinces. But he was grateful for this new life in Port-au-Prince because in 1974, for the first time in his twenty years, Dieudonné Lamothe was no longer always hungry.

Another new arrival into Port-au-Prince was twenty-four-year-old Dinois Jeanty, from the rural hamlet of Fond des Blancs. His father owned several acres, but the land was not fertile and squatters battled the rightful owners for the privilege of farming outlying plots.

Jeanty was a simple man, small and slightly crippled, with a dragging right leg. He was devoutly Catholic and had been raised to fear and mistrust vodoun. He was totally illiterate, but kindly and affectionate, and he enjoyed the bustle and the activity of Port-au-Prince. He was also very lucky, and through his friendship with a neighbor he landed a job. Only a month after he arrived in Port-au-Prince, Jeanty was Colonel Roger St. Albin's new houseboy, earning room and board and $50 a month.

These two were among the luckier ones, Lamothe with enough food on his plate and Jeanty with $50 a month to help his family back home. Countless others fared much worse.

Out in Lestère, Orestil Louissaint lived always on the edge of fear. It had begun when he refused Papa Doc's invitation to become a Macoute. Then there had been the reneging on the huge debt for Duvalier's gas bill, the loss of his house in Port-au-Prince, the continual harassment at his gas station and the death threats against himself, his wife, and his fourteen children.

The individual who most hated him was the ferocious Zacharie Delva, the ex-sidewalk vendor now second only to Duvalier in power. Delva was so warped and cruel a man, he terrified a nation, and when villagers heard the sirens on his black limousine—the vehicles foreigners surreptitiously called "Macoutemobiles"—they shut down the town and hid, quavering, in their houses.

Delva's vodoun *cérémonies* were legendary, including the one he had held on the steps of the Catholic cathedral in Gonaives. So was his sexual appetite, and he forced scores of men, many heterosexual, to couple with him under pain of torture or death. He also delighted in humiliating others, and after moving his bowels bent over and ordered other men, especially officials, to wipe his anus.

Delva's home base of Gonaives was frighteningly close to Lestère, and Louissaint was in constant danger. Delva never forgave him for knowing him in the old days, when Louissaint had bought cola from him as he pushed his primitive ice-filled cart along the Boulevard Bi-Centenaire. Now Delva's favorite tactic with the formidably respectable Louissaint was to order him to join the Macoutes; each time Louissaint refused, punishment followed. In 1973 the punishment was thirteen days in Fort Dimanche, where Delva sent him to die. Louissaint's sister-in-law saved him, but she could not prevent his reincarceration. As long as Duvalierism tolerated Delva in its hierarchy, Louissaint knew men like himself would never be safe.

In Port-au-Prince, Jean Joseph Charles could never forget his eighteen months in Fort Dimanche, nor the humiliation of his release. When he walked out of the gates with visible joy they rearrested him. "Who do you think you are to bounce out like that?" a soldier shrieked, and a humbled Charles spent another two weeks in prison before, shuffling and stone-faced and staring down at the ground, he slunk away from the nightmare. Now, reliving every minute, he was busily writing his memoirs, jotting it down on envelopes, in scribbles on paper bags. It was the story of his life, and he called it *Soul in Panic*.

Charles knew he was in trouble when he returned home to his shabby room in Pétionville after an evening of deep discussion in a coffee shop. Hovering on the sidewalk just outside the entrance were men unmistakably Macoutes, and before they had spotted him Charles beat a prudent retreat. Hours later, homeless and nearly penniless, he ventured back. The Macoutes had left, and for want of an alternative he entered his room and dropped into his bed.

They arrested him the next day, early in the morning. The interrogation took place in the Pétionville Barracks, and daily for two weeks they beat, cuffed, cursed, and questioned him: "Why are you plotting against the President? What friends of yours are in the plot? What are you planning to do, and when?"

Jail-wise and fatalistic, the "soul in panic" did not panic. Instead he answered modestly and correctly, refused to name names, repeated over and over what was the truth. He was an artist, and he made his living painting and sculpting. It was not much of a living, but it enabled him to pursue his obsession, inventing the perfect art form to convey human experience in all its dimensions. Finally, disgusted but convinced, his jailors released him. When Charles reached his little room he saw that they had ransacked it. He closed his eyes before he checked to see if his worst fears were true. They were. The Macoutes had not only removed every last one of his paintings, they had also stolen his sole copy of *Soul in Panic*.

Worse, much worse, than any other prison was the death house of Fort Dimanche. "Although at least 150 political prisoners are still held in the Fort Dimanche prison, most have been there since the previous regime," *The New York Times* declared, citing the assurances of a foreign diplomat that things in Haiti had changed. "Those who have gone to jail under Jean-Claude were all involved in some concrete anti-Government activity," the diplomat explained. "No one has been arrested for his ideas." The diplomat was mistaken. In Jean-Claude's Haiti, people were arrested because of ideas, associations, and just plain bad luck, being in the wrong place at the wrong time.

On June 21, 1975, Lionel "Ti-Jé" Woolley and several other Tonton Macoutes stormed into the home of a mild-mannered, middle-aged agronomist named Hector Estimé and arrested him. As Estimé watched helplessly they ransacked the house and grabbed all his papers and books. They pushed him into a Peugeot and drove him to Dessalines Barracks.

Hector's brother Rameau, the one-time Justice Minister whom Papa Doc had already imprisoned twice in Fort Dimanche in 1967 and again in 1970 while he was still a minister, was also arrested, as was their cousin Wiltern, walking in broad daylight.

At the barracks, Hector, Rameau, and Wiltern were thrust into a tiny airless cell and forced to stand facing the wall for four hours. Then Luc Désyr, Lionel Woolley, Colonel Jean Valmé, Colonel Albert Ti-Boulé Pierre, Captain Emmanuel Orcel, and Captain Raymond Cabrol arrived to begin the torture session that would be repeated for fifteen consecutive days. The military men, Valmé, Pierre, Orcel, and Cabrol, did the actual torturing, spelling each other as they battered the trio with batons, demanding that they reveal details about an alleged plot against Duvalier, especially the names of the plotters. When the Estimés did not talk they moved them to the basement of the palace, where the military foursome supervised a torture session lasting from 1 to 10 p.m.

It was Hector's first introduction to the jack, wrists and ankles bound together, body bent over a stick. Then, helpless to ward off the blows, he, Rameau, and Wiltern were beaten to the rhythms of each other's shrieks and pleas for mercy. Throughout, Luc Désyr indulged in his passion for recording torture sessions, a pleasure he had shared with Papa Doc when the dictator was alive, the two short, homely, bespectacled men listening and chortling together as they played and replayed the agonies of their fellow Haitians.

"Break his fingers!" Désyr ordered clearly. "Hit him harder." Over a decade later, when that particular tape was found in Désyr's home, Hector was to have the curious experience of reliving again those moments.

The Estimés still refused to talk, and though Hector suspected that Rameau and Wiltern had been plotting, he had not, and so had nothing to reveal no matter how terrible the torture. Rameau, so severely beaten he could not walk, had also remained silent, and so had Wiltern.

A week later the trio was transferred to Fort Dimanche, Hector to Cell 7, where he was face-to-face with Wiltern, and Rameau to Cell 1. Thirty to forty men shared each cell, sleeping in shifts at night on little bug-infested straw mats, always fighting for air in the steaming, unventilated fortress.

In ragged shorts, shoeless, the men milled about their cells, talking or praying, dehydrated, starving, watching their bodies decay and waiting for almost certain death. When his brother Rameau and six months later his cousin Wiltern died, Hector knew immediately. Prisoners shouted out the news, sang funeral dirges, then banged on the gate to summon the guards, who came grumbling down to fetch the latest corpse.

That they were dying did not exempt prisoners from torture, and some men scarcely alive were taken out and beaten. Then their cell mates would doctor them.

Each morning the previous day's bodies were buried in shallow graves at the back of the fort, and at night Hector could hear dogs digging up the bodies to finish off what little meat remained on them. Over the course of the two Duvaliers' regimes Rameau and Wiltern were just two of at least fifty thouand men and women who died at Fort Dimanche and were buried in the shadow of its infamous walls.

Few prisoners were political objectors, Hector knew. Most were peasants without any political ideology at all, sent there by vengeful Duvalierists who often followed their victims into the same death cells. If only the outside world knew what was happening, Hector and his cell mates used to lament. Why did the cowardly "Plop Plop," the men's nickname for the despised Colonel Enos St. Pierre, the officer in charge of the fort's political prisoners, refuse to tell Jean-Claude what was really happening? Plop Plop was worse than a murderer, he was a moral coward, Hector often reflected. And with every day that went by he saw more innocent victims thrown into the cells to take their places beside the dying, and to replace those who were already dead.

*   *   *

Young Bobby Duval was such a victim. Bobby was the tall, athletic son of an educated and prosperous mulatto family. At the height of the Duvalierist terror in 1964, Bobby's father had moved his young family to Puerto Rico. The move had been precipitated by a schoolboy incident that in another country might have resulted in a black eye but in Haiti could well have caused Bobby's death.

One of his classmates was a government minister's son, and when in a schoolyard squabble he slapped Bobby in the face, Bobby retaliated. Immediately political realities surfaced, and Bobby was warned not to bother the boy. Enraged and insulted, he taunted the boy's chauffeur instead. But the chauffeur was a Macoute, and the minister was alarmed enough to visit M. Duval. "You'd better make sure your son stops harassing that chauffeur," the minister warned. "He's angry, and I can't control or be responsible for anything he might decide to do." M. Duval read the writing on the wall and soon afterward settled his family in Puerto Rico.

Bobby integrated happily into his new school, but the Haitian community was strong and his family maintained close links with it. When Bobby was thirteen he went to see *The Comedians* and stared transfixed at the movie version of his own experience, when as a ten-year-old student he had sneaked out of Petit Séminaire St. Martial to attend the execution of Marcel Numa and Louis Drouin. The crowd had been packed with public school children forced to attend, so nobody noticed one private school child hovering alongside them. Now, reliving that nightmarish scene, Bobby knew he could never forget his Haitian roots.

After high school at Valley Forge Military Academy, a business course at Nichols College in Boston, and then a bachelor's degree at Concordia University in Montréal, Bobby Duval was ready to return to Haiti. It was 1975, he was twenty-two, and, as everyone knew, the Haiti of Jean-Claude Duvalier was a nation geared to liberalization and economic development. Perfect, Duval thought, to put into practice all the business theory he had learned abroad. Within months he had opened Haiti's first tire retread operation, and all his faith in his native land seemed justified.

Then on April 20, 1976, Lionel Woolley and three Macoutes went to his factory and arrested him on charges of trying to overthrow the government. For one day he was interrogated at Dessalines Barracks, where he learned there had been a shooting incident in the Carrefour slum and they suspected him of involvement in it. They did not beat him, just asked him questions. Then, without charging, trying, or sentencing him, they moved him to the National Penitentiary to wait for whatever might happen next.

The day he arrived he tried to kill one of his cellmates, the young man who had named him to the Service d'Information as an anti-Duvalierist plotter. Finally the guards had to transfer him to a different cell because he wouldn't stop his murderous attacks.

When Duval entered the fort he was a strapping 180 pounds and in prime condition after a lifetime of soccer and hiking. In his new cell, still strong, he spent the first few weeks helping weaker prisoners, carrying them to the showers when they could no longer walk. But Fort Dimanche snuffed one like a candle, and before too many weeks had elapsed even his well-trained body had begun to decline, so that by the time Duval left the fort a year later he could no longer walk, and it took all his strength merely to lift his forearms a few inches into the air.

Duval kept alive by sheer mental effort, invoking the reserves of the human mind and spirit, refusing to die. He kept himself busy, awakening every day enthusiastic for what lay ahead. You had to keep your mind going, he knew, for the whole key to existence was in the mind. Duval saw other men go mad and hasten willing death, throwing away their food, scorning life. But food was precious, and Duval wasted not even the most pitiful morsel.

Duval's greatest pleasure lay in talking to his cell mates, most of them peasants, and at least 60 percent of them innocent people who were to die without ever understanding why they were in prison. They and the others, the 10 percent Communists and the strong contingent of Duvalierists, had plenty to offer a thirsting young mind, and as long as he lived Duval listened.

One of the best storytellers was Jean Julmé, once Papa Doc's Interior Minister, who never failed to provoke Duval into laughter. Skinny, near death, the old Macoute still spent hours boasting about his feats under Duvalier. Killing people was his business, Julmé used to tell his cell mates, and a beautiful thing it was, because killing represented the summit of political power.

Now near naked and dying in a filthy prison cell, Julmé remained obsessed with regaining the political power he had lost. He was in Fort Dimanche for plotting a coup d'état against Jean-Claude, distributing tracts with his own photos all over the Artibonite. "I still intend to become President," Julmé would declare. "Today I'm closer than ever to power because international pressure is on the government to release me. Tomorrow, who knows? It might easily be Jean-Claude crouching right here in this cell with you."

When Bobby was not listening he was teaching in the prisoners' improvised "school," held in the cell. He conducted daily classes in business administration and English, and attended classes in architecture and medicine. A man who wanted to live had to be his own doctor, Duval knew, for though a Dr. Craven came every two months, the men were terrified of him, knowing that the doctor had executed eight prisoners by lethal injections.

Duval greatly enjoyed the limited leisure time his other activities permitted him, especially chess and dominoes. Of course you had to play carefully because the board and pieces were fragile, molded from clay improvised from bread and potatoes and dyed black and white with coffee and lime peeled from the walls.

Toward the end, Duval watched tuberculosis advance through his body, the big bumps on his chest and stomach signaling that his insides were eating up his skin, announcing impending death.

Of course he knew they wanted you to die that way, consumed by disease. That was why they scheduled showers for 2 a.m., waking feeble men from broken sleep to shuffle their wet bodies down an unprotected corridor whipped by the chill night wind, TB the price for a few seconds of a few drops of water without soap, leaving you always dirty and cold.

In all ways prison was a new dimension of life, with every aspect magnified. Duval had never been a religious man, but in the fort he prayed five times each day. And every time a prisoner died the religious ceremony the men improvised provided sustenance for his hungering soul.

Back in April in the National Penitentiary, Lucien Rigaud had seen Bobby Duval, but only from a distance, because Duval was with the political prisoners, while Rigaud was in with the common criminals. Rigaud's great financial success was at the root of his problem, and in envy-ridden Haiti wealth ultimately made him more enemies.

On December 26, 1975, Rigaud heard an intruder at his window and leapt out of bed to stare directly into a man's startled eyes. He grabbed his empty .22 pistol and, wearing only underpants, ran out and down onto the street. The intruder fled, but Rigaud saw him stop to fire two shots at someone who had appeared in his path.

Rigaud dropped to the ground, then returned home. Later he ventured back outside, and to his horror discovered the still-warm body of Solon Marcellin, for thirty-two years the handyman for the Rigaud family, in a bloody heap on the road.

At the Pétionville police station, where he went to report what had happened, Rigaud recognized a policeman as the man at his window and realized he was in serious trouble, the victim of a conspiracy rather than a burglary. The next day the Pétionville commandant, Major Jean-Claude Guillaume, arrested him. For five days Rigaud sat or stood, eating nothing, for fear of poison, and saying nothing.

Outside, Claire-Lise managed to have him transferred to the penitentiary in Port-au-Prince, where Rigaud confided to Commandant Colonel Francis Charles that the intruder was a Pétionville policeman whom he identified from a jumble of police files as Berthany Innocent. Charles did a fingerprint test on Rigaud's window louver, and Innocent's prints were on it. Then a ballistics test showed Rigaud's pistol had not been fired for six months, proving he could not have shot Marcellin.

Brought in for questioning, Innocent not only admitted his role in the break-in but also named two colleagues, Sténio Bellevue and Cedmé Achner. Charles arrested all three, and Rigaud left the prison, now certain that he had been the target not of a burglary but of a high-level police assassination. "Carry a gun at all times," advised Colonel Charles. Rigaud, one of Haiti's finest marksmen, did not have to be told twice.

The pressure on Rigaud mounted when the commandant of the Pétionville Macoutes, Paul Véricain, issued a VSN card in the name of the dead Solon Marcellin, then, in St. Peter's Cathedral, proceeded to give the handyman a state funeral attended by at least two thousand Macoutes in dress blue uniform. Rigaud understood the ploy; in Macoute-ridden Haiti he was being set up as a Macoute killer.

Meanwhile, Major Guillaume had also undertaken a harassment campaign that included throwing Claire-Lise into a common jail cell from which she emerged days later infested with lice.

Lucien Rigaud's turn was next. Despite full confessions from two of the accused policemen, a military investigation team cleared all three and soon after they received promotions. Major Guillaume had engineered this abortion of justice in a personal interview with the President during which he broke down, arguing that disgracing his men—and therefore himself—could only lead to a weakened military. "We're the ones who protect you," said Guillaume. "If Rigaud can get me, Mr. President, then don't you see he can also get anyone else, including you?" Jean-Claude saw the point and ordered the three self-confessed offenders exonerated and promoted.

Rigaud was arrested and, as he had feared, charged with murdering Marcellin. For nineteen days he was imprisoned in a filthy *cachot* so tiny he could not stretch out even to sleep. During those days Claire-Lise managed to get through to the President himself. She had an excellent contact, Nicole Rousselet, a Frenchwoman she had met in Swiss boarding school. Blond, long-tressed Nicole was also Jean-Claude's lover, and for months he kept her in the Royal Haitian Hotel, visiting her daily and promising marriage and a future life away from Haiti, in Monaco. Nicole did her best to intervene on Rigaud's behalf, forcing Jean-Claude to listen to a tape Claire-Lise had recorded of the entire sequence of events. Jean-Claude refused to free Rigaud, but at Nicole's insistence he finally ordered him transferred to the National Penitentiary.

Before the transfer soldiers hauled Rigaud out of the *cachot* and dumped him onto the barracks floor, where he lay for four hours before regaining enough strength to stand up. "That light-skinned guy must be a werewolf to survive," he heard a soldier comment. As Rigaud lay there, full-bearded and black with filth, people were pushed past him on their way to and from various cells and interrogation rooms, and he saw men and women with broken heads and raw, bleeding flesh.

He also saw one man he knew, a mulatto businessman named Ernest Bennett, a coffee exporter who had served time under Papa Doc for bad debts and financial shenanigans. Rigaud noticed that Bennett was not handcuffed like the others but merely stood up against a wall while Colonel Jean Valmé boxed his ears four times and spoke menacingly in a low voice.

Later, in the National Penitentiary, Rigaud soon learned that Jean-Claude had added a new dimension to his transfer order: "Transfer Rigaud, and put him in with the common prisoners," Jean-Claude had instructed. "And then make garbage out of him, turn him into a vegetable."

But for eighteen months Rigaud defied him, buying and bribing his way to safety and small creature comforts, paying other prisoners to guard him at night so he could stretch out on a cot and have a night's sleep. And with Claire-Lise on the outside involving Amnesty International and the Swiss and American embassies, Rigaud was also protected from beatings and torture.

Starvation and brutality were everywhere, and 95 percent of the men had only prison fare to eat. Though the penitentiary commandant, Colonel Louis Charles, received a daily allowance of $5,000 to feed his more than two thousand charges, he preferred to starve them and pocket the money. The four BMW's this blood money had paid for he stored in the prison courtyard. The General Hospital's morgue truck came daily to collect corpses that were dumped into a pit on the Morne St. Christophe.

Rigaud was appalled at the plight of the political prisoners. Among them, Rigaud learned, was a sixteen-year-old boy arrested a decade ago with his father. The father had long since died, but the boy remained in prison, a forgotten, innocent tragedy.

But that boy was neither the only nor the youngest child in the prison, and to Rigaud, with young children of his own, this was the filthiest aspect of an intolerable system. Every two weeks the guards would open the cells and push into them the *cocoyers,* the terrified eight- and nine-year-old boys who lived and slept on the streets, earning money by washing cars and begging. The guard's pimped them to desperate men, and those who could pay for the privilege raped the children, who all became so infected they had to be replaced every two weeks. Many died in prison, smothered to death in the *cocoyer* cell so small they were piled one on top of each other.

Duvalierist Haiti was about contemptuous disregard for human rights, about cowardice conquering morality and decency. It was also about greed and the perversion of values, an ongoing marathon for fortune that dominated government and individuals, sapping them of all moral direction and worth. The 1975 Audubon stamp scandal illustrates beautifully to just what lengths Haiti's leaders would go in their frenzied quest for easy money. The scandal was an almost perfect crime, and only the most unexpected of coincidences uncovered and revealed it.

The architects of the stamp scandal were Jean-Claude's sister Nicole, his ambassador to Spain, General Claude Raymond, formerly his chief of staff, Internal Revenue Chief Franck Sterling, Port-au-

Prince Airport Security Chief Gabriel Brunet, and Haitian Consul in Miami Eugène "Sonson" Maximilien. Jean-Claude himself was excluded from the scam, and in fact his sister Nicole warned all the others that they were dead men should any of them ever reveal her role in the affair.

The scheme was simple. Fake Haitian stamps, exquisite renderings of bird watercolors by native son Jean-Jacques Audubon, were printed in Russia and placed on world philatelist markets. But philatelist societies require authentication of all stamp issues that they promote. The schemers resolved this obstacle by bribing the State Press director to print a single issue of the official government *Moniteur* announcing the Audubon stamps and validated it with the forged signature of the appropriate Haitian Commerce Ministry official.

The Philatelist Society in Switzerland was satisfied with the apparently genuine *Moniteur*, endorsed the Audubon stamp issue, and began to advertise it to stamp collectors the world over.

The schemers next bribed Haitian postal officials to authenticate the stamps with a first-day-of-issue postmark. Then they delivered them to a Miami Springs bank entrepreneur for selling them, and began to rake in small fortunes. Nicole Duvalier's share, $4 million, was the largest.

But an avid Haitian stamp collector who was the Commerce Ministry lawyer responsible for approving all stamp issues received an advertisement for the Audubon stamps. Perplexed and suspicious, he notified the Philatelist Society, which forwarded him a photocopy of the fake *Moniteur*. The official whose name had been forged denied any knowledge of the *Moniteur* or the stamps, and soon a national and then an international scandal erupted.

Jean-Claude Duvalier's advisers convinced him that a public trial was essential to cool scorching international disapproval, and so in Haiti's first live televised trial, a phalanx of Duvalierist officials confessed their guilt, accused their fellows, and were sentenced to jail. The international collectors were satisfied, and the publicity resulting from the trial gave the stamps additional value. The principal players in the scheme all escaped unscathed, and Nicole Duvalier's name was never mentioned. Some officials found guilty were innocent, but Jean-Claude rewarded them handsomely for their compliance in agreeing to be scapegoats. They were released early from comfortable jail cells and given money, jobs, and cars.

*   *   *

In 1976 Dieudonné Lamothe thought he had found a unique way to escape from *la misère* after he placed second in a six-kilometer race and began training to qualify for Haiti's national Olympic team. He had learned that Olympic athletes were given visas and plane tickets to Canada. Once in Montréal, he would go to live with his cousins and begin to live the decent life his Haitian birthright had denied him.

But when Lamothe arrived in Montréal his cousins begged him not to ruin his future as an athlete by disappearing into the nether world of illegal immigrants. Bitterly disappointed and torn by indecision when he learned that two other Haitians on the team were not going home, he ran the five thousand meters in an anguished haze, finishing eleventh out of fifteen. Then, heeding his cousins' advice, he got back onto the plane to Haiti and returned to confront *la misère*.

On December 24 out in Léogane, in the Duvalier family peristyle, Simone Duvalier and her mother, Clélie Ovide, arrived in a convoy of cars and trucks carrying coal pots and goats and chickens and other foods for sacrifice. They arrived at 4 a.m. and went home again at midnight, for December 24 was vodoun's most important ceremony and, as both women fervently believed, neglect of the *loas* inevitably brought disaster.

The President-for-Life had accompanied his mother, but he observed her religion less rigidly, and while the others danced in frenzied possession under the sacred *mapou* tree, Jean-Claude quietly slipped off down to the refreshing shallows of the river and paddled around.

The goats were slaughtered in ritual sacrifice, their bleating protests suddenly silenced. Chickens were roasting, and succulent morsels of greasy black pig, spiced cornmeal, and other Creole delights simmering in the huge coal pot sunk into a deep round hole.

As the day wore into evening Haiti's First Lady danced, her white slacks muddied as she flung herself about, surrendering herself to the *loas* who claimed her and drove her to shake with renewed frenzy. A particularly powerful *loa* surged through her, and though she was nearly sixty years old, Simone Duvalier flung herself downward onto the ground, balanced herself on her hands, and danced upside down under the *mapou* tree.

Jean-Claude, munching on tasty grilled *griot*, watched his mother impassively. Though he understood the importance of magic, he preferred to serve the spirits vicariously, providing the appropriate sacrifices, hiring the most powerful *houngans* and *mambos* to pray and sing and dance, practicing his religion as he did his presidency, little involved, indifferent, dependent on others to get the job done. By midnight the ceremony was over, and the First Family, sated with spiritual communion, returned to the palace to preside over another year of Duvalierism.

8 JEANCLAUDISM, 1977–79

T HE INAUGURATION OF CARTER AS U.S. PRESIDENT ALSO inaugurated a new awareness of human rights in Haiti. By early 1977 Haiti was still the poorest country in the Western world, and Duvalierism kept it that way. But in return for the misery, poverty, and pitiful underdevelopment that it bartered for the millions in aid money that had become Haiti's most important source of revenue, Jimmy Carter demanded that human rights be respected, improved, investigated.

Jean-Claude and his government were to have many bad moments under Carter, who announced his new foreign policy would be "democratic . . . based upon fundamental values." Central to these values was a genuine commitment to human rights, and this man who owed his margin of victory to newly enfranchised black Southerners meant business. He signed the Inter-American Convention on Human Rights, focused international attention on the issue, and, most effectively, withheld aid from nations failing to measure up to specific internationally approved criteria.

Haitians were not slow to get the point. Peasants with just the vaguest notion of what Carter represented sported Jimmy Carter T-shirts, while newspapers and revues routinely printed long extracts from his speeches, messages, declarations. The more daring of the media, including Creole radio stations, even criticized the government, though never Jean-Claude.

During the Carter era Henri Bayard was Haiti's most powerful government minister. He had long been influential, but after Jean-Claude resolved the Audubon stamp scandal by ousting Fourcand, Bayard reigned almost supreme. Under his guidance the presidency was given a new thrust, at least for propaganda purposes, and Jean-Claude was portrayed as President not merely of Haiti's French-speaking elite but also as a man of the people. On April 22, 1977, in a speech to the nation commemorating his sixth anniversary in office, Jean-Claude thrilled Haitians by speaking in proverb-peppered Creole, his first official speech ever in that language.

The second aspect of the new Duvalierism was a much-heralded liberalization, a thaw in the old repressive policies regarding political prisoners, freedom of speech and of the press. "I alone can blow the winds of liberalization," Jean-Claude declared. To Haitians sweating under the weight of Duvalierist oppression, however, the winds he blew provided little relief.

In the National Penitentiary, Claire-Lise Rigaud still visited Lucien every day, but finally she felt she could not continue, unable to bear the increasingly vulgar body searches as grinning guards inspected her breasts and peered and pried at her genitals, saying they were looking for weapons. Enraged, Lucien Rigaud bought himself a transfer to the General Hospital, where his wife could visit him without humiliation. After three weeks, however, he learned that Jean-Claude intended to send him to Fort Dimanche for execution. Rigaud acted immediately, Claire-Lise his main resource. He told his guards he was broke and needed to sell his car, and so he had asked his wife to bring it to the hospital and leave him the keys. When she arrived she offered each of the guards a doctored soft drink, then, as they were thirstily drinking, handed Lucien the car keys and a packet of money and left.

Soon the Valium-drugged guards were asleep. Rigaud plumped up pillows until they resembled his sleeping form, dressed, and slipped out of his room. Until he reached the street where Claire-Lise had parked the car, he simply bribed everyone else he encountered. Then, free after so many months, he slipped behind the wheel and drove off. Minutes later Rigaud arrived at the Mexican Embassy, where he sought and obtained political asylum.

Claire-Lise was not so lucky. Major Guillaume arrested her and forced her to watch a woman beaten so harshly that she could no longer stand up. Claire-Lise was then released and began to receive anonymous death threats. Finally she packed up her three children and fled home to Switzerland to wait for her husband.

For the next eighteen months, until Lucien Rigaud also fled Haiti, he and Claire-Lise kept up pressure on Amnesty International and other human-rights organizations so that he, and thousands of other political prisoners in "liberalized" Haiti, would not be forgotten.

They were not forgotten, and the Americans, Amnesty International, and other human-rights organizations kept up the pressure on the Haitian government. One immediate consequence was that on September 22, 1977, the twentieth anniversary of Duvalierism, Jean-Claude ratified the Inter-American Convention on Human Rights. He also liberated 104 more political prisoners. This time Bobby Duval was included, but only because President Carter had written directly to President Duvalier saying he was personally interested in seeing the dying young man set free.

Duval was in the final stages before death. He could no longer stand up. The young, athletic man had shriveled to a ninety-pound skeleton. Duvalier's henchmen dared not release him in that condition. Instead they transferred him to the penitentiary and then Dessalines Barracks, and for three months nursed him back into the health they had destroyed. Three huge meals a day ballooned him up to 220 pounds. Medicines reversed and repaired most of the organic damage. In the last month, when he was nearly normal, his parents were allowed to visit and to bring food from home. By the time he was freed he looked—though he did not feel—healthier than ever, and he walked through the prison gates to return to the bourgeois life from which he had been snatched away.

Once Duval and Duvalier were both guests at the same party. Duval remained composed, though he knew Duvalier knew who he was; Duvalier was equally impassive. Over the heaped platters the two young men cast covert glances at each other, but neither spoke.

But Duval never forgot what had happened, and though he knew it was risky, he testified before the U.S. Congress about human-rights abuses inside Haitian prisons and about the tricks, recounting the time he and the other prisoners had been transferred in a container to the military base in suburban Frères while a Red Cross investigation team inspected the prisons. When the Red Cross people had gone, the prisoners were returned to their spruced-up cells in the same container.

Jean-Claude also honored Duvalierism's twentieth anniversary with the unveiling of a spectacular new ideology, a policy of economic development he announced with straight-faced pride as Jeanclaudism. "Jean-claudism," Jean-Claude explained, "is the Duvalierist Revolution that, its explosive phase achieved, enters into its economic phase to finish its work because it is evident that a revolution cannot know success unless it completely assures the rehabilitation of the suffering masses." Duvalierism having won the social battle, Jeanclaudism would now fight the economic battle. "The Gospel of Christ did not destroy the Old Testament," Jean-Claude reminded his people solemnly. "On the contrary, it came to explain it, to complete and realize its promises."

However, after introducing Jeanclaudism to the mass of Haitians in the first major speech he delivered in Creole, Jean-Claude seemed to cast doubt on the success of his father's great social revolution. "The Haitian detests himself and hates himself and he cultivates faults and negative qualities because he has the spirit of contradiction in him," he declared. "He does not love truth, and is blind to its clarity. The Haitian prefers instead the shadowy zones of existence where obscurity triumphs, and he lives in the absurd because reason and logic anger him. The Haitian searches for himself without finding himself, and he is still searching."

To Americans, however, he tried to portray a different picture of Haitians and Jeanclaudism. In an article published in English for foreign consumption, he wrote,

> We Haitians are descendants of downtrodden tramps who fell down, made naked by sun and guns. We Haitians advocate plain truth. We cannot be, at the same time, humanists and racists, universalists and particularists. We cannot repudiate the human condition. Our Haitian democracy calls for the dignity of the human condition against the stream of violence in all its multiple aspects: oppression, servitude, assimilation and alienation; despair and humiliation, scarcity, squalor and ignorance. What a gallant example Haitians offer to a world frightened into hysteria by conflagration, and torn asunder by civil strife and general indiscipline."

This remarkable piece ended on a triumphantly upbeat note: "This is the Haitian Progressive Order I have set up under the aegis of Jean-claudism and which I invite all of you into."

The reality of the Haitian Progressive Order combined elements of the "absurd" or illogical and unreasoned nature of Haitian life, the cynicism of two decades of unprogressive, degenerate dictatorship, and the attempts of individual Haitians to fan the embers of freedom with the winds of Jeanclaudist liberalization.

Most absurd of all, the incarnation of Jeanclaudist cynicism, was the Luc Nerée incident, when Tonton Macoutes publicly attacked one of Haiti's most upright Protestant leaders on his way home from church and beat him so savagely that he required brain surgery to save his life.

The Reverend Luc Nerée was one of Jimmy Carter's most fervent admirers, and when Carter replied personally to a letter he had written, Nerée delightedly ripped off the signature and reproduced it under a translation of Carter's inaugural address he published in *Hebdo-Jeune Presse,* his son's newspaper. Three months later Interior Minister Aurelien Jeanty declared Nerée one of the government's most dangerous enemies. In a personal interview, when Nerée protested, Jeanty angrily accused him of being an American FBI agent and posted Macoutes, including one disguised as a candy seller, to spy on Nerée's house in the huge compound of his Aid to Children Mission, where he daily fed, clothed, educated, and ministered to hundreds of slum children.

Nerée retaliated by printing an account of his interview with Jeanty in *Hebdo-Jeune Presse.* Jeanty was furious. He called Nerée a madman and gave orders to his goons to chase off the streets all the little boys who hawked the newspaper.

Then in December 1977, when his son was out of Haiti, Nerée revealed that Jeanty had issued a directive ordering rural Macoutes to beat up peasants they considered politically recalcitrant or hostile. François Duvalier had created the VSN to guarantee national security, Nerée wrote, but instead many Macoutes killed, beat, and robbed people, betraying the original purpose of their mission. To serve the best interests of the country, Nerée concluded, the VSN should be made subservient to the army.

Minister Jeanty summoned Nerée to his house. "You are sabotaging the country," Jeanty told him angrily. "Nobody will come here anymore and the economy will be destroyed. The only thing I'm asking of you, Nerée, is that you tread softly." Jeanty terminated the interview on a menacing note: "I'll be watching the next issue of *Hebdo-Jeune Presse.* And if you think President Carter can do anything for you, you're greatly mistaken."

A shaken Nerée returned home and ventured outside only to preach or to lead a Bible class. One night as Nerée and his sister-in-law were driving away after a Bible class, two Macoutes slammed their car into Nerée's. Then, as horrified members of his congregation watched, the two men yanked Nerée's sister-in-law from her seat and flung her under the car, where they kicked her unconscious. Nerée, fighting for his life, clung to the steering wheel. A Macoute grabbed his necktie and strangled him until he fell out of the car.

Other Macoutes joined the first two, and all kicked at the prostrate pastor, pounding him with brass knuckles until blood streamed down the pavement, and frightened Baptists stood wailing and calling on God to come to the rescue. A policeman appeared but hastily retreated when he saw what was happening. The Macoutes shouted at a passing *tap-tap* to run Nerée over and finish him off, but the driver swerved and sped away.

Nerée heard a voice say, "You might as well stop now. The pastor is dead." He understood that feigning death was his only salvation. Only inside the safety of the General Hospital did he dare move and let the doctors know he was alive.

The doctors protected him, and Nerée survived. His son, who had returned from Europe, tried to stave off further attack by informing the world what had happened. He called the American ambassador and local radio stations and went around to the daily newspapers with details. His strategy worked, and Jean-Claude was subjected to immediate international pressure to explain what had happened. Yet despite a plethora of witnesses to the Nerée incident, the government exonerated the Macoutes and blamed Nerée.

"In effect, this is what happened: (a) a car accident (b) an altercation (c) a brawl," said an official statement. "Wanting to establish a cause and effect link between the appearance in *Hebdo-Jeune Presse* of an article with a virulent attack against the VSN is to appeal to simple coincidence."

The Nerée incident had several important consequences. It tested the sincerity of Jeanclaudist liberalization and also the mettle of the Haitian press. At the trial of Nerée's assailants, held three months after the incident, Public Prosecutor Rodrigue Casimir asked for sentences of three years, a ludicrous punishment for an assault that had nearly killed Nerée. In court the convalescent Nerée refused to identify his aggressors, declaring that he forgave them, "for they knew not what they were doing." The fact was, he knew they were all related to either Interior Minister Jeanty or Macoute chief Madame Max Adolphe. At trial's end Escarmé Joseph and Wesner Pétion each received two-month sentences, which they served only in the day, being released at night to go home. Their sentences more than justified Nerée's caution in refusing to cooperate with the "prosecution."

The Haitian press acquitted itself much more honorably than did the government. Most cowardly were the government-subsidized *Le Nouveau Monde,* which refused to discuss the Nerée affair because it lacked information, and *Le Matin,* which published the government's version. *Panorama* called the attack "brutal and premeditated," while *Le Nouvelliste,* dean of Haitian papers, expressed courageous disapproval. Most outspoken of all was *Le Petit Samedi Soir* editor Dieudonné Fardin, who announced on the cover, "We have chosen to speak," and inside gave a full account of the incident, including a severe criticism of the government communiqué. "Such declarations may produce other 'accidents,'" Fardin pointed out bitterly.

The Inter-American Press Association came to its own conclusions, reporting that the Nerée affair proved that Jeanclaudist liberalization was fake. Haitian journalists, the report continued, had to develop a sixth sense about how far they could go without violating certain taboos. Survival meant they could never attack Duvalier, his family, or the legitimacy of the presidency-for-life. They could never mention corruption in high places, and they could not criticize the VSN. Luc Nerée had broken the latter taboo, and he had paid the Haitian price.

A muzzled press usually means a vulnerable government. To ensure that its secrets remained secret, Haiti's government adopted the policy of all repressive regimes: "Kill the messenger."

One day privately owned Télé-Haiti found a way to deliver that message through a messenger even Jeanclaudism would not think to kill. He was that oddity, a Haitian peasant who had survived ninety years of *la misère* as regime succeeded regime: government by *caco* bandits, the American occupation, Estimé's black populist "Revolution," and now, in his final years, the government of economic development called Jeanclaudism. As thousands watched him, Gros-Jean, at ninety untouchable and unforgettable as the incarnation of Haiti's sad decline, uttered through toothless gums a story of hardship salted with tragedy, despair, and a hopeless prognostication for the Haitian human lot.

Gros-Jean had spent a joyless childhood in Cavaillon. Then in 1917, after the American Marines intervened and occupied Haiti, he joined boatloads of other Haitians and set out for Cuba. For eighteen long years he cut Cuban sugarcane, dreaming as he worked under the blazing foreign sun of the day he would return to Haiti with enough money to build a little house, to plant his own vegetable garden, and, in his courtyard, to tether a few black pigs, perhaps even a goat or a cow. For eighteen years he scrimped to put all his savings into the *banco de colonos* in Cuba. Then in 1935, when Cuba expelled tens of thousands of its black Haitian cutters, Gros-Jean and the others discovered the *banco de colonos* would not pay them.

Gros-Jean left Cuba middle-aged, weakened in body, and without a cent to realize his dream. Back home he discovered that soil erosion and overpopulation had made poor Haiti even poorer, and after another lifetime scrabbling for existence, Gros-Jean faced death without a single comfort, without hope, without memories of anything that was not painful.

The message was grim and a reproach to a long line of Haitian governments, yet in statistical, abstract form, minus the human factor, Gros-Jean's Haiti was Jean-Claude's message and selling ticket, the justification for Jeanclaudism's new developmental thrust. Even misery had a price, and Jean-Claude had for sale deforestation, eroded soil, decreasing crop production, a critical lack of infrastructure, a nation of roads mostly impassable except by Land-Rover or intrepid mule. Demographically, he could point to his people, a burgeoning population riddled with chronic poor health, high infant mortality, unemployment and malnutrition, widespread illiteracy. For developmental purposes, raped and ruined Haiti was virgin soil, and to keep the foreign-aid millions and legions of NGOs rolling in, all that was needed was to market it.

Reforestation was one such potentially lucrative developmental area, and Jean-Claude and Simone devoted days to planting saplings and encouraging other projects. On his twenty-seventh birthday Jean-Claude even received a nursery of one million saplings in the arid Ti-Tanyin region, though by the time he turned twenty-eight most of these had died. "Our land is exhausted, denuded, its mountains, hills and valleys haunted by the specter of desolation and inhospitality," Jean-Claude solemnly proclaimed. "Once Haiti exported wood. Now we import Formica."

Agriculture Minister Edouard Berrouet, a mulatto agronomist who had quickly shed his socialist leanings when Papa Doc gained power, also mounted ambitious reforestation campaigns. He declared a state of emergency in the Forêt des Pins and outlawed hunting of all species threatened with extinction. "Hunger is now permanent," Berrouet warned, and the money flowed into his department's coffers.

"Haiti is squeezed between a desperate long-term need to rehabilitate an environment already devastated, and a short-term imperative to feed a needy people," said Rice Odel of the Washington-based Conservation Foundation. A sympathetic world responded, though the haphazard reforestation programs all failed to keep pace with deforestation.

At the height of reforestation, 30 million trees were planted annually, of which about one tenth survived, while 60 to 100 million were cut down. The Duvaliers, indifferent to the crisis, preached reforestation only as a way to attract aid money to steal. At the same time they granted forested properties to friends and relatives who stripped them and sold the wood to poor peasants for charcoal. Meanwhile periodic droughts continued to ravage the land, and foreign donors rushed emergency gifts of food over and above their normal quotas to feed starving peasants.

One important loss from the eroding soil was coffee, Haiti's chief export crop and an important source of foreign earnings. Production of the highly regarded Arabica coffee, descended from a tree stolen in 1723 by Gabriel Mathieu de Clieu from the royal Jardin des Plantes in Paris, continued to drop almost yearly. So did production of sugar, rice, and beans, to the extent that about one quarter of the agricultural country's foodstuffs had to be imported, and the percentage rose yearly. Worse, much imported food, especially donated goods, competed directly with local agriculture, undercutting it in price and quality. Often peasants abandoned farming altogether when their former customers began to obtain food elsewhere, either free or at unbeatably cheaper prices.

In a few limited areas Jeanclaudist developmental programs had modest successes. This was particularly true when Haiti's richest resource was used—its vast pool of laborers eager to work for $3 daily. They also worked hard, were reliable, and, despite illiteracy, easily trainable. Cheap and productive, the Haitian work force in a newly nonviolent society was an easy sell. Jeanclaudism guaranteed that trouble-making labor unions would not intervene to muddy the waters and also offered foreign clients ten-year tax holidays and total freedom to re-export their profits. The only drawbacks were the kickbacks to Jean-Claude and a host of government officials. Overall, a very attractive setup, and many foreign manufacturers opted to come to Haiti.[21]

Very soon Port-au-Prince had about 240 assembly plants, most American-owned. Their sixty thousand mainly female employees assembled electronic components, textiles, and all the baseballs used by the American and National Baseball leagues. Since every employed Haitian feeds at least five others, the assembly industries can be said to have fed over one-third of a million people, albeit inadequately. However, the industry as a whole contributed little to the government revenue and relieved only slightly the crushing need for employment nationwide.

Tourism was another modest success, with foreign visitors lured by the Jeanclaudist facade of liberalization and by the end to public terror. Cruise ships returned, and in 1977, one of its peak years, the number of tourists reached a total of 167,260, although this figure also includes businessmen, development and foreign aid workers, and missionaries. Over in secluded Montrouis, the Club Méditerrané opened a branch, where thousands of tourists a year could enjoy Haiti without being exposed to its terrible poverty or its eroded soil. However, Club Med represented little financial advantage to Haiti, for Jean-Claude granted it franchise privileges and the club imported almost everything, including food, and employed Haitians only as menials.

Construction projects, all foreign-financed, also paved roads connecting Port-au-Prince to provincial cities, so that the 170 miles' distance between the capital and Cap Haitien no longer took eight hours, and the trip to Jacmel no longer involved crossing a hundred fords. But throughout the republic 2,400 kilometers of rugged road remained unpaved, much of it impassable during the rainy season, and most money donated for roads was squandered through incompetence, embezzlement, kickbacks, and government corruption.

Not surprisingly, and despite massive propaganda extolling Jeanclaudism's successes in the development area, Haitian society remained virtually unchanged. Business and commerce were controlled by the same three thousand families who traditionally ran them, and their annual incomes of more than $90,000 contrasted glaringly with the $720 of the factory worker. Jean-Claude personally earned a mere $24,000 yearly, but he supplemented that with $1.5 million expense money for his presidency and millions more from other sources, including unreported government revenues, kickbacks, and extortions from foreign aid and compulsory gifts from grateful local and foreign businesses.

For propaganda purposes Jean-Claude also took sporadic personal interest in various projects, even riding horseback through the countryside to see for himself what was really happening. Edouard C. Paul, who in 1969 had sent Cayes literacy worker Pierre Denis to his death, announced, "We are living now what we may call the era of the Haitian people, because a leader loves them and devotes himself body and soul to give them back the life they thought was lost."

In fact, during this period of self-congratulatory rhetoric and modest development, two things happened that swiftly put an end to any hope, however slight and illusory, for Haitian economic salvation. The first was the discovery, in the neighboring Dominican Republic, of African Swine Fever, or ASF. The second was the discovery, in the United States, of the new and incurable disease identified as Acquired Immune Deficiency Syndrome, or AIDS.

ASF is an AIDS-like virus, infectious and incurable, which kills its porcine victims within forty-eight hours of the first symptoms but has no effect on humans, even if they eat contaminated meat. The ASF virus gets into the animal's respiratory apparatus, propagates in tissues, liquids, and secretions, and is communicated by ticks, direct contact, or by contaminated food. It is an exceptionally resistant virus and can live in soil up to 23 degrees centigrade for 120 days. It has been detected in treated hams, bacon, and sausages even after six months in a refrigerator.

ASF is thought to have originated in Africa, contracted by wild hogs which spread it to domestic herds. By 1971 ASF had crossed over to Cuba, seven years later to Brazil, and on July 8, 1978, its presence was confirmed in the Dominican Republic. On July 14 Haiti went into action. She closed all land routes to the Dominican Republic and instituted quarantine measures such as disinfectant foot baths at ports and airports. At a cost of $60,000 Haitian officials created a fifteen-kilometer swathe along the border from the Bay of Mancenille to Anse-à-Pitre and killed every last one of the 26,671 pigs in it. Drastic though this was, it did not eradicate ASF, and by early 1979 the disease had killed 30,000 pigs in the Artibonite, and then it spread to Kenscoff and various other parts of the country. New and more drastic action had to be taken.

In fact, had Haiti been left to her own resources, she undoubtedly would have done what she usually did—little or nothing. Spain and Portugal, both chronically infested, control but do not eliminate by defining buffer areas and slaughtering all animals within them. Several African nations do even less, and after cyclical deaths ASF eventually kills only 20 percent of the herd, a tolerable loss for their subsistence peasant economies and for Haiti's. However, it is disastrous for the North American-style industrial pig farming, with high volume and low profit margins, and so when ASF showed up in the Dominican Republic and Haiti, the United States and Canada put immediate and tremendous pressure on their governments for total eradication, and followed it up by planning, financing, implementing, and supervising the program. By February 1981 there was not a single pig left in the Dominican Republic, and the North Americans insisted that Haiti too undertake total eradication.

Haitians and their leaders also had no inkling of the havoc that would be wrought by the advent of AIDS, a problem that for a time the world would blame on Haiti and accuse her of exporting, and punish her by officially listing her people as one of the "four H's" at high risk of AIDS: homosexuals, heroin addicts, hemophiliacs, and Haitians.

Both ASF and AIDS brewed in the underground of the nation's life, and were more destructive to Haitian society than the critical articles and news commentaries whose authors were so ruthlessly crushed. But because they understood nothing of this, Jean-Claude and Jeanclaudism continued as if their worst enemy was Jimmy Carter and their greatest fear that he would be reelected.

By 1979 that fear was lessening. Carter was in serious trouble in the areas of inflation, by then double-digit, the energy crisis, and the humiliating failure to rescue fifty-two American hostages held in Iran.

Few people watched his downfall with more joy than Duvalier, who would later throw a madcap champagne party at the palace when Reagan swept the polls in November 1980. Now in his late twenties, Jean-Claude perceived that his most pressing problems were to gain independence from his mother and to push the Jeanclaudists to victory.

It was with his friends that Jean-Claude finally developed the urge to stand up to his mother and control his own life. It was not from lack of self-esteem but rather from sheer inertia that he had let her usurp his role. After all, he knew he was the greatest, because everyone around him constantly told him so.

This mania for winning extended to everything. The President could not bear to lose even games of chance. Though his friends flattered themselves that they did not flatter him, they knew better than to let him lose at their games. And he was tireless, so nearly every party presented an identical 4 a.m. scenario: men and women sleeping on chairs, sprawled on couches, and even on the floor because Jean-Claude refused to call it a night.

These parties were Jean-Claude's sole preserve. His mother almost never came, and if she did, it was at his special invitation. For this reason he attached great importance to them, devoting considerable care to planning, especially the guest lists. His friends drafted preliminary lists, which Jean-Claude then carefully checked, adding names and sometimes dropping them, "I'm sleeping with his wife," he'd say matter-of-factly, and a name would be crossed off.

Jean-Claude's clothes reflected a conservative bent, and also his obsessive one-upmanship. Everything he owned was tasteful and well made, and it was also just that much better than anyone else's. His shoes were made-to-order, his ties $250 apiece, his suits and shirts exquisitely tailored, and everything was imported. He owned a great deal of jewelry, most of it gifts, but wore only a ring and link bracelet to set off his manicured hands, and sometimes a gold chain, but only at the beach. The man who appeared so absurdly fat and blankly moon-faced in photographs cut a much livelier figure in life, dancing lightly and laughing with his friends, immaculate, polished, controlled.

Parties, sports, and evenings spent watching movies in the palace's private viewing room were Jean-Claude's real world, but sometimes he ventured into politics from a nagging sense of duty as well as pressure from palace officials, and as the years went by, to try to regain from his mother the power he had allowed her to assume by default. He was not motivated enough to attend cabinet meetings, but he authorized constant cabinet changes, vacillating between this faction and that, firing, hiring, restructuring, sowing insecurity and provoking in his ministers a scramble for instant wealth before the ax fell on their necks too. In the fourteen years of his regime, Jean-Claude went through about three hundred ministers, a crowded field considering the limited number of cabinet posts to fill. In 1972 there were only eleven ministries, with a few others added later, including the development-minded Ministry of Planning. "Minister of the Month Club," some insiders wisecracked in private about the continual cabinet shake-ups. "*Cabinè té tombé,*" the Creole peasantry exclaimed. Another cabinet has fallen.

In 1979 Haiti's farcical legislative elections provided Jean-Claude an unexpected opportunity to hit back at his mother. To show the world, and in particular the Americans, how wildly popular Jean-Claude was among his people, his government decided to orchestrate "elections" that would appear democratic through the wide range of candidates who presented themselves to the electorate.

In fact the National Assembly in no way resembled the model described in the Constitution: fifty-eight democratically elected congressmen who meet publicly from April through June, and have the power to declare war if the executive recommends it, approve or disapprove international agreements, initiate legislation, revise the Constitution, and to function as a high court of justice. The reality was an Assembly of cowed yes-men who rubber-stamped presidential laws and decrees and spent their time making speeches about the splendid achievements of the regime.

In preparation for the elections the palace hand-picked all the candidates, giving voters the choice between committed Jeanclaudists, devout Jeanclaudists, and virulent Jeanclaudists. But unexpectedly, two determined anti-Duvalierists announced their candidacies, and the regime had a real contest on its hands. The first was feisty Protestant pastor Sylvio Claude, who tried courageously but quixotically to pit himself against Madame Max Adolphe, the Tonton Macoute chief, and also the incumbent deputy for her hometown of Mirebalais. Unthinkable and intolerable. The regime retaliated swiftly; Claude was beaten, arrested, taught on the instant one cardinal tenet of Jeanclaudism—whoever opposes Jean-Claude is an enemy of the state. Forcibly exiled to Bogotá, Colombia, an embittered but stubborn Claude watched Madame Max sweep to undisputed power, and began to plan his next move.

In Cap Haitien, far from Port-au-Prince's strangulating grip, the second candidate proved more recalcitrant. His name was Alexandre Lerouge, better known as "the Lerouge Phenomenon," and he soon took over and controlled the elections. The Phenomenon was a humble customs clerk without money, influence, or backing.

To the astonishment and delight of Cap Haitien residents (Capois), Lerouge openly campaigned on an independent, anti-Jeanclaudist platform. Radio stations rushed reporters up from Port-au-Prince, and for the first time in memory Haitians could hear men-in-the-street interviews about their favorite candidate, the uncompromising, unstoppable Lerouge. Capois swarmed to his support, and sheer public exposure protected him from flabbergasted palace officials who reluctantly discarded killing or arresting him as an acceptable option.

Finally Simone Duvalier intervened by providing a rival candidate she and the old-guard Duvalierist "Dinosaurs" believed could beat Lerouge, given a little palace help in ballot counting, of course. The man she chose was Claude Vixamar, former Cap Haitien prefect and impeccable intellectual, professor of law and French literature at local Cap Haitien schools. Already strong-armed by Simone to serve as Under Secretary of State for Information, the erudite Vixamar, unhappily lodged in an $8-a-day room at the Auberge de Port-au-Prince, now received another summons. "You're going to run against Lerouge," Simone informed him. Vixamar was aghast and declined the invitation. But this was no invitation, it was an order, and Vixamar walked out of the palace a candidate.

His campaign was brief, as he was parachuted in at the last minute. Its most notable moment came when Simone sent truckloads of soldiers, Léopards, and Macoutes to Cap Haitien to stump for him and to distribute thousands of "Vixamar for Deputy" T-shirts. The Capois crowd, virtually all pro-Lerouge, shouted their outrage, snatched up all the T-shirts, then wore them inside out and paraded through the city shouting, "Long live Lerouge!"

Election Day arrived hot and happy, with a huge turnout for Haiti's usually stolid elections. At every polling station Lerouge's partisans monitored the ballots, asking voters whom they were voting for and then tabulating the results. By 11 a.m. their unofficial tally was Lerouge 27,000, Vixamar 900, and they declared Lerouge elected. Mardi Gras bands poured out into the streets, and until late into the night people danced and sang and celebrated this wonderful event, the fair election of an antigovernment deputy who for three months a year would sit in the impotent National Assembly with fifty-seven Jeanclaudist stooges and, in his own person, provide the nation its sole voice of freedom.

When officials arrived to cart the ballot boxes back to Port-au-Prince, the people refused. Count the ballots here in Cap Haitien, they insisted, and on new orders from the palace, it was done accordingly. The final vote was 34,800 for Alexandre Lerouge and 3,400 for Claude Vixamar. The Lerouge Phenomenon had carried the day, and Haiti's maturing President-for-Life had struck a successful blow for independence from his mother.

Foreign observers were little impressed, understanding the Lerouge Phenomenon to be just that, and unlikely to be repeated. Much more significant, from their standpoint, were the recent revelations of Wendell Rawls, Jr., in *The New York Times Magazine*, with its chilling title and subtitles: "*BABY DOC'S HAITIAN TERROR: Why have we resumed sending foreign aid to Haiti, when beatings and deaths are still daily events in its crowded prison? Just ask Lucien Rigaud. . . .*"

Lucien Rigaud was a phenomenon of a different ilk, and like Lerouge, he refused to be silenced. Jean-Claude took his case both seriously and personally, knowing how well connected Rigaud was, and because he had been warned that Rigaud had threatened to kill him, even at the cost of his own life.

Two weeks after he arrived at the Mexican Embassy, a bored Rigaud was gazing out the window when he saw Jean-Claude cruise slowly down the street to the Craan Business School just opposite the embassy, then stop his car to ogle the young women going in and out of the building. Suddenly he turned and spotted Rigaud. Their eyes met, and Rigaud grinned wickedly. Jean-Claude paled, started his car, then nearly smashed it in his haste to speed away.

Months later, transferred to the ambassador's residence in Musseau, Rigaud surreptitiously entertained a guest who had twice sneaked into his room in the dead of night, his entry secured by the bribes that smoothed Rigaud's way everywhere in corruption-riddled Haiti. The men talked until just before dawn, with Rigaud telling his story and showing journalist Wendell Rawls, Jr., all his documents, including the signed confession of the two policemen involved in the first bungled attempt to kill him. Weeks later *The New York Times Magazine* appeared with Rawls's article in it, an analytical account of Rigaud's saga, and a searing condemnation of human rights in Jeanclaudist Haiti.

Immediately and repeatedly, Jean-Claude contacted Rigaud, offering him safe-conduct if only he would remain silent and warning him that he would spend another twenty years in the Mexican Embassy if he did not. Rigaud agreed not to talk, pretending to believe he would be given safe-conduct. Then one night he threw away all his belongings, hid in the little stairwell containing the swimming-pool filter, and listened in cramped amusement when the alarm was given that he had escaped. In the all-out campaign to find him, the safest place was right where he was, and only after the SD came and arrested all the servants for questioning about his escape did he simply stroll outside under cover of night and make his way by *tap-tap* to Montrouis, to the Kyona Beach resort where he stole a sailboat and sailed off into the dark sea.

Rigaud had never sailed before and, seasick and sunburned, he drifted helplessly for three days until he sighted land and washed up at Guantanamo Province, Cuba. At the U.S. military base there Rigaud identified himself, and within days an official plane arrived to carry him off to Washington. There he testified about his adventures in Haiti and his dealings with Congressman Flood, and wired money to the owner of the sailboat he had stolen. Then he joined Claire-Lise and the children in Switzerland.

Back in Haiti, Jean-Claude was furious. Rigaud and his big mouth had flown the coop, and now Washington had begun an investigation into the congressional influence peddling that Haiti—and Jean-Claude—relied on and thrived on. "Rigaud's story . . . raises serious questions about the propriety of America's resumption of foreign aid to a country where conditions may not have improved sufficiently to warrant it," Rawls had written, "and it suggests that Congressional corruption rather than altruism may have led to that resumption. The United States Justice Department wants to question Rigaud in this country as a key witness in investigations of Pennsylvania Representative Daniel J. Flood and possibly others on Capitol Hill who may have peddled Congressional influence in the distribution of foreign-aid funds for Haiti."

Despite Haitian apprehension, American funds did not dry up. Though the State Department took the Rigaud affair very seriously, too many vested interests hampered efforts to act on it. As Lucien Rigaud confided to Wendell Rawls, too many Americans and Haitians had stakes in keeping human-rights abuses and corruption under a lid. Too many officials were on the take, and too many people had to be fooled. American companies such as Reynolds Aluminum, Rawling Baseballs, and hundreds of others taking advantage of Haiti's low wages and proximity to the U.S. would certainly react unfavorably to documented accounts of human-rights abuses. And for the fledgling tourist industry, bringing precious American dollars into the country and keeping alive Haiti's wonderful art and artisanship, pottery, weaving, and basketry, revelation of tortures and brutal prisons might well be the beginning of the end.

An even more important consideration was Haiti's non-Communist stance, an American foreign policy priority that supersedes all others, including human rights. Even Carter backed away from disowning countries guilty of human-rights abuses when overall national policy dictated. Rod Prince, a British political scientist and author of *Haiti: Family Business,* asks why the Americans tolerated three decades of Duvalierism, and answers the question succinctly:

Washington has made it plain enough . . . that its preference is for conservative pro-business regimes which respect the norms of elected parliamentary government. Equally, it supports anti-communist minority undemocratic regimes in preference to unknown dangers, such as social upheaval and the possibility of revolutionary regimes or even radical nationalist regimes taking power. To a considerable extent, great survivors like the Duvaliers owe their continued hold on power to this ingrained fear of change on the part of the U.S.

Cuba, fifty miles away, was the Duvaliers' most potent argument for continued American support for their virulently anti-Communist regime.

The reassuring nonconsequences of Lucien Rigaud's carefully documented charges about the true face of his country and its methods of obtaining and dispersing foreign aid greatly cheered Jean-Claude. So, by late 1979, did daily news of Carter's losing battle to retain his people's confidence. As the Jeanclaudist government became less concerned about concealing human-rights violations, a courageous opposition movement made desperate attempts to save the situation and to prevent Haiti from completely abandoning the liberalization path Jean-Claude now openly strayed from.

The most significant opposition activity came when both Sylvio Claude and Grégoire Eugène, returned from exile, founded independent political parties. Claude's was the Christian Democratic Party of Haiti, Eugène's the Christian Social Party of Haiti. At the same time Eugène published *A Plea in Favor of Political Parties,* snapped up in local bookshops, in which he declared that democracy like nature abhorred a void, and yet a void was precisely what single-party systems created.

Jean-Claude was personally and profoundly disturbed by the birth of Haitian political parties. On July 25 he summoned his former tutor Eugène to his house at Desprez. The presidential note was delivered as Eugène sat adjudicating oral exams at the law faculty. He read it, then stood up and loudly addressed the startled students. "Wait for me," he urged them, hoping to prevent any "disappearance" Jean-Claude might have in mind for him. He added for good measure, "As it's the President who's sent for me, I have to go, but wait for me, I'll be back in an hour. And please, tell the other groups to wait."

At the elegant mansion in Desprez, alone except for the microphones Eugène felt sure were concealed somewhere, Jean-Claude met him at the stairs and inquired politely, "Professor, how are you?"

"I'm fine, thank you, but the country is in dreadful condition," Eugène responded, and launched into a tirade about Haitian injustice, inequalities, and corruption. "They use the city cistern-cleaning trucks to clean the road in front of your house half an hour before you leave so you won't get dust in your face," he raged. "And while they're waiting for you, and sometimes it takes hours, they don't even get fed. Slaves at least used to get fed."

Jean-Claude listened with polite incomprehension before he finally interrupted to get to the crux of the meeting. Without subtlety or any apparent sense of irony, the President offered Eugène a house and $40,000 cash in return for dismantling his new political party. Now it was Eugène's turn to stare blankly. "No, no," he said firmly.

Jean-Claude treated the Christian Democratic Party of Haiti's founder, Sylvio Claude, a rugged man of the people, more brutally. On August 29 Claude and his daughter Marie-France, the party's vice president, were at party headquarters when two men appeared and asked to join up. So convincing were they that PDCH guards invited them to speak to Claude, who enthusiastically discussed his party's platform until suddenly one held a knife to his throat. Claude fled, but not before he was shot and wounded in the left ear. Hours later, still at large, he was arrested by the SD on the Rue Courte, near the cathedral, and eventually charged with "subversive activities," unspecified but undoubtedly referring to a PDCH meeting three days earlier that had ended with wild anti-Duvalierist cheers.

But the regime did not want Claude in jail; they wanted him out of Haiti. Though a court exonerated him, the government kept him under lock and key, then tried to force him onto a plane for Quito, Ecuador. The stocky little pastor made such a public commotion at the airport, however, that his captors angrily returned him to the penitentiary. Immediately, and equally angrily, the PDCH issued a press communiqué complaining of "intense pressure put on him to accept immediate banishment." Added the PDCH grimly, "Mr. Claude received a visit in the prison from the Interior and Foreign Affairs Minister, who confirmed that the United States, France, Brazil, and Mexico are prepared to accept him as an exile."

Claude refused to cooperate. "The Political Bureau of the PDCH protests energetically against such illegal and anti-democratic maneuvers and demands the liberation of Mr. Sylvio Claude since the law has no further charges against him." But the Jeanclaudist government was above the law, and so Sylvio Claude had to languish in prison, humiliated, severely abused, and determined not to surrender.

Liberalization was now openly flaunted, and human rights practiced mainly in the breach. American missionary Joel Trimble discovered this firsthand in the dusty little town of Belladères, whose army commandant, barefoot and in Bermuda shorts, threw him into the local prison's underground dungeon for several hours. Trimble had come to Belladères to interpret for a CARE mission planning to pave the area's roads, and the officer decided his attitude was disrespectful. Inside, Trimble spent hours praying over a dying prisoner, jailed then battered so savagely he lay like a rag doll in bloodied mud. His crime, Trimble learned from other prisoners, was surrounding his garden with poisoned thorns to stop the nightly thieving that was ruining him. By the time Trimble was released, the man died in his arms, groaning a sinner's prayer of repentance.

The incident had an ironic aftermath. For reasons Trimble never learned, the commandant was discharged from the army. In disgrace and desperation, brooding about his dismissal, the ex-officer must have concluded that Trimble had been responsible. Months later, visiting his mother in Rochester, New York, Trimble opened a much-forwarded envelope and read with hilarity and wonder, "Honorable M. Joel Trimble, I now realize how wickedly I have treated a noble man like yourself, and do not blame you for having me fired from the army. Please, Sir, come back to Haiti and intercede for me with your powerful friends so that I may be reintegrated and resume my military command."

Another chilling example of Haiti's fundamental disregard for human rights came when the Interamerican Commission on the Rights of Man, an OAS group that had inspected Haiti's prisons, released a report on Fort Dimanche that included a partial list of 151 prisoners who had died or been executed in recent years, most in 1975 and 1976.

The Haitian government, apprised of this list, responded on October 6, 1978, that though it provided medical and other care to inmates, some simply could not endure imprisonment and, deplorably of course, they died. Others on the list, the note continued, were dangerous terror-ists, and several had lost their lives in armed shoot-outs with the forces of law and order. Asked to identify these terrorists, the government maintained total silence. Then on December 7 it issued a new statement charging that many names on the commission's death list were actually fabricated, and that no such people even existed.

The commission also demanded information from the government about the executions it had documented and described in detail. "The method of execution is barbaric. These last few years they do not waste bullets to execute prisoners. They make them advance one by one in the night towards the sea and strike them down with a club at the nape of the neck, like dogs. The dull thud of the blows of the club can be heard even in the cells." But the government furnished no information, instead deny-ing that any executions at all had taken place between 1974 and 1976.

The commission report, based on investigations and the testimony of hundreds of prisoners given amnesty, described all facets of prison life, beginning with the introduction to the fort, the grotesque physical examination of the nude prisoners "not for medical purposes, but to humiliate them." The filth and contamination, the overcrowded cells, which necessitated sleeping in shifts, the unspeakable food, above all the callous brutality of the keepers were all documented. "We don't stop people from dying," the commissioners quoted jailer Enos "Plop Plop" St. Pierre, Jean-Claude's personal nominee. "If you are tired, stick your head in the bucket of shit. Kill yourself. Anyway, you know you are al-ready dead."

The commissioners also accused the Haitian government of brazen lying by repeatedly assuring them that Jean-Claude had closed Fort Di-manche in 1977. The truth was, the commissioners said, the section called "Nirvana" alone had been closed, and then only to construct more solitary confinement cells. They also revealed that they were now aware of Haiti's pre-inspection precautions: prisoners transferred and hidden elsewhere, cells cleaned and painted, food improved, prisoners coached by Colonel Louis Charles and Major Emmanuel Orcel of the SD. In fact, so many precautions had been taken that when the commission visited the barracks in Jacmel and Cap Haitien, they found not a single political prisoner.

The final blow to Haitian liberalization was November 7, 1979, Black Friday. Black Friday began as a giant meeting of the Human Rights

League, founded in 1978 by Jean-Claude's former tutor Gérard Gourgue. For two weeks radio and TV had advertised the meeting, and in response three thousand men and women crowded into the vast hall of the Belgian Salesian Brothers compound in the heart of the teeming slum of La Saline. By 4 p.m. the courtyard was packed with cars, while outside irate *tap-tap* drivers cursed and blasted their horns at these traffic-snarling invaders. The cause of all this commotion? A speech entitled "The Political Climate and Human Rights," to be delivered by Gérard Gourgue.

After a brief introduction by the league's vice president, Irma Rateau, Gourgue picked up the microphone. "I would ask you to keep calm and to observe discipline so you won't become unwitting victims of provocation against you," he began. The excited crowd hushed, and after a minute of silence Gourgue spoke again.

"First, this conference on the political climate and human rights is dedicated to those whose lives were snuffed out and souls destroyed by the violation of those rights." Gourgue added, "I dedicate it also to the Armed Forces of Haiti, apolitical, institutionalized, put in place to assure public order and to protect human rights." Suddenly piercing cries cut through the packed hall: "Vive Duvalier!" "Long live Jean-Claude!" "Jean-Claude-for-Life!"

The panic was instant and contagious, and frightened people began to file out of the hall, anticipating trouble. "I demand that the law enforcement agent sent by the government of the Republic to assure the safety of all of us in this hall come forward and show himself," Gourgue shouted above the rising din. The Duvalierist provocateurs shrieked louder, followed by the sound of smashing chairs. Men and women screamed in terror, fleeing, trampling others, stampeding toward the one door left open to escape the blows of the band of Macoutes who attacked while policemen stood by and did not intervene.

Clovis Désinor, the long-time Duvalier minister turned anti-Jeanclaudist private citizen, remained where he was, arms folded, and refusing to run for cover. "Only sheep run," he said contemptuously to the former President, Franck Sylvain, who clung to him in fright. The real truth was, Désinor's bad leg made it impossible for him to run.

Inside the hall the damage was appalling, the floor littered with wounded men and women and piles of broken furniture. The toll was heavy. Gourgue had been brutally beaten and suffered multiple hematomas on his face, neck, and trunk. A Macoute had clubbed Madame Gourgue's breasts, then crashed a chair down onto her skull. Grégoire

Eugène, another prime target, had hidden in a tiny antechamber, but the Macoutes found him there and only the appearance of Major Claude Jean saved his life. Radio Metropole news analyst Dr. Georges Michel, the young doctor with an encyclopedic memory, had suffered a fractured skull, multiple contusions, and been left for dead. Constant D. Pognon, who believed God had destined him to become Haiti's President, slumped to the floor, his tape recorder in smithereens.

Foreigners were not spared. Two members of a Canadian aid delegation were beaten. An American political attaché was punched. Ragnard Arnesen, OAS representative in Haiti, was bloodied. Mme. Claude Lemonge, press attaché at the French Embassy, had her eye blackened. Frederick Thomasheck from the German Embassy was struck several times.

The Haitian government's reaction was predictably cynical. "Fights had broken out between different members of the audience," declared an official communiqué, "and despite timely police intervention, there had been some injuries and material damage."

Those who had attended Black Friday's meeting left it in full knowledge of what they had come to find out. Jean-Claude had been told and firmly believed that groups such as the Human Rights League could bring down his government, and so when any of his subjects dared speak out in favor of freedom, he responded with cracked skulls, imprisonment, and exile.

And yet even in Haiti's blackest moments, glimmers of light pierced the darkness. Years after Pastor Luc Nerée had been attacked and nearly beaten to death, Duvalier's security chief, Luc Désyr, another Baptist, limped up to him after Sunday service at Quisqueya Chapel. "My dear Nerée," Désyr said confidentially, "I've come to tell you something very interesting about your ... your incident. Did you know that the guys mixed up in that affair are now all dead?"

The two Baptists stood facing each other in the modern chapel, Nerée listening raptly as the older man counted off on his fingers the fates of all five of the Macoutes involved. One young man, a relative and favorite of Madame Max Adolphe, had died in a motorcycle accident on his way to Mirebalais. Another shot himself to death as he cleaned his gun. Two more had died together in a car accident, though their woman companion was not hurt. The man who had smashed Nerée's head had crushed his own skull against an electric pole.

Even Interior Minister Aurelien Jeanty was dead, and in such a

manner as to make even the most irreligious wonder about divine intervention. Jeanty had gone, revolver in hand, to collect rents from one of
his slum properties. One tenant was a young man who implored Jeanty
for more time. For reply Jeanty pulled out his revolver. The young man
raised his hands and retreated quickly into the house, saying perhaps he
could borrow from someone. He returned with his own gun and shot
Jeanty.

Jeanty did not die, and in the air-conditioned comfort of Canapé
Vert Hospital was recovering nicely after surgery to remove the bullet.
One day the door to his room opened, and in walked one of his mistresses, carrying a bouquet of flowers to cheer him. But his joy was
short-lived because his wife suddenly appeared, recognized the other
woman, and chased her from the room. Jeanty attempted to intervene,
tearing his I.V. from his arm and ripping off his bandages as he lurched
after the women. The combined effect of his rage and physical efforts
were too much for him, and that night Aurelien Jeanty died.

Twenty-two years of Duvalierism had taken their toll. Jean-Claude
said it himself in a major speech to the nation. "My government's most
difficult preoccupations are three, the energy crisis, the food crisis, the
water crisis." He was telling the literal truth. After enduring two decades
of Duvalierism, Haiti had run out of energy, run out of food, run out of
water. Droughts, crop failures, and famines had become chronic. Misery
abounded, and so did people, their unstoppable birth rate outweighing
the tragically high infant mortality.

Increasingly the way to escape the misery was to escape Haiti itself.
Desperate men and women took to the sea in boats, in numbers so large
that every month a thousand arrived alive in Florida, and at least a thousand and probably more died en route. Those who played it safer and
went overland to the Dominican Republic were not much better off.

In Gonaives one woman's plight summed up and condemned an
entire regime. After she had given birth to her eighth child, the woman
simply strangled it. When she was arrested and brought to the police
station, she admitted what she had done, explaining that she had been
obliged to kill her eighth child so that seven others could live. Lucid and
serene, she told her jailers, "I did it so he wouldn't have to live gnawed
by pain and hunger, and I did it so that he wouldn't starve the other
seven, who already have little enough to eat."

But for many in fatalistic Haiti the situation could not be otherwise, for Duvalierism meant misery, and Duvalierism might go on forever. It had gone on for twenty-two years, after all, and in Duvalierist mysticism twenty-two was a magic number. Why? Because twenty-two years ago Papa Doc Duvalier had made a pact with the Devil, who granted him absolute power, and that pact endured until September 22, 1979. Once renewed, it would continue for another twenty-two years.

Simone Duvalier, most Haitians believed, had undertaken to renew that pact on behalf of her son, Jean-Claude, before it expired. But when she contacted the *laos* and asked them to intercede for her, they informed her that Jean-Claude at twenty-seven was too young, for the Devil dealt only with those who, like Christ, had lived at least thirty-three years on this earth. Nor could she, his mother, make the pact on his behalf, unless she did so as his wife, wed to him in a mystic marriage.

Simone did not hesitate, so the story went, and in July 1979, two months before it was too late, wed her own son in ritualistic vodoun rites. Once the marriage was validated, by vodoun rituals in the palace and by Catholic rituals in the provinces, Simone contacted the Devil. Then, on behalf of Haiti's President-for-Life, she negotiated another twenty-two-year pact by which Jean-Claude, like his father before him, would keep control of the ravaged nation until September 22, 2001.

"After Duvalier, Duvalier!" How was a weary nation to fight its preordained lot?

9 JEAN-CLAUDE AND MICHÈLE, HONEYMOON

A YEAR LATER JEAN-CLAUDE REALLY MARRIED. HIS BRIDE this time was Michèle Bennett, a young woman soon to gain world notoriety for her reckless squandering of Haiti's public revenue, her close links with sordid drug dealing, and her contemptuous disregard of the six million people she and her husband ruled over. And in the Duvalierist world where *noirisme* still remained a crucial issue, light-skinned Michèle was the antithesis of the "authentic" Haitian woman Papa Doc's dark doctrine had idealized.

Jean-Claude first met Michèle in 1962 at Collège Bird, where both were students in the sixth grade. Jean-Claude was a timid, gawky eleven-year-old known as "Fat Potato" and "Baskethead" because of his enormous size but popular because he was friendly and without affectation. Michèle was twelve, a lanky, long-haired, vivacious beauty with a boisterous laugh, a foul mouth, and a "reputation." Jean-Claude was one of the few who did not try to take advantage of it. He simply fell deeply in love, and while other boys disappeared with her into empty classrooms, bathrooms, and closets, Haiti's fat dauphin contented himself with ogling.

The young Duvalier's fascination with Michèle terrified her father, Ernest Bennett. For one thing, Papa Doc had already imprisoned him for bad debts and financial misdoings. For another, Michèle was irrepressible, and Bennett knew how terrible the consequences could be if Papa Doc took offense at one of her smart-mouthed remarks. In Duvalierist Haiti nobody was exempted from the terror, including children. Even the schoolyard supervisor at Collège Bird had nearly died of fright the day Jean-Claude tumbled down in a ball game and another child had shouted, "Duvalier has fallen!"

Michèle was still at Collège Bird on the Friday morning when Clément Barbot's men shot and killed Jean-Claude's chauffeur and bodyguards as he and his sister Ti-Simone stepped out of their black limousine. Teachers rushed the shaken children into a separate room where they waited alone until the palace was notified. The next year Papa Doc transferred Jean-Claude back to St. Louis de Gonzague, while Bennett sent Michèle, sassy, irreverent, and without a word of English, to the safety of St. Mary's School in Peekskill, New York. From then until she returned to Haiti as a divorced mother of two, Jean-Claude never saw or contacted her again.

When Michèle resurfaced she was Madame Alix Pasquet, a wife of a man whose father had tried to kill Jean-Claude's father, and who had instead been killed by him. Michèle and the handsome playboy Pasquet married in 1973, and before their 1978 divorce, had two sons, Alix and Sasha. After the divorce Michèle returned to her parents with the children. In New York she had worked in the garment district for a firm that manufactured bedroom slippers for large-footed ladies. In Port-au-Prince she joined her sister Chantal as a secretary in their father's export business, controlling truck drivers and shipments of coffee and cement.

Off-hours, Michèle led an exhausting social life, passionate and high-living. As one affair after another ended in disappointment, Michèle plunged into deep depressions. Several times she toyed with suicide, once swallowing so many sleeping pills she had to be hospitalized.

Unstable, overwrought, and desperate, the young divorcée became more and more promiscuous. The young men of Haiti's snobbish elite seduced and were seduced, then crawled out of her bed to report. Michèle, destroying her own chances of acquiring a decent husband or of being accepted into top-drawer Haitian society, won instead a reputation for sexual prowess, as her ever-lengthening list of lovers talked about this back-street girl so common in the drawing room but so magnificently sensual in bed.

It was precisely this reputation that prompted Jean-Claude's friends to invite Michèle to the Duvalier ranch for an afternoon of swimming, partying, and easy casual sex. After eight years in power, Jean-Claude had all but exhausted Haiti's supply of willing and available women, and his friends were increasingly hard put to supply suitable new candidates.

Michèle accepted eagerly and brought her little sister Joan, the pretty, plump, dark-skinned girl so different from the other Bennetts that her true parentage was a subject of gossip. Dining at the ranch that afternoon, Michèle and Joan sat on either side of Jean-Claude, fondling him under the table with teasing fingers, each sister outdoing the other in her audacity.

Then, escalating to grown-up adventure, Jean-Claude and Michèle disappeared into a bedroom, where they spent hours together while Jean-Claude learned firsthand that Michèle deserved her reputation. When finally he had had enough he emerged from the bedroom, walked over to his friends, and in his uninflected nasal voice uttered the verdict that would have major implications not merely for his own life but for Haiti and its six million Haitians. "Hey, guys," said the President-for-Life with a little grin they had never seen before, "Do you know what? I've finally met my match!"

Their sex life was passionate and like nothing Jean-Claude had ever experienced. Michèle became more daring, and Jean-Claude could not hide the scratches all over his body. "I keep falling off my motorcycle," he used to stammer in reply to his friends' teasing. "She's tough," he added admiringly. "A very tough girl."

Michèle became his steady girlfriend, though he was not faithful to her. Fidelity was not part of his gang's code, and it never occurred to him that he couldn't also have as many other girls as he fancied. But Michèle, arrogant and imperious with this new boyfriend she knew loved her, became hysterical when she discovered he was cheating on her. She sped up to the ranch in her Simca Matra sports car and at the top of her voice shrieked at Jean-Claude, oblivious to the guards standing sentinel at the entrance. Then before the astonished Jean-Claude could reply, she reversed in a squeal of gears and hurtled back toward Port-au-Prince.

Jean-Claude, who had spent his life hearing how wonderful he was, took the incident to heart. "No more fooling around, guys," he told his friends. "I'm going to be faithful to Michèle." He laughed and shook his head. "She's dangerous!"

As she became more and more a permanent fixture at the ranch and at the house in Desprez, Jean-Claude's gang's uneasiness increased. What was he doing, dating this slut that everybody else had already slept with? She was so coarse that their own girlfriends refused to associate with her, and yet Jean-Claude, at the marriageable age of twenty-seven, seemed mesmerized. He even seemed to forget how he had met her, and how she and Joan had both caressed him under the table. In fact, Jean-Claude now referred to Michèle as if she were a saint, the purest of virgins who somehow had had two children. Still, he could not forbear mentioning her stupendous sexual drive, the heartbeat of their relationship.

Simone, less direct than her late husband, merely tried to exile the usurper, but when Macoutes arrived to escort Michèle to the airport, she refused to go with them. She flew into hysterics and phoned Jean-Claude, threatening, pleading, enraged. Simone had made a serious error. Jean-Claude confronted his mother angrily, then countermanded her order to have his girlfriend exiled. He loved his mother but he also deeply resented her domineering ways. Now, as Simone quickly discovered, in any conflict with Michèle, Michèle inevitably emerged the winner. As winter turned into spring, harsh words became the order of the day in the palace apartments, as the President and First Lady quarreled with increasing vehemence.

Michèle did not make things any easier. She put unrelenting pressure on Jean-Claude, her hatred as implacable as Simone's. In the little notebook in which she preserved details of all those who offended or slighted her, Simone's name figured in capital letters.

Marrying Michèle was the most important decision Jean-Claude had ever taken in his life. Virtually all his family, friends, and palace councillors opposed the idea. His mother spoke bitterly against Michèle, reminding Jean-Claude of her unsavory reputation, her discreditable family, and her two sons, Alix and Sasha, grandchildren of the man who had tried to assassinate Jean-Claude's father.

Palace advisers, both Duvalierist and Jeanclaudist, warned repeatedly that marrying a mulatto, especially that mulatto, would have political implications that would erode the immense popularity and power base they had painstakingly helped Jean-Claude build up.

But countering all these urgent appeals to wait, to reflect and consider, to do the manly thing and give her up, was Michèle herself, her greatest weapon the lithe little body that was so in tune with Jean-Claude's obese one that when they were together he forgot mother and sisters, forgot his father's Black Revolution and pogroms against Haiti's mulattoes, forgot friends and years of friendship, and knew only that he loved Michèle, could not live without Michèle, and must marry Michèle.

Government officials realized the strength of his determination and the futility of opposing it only after the March 1980 incident at the Hotel Mont Joli. UNESCO General Secretary Amadou Mata M'bow, whose wife was Haitian, was coming to visit the Citadelle to examine it and make an international plea for funds to restore it. Jean-Claude would accompany him on his three-day trip to Cap Haitien, the longest trip he ever made outside of Port-au-Prince during his entire regime. Chief of Protocol René Hippolyte reserved the entire Hotel Mont Joli for the Haitian and UNESCO dignitaries and arranged for Jean-Claude to stay in the lovely gingerbread home of Dr. Carlet Auguste, Haiti's ambassador to Germany.

A day before Jean-Claude left for Cap, the desk clerk at the Mont Joli was approached by a slender, heavily made-up young woman with stained teeth and eyebrows plucked into a surprised arch. She identified herself as Michèle Bennett and asked to check into the Honeymoon Suite. The clerk consulted the books and saw that Michèle had indeed made the reservation, but she had to explain that Protocol had taken over the whole hotel and, unfortunately, Michèle could not have the Honeymoon Suite or any other room. Michèle stood her ground and argued with increasing anger, and finally the clerk summoned Hippolyte to deal with her.

Hippolyte arrived with General Claude Raymond, then Haiti's Interior Minister, but on recognizing the notorious Michèle Bennett, Raymond cut short her explanation and shouted furiously in Creole, "You damned little slut! Do you think you can chase the President all over the country just like that? How dare a cheap trashy number like you hound him like that! Don't you understand that he's the President?"

Michèle understood only too well, and within minutes she was sobbing her tale of frustration and humiliation to the palace. Immediately Jean-Claude phoned the Mont Joli and ordered the clerk to give Michèle her room. Later, as the story spread around Cap Haitien, Ernest Bennett mentioned complacently to a few friends that in the not very distant future his daughter was going to be someone everyone in Haiti would have to reckon with.

The reckoning started even before. Within a week of Jean-Claude's return to Port-au-Prince from the M'bow visit, he fired René Hippolyte, Claude Raymond, and, for good measure, Information Minister Jean Narcisse, who had organized the tour. He also sacked two colonels at army General Headquarters for comments they had made and others had dutifully reported to the palace: *noiriste* Franck Romain had cursed Michèle and demanded to know what the hell Jean-Claude thought he was doing associating with that mulatto bitch. Colonel René Prosper too had condemned Michèle, not for the fairness of her skin, but for the scarlet of her reputation. If Jean-Claude's intimates had not clearly understood before how he felt about Michèle, they did now.

Though he had seldom bothered himself about his government's functioning, never attended cabinet meetings or displayed any enthusiasm for or even interest in affairs of state, Jean-Claude Duvalier was nonetheless the President-for-Life. When abruptly he shed the docility born of lethargy and asserted himself on this one crucial issue, Duvalierists and Jeanclaudists alike came to the unhappy realization that, thanks to their own efforts, he had the power to do whatever he wanted, including marrying Michèle Bennett. Furthermore the Duvalierist system left them with few options—kill him, oust him, or swallow his decision and pray that it could somehow be contained within the confines of Jeanclaudism.

It finally took Foreign Affairs Minister Edner Brutus, one of the leading Dinosaurs, to repair the breach. He went to old friend Simone and persuaded her to abandon her hopeless fight to stop the marriage. The bitterness the marriage was creating could end up splitting the palace into warring camps, and could even destroy the foundations of the Duvalier regime. "My best advice is to accept that Jean-Claude is going to marry Bennett, and to put as gracious a face on it as you can," he declared.

Simone, fighting for her political life, realized that only in accepting defeat could she even hope to salvage her position. She accepted her son's marriage and, in a gracious about-face, stood as the matron of honor.

Even after Simone gave up the battle, her mother, Clélie Ovide, tried to convince Jean-Claude to cancel his plans. Three weeks before the ceremony she sent for her grandson. "You loved Michèle Bennett when you were schoolchildren together," she reminded him. "But your own father was totally opposed to the girl because of her family, and you know that both he and the Bennetts made sure she was sent away so you'd never have anything to do with her again."

Jean-Claude listened politely, his face impassive. Then he leaned forward slightly and spoke with quiet emphasis. "Before I'd give up marrying Michèle, I'd resign as President, Gran," he said.

Michèle believed she knew what was really bothering Simone's old mother, and decided to try to win her over. Sitting prettily in the same chair Jean-Claude had sat in days earlier, Michèle said the magic words she thought Clélie wanted to hear. "I only want to marry Jean-Claude," Michèle said with wide-eyed insincerity. "I don't have the least desire to become First Lady." Clélie nodded and said nothing, but soon her eyes closed, and the houseboy hovering beside her came and ushered Michèle to the door, then scooped tiny Clélie up in his arms and carried her off to her bedroom.

April 29 was the date of no return, when Jean-Claude publicly committed himself to Michèle. Télé-Nationale and Radio National repeated the news three times: Mr. Jean-Claude Duvalier, President-for-Life, was engaged to marry Madame Michèle Bennett. The news hit most Haitians like a bombshell, as even the humblest peasants soon learned that the intended bride was a divorced mulatto and that her first husband had been the son of the same Alix Pasquet whose abortive invasion had inspired Papa Doc to create the Tonton Macoutes.

The couple faced but then quickly ironed out a few obstacles, the principal one the question of a Catholic wedding. Michèle was a divorced woman, and without an annulment from Rome could not be given Catholic rites. But dictatorships can achieve much that freer systems cannot, and not for nothing had Papa Doc cowed Rome and won the right to name Haitian bishops. As luck would have it, Michèle's mother's cousin, Wolff Ligondé, was the Duvalierist Archbishop of Port-au-Prince, so without much difficulty he was persuaded to marry the young couple himself in the Cathedral of Port-au-Prince.

The wedding, listed in the *Guinness Book of World Records* as one of the world's three costliest, was certainly the most spectacular Haiti had ever seen and a harbinger of things to come. It cost an estimated $3 million, which included $100,000 for a display of fireworks that even the poorest Port-au-Princien could gaze up into the night sky to marvel at, and an unspecified small fortune to Monsignor Ligondé to refurbish the decaying old cathedral in rich tropical tones of pale yellow and orange.

The wedding itself had more the flavor of Hollywood than of Haiti, as garish military costumes mingled with extravagant dresses, all in startling contrast to the black and white costumes of the bride and groom. Michèle wore an elaborate white Givenchy gown with an unbecoming headpiece that stood up around her head like a giant tattered snowflake and defeated the efforts of the hairdresser she had flown in from Paris.

The mass was sung, the vows exchanged, and Michèle emerged into the dark Port-au-Prince night to a thunderous 101-gun salute and a new career as Madame Michèle Bennett Duvalier.

Afterward the Duvaliers entertained friends, family, and officials at a lavish reception, while on the streets hundreds of thousands of the hungry poor were feted with free soup and rum and wore free T-shirts with a photo of the smiling Jean-Claude and Michèle on them. Michèle Bennett had accomplished a feat worthy of celebration: she had parlayed her exquisite legs, lustrous long hair, tarty good looks, and inspired sexuality into a home in the National Palace. Once the fireworks were over and the last champagne bottle uncorked, she had to take up the second stage of her campaign. She had won the battle to become Madame Jean-Claude Duvalier, but never for an instant did she forget that Simone and not she still held the title and position of First Lady of the Republic.

The wedding accelerated the decline of Duvalierism, at the same time reorganizing the governmental apparatus and radically changing its personnel. The marriage also reunited many of the old *noiristes* who had fallen from favor under Papa Doc with those who survived until the advent of Michèle. Clovis Désinor was the most important of them, and Michèle had early on understood that Désinor, the dean of *noiriste* intellectuality, would be either a powerful ally or a powerful enemy. Just before the wedding she had visited his big white house in Canapé Vert, embraced him affectionately, and called him "Papa Clo." When the wedding was announced she sent her mother, Aurore, and Désinor's onetime friend Simone Duvalier to invite him. Désinor saw through it all, countered flattery with gallantry, then sat down at his writing table and, on behalf of his entire family, refused his invitation to the wedding. "Politically, a stupid move," Désinor repeated privately to friends and family. "Jean-Claude simply hasn't enough education. A mulatto woman like that! Why couldn't he have found a decent black girl from his own class to marry?"

General Gérard Constant, former Papa Doc chief of staff fired just months before his friend Désinor, also disapproved of the wedding. Nevertheless he attended, slightly mollified to receive an invitation to the reception as well as the church. However, the once-honored chief of staff found himself excluded from the head table that had always been his accustomed place and was obliged to circulate like an ordinary citizen. Constant glowered, refused to eat, and then, hungry and in full sulk, insisted on leaving early. The wedding had made the regime another important enemy.

The wedding also focused popular discontent on Michèle, on her color, and her past. It was an easy step to declare that Jean-Claude had erred in marrying her, and then to add that Jean-Claude erred in many things, and that perhaps he ought not to be President at all. This line of thinking took years to develop, but its origins can be precisely dated—May 27, 1980, the day Jean-Claude took as his wife the hated Bennett.

In her big house, also in Canapé Vert, Clélie Ovide, Jean-Claude's maternal grandmother, was heartsick. She had not gone to the wedding, pleading illness and old age. But the real reason was that Clélie knew that Michèle would be the ruin of her family.

Dinois Jeanty, whom General St. Albin had brought to be her houseboy two years earlier, was just as distressed. Between himself and the fragile old lady a strong bond of affection had sprung up, for neither could speak a syllable of French nor read or write a single word, even in Creole. Often as he sat spoon-feeding her the mush that was all she could tolerate, Clélie would reminisce about her son-in-law, François, and shake her white head sadly as she thought of how angry he would be to see his Benjamin marrying that hussy Michèle Bennett. How wrong Jean-Claude was to choose a mulatto and not a Haitian for a wife, she would sigh, for it could only lead to destruction, and no amount of prayers and magic incantations could charm away the evil that Clélie foresaw was about to befall the Ovide family.

All Clélie's worst fears were realized. Before a year had passed Michèle had revenged herself on the Ovide family with a viciousness that stunned even Haitians hardened to their rulers' excesses. Meanwhile palace officials engaged professionals to give the President's new wife lessons in public behavior and personal grooming. They taught her not to lift her elbows and scratch her armpits. They rehearsed her in sitting with her legs crossed so that her underpants did not show. They insisted that she stop chewing on her sunglasses during long ceremonies and speeches. They convinced her that her overplucked eyebrows and excessive makeup were inappropriate.

Slowly the palace created for her an entirely different image, that of a small, sweet, simple girl, modest and unassuming, as devoted as her husband to the economic betterment of Haiti's long-suffering people.

To give credence to this lie, Michèle now accompanied Jean-Claude everywhere, including the provincial *tournées,* and the Jeanclaudist *L'Assaut* raved about her, "Simple and discreet as a smile, she chooses to accompany her husband to the provinces for her first post-nuptial *tournée.*" She was also beside her husband in every photo, her dresses tasteful, jewelry simple, lovely long hair pulled into severe buns or brushed into shining girlish tresses. "A simple heart, the depositary of Jeanclaudist humanism," enthused *L'Assaut.*

During the first months, while she and her mother-in-law were still fighting their terrible war for control of the palace, Michèle had to share Simone's public glory, sitting between her and Jean-Claude at ceremonial functions while photographs of these chilly sessions were captioned "Between mother and wife, the son embodies hope," and "the Wife, totally devoted to the Revolution, while the Mother's accents continue to nourish its flame." Behind the scenes Michèle was attacking on every flank, and before a year had elapsed she had the supreme satisfaction of being named First Lady while Simone was demoted to "The Guardian of the Duvalierist Revolution."

The in-palace warfare was incessant and obscene. Now safely married, Michèle turned into a living hell the palace that had been Simone's home for twenty-three years. She could never forget the older woman's attempt to exile her. She began by firing everyone she felt sided with Simone, and soldiers, maids, ministers, and public officials alike fell victim to her ax. Decades of tradition and memories were as ruthlessly destroyed as Michèle undertook her own renovations. She built elaborate living quarters and designed for herself a black-laquered office. She even remodeled Jean-Claude, forcing him on to a diet and forestalling any cheating by threatening the palace staff: "Anyone who provides him food will wish they'd never been born."

Next she pared away at all Jean-Claude's friends, and by July, two months after her marriage, she had booted out those he had been inseparable from for so many years. First, and unforgivably, they did not approve of her. Second, and just as unforgivably, Jean-Claude was too attached to them, and to Michèle this made them rivals. Even Ti-Pouche Douyon was banned, keeping his title and salary as private secretary but not his job. So from virtual exile in Miami, Ti-Pouche concentrated on building a personal fortune buying and selling Haitian art and acting as intermediary whenever Jean-Claude needed one for business transactions outside Haiti.

Her victims were legion, but Michèle reserved her full fury for Simone. Jean-Claude cheered her on, using her as a shield between himself and his mother. In fact, this was one of Michèle's many attractions—that since their first moments together she had always encouraged him to snatch back the authority his mother had usurped and he had surrendered. Just weeks before the marriage, and still triumphant over his handling of the Hotel Mont Joli incident, he had let Michèle show him a much more spectacular way to flex his political muscle and to show his mother—and himself—that he could and would defy her.

The incident involved Simone's good friend Madame Horace Coriolan, Tonton Macoute commandant of the mountain region of Kenscoff. When Madame Horace pitted herself against an idealistic, community-minded young priest, she unwittingly set the stage for a contest between Simone Duvalier, who was still the First Lady, on the one hand, and the President-for-Life, Jean-Claude Duvalier, and his fiancée, Michèle Bennett, on the other.

Father Occide Jean, better known as "Père Cico," was a thirty-four-year-old, blue-jeaned, Afro-coiffed Haitian who had been assigned to the backward Kenscoff parish in November 1975. Starting with nothing but the three pennies he found in the church treasury, he appealed to his parishioners' pride, encouraged them to set up self-help projects and cooperatives, and named these enterprises "Afè Nèg Koumbit"—Black People's Business Cooperative.

Before long Afè Nèg Koumbit bottled soft drinks, ran canteens and bus services, and provided refrigerated facilities and dormitories to vegetable sellers who had always before slept outside on the streets. As its people picked themselves up, Kenscoff too began to shine, with public trash cans and benches and cleaner streets than anywhere else in the notoriously filthy republic. Profoundly suspicious of this near-miraculous transformation of their mountaintop, Kenscoff's Duvalierists and Tonton Macoutes could find only one explanation—Père Cico, they charged publicly, must be a Communist.

Now that they had his number, it remained only to rid Kenscoff of him. At 7:30 on Wednesday, April 2, 1980, Père Cico was in his cassock in the confessional, hearing and absolving the sins of a long line of penitents. Suddenly four young women burst into the chapel and began to shout blasphemies and obscenities. Cico tried several times to persuade them to leave, but when they absolutely refused, his patience snapped, and he reached out and smacked one of the young intruders hard on her sassy mouth. A free-for-all ensued, and blood ran down several faces, including Cico's. Unorthodox behavior, undoubtedly, especially for a priest in his own chapel. Unforgivable too, it seemed, for the four girls were Madame Horace's nieces, sent expressly to disrupt Père Cico's religious ministrations.

Macoute-ridden Haiti stirred with excitement. Cico, the hippy priest who slapped wrongdoers, was recalled to the archbishopric of Port-au-Prince for punishment. Madame Horace, relying on her powerful friend Simone Duvalier, celebrated in smug victory in Kenscoff.

But the unheard-of happened, and Jean-Claude Duvalier intervened, ordering Archbishop Wolff Ligondé to send Cico back up to Kenscoff. Home again, the triumphant Cico publicly forgave those who had trespassed against him: "Forgive them, O Lord!" he cried to his cheering congregation. "Forgive them, for they know not what they do."

Down in Port-au-Prince, however, Michèle knew what she was doing, and in championing Cico over Simone's friend Madame Horace, she had scored an important psychological victory for Jean-Claude against his mother's power. Just to make sure everyone understood the point, she sent her husband-to-be up to Kenscoff, where he publicly toured Afè Nèg Koumbit facilities, shook hands with Père Cico, and spelled the end to Madame Horace's power.

In an ironic aftermath the newly wed Duvaliers befriended Cico, encouraging his projects so enthusiastically that he became their greatest ally. He even joined the Tonton Macoutes on Tonton Macoute Day, paraded publicly in Macoute blue, saluting Jean-Claude and spouting Duvalierisms as fluently as Scripture.

At the end Simone Duvalier's downfall was anticlimactic. She simply gave up, defeated by Michèle and the daily degradation. The blue-and-green African parrot was a case in point. After she imported it Michèle taught it to speak, then installed it outside Simone's bedroom so that every daybreak the older woman woke to the parrot's raucous "Fuck you! Fuck you!"

Marie-Denise also hated Michèle, but ultimately even she deserted her mother. Years earlier, Marie-Denise's husband, Max Dominique, had left her to live with her sister Simone in Miami. He had also retained control of the lucrative cocoa-exporting monopoly Papa Doc had granted Marie-Denise. Bitter and humiliated, Marie-Denise had fought and failed to regain the rights to the cocoa trade, and in her losing battle with her ex-husband, her mother had sided against her.

Simone had also failed to support her eldest daughter in other palace dramas, and now, in the most critical power struggle ever, Marie-Denise preferred to throw in her lot with her brother, even if that meant accepting Michèle Bennett as his wife.

Simone, stoic in grief, maintained stony silences and finally understood that life as she had known it was over. At last, before she was demoted from First Lady to Guardian of the Duvalierist Revolution, she packed her belongings and moved to the lonely peace of her house in Canapé Vert, where she deteriorated so badly that Clélie had to send food to her until Clélie herself died on May 12, 1981.

Voluntary exile to Canapé Vert was not victory enough for Michèle. Now Simone had to suffer more. Michèle attacked just where old Clélie had feared, and she swooped down on Ovide people, sending soldiers and Macoutes to escort them first to the *cachots* of Dessalines Barracks to meditate and suffer, and then to the airport into exile. The second First Lady was thorough, and by the time she had finished, Simone had endured the exile of ninety-six Ovide family members, every relative she had in Haiti.

On the day Adèle Ovide, the last of the ninety-six, was forced out of Haiti, a bedraggled Simone made her final trip to the airport. She wore no makeup or jewelry, and her dress was as plain as a housemaid's. Nobody greeted or saluted her and she stood in silence, watching as Adèle too disappeared into the waiting room. Only the airport chief, Ti-Son Mackintosh, walked up and bowed his respects. Then, forlorn and beaten, the Defender of the Duvalierist Revolution directed her chauffeur to the Dessalines Barracks, where she got out of her blue Peugeot and presented herself to an embarrassed SD Chief Colonel Jean Valmé.

"You've sent away all my family," Simone said quietly. "I'm the last one left, so I'm sure you must want me next. I'm saving you the trouble of coming for me. Here I am. You can arrest me right here and now."

Valmé, embarrassed and shocked, called the palace and explained to Jean-Claude that his mother was sitting on a bench in the police station demanding to be arrested. "Let her sit there," Jean-Claude said shortly.

Valmé returned and told the elderly woman to remain where she was. Hours later, as she waited immobile and silent on the hard wood bench, Valmé received another call. "You can let her go now," Jean-Claude ordered. "Tell her to go home."

Simone went home, while Michèle stayed in the palace with her husband. The contest was over. Slowly, as months crept into years, the Ovides made timid sorties back home, and the number on foreign soil dwindled. Simone began to eat again, and even made infrequent visits to the palace. Gradually life for the Ovide family returned to normal. But few other Haitians had this luxury of secluding themselves to brood in lonely despair, for their lives went on and they kept constant company with *la misère*.

On August 5 Haiti was struck by a hurricane that meteorologists soon baptised "Allen the Goliath." Allen had the fastest landspeed measured in two hundred years, and in Haiti left more wreckage than even Hazel in 1954.

Allen hit first along the Dominican border and raced toward the south, uprooting coffee and cacao trees replanted after Hazel had destroyed them in 1954, drowning fishermen, leaving 835,000 people homeless, killing 220 humans and thousands of small domestic animals, so that the stench of decomposing carcasses polluted the damp air for weeks afterward.

To despairing Haitians, God had opened up the skies and pounded them in merciless retribution for the evil and corruption that stalked their land. More and more, they dreamed of leaving it.

By the time Jean-Claude married Michèle, about 1.5 million Haitians lived as expatriates, a number equal to 25 percent of those in Haiti. The exodus had begun long before Duvalier, in response to the hard life at home and the relative ease of finding menial work abroad. But under the Duvaliers the numbers soared as Haitians fled death, whether in the form of torture, execution, or sheer starvation. Of these, three hundred thousand endured only marginally better existences in the Dominican Republic, where 90 percent of all cane cutters were Haitian. Another thirty thousand had little more to be thankful for in the Bahamas, where one-time warm welcomes had turned to overt hatred for these desperate men and women. More fortunate were the four hundred thousand who had reached the United States, and the smaller numbers settled in various other parts of the globe: forty thousand in Canada, six thousand in France, and six thousand throughout Africa.

But touching foreign soil was by no means a final solution for the world's newest nomads, because for hundreds of thousands forcible repatriation was always around the corner, except in the Dominican Republic, where enslavement was a much likelier hazard. According to heartrending testimony from hundreds who escaped, stories corroborated by the London-based Anti-Slavery Society, Dominican soldiers routinely rounded up illegal Haitians for forced labor in the sugar fields, the core of the nation's economy.

Captured, they earned $1.50 a day, from which employers often deducted the cost of miserable meals. They slept on the floor and, in the words of a Dominican foreman who used them, "lived like animals." The huge cane plantations were surrounded with barbed wire, armed guards, and dogs, and the cutters could not leave until the season was over. Even then they were often released without enough money to return to Haiti, trapped in this inhospitable country that despised their color and called them "Congos," the lowest of the low.[22]

Haitian life in the Bahamas was scarcely better. The ongoing hostility of Bahamian citizens and authorities had provoked two concerted attempts to rid the Commonwealth of Haitians, once in 1974 and again in 1978 when they were hunted down in the streets, imprisoned, beaten, then deported. At any given time in Nassau's Fox Hill prison, 900 to 1,500 Haitians occupied cells designed for 600, and as fast as inmates were deported, new ones took their places. Even for Haitians resident for as long as twenty-five years, there was no security. Bahamian-Haitian tensions escalated, and in November 1980 came to a head in the Cayo Lobos tragedy.

Ironically, the tragedy began on the mystically significant twenty-second of September 1980, the twenty-third anniversary of Duvalierism. On that day 116 Haitian men, women, and children who could endure no more poverty and hopelessness clambered into a derelict boat and set sail for Miami. Forty kilometers off the coast of Cuba the boat began to list, and its captain managed to steer it toward a tiny island where its frightened passengers spilled out. This was Cayo Lobos, a deserted appendage of the Bahamian Commonwealth. Moaning, hungry, and thirsty, the boat people realized Cayo Lobos was less hospitable even than Haiti, without coconuts, fruits, shelter, or water, with nothing but blazing sun and parched soil.

That night their captain sneaked off to the boat and sailed away, abandoning his charges. One died, then another; soon five were dead. In early October, Gilner Gérard could take no more and plunged into the sea. He swam toward death, but miraculously, a fishing boat saw and rescued him. On October 23 the Bahamian government returned Gérard to Haiti, where his horrifying description of his compatriots' plight was carried on Télé-Nationale and on several radio stations.

The news rocked the Haitian public, but not Jean-Claude and his government—the Bahamian government had alerted Haiti, and when no response was forthcoming, notified them twice more. Americans flying in a small pleasure craft had spotted the Cayo Lobos survivors, and had not merely informed the Bahamian government, but also returned to drop down boxes and cans of rations, which saved the Haitians' lives. Meanwhile, in Haiti, the Jeanclaudist government finally responded to the Bahamians: "We have no boats to rescue these people. Do with them what you will."

The Bahamians did just that, arriving in a coast guard cutter to rid even this desolate portion of Bahamian soil of the people the editor of the *Bahamas Guardian* called "the pariahs of the Caribbean." But these particular pariahs had pulled up and sold their last stakes to leave Haiti. They refused to board and stoned the cutter. When the Bahamians landed anyway the Haitians linked arms in a human chain and stood the ground that was not even theirs. The Bahamians launched tear gas, until the weakened Haitians writhed on the ground. Then they beat them, clubbing them with machine guns, rifle butts, nightsticks. Finally the Haitians were shoved onto the cutter. That was how it happened, and a CBS film crew was on the spot, filming each horror-filled minute for that night's newscast. On November 16, accompanied by another Bahamian warship to make sure they did not escape, the Cayo Lobos boat people were returned to Haiti.

The Jeanclaudist government, furious and humiliated that these wretches had exposed to the world the depths of their misery, swallowed its rage, invited foreign journalists to greet the Cayo Lobos survivors, then planted fake survivors, who strode down the gangplank shouting, "Vive Jean-Claude Duvalier! Duvalier for life!" Later the real survivors were whisked away, several on stretchers, many tubercular, all in poor condition. To begin their lives over again, announced the government spokesman, each would be given $40.

For conscientious Haitians, the Cayo Lobos tragedy was a breaking point. Grégoire Eugène headlined the November 21 issue of his party's *Fraternité,* "Special: The Cayo Lobos Affair, A National Shame, Will

Not Be Filed Away," and he followed this on November 27 with "Cayo Lobos: the File Remains Open Forever."

Eugène launched the most direct, bitter, and reasoned attack on Jean-Claude's government ever seen inside Haiti. The government should have leapt to the rescue, requisitioning boats if need be, and "that does not exclude the presidential yacht," Eugène added.

Eugène also sounded the alarm of what he called "a certain disquieting Haitianophobia," akin to anti-Semitism, which the Bahamians and Dominicans no longer bothered to hide. "If we don't watch out," Eugène warned, "we'll find ourselves one day or another confronting a massacre, a re-play of the Dominican Vespers of 1937. . . . Doesn't the sad memory of those Vespers make the Haitian government tremble?" Indeed, "Might Haitianophobia so exasperate the Bahamians as well that they resort to murdering them?"

Eugène did not rest his case. The responsibility for Haiti's boat people, who by their sheer volume provoked the United Nation's intervention and caused considerable problems for the unwilling host countries, was Haiti's own. The solution, he spelled out, "is to provide means to allow Haitians to live a decent life in their own country."

Jean-Claude and his councillors read with disbelief. The kick of the champagne they had downed in wild celebration of Carter's November 4 defeat was still a bubbling memory, the climax to months of a repressive wave extinguishing the last breaths of liberalization. Eugène and his colleagues had failed to learn the lesson recently administered to other outspoken journalists. The time had come to dispense with lessons. On November 28, the day after his second article appeared in *Fraternité,* Macoutes arrived at Eugène's house and took him to Dessalines Barracks. Then on December 2 he was driven to the airport and forced onto a plane for New York. The post-Carter, Jeanclaudist crackdown had begun.

The crackdown ended a troubled period when protesters had still dared take to the newspapers, the airwaves, the streets. Disturbing antigovernment, antiauthoritarian outbreaks had erupted in Cap Haitien, Cayes, and Gonaives. But not for long.

"I alone can blow the winds of liberalization," Jean-Claude had boasted. "No one else can be put in power to blow the winds more strongly than I do. Never." Duvalier stripped Haiti of virtually all its most outspoken critics, its journalists, its political and syndicalist leaders. He and Michèle now sat firmly at the helm, and the rich became richer, the poor poorer. And with escalating speed, the nation rushed along its calamitous route toward disaster.

Despite the risk, Haitians in growing numbers joined the ranks of the boat people, a word now in full currency in Creole and pronounced "bot pipple." Transporting them had become a thriving business, with the tiniest, leakiest vessels cramming wretched pioneers into their hulls for prices ranging from $100 to $2,000, payable in advance. For the privilege of attempting to sneak into a foreign country to pick fruit, sweep floors, or scrub toilets, entire families pitched in and sold land, animals, all their belongings as a final investment to send one family member to save their collective life.

A deal was struck, and for his new life in Miami the escapee bundled up a change of clothing, a Bible, a precious photograph, a bottle of water, stalks of sugar cane and dry sheets of cassava bread, the Haitian matzoh. Then, in the dead of night, he climbed into a boat with hundreds of others, all praying God they would fall prey to neither the fat, knowing sharks that followed their passage, the American patrols with their radar, or the captains who once on the high sea killed all their passengers, dumped them overboard, and returned to Haiti, where more victims lined up to pay for a passage out.

The larger freighters, forty to seventy feet long, usually made for the Bahamas before striking out for Florida. If they arrived, their passengers simply jumped off and swam ashore. This sophisticated transport cost between $2,000 and $3,000, putting it out of the reach of most Haitians, who do not earn that much in a lifetime. The smaller sailboats, charging less, sailed west to nearby Cuba, where the Cubans—to be rid of them and also to annoy the Americans—fed and watered them, repaired their boats, then pointed out the Florida coast.

No one could calculate the chances of surviving, for no one knew how many set out, and the Americans had only the roughest notion of how many arrived. But compassionate American Coast Guard personnel wrote accounts of empty boats they encountered, their passengers all drowned, and of boats with specially constructed cubbyholes where crews hid their wretched cargo whenever they ran into American search vessels, cubbyholes from which few children ever emerged alive. And for those who beat the odds and landed alive, another fate awaited them— arrest, jail, repatriation.

As more and more boat people poured in, Americans began to feel twinges of Haitianophobia. Floridians especially resented this influx of helpless blacks, and though official U.S. policy toward light-skinned and literate Cubans was very warm, resistance to the fleeing Haitians increased. With Ronald Reagan in Washington, much stricter measures against illegal Haitian immigrants were taken.

Arrests and detention of large numbers of them became so commonplace that in Florida, where 23,000 Haitians entered illegally between January 1980 and September 1981, and an average of 1,259 per month during 1981, they even had their own prison, Krome Detention Center. The administration defined the Haitians as economic refugees ineligible for residency and jailed them until deportation orders could be processed. In Krome thousands waited, depressed and demoralized, while an overflow of nearly eight hundred were transferred to Fort Allen in Puerto Rico, which had agreed to accommodate them.

Fort Allen was a tropical nightmare. Twelve-foot-high chain-link fences surrounded them, with large fishhooks embedded in the wire so that any Haitian foolish enough to attempt escape would be ripped to shreds. The Haitians were housed in canvas tents, twenty in each one. They were protected from mosquitoes by torn screening and had no chairs, tables, closets, lockers, hangers, racks, or even pegs to store their meager possessions. Sanitary facilities consisted of cold-water sinks and showers and communal toilets, outside the tents, behind sheet metal.

Fort Allen boiled in the sun, and without trees or grass or shelter, the Haitians either sweltered or else sought refuge in the stifling tents. They ate adequately, but some of the men developed gynecomastia, or enlarged breasts. New York Congressman Robert Garcia remarked after his visit there, "The only difference between Attica and this place is that at one you have concrete walls and at the other barbed wire." Added Congresswoman Mary Rose Oakar, "[Fort Allen] was very much like a concentration camp. These poor people are living, caged animals. Their souls are being taken away."

In his concern to find a solution to the problem, Florida's young Governor Bob Graham traveled to Port-au-Prince to discuss it personally with Haiti's young President Jean-Claude. "Extremely positive," Jean-Claude described their encounter, at which Graham conveyed an ultimatum from the U.S. government: stanch the flow or else permit us to do so, if necessary by force of arms. Florida's economy was reeling under the influx of Cubans and Haitians. International political considerations forced them to admit the Cubans. Against the Haitians, however, the Americans could and did do battle.

Tragedy lent them ammunition, as world repugnance against the boat-people phenomenon grew. This was fueled when thirty-seven Haitians were drowned within yards of shore at Fort Lauderdale, and on TV screens everywhere the world could see their naked bodies lying still and contorted on the hot white sand. Rumors that the boat-people business was as inhumane as Haiti itself were confirmed with the revelation that two captains murdered ninety of their passengers, throwing them overboard to the sharks.

In September 1981, the month before these latest Haitian scandals, U.S. policy had been formally translated into a bilateral U.S.-Haitian agreement authorizing the Americans to patrol the waters between the two republics and to intercept and return to Haiti any illegal immigrants, using armed force if they had to. The Haitian Migrant Interdiction Operation (HMIO), which cost the Americans about $2 million monthly, employed a full-time coast guard cutter in the Windward passage between Haiti and Cuba. It also involved air support and used helicopters deployed from the cutter, fixed-wing HU-25A Falcon jets and HC-130 Hercules aircraft based in Guantanamo Bay.

Though the agreement was bilateral, the Haitian navy was too poorly equipped and trained to assist. Its patrol boats were too small for offshore patrolling and it lacked coastal stations and communication. As a result its sole function was to assume custody of seized vessels once the Americans had captured them.

In Haiti the Jeanclaudist government publicly praised the boat people for their courage and enterprise, not entirely hypocritically—after all, those Haitians who did manage to work abroad sent home about $100 million yearly to their destitute relatives. Diasporic Haitians were the nation's most important source of foreign exchange, and did more than all foreign-aid programs combined to help their people, in some cases keeping entire villages alive.

On the other hand, the boat people's wretchedness was a humiliation and a slap in the face of Jeanclaudism, so in typical fashion the regime struck out, blaming everything but its own dismal failures for the crisis. Spokesmen blamed the Americans for not issuing entry visas, and exploitive boat owners were accused of selling seats in unsafe vessels. They even suggested that many boat people were not Haitians but actually disguised Cubans trying to infiltrate the U.S. to implant communism there. Everyone was guilty, except the innocent government of Haiti.

The next ploy was to shock would-be boat people, and on November 6 the corpses of twenty-three of those drowned at Fort Lauderdale were repatriated, and on Jean-Claude's personal instructions the funeral salon was opened to the general public. From everywhere people streamed in to look, especially peasants from the main embarkation points hoping to identify missing relatives.

"Their faces were not gay," reported the Jeanclaudist bulletin *Information*. "Gleams of pity and sadness etched their faces and on others was despair, shame, anguish and horror of the future." Every one of the twenty-three corpses went to prove, *Information* concluded, that Jeanclaudism's policy of economic development was the right one, and all Haitians should make common cause in supporting it. If viewing corpses was not lesson enough, the government also greeted some repatriated Haitians harshly, imprisoning and beating them, often fatally.

Despite the Jeanclaudist "economic revolution," Haiti's economy had never been worse. Crop failures and meager harvests were so common that despite importation of foreign rice and other foodstuffs, people continued to starve. But even in the face of such misery, the worst aspects of Jeanclaudism were in full operation.

Haitians now paid triple for their cooking oil because of a monopoly scam that netted millions for a few in Jean-Claude's favored circle, and much worse lay in store for the people. By 1981 the eradication of all Haitian pigs was just around the corner, and on July 21, 1981, the Haitian government signed a contract with the Inter-American Institute for Cooperative Agriculture (IICA) to organize and execute the U.S., Canada, and Mexico-funded Program for the Eradication of Porcine Swine Fever and Development of Pig Raising (PEPPADEP).

Haitians had an estimated 1.2 million pigs, degenerate, long-legged, long-snouted descendants of those imported by centuries-earlier European settlers. Pigs were peasants' animals, and even the poorest raised one or two. They required no piggery or special care and lived tied under trees in the meanest courtyard. They ate anything and everything and turned even human excrement into protein and fat. They required little water. They developed slowly, reaching their full weight of eighty to a hundred pounds in two years, and birthed only a few piglets. But as the traditional oil-fried, spiced *griot*, their meat was Haiti's favorite, and their high-calorie fat content gave calorie-deprived Haitians nutritional benefits as well.

These Creole pigs were also the backbone of the peasant economy, the "bank" they drew on for life's emergencies: October school fees, illnesses, weddings, baptisms, and deaths. A pig was slaughtered and sold, another crisis averted, and groveling about in the dry mud courtyard a piglet was munching banana peels and garbage, providing for another tomorrow.

PEPPADEP, the program to eradicate every last one of these Creole pigs, would be the most devastating blow struck impoverished Haiti, but until there actually were no more pigs, the consequences of PEPPADEP were neither understood nor predicted.

In face of all this misery, Haiti's newest Duvalier decided to launch her own program of social works, an ambitious attempt to alleviate at least a small part of her people's suffering. On January 15, her birthday, Michèle announced the creation of the Michèle B. Duvalier Foundation, which would build clinics, orphanages, schools, and a hospital. It sounded virtuous, for in her first flush of power Michèle was sincere in wanting to make an impact on her country. Within a few weeks of her marriage she visited the Reverend Luc Nerée's Aid to Children headquarters and asked for a tour and detailed information as to how he had single-handedly accomplished so much.

"God says, 'Suffer the little children to come unto me,'" Nerée told her, "and that is just what we do." Every day special buses brought children to the compound, where they sat down to a nourishing meal of rice and beans or macaroni and cheese. If they were sick, the clinic charged only a minimal fee, and three staff doctors and twelve nurses and aides provided all treatment and medicine necessary, saving hundreds of lives. But Nerée also sought to develop self-respect along with good health in the children and required them to appear scrubbed and brushed and groomed. Since most owned only raggedy clothes, he had semiannual distributions, with each girl receiving two dresses and each boy two shirts and two pairs of pants. Once a year they all received what was even more precious, a new pair of shoes, and at Christmas, carefully wrapped gifts of crayons and coloring books, balloons and other wonders contributed by American Baptists.

Michèle was so touched, she contributed $2,000 on the spot and gave Nerée her palace number to call whenever he had a problem. Twice he ran out of sugar, and each time the palace delivered sacks of it hours after his calls. Michèle returned several times to visit Aid to Children and impressed Nerée as utterly sincere in her concern for him, his work, and the five hundred children in his care.

Despite her interest in this work, Michèle's most outstanding and expensive charitable project—her Bon Repos Hospital—was not originally designed for children. Instead she had toyed with Haitian Cancer Society president Dr. Chevalier's suggestion that she build a private operating wing, the best in the whole Caribbean, for her own personal use, for any surgery she might need. The idea attracted her, but when she mentioned it to Health Minister Dr. Gérard Désir, he ridiculed it and warned her that the entire country would laugh at her and Jean-Claude if she did such a preposterous thing. Why not build a charitable hospital instead? he urged her. Her sons' pediatrician, Yves Jean-Pierre, agreed, adding that it should be for children. Dr. Désir approved but proposed a maternity wing too, so that the mothers would have prenatal care as well. Michèle liked the notion, and her famous Bon Repos Hospital was conceived.

But it was not until 1983 that the scandal-plagued institution opened its doors. Until then Michèle busied herself with social works, throwing herself so wholeheartedly into visiting the schools and clinics she patronized that no less saintly a personage than Mother Theresa praised her to the heavens, saying, "I have never seen the poor people being so familiar with their heads of state as they were with her. It was a beautiful lesson for me. I've learned something from it."

On the tenth anniversary of Jeanclaudism, Jean-Claude presided over a nation of millions who tilled eroded soil, relied on capricious gods, and struggled against corruption, injustice, and incompetence.[23] His country was such a catastrophe that many Haitians and foreign observers privately predicted his regime's downfall. But Jean-Claude knew better than that, and in his evaluation of a decade of government found nothing but good things to say. In fact, as befitted the exponent of the New Testament of Duvalierism, he used the occasion to introduce the Credo of Jeanclaudism.

"I believe in Jeanclaudism living and wise," the litany began.

Nourished with the eternal philosophy of the illustrious Father of the Revolution, enlightened by the years of experience of an attentive mother, whipped on by the dynamic goodness of an intelligent wife always lovingly drawn towards the lot of the humble . . . I believe in Jeanclaudism, democratic and strong, capable of confronting subversion and installing peace and liberty on Haitian soil. . . . I believe in Jeanclaudism, the firm spirituality of the new era, which makes hearts beat, swells chests and harmonizes the national song in a single choir to cry out, "Long Live Jean-Claude Duvalier for Life!"

10 MARRIAGE

BERNARD SANSARICQ DID NOT PROFESS THE CREDO OF
Jeanclaudism. Deuteronomy's chilling "Punishment for the sins of
the fathers shall be visited unto the third or fourth generations of
those who hate me" more aptly expressed his sentiments. That was why
Sansaricq, from the Cayes branch of the Sansaricq family massacred in
the Vespers of Jérémie in 1964, spent January plotting another armed
invasion of Haiti.

Sansaricq lived in Fort Lauderdale, Florida, and operated a gas station in nearby Davie, but this was a sideline to his obsessive attempts to
overthrow Duvalier, first the father and now the son. Sansaricq was also
a skilled anti-Duvalierist fund-raiser, and by January 1981 had amassed
a large enough sum for an invasion attempt. Some of it had been donated by anti-Duvalierist Haitians and Americans, the rest by investment-
minded companies to whom he had promised mineral rights as soon as
he conquered the republic and set himself up in power.

Sansaricq and his band of thirty-nine moved from Florida to South
Caicos, where he leaked his plans to the press. Alarmed and annoyed,
Turks and Caicos officials ordered him to leave. Sansaricq hired a six-
seater seaplane and in two hops transported eight of his men to the
beautiful Haitian island of La Tortue, better known both now and in
pirate days as Tortuga, where British buccaneers kept women, wine, and
supplies.

Tortuga is six miles offshore from Port-de-Paix, an odd tactical
choice for launching a mainland invasion. Many suggested that Sansaricq selected it precisely because he never intended a genuine invasion,

merely a grandstanding gesture to justify money already raised and spent and as a tool for future fund-raising campaigns. This supposition was strengthened when Sansaricq himself refused to board the boat he rented for the twenty-five men still on South Caicos. One of the twenty-five, Jean-Claude Bernard, whose cousin Blondel Bernard was on Tortuga, took matters into his own hands, waving his .45 at Sansaricq until he reluctantly climbed aboard. Bernard himself, thoroughly disgusted, then defected and returned to Miami.

Near Tortuga, Sansaricq pulled out his own gun, shot and disabled the motor, and punctured the floorboards so that the *Caicos Cloud* began to take in water. The ruse worked, the men had to radio an SOS, and Sansaricq watched thankfully as the U.S. Coast Guard cutter *Gallatin*, patrolling eight kilometers north, sent them handcuffed to Miami, where they arrived and were arrested, and their thirty-three guns, twenty-two pipe bombs, and 5,320 rounds of ammunition were confiscated. Sansaricq was soon released on $600,000 bail, furnished by grateful supporters, and he returned to his anti-Duvalierist rhetoric and renewed fund-raising.

But there were still eight Haitian rebels abandoned on Tortuga, and these determined to fight it out, even to the death. Their leader was Richard Brisson, from a mulatto professional family. Another was Wilner Parisse, who enjoyed the reputation of being possessed by a *loa* and hence invulnerable. The rebels began well, commandeering a jeep from Canadian missionary Father Chabot and forcing him to drive them to the village of Hauts Palmistes, 1,200 feet atop the crest of a mountain. Secure in their mountain perch, the rebels waited.

Alarmed that the invaders had not been dislodged, Jean-Claude dispatched Léopard commander Colonel Acédius St. Louis to reinforce the regular troops and Macoutes. But so nervous were the soldiers that they fired at everything that moved, including one another, and the deaths they caused were all on their own side. Then one of the rebels felt hungry and sent a peasant to fetch him some bread. The man returned with a squad of twenty Léopards, but Wilner Parisse leapt out and shot one dead. The troops panicked; Parisse was supernatural and they could not overpower him. Soldiers begged off sick and a dozen had to be sent home.

Finally Jean-Claude called on his assistant chief of staff, Brigadier General Henri Namphy, then weekending at his country retreat in Camp Perrin. Namphy summoned his personal friend and comrade in arms

Colonel Williams Regala and mustered soldiers from the Thirty-sixth Tactical Division of the Dessalines Barracks.

In Tortuga, Namphy ordered his men to surround the invaders, to block off all paths of escape, and then sit down in the shade and play cards. Attacking up the mountain was futile and would cost lives. Prowling around would do the same. But waiting until the boiling sun, hunger, and thirst drove the rebels out of their protected hiding place was guaranteed to work.

On January 21 five of the eight emerged shooting, maddened by the scorching heat, and the soldiers easily killed three of them. One more was beaten to death by peasants. A group of Léopards captured Parisse, wounded in the leg, and took him to a hut where they fed him spaghetti. As Parisse ate he smiled at his captors and said, "Listen to those drums. It's been a long time since I heard my people's drums." He added, taking another bite of spaghetti, "I know you're going to kill me, but even at the end we have to enjoy ourselves, isn't that so?"

A Léopard grabbed him in a stranglehold and with his other hand stabbed him over and over until Parisse fell to the ground. The three other rebels in Hauts Palmistes surrendered and were taken to Port-au-Prince. There Jean-Claude ordered them to the palace, where he personally questioned them, had them tortured and executed. Interior Minister Edouard Berrouet issued a communiqué advising the Haitian public that all eight invaders had been killed on Tortuga.

Equally untrue was the official death toll on the government side, given as two Léopards and one Macoute. The truth was, many Léopards and Macoutes were killed, all but one shot in error by their own side as they thrashed about on the mountain.

On January 26, to give credence to the official lie, a huge state funeral was held for Eliézar Damas, the one acknowledged Macoute casualty. High-ranking army and VSN officers, Jean-Claude's latest cabinet ministers, and top government officials all attended. But the death they really mourned was not Macoute Damas's but the myth of the Léopards' superiority, for in their first real action, against eight trapped civilians, the Léopards had performed miserably, a disgrace to the national pride.

The Sansaricq fiasco claimed many victims, exposed dangerous incompetence in the Léopards, and sparked hopes in disillusioned Haitians that other, more committed and serious rebels might appear. They did, but were never strong enough to dislodge Jean-Claude. Ultimately,

Jeanclaudism did itself far more damage than all these failed quixotic missions together.

The comical-sounding PEPPADEP was the name of Haiti's next tragedy. Nationwide porcine blood tests had showed 22.86 percent of Haiti's pigs infected with ASF, an epidemic rate. The Creole pig had to die.

The slaughter began in May 1982 and lasted eighteen months. Creole-speaking American veterinarian Dr. Bob Amelingmeier headed PEPPADEP field operations under orders of Canadian Dr. Guy Meilleur and Haitian Dr. Robert Joseph. Four hundred young French-Canadians and Americans, divided into fourteen brigades, with 110 vehicles, were responsible for registering every pig in even the remotest hamlet, paying $40 for a large pig, $20 for a medium, and $5.00 for a piglet in cash, which in the safe Haitian countryside they carted about in wads in their backpacks. Of an estimated 1.2 million pigs, PEPPADEP killed 380,000, paying out $9.5 million for the right to slaughter them. Most others were slaughtered by their owners, who hoped to sell them for more than the PEPPADEP rate.

Unlike the neighboring Dominicans, who defended their pigs with violence, the Haitians resisted by hiding them away in mountains, in caves, in pits dug deep and covered with banana leaves and vegetation. Presidential Guard Commandant General Gracia Jacques openly kept scores on his farm. Most surviving pigs were owned by Macoute chiefs, in Haiti above the law and untouchable.

In Cayes-Jacmel *houngan* Lucien Charles had already decided that PEPPADEP would not touch a single one of his herd of 150 pigs. He knew, as everyone did, that many peasants trustingly led their pigs to slaughter, then received no compensation. He had no intention of being one of them.

PEPPADEP did not get Charles's pigs, the gods did. In his great central courtyard he made ritual preparations and the sacrifices began. Long into the nights and days that followed, his peristyle reverberated with the sounds of Petro drums and chanting, and out in the courtyard the wonderful fragrance of roasting pig tantalized the hundreds who came to serve the gods and gorge themselves as they communed with them through human appetite.

Afterward, in his five other peristyles, Charles sacrificed scores more, until his herd was eradicated, and he wondered what punishments the gods would wreak on him next November, when during the important ceremonies for Baron Samedi he had no black pigs to offer him.

The effects of PEPPADEP snowballed long after the project ended in December 1983. Haiti's disastrous economy continued to nosedive. The agricultural sector in particular had been hard hit by Allen the Goliath, but there already existed several critical problems: erosion and the loss of topsoil; lack of infrastructure, technical and financial backup to rationalize irrigation, drainage, and transportation projects, the need to stock essential products; and demographic density, with as many as five hundred people crammed onto each square kilometer. "Agriculture employs 80 percent of our people," Jean-Claude declared solemnly in a speech to the Legislative Assembly, "but its participation in the GNP is only 35 percent."

Ernest Bennett rushed economic disaster forward at an even faster clip. Though agriculture was crucial to the economy and to Haiti's foreign earnings, nobody stopped coffee exporter Bennett from diverting from the state and into his own pockets every cent he could. Once Michèle was ensconced in the palace, her father not only muscled his way to domination of the coffee market but he enjoyed exemption from the export duties that were such an important source of revenue to the Haitian government, and one that all other exporters always paid.

That the Bennetts would go to amass fortunes on the backs of a desperate people is as much a lesson in human depravity as it was the final nail in the coffin of the dictatorship. One out of dozens of illustrations is the Mexican oil scandal.

In 1982 Mexico sold Haiti, on terms more generous than most foreign aid, $11 million of crude oil repayable over twenty years, with several years of grace. Haiti's only immediate obligation was to refine it, and so tankers were sent to the refineries of Curacao. But Bennett, seeing in the Mexican crude oil the chance to make easy millions, intercepted it, then negotiated and sold it to South Africa, oil-starved by an Arab embargo, for $7 million.

The Black Republic had now lost her precious oil to white-ruled South Africa, but not her debt to Mexico. Interpol became involved after South Africa paid its benefactor Bennett by transfer. The bank receiving the order alerted Interpol, which in turn demanded to know the reason for the transfer of such an enormous sum. The scandal became public, and Interpol blocked the money. South Africa kept its oil, but Mexico and not Ernest Bennett got the $7 million, and Haiti, which had never received a drop of the precious fuel, was released from its Mexican debt.

Most of Bennett's other deals were ongoing. With the connivance and protection of his daughter, he also sold his services to the international drug trade. In the 1980s cocaine was the right stuff, and Ernest Bennett quickly set himself up as Haiti's most important link in the Colombia-Haiti-U.S. cocaine traffic, soon winning the title "The Godfather." But until he founded Haiti Air and began to fly international routes in 1985, Bennett confined his activities to warehousing drugs, fueling drug planes, and coordinating transfers from one vessel to another as drug runners arrived to make another leg of their journey.

Bennett's corruption, however, was a minor debacle in the course of Jeanclaudism, a system of repression that benefited the ruling Duvaliers and a tiny upper crust and through brute force and nonstop national brainwashing kept iron control over the nation's coffers, its administration, and its people.

François Duvalier had not begun obsessed by money, but by the time Duvalierism evolved into Jeanclaudism, enrichment was its primary object, and Duvalierism provided for the greedier Jeanclaudists the perfect vehicle to bleed the national treasury.

At the heart of the system, with its archaic structure, convoluted accounting procedures, and decentralization, was the Duvaliers' inability to acknowledge the autonomy of state funds and properties. The New York law firm Stroock & Stroock & Lavan, charged with reclaiming the moneys the Duvaliers stole, said,

> The Duvaliers treated Haiti as if it was their private property. Their dictatorship did not permit them to make a distinction between the goods of the State and those of the Duvalier family. They behaved as if Haiti was their feudal kingdom and the coffers and revenues of their State their private property. The distinction between the Public Treasury and their private goods scarcely existed. The distinction was ignored to the point that the Duvaliers had blank check books for drawing on funds.

The system was breathtakingly simple. On the blank checks the Duvaliers would simply write the account number of a government department, the name of the beneficiary—often "Cash"—and endorse and cash the check. This economic despotism extended to all government departments, and the Duvaliers routinely raided all these agencies: (1) the Finance Ministry; (2) Tobacco Authority, which controlled the price stability of essential goods by buying and selling them; (3) the Flour Mill; (4) the State Lottery; (5) the State Gambling Commission; (6) State Automobile Insurance; (7) Teleco, the phone company; (8) Electricity of Haiti; (9) Cement of Haiti; (10) National Bank of Credit; (11) Tax Department. Simply, the Duvaliers had at their disposal the entire resources of the nation.

Another aspect of the Haiti/Duvalier finances was a system of establishing "extra-budgetary" accounts controlled by trusted Duvalier cronies. Frantz Merceron, the Finance Minister, alone oversaw extra-budgetary accounts worth $70.7 million. These moneys were siphoned from regular government revenue, and Duvalier drew on them by writing checks to himself, his family, and friends. Checks as large as $6.8 million were written.

Another form the embezzlement took involved forcing government agencies to write checks to three dummy agencies bearing the charitable-sounding name "Social Works," one for Jean-Claude, one for Michèle, and one for the newly rehabilitated Simone. Though "Social Works" had no bank account, the Central Bank honored checks with any one of these three signatures.

Michèle also had her real foundation, and government organizations regularly issued checks to it. Michèle endorsed them and usually withdrew them in cash or deposited them directly into her personal account. Not that the Duvaliers were needy even on paper. Despite Jean-Claude's small salary, the national budget provided for an average annual sum of $1.5 million for the expenses of his presidency, and Michèle had a monthly salary of $100,000.

But Michèle sometimes overspent. In 1983, when she had a bank overdraft of $284,617.25, her friend Merceron had an identical amount credited to her account. It was not that she was broke, but she preferred to keep her money outside Haiti. Soon after her marriage, for instance, she deposited $14.3 million in her personal account at New York City's Irving Trust.

Gourde-rich, the Duvaliers still had the problem of converting their money to greenbacks, negotiable anywhere. Central Bank Governor Jean-Claude Sanon aided them, cashing their gourde checks in dollars drawn from the Central Bank, repository of Haiti's hard currency reserves. The Duvaliers then entrusted them to "mules" such as Victor Nevers Constant, murdered by Haitians in Paris before he could stash the cash into the Duvaliers' bank accounts. The mules carried the money in suitcases to foreign countries, religiously declaring their cargo to customs officials, specifying who owned it, then depositing it into U.S., Swiss, French, and other banks. Over three decades the entire Duvalier clan and virtually all their associates built up gigantic fortunes, while the people of Haiti still earned an average of less than $300 a year in the cities and $150 or less in the countryside—annually.

The Duvaliers had been greedy long before the advent of Michèle, but she escalated avarice to new levels. In 1981 an International Monetary Fund team discovered that Jean-Claude had obtained $20 million from government revenue for his own personal use in December 1980, soon after his wedding. The team also found that $16 million had disappeared from different government accounts during the first three months of 1981. Few Haitian officials raised their eyebrows at this, for Haitian ministers traditionally worked with drawers full of cash in their offices, and money being carted about in sacks was commonplace. As state embezzlers the Duvaliers were right in line. It was only the staggering amounts that seemed outrageous.

Michèle attended all cabinet meetings and forced Jean-Claude to accompany her. She intervened actively in the government and soon dominated ministers and directed policies.

Michèle was equally ambitious for her palace, and spent fortunes obliterating all traces of Simone Duvalier's staid conservatism in favor of her own self-conscious trendiness. Michèle mixed styles, blending modern and antique, the finest Egyptian art and African elephant tusks, furniture copied from European palaces. Apart from some native art, she de-Haitianized the palace, even sending to Florida for the fresh flowers that cost her people $50,000 a month.

Michèle and Jean-Claude's private, two-story palace apartment had thirty-foot ceilings and hermetically sealed doors. Apart from the bedroom wing, with its interior balconies and bathrooms with gold and lapis lazuli fixtures, there was a medical suite, a beauty parlor, and a kitchen with all-computerized equipment.

Michèle took the same approach to her own decoration, dressing to suit a model she invented for her status as First Lady. "Of *course* I spend money on clothes," she once said indignantly to an American journalist, Bella Stumbo. "How do they *expect* the First Lady of Haiti to look?" Probably like Simone Duvalier—reasonably chic, moderately bejeweled, a typical matron of the Haitian elite. Certainly not like Michèle, spectacularly adorned from closets full of Valentinos and Givenchys, clacking about on spike-heeled Susan Bennis Warren Edwards shoes at $500 a pair. Michèle ordered jewelry as she did everything else—in bulk, by the dozens, scores, boxloads. One order, to the Caribbean jewelers Spritzer & Fuhrmann, was for $200,000.

Not all of Michèle's money went into her own coffers. At first, seduced by the fantasy that she would become Haiti's Evita Perón, she built clinics, cut-rate pharmacies, schools and hospitals for the poor. "I know I am often compared to Evita Perón," she liked to say, though few ever made the comparison. "Even before I became First Lady," she confided to Bella Stumbo, "I was conscious of the needs of my people. When I married the President, I knew I had a chance to do something important for them. . . . I am a social worker at heart, and always have been."

At first this flattering self-evaluation was shared by others—hadn't Mother Theresa raved about how much her people loved Michèle? But one or two years after her marriage, Michèle's reputation as a "dragon lady" was already well established. This period of escalated extravagance came after Michèle felt she had secured a permanent place in the Duvalier First Family, when on January 31, 1983, she gave birth to her third and Jean-Claude's first son, François Nicolas Jean-Claude Duvalier.

Jean-Claude and Michèle never felt twinges of guilt or even doubt about what they were doing, how they were living. "It was the custom of the country," Jean-Claude explained to Barbara Walters a few years later. "My husband and I . . . we have what you call our hands clean," added Michèle. "I don't think we did anything wrong." But foreign lenders did not share this view, and in the first year of their marriage the Duvaliers fought hard to keep up the level of foreign aid, essential to their parasitical survival.

The IMF was particularly difficult, and then Canada canceled a major rural development project after revelations of scandalous mismanagement and theft of funds. In October 1981 the U.S.'s new ambassador Ernest Preeg condemned Haiti's failure to make a "credible start" to economic reform. Finally Jean-Claude agreed to appoint a new Finance Minister and give him carte blanche to implement a wide array of fiscal reforms.

The new minister was World Bank official Marc Bazin, recommended by the reform-minded planning minister Pierre Sam and generally approved by the international lending community. Bazin arrived to discover that his Jeanclaudist colleagues had no intention of cooperating with him.

Bazin, stubborn and confident, was determined to succeed despite the obstacles. He tackled the tax and banking systems, introducing the novel notion of accountability into them. He also imposed import quotas on selected items such as luxury cars and tried to prevent the smuggling so nonchalantly accepted that street vendors displayed smuggled goods on every downtown sidewalk.

But corruption even touched Bazin personally, because as minister he was expected to authorize transfers of large sums of money outside Haiti, some to the Duvaliers' Swiss bank accounts, some to the U.S. where it was reportedly donated to American politicians as campaign funds. Finally he drew the line at continuing to allow Ernest Bennett to avoid paying his taxes. Michèle was furious at Bazin's audacity but the final straw was when he objected strenuously to the appointment of Dinosaur Antonio André as Central Bank governor. "It's him or me," Bazin informed Jean-Claude. Jean-Claude chose André, and in July, only five months after he had entered the cabinet, he fired Bazin. A disillusioned and disgusted Bazin returned to the World Bank, convinced now that under the Duvaliers, Haiti was beyond saving.

The Duvaliers also sacked another reformist technocrat, Minister of Planning Pierre Sam, descendant of Tiresias and Vilbrun Guillaume Sam, co-owner of the Hotel Oloffson, and an international agronomist who had spent two decades of Duvalierism in exile. Duvalier had summoned Sam home in 1981 and invited him to become Minister of Planning. Sam hesitated, extracted the promise of a free hand to implement streamlining of the country's administrative structures, and accepted the job so he could exercise pressure on the sluggish government from within. This strategy included bringing in Bazin, but the government did not appreciate Bazin's sweeping reforms, and his mentor, Sam, also lost his job. One day Sam heard on his car radio that a new minister had been installed. He continued on to the palace, politely greeted his successor Claude Veil, and began life as a private citizen.

In 1982 Haiti's bleak economic outlook translated statistically into an import/export imbalance of $137 million, and $48 million more was transferred out of Haiti than into it. Treasury expenditures exceeded revenue by $38 million, leaving an overall treasury deficit equal to 2.5 percent of the GNP. The gross domestic product shrank 4.7 percent and, thanks to Hurricane Alex, which wiped out half of Haiti's coffee trees, only $45.1 million worth of coffee was exported, compared to $66.8 million in 1980.

Tourism, next only to coffee and cash remittances from the diaspora as a foreign exchange earner, had also taken a nosedive. Seventy thousand American visitors dropped to ten thousand, and Americans accounted for two-thirds of Haitian tourism. The industry's worst foe was AIDS, or fear of AIDS, because in 1982 the deadly disease was first especially associated with Haitians.

Pathologists at Jackson Memorial Hospital in Florida noted that a dead Haitian's brain showed evidence of toxoplasmosis. This was, writes David Black in *The Plague Years: A Chronicle of AIDS, the Epidemic of Our Times,* "a clue from the grave, as though a zombie, leaving a trail of unwinding gauze bandages and rotting flesh, had come to the hospital's Grand Rounds to pronounce a curse." Now alerted to the connection, doctors discovered that disproportionate percentages of Haitians carried the disease, and AIDS stamped Haiti's international image as political repression and intense poverty never had.

Jordan Maxwell, a Canadian businessman returning to Montréal, described how an immigration official dropped his passport as soon as he heard the reply "Haiti" to a routine question about residence. In New York City travel agency computer services warned prospective visitors, "Travel to Haiti not advised."

Jean-Claude's government responded to the AIDS charge by closing down Port-au-Prince's many gay bars and hotels, most catering to foreign guests. Then it expelled homosexual American diplomats. On the AIDS issue, as on no other, Haitians united, unanimously condemning the Atlanta Center for Disease Control's inclusion of Haitians on the high-risk-for-AIDS list. Several Haitian hotel owners even seriously considered suing the ACDC for the amount of the business they had lost.

Terrified of contracting AIDS, and aghast at the misery of the wretched people washed up dead and alive on Florida's shores, former Hotel Oloffson guests stayed away from Haiti. And in their large private quarters, Oloffson directors Al and Suzanne Seitz had a special reason for sadness, for Al was dying of pancreatic cancer.

The Presidential Palace in Port-au-Prince was severely damaged after the January 12, 2010, earthquake laid waste to Haiti's capital.

Downtown Port-au-Prince ravaged by the quake. Most of the city was left in ruins.

René Préval takes his seat in Parliament as the new President of Haiti after taking the oath of office May 14, 2006, in Port-au-Prince.

Floods ravage southeastern Haiti, 2004. Unchecked deforestation and erosion caused catastrophic natural disasters.

President Bill Clinton greets President-in-exile Jean-Bertrand Aristide in the Oval Office on October 14, 1994, the day before a U.S. government plane restored him to Haiti.

A client of Fonkoze, Haiti's alternative bank for the organized poor. Fonkoze helps women, the backbone of Haiti's economy, struggle out of poverty with microloans, and teaches that political democracy cannot survive without economic democracy.

This $600,000 check written to the bank from President Aristide's official Secretariat account enabled the depositor to get cash. Central Bank officials told investigators such transactions were "business as usual."

In 1987, an angry crowd in downtown Port-au-Prince captured and set a suspected Macoute on fire, Père Lebrun style.

Anne-Denise Cius holds a photo of her son, Jean-Robert, murdered by soldiers as he stood beside a priest in the courtyard of Immaculate Conception College in Gonaives.

U.S. Ambassador Clinton Knox with "Papa Doc" Duvalier. Knox also gave Duvalier relics from the historic moon landing, shared by the U.S. with friendly nations.

Newlyweds Jean-Claude and Michèle in May 1980, just as she forced him onto the diet that helped him shed 70 pounds.

Toussaint Louverture created a stable agricultural economy and reconciled blacks, whites, and mulattoes. He is revered as "the first West Indian" and "the Great Liberator."

The ruins of the Citadelle La Ferrière, one of UNESCO's wonders of the New World. The Citadelle took fifteen years to construct and could house five thousand men.

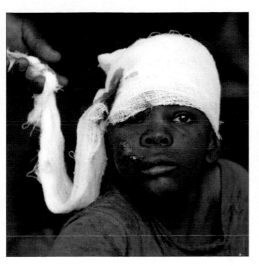

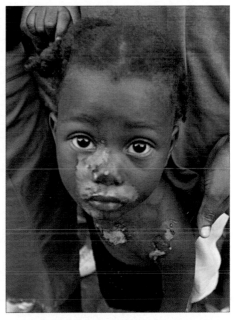

A traumatized young earthquake victim is treated at an ad-hoc clinic installed at the United Nations Stabilization Mission (MINUSTAH)'s logistics base.

A week after the earthquake, a small girl waits in line for food and water distributed by Brazilian MINUSTAH soldiers in Port-au-Prince's Cité Soleil slum.

Tent city for Haitians displaced by earthquake, outside Gheskio Field Hospital on the grounds of private Quisqueya University, Port-au-Prince.

Children in the Pétionville Golf Club tent camp run by Sean Penn build their Barbie doll a tent-house just like theirs. It even has a scrap of carpet.

Life goes on as children jump rope in a rubble-strewn street in the Delmas 32 neighborhood of Port-au-Prince, seven months after the earthquake.

It was Mardi Gras, Al's last. In the close, humming air Suzanne could feel suppressed excitement, as Haitians waited for the annual celebration where care was forgotten, sadness temporarily laid aside. For weeks the vodoun drums had been rolling nightly, punctuated by singing and the grating bellow of the conch as irrepressible Africa prepared for penurious Christian Lent.

One of the few guests still unafraid to visit was Mick Jagger, whose song "Emotional Rescue" had been written on a previous visit to the Oloffson. Now, with model Jerry Hall, he had come to study the music and movements of Haiti's famous Carnival. They sat at the bar, chatting idly and waiting for dusk and the onset of the last night of celebration. They knew about the once-boisterous Al, now lying in his huge bed, without the usual noisy fun, the annual surrender to Carnival magic.

"We can't have that then, can we?" Jagger decided suddenly, and slipping down from his stool, led Jerry, Suzanne, and family friend Gareth Browne over to the Seitzes' cottage, where they marched into the bedroom.

"Lovely to see you," he greeted the dying man.

"Been a long time," Al replied gruffly. Then his eyes widened as Jagger proceeded to crawl into bed with him.

"Come on, there's room enough for friends," Jagger admonished the others, and in another minute Jerry and Gareth Browne and Suzanne were all tumbled together in the outsized bed, pressed around Jagger, who lay cradling Al in his arms.

Suzanne and Jerry saw the pleasure that flooded the dying man's face. When Al was tired and comforted, Jagger gently released him and everyone rolled out of bed. Afterward they went downtown to Carnival, where in front of the palace hundreds of thousands of Haitians danced and sang for three joyous days, celebrating life, forgetting death, obliterating the true face of Haiti.

A few blocks away from the genteel decay of the Oloffson another family drama was being played out that provoked not emotional rescues and reconciliation but rather put one man in jail, overthrew a cabinet, and once again exposed Haiti's ugly underside to the outside world. Specifically, on March 26, 1982, Michèle Bennett's younger brother Franz was arrested by American federal agents in San Juan, Puerto Rico, and charged with possession of cocaine and plotting to smuggle drugs.

Franz was involved in all aspects of the trade, including using it. A confidential U.S. Drug Enforcement Agency file, dated May 1982, subsequent to Franz's arrest, elaborated:

> Reportedly, several large narcotic trafficking organizations based in Haiti utilized Bennett's fuel concession at Duvalier International Airport in Port-au-Prince to refuel private aircraft while smuggling cocaine and marihuana from Colombia to the United States. Haiti is used as a storage depot and transshipment point for narcotics destined for the United States. It is alleged that military personnel guard the storage depot and that Bennett was insulated from arrest in Haiti since his sister is married to President Duvalier. Bennett . . . also had been smuggling approximately 40 kilograms of high quality cocaine per shipment in false bottom suitcases aboard an air taxi service from Port-au-Prince to Miami via Nassau. [The air taxi was B & G Air Taxi, which stood for Franz Bennett and Christian Guichard, his business partner, whom father Ernest teamed up with after Franz was jailed.] During negotiations in San Juan, Bennett offered undercover agents safe passage for a drug-laden aircraft through Port-au-Prince in return for $60,000. Bennett was arrested when he accepted $25,000 and samples of cocaine for the balance. Reportedly, the President's wife, Michelle Bennett Duvalier, has intervened on her brother's behalf and is trying to persuade Haitian officials that Franz is innocent of any drug offense.

Franz himself made Michèle's task uphill work, for his conversation with the federal agents he thought were members of a drug ring had been recorded. Moreover, to the question as to whether Jean-Claude was aware of his activities, Franz had replied promptly and with apparent surprise—of course Jean-Claude knew. Furthermore, Franz added, he could guarantee safe passage of cocaine and heroin through Haiti without police interference. He agreed to handle monthly shipments of fifty-five kilos of cocaine, worth $2 million each, a deal clearly recorded on the tape.

Back in Haiti, Franz's arrest threw Michèle into hysterics. It was impossible to think of her little brother doing time in an American prison, as if he were a common criminal. He simply had to be released, and she vowed to do anything and everything she could to bring that about.

Jean-Claude too was afraid of the explosive temper, the iron will, and also of losing her, his wild-maned, supple little wife. So when she decided to get her brother freed, the President had to disregard any other considerations and do as his First Lady desired. In no time at all Michèle had caused another cabinet to fall.

Ricot and Edith Bayard had invited Jean-Claude, Michèle, and a coterie of their friends for dinner. As soon as the Duvaliers arrived Bayard beckoned Jean-Claude and asked to see him alone, upstairs. Bayard went straight to the point. He had just received a phone call from Georges Léger, Haiti's ambassador to the U.S., whom reporters were hounding about the Franz Bennett drug scandal. Léger, an experienced diplomat and lawyer, had consulted topflight American lawyers, and on the basis of their advice and his own strong instincts, he counseled the Haitian government to wash their hands of the affair and to allow American justice to take its course.

When Jean-Claude went back downstairs he took Michèle aside and repeated the conversation to her. "And do you mean that you allowed that man to tell you my brother should go to jail and yet you didn't fire him on the spot?" she responded. "Come on, Claudi. We're not staying here another minute."

"*Cabinè té tombé,*" Haitian tongues soon wagged. ("The cabinet has fallen.") For advising him not to risk his presidency for a drug smuggler caught red-handed, Jean-Claude fired Bayard. For agreeing with Bayard and listening to the cassette without giving it to him, Jean-Claude also fired Berrouet and Pierre-Louis.

In Haiti the Duvaliers could fire one minister after another, but they discovered that pressuring the Americans was far more difficult. After Jean-Claude and Michèle failed to convince, bribe, or otherwise cause American officials to release Franz, they decided to resort to trickery. Franz had been granted bail of $2 million cash. All they needed was to post that bail, then spirit Franz back to Haiti, where the Americans could never touch him. Accordingly, they went to Major Fritz Romulus and demanded that he authorize a passport with Franz's photo but not his name. Romulus refused, and said he could not do it.

The Duvaliers obtained the false passport elsewhere, but before sacrificing $2 million for bail they intended to forfeit, they obtained a bail reduction hearing at which Franz's lawyer asked for bail to be reduced to $45,000, because that was all the Bennett family could raise. The judge, rightfully skeptical, denied the motion, and Franz returned to jail. Subsequently bail was canceled altogether, and Franz had to remain behind bars until his trial.

In the United States the twenty-eight-year-old Franz, casual in a white T-shirt, designer jeans, and brown sandals, faced trial calmly and pleaded innocent to all three charges. He was found guilty and sentenced to four years in a federal penitentiary.

Back in Haiti the power vacuum left by the ouster of the powerful Bayard clique who had run Haiti for so many years was immediately filled by Dr. Roger Lafontant, Jean-Claude's new Interior Minister. Years later, testifying in a Canadian court, Lafontant's three daughters described their life with him as "brutal and humiliating," and said they were applying to legally change their surname. With the advent of this sinister physician, who saw himself as another Papa Doc, a new and terrible chapter in Haiti's litany of misery now began.

Michèle was also doing her utmost to fill a vacuum—that of a successor to her husband's presidency. Until she had produced an heir to the Haitian throne, the ever-insecure Michèle would not feel in control. Adding to her anxiety was her December 1981 miscarriage of a baby boy, and so through her next pregnancy she traveled to Miami's Mount Sinai Hospital to be sure she carried to full term. But Haiti's dauphin had to be born in his kingdom, and so it was in Canapé Vert Hospital and not Mount Sinai that François Nicolas Jean-Claude Duvalier II first saw the light of day.

The newest Duvalier arrived on January 31, at 7:22 in the morning, weighing a healthy seven pounds eight ounces. Jean-Claude was with his wife in the labor room, nervous and awkward in a medical gown and bonnet.

Canapé Vert Hospital had been prepped for the presidential delivery, and days earlier secret servicemen had combed it inch by inch. Macoutes in sunglasses and military guards stood everywhere, and an antiaircraft gun had been positioned at the outside doorway. These precautions were necessary, for the year 1983 had opened with violence when the Hector Riobé Brigade had attempted to bomb Jean-Claude and Michèle, about to give the world another Duvalier.

The brigade was named after a young man whose father Papa Doc had murdered in 1963 and who in revenge had barricaded himself in Kenscoff and picked off all the Macoutes who tried to capture him. When Riobé saw his mother coming to ask him to surrender, he turned his pistol onto himself and committed suicide.

Like Riobé, brigade members were both brave and fearless and took mortal risks to get at the Duvaliers, bombing Port-au-Prince with tracts and trying to bomb the Duvaliers in the palace with explosives. On New Year's Eve, at 3 a.m., a blast shattered a red Hyundai Pony parked at the corner of the Rue des Casbernes and the Rue de la Réunion, not far from the palace. Windows in the neighborhood broke, and a thick smoke blanketed the sky. Had it not been for the blazing car, nobody would have realized a bomb had exploded. They would have assumed the detonation was one more rowdy Macoute shooting his Uzi in the air to celebrate the New Year. Inside the Pony a brigade member, Allan C. Mills, a black American of Chinese-Jamaican extraction, was in shreds, and three passersby died.

The bomb had been intended for Jean-Claude and Michèle. For weeks afterward security throughout Haiti was tightened. Macoutes and soldiers mounted roadblocks and systematically searched all cars, but despite their vigilance two more bombs were discovered near the palace.

When the deadliest attack came, however, it was struck by the Roman Catholic Pope, John Paul II. Michèle and Jean-Claude had long anticipated the Pope's visit. In the wake of financial scandals, rising murmurs of criticism, the made-in-Haiti AIDS curse, floods, hurricanes, and disaster, they believed the papal visit would sanitize Haiti's image as nothing else could. Michèle threw herself into receiving the Pope as a First Lady should. One preparation was to authorize her close friend Johnny Sambour to spend $4 million, which she withdrew from various ministries, to redecorate François Duvalier airport. She forced a reluctant Roger Lafontant to marry his live-in mistress, Gladys Murad, insisting that unless he did so he could not stand in line to shake hands with His Holiness.

Jean-Claude spent more than money. Pope John Paul would come only, Church officials informed him, if he agreed to relinquish one of the powers his father had wrested from a more cowardly Vatican in 1964. Specifically, Jean-Claude had to restore to Rome the right to name bishops and the archbishop. And he had to do so publicly, in front of hundreds of thousands of wildly cheering Haitians. It was a huge price, but he decided to pay it.

John Paul accepted the invitation and began to do his homework, learning enough Creole to speak to the throngs of Haitians who turned out to greet him in the only language most understood. And he knew what to tell them, knew all about *"la misère"* and that life in Haiti was scarcely any life at all. Posters portraying the Pope and the Creole legend *"Men mwa. Koté nou?"* ("Here am I. Where are you?") were plastered all over Port-au-Prince to ensure maximum attendance for the great day.

Wednesday, March 9, the crowd gathering to welcome the Pope numbered in the hundreds of thousands. By early morning they had begun to arrive, peasants in bright cottons carrying flowers, wearing tropical garlands. Mingled with them were nuns in their blue-and-white habits, who could scarcely contain their elation, and calm military officers in full-dress uniform. Security officers disguised as journalists walked up and down with notebooks and roving eyes.

At 11:50 the Duvaliers' black, six-door Mercedes 600 screeched to a halt on the north side of the airport, amid the wail of sirens from the accompanying security vehicles and motorcycles. Michèle and Jean-Claude stepped out, Michèle in severely tailored beige, hatless, her hair shiny in a chaste bun. Jean-Claude looked trimmer than usual. The Duvaliers entered the presidential peristyle especially constructed for the occasion. Then they too waited.

Radar swept the air from on top of the airport, where soldiers in olive green stood sentinel, and a little helicopter flew in a monotonous circle. Suddenly, at 2:10, a deafening cheer rose from the sea of humans who forgot their thirst, the blazing midday sun, and knew only that the Pontiff had come all the way from his country to visit them. All eyes were fixed toward the Gulf of Gonave as the Alitalia DC-10 glided into sight and then slammed hard onto the ground, raising clouds of dust. The orchestra and the Haitian choir began to sing *"Tu es Petrus"* as the jet doors opened and Monsignor Wolff Ligondé and the papal nuncio disappeared inside. Suddenly John Paul himself appeared, turned, and with outstretched arms directed the singing. Then, beaming and blessing the people, he descended the ramp, deliberately walked across and off the red carpet, and knelt down and kissed the Haitian earth.

Haitians shouted with joy. The Pope's cap fell off and someone ran to hand it to him. Jean-Claude welcomed his illustrious guest with extravagant words: "Around me rises up the Haitian nation in its entirety, united in the same elation of enthusiasm, communing with the same religious fervor, to acclaim Your Holiness and to receive your message of love, peace and justice." In tribute to John Paul's Polish origin, Duvalier also praised the Polish-Haitians "who had not hesitated to join the ranks of the revolting slaves."

For thirteen long minutes the Pope listened, his left hand shading his face. When it was his turn he read his speech in Creole, carefully pronouncing the strange sounds. "There must be a better distribution of goods, a fairer organization of society, with more popular participation, a more disinterested conception of service on the part of those who direct society," he declared.

"I appeal to all those who dispose of power, of riches, of culture, to understand their urgent responsibility towards all their brothers and sisters," he added. And to thunderous applause that was to echo for years: "Where are you?"

"Here we are!" roared the people.

"Things have got to change here!" John Paul cried, and told the Haitian people that he and the world knew all about Haiti.[24]

Some portions of the real Haiti the Pope had described were hidden from him, cleaned up by express order of the Duvaliers. As he passed along the Avenue Marie Jeanne, John Paul did not see the sidewalk vendors who always sold there, their wares piled high on greasy wooden tables. The beggars and cripples had also been sent packing, deprived for one day of their preferred begging spots at the stoplights along the wide street. The sidewalk had been whitewashed, and Avenue Marie Jeanne sparkled as never before.

Once downtown John Paul made a brief stop at the palace, taking the littlest Duvalier into his arms and blessing him. He returned to the airport through darkness and flew off into the night.

The Duvaliers never recovered from the Pope's visit. The whole country buzzed with his sensational message: "Things have got to change here!" A new spirit of radicalism was born in the land.

Contemptuous of mounting criticism, in 1983 Michèle opened her Bon Repos Hospital, the tragicomic microcosm of all that ailed

Haiti. Bon Repos, in the district of Croix des Bouquets, was well conceived and represented the epitome of Michèle's "Evita" fantasy. It was
a maternity-pediatric hospital with 168 beds and two out-patient clinics that treated 150 patients daily. In its medical-social complex it contained a school for three hundred students taught by six teachers, an
excellent ratio by Haiti's appalling teacher-student standards, a chapel
for spiritual needs, and a canteen. Bon Repos employed 375 people,
the canteen twelve. There were residences for twenty nurses and for
eight interns. Impressive on paper. Unfortunately, the reality was far
different.

The hospital's physical plant was offered to Michèle by the State
Flour Mill as a gift. It had already been a juvenile delinquents' home that
had never received a single delinquent and an old-age home whose inmates were evicted when Bon Repos was born. Bon Repos had to be
completely rebuilt, and despite vast outlays, the work did not proceed
properly. Michèle finally fired the engineer and hired in his stead Colonel
Samuel Jérémie, Jean-Claude's childhood chauffeur and now head of the
notorious Anti-Smuggling Brigade and the State Stores. At last, and at
the enormous cost of $4 million, the building was finished and opened.
It was built with cement mixed with sand from Source Puante—"Stinking
Spring"—only meters away, and the cement this produced was of such
poor quality that the walls cracked almost immediately into great spi-
dery patterns, and worse, the cisterns and reservoirs leaked, and what
water there was stank and was full of microbes.

Michèle never noticed, though she took great genuine pride in her
hospital and with her sister Joan visited it almost daily. American journalist Bella Stumbo accompanied Michèle on a visit to Bon Repos.
Stumbo saw a genuine performance, Michèle playing Evita. She did not
see crucial elements that were normally part of the daily performance,
when Michèle played doctor. Michèle constantly told her friends she had
always wanted to be a nurse, but at Bon Repos she acted as if she thought
she was a doctor, always striding about in a blue medical gown, a stetho-
scope around her neck. She even made medical judgments, and would
order imperiously, "This one's been on serum long enough. Remove the
I.V." At another bedside: "The dosage is wrong. Reduce it." Doctors had
to jump at her orders, and she fired anyone for the least sign of rebellion
or even astonishment.

Most who remained on the staff grew cynical and developed their
own scams. Thieving was rampant as workers raided Michèle's well-

stocked hospital. The medical care also failed to reflect the high standards Michèle both hoped and assumed it had. Doctors operated unnecessarily to earn an extra $20 and $30 for a Caesarian or hysterectomy on top of their regular salaries. The water used to bathe patients was so germ-ridden, it caused serious infections. And when patients appeared to be dying the staff rushed them to the General Hospital so they would not be criticized for having so many deaths on their hands.

And even Michèle could not resist using Bon Repos to steal. Businesses, friends, Tonton Macoutes, army officers, everyone had to give. She kept Bon Repos generously financed, but she made sure Bon Repos reciprocated just as generously. And after the Duvaliers fled, government agents announced they had discovered 330 pounds of cocaine stashed in the Bon Repos pharmacy, part of a Bennett cache waiting for transshipment.

After the Pope's visit Haiti returned to its sullen, deteriorating norm. Hunger drove people into the streets. Repression made mere memory of liberalization. Palace politics took on new and omnious dimensions as Michèle and newly powerful Lafontant intrigued against each other and continually clashed, leaving Jean-Claude in the middle, buffeted this way and that, torn between adored wife and stern father figure.

Adding to the sense of insecurity was Jean-Claude's poor health. Though Michèle had solved his weight problem, she could not cure the agonizing arthritis that attacked his knees, wrists, and hands so severely that he could not walk or lift his hands. Several virulent attacks of the disease forced him into a wheelchair, and instead of sports he had to spend hours at painstaking physiotherapy. Doctors were consulted, and the latest rumor to traverse Haiti was that Jean-Claude had an incurable disease, dared not leave the country for treatment for fear of a coup d'état, and within a matter of months would be dead. Only after proper diagnosis and medication so improved his condition that he began to walk, then swim, did the rumor die.

Only one thing was certain. The Duvaliers loved Duvalierism, which continued to enrich and honor them. Consequently, on August 27, 1983, when François Nicolas Jean-Claude Duvalier II was not yet seven months old, the Legislative Assembly was forced to rubber-stamp a new Constitution:

The President-for-Life of the Republic, the Citizen Jean-Claude Duvalier, has the right to designate as Successor, any citizen fulfilling the conditions set out in article 102 of the present constitution. The designation will be made by a proclamation of the President-for-Life, who by a decree, will convoke the people in their assembly to ratify his designated successor.

11 THE DYNASTY FALTERS

LATE ONE NIGHT IN OCTOBER 1983 MADELEINE BAZILE Pierre-Louis lay brooding on her cot, recalling the day men came and killed her two pigs, smashing their heads with clubs so they shrieked high eerie shrieks and then died. Soon the mountain hamlet of La Reserve wakened again as her own inhuman shrieks pierced the chilly mountain air and her neighbors cursed Madeleine Pierre-Louis, whom their shared misery had driven mad.

Madame Pierre-Louis was a hardworking woman with a tiny boutique where she sold cola and cigarettes and cheap rum. Now she shouted every night, "My pigs! My pigs! Give me back my pigs!" because her children could no longer go to school. When exhausted neighbors came to remonstrate she grabbed stones from the eroded hillside and hurled them. "My pigs! Give me back my pigs!"

One night she hurt a man badly, and her family bound her with ropes. In lucid moments she pleaded and promised, but as soon as they untied her she stoned them and bit and fought and cursed.

The next step was Beaudet Mental Asylum, and for two weeks the village slept. Contrite and docile, Madeleine Pierre-Louis returned home. Her friends, who also had no pigs or money to educate their children, greeted her warily, and four nights later she began to scream again, "My pigs! My pigs!"

Madeleine Pierre-Louis's despair was echoed throughout Haiti, background music to the final years of Jeanclaudism. Just like her, Haiti too had lost control. In the palace the incompetent Jean-Claude and Michèle invented a new system to try to salvage the deteriorating nation, promoting a small clique of trusted advisers above all others and labeling them "super ministers." Bewildered and frustrated by a Haiti gone wild, the Duvaliers relied heavily on these super ministers and increasingly spent their time gorging themselves on comforting drugs, Saturday night orgies, buying binges, and assaults on the national treasury unparalleled in Haitian history.

Increasingly, church and state conflicted, and though the state won every round, each victory was pyrrhic, and the defeated Church emerged stronger. The people too, millions of Madeleine Pierre-Louis's, were so hungry and hopeless that they ceased to worry about waking the neighbors, grew contemptuous of government and sickened by its false promises. In the end they knew that they no longer had anything to lose.

The super ministers sprung on the nation in November 1983 were Dr. Roger Lafontant, Frantz Merceron, Jean-Marie Chanoine, Alix Cinéas, and Théodore Achille. The two most influential super ministers were Lafontant and Merceron, the former Jean-Claude's favorite, while Merceron was Michèle's. Lafontant and Merceron despised each other. They were studies in contrast, with common denominators of greed, immorality, and unscrupulousness. Lafontant, the Interior Minister, was an old-style *noiriste* who saw himself as a modern, improved Papa Doc. "I am a man of principle and never compromise the sacrosanct principles of the Duvalierist Revolution," he said after he had used Ricot Bayard's ouster to claw his own way back into power.

Lafontant was also a Macoute, and with Papa Doc-like tactics— bulging envelopes of money, favors and weapons sprinkled like confetti—he cemented his personal popularity among the Macoutes, improving their morale and forcing the nation to pay homage to them. Brutal and as indifferent to foreign opinion as Papa Doc had been, Lafontant deepened Haiti's climate of fear with new disappearances, tortures, and murders.

Merceron, the Super Finance Minister, was entirely different. A suave, Paris-educated mulatto, Merceron succeeded the deposed Marc Bazin as Finance Minister and made it his business to continue some of Bazin's reforms, keeping the IMF happy. Basically, Merceron ensured that Haiti kept to her schedule of loan payments. Whatever else could be said about the country, it had one of the Third World's best records for honoring debts.

Merceron was as brilliant as he was unscrupulous and for over two years adroitly juggled a financial time bomb. Merceron's unsavory personal life had given him valuable practical experience when he had sacrificed his young French wife and their baby to marry a much older and exceedingly rich Canadian widow.

Among the other super ministers one would play a most significant role in Haiti's internal politics—Alix Cinéas, a longtime minister and able engineer. Personally, Cinéas was a moderate who had intimate ties with the Duvalier family, both Papa Doc and Jean-Claude. So had his brothers Fritz, a doctor who served as a Duvalierist ambassador, and Ernest, an engineer. Another super minister, Jean-Marie Chanoine, was a personable and talented man, adept at political survival, and widely credited with a voracious sexual appetite for both men and women. Théodore Achille, who had risen to prominence as the defense lawyer in the Audubon stamp scandal, became Michèle's favorite lover, though he continued his affairs with other women.

As Jeanclaudist ministers operating within the Duvalierist framework they had shared priorities. One of the first was manipulating the legislative elections scheduled for February 12, 1984, which had to appear democratic and fair to foreign eyes, but under no circumstances could actually be democratic or fair, for anti-Duvalierists could never be allowed to win.

Fooling the world was the super ministers' most important concern, so the ministers stamped out all the dangerous candidates. Grégoire Eugène was such a man, and they barred him from returning to Haiti until February 22, a fortnight after the polling. Other candidates were threatened and warned. Sylvio Claude was convicted in 1982 and sentenced to six years in jail, pardoned months later, placed under house arrest, hauled in again, beaten, released, forced into hiding, then rearrested after the SD tortured his daughter until she revealed his whereabouts. Alexandre Lerouge in Cap Haitien was threatened and slandered, and other potential anti-Duvalierists warned off from attempting to run. As a result the main choice among the 307 candidates was between degrees of Duvalierism, with each man boasting of his own fierce commitment to the great revolutionary cause.

Just in case these compromised candidates were not guarantee enough, the elections were rigged. In Ganthier, which ran a typical election, Tonton Macoute commandant and mayor Raoul Vil distributed two thousand electoral cards to a dozen of his cronies, and in a marathon of inventiveness they filled in two thousand fictitious names. The cards came in handy, because Election Day brought the distressing news that voters were passing over incumbent and Duvalier favorite Edner Cadet in favor of independent Duvalierist Etzer Racine, so scores of pseudo-electors armed with false cards exhausted themselves running from poll to poll, voting for Cadet. Throughout Haiti similar frauds were perpetrated, and genuine voters were intimidated and bribed to vote for the presidential favorite.

Unimpressed, foreign observers dismissed the elections, and continued to cry out for reform. Some even proposed that the presidency-for-life be abolished and that the presidency be made elective. But no amount of foreign aid could force Jean-Claude to concede.

"The Presidency-for-Life was the choice of the people," he said in a March 1984 interview.

> I was designated in 1971, as was Dr. François Duvalier in 1964, by the Haitian people in full exercise of their sovereign rights and in line with a long tradition dating back to our earlier history. . . . The Haitian president-for-life was the result of a free choice of a group of men aspiring profoundly for the stability so necessary to build progress in common, whereas for other countries presidents-for-life for the most part are the result of wars or quests for power by ethnic groups.

On May 11 Super Minister Lafontant translated this hard line into action, banning all except Jeanclaudist political parties and all publications and articles critical of the regime. On May 21, after police beat a pregnant woman to death in volatile, hungry, pigless Gonaives, thousands took to the streets shouting antigovernment and anti-hunger slogans. For two days the riots continued as protesters battled government troops, who shot and killed at least forty.

Along with these soldiers Jean-Claude sent Super Minister Cinéas and Agriculture Minister Nicot Julien as special envoys to find out what was causing the Gonaives uprising. "The people say they are hungry and refuse to endure any more misery," they reported. "They say ever since you married Michèle the situation has gone from bad to worse, and they blame her and her father for ruining the country. And they say they'll take to the streets against you, Excellency, unless you agree to divorce Michèle, and expel both her and Ernest Bennett from Haiti."

Jean-Claude listened, reported to Michèle, and abruptly fired Ci-néas and Julien. When a week later 25,000 people rioted in the streets of Cap Haitien, he sent tough-minded Lafontant in to supervise the military operations. Hunger was also the issue in Cap Haitien, and had provoked the people to riot after Haitian officials in charge of CARE warehouses sold food on the streets rather than distributing it free to the poor. The Cap Haitien prefect, Auguste Robinson, trying to calm the protesters, denounced the sales but the riots continued, and during an entire day troops shot at the people, killing dozens and wounding at least fifty.

Learning nothing from either Gonaives or Cap Haitien, Lafontant clamped down further. In two swoops in June and November he ordered hundreds of opponents arrested, including journalists, political leaders, unionists, and Catholic Church members.

Sylvio Claude was back in hiding, while his daughter Marie-France fled to Europe. Grégoire Eugène, returned from exile for less than four months, was also a target. On June 19, five days after he published an issue of *Fraternité,* police arrested him, pushed him into a car, and took him to Dessalines Barracks, where he was forced to stand facing a wall for five hours. Eugène was released the next day into house arrest, after immediate intervention on his behalf by the American Embassy. From then until September 23, SD agents guarded his house and arrested each of the twenty-five people who attempted to visit him.

In July 1984 Lafontant transformed a routine nightclub tragedy into a power struggle between Macoute and civilian, between black and mulatto, between himself and Michèle Bennett. On the evening of July 12 Lafontant's Macoute bodyguard, Pierre Lavilla, with time on his hands because Lafontant was in Israel, appeared at the posh Haitian King's Club with a prostitute on each arm, the trio wearing shorts and T-shirts. The light-skinned and pregnant receptionist expressed surprise at seeing such improperly dressed clients, and immediately Lavilla said, "It seems you don't like our clothing."

The receptionist recovered quickly, and she left quickly to fetch her fiancé, Michel Baptiste.

Lavilla lurched into the club and began to drink, talking at the top of his voice about how light-skinned people mistreated blacks. Michel Baptiste tried to pacify him, but Lavilla took out his gun and threatened him.

An army lieutenant who knew Lavilla gently escorted him outside, but when the drunken Lavilla reappeared waving his gun, Michel Baptiste slipped out to summon the police.

In the club a frightened waiter told Michel's brother and co-owner Erick Baptiste that someone had tried to kill Michel. Erick put his .38 in his belt and went to rescue his brother. Lavilla grabbed him by the arm, shouting that the club had hired a white woman to prevent blacks from entering and that he had to find the girl and beat her, to teach her a lesson. Then he aimed his gun at Erick's head. Erick shot him in the wrist to disarm him, Lavilla tried again to blast him, and Erick fired four more shots. The last one caught Lavilla in the jugular, and he slumped to the ground dead.

Erick Baptiste soon learned he had just killed a Macoute, and not just any Macoute either, but Lafontant's bodyguard, inherited from Marie-Denise Duvalier. He was subsequently accused of plotting against Lafontant and imprisoned in Dessalines Barracks as a political prisoner.

Meanwhile, Macoute chief Hervé Jeanty and Police Chief Colonel Ti-Boulé Pierre had driven over to the King's Club. Edith Clergé, the receptionist, terrified, agreed to talk to Pierre, but as she climbed into the police car Lavilla's colleague Michel Mirabeau shot her several times in the back. Ti-Boulé shouted the order to take Mirabeau, who hid behind a cement pillar and yelled, "If anyone moves, I'll blow him away."

Jeanty calmed Mirabeau down, and Ti-Boulé drove Edith to the General Hospital. But just then Lavilla's body was brought into the hospital morgue, and Edith's life was again in danger as angry Macoutes gathered. She was rushed to Canapé Vert Hospital and into surgery. Her baby was saved, but several metal shards remained imbedded in her back.

At Dessalines Barracks Erick Baptiste's situation worsened when Super Minister Lafontant returned from Israel and ordered a state funeral for Lavilla. Terrified, the Baptiste family enlisted the aid of fellow coffee importer Ernest Bennett and his daughter Michèle. Michèle, pregnant again and in combat with Lafontant, had Erick Baptiste transferred to the relative security of the National Penitentiary. In early October a police inquiry and a criminal court trial exonerated him. On October 9 Baptiste was freed. But this was Duvalierist Haiti, and Lafontant ordered Baptiste reimprisoned. Forewarned, Baptiste promptly took refuge at the French Embassy.

Old Léon Baptiste again begged Ernest Bennett to help. Bennett called Jean-Claude, who refused to intervene, but at Lafontant's urging he phoned Baptiste and offered him safe-conduct, coupled with the threat that this was his last chance to accept.

First Lady Michèle left her husband in an attempt to force him to dump Lafontant. It's either Lafontant or me, Michèle warned. But because of her love affair with Théodore Achille and persistent rumors that the child she was carrying was his, not the President's, her position was shaky. Jean-Claude refused to fire Lafontant, and at last a very pregnant and sullen Michèle returned to the palace of her own accord.

Erick Baptiste finally gave himself up, because his whole family was now in hiding, and he feared for their lives. But instead of the safe-conduct Jean-Claude had promised him, he was thrown back into jail. Months later the Supreme Court again freed him. The Baptiste family attributed this decision entirely to the moral pressure the Americans and Amnesty International put on the regime to respect Baptiste's human rights.

Lafontant, however, charged that the Baptistes had bought the Supreme Court justices, and convinced Jean-Claude to fire the Justice Minister, the Attorney General, and the Supreme Court judge. They had tried to render justice, and Lafontant was not going to let them get away with that.

In August 1984, during the Los Angeles Olympics, a uniquely Haitian drama unfolded. In June the Haitian Ministry had notified marathoner Dieudonné Lamothe that he would be running in August's Olympics. Lamothe was elated and began serious training.

Lamothe had problems other international runners could not even imagine. His coach, hired because his father was a food taster in the palace, was amiable but seldom worked with him. Lamothe had no money for a special runner's diet, no masseur to pummel out the aches and injuries of a day's running. He could not even afford proper running shoes, and because he had failed to win the 1982 marathon in Cuba, the Sports Ministry refused to buy him a pair.

As he trained Lamothe also brooded, hoping at least for enough money to leave his wife and baby son provided for while he was in Los Angeles. But as departure day approached and he still had no money he grew desperate and threatened his coach that he would refuse to go. The coach was afraid of losing out on his own free trip to Los Angeles. "You'll get $500," he promised.

Meanwhile, Ministry officials kept telling Lamothe how much they expected from him, and the coach said half jokingly, "If you don't win, you can't come back to Haiti." Lamothe did not want to live anywhere but Haiti, and the coach's threat worried him. "Okay, I'll try to win a medal," he replied, but he knew that it would take a miracle for an untrained, badly nourished runner like himself to win.

July 26 was his thirtieth birthday and the day of departure. There was still no money, and the utility company had threatened to cut off the electricity. At 6 a.m. Lamothe summoned up all his courage and presented himself at the home of Serge Conille, the Sports Minister. Conille received him in his bathrobe and heard him out. "Running is a Haitian sport," Connille commented at the end. "I'll take care of your family." On the strength of that promise Lamothe returned home, packed his things, including the pair of Nikes he had borrowed from a friendly American electronics factory manager, and kissed his wife, Carole, goodbye.

At the airport the other members of Haiti's Olympic team were waiting, fencers and tennis players, all mulatto. In face of their self-assurance and elegance, Lamothe was mortified at his own pathetic suitcase, tattered and broadcasting his poverty. He was handed an envelope with $250 and was told that Carole would be given another $250 that day.

At the Olympic village the other runners knew he was nothing, and even the French-speaking Africans he had hoped would be friendly rebuffed his attempts at conversation. Lamothe's worst experience was in the free cafeteria. The food was so delicious and plentiful that he heaped his plate. He knew it was wrong, but after a lifetime of hunger, he could not resist.

The day of the race, six pounds heavier, Lamothe donned his borrowed shoes and took his place in the stadium. He knew he could not win, that his poor training and physical condition would dictate his race. But suddenly the surging excitement of the crowd charged him, and he thought, "I can win!" When the starting gun sounded he started off with all the confidence of the best-prepared runner.

Until eighteen kilometers, when his heart pounded and his legs hurt, and he knew he had to slow down. He had also discovered that humidity, rare in Haiti, was not the terrible coldness he had imagined, but rather a debilitating steaminess that was now sapping him, making it difficult for him to breathe.

At thirty-two kilometers other runners had already finished, and their times were posted by the roadside. No honorable place was possible. Sheer survival was now the question. His struggle was evident, and an ambulance cruised alongside him. He began to walk and run, and in a haze of pain wondered if he would even be allowed to enter the stadium, because there was a three-hour limit.

By thirty-five kilometers two stretcher bearers ran beside him, sometimes falling behind to catch him should he collapse. Only the strongest forces kept his disabled body going—images of Haiti, the faces of his people, the consequences for him if he did not finish.

The marathon was over. Dieudonné Lamothe was the last man to enter the stadium. Suddenly on television sets the world over announcers exclaimed, "Wait! Here's another runner! Who is it? It's . . . it's Haiti!" And to the roars from hundreds of thousands of encouraging spectators Lamothe ran that last lap, suddenly bolstered by the illusion of strength, strong again, the Haitian runner who had finished the race.

It was over. He bought souvenir T-shirts for Carole and his little son and tried to forget the marathon. Nobody met him at the airport, and he arrived home to find the electricity cut off, for Carole had not received the promised $250. The young couple sat in darkness with their child, and husband confided to wife his saga of humiliation and endurance, a typical Haitian story in which the hero's choices are not victory or defeat, but survival or death.

School opening that October, the first after PEPPADEP's final eradication of the nation's pigs, revealed that registration had plunged as much as 40 to 50 percent. Street vendors of cheap notebooks and pencils went hungry. The Lebanese and Syrian drygoods merchants had unsold stockpiles of checkered cotton for the traditional Haitian school uniforms. Deschamps Printing Company's orders for Creole and French textbooks plummeted. All over Haiti children stayed at home, understanding that something was happening to them and that hard times were suddenly much harder.

Erosion was advancing so inexorably that in December 1984 the Interior and Agriculture ministers issued a joint communiqué announcing the death throes of Pic Macaya in the South, which had 300,000 Haitians dependent on its natural reservoirs for their water. The great hydroelectric Peligre dam in the central plateau was dry and clogged with sludge from the topsoil that had poured into it. Blackouts shut down businesses and frazzled the nerves of those who could not afford generators. Huge oil trucks converted to haul water sloshed along the roads of Port-au-Prince in caravans as people paid up to $80 for three thousand gallons of undrinkable water to flush their toilets and wash their clothes.

Haitian soil was so exhausted and poor, it could produce only .90 units of rice per hectare whereas the Dominican Republic produced 2.67, Mexico 3.28, the U.S. 5.04, and wonderfully fertile Spain 6.04. Haiti could grow .67 units of corn to the Dominican Republic's 2.10, Canada's 5.38, the U.S.'s 6.35. Its sugarcane grew at 49 units compared to the Dominican Republic's 62.35, the U.S.'s 80.51, and Spain's 100. And coffee, Haiti's chief export crop, grew only .25 units whereas the Dominican Republic grew .31, Guadeloupe .95, and Mexico .75, statistics as dry as the eroded land that was starving Haitians.

Macoutic Duvalierism had transformed Haiti into an unproductive catastrophe, and its hardworking people into a nation of beggars. To keep their system functioning, Jean-Claude and his Macoutes were the biggest beggars of all. But unless the regime made serious and genuine improvements in its human rights, permitted free elections and a free press, and established fiscal reforms, the U.S. had every intention of withholding some of the aid money that was by then 70 percent of Haiti's national budget.

In early 1985 Catholic priests led thirty thousand people through the streets of Port-au-Prince shouting, "Down with hunger! We have had enough of *la misère!*" That same year, Jean-Claude finally admitted he had a big problem. It was the giant reduction in American foreign aid, from $44.6 million in 1984 to $34 million in 1985.

The regime's business rushed on. Lafontant had orchestrated a new reign of terror. Once again the prisons bulged, and new exiles swelled the diaspora. Within Haiti the Macoutes swaggered with the confidence of those who know they are truly appreciated, and they had as tangible proof the envelopes Lafontant dispersed among them just as grandly as Papa Doc had, and much more generously, because Finance Minister Merceron kept Lafontant so plentifully supplied.

July 29, 1985, Tonton Macoute Day, was one of Lafontant's most important triumphs. On that day the Macoutes were honored by Jean-Claude and his whole cabinet, all sporting brand-new blue Macoute uniforms.

Downtown in the streets, exuberant Macoutes had such a fine time at their national party that they shot twenty-seven people, many asleep in their beds.

Merceron in the Finance Department was as domineering and successful as Lafontant in the Interior. He met Michèle's most outrageous demands cordially, never failing to satisfy them. He also coordinated the efforts of the Duvaliers' legal advisers in transferring and hiding away their money in foreign accounts, setting up dummy corporations and holding companies, carefully hiding the traces so that in case of eventual trouble, the Duvaliers would be protected. Merceron helped himself generously as well, and made similar arrangements for his foreign caches, as did all the other ministers. He made sure that he—and he alone—shared with Michèle and Jean-Claude the power to sign checks on their private accounts.

Merceron also continued to administer Haiti's finances. He did so efficiently and unscrupulously, stripping the treasury, inventing new ways to plunder. Teleco was Haiti's largest foreign exchange earner and he milked it dry of the American dollars it earned in reciprocal arrangements with foreign telephone companies. He also added a $1.40 surcharge and 10 percent sales tax on every long-distance call.

He closed down SODEXOL, jointly owned by the government, Duvalierist cronies and an Israeli-Panamanian consortium, which had a monopoly on supplying cooking and industrial oil, and opened in its stead ENAOL, a state-owned operation that performed the same functions. The price of cooking oil to the Haitian consumer rose again, and through ENAOL Merceron was able to garner millions more for Jeanclaudist needs, which included his own. He added a $1.00 tax to every bag of cement sold by the state cement factory and $.94 to every bag of flour from the Flour Mill, and from the proceeds sent monthly $175,000 to Jean-Claude, $25,000 to Michèle, and $20,000 to newly rehabilitated Simone Duvalier.

He also opened Darbonne, a sugar mill that in 1980 the IMF, World Bank, and Inter-American Development Bank had recommended should not be built. Darbonne was a typical Jeanclaudist scam, a grandiose scheme designed to convince Jean-Claude of a project's feasibility, enlist his aid in financing it, whether by local or foreign moneys, and then to steal millions before the project ever saw the light of day.

Darbonne was a giant mill custom-designed by Idi Amin for Ugandan cane production. Before its Italian manufacturers had delivered the order, Amin had to flee Uganda, leaving the Italians with one unsold custom-designed sugar mill on their hands.

Enter Haitians on the snoop for just such opportunities. On the initial purchase price alone millions could be made. Jean-Claude was easily convinced of the viability of the scheme, and the Haitian government financed it and guaranteed it 100 percent. At first Finance Minister Hervé Boyer wanted to put the mill in the Artibonite Valley, until his experts informed him that rice and not sugar was grown there, forcing him to look about for a new location. The Central Plateau was considered and rejected. Finally sugarcane-growing Léogane was settled on, and under Merceron the mill became operational, against the advice of the world's largest lending institutions and at a cost to the Haitian government of $100 million.

Darbonne was designed to process Uganda's vast sugarcane production. Haiti's inferior one at full production could only keep Darbonne 40 percent functional. Additionally the scheme nearly ruined the old Haytian-American Sugar Company (HASCO), whose railroad to the Léogane sugar fields was ripped up to ensure that Darbonne and not HASCO bought all the local sugar. Once again Haitians watched as workers ripped up railroad tracks, halting the famous sugarcane train that ran through the heart of Port-au-Prince, spilling big stalks that children delighted to grab and suck, staving off the pangs of hunger.

The Duvaliers were spending all that Merceron could raise. The news worsened daily, with mounting foreign criticism, aid cuts, internal dissension, and waves of popular unrest. Sheer prudence dictated that as much money as possible be stashed away abroad. Michèle in particular was under heavy attack, and from every niche of society, from high-level palace and army colleagues, friends, and relatives, Jean-Claude heard the litany first chanted in Gonaives: divorce Michèle, exile her father. Michèle's insecurities were seriously fueled. Her obsessive fascination with Théodore Achille was reminiscent of her pre-Jean-Claude days. The gossip she provoked among palace staff whenever she met Achille caused widespread speculation about the paternity of Michèle Anya, the baby she gave birth to on December 1, a year after Nicolas was born.

While Haiti groaned, Michèle, with a trail of her acolytes, prowled the luxury shops of New York and Paris. The famous French jeweler Boucheron and the Shah of Iran's sister, Princess Ashraf Pahlavi, flew to Haiti to sell her jewels, and Michèle made their trips worthwhile, choosing millions of dollars' worth of gems. She bought fur coats and a special oversize refrigerator to insulate them against Haiti's tropical climate.

While his daughter tried to spend away her unhappiness, her father built himself a new empire. Ernest Bennett was as great a liability to Jean-Claude as Michèle was, but far from toning down his activities and keeping a low profile, Bennett inaugurated his most scandalous scheme when on May 27, 1985, he opened his own airline. Haiti Air was a real passenger airline, run with a plane rented from Irish Airlines Aer Lingus. This dimension satisfied Bennett's pride—he was the owner of Haiti's only national airline. But airlines are notorious money losers, and Bennett's incompetently managed one was no exception. Fortunately for him, his daily $30,000 loss was a mere inconvenience. He had a much more lucrative sideline in which Colombian drug kings and not Aer Lingus were his partners.

The Bennetts had been drug-running since 1980, and with their associates had moved hundreds of millions of dollars' worth of cocaine into the U.S. Haiti Air gave Bennett the opportunity to not only warehouse the drug for his Colombia partners, and to coordinate transshipments, but also to run it himself. He had huge quantities to sell, because as "The Godfather" for four or five Colombian drug rings, Bennett usually received payment in cocaine.

The scam was uncomplicated—a dictatorship can slice through red tape. Through Colombia drug kings Pablo Escobar and Carlas Lehder the cocaine was distributed to "mules." Some were pilots who flew it to one of Bennett's several clandestine airstrips. When Haiti Air opened, more cocaine was poured into Haiti crammed in the suitcases of Colombian pseudo-tourists. These mingled with real tourists, who flocked to Haiti via Avianca on a Club Med special $699 one-week trip. The scam began when Club Med luggage was loaded directly onto buses without customs checks—Bennett and bribery arranged this with Port-au-Prince Police Chief Colonel Jean Valmé, and after 1983 with Colonel Ti-Boulé Pierre, successor to Valmé, whom Michèle had fired for slapping her father in 1976.

The cocaine was collected by a Frenchman, Hervé Hardy, and distributed to certain of the Haiti Air stewardesses who moved it to New York and Miami, as they did most cocaine Bennett received. A certain amount was also kept for local consumption, and at his Pétionville home Hardy distributed it to Haitian dealers so the elite users could buy at home. One important dealer was Marvin Cardoza. Another was his friend Ti-Ernest Bennett, one of Michèle's brothers. When the Bennetts were in on a good deal, they liked to share it with other family members. When the Duvaliers left Haiti, cocaine shipments were found at Michèle's Bon Repos Hospital, her vacation home in Fermathe, her father's Lada-Niva car dealership, and even in the palace, along with hundreds of syringes and coke pipes.

Playing for time, out of his depth, zigzagging crazily as he followed advice showered on him from all sides, Jean-Claude announced on April 22 that he had decided to appoint a Prime Minister and legalize the functioning of political parties, banned since Lafontant's May 1984 decree. This announcement was received with hope liberally tinged with skepticism, but for some weeks it staved off the gathering storm. Then Jean-Claude ruined this slight advantage by allowing Lafontant to convince him that a national referendum on his presidency-for-life would set that sensitive issue to rest, both inside Haiti and outside, particularly in the United States. Accordingly and with great fanfare, Jean-Claude announced the contents of the questionnaire and immediately brought down on himself a deluge of ridicule.

Designed by the unsophisticated Lafontant, the referendum questions were not subtle. Citizens had to vote yes or no that (1) they ratified Duvalier as President-for-Life with the right to name his successor; (2) they wanted the office of Prime Minister created, which a member of Duvalier's majority party would fill, and which would be subordinate to the presidency-for-life; (3) they agreed the executive power should dominate the legislative, allowing the President to dissolve Congress in case of conflict; (4) they wanted legalized all political parties that recognized Duvalier's status as President-for-Life, had at least eighteen thousand members, and had neither international nor foreign affiliations that were political, syndical, or religious—in a word, that were neither Communist, socialist, nor Christian.

The newly radicalized Catholic Church, ti-l'église, the people's church, responded immediately, and Radio Soleil—Radio Sun— denounced the referendum as a crude attempt to eliminate the Catholic Church from Haiti's political life. In Sunday sermons enraged priests denounced the referendum in even stronger terms. "There is only one man who holds office for life," thundered Father Yvan Pollefeyt. "He is Jesus Christ!"

"We will never allow the Church and its Marxist priests to run this country," retorted Roger Lafontant. Haitian government spokesman Guy Mayer stated, "We have no proof, but maybe they might have been educating guerrillas." Government Radio National warned the people, "Don't listen to Radio Soleil!" In consequence, dials all over the nation were immediately turned to Radio Soleil as people listened, curious to find out what they were not supposed to listen to.

On Sunday July 21, the day before the referendum, Macoutes broke into Petit Séminaire St. Martial in downtown Port-au-Prince, climbed to the priests' residence, and burst into the room of a seventy-eight-year-old Belgian priest, Albert Desmet. They beat and tortured him so savagely that he lost an eye, and two days later died in St. François de Sales Hospital.

The Macoutes had made a mistake. They had killed the wrong man. Their target had been Father Triest, Radio Soleil director, not the senile pensioner. Roger Lafontant had made an even worse mistake. For a regime desperately fighting to stay alive, the premeditated butchery of an elderly foreign priest was intolerable. Desmet's murder was officially blamed on thieves, but the people knew better. Lafontant was out to kill his opponents.

On Referendum Day Haitians stayed at home. Streets everywhere were empty. Jean-Claude, at the wheel of a white Audi, visited dozens of polling stations, Michèle beside him, with two bodyguards with machine guns in the back seat. Behind, two cars full of armed men followed. Only at City Hall, where Port-au-Prince mayor Colonel Franck Romain had organized a street festival with free rum and music, was there any sort of turnout, and only there was Jean-Claude cheered. Lafontant tried to bolster the vote by ordering soldiers and Macoutes to grab people on their way to work and force them to vote. Some voters were captured this way, but still the turnout was less than 10 percent.

Despite his bleak defeat at proving popular support, Jean-Claude had deluded himself that the people wanted him to remain President-for-Life. The people of Haiti had turned out in droves, Lafontant declared, and by a vote of 99.98 percent had confirmed Jean-Claude in his presidency-for-life. The regime, already brutal, had now made itself ridiculous.

But the joke was not over, and on July 24 Lafontant expelled three Belgian priests, Fathers Hugo Triest, whom he would have preferred to kill, Yvan Pollefeyt, curé of Pointe à Raquette, and Jean Hostens, curé of

Montrouis. They were the first clergymen expelled from Haiti in fourteen years.

The regime was also under attack by the politicians. Defiantly, Grégoire Eugène published a second little green book. *The Haitian Miracle Is Possible: A Plea for Development* hit the streets and bookstores on July 22, Referendum Day. "Unconditional partisan of political pluralism, I persist in hoping that in spite of all the resistance against it, all the forces of inertia, our political system will be inspired, sooner or later, with democratic free play and will lead the country to experience the only formula that can pull it up from the lowest step of the ladder of development," Eugène wrote.

From Duvalierist forces at odds with Jeanclaudism's incompetence and growing brutality another voice spoke out against the presidency-for-life and in favor of presidential elections: "Our young people aged less than thirty-two, who today represent about 50 percent of the Haitian electorate, have never enjoyed their legitimate privilege of choosing the Leader of the Nation," declared Clovis Désinor. In fact, Désinor hoped that they might choose him. In 1985 he took the giant step of announcing that he too was forming a political party.

On October 3 Désinor went further, issuing a communiqué urging support of Grégoire Eugène's position on the functioning of political parties. And after a decade of refusing to join forces with the "Band of Five" anti-Duvalierist opposition leaders, Eugène, Hubert de Ronceray, Sylvio Claude, Alexandre Lerouge, and Constant Pognon, Désinor decided the time had come to join them. "It is evident that the intended political liberalization has been extinguished," he wrote. Jean-Claude had had his chance. Now he had to go.

Jean-Claude countered with the rival National Progressive Party, founded by such Duvalierists as Madame Max Adolphe, Saint-Ange Bontemps, Luckner Cambronne, Ti-Pouche Douyon, all the super ministers, a contingent of powerful Macoutes, and relatives and friends frightened that if Jean-Claude fell, so would they.

The farce continued as Jean-Claude solemnly thanked the founders of the new party. "Because Jeanclaudism feeds at the doctrinal source of Duvalierism, the Economic Revolution and the process of democratization inaugurated in 1971 are merely the offshoots of the Political Revolution accomplished by my father." Regretfully he declined accepting their offer of the PNP leadership. "The new political system approved by a crushing majority of citizens last July 22 prevents me from being a Party Chief. I must remain, as Chief of State of the Nation, an impartial umpire between all political groups." In face of disaster, Haiti's Nero played not the fiddle but the fool.

In mid-September Jean-Claude fired Roger Lafontant. The murder of Father Desmet, the expulsion of the Belgian priests, the new rash of arrests and repression set the stage. The coup de grâce was delivered by Super Minister Frantz Merceron, who had been accumulating a dossier on Lafontant and now struck when the timing was best. "Have you any idea how much Lafontant is costing you, Mr. President?" was the essence of Merceron's case. Jean-Claude had not, and so the methodical Merceron pulled out files in which he had recorded the millions Lafontant had required to keep his elaborate Macoutic empire in well-heeled operation.

To Jean-Claude this was the final betrayal. Not only had Lafontant given him monstrously bad advice, he had also rifled the national coffers on a positively Duvalieresque scale. And because of him those coffers were at increasingly serious risk. Outgoing USAID Director Peter McPherson had repeated at an airport press conference as he left Haiti, "I spoke to [President Duvalier] about our unceasing preoccupation on the subject of human rights and freedom of the press. . . . Progress in the domain of democratization is a condition of American economic aid to all countries, and that includes Haiti." The Americans had been every bit as unimpressed by official "proof" of Haiti's scrupulous observance of human rights as the International Human Rights Commission in Geneva.

Fired, Lafontant did not panic. Instead he arranged for a bomb to be found on a Port-au-Prince-bound Haiti Air flight, then announced his "discovery" to the palace, certain that out of boundless gratitude, Jean-Claude would restore him to power. Lafontant hoped as well to cast suspicion on Ernest Bennett and even to engineer his downfall. After all, Haiti Air belonged to the impertinent mulatto usurper. Why shouldn't he be blamed for blowing up his own plane?

Lafontant miscalculated. Jean-Claude not only did not believe him, he reacted furiously to the setup. On October 4 passengers at François Duvalier International Airport were startled when a sea of soldiers appeared, escorting to the waiting Eastern Airlines Boeing jet Roger Lafontant, his wife, Gladys Murad, and his two Macoute henchmen, Michel Mirabeau and Jean Dérac.

"Dr. Roger Lafontant forgot only one thing," commented *Le Petit Samedi Soir.* "Haitian politics is a cruel mother who devours her own children." "What airline did they put Roger on?" was the latest Haitian riddle, "Cold Air" the response. Now it would be from his Canadian exile in Montréal, where he operated a fleet of taxis, that Roger Lafontant continued to plot his coup d'état against Jean-Claude Duvalier.

With Lafontant gone, Alix Cinéas returned to the cabinet, but his personal reflections during his seventeen months in disgrace had transformed him from a loyal Duvalierist to a secret dissident committed to ousting Jean-Claude. He had watched starving people protest and die in Gonaives. He had discussed with a few close friends the scandalous goings-on in the palace, where the President-for-Life and and the First Lady took drugs and cheated on each other. He had watched as the Bennett family and their cronies tore the country apart.

The conspiracy had taken final form one cool evening in the mountains of Laboule, at the home of Gérard C. Noel. The Jérémie-born lawyer sat drinking and idly chatting with his guests and close friends Lieutenant General Henri Namphy, Duvalier's army chief of staff, and Colonel Williams Regala, inspector of the armed forces. Suddenly he burst out in Creole, "Instead of wasting our time talking shit, why don't we do something about cleaning the shit out of the palace?" Over their rum glasses Namphy and Regala exchanged glances, then turned to Noel and began to talk. By evening's end the three men were still in deep debate about the logistics of forcing Duvalier out. The conspiracy, long brewing among dissident military officers, had now crystallized into the concrete planning stages.

Henri Namphy, who within a year would replace the man he was now plotting to overthrow, had never approved of Jean-Claude as Haiti's President. In the late 1970s he had caused something of a sensation at a party when someone made a reference to Duvalier. Too much rum had loosened his tongue and Namphy silenced the entire room by retorting, "Fuck Duvalier." Apparently the widely repeated incident stopped short of Jean-Claude's ears, and Namphy continued to serve as a senior officer increasingly shocked by the Duvaliers'—and later the Bennetts'—uncontrolled greed. He was just as disturbed by the swift rise to power of Roger Lafontant and the consequent triumph of the Macoutes over the army. (Lafontant harbored a deep and mutual hatred for Namphy, who warned his immediate family that he was a volatile and deadly enemy.)[25] Noel's outburst that evening in Laboule was simply the articulation of what Namphy and certain fellow officers had long agreed among themselves. To continue in blind support of Jean-Claude Duvalier had become more treasonable than to turn against him. "The army, it's the people," went the Creole adage Namphy liked to quote. In wantonly firing officers and undermining the armed forces, Duvalier was also destroying the people—and the nation.

Namphy, conservative and conventional, did not find it easy to accept that patriotism demanded disloyalty to his President. Even in the darkest days of Papa Doc he had declined to join any of numerous plots to overthrow or assassinate the dictator. For one thing, in a divided army, he had been a member of a pro-Duvalierist faction. He also believed that the elder Duvalier was Haiti's legitimate President, and that the essence of the Revolution he preached was fundamentally sound, despite abuses in its practice. Now, as commander in chief, he gave the armed forces top priority in any decisions he made.

In the past two years Namphy had refused to join Lafontant, his longtime enemy, in overthrowing Jean-Claude. Infuriated by Lafontant's audacity in claiming the presidency, and repelled by the prospect of the Macoute-ridden regime he would certainly establish, he declined to participate. Even in exile in Montréal, Lafontant plotted to replace Namphy with a more compatible chief of staff, such as Ti-Boulé Pierre, who would help him get rid of Jean-Claude so that he could assume the presidency himself.

The conspiracy that took shape at Gérard Noel's was predicated on no man's grandiose ambition—only on the inescapable realization that Jean-Claude Duvalier had to go. Namphy and Regala, with their military and civilian allies and the American officials who encouraged them, all agreed in principle that no new dictator would replace the old one and that democratic elections would be held as soon as possible. In the interim a benign provisional government would oversee the difficult period of transition. Above all else, they vowed that the process would be bloodless.

These admirable sentiments were never translated into a detailed post-Duvalier scenario for the highly complex society whose functioning depended on its intricate power structure and relationships. What would be done about the tens of thousands of the most violent of the Tonton Macoutes and hard-line Duvalierists whom the regime had encouraged to brutalize their fellow Haitians and whom their victims could never pardon? What would be done about genuine revolutionaries, many in the Catholic Church, and others either silent, underground, or in exile? What would be done to right old wrongs?

None of the conspirators were revolutionaries. At most they were motivated by mild reformism, the reactive anger of privileged Duvalierists disgusted at Jeanclaudist excesses, seeking to restore some measure of independence to the Haitian armed forces and to halt the looting that had very nearly emptied the national treasury. Because this was the extent of their ambition they saw no need to make common cause with men such as Sylvio Claude, Grégoire Eugène, or Hubert de Ronceray, who had devoted years and risked their lives to fighting not merely Duvalier but Duvalierism itself. And they hated and scorned leaders of the popular movement already roiling among the people of the ever-expanding cities and the countryside.

The restricted scope of the anti-Jeanclaudist conspiracy was even more clearly delineated when, in the months to come, its leaders failed to recruit or even dialogue with those leaders. Even after the people rose in waves of uprisings in late 1985, the conspirators never sought to channel or coordinate the rebellions, though they were quick to use each renewed outburst as ammunition to convince Jean-Claude he had to leave.

Inside Haiti the months of unrest and rebellion preceding Duvalier's overthrow were generally referred to as "the Revolution," but like the Duvalierist social and economic revolutions, it was no revolution at all. It was, in grand Haitian tradition, a Duvalierist housecleaning led by Namphy and other officers and civilians who knew how frequently presidents had been military men, and also how frequently military men had overthrown presidents.

Until he replaced Jean-Claude Duvalier on February 7, 1986, Henri Christophe Namphy seemed a most unlikely candidate to assume the Haitian presidency. Inside Haiti he was known as a competent and brave officer who drank to excess, apparently without ill effects, and who had endeared himself to the populations of Cayes and Cap Haitien by saving civilian lives when he was military commandant of each district. Outside Haiti he was not known at all, and foreign diplomats had to rely on personal encounters with him for information. The picture they usually painted after meeting Namphy was of an honest Haitian who was polite but not overly friendly, a man who wasted no time in small talk. These assessments were fair ones, but they touched only the surface of this emotional, short-tempered, and close-mouthed Haitian general suddenly catapulted into world prominence and, within two years, international ignominy.

Henri Namphy had been a twenty-four-year-old lieutenant when François Duvalier was elected in 1957, a hardworking officer who rose steadily through the ranks. He consistently avoided the dangerous arena of politics and confined himself to struggling to abide by Duvalierism without compromising his basic personal principles.

Namphy was known among Haitians for refusing to fire on civilian crowds even if this meant defying Papa Doc. Namphy had never asked Duvalier for a personal favor. Papa Doc had once commented on this with some displeasure, for he liked to obligate people to him by granting them special privileges. "How is it that none of your family works in the government?" he'd demanded. "Why is it that you've never needed to ask me for any help for them?" But Duvalier forgave Namphy his independence. "I never worry about Ti-Blanc's loyalty," he confided to his intimates. "I know that his ambition stops at too many women and too much rum."

Papa Doc's assessment failed to recognize the extent of Namphy's professional ambition, but he was accurate about his passion for dallying with the ladies and drinking with the boys. Namphy's philandering was not exceptional among Haitian men, and although he fathered a daughter in the 1960s, he did not marry until middle age.

Papa Doc apparently accepted the drinking and made no attempt to reproach him for it. Instead, when Namphy did a stint in the Palace Guard, the President simply had a small refrigerator installed in his office so that Ti-Blanc would have a constant supply of soft drinks to dilute the rum; as a medical doctor, Duvalier worried that Namphy's liver could not metabolize so much alcohol.

Papa Doc's death and Jean-Claude's ascendancy to the presidency changed little for Namphy, except that he and his fellow officers enjoyed the new security of knowing that their physical survival was no longer an issue, as it had been throughout the elder Duvalier's rule. But like so many others, Namphy disapproved of the young President and kept their relations correct but formal. Namphy became acting chief of staff when the ailing General Roger St. Albin was diagnosed as terminally ill with cancer, and in early 1984, when St. Albin died, he succeeded him as chief of staff. Despite these promotions, Namphy stayed away from the palace except on business, attending only those ceremonial functions that absolutely required his presence.

The glittering social life of the palace held no attractions, but the lively banter and discussion at his mother's small bungalow did. In 1982 Jeanne Namphy had returned from New York, where she had toiled as a nurse's aide for twelve years until she saved enough money to fulfill a longtime dream—to buy her own home in Port-au-Prince. She settled into her modest new two-bedroom house, filled it with tropical plants and photographs of her five children, brought her centenarian mother, Sé-Rose, to live with her, and settled down to retirement.

The pious and plain-spoken "Mammy Jeanne" drew people toward her. She regularly entertained visitors, ranging from the highest to the lowest, and her small living room resembled a modern Haitian version of France's eighteenth-century salons.

Mammy Jeanne was also once again an important and stable part of her oldest son's life. Several times a week one of the army's official vehicles would park in front of the iron gate where Jeanne's mongrel Poppy patrolled. Inside the house sat Haiti's chief of staff, sampling his mother's homemade soursop ice cream or her cashew chicken, the traditional dish in Haiti's North.

In 1985 Namphy resolved his difficult personal life, ending in divorce court his long-troubled marriage to the outspoken Gisèle Celestin. World-traveled and much more sophisticated than her husband, she had continually warned him that the men who congregated every weekend at his country house in Laplaine—to which she was not invited—were only using him, drinking his liquor and giving him bad advice.

At the end, Namphy returned home only to change his clothes and spent almost all his nights in his country house in Laplaine. After he and Gisèle divorced, he moved from the Laboule house to Laplaine, on the outskirts of Port-au-Prince, and settled into family life with his mistress, Gabrielle, whom he later married, and their young daughter, Melissa. Gaby, small and pretty with a wistful smile and huge dark eyes, was an undemanding woman who shared Namphy's plain tastes and was devoted to and fiercely protective of him. Though she did not drink, she enjoyed the long evenings spent outside chatting with his gang of friends on the gallery of the chalet-style farmhouse. During quieter times Namphy read his way through his impressive French- and Spanish-language library. He was no intellectual but he kept well informed about a broad range of subjects and was deeply versed in the history of Haiti.

When Namphy embarked on the campaign to oust Duvalier, the newfound serenity of life with Gaby and Melissa helped him take another important decision. To see him through the long grim months ahead, Namphy made a supreme effort to give up liquor.

Sober, personally happy, and convinced that what he was doing was right, Namphy began sounding out fellow officers, so that a core of key men would be counted on to assist in a bloodless ouster and not take up arms in final defense of the President. Longtime friend Williams Regala, the brilliant and cynical *noiriste* colonel who had been at Namphy's side the night Gérard Noel first urged them to act, worked with him. Together they lined up recruits, finding a fertile field in the ranks of former officers fired by Jean-Claude, often because Michèle did not like them or because Roger Lafontant had engineered their dismissal in an attempt to purge the army of his enemies. These ex-officers almost uniformly despised Jean-Claude, and an important part of Namphy's and Regala's strategy was to have them reinstated in the army. At the same time they engineered the revocation of officers they considered rivalous and Macoutish, and unlikely to support them. Among them were Colonels Samuel Jérémie, Emmanuel Orcel, Albert Ti-Boulé Pierre, and Raymond Cabrol.

Ironically, Henri Namphy considered himself a sincere democrat, and in Haitian terms he was. He had long enjoyed a reputation as a "democratic" officer, but what this actually meant was that Namphy was not at all snobbish and, despite his light skin, chestnut hair, and green eyes, fraternized as intimately with blacks as with mulattoes.

Namphy was the only one of Mammy Jeanne's children who spoke almost no English, and though his first wife, Gisèle, was a travel agent, he showed little interest in traveling anywhere outside of Haiti. His French and Spanish were excellent but he preferred to speak Creole, in which he could express himself as crudely as any common soldier, "Fuck him" being a staple of his vocabulary. He was a soldier's soldier and a Haitian's Haitian, and in his world, that made him a "democrat."

Furthermore, although he had thrived under Duvalierism and had never voted, he insisted that democratic elections, freedom of speech, the press, syndicalism, and religion would be essential in the new post-Duvalierist Haiti. But as soon became clear, this newly embraced ideology was largely a ploy to assuage the Americans who made it part of their negotiations that led to Duvalier's ouster.

*   *   *

The plot soon included several American officials who offered guarantees that the U.S. would recognize a military-civilian coalition government as Haiti's new ruling body as soon as Duvalier was gone. Friendly Americans, including Ambassador Clinton McManaway, Jr. went even further. The U.S. would help in the ouster and its aftermath, if democracy—as always undefined—and not a new dictatorship was really the conspirators' goal.

In the civilian world one of the most important conspirators was Alix Cinéas. Cinéas had many friends in the military. He was also very close to the Duvalier family, and despite Jean-Claude's initial anger at him as the bearer of bad tidings from Gonaives, he remained the Duvaliers' trusted councillor about matters personal and political and was constantly summoned to the palace. Cinéas's main role in the conspiracy was a subtle one—to use his considerable influence to convince Jean-Claude that he must leave Haiti.

Meanwhile, in a parallel development, the Catholic Church's growing anti-Duvalierists campaign facilitated the.conspirators. Since March 1983 the Church had been speaking out against the regime's abuses, defying the government, challenging Jean-Claude, rousing Haiti's millions of Catholics. Radio Soleil grew daily more strident in its anti-regime attacks. The bishops took a stand, with Jérémie bishop Willy Romélus fearlessly speaking out. In the traditionally independent North, Bishop Gayot did the same. Haitian and foreign priests also spoke out, inspired by liberation theology and also disgust at the endemic corruption, and Sunday sermons were as much about politics as God.

The volatile people of Gonaives rose up first. On October 30 Gonaives police arrested Pollux Saint-Jean, recently returned from Miami to devote himself to anti-Duvalierist activities. Specifically, he was a member of a left-wing rebel group headed by Dr. Lionel Lainé, killed in late October after the SD surprised him in the Nan Waney slum of Port-au-Prince. Saint-Jean's arrest provoked demonstrations, minor but a harbinger of things to come.

Michèle too fueled the popular fury in Gonaives—and elsewhere—by embarking with a party of two dozen on a European shopping expedition that cost the hungry nation $85,000 in first-class plane tickets alone. The total cost of her purchases of furs, clothes, paintings, and other artwork was $1.7 million, and in anticipation of her financial needs for the trip, obliging Finance Minister Merceron dug into the nation's foreign reserves.

Afterward fuel tankers refused to stop in Haiti because the government had no foreign currency to pay them. *Tap-taps* and *camionettes* (public vans) and taxis and private cars lined up for hours for small rations of gas and diesel. As transportation problems grew, food shipments to the hungry countryside lagged, and starvation was the consequence. These shortages caused sporadic riots and uprisings, as desperate people no longer had anything to lose.

Michèle believed the real problem was that she and Jean-Claude were misrepresented. One of the projects that had made Michèle even more misunderstood had been her famous 1984 *tombola*. Time had not diluted the popular rage at the *tombola*, a feast so extravagant it stunned even Haitians accustomed to her excesses. "If Nero were to come back to earth and throw a party, this was the party he would throw," exclaimed the renowned Haitian painter Bernard Séjourné, who was a guest. The *tombola*, at $500 a plate, was a fundraising event for the Bon Repos Hospital. To spur attendance at the lavish party, Michèle raffled off fabulous jewels as door prizes, the perfect adornments for her guests' couturier gowns. She herself was spectacular in a rhinestone-studded gold gown with a diamond-and-sapphire necklace and matching earrings so heavy that they hung down from her lobes like a pair of flashing spare ears.

After her hundreds of guests dined on the sumptuous fare and sipped the finest champagne, Michèle and Jean-Claude led the dancing, Michèle's lovely body sinuous and graceful, Jean-Claude, in white-on-white, light-footed and smiling. The raffle tickets were drawn, and the winners displayed their dazzling prizes.

The *tombola* was of course in the best of causes, Michèle's foundation. The clash of luxury with the daily grinding misery they could not escape maddened the viewers watching the public television sets, and in Gonaives, on November 27, a peaceful demonstration of children and young people marched from the grim, parched slum of Raboteau, protesting against hunger, against the misery of their lives. By 11:30 a.m. all schools except one closed their doors, and parents rushed about gathering up their children. At every crossroads demonstrators burned tires. The air of Gonaives hung black with protest. Soldiers fired in the air, dispersing people who ran away and then reformed. Everywhere anti-Duvalierist placards appeared, and from thousands of chanting Haitians rang the strains of newly coined anti-Duvalierist songs.

*   *   *

On November 28 in Gonaives, twenty-year-old Jean-Robert Cius rose from the bed he shared with his fourteen-year-old brother Joseph in their home in dusty Raboteau. Jean-Robert was a student at the College of the Immaculate Conception. He was also his mother's, Anne Denise Hilaire's, joy and her family's brightest hope. Since his father had fled into exile fourteen years earlier after being imprisoned for distributing anti-Duvalierist tracts, young Jean-Robert had been his mother's confidant, trying to assume the burdens his father had left behind.

This Thursday morning Jean-Robert quickly ate his breakfast, kissed his mother goodbye, and set out for the college. Anne Denise would never see her son again.

That Thursday Gonaives erupted in antigovernment riots. Demonstrators roamed the streets, and at 10:15 they arrived at the college to invite the students to join them. The school yard emptied, and only forty boys remained. Father Rosaire Guévin, the school's Canadian director, decided to send them home. Jean-Robert gathered up his books and walked outside, but when he saw a police truck speeding toward the college, he ran back inside to stand close to Father Guévin. The policemen, shouting that they were dispersing demonstrators, fired directly on the students.

Beside Father Guévin, Jean-Robert fell. Two policemen ran over to him. "Kill him," shouted one. But the other refused, and Father Guévin rushed Jean-Robert to the hospital, where he died.

Jean-Robert was not the college's only victim. After he was shot, Makenson Michel had fled the schoolyard. Macoutes followed and caught up with him in front of a coffin-maker's shop, then beat and stabbed him to death with bayonets.

Daniel Israel, son of a Macoute and a member of a secret anti-Duvalierist group, was attacked by Macoutes as he stood across from the school. "You can't shoot children!" he shouted. But they could, and Daniel fled for his life down a tiny alley, through a maze of huts, past a thick mango tree. The Macoutes followed him, shooting, and the walls of the houses and the tree were pitted with bullet holes. Just before he died Daniel turned and begged for his life. "Please don't shoot me," he cried. "You know my father!" They shot him where he stood.

Jean-Claude Duvalier sent the three families condolences and envelopes of money. The mourners spat at the one and refused the other. "You want to pay for killing our children?" a mother shouted. "Do you think they are pigs?"

12 THE FINAL DAYS OF DUVALIER

J AIL CELLS WERE ONCE AGAIN FILLED TO OVERFLOWING AS
journalists and dissidents of all stripes were arrested. Those still free
now spoke out in furious protest, with Grégoire Eugène, Rockefeller
Guerre, Gérard Gourgue, and Aubelin Jolicoeur leading the chorus. Radio Soleil and Protestant Radio Lumière broadcast their words and denounced Duvalier.

The regime, panicking at the message, killed the messenger. On December 5 Duvalier ordered Radios Soleil and Lumière shut down for giving "alarmist" news. All other private stations then joined in a voluntary news blackout, leaving only Radio Nationale on the air. Haitians with shortwave bands turned to foreign-beamed Creole broadcasts for their news. Some listened to Voice of America, others to Radio Moscow.

A great silence fell over Haiti, but soon other voices dispelled it— the shrieks of rioting mobs, the ringing words of priests from their pulpits, the buzz of millions of private conversations, the cries of prisoners.

On December 24 the Catholic Bishops' Conference issued its Christmas message to the nation. "It's time to say no to lies, yes to truth!" the bishops declared. "No to servility, yes to liberty. No to selfishness, yes to sharing. No to torture, yes to respect for man. No to violence, yes to dialogue. No to injustice and abuses, yes to justice. No to hatred, yes to love."

Millions of Haitians heard the message and rejoiced. In the palace the Duvaliers heard it with different ears. Infuriated, they sent a high-ranking official to scold Michèle's uncle, Archbishop Wolff Ligondé, forced by peer pressure and moral persuasion to co-sign the document. "How could you sign such a thing when you have a relative on the other side?" was Michèle's angry message.

Old Duvalierists, *noiristes* now considered moderates in comparison with the voraciously greedy Jeanclaudists, were summoned back to prop up the failing machine: the once-popular and long-retired Pierre Merceron, Dinosaur ex-minister Adrien Raymond, brother of General Claude Raymond, and Georges Salomon.

The only one of the trio who would play an important role in the final days was former Ambassador and Foreign Affairs Minister Georges Salomon, well known for his probity, mildness, and erudition. The distinguished elder statesman, a direct descendant of President Lysius Salomon, knew the regime was in its death throes. In face of the national crisis, Salomon decided patriotism obliged him to sacrifice his personal life and reputation to ease Papa Doc's inept son out of office. The reward would be, he hoped, Jean-Claude's dignified retreat and, above all, no bloodshed.

By early January, however, the death toll began to climb. On January 6 and 7, seven cities erupted in antigovernment demonstrations: Gonaives, Petit Goave, Cayes, Jérémie, Miragoane, Cap Haitien, and Léogane. In Gonaives a man was killed while watching troops fire on a crowd of demonstrators. In Petit Goave protesters burned down the customs house, the tax bureau, and the water company office.

The uprisings, timed to coincide with school reopening on January 7, kept Haitian schoolchildren at home. On January 8, despite agonizing personal indecision and only after bitter cabinet debate, Jean-Claude ordered the schools closed. If they could only be reopened by violence, went the prevailing logic, best close them by governmental decree and undercut one of the opposition's most sensitive areas of protest. So more deaths by bullets were avoided, but no tally was taken of the victims among the almost eight hundred thousand children relying on school feeding programs for their one daily meal.

On January 9 Jean-Claude turned in desperation to his father's realm of inspiration—the priests of the Haitian vodoun gods. A dutiful practitioner who routinely visited his personal *houngans* in the peristyles in Croix des Bouquet, Léogane, and Diquini, up the road past Katherine Dunham's and the Habitation Leclerc, Duvalier now felt he needed more forceful guidance. On January 9, at 6:30 p.m., he telephoned vodoun priest Max Beauvoir. "This is Jean-Claude," Beauvoir heard, and immediately recognized the President's nasal voice though he had never met him. Calm as ever, Jean-Claude asked Beauvoir for his guidance during this critical period in the national life. Equally calm, Beauvoir asked for a week's delay so that he could provide that advice after proper reflection.

Jean-Claude agreed, and at noon on Thursday, January 16, the handsome, debonair Beauvoir, a Paris-educated chemical engineer and deeply learned in vodoun after years spent apprenticing in rural peri-styles, brought a delegation of seven senior *houngans* to the palace, where Jean-Claude and Michèle met with them.

Led by Beauvoir, they talked to their President for more than two hours, pounding him with a list of grievances ranging from universal unemployment, endemic corruption, widespread degradation, and mis-ery. If Jean-Claude had still imagined he retained some grass-roots popu-larity, these *houngans* disabused him of the notion. Beauvoir told him gravely, explaining the national turmoil, "Since March 1985, the spirits have wanted you to leave."

"I am lost," Jean-Claude replied. For fourteen years, he told the assembled priests, his advisers had never mentioned that his people were complaining about their suffering. The biggest shock of all to him was the message that the *loas* wanted him to leave.

Similar messages began raining down on the President from less esoteric domains. The Haitian Catholic Episcopal Conference, the Hai-tian Human Rights League, the Haitian Committee of Members of Reli-gious Orders, the Representatives of the Protestant Churches, and the Haitian Medical Association all publicly condemned him and demanded immediate redress of the nation's grievances.

But it was the Haitian Industrialists Association (ADIH) condem-nation that infuriated Jean-Claude. After noting the reign of tension and fear throughout Haiti, and the continual eruptions of popular dis-content, the industrialists blamed Duvalier and his failure to implement democratic structures for their own current problems: bad press in for-eign media, harming the chances for attracting future investment, can-cellations of orders from foreign contractors, on which the industrialists were almost entirely dependent, and their fear that the sixty thouand jobs their factories provided were in jeopardy, and with them, the three hundred thousand people whom those jobs fed, clothed, and kept alive.

Unfair! raged Jean-Claude, so angry that he even interrupted emergency cabinet sessions to harp on the ADIH communiqué. He had given the industrialists priority over all other businessmen, Jean-Claude reminded everyone, and they had raked in fortunes from all the tax holidays, franchises, and other benefits he had lavished on them. But what had they provided in return? Only sixty thousand jobs, a mere bagatelle when Jean-Claude had been certain they could create a million. Instead of investing their own hefty profits into business, they (Duvalieristically) built beach houses and bought luxury cars and traveled. They had not, Jean-Claude believed, returned to the people the advantages he had entrusted to them as vehicles for his economic revolution. Now, when they turned on him with self-righteous anger, he felt their betrayal was undeserved.

The people were also betraying him, telling their President they no longer loved him, openly rebelling against him. They improvised road-blocks of rocks and boulders and lay behind them in wait for motorists. Woe to owners of jeeps and Pajeros, favored by the Duvaliers as gifts to supporters and as bribes to convert those who were not. These were doused with gas-oil, $3.00 a gallon, and ignited. More acceptable vehicles were spray-painted "Down with Duvalier," the slogan motorists were forced to utter before being turned loose to return to the capital in their rolling graffiti.

The death toll rose slowly and inexorably. Tracts appeared overnight in the streets to disappear just as suddenly. They stated the undeniable truth—the Duvaliers had raped the Black Republic until it lay bleeding and exhausted. The tracts also attacked on other fronts—that homosexual *"macici"* Jean-Claude must go! For good measure, Michèle Bennett was branded a lesbian.

Every morning brought new horrors: children arrested in a church in Cayes and beaten, markets closed down so the price of food sky-rocketed. In the Martissant slum next to Port-au-Prince the nights were punctuated with the blasting of machine-gun fire as Macoutes shot up neighborhoods and neighbors. So many were struck by stray bullets as they lay sleeping that residents took to lying under rather than in their beds.

Strikes closed stores and markets and rocked the leaky ship of state. The price of American money rose higher and higher on the black market as frantic Haitians unloaded their *gourdes* and fled. Rumors flew from one end of the country to the other: Lafontant was landing to oust Jean-Claude, Lafontant was dead, murdered on the streets of Montréal.

Jean-Claude's son Nicolas was also dead, a victim of surgery to cure the condition that had caused his retardation.

People repeated an old Haitian joke. Jean-Claude has just married the detested Michèle, the story goes, and in honeymooning with her has ended his nine-year honeymoon with the Haitian people. He is in a helicopter, while below him thousands of peasants wave their arms at him and shout. "I can't hear what they're saying," Jean-Claude complains to his pilot. "Go lower, I want to hear what my people are calling out to me." Reluctantly the pilot loses altitude until finally Jean-Claude can hear the collective voice of his people. "Jump!" they are shouting in unison. "Jump, Jean-Claude, jump!"

Even as they betrayed him Jean-Claude was again betraying his people, trading nineteen thousand of them for $2 million. The victims were the cane cutters, and as he had every other year, Jean-Claude sold his people's backbreaking labor to the Dominicans.

The Dominican Sugar Council asked that hiring for the 1986 *zafra* begin in mid-January, and specified nineteen thousand Haitians. Before Duvalier authorized the hiring halls to open, he wanted his money. On January 18 he got it, in two leather suitcases hand-carried to the palace by Hervé Denis, Haiti's ambassador to the Dominican Republic, who arrived in a chartered jet with three Dominican sugar officials. Alone with Duvalier in his office, Denis handed over the money, then chatted for thirty-five minutes. Afterward he informed the waiting Dominicans that all was well and that he had instructions to visit Police Chief Ti-Boulé Pierre to iron out details with him so the mammoth hiring process would go smoothly.

The hiring began in Léogane, began badly, and ended worse. The year before, for the first time ever, there had been wide-scale Haitian opposition to the *zafra*. It had sprung up after the National Bank of Agricultural and Industrial Development (BNDAI) replaced the Central Bank as the organizer for exchanging pesos into *gourdes* at the border. Instead of the usual routine business transaction, the BNDAI harassed the men, forcing them to strip and submit to a body search in case they had concealed money. BNDAI officials then stole the pathetically few pesos they had earned, leaving the cane cutters to return to their starving families still penniless after more than six months of backbreaking labor. Next year, vowed the legions of ragged and penurious cutters, we will refuse to go.

But when next year became this year, desperation changed their minds, and by the thousands they turned out to register. Instead of the usual ten halls, only the interior of the Léogane market had been reserved, and five thousand men together fought to enter its two doors, pushing, shoving, creating panic. Others boycotted the hiring but surrounded the building, protesting the inhuman conditions of the *bateys*. The army arrived to calm matters, followed by Tonton Macoutes, who attacked protesters, provoking full-scale riots. Twenty-six people were killed. Léogane, in open rebellion, caused the government to move the hiring center to Jacmel, but Jacmeliens refused to cooperate. "If it's not good for Léogane, it's not good for Jacmel!" they protested.

Soon afterward, with bets placed everywhere on how much longer Duvalier could retain his power, Ambassador Denis conveyed to him the Sugar Council's request that he return the $2 million for the abortive hiring. But Jean-Claude only took money, he never gave it back. In any case, it was long since out of Haiti and safely in a foreign bank account. Meanwhile the unemployed cutters starved, and in the Dominican Republic the sugar planters rounded up illegal Haitians and forced them into the *bateys* in place of the nineteen thousand they had paid for and not received. They also encouraged and helped Haitians to cross the border "illegally" to cut cane, and out of desperation many did so.

The timing was now ripe for the military conspirators to attempt the most delicate and difficult part of their strategy, and also the most crucial. This was to make contact with key Tonton Macoutes and convince them that it was essential that even they, the cornerstone of Duvalierist power, would benefit by Duvalier's departure. What made the prospect so dangerous was not only that the conspirators had to succeed but that they had to ensure that the subject of their talks be guarded in absolute secrecy.

Approaching the Macoutes was dangerous in the extreme. After twenty-eight years of Duvalierism, they and not the army were the strongest armed force in the nation. They totaled about fifty thousand registered members, many of them also in the army, and untold numbers armed. The Haitian armed forces, however, emasculated, divided, and subservient to Duvalier, numbered only seven thousand, including army, police, coast guard, air force, fire department, Palace Guard, and the Corps of Léopards. The mass of enlisted men were also poorly paid, earning as little as $86 a month. They were also in poor health and frequently so malnourished they slept on duty. Only the highest-ranked officers enjoyed reasonable salaries and generous living allowances. They were also in a position to siphon off funds for supplies and equipment, and in a variety of other ways could embezzle military moneys to enrich themselves.

Macoutes were almost invariably better off than mere soldiers. Their commandants and officers lived opulently, and the rank and file were at least able to feed themselves adequately, because even the humblest Macoute had life-and-death powers over his countrymen.

Yet the very strength of the Macoutes made alliance with them necessary. Even if they refused to cooperate, at least their neutrality had to be assured. But Henri Namphy, known for his hostility to Astrel Benjamin and other leading Macoutes, was not the man to conduct the negotiations. Williams Regala also declined, though he had an entrée to Macoute chief Elois Maitre, whose daughter Gladys was one of his friends. Ultimately the job was done by old Duvalierist Clovis Désinor, brought late into the plot by a civilian conspirator, a Haitian businessman whose role in Duvalier's ouster was as liaison between the influential Désinor and American officials.

The scheme to oust Jean-Claude delighted Désinor. He had spent fourteen years brooding over his own precipitous dismissal in 1970, made more bitter because he had always believed he and not Jean-Claude had been the rightful successor to Papa Doc and the black populist Duvalierist Revolution. Désinor immediately recognized the need for Macoute concurrence. He contacted Commandant Madame Max Adolphe and invited her to sit down with him in a deadly serious discussion.

Madame Max was stunned by Désinor's revelation of the plot and greeted it with complete hostility. She saw no reason to lend her support, demanding to know why the Macoutes, totally bound up as they were in a symbiotic power relationship with Duvalier, should wish to amputate what amounted to their own head.

Slowly, Désinor persuaded her. Haiti under Jean-Claude was finished, he argued, and Jean-Claude himself was barely treading water. The fact was, he disclosed, the Americans, who had for twenty-eight years propped up the Duvalier regime, now desperately wanted him out. To achieve that, they were prepared to support an interim military government that would preside over democratic elections and then step down from power in favor of an elected President. This meant, Désinor continued, that the Americans were also prepared to make basic concessions to those parties who provided valuable help in the complicated ouster, such as Madame Max herself, chief commandant of the Tonton Macoutes.

The American blessing to the enterprise shocked Madame Max. That these staunch allies had changed tack impressed her strongly, and finally convinced her. So did Désinor's warning that her refusal to cooperate would inevitably lead to a bloodbath, for if the Macoutes defended Duvalier against the army and the enraged population, the explosion of violence that would follow would be nothing less than a Haitian holocaust.

Once the prospect of civil war might have challenged Madame Max. Now, a widow and grandmother in her sixties, she was without the fire that once made her Duvalier's head Macoute and dragon lady. She was still smarting from the public humiliation of her forced retreat from Macoute Headquarters in Kenscoff only two months earlier, on October 21, soon after her archrival Roger Lafontant had been exiled. Madame Max had driven up the mountain in company with other top Duvalier officials to replace the three top local VSN officers, all of them Lafontant appointees. Instead rebellious Macoutes fired warning shots, and the once-omnipotent Madame Max was obliged to return to Port-au-Prince without installing her own Macoutes in Kenscoff.

Old Rosalie Adolphe listened to older Clovis Désinor, and before long she was convinced that the only sensible way out of Haiti's current crisis was for the Macoutes to remain neutral and, when the time came, not to prevent Jean-Claude from leaving Haiti. She agreed to contact several of her key officers and, with them, guarantee that Jean-Claude could safely flee.

However, until the final moments the rank and file could not be allowed to know what was happening—impossible to reason with so many thousands that their interests lay in allowing themselves to be abandoned by the man whom they regarded as their savior. An integral part of the plan was for the post-Duvalier government to protect the Macoutes in return for their cooperation. Obviously the small army could not guarantee such protection to every man in blue who swaggered on foot through the village or city neighborhood of his private bailiwick. It was unfortunate, but the big Macoutes had to gamble with the safety of the little Macoutes, trusting only that the army would fulfill its promise to safeguard as many of them as it could, and that not too many would fall victim to the post-Duvalierist popular vengeance. In the meantime it was essential to keep news of the deal away from the Macoute majority.

Once she had acceded to Désinor's urging and agreed to commit the Macoute leadership to the anti-Duvalier conspiracy, one of the conditions Madame Max demanded was a guarantee that the Americans would honor her visa to the U.S., where her son lived in St. Louis, Missouri, and where she had a close friend, a former Fillette Laleau, in Florida.

At first the Americans were adamantly opposed to even meeting with Madame Max. "She's a Macoute!" exclaimed one angry official. "She's a monster!"

The Haitian businessman acting as liaison shrugged off their objections. "She's also our only hope of kicking out Duvalier," he pointed out calmly. "If the Macoutes decide to keep him here as a puppet or even as a hostage, you'll have a civil war on your hands and enough blood will flow to drown us all."

His words were unanswerable, and in December Madame Max made the first of three visits to the American Embassy, down by the ocean on palm-studded Harry Truman Boulevard. The second one was in mid-January, and the final one a week later. The details of the agreement struck were held in confidence. It was understood, however, that the Americans fought grimly before accepting any of Madame Max's conditions, but that on her second visit the Macoute chieftain had warned them, "I'll return one more time. We'll either agree or we won't. But whichever it is, it will be my last visit here."

Another round of the discussions took place in a mansion high in the mountains above Port-au-Prince. There Clovis Désinor met with the U.S. Embassy's commercial attaché, Aubrey Hooks, widely believed to be a CIA undercover agent, and Larry Rosen, and USIS spokesman Jeffrey Lite. The talks were strained, with the Americans visibly swallowing their distaste for the proceedings. The object was for each side to assure the other of genuine cooperation during the complicated maneuvers to oust Duvalier, for each represented important interests indispensable to the operation.

Early on, Désinor told his intimates he believed the Americans favored him to head the provisional government that would follow Duvalier, though he said they had also mentioned the name of Marc Bazin, Jean-Claude's shortlived Finance Minister, in the same context.

In addition to his invaluable assistance with regard to Madame Max, Désinor provided much sound tactical advice. He explained to the Americans how certain cuts in food donations to the countryside would provoke immediate and extensive rioting as panic-stricken peasants protested. The consequence would be short-term misery but long-term alleviation, Désinor reasoned, for the impact of the terrible uprisings would help rid Haiti of Jean-Claude and all the sooner place it in benign protective custody—his, he believed.

In other offices and in other parts of Port-au-Prince, General Namphy was meeting with other Americans, including Ambassador McManaway, with whom he would develop a friendship. Though Namphy spoke and understood virtually no English, the Americans spoke French and felt they were communicating effectively with the Haitian general with the anxious eyes about how and when Jean-Claude's ouster would take place and what sort of government would replace him. It was generally understood that the only guarantee for a bloodless transition after Duvalier left was the army—and General Henri Namphy, chief of staff, was in effect the army. In less troubled times a President's successor would be the Chief Justice of the Supreme Court, but in late 1985 and early 1986 nobody doubted that the gun was mightier than the gavel.

On January 20, in face of ever-mounting popular protests, the government asked an OAS human-rights investigative team to postpone its upcoming visit. On the same day the new Information Minister, Adrien Raymond, made the rounds of the newspapers to detail Jean-Claude's new policies of liberalization and democratization. In the circumstances these were ridiculous and irrelevant, and by January 26 Haiti was in full rebellion. In Cap Haitien on that day thousands of people paraded through the streets shouting, "Down with Duvalier! We're going to be the ones to strike the final blow!" Later the protesters regrouped and stoned Cap Haitien's radio station, shouting that it broadcast only pro-Duvalier propaganda.

The Cap Haitian protests continued, with most of the town's seventy-five thousand citizens participating. One man died and twenty-six people were wounded as soldiers and Macoutes patrolled the streets, fired into the air, and attacked with clubs. Protesters clogged the main streets and stoned the men in olive green and in blue.

Unsuspecting foreign tourists caught downtown during the heat of battle rushed back to their cruise ship, which lifted anchor and sailed off.

Despite the gravity of the situation, an air of unreality permeated the uprisings. Misery had provoked them. Religious and political figures and daring journalists had articulated grievances and encouraged them. But only individual local leaders had emerged to organize and direct each collective outburst without benefit of national coordinating committees, and no national plan was elaborated. To this game another dimension was soon added—looting. Food warehouses, orphanages, schools, hospitals, and stores throughout the nation were attacked and emptied as men and women carried off every last ounce of the supplies that fed hundreds of thousands daily.

In the palace Jean-Claude learned with disbelief that the uprisings were continuing with full force and that spokesmen for the rebelling population of Cap Haitien had publicly threatened to strike the final blow. Papa Doc had often enough repeated the classic Haitian adage—"If Port-au-Prince rises up, smash their heads with *cocomacacs*. If Gonaives rises up, buy them off with *gourdes*. But if Cap Haitien rises up, pack your suitcases and go."

Shaken and furious, the President had condemned his rebelling people to death, personally telephoning Lieutenant Colonel Renaud Mompoint in Gonaives, Lieutenant Colonel Jodesty in Cap Haitien, and other commanding officers throughout Haiti and ordering them to fire on demonstrating crowds. "Massacre them if they take to the streets," he shouted to one officer after another.

But Mompoint, Jodesty, and others had subsequently phoned General Namphy at Army Headquarters, and in every case Namphy had countermanded the President's orders. "Hold your fire," he had instructed the officers. "The Haitian army must not fire on its own people."

It was all going according to plan. Obeying General Namphy and disobeying President-for-Life Duvalier, the army remained passive as uprisings continued. On January 29 soldiers stood by watching as thousands stormed Cap Haitien's CARE warehouse, fighting with one another over gigantic oil canisters and fifty-kilogram sacks of wheat. "Long live the army!" looters shouted. A few incidents marred the general enthusiasm, but more and more the desperate people looked to the military to lead them, to save them—at least temporarily.

In Port-au-Prince, Jean-Claude made important moves. He disbanded the hated SD, his secret police. He sacrificed three Macoutes in Gonaives, whose arrests for the November 28 murders of three schoolboys were announced. He fired the most brutal army officers and reintegrated into the army many of the moderates whom Lafontant and Michèle had driven out. As measures to salvage his position they were ineffective. But as moves that strengthened the hand of those working against him they were perfect.

Among the colonels fired were Albert Ti-Boulé Pierre, Raymond Cabrol, Emmanuel Orcel, and Samuel Jérémie, men so compromised by the regime it was believed they would fight to the death to preserve it. Reintegrated were Lieutenant Colonels Prosper Avril, Gérard Lacrête, Acédius St. Louis, and Fritz Romulus. Promoted to full colonel were Avril, Lacrête, and St. Louis. Increasingly the key military units were commanded by men who would refuse to fire on the people for the sake of saving Jean-Claude Duvalier's hide.

As the situation worsened Jean-Claude slept less, drank more coffee, and calmed himself with drugs. Black circles rimmed his eyes, and he took to using cucumber compresses for relief. Officials arrived at the palace at all hours without any good news and tried to persuade their disoriented President to focus on the key issues: either pledging true democracy, which meant immediate presidential elections, fleeing Haiti, or smashing the rebellion with all the force the Macoutes and the army had at their disposal.

Jean-Claude continued to reject all three options. The presidency-for-life was not negotiable. Instead he worried about whether the Americans were planning to invade Haiti and instructed Foreign Affairs Minister Georges Salomon to consult with the various foreign chancelleries to discover if they would support the U.S. in a Grenada-style operation. They would not, Salomon reported, but still Jean-Claude fretted, worrying aloud about American ships harbored near Port-au-Prince and about reports of military planes at the ready in South Carolina.

In Port-au-Prince itself he coerced stores to reopen, sending Macoutes to intimidate owners into unlocking their doors, threatening them with jail and confiscation of their property if they refused. Shops opened under duress, but in the huge markets that are the heartbeat of the Haitian economy and life, "Madame Saras," the market women who supply the smaller vendors, stayed in the countryside, frightened they might not be able to make it back home. The few who ventured to the markets found hordes of buyers, and prices for even flabby vegetables and wormy rice soared as panicky shoppers competed for whatever food they found.

By the end of January the uprisings had become more ferocious, with deaths on both sides. Increasingly, Macoutes were the targets of attacks. In the provinces thousands of the men in blue disguised themselves as women and fled to the VSN Barracks in Port-au-Prince, just meters from Dessalines Barracks.

The Léopards in Gonaives, stationed there permanently since November 28 and now commanded by moderate Colonel Fritz Romulus, disarmed the Macoutes just as they were about to open fire on a crowd of protesters who massed in front of their barracks, taunting them and waving little American flags.

The pressure was on the Duvaliers to leave. Jean-Claude toyed unhappily with the idea, while Michèle rejected it utterly. "I married the President, and I'll leave the palace in a coffin," she snapped. Yet from foreign embassies came confirmations that the Duvaliers had requested asylum, and Greece and Spain both reported rejecting them. Odd countries for the Duvaliers to have chosen—socialist, unsympathetic to deposed dictators, and both without any known Duvalier holdings. Even odder, mused Foreign Affairs Minister Georges Salomon, was that the Duvaliers had not followed regular channels and instructed him to sound out various embassies. Probably, he reasoned, Michèle had personally put out these bizarre feelers to prove to Jean-Claude that nobody would accept them. Salomon would have found them a haven; that was why Michèle did not approach him.

In Montréal, Roger Lafontant had been plotting a coup d'état. He spent hours on the phone with Haitian relatives, friends, and followers, detailing his plans, culling support, giving instructions. He intended to return as a perfected Papa Doc, and at a time when they were running for their lives he let the Macoutes know he would soon be home to rescue them. Lafontant could also count on the army officers recently fired: Ti-Boulé, Cabrol, Orcel, perhaps Jérémie, the biggest thief of all. But what he could not count on was the upper-level Macoute command. As Interior Minister he had challenged Madame Max's power and undermined her as much as he could, and now that she and not he remained in power, he would pay a heavy price for his arrogance toward her and the Macoute leaders loyal to her.

Jean-Claude, knowing nothing of the treachery on his doorstep, was obsessed with Lafontant's machinations in Montréal. His spies brought him taped conversations of Lafontant's calls, and with angry fascination he heard Lafontant advise relatives where he had hidden weapons and what to do when the time came for his invasion. A hodgepodge of vinyl valises and boxes and an arsenal of weapons seized from Lafontant's mansion in Port-au-Prince's elegant Peguyville suburb now lay heaped in a passageway in the palace. The relatives, however, were released. Their interrogation had made it quite clear that they had never cooperated with Lafontant and wanted no part of his plots.

The day after Lafontant's house was searched, Jean-Claude was hit with another crisis—the U.S. announced its decision to block $26 million in aid money until Haiti could prove it had shown progress in the field of human rights. "With the unwarranted shootings and beatings that are taking place, it is clearly impossible for us to proceed with a determination that [human rights] progress is being made," said a State Department official.

Rumors now flew that the Duvaliers were leaving. Servants reported seeing dozens of packed suitcases in the hallway; they did not know they were Lafontant's. Ambassador McManaway and U.S. Embassy officials were in continual telephone contact with the palace, and when on the afternoon of January 31 McManaway received a call to go to the palace, most in Port-au-Prince quickly knew about it.

At 5 p.m. the deputies were ordered to gather at 8 p.m. at the National Assembly to debate the crucial issue of a state of siege, which three days earlier they had been unable to decide on. By the time most of them had been located and begun to work, it was already 10 p.m. Despite the late hour, the discussion was interminable. For the first time since their "elections" the deputies spoke and acted like independent beings, and because they were all aware of the historic nature of the decision under consideration, they had no intention of making an historic mistake. At 1 a.m. they decided to send a delegation of ten to the palace to see the President.

Public Works Minister Alix Cinéas accompanied them, and at 1:30 Jean-Claude and Michèle received them, Jean-Claude haggard, his face gray and drawn, Michèle watching with blazing eyes. The deputies begged the President to agree to announce presidential elections as an alternative to a state of siege. Michèle cut them short. "Never will my husband consider presidential elections," she informed them in tones that left no doubt of her resolve.

At 2 a.m. on TV screens across Haiti insomniacs watched a computer message flash across Télé-National's screen. "Stand by for an important announcement," it said. Within minutes thousands of telephones rang as Haitians wakened one another to share the news that the Duvaliers had left the country.

In those bleak hours before dawn the exhausted President suddenly succumbed to the hopelessness of his position. Even the docile deputies had come to challenge him. He and his government had lost control, and in those despairing moments he admitted defeat. He would leave while he still could.

A dozen times already Jean-Claude had made the same decision and then changed his mind, giving in to Michèle, who furiously ordered him to stand firm and fight. Earlier that day, during one of his frantic mood swings, Jean-Claude had arranged for a plane. Now, after a few quick phone calls, he reactivated his earlier arrangements, alerted a few relatives and friends. Then, quietly and quickly, Jean-Claude and his little convoy sped along the silent streets of Port-au-Prince and out onto the airport road.

Despite their stealth and the lateness of the hour, they did not leave unobserved. Frank Russo, the pseudonym for a State Department official who for days had shuttled back and forth between the embassy and the palace, saw them drive off, a carload of army officers leading them. Russo immediately passed that information to the U.S. Embassy. In Washington, American officials trying to confirm the news that the Duvaliers had left were unable to contact sources at the airport. The army had jammed all communications. Reviewing and analyzing all the cables and phone calls already received from Port-au-Prince, the Americans concluded that the Duvaliers had fled.

They had not. Jean-Claude had again changed his mind. The person responsible was Colonel Prosper Avril, accompanying them in the same car, while General Namphy and other officers preceded the Duvaliers in another vehicle.

"It's certain that I have to leave?" Jean-Claude queried, as always seeking reassurance.

The mild-mannered Avril, the Duvalier family adviser for so many years it was said he knew more about their finances and secret accounts than they did themselves, hesitated. At this crucial interval he said the words that literally turned the indecisive Jean-Claude around in his tracks. Avril implied that it was still possible for Jean-Claude to regain control of the situation.

A plausible explanation for Avril's behavior is that he felt so compromised by his years as faithful and clever account-keeper for the Duvaliers that he foresaw only grave trouble for himself the minute the Duvaliers were no longer in power to protect him. He had with several other officers endured over two years of Jean-Claude's official displeasure when Dr. Roger Lafontant's influence was paramount in the palace and he had been abruptly retired. Recently, however, he had been reintegrated into the army and was afraid that his colleagues might fail in their plan to succeed, and that Lafontant, then rumored to be on the eve of an invasion, might use Jean-Claude's flight to mobilize the Macoutes and seize power himself. Such a suggestion would have been enough to galvanize the vacillating President into furious action. In whatever terms he couched his remarks, provoking Jean-Claude to change his mind, Colonel Prosper Avril set into motion a terrible chain of events.

Now that he had decided not to leave, Jean-Claude was obsessed with hiding all traces of his return to the palace. It is widely believed that he wanted the plotting Lafontant to think he had fled, so when he landed and attempted to take over the palace, Jean-Claude sent away the waiting plane and ordered the tower not to record any communication with it. But he was too late, because everywhere in Port-au-Prince people already knew. They had rushed outside and climbed onto rooftops and they had seen the plane leave, the big unscheduled jet hurtling away from Haiti, and they were sure Jean-Claude was on it.

On the way back to the palace the Duvalier motorcade narrowly avoided an accident with a young Haitian couple. From one of the vehicles a bodyguard leaned out and machine-gunned the man and woman to death. The double murder had been to prevent witnesses reporting that they had seen the Duvaliers out on the road at this hour of the morning.

The young people died for nothing. Lafontant, learning at the last minute that Duvalier was still in the country, canceled planes he had chartered for the invasion. And before the Duvaliers arrived back at the palace, Port-au-Prince residents with ham radios were listening to announcements from the U.S. that Jean-Claude had fled. Within hours Haitians all over the nation had wakened from troubled sleep, jumped out of metal cots, from sleeping mats, from strips of cardboard on city streets. "Jean-Claude is gone!" echoed in the dusky streets of the city.

At 4 a.m. the National Assembly voted almost unanimously in favor of a state of siege.

In the cool hills of Pacot, newsman Gabriel Guerrier awoke to the gentle sounds of Haitian morning. For more than two weeks he had been living at Radio Cacique, sleeping in an upstairs room overlooking the courtyard and the stately old gingerbread house that belonged to the station's owner.

He made a pot of strong coffee and started to jot down ideas for his news broadcast. He fiddled with the radio and began to monitor the shortwave that would provide him with almost all the news he would give.

The phone rang just before he was ready to go on the air. "My God, Guerrier, are you crazy?" he heard a familiar voice. "Get out of there, get out as fast as you can! Haven't you been listening to Radio Nationale? The Assembly's voted something called a state of siege, and as of 4 a.m. they've closed you down, along with Soleil and Lumière."

The warning phone call had come just in time. Guerrier heard a car door slam on the quiet residential street and a minute later the banging of Uzi butts against the metal gate. He raced out into the garden and behind the station, and despite his short stocky frame, vaulted over the back fence with the ease of desperation. By the time the six Macoutes forced open the padlocked gate, Radio Cacique was deserted, Gabriel Guerrier was in a chicken coop blocks away, and on his desk in the modest studio a half-finished cup of coffee still gave off vapors of heat.

At 7:23 a.m. White House Spokesman Larry Speakes thought he knew that Jean-Claude Duvalier had fled. In the Old Executive Office Building next door, Lieutenant Colonel Oliver North was furious at the news. His own Haitian sources had informed him that Jean-Claude had taken with him "our money," about $12,000 kept in a secret account in a Haitian bank and destined for the Nicaraguan *contras*. North grabbed a telephone and, according to journalist Jack Anderson, tried to contact intelligence sources to confirm whether the Duvaliers had absconded with his secret funds.

At 7:23 a.m. in Haiti thousands listening to shortwave radio reacted differently to Speakes's announcement. "This morning at about 2 a.m., the former President of Haiti, Jean-Claude Duvalier, with several members of his family and entourage, left Haiti." Confused Haitians heard, and they continued to rejoice. The state of siege was a mere ploy. The truth was, they knew in their hearts, Haiti was finally liberated.

Down in the La Saline slum an excited crowd was gathering.

They began to march, chanting religious songs and political slogans. They also heard the news that blared from hundreds of portable radios. "State of siege," the newsman repeated over and over. But the Duvaliers had already fled, some said. The crowd was confused, and the calm mood was replaced by hysteria.

Down on the Rue du Magasin de l'Etat, Emmanuel "Toto" Albert, news director of Radio Nationale, stood in the sound studio with his distinguished guest. In front of the microphone sat Jean-Claude Duvalier, thinner than usual, casual in a beige sport shirt and trousers.

"I'm ready," said the President. He drew a deep breath, then in the nasal Duvalier voice gave lie to the news that had sent his people spilling into the streets with joy. "They have been saying since two o'clock this morning that I flew away," the President intoned in Creole. "Such a thing is not true, understand?" The thin voice hardened. "The President is here, stronger than ever, as strong even as a monkey's tail."

The thousands marching through the squalor of downtown Port-au-Prince heard Duvalier's statement and were no longer the same people who had come to march in docile protest. A block away was a school building, and as they screamed that building came to represent Duvalier himself. With howls of rage they picked up the stones that in eroded Haiti lie everywhere like exposed bones, and before Macoutes could come to shoot them they pulverized thousands of school benches, smashed the scarred blackboards, made a giant bonfire of the tattered textbooks and added to the flames everything they found.

Downtown, Jean-Claude and Michèle began a whirlwind *tournée*. Surrounded by Macoutes with Uzis and automatic rifles, Jean-Claude and Michèle sped the short distance to the Croix des Boussales Market. The sight of the jumble of vegetables and the mainly female presence was reassuring. "I'm going to get out," Jean-Claude decided.

"Good morning," the President greeted the market women. He smiled and they rewarded him with spontaneous cheering, confused by the sudden appearance of this pleasant young man who did not seem at all the menacing and vicious dictator everyone talked about. "Long live Jean-Claude!" they shouted, and Jean-Claude leaned over gratefully and shook the hands they tried first to wipe clean on their grimy skirts.

"But, he's red-skinned!" a woman cried out suddenly, amazement conquering caution. "Why, I thought he was black!"

"It's true," another woman took up the cry. "The President isn't black, he's just as red as an apple."

The First Couple made several more stops. Michèle, smiling tightly, chic in a fresh beige jumpsuit, her long hair in one single braid, remained at the wheel. "As you can see, I am still here," Jean-Claude said over and over. "I am staying here, and I intend to remain President for life as constitutionally guaranteed."

Back at the palace Michèle clung to her husband's arm. "As you can see, we're still here," she volunteered in English to the horde of foreign journalists clambering for interviews. They scribbled down her words, and a few noted how the terrible days had seamed deep lines everywhere on her thin elegant face.

At 9:30 a.m. Larry Speakes corrected his earlier announcement. The Duvaliers had not fled and Haiti was still under their control. "The information is that there is no change of government, and martial law has been declared and all nongovernment radio stations closed. There are reports of sporadic gunfire and looting and heavy military presence in the streets." The false departure was now a matter of history.

At the presidential dining-room table Foreign Affairs Minister Georges Salomon sat hunched over a pad of yellow legal paper. That afternoon Jean-Claude sat gravely in his palace in front of hot TV lights and cameras and read Salomon's speech, he and his people hearing it together for the first time.

> I understand your impatience in face of the material difficulties that assail you and I share your legitimate aspirations to improve the conditions of your lives. . . . I know that the per capita income is modest. I know also that the distribution of wealth is unequal and sometimes even shocking. I solemnly propose to you today a new order of society in which will be invested, under strict and rigorous control of which you will be yourselves both judges and beneficiaries, all the means and resources of our economy. This project which has been elaborated by our most qualified technicians is already prepared.

The false departure inaugurated new rounds of violence as Haitians, joyous that Jean-Claude had fled, turned against his henchmen, smashing and looting property and torturing and killing whomever they could catch. Discovering they had been deceived and Duvalier was still in the palace, they continued to fight.

Up in the pine-studded hills of Fermathe, mobs attacked the Duvaliers' vacation home. They stripped it of all its expensive furniture, smashing the elegant fixtures in its six bathrooms and stripping from the ceilings and walls crystal chandeliers, lamps, even wiring. The newly coined term *déchoukaj*—uprooting—was being refined and practiced.

In Petit Goave mobs attacked Macoutes' homes, beat a Macoute mercilessly, and with machetes hacked off his legs and paraded the howling dying creature through the streets of the town.

Léogane was the site of the most ferocious excesses. By early morning a crowd euphoric at the news of the Duvaliers' flight gathered and decided to avenge themselves on the town's Tonton Macoutes. Marching together by the hundreds, they smashed homes and ravaged fields. They also attacked the substantial properties of Colonel Samuel Jérémie, retired in the purge of Dinosaurs and fired as chief of the Anti-Smuggling Brigade, a post he had used to extort millions from importers large and small.

Jérémie had acquired sizable farmlands in Léogane and was a serious banana and sugarcane planter. The crowd arrived, beat Jérémie's watchman unconscious, razed the depot where he stored his crops and farm implements, and carried off pieces of the roof for their own use. They also destroyed the cane and banana fields. Then they continued on to attack other homes and other properties.

Word of the *déchoukaj* soon reached Jérémie in Port-au-Prince. Livid, he stormed into the palace and demanded assistance from Colonel Max Vallès, presidential guard commander. Vallès refused, explaining that every hand was needed to quell uprisings in the capital. He referred Jérémie to Macoute commander Hervé Jeanty, whose assistant provided him with three men. En route to Léogane, Jérémie stopped at the Gressier VSN headquarters and gathered reinforcements. Then with two jeeploads of Macoutes, Jérémie raced through Léogane and along dirt roads until, in the hamlet of Belloc, he found the mob he had come to settle accounts with.

Belloc is a bucolic hollow in the heart of sugarcane country. At 5 p.m. that Friday its residents, drinking in the spectacle of three hundred singing marchers, suddenly saw Samuel Jérémie's convoy slam to a halt in front of little Ste. Famille Church. The Macoutes leapt from their jeeps and began to spray the marchers with bullets. The wounded hid behind trees, crawled onto porches and houses, and dragged themselves into the dense cane fields. The Macoutes followed them, shooting. Silence fell.

But Jérémie was still not satisfied, and for half an hour he strode up and down the road, taunting everyone he saw, threatening them with death. "You think it's smart to wreck my fields?" he shouted. "Do you want to come out here and grin at me in my face?"

Finally his fury was sated, and he climbed back into his jeep, followed by his Macoutes. As soon as they drove off, the people of Belloc began to assess the damage. Corpses were everywhere, lying in pools of blood. Wounded men and women crawled toward safety, leaving trails of scarlet behind them. They took only the most gravely wounded to Ste. Croix Hospital. The others they cared for themselves, not wanting to identify themselves to the authorities. The dead they carted away and buried secretly, without death certificates, to avoid reprisals for being related to Jérémie's victims.

Estimates of the dead ran as high as fifty. American-run Episcopalian Ste. Croix Hospital alone admitted twenty-four wounded, and in huts everywhere relatives nursed other victims. When news of the massacre reached the palace, Jean-Claude Duvalier was so furious that he ordered Samuel Jérémie arrested. His longtime childhood chauffeur and family confidant had just dealt another blow to his staggering regime.

The false departure signaled the final moments of the regime. The conspirators, cheated of victory at the last minute on January 31, now had little to do but wait, as ordinary Haitians stepped up their pressure on Jean-Claude to leave. Outbreaks of serious violence occurred in provincial cities one after another. Mobs sacked government buildings, schools, private homes, institutions, and charitable installations and projects, most foreign-run and -financed. They burned cars and trucks and equipment. They emptied warehouses and razed fields, uprooted maturing crops, saplings, trees. In unthinking fury they rampaged, destroying even sources of their own livelihood.

They made special targets of the Macoutes, smashing their homes, stoning and roasting them alive. Private property was seldom destroyed in error; only properties thought to belong to organizations rather than individuals were indiscriminately savaged, with Taiwanese rice projects in the rice-growing Artibonite province ruined, French and Belgian agricultural projects pillaged, and American food distribution programs raided nationwide.

Wherever they could the beleaguered Macoutes attacked full force. The army did not, often standing back with crossed arms while mobs smashed property, intervening mainly when the targets were human. "Long live the army!" people cried. The men in olive green had never been so popular.

The Macoutes massing in Port-au-Prince were in no such mellow mood. Their lives were ruined, and they grew more and more restless as rumors proliferated that Jean-Claude was about to leave them to their fate. At least in Port-au-Prince they felt safe, and to show how invincible they still were they shot a mechanic to death before the eyes of horrified foreign reporters after Sunday services on February 2. But the other side of the coin was the implacability of popular fury against them, and a Macoute caught alone by a rampaging mob wisely shot himself in the head, also in front of a foreign newsman.

Journalists were barred from the provinces and could only glean news from Haitians and foreigners escaping into Port-au-Prince. Phone lines were cut to calm the people, but the extravagance of rumors spread in place of news inflamed them even more. The people of Cap Haitien had cut off their Prefect Auguste Robinson's head and stuck it on a post, the people of Port-au-Prince repeated to each other. In Jacmel every single Macoute in town had been killed, except one wounded man who had made it into Port-au-Prince to tell the tale. Michèle was already in France, in New York, in Miami. Jean-Claude was going to divorce her, was mad at her for ruining his government, had only used her to cover up his homosexuality. But Michèle didn't care, the rumor-mongers declared, because she was a lesbian, smoked marijuana and had her eyes on buxom Carmen Christophe, owner of the Carmen gambling bank chain and a re-born Christian.

In the palace Duvalier followed the news obsessively, for the false departure had plunged him back into the nightmare of evaluating his options. He was especially influenced by American thinking about Haiti. When Senator Dave Durenberger, chairman of the U.S. Senate Select Committee on Intelligence, requested the OAS to send in troops to quell mounting violence in Haiti, Duvalier was furious and agreed with Foreign Minister Salomon's assessment of the request as ridiculous.

Yet, despite their disdainful comments, Duvalier and his ministers worried constantly about American intervention. Therefore, Secretary of State George Schultz's comments on a *Good Morning America* TV interview badly shook Jean-Claude. Defining Haiti's basic problems as poverty and illiteracy, Schultz elaborated, "We believe, as is our view around the world, that the way to start out of these problems is to have people running the government who are put there by an electoral kind of process. We are calling for the type of government there and elsewhere that is put there by the democratic process."

Jean-Claude reacted angrily to Schultz's declaration. Salomon, who had already typed out his letter of resignation and carried it around in his pocket, was rapidly exhausting his reservoir of patience. When Jean-Claude demanded that he arrange for an immediate dialogue with the Americans about the Schultz declarations, Salomon almost handed him the letter. "I don't see in the declaration any invitation to dialogue," Salomon said brusquely. But Jean-Claude and Michèle were fixated on the Americans' disapproval, rather than the crucial issues at hand.

Underlying the Duvaliers' anger was their realization that if presidential elections were not held, they would have to go—that is what Schultz meant. Larry Speakes's premature announcement of their earlier departure was further confirmation that the Americans were now longing to see them out.

The Jamaican government, acting as informal emissaries for their close allies the Americans, spelled it out in even clearer terms when Prime Minister Edward Seaga sent his silver-haired and silver-tongued mulatto Social Security Minister Dr. Neville Gallimore to convince Duvalier to leave. Gallimore already knew Michèle's sister Joan, and once when Michèle had visited Jamaica he presented her with three pedigreed goats from his private herd.

On this latest mission Gallimore saw Jean-Claude twice. The first time, after warmly embracing the distraught Haitian, he spent three hours discussing the President's options, Joan acting as interpreter. Gallimore told Duvalier he could either stay and crush dissent brutally or he could leave. Duvalier responded by complaining about what was happening in his country. "He said there were agitators out there causing trouble," Gallimore reported. "He said all the aid he was promised hadn't come. He was blaming everyone else. I told him that the people were attacking him not with machine guns, but with sticks and loud voices," Gallimore continued. "There was no single leader. I told him the international community wouldn't take kindly to those people being shot down."

Michèle attended the Jamaican's second and final meeting with Jean-Claude, her mood grim after a morning tour of the capital revealed most stores and businesses had shut down. Gallimore tactfully did not mention the burning countryside and growing piles of corpses and replied that politics always has its peaks and valleys. That night their friend and minister Daniel Supplice left a scribbled message at Gallimore's hotel saying that Duvalier was willing to relinquish the presidency-for-life, serve one term in office, then hold elections. Later young Supplice arrived in person and told Gallimore that Duvalier was willing to leave but needed time to make final arrangements.

As they debated, hesitated, as Haiti boiled and erupted, the Duvaliers came to realize they had no real choice. Above all the American attitude swayed them, and they understood that Gallimore's mission was not a powwow between two Caribbean brothers but a maneuver to urge the American position.

Jean-Claude had only once left Haiti, on a childhood trip to France. Leaving was a tremendously difficult prospect, wrenching him from what had been a paradise on earth. His last attempt to leave had been a last-minute decision to avoid further trouble, further bloodshed. But the savagery of the people's premature celebration of his going away had embittered Jean-Claude. Whether he stayed or decided to leave, he would first of all punish those who had brought him to this terrible pass.

Michèle was if anything more bloodthirsty. "If I have to leave, I want to walk in blood from the palace to the airport," she declared.

But the plotters had united against that very contingency, and whenever the Duvaliers wavered and seemed to incline toward staying, they increased the pressure on them to make them leave quickly, without shedding more blood.

The race was against time. Carnival was scheduled for February 12, when millions of Haitians would take to the streets, unfettered, unafraid, a singing, dancing mass that could swiftly turn from revelry to violence. In Haiti's current unrest, the psychology of the crowd could metamorphose the people into the raging warriors of their ancestors. In February 1986, Carnival would be the perfect catalyst to transform rebellious uprisings into full-scale revolution, and once again the streets of the Black Republic would run red.

*   *   *

The dénouement came on Wednesday night, February 5, at a family summit meeting at Ernest Bennett's house. Bennett had liquidated much of his Haitian holdings, including his SONAVESA, and Haiti Air was up for sale. The Bennetts were on their way out, and the meeting was to plan a strategy to coordinate their final moves.

The Bennetts were a close family, and they had always collaborated in their business ventures. The scenario they painted was brutally clear. The Duvaliers had lost the support of all the key elements propping up their regime: the Americans, the army, the Haitian elite. The Americans issued ominous warnings. The army exercised restraint when its orders were to repress. In the industrial and commercial heartland of Haitian commerce, the American-run factories alone functioned, but only to fulfill orders, not to support the regime. Only Macoutes were still loyal and, as far as the Bennetts knew, willing to defend the Duvalier dictatorship.

The meeting ended with unanimity. The Duvaliers and the Bennetts had to go. But Michèle and Jean-Claude vowed that before they left they would settle their accounts and guarantee that whoever succeeded them would find the presidential throne uncomfortable indeed.

That night at the palace the lights burned late. The Duvaliers summoned Ernst Simon, one of the *houngans* traditionally called to the palace, and Michèle ordered a *cérémonie* to curse the presidential bed so that the next person occupying it would die a horrible death there. Houngan Simon afterward described the ritual he performed. This particular one required two unbaptized babies, and with time a crucial factor, Simon sent to the General Hospital nursery for them. Normally he used other sources and paid only $40 for sacrificial babies, but under the terrible pressure the Duvaliers were putting on him, he had to resort to a hospital contact who demanded $400. Simon's supplier removed two newborns from the filthy, untended nursery where the tiny corpses of newborns, dumped into hampers, were gnawed by rats. The mothers of the two infants sacrificed would be notified that their children had died; in death-ridden Haiti, they would accept this unquestioningly.

But one of the babies delivered was a girl, and Simon angrily refused to accept her. The gods were quite clear on the matter—they would respond only to two males, unbaptized. Back to the hospital went the girl, replaced within half an hour by a boy.

The *cérémonie* took place behind closed doors, with only the Duvaliers and Simon presiding. Hours later, the incantations and prayers chanted, the sacrifice offered and accepted, *houngan* Simon tiredly bundled up for secret burial the dead infants, reeking and sticky with rum and pocked with morsels of chopped herbs. The Duvaliers spent the night in Michèle's room and slept better than they had in weeks, secure in the knowledge that they had doomed anyone trying to usurp the place that was rightfully theirs.

Early on Thursday, February 6, Jean-Claude called Georges Salomon in. Salomon found him more relaxed than usual, the dark smudges under his eyes less severe. "Join me for breakfast," Jean-Claude invited. Then he began to recount how last night Macoutes had kidnapped six nuns from the Emilie Sigueneau old-age home where his father had once worked, not far from the Léogane Leper Complex. "Do you realize what international reaction will be if those sisters are killed?" Jean-Claude demanded. "I've ordered two detachments of Presidential Guards to scour the roads and search every car until they find them."

Then he turned to what was uppermost in his and everyone else's mind. "The fact is, Minister Salomon, we are finished here," he continued. "We must leave before Carnival, before more people are killed." Salomon raised his eyebrows inquiringly. Jean-Claude hesitated briefly, then added laconically, "Tonight."

At 2 p.m. Salomon called the U.S. and the French embassies. Their ambassadors arrived at the palace twenty minutes later, surprised only at the speed of the decision. The French ambassador particularly was alarmed at their haste. It was already nighttime in France, and that would further complicate arrangements. It also meant that it would have to be the Americans, their Guantanamo Bay base less than an hour away from Haiti, who furnished the getaway jet.

At 6 p.m. Salomon urged Jean-Claude to form a government to succeed him. "You can't leave the country in disorder after building it up for fifteen years," Salomon said smoothly. Jean-Claude shrugged. He picked up his pen and began to write. "Henri Namphy, Williams Regala." He paused, then said, "All right. Gérard Gourgue, Max Vallès, Alix Cinéas."

Salomon typed the list. "Now you'll have to advise Namphy," he told Jean-Claude.

"Not yet," Jean-Claude demurred. "I'll tell him later, at 8:30."

"No!" Salomon exclaimed. "You can't leave it till the last minute like that. He's got to get over the shock. He'll need to make preparations, arrange security from here to the airport." Then, peremptorily: "Call General Namphy," he ordered a palace official. Jean-Claude said nothing, and before long Namphy arrived, accompanied by Regala, Avril, and Vallès. Alix Cinéas and Michèle and a few other officers and civilians joined them soon after.

Salomon left them closeted in Jean-Claude's office while he went off to prepare passports for those who would accompany the Duvaliers, snipping and gluing photographs, completing documents. Later he had to go to the chancellery to meet with McManaway about the final details: What was the limit of passengers and luggage on the plane? Could the Duvaliers carry handguns? Salomon had a heavy agenda before him.

Inside Duvalier's office what began as a momentous meeting quickly became historic confrontation. Before informing his chief of staff that within hours he was to succeed him, Duvalier had other accounts to settle. Topping his list was army insubordination, the reports of the systematic refusal of soldiers to fire on the rebelling people as he had personally ordered, and Duvalier handed Namphy a long list of the names of officers to be executed for treason. Namphy took the list and carefully put on and adjusted his reading glasses before he glanced down at the columns. His bulldog jaw was set hard, his lower lip thrust out defiantly. Then he reached for a pen and added another name.

"*Men mwen*," he said succinctly in Creole. ("I'm here.")

Jean-Claude read and saw with angry astonishment that at the top of the list Namphy had written out "Lieutenant General Henri Namphy." As Duvalier stared at him Namphy added, "Put your own name down too, Mr. President. You're a wicked man."

Suddenly Jean-Claude understood everything. "It was you who countermanded my orders?" he demanded.

Henri Namphy stood firm. "Yes," he replied. "You have to leave," he added, his eyes fixed coldly on the President's haggard face.

Michèle's dark eyes blazed. "Kill him, Jean-Claude!" she shrieked, and bolted over to where Namphy stood, lifting her arm to slap his face. Williams Regala grabbed her arm and twisted it behind her back, immobilizing her. "What are you waiting for, Jean-Claude?" Michèle cried, her eyes streaming with tears of rage. "Shoot him! Kill him, you fucking queer!"

Jean-Claude reached for his .38, but before he could aim it Regala attacked him, then pinioned both Duvaliers together. At last Prosper Avril moved too, and with visible reluctance handcuffed Jean-Claude's hands behind his back. Then Regala, caressing his revolver, spoke for the first time. "If Henri Namphy has so much as a headache," Regala warned them in his measured tones, "the army is already in position to blow the pair of you away."

But Michèle, hysterical, would not be silenced. Outside the office door were a dozen Macoutes who would kill anyone who tried to harm Jean-Claude, and she decided to alert them. Just as she opened her mouth to scream, Avil made a split-second political decision and leapt at her, slugging her hard on the jaw, knocking her out cold. Yards away, out in the hallway, the Macoutes stood by idly, unaware.

Jean-Claude, shaken and ashen-faced, turned to his councillor Cinéas. "Is it true, Alix?" he asked pathetically.

Cinéas nodded. "It's true. You have no alternative. You have to leave. You no longer have any say in the matter."

Jean-Claude had no hope that the five-man council who had now succeeded him would permit him to authorize the Macoutes to begin the mass executions of disaffected youth he and Michèle had intended. The lists were already in his possession, prepared by Macoute leaders in each neighborhood of Port-au-Prince. Each list contained a hundred names, and for each one submitted Jean-Claude gave in exchange a Pajero jeep and $2,000. Macoutes eagerly manufactured lists. Throughout Port-au-Prince thousands of young men and women had never been in such danger of dying. By merest luck the events in Jean-Claude's office provided their reprieve.

When the meeting finally ended the Duvaliers were released under discreet but armed guard. Regala had threatened to keep Jean-Claude handcuffed, but it was no longer necessary. He would cause no more trouble. Both he and Michèle, conscious again, finally understood. Now they wanted only to pack as much as they could and leave the country in which they no longer had a single friend. As they left Jean-Claude turned to Namphy. "Look after the officers in the 1972 graduating class," he said, his voice breaking slightly with unaccustomed emotion.

Georges Salomon, unaware of what had just happened in Jean-Claude's office, rushed back to the palace to report the conditions that Ambassador McManaway had outlined to him. The Duvaliers, so recently humiliated, reacted furiously. Not to carry firearms? A limit of two suitcases each? Submit to metal detectors? Did the Americans think they were animals?

The Americans, sharing the minister's anxiety to see the Duvaliers off, made more compromises. They could bring their firearms in a sealed box. They but none of the others in their party would be exempted from being searched at the airport. If they wanted to increase their luggage allowance, they could trade off passengers for suitcases.

The Duvaliers cheered up. Although it meant sacrificing friends and relatives to their fate, they dropped eleven names from the passenger list. Two of those eliminated were Michèle's old grandmother, confined to a wheelchair, and her grandfather, Georges Bennett, abandoned without even being advised of what was in store.

Michèle was as serious a packer as she was a shopper, and into a mountain of Louis Vuitton and Gucci suitcases she stashed away the booty from over five years of presidential sprees. Soon she discovered she needed more space and rushed into Jean-Claude's room, where his valet, André Leclerc, stood weeping as he packed the President's clothes. Michèle interrupted his sorrow, ordering him to unpack most of her husband's clothes so she could stuff the suitcases with paintings, a silver service, antique crystal candlesticks, and other valuables. Leclerc refused, but under a barrage of threats he gave in and did as she said.

Jean-Claude was not as interested in what he carted off to France as what he disposed of in Haiti. Picking up the phone, he finished unfinished business and ordered the executions of Samuel Jérémie, Ti-Boulé Pierre, and Madame Max Adolphe. These were the people whose brutality he believed had scarred his regime, ultimately destroying it. "They got me into this mess," he said to several palace guards. "I'm going to kill them."

Just after he had given these last-minute execution orders, Jean-Claude received the news that the Presidential Guards had located the six kidnapped nuns and returned them to the Emilie Sigueneau home. He immediately phoned the old-age home and in a long phone conversation comforted them about their ordeal.

Then he picked up a pencil and one of Georges Salomon's yellow legal pads and laboriously composed the farewell speech he would leave for his people on a TV cassette. "After thorough consideration of the situation, I have been unable to hope that my remaining would spare my people this nightmare of blood. This is why I am willing to go down in history with my head held high and with a clean conscience."

*   *   *

Earlier that afternoon many Duvalier cronies had left: several of the Bennetts, including Michèle's unstable sister Chantal Moura, the Pasquets, Jean-Marie Chanoine, Jean-Robert Estimé, and Macoute chief Lionel Woolley. Théodore Achille forced Eastern Airlines to bump a passenger already seated so his friend, Farida Sassine, could board, and left his wife, Lisi, and their three children in Haiti to whatever fate might overtake them.

Tonton Macoute chief Madame Max, who made good her promise to control the men in the VSN Barracks, waited a little too long. Notified only late Thursday that today was the day, she raced downtown to withdraw money from her huge savings account but the bank had already closed. Back at her Pétionville home she packed a few suitcases, then called her staff together. Duvalier is leaving, she told them. Then she bid them goodbye and waited for the soldiers to escort her to Dessalines Barracks, where she took refuge until the plotters, taken off guard by the swiftness of Duvalier's decision, could help her flee Haiti.

Unlike Michèle, Madame Max had had too little time to pack. She had to leave her treasures behind, including her well-thumbed pornography collection with titles such as *Tyrannical Mistress* and *Painful Love*.

At the palace the more fortunate Duvaliers finally finished packing. Their suitcases were stashed away behind the elevators, where the servants could not see them. They showered and dressed for the flight, Michèle taking special pains with her makeup because she was menstruating and a tiny pimple had popped out on the tip of her nose. She was too rushed to do her hair, but wrapped a white turban around it, her trademark.

It was time to go to the airport. The plane was to leave Haiti at 2 a.m. But Michèle had a much better idea, and she and Jean-Claude decided to throw a midnight champagne party for their closest friends. The party was high-spirited and amusing, the fittingly trivial exit of the irresponsible tyrants who had by whim, fancy, and meanness wrought havoc in the lives of so many people.

Before they left the palace Jean-Claude made a last phone call. It was to Fort Dimanche, where he had transferred his old chauffeur, childhood confidant, and most loyal officer. "Have you executed Samuel Jérémie?" he demanded.

"Yes, Excellence, I have," the officer lied, breaking out in a terrible sweat. It occurred to him that Jean-Claude might not believe him and come to check in person.

At 2:13 two carloads of Duvalier and Bennett relatives sped through the airport gates. For the next hour trucks arrived, loaded with Louis Vuitton and Gucci luggage. Finally the Duvaliers arrived, preceded by carloads of army officers, including an exhausted and taut-nerved Lieutenant General Henri Namphy. Jean-Claude came after, at the wheel of his light gray BMW. Michèle sat beside him, theatrically smoking a cigarette and blowing smoke in the direction of the horde of photographers and reporters who ran alongside.

Their secret was not secret, CBS having earlier announced that Duvalier would flee within twenty-four hours. Even without CBS and American intelligence contacts, Haitians had their own leaky sources, and when the Duvaliers left it was to the popping of flashbulbs, shouted questions they refused to answer, and a last chance for Michèle to display her contempt for those she was leaving behind.

Quickly and quietly the Duvaliers boarded the plane, with three bodyguards and nineteen other family members, including Simone Duvalier, the Guardian of the Duvalier Revolution. Few appeared as calm as Jean-Claude and Michèle, and some were weeping. What the Americans did not know was that both Michèle and Jean-Claude now carried handguns, provided them earlier by the officer responsible for arranging the motorcade and its route. At his final meeting with Duvalier, he had handed over the weapons. He had also informed the President that there were two Uzi submachine guns hidden under the front seats of the presidential BMW.

At 3:47 a.m. the C-141 lumbered down the brightly lit single runway of François Duvalier International Airport. It picked up ground speed as it came parallel to the central terminal building, then slowly lifted its nose skyward. The din of its giant engines all but drowned out the joyous shouts of the throngs of people at the airport to celebrate this historic night.

The big plane was quickly reduced to a pattern of blinking lights as it climbed farther into the deep blackness of the tropical night. Upward of two thousand pairs of eyes followed its airborne course as the C-141 banked sharply and slowly circled Haiti's capital city. A few gasped when it appeared for an instant that the plane was preparing to land again. Their alarm was false, and suddenly the C-141 banked again, and in its silhouette of lights shot upward into the eastern sky.

At nearby Fort Dimanche the duty officer who had not executed Samuel Jérémie stared up into the night and heard the roar of the jet. He closed his eyes and made the sign of the cross. "Thanks be to God, I'm liberated," he said fervently. Jean-Claude Duvalier was gone, and a terrible era in Haiti's bloody history was over.

13 THE LEGACY: DUVALIERISM WITHOUT DUVALIER

B Y DAYBREAK ON FEBRUARY 7 HAITIANS WARY OF FALSE departures had reassured themselves that last week's lie was this week's truth—Duvalier had gone and Haiti was free. By 9 a.m. millions spilled onto the nation's streets, waving victorious palm leaves, blowing conch shells, banging pots and metal lampposts, singing and chanting and shouting, improvising frenzied dances, inexhaustible in their joy.

Tired soldiers were targets of their collective love. Men saluted them exuberantly, a few even kissed their feet. Women as newly liberated as Haiti flung themselves onto the men in olive green, thanking them for helping to scrape off the Duvalierist filth.

Euphoria turned quickly to vengeance, and Papa Doc and his Tonton Macoutes were principal victims. Yet when his people filed wrathfully into Port-au-Prince's crowded cemetery armed with iron bars and rocks, Papa Doc must have been laughing in some other grave, for the marble-tiled crypt inscribed with his name was empty.

Most villains were still alive, however, and the blood Madame Max had predicted her Macoutes would shed began to redden the streets. A few, unaware that Duvalier had fled, were caught and killed in uniform, often by children as well as adults. At least one had his legs hacked off with machetes before he was roasted alive "necklace" style, immobilized in a rubber tire, doused with gasoline, then set ablaze, his charred corpse later paraded about on a tree branch like a pig on a spit. In one Port-au-Prince street excited children played soccer with a human head. In Léogane a Macoute chief was pinioned for a mass beating. When he was pulpy the mob gouged out his eyes and hacked off his head, then stuck it on a pole and danced around it.

The joy of celebration was drowned out by reprisal and revenge. Before the death and damage tolls mounted further, the army declared a 2 p.m. curfew. Liberated Haiti feted under the gun, trapped behind the private walls of its mansions, houses, and huts. From radios and TV screens the people learned that their new rulers were five men called the National Council of Government, and their new president was Lieutenant General Henri Namphy. The other members were Colonel Williams Regala, Colonel Max Vallès, and civilians Alix Cinéas and Human Rights League founder Gérard Gourgue. Colonel Prosper Avril was the government's official adviser. Haitians heard the news and most cheered; the CNG had their approval if not their blessing, and what mattered more than anything was that Duvalier was gone.

The CNG also had Duvalier's approval, because it was his handiwork. In a novel sort of pre-ouster debriefing, he had handpicked its members, with the exception of Gourgue. Few people knew this though many guessed, and from the beginning people worried that Duvalier and not Duvalierism had gone. Certain vodounists were apprehensive about their safety from militants in the Catholic and Protestant churches. Ti-Legliz, the Catholic Church's activist liberation movement, doubted that the likes of Namphy, Regala, Vallès, and Cinéas would give the people what they had battled to win. Disgruntled Haitians in the million-strong diaspora shouted openly, "Duvalierism without Duvalier!" and challenged the government's legitimacy.

The new Haiti was cleansed literally and figuratively. Names were changed. Avenue Jean-Claude Duvalier became Avenue Jean-Paul II. Duvalierville reverted to its pre-Duvalier name of Cabaret. François Duvalier International Airport became Port-au-Prince International Airport. The gruesome Port-au-Prince slum of Cité Simone (a grotesque memorial to Simone Duvalier) was misnamed Cité Soleil—Sun City. The millions of little paper Duvalierist flags that crisscrossed streets and buildings like black-and-red cobwebs were torn down and shredded, and soon millions of liberated Haiti's red-and-blue flags replaced them. As fast as prisoners and seamstresses could stitch them, new flags were raised over public buildings.

The palace was no longer forbidding. The government used only its administrative wing, and at night President Namphy went home to sleep in his own bed. The street in front of the palace, long closed to pedestrians, was reopened, and adventurous Haitians strolled past or lolled against its iron fencing, relishing the experience.

In March citizens banded together in local community councils. Then, armed with brooms and shovels, men, women, and children transformed Haiti's filthy cities into gleaming meccas, digging out tons of accumulated offal, scooping out clogged gutters, beautifying their world. They painted the curbs of crumbling sidewalks with patriotic red and blue, and planted flowers in old cans and inner tubes. "We cleaned out the government," they shouted, "now we're cleaning the country."

The outside world looked on and cheered. The Duvaliers had left only enough in the treasury to pay the army for one week, and so the U.S. hastily released $25 million in blocked aid money. The new government had freed all Haitian political prisoners and was correcting human-rights abuses, the Americans said. And optimistically the Haitian government retained New York lawyers Stroock & Stroock & Lavan to reclaim the moneys the Duvaliers and their cronies had stolen, estimated in the hundreds of millions.

In the new climate of freedom, democratic plays, poetry, and songs flourished. Radios repeatedly aired "When I See the Sun," the anti-Duvalierist movement's catchy resistance song. The film of Graham Greene's *The Comedians* played for the first time in Haiti.

One month after Duvalier's flight a cheering crowd of twenty thousand, including General Henri Namphy and the CNG, crammed Sylvio Cator Stadium to celebrate a Creole mass that opened Misyon Alfa, a program to teach 3.5 million Haitians, over 90 percent of the nation's adults, to read and write within five years. Misyon Alfa would operate in Creole, cost $24 million, and was one of the most ambitious literacy programs in the world.

Exiles flooded back home. Two were former presidents. Daniel Fignolé, terminal cancer slashing lines on his face, hinted he would once again run for President and soon died. General Paul Magloire, strapping and hale at seventy-eight, received national honors at the palace.[26]

Political hopefuls arrived from every corner of the diaspora: Louis Déjoie, a portly building contractor and son of the man whom François Duvalier had defeated in 1957; René Théodore, leader of PUCH, the United Party of Haitian Communists; Marc Bazin, now dubbed "Mr. Clean" after his famous failed attempt to reform Haitian finances; rotund Leslie Manigat, an intellectual briefly jailed under Papa Doc and author of several respected analyses of Haiti's sad political history.

Renegade Coast Guard Commander Colonel Octave Cayard returned with over a dozen men who mutinied with him in 1970. "Exile was a nightmare," wept Cayard as hundreds cheered and soldiers saluted him. Journalists too came home, many exiled in the 1980 purge. Jean Dominique, Evans Paul, and Anthony Pascale, better known as Kompè Plim and Kimpè Filo, paraded back through streets decorated with wall graffiti welcoming them.

But the Haitian public had not forgotten the Macoutes and with increasing vehemence demanded that they be tried for crimes committed under the dictatorship. Soon an ominous rumor circulated, charging that the army was enlisting Macoutes. When Colonel Prosper Avril told foreign reporters the army would deal with Macoutes by transforming them into soldiers, he transformed rumor into fact. What he failed to mention was that the Macoutes in question were powerful and well-connected, and that they were being absorbed into the army's command structure.

The honeymoon between Haitians and their new government ended when the latter helped Colonel Albert Ti-Boulé Pierre flee to Brazil and tried to do the same for Duvalier Security Chief Luc Désyr. Désyr was already aboard an Air France jet when a stewardess alerted a radio station, which broadcast the news and drew an immense crowd to the airport. Air France surrendered Désyr to the army, but the incident provoked a bitter public outcry that the government was protecting Duvalierists. Justice Minister Gérard Gourgue agreed and, in protest, boycotted General Namphy's ceremonial raising of Haiti's new red-and-blue flag at the National Palace.

Then on March 5, without consulting or notifying his colleagues, Gourgue released all prisoners in the National Penitentiary, and 238 convicted thieves, rapists, murderers, and drug dealers filed through its mustard-colored courtyard to freedom. Gourgue justified this on the grounds that some prisoners had been jailed by Macoutes and had never stood trial, while others suffered gangrene from untreated wounds. But he had only freed prisoners in Port-au-Prince, not the provinces. An ugly rumor spread and persisted that Gourgue had accepted $67,000 from the family of jailed drug trafficker Marvin Cardoza, a colleague of Franz Bennett, jailed in December 1985 after he was caught in Cayes with 790 pounds of cocaine. Reporters hounded

Gourgue with questions about the rumors. Haitians blamed him for contributing to Haiti's post-Duvalier crime wave.

Two weeks later Gourgue resigned. "I've been considering it ever since Ti-Boulé left Haiti," Gourgue said. Looking tired and strained, he added that the government had not the means to satisfy the legitimate demands of the people.

Gourgue's resignation was a critical blow to the government, which lost its only non-Duvalierist member. Namphy never forgave him and henceforth referred to him as a *vagabond,* a bum. Gourgue's resignation, however, provoked major government changes. Under unrelenting pressure, Namphy fired his most Duvalierist colleagues, Avril, Vallès, and Cinéas. Haiti's new government now consisted only of himself, Regala, and civilian lawyer Jacques François. That afternoon gunshots rang out and burning tires blackened the sky of Port-au-Prince as antigovernment protests erupted for the second day.

The jubilation of liberation had evaporated in the bitter awakening to Haiti's grim realities. Indeed, apart from the freedom to decry the new rulers, what else had changed? Hunger still ravaged the land. Almost every night thieves murdered innocents and plundered their homes. Devout ladies had gold crosses ripped from their necks on the very steps of churches. The nation's few thousand policemen were paralyzingly ineffectual against the rising crime wave. Among the wealthy the demand soared for Rottweilers and Dobermans, security guards and guns.

The countryside too groaned as *houngans* and *mambos* were murdered. Many of the victims had been Macoutes. Others were reputed to be evildoers or werewolves.[27] Some were killed so cynical neighbors could steal their belongings.

But some were targets of the religious frenzy of charismatic Catholics and Protestants who seized on Duvalier's downfall to uproot the traditional religion. Both Protestant and Catholic priests revived the "renunciation" rituals of the American occupation, intimidating *houngans* and *mambos* to publicly renounce their beliefs.

Also in the countryside the new "white" North American pigs introduced to replace the old Creole pigs provoked a burning political issue. These pampered breeds, the only ones now allowed, could survive only in cement piggeries and required adequate water and protein and vitamin-enriched pig feed. The U.S. and Canada, terrified of a recurrence of ASF, kept tremendous pressure on the Haitian government to resist demands to import Creole pigs. Only bourgeois Haitians, who had sufficient capital to raise these heavy-weight, large-littered animals with cost efficiency, sided with the North Americans.[28]

Haiti boiled with discontent. The government was fast losing both popularity and credibility. It refused to act on the nation's crucial issues, including reforestation and the pursuit of Duvalierist criminals. The justification for its inaction was its temporary mandate, yet it also declined to announce an election schedule. The people, still hungry and again angry, protested through strikes, work stoppages, and street demonstrations.

Henri Namphy, so recently a national hero, collapsed under the stress and longed to resign. His doctors ordered a week of complete rest and banned him from seeing TV or newspapers or listening to the radio. The news he missed was not reassuring. And foreign diplomats complained privately that Namphy's government was sluggish, responsive only to violent pressure, secretive, and inefficient. They were alarmed by its refusal to set an election date and continued to support it mainly because they saw no alternative.

Namphy recovered to face his worse crisis yet—the reemergence of the Macoutes. To serve notice that they were still a force to be reckoned with, the Macoutes, led by ex-Colonel Franck Romain and Paul Véricain, provoked a tragic incident that led to seven civilian deaths and seriously undermined the military government. They chose a massive memorial march to Fort Dimanche and infiltrated thousands of roughly dressed young men among the carefully groomed mourners, many of them elderly men and women whose relatives had died in the fort. Jeering at march organizers, they pushed past an army cordon into the forbidden grounds of Fort Dimanche.

Panicky soldiers fired live ammunition and then tear gas at the huge crowd. Three people were shot to death and three were electrocuted, as gunfire cut electric wires that then fell on them. A seventh, clutching his torn belly and begging horrified onlookers to save his life, died later during surgery in the General Hospital. Dozens more were bruised, thousands were frightened. The outside world and Haiti's millions learned with outrage that the army had shot at people attempting to lay wreaths and plant flowers to honor the unmarked graves of fifty thousand victims of Duvalierism. For once the government moved. Within days both Franck Romain and Paul Véricain were arrested and charged with murders committed under Duvalier.

But Fort Dimanche was a catalyst for popular discontent, and also catapulted Jean-Bertrand Aristide into the public eye, thanks to his riveting live radio eyewitness account. Street riots, general and partial strikes, demonstrations and strident public outcries against the government finally produced an official reaction. With acrid smoke still fouling the night air and soldiers breaking down barricades throughout Port-au-Prince, a beleaguered General Namphy appeared on radio and TV and announced that in November 1987, Haitians would go to the polls following which, on February 7, 1988, the government would resign in the elected President's favor.

The government also conceded to popular demands for judgment of Duvalierist criminals by tossing Samuel Jérémie, Luc Désyr, and Edouard C. Paul into the hands of justice. Each symbolized the worst sort of Duvalierist criminal, and each had burned his personal political bridges, putting himself outside the magic circle of those the government had pledged to protect.

Samuel Jérémie's eighteen-day court-martial convicted him of torturing and killing a black belt karate expert, a man beaten so savagely that his heart, spleen, liver, lungs, and kidneys had hemorrhaged. Blinking back tears, Jérémie heard his sentence: fifteen years and dismissal from the armed forces.

Luc Désyr was tried in the courtroom of newly appointed Judge Antoine Jean-Charles, whom Désyr had interrogated in the palace in 1964. The trial lasted eighteen hours, with one juror frantic about leaving his business unattended, escaping from the courtroom only to be caught and hauled back inside. After an eighteen hour marathon of a trial, the jury found Désyr guilty of illegally arresting, torturing, and killing Jean-Jacques Dessalines Ambroise and his pregnant wife, Lucette Lafontant, in 1965, and of illegally arresting and torturing Emmanuel Ambroise in an earlier incident. Judge Jean-Charles immediately sentenced Désyr to death, later commuted to life imprisonment since Haiti has no capital punishment.

Days later, and despite irrefutable evidence establishing his guilt, Edouard C. Paul was convicted, with extenuating circumstances, only of complicity in the 1969 murder of literacy worker Pierre Denis and received a mild three-year sentence.

There were no more major trials of Duvalierist criminals. Justice Minister François Latortue qualified as merciful the government's failure to prosecute. "In any other country just emerging from thirty years of despotic rule, a man as evil as Désyr would never be judged, just taken out and shot," Latortue declared. "[W]e wanted an end to butchery, we did not want to begin the new regime doing the same things the Duvaliers and goons like Désyr did." Most Haitians, however, believed that pressure from and complicity with still-powerful Duvalierists was the reason no more trials had been scheduled and why criminal charges against Franck Romain and Paul Véricain had been dismissed—for lack of evidence.

Outside the courtroom the government had some small economic successes. Finance Minister Lesly Delatour restructured the nation's finances and eliminated numerous areas of corruption. Soldiers received salary increases, with base pay raised to $130 monthly. Civil servants' salaries also rose as moneys previously embezzled were redistributed. Commerce Minister Mario Celestin, Namphy's ex-brother-in-law, set lower prices on many essential goods.

But these improvements were slight, and Haitian life continued to deteriorate measurably. The closure of the state-owned Darbonne sugar mill and ENAOL cooking-oil plant, Duvalier scams that drained millions of dollars annually from the national revenue, undercut private industries and raised consumer prices, provoked a general furor. Twelve thousand assembly industry jobs lost during post-Duvalierist rioting were not replaced. Gangs raided foreign food distribution warehouses, forcing feeding programs to cut back to less than 400,000 the number of children fed compared to about 800,000 during the final years of Duvalier. Smuggling, which officials tolerated or participated in, was also assuming monumental proportions, lowering prices but destroying local businesses and the customs duties that were one of Haiti's most important sources of revenue. And in June about 250,000 were left homeless in terrible floods that struck the South, destroying crops and killing livestock.

As if this were not enough, American policy-makers successfully pressured the new military government to do what the Duvaliers had refused to: remove the 50 percent import tariffs on rice and other foodstuffs, part of the grand scheme to restructure Haiti's economy. It helped that Finance Minister Delatour, an advocate of neoliberal economics including open markets, supported these measures and cooperated with American policy-makers to lay the groundwork for a drastic revamping of the economy. Henceforth, Haiti would become an assembler of cheap goods for American, Canadian and other foreign markets, and a hungry importer of those nations' foodstuffs.

By the summer of 1986 Haiti was back on the brink of disaster. Namphy, again close to a breakdown, implored his critics for more time to redress grievances. His former schoolteacher Simour Roman pleaded for him. "I have just come from the palace," Roman told a meeting of angry opposition leaders. "Henri Namphy is a man close to tears, who can't sleep." But Haiti was a nation of men and women close to tears, who could not sleep, and the crowd shouted Roman down.

In the tense atmosphere before July 29, formerly celebrated as Tonton Macoute Day, wild rumors spread about a Macoute coup d'état or, alternately, a nationwide *déchoukaj* of remaining Macoutes. In response twenty-eight political, human-rights, and workers' groups allied to form the Liaison of Democratic Forces to coordinate opposition to the government.

A new crisis erupted in mid-September, precipitated by the "disappearance" of Charlot Jacquelin, a Misyon Alfa literacy teacher. Witnesses claimed Jacquelin was arrested for his part in the recent murder of a soldier, but the army, duplicitously, denied any knowledge of the arrest or of Jacquelin's whereabouts.[29] Jacquelin's "disappearance" became the rallying point for anti-government protests, and everywhere posters and car stickers appeared demanding, "Where is Charlot Jacquelin?"[30]

The popular outrage at the government culminated in a massive boycott of the October 19 elections of an assembly to draft a constitution, the essential first step to establishing democracy. But the government decided to name twenty of sixty-one of the assembly members, with only forty-one to be elected. The nation rebelled, and only 6 percent of eligible voters turned out. The assembly met anyway and hammered out a constitution that eventually won overwhelming support.

On the political scene hard-core Duvalierists formed the Union of National Entente Party, known as PREN, and announced they would field a candidate in November 1987's presidential election. PREN headquarters were at the country home of former Duvalier Chief of Staff General Claude Raymond. The party's platform was a return to the black populism that Dumarsais Estimé and François Duvalier had ridden to power. Clovis Désinor was rumored to be the probable candidate, and Jean-Claude Duvalier was said to have contributed $13 million to finance the party.

The creation of a Duvalierist party nine months after Duvalier's famous flight provoked a national panic. On November 7, fifty thousand people demonstrated in Port-au-Prince. The Liaison of Democratic

Forces organized the protest, aided by the Catholic Church, and at 11 a.m. church bells rang, car horns honked, pedestrians banged with shoes against lampposts and metal fences, and youths shouted antigovernment slogans. The provinces also protested with days of strikes and marches, until the government pressured the Duvalierists to disband their party.

Namphy delivered another address to the nation-in-crisis. "During your demonstrations I saw, heard and understood you," the general said. "Like you we want to see the terrifying system of Macoutism disappear forever. I have lived in my skin your anguish at the possible return of the old system that raped and villified the country."

But PREN's abrupt self-destruction did not ease opposition pressure on the government, for Duvalierists still held powerful official positions, Macoutes operated more and more openly, and the government's administration continued, inefficiently and ineffectually. General strikes continued to paralyze Port-au-Prince and the provinces. Two protesters in Cité Soleil, carrying a coffin representing the death of the government, were shot and killed by police. The next day Interior Minister Colonel Williams Regala issued communiqués banning all protests leading to public insecurity and violence.

The political scene remained chaotic. An estimated two hundred presidential candidates had emerged, often with virtually indistinguishable platforms. There were myriad politically active workers, human-rights, feminist, rural, professional, youth, and commercial groups, which routinely quarreled and splintered, adding to the confusion. Even the Church was divided, with the activist priests of Ti-Legliz on one side and the nonpolitical traditionalists on the other.

Through intense politicization programs in the countryside, Ti-Legliz workers recruited cadres of peasant workers, worked and lived with the people, and quietly gained their confidence through small, local, desperately needed projects: a clinic here, an irrigation ditch there, roads connecting agricultural communities to previously inaccessible markets. These men and women operated under the leadership of a group called Tet Ansamn, the Creole expression for "Solidarity," and they were laying the groundwork for radical social reform in the countryside, where 76 percent of Haitians then lived, as well as in the cities.

Ironically, the Communist Party, under soft-spoken René Théodore and his affable secretary general, Max Bourjolly, participated in the political maelstrom as moderates. They kept low profiles and defended moderate positions, apparently to make themselves palatable to Haitian society so that they could win Haiti through democratic elections, not in the first round but in subsequent ones. Given the hopeless condition of most Haitians, many dispassionate observers agreed that Communists could eventually conquer through the polls.

One year after Jean-Claude Duvalier fled, President and General Namphy remarked at a palace press conference that Haiti was not ready for democracy. "Democracy can't come tomorrow, we need to work to install it." Namphy listed freedom of the press and speech and his electoral calendar and his government's achievements and admitted that its first year of office had been troubled. "Savage strikes . . . cost the loss of more than twelve thousand jobs, public demonstrations . . . upset commerce, schools and government services. This cacophony . . . would have made it difficult for any authority to operate."

Haitians observed the historic day with resignation and bitterness. At an official ceremony General Namphy, Colonel Regala and other officers arrived in Jean-Claude Duvalier's $65,000 Maserati, and all carried submachine guns. Troop carriers patrolled the streets. The joy that had accompanied Duvalier's flight a year earlier seemed an aeon away. The man had gone but his *marassas* remained.

Brazil refused to extradite Ti-Boulé. The government fired four cabinet ministers, three of them hostile to Duvalierists and relatively efficient. Only the departure of General Jean-Baptiste Hiliare, a former National Penitentiary director who starved his charges, was not regretted. Ex-Education Minister Rosny Desroches was a progressive thinker. Justice's François Latortue had pursued Duvalierist criminals. As Health Minister, Michel Lominy had shut down the General Hospital's AIDS-infested blood bank and designated the Red Cross, with its U.S. laboratory testing facilities, as Port-au-Prince's only blood bank.

Suddenly public attention was riveted elsewhere, to the newly drafted Constitution, which was written in both Creole and French, and elevated Creole to the status of official language. Ironically, this complex document, composed by government appointees and citizens whose election had been overwhelmingly boycotted, was to become the new political bible whose truths, if implemented, would save the nation.

The Constitution was written in haste by inexperienced laymen trying to solve political problems by forestalling them. It provided for a bicameral legislature, a President, and a Prime Minister chosen from the majority party. The Prime Minister and the President would share the power of appointing ministers, a provision meant to safeguard against power-hungry presidents. Instead, it locked the President and Prime Minister into adversary positions and almost guaranteeed future political deadlocks.

The Constitution also tackled the now-unloved and divided military. One of its highly controversial clauses separated the police from the armed forces and described a special police training academy. It decreed that soldiers could be tried by civilian rather than military courts for criminal offenses. The public applauded these changes. The army hated and feared them.

The Constitution, published in both Creole and French, elevated Creole to the status of official language. And the Mole St. Nicolas, mentioned for decades as a possible site for an American military base to replace Guantanamo when its lease expired, was claimed forever for Haiti. "The Haitian Republic's land is inviolable and can never be given up by any Treaty or Convention," the Constitution declared.

But the most crucial articles were those governing elections. A Provisional Electoral Council was created to supervise the elections. The council would have nine members, each chosen by a representative sector of society: the Catholic Church, the Protestant churches, the government-appointed Consultative Council, the Supreme Court, human-rights organizations, the Association of Journalists, the National Council of Cooperatives, the university, and commerce and industry. The council would be independent of the government and the absolute authority on election issues.

But it was the famous Article 291 that excited and galvanized the country. That article empowered the council to disqualify from political office for ten years anyone accused by public clamor of having murdered, tortured, or embezzled under the former Duvalier presidents or of having supported their regimes "with excess of zeal."

The next step was a national referendum on the Constitution. On Sunday, March 29, over one million Haitians showed up, waiting patiently in long lines for their moment at the polls. Many were voting for the first time. To circumvent the problem of illiteracy, ballots were color-coded—white for yes, yellow for no. Officials gave each voter one of each so that he could vote with one and discard the other, secretly. But it was not a secret vote, because many people, fearing the government would cheat, wanted to prove that the vote had been a massive yes and openly displayed the ballots they cast.

The final tally was 99.98 percent yes votes, and countless voters volunteered to journalists and observers that it was article 291 that they were supporting. Many of those no voters were soldiers.

The national euphoria at having had a virtually perfect election soon evaporated in the realities of the desperately poor country. The 225,000 new "foreign" pigs were starving, often to death, with sows losing entire litters they had no milk to suckle. The immediate cause was the shortage and consequent skyrocketing price of wheat shorts, the cheapest and most plentiful feed. Massive uncontrolled smuggling of cheap rice from Miami allowed peasants to eat rice more than bread, hence the drastic cut in flour production.

Smuggling also dealt the economy another crushing blow when the Haytian American Sugar Company (HASCO), Haiti's largest private employer, closed its doors with 445,000 hundred-pound bags of unsold sugar, unable to fight floods of sugar sneaked in from the Dominican Republic. HASCO's closing put into financial crisis between 280,000 to 300,000 people, the number supported by the 3,500 laid-off workers and the 30,000 to 40,000 small planters who supplied HASCO's sugarcane. Weeks earlier, smuggling also forced the closure of sugar mills in Cayes and Cap Haitien.

Bit by bit Haiti's major businesses were shutting down, contracting, or suffering severe losses. Business reeled under a new blow in mid-April when Gérard Dumont, Haiti's largest *gourdes*-to-dollars money changer, absconded with an estimated $20 million.

Further eroding the economy was erosion itself, as heavy rains destroyed roads and killed pedestrians and drivers caught on main city streets by churning waves that dashed them down ravines and smashed them against walls. Decayed roads deteriorated further. Crops were lost, topsoil swept into the sea. In a joint message Haiti's Catholic bishops called Haiti's ecological, economic, and social conditions "national disasters" and added that "nobody seems to be worried, neither public officials, nor the unaware public. . . . These disasters menace our fledgling democracy," the bishops concluded.

Against this backdrop of national deterioration, Haiti's political life unfolded. With presidential elections six months away, registration began. Thirty-five candidates deposited the required $1,000 and submitted lists of two thousand supporters, so Haiti faced its first democratic election in three decades with a slate of would-be presidents large enough to staff a continent of nations, while candidates for senatorial, mayoralty, and legislative posts went begging. In the nation where people joke that every Haitian wants to be President, very few politicians were willing to stoop to being anything less.

On May 21 the new electoral council was sworn in and its spokesman, Ernst Verdieu, pledged the council would uphold Article 291 of Haiti's new Constitution and ban from political office any Duvalierist supporters or collaborators.

Most of the councillors were as marked by Duvalierism as the government members. Only Dr. Ernst Mirville and Ernst Verdieu, who had spent most of the Duvalier years in Montréal, seemed untainted. But several councillors had become anti-Duvalierist activists, and from the beginning they were headed on a collision course with the increasingly reactionary government.

The clash came without warning, initiated by the government just as it was about to emerge triumphant after an unsuccessful antigovernment general strike. The strike had been called by Haiti's most important trade union, the Autonomous Central of Haitian Workers (CATH) in support of a long and unrealistic list of demands, including the repatriation of three hundred thousand Haitian cane cutters in the Dominican Republic.

The CATH strike call generated little support and much resentment and failed to shut down most businesses and markets. Then as the strike sputtered into a second day, the government snatched defeat from the jaws of victory by issuing three decrees, one of which precipitated the worst political crisis since Duvalier had fled. In that decree the government seized partial control of the electoral process from the council, thereby violating the Constitution and also the psyche of the Haitian people. Even squabbling politicians met to plan common strategy. Instead of backing down, Information Minister Jacques Lortie inflamed the situation by snapping angrily at journalists, "The government issued the decree so we could have elections. Whether the decree is unconstitutional or not does not concern us." Though this remark cost Lortie his job, he had accurately expressed the government's position.

The Electoral Council condemned the government and vowed not to participate in any elections based on the offending decree. It took two weeks of social and economic breakdown, widespread rioting with a score of civilians, including a nine-month-old baby, shot dead by soldiers, dozens more wounded, small businesses ruined, and a people's collective joy at the prospect of democratic elections collapsed before General Namphy backed down, on television, and promised to rescind the unconstitutional electoral decree. It was too late. The opposition, now loosely united in an umbrella group of fifty-seven organizations known as "The 57," vowed to continue striking and protesting until the government resigned.

Then the council resumed talks with the government and announced it was working on a new electoral law. With the election process apparently restored to the council's jurisdiction, most strikers returned to work. The protest movement (but not army violence) seemed to be losing steam.

The council refueled it, breaking off its discussions with the government and suspending work on its new electoral law to protest army violence. In separate statements both General Namphy and Colonel Regala urged resumption of the talks. It was the last time they would call for conciliation, and they never forgave the council for spurning them.

"The 57" urged the council to maintain its tough stance and orchestrated new strikes and antigovernment marches designed to force the government to resign. But as in the past the opposition leaders lost credibility because they could not answer the crucial question: Who would take over if the Namphy government was forced out?

In the midst of the violence and political chaos, a torrential rainstorm lashed Port-au-Prince. Topsoil from the mountains caked the streets. Heavy winds toppled trees and utility poles and uprooted rocks, blocking roads. At Port-au-Prince cemetery the earth buckled, exposing and opening coffins, loosing bones and rotting clothing onto the streets and courtyards of nearby houses. At least thirty died, including some of the city's two hundred thousand homeless who had climbed into crypts in the cemetery after they saw people drown on the sidewalks they usually lived on. "God is angry at Haitians," the people told each other fearfully. Vodoun priests agreed, saying the gods were displeased with the turmoil of the past three weeks.

On July 14 "The 57" called for a new general strike. Many presidential candidates opposed it and said that only elections could extricate Haiti from its condition of perpetual crisis, but "The 57" overrode them, and the public supported "The 57." "Burn tires, burn tires, we have no other arms, until we get a revolutionary popular government!" exhorted fiery Father Jean-Bertrand Aristide. Bishop Willy Romélus urged Catholics to strike until the government resigned.

On the ground, soldiers vacillated between energetic intervention and complete indifference in face of anti-government protests and rioting. Sometimes they shot and killed, arrested protesters and seized journalists' films and cassettes. Other times they stood by, indifferent. Meanwhile, their high command was preoccupied only with revamping the army. The result? The creation of a new level of general, and an increase to sixteen the number of generals who could be named. Shortly afterward, Colonel Williams Regala was promoted to Brigadier General, bringing to three the actual number of Haitian generals.

Then the government issued a decree cracking down on public demonstrations. Simultaneously the council refused to submit its new electoral law until its budget was approved, and the government refused to consider the budget until it had the electoral law in hand. The electoral law had now become a hostage between rival authorities.

Worse was to come in the form of a massacre in the remote, isolated district of Jean-Rabel, 150 miles northwest of Port-au-Prince. The massacre was the climax to years of struggle between Tet Ansamn, the agrarian reform group led by Ti-Legliz, and landowners large and small. In Jean-Rabel, Tet Ansamn was led by Haitian priest Jean-Marie Vincent and his Swiss lieutenant, Paola Eten. Operating out of a vast stone structure like a modern-day single-storied medieval fortress in the tiny arid hamlet of La Coma, they undertook vitally needed public projects, encouraged cooperatives and organized peasant agro-political groups known as *gwoupman*. They also denounced American food donations as a tool to enslave the people by creating dependence on handouts. By 1986, when Duvalier fled Haiti, an estimated eight to ten thousand of Jean-Rabel's seventy thousand people were Tet Ansamn members.

After Duvalier left Haiti, Tet Ansamn turned from local projects to radical land reform and began surveying and forcibly redistributing private property. They also encouraged sharecroppers to occupy state land and to refuse to pay rent to large landowners whose land they worked.

The inevitable happened. The Catholic hierarchy disowned Tet Ansamn. Small landowning peasants joined the larger landowners—an alliance known as *anti-gwoupman*—to fight Tet Ansamn. Violent conflicts erupted. Houses, clinics, and schools were torched. Crops were destroyed. Victims sued aggressors in court, and Jean-Rabelians repeatedly appealed to the army and government officials for help. None responded.

On July 23 Tet Ansamn leaders rounded up more than 1,000 *gwoupman* peasants armed with clubs and machetes to confront an even greater number of anti-*gwoupman* militants, who routed them. Survivors hid, but those who fought back were slaughtered, a few by decapitation. How many died? An anti-*gwoupman* leader boasted that 1,042 "communists" died. Tet Ansamn leaders claim no more than 100 to 120 died. Government investigators reported at least 225 victims.

The Jean-Rabel Massacre exposed simmering and fundamental discontent in a nation where population density is greater than India's, four million cultivate tiny plots of eroded soil that cannot sustain life, and less than 3 percent of landholders own large farms. Throughout Haiti the same scenario exists, and on La Gonave island a similar land dispute has since left eight dead.

Port-au-Prince reclaimed national attention when antigovernment protests and general strikes broke out again. The death toll, already at twenty-three since the outbreak of violence in June, climbed again. On July 29, Tonton Macoute Day, ten died and thirty were wounded in front of Teleco as soldiers, obeying orders to defend the nerve center of the nation's telecommunications system, opened fire on a group of demonstrators.

On August 1, in a macabre tragedy of errors, protesters attacked a garbage truck laden with the corpses of indigents from the General Hospital. They believed the bodies were riot victims and tried to kill the driver. Soldiers arrived and shot and killed three. A young man fell and died between sacks of rice, a vegetable vendor collapsed onto a basketful of lettuce, and a graying, middle-aged man bled to death on piles of oranges.

The death count was up to thirty-seven when armed men in Léogane hacked to death a moderate centrist presidential candidate, Louis Eugène Athis, and two of his colleagues, then burned their bodies. The government did not investigate the killings, and opposition critics charged it with covering up a police-sanctioned crime. Haitians began to observe a voluntary curfew. By 9 p.m., the streets were empty.

Three months before the elections Ti-Legliz spokesman Father Jean-Bertrand Aristide galvanized packed congregations with his diatribes against the government. His nervous Salesian superiors transferred him to a rural parish, then relented after youthful supporters went on a hunger strike to protest the transfer.

Triumphant, Aristide urged Haitians to overthrow the government and added, "Part of our mission is to destroy the capitalist system. Socialism is closer to the Gospel than either capitalism or communism."

On August 23, as Aristide spoke at a religious service near St. Marc, gunmen started shooting. The young priest escaped and was spirited away with other priests in a five-vehicle convoy heading back to Port-au-Prince. Despite a raging tropical storm, soldiers stopped and searched the car, then waved it on after the driver was identified as Joseph Burg, a Canadian monk.

A hundred meters farther, at another barricade, six civilians shouting "Communists!" began stoning Burg's car, smashing the door, the windows, and the headlights. When a rock hit Brother Burg, he floored his gas pedal and drove away, guided only by jagged bolts of lightning. Only later did Burg discover that Father Jean-Marie Vincent of Jean-Rabel had had his head gashed open and a bone smashed. Two other priests were injured, and Aristide was in a state of shock. Information Minister Gérard Noel condemned the attacks on the priests, but the government undertook no investigation. It began to appear as if in Haiti, Macoutes could again operate with impunity.

So too could they in France. After France's initial and transparently perfunctory attempts to convince them to find some other refuge, the Duvaliers settled happily into opulent exile. They rented a home from Mohamed Khashoggi, son of Saudi Arabian arms dealer Adnan Khashoggi, in the hills of Mougins, near sunny Cannes. When they did not feel like dining out, they ate meals catered by the Moulin de Mougins, Roger Vergé's three-star restaurant. Jean-Claude claimed to be studying law, but in fact he spent his time much as he had in Haiti, partying and enjoying the company of beautiful young ladies introduced to him by one of Michèle's brothers, broke and grateful for Jean-Claude's generous financial support.

Simone had long fled Michèle's home to move in with her daughter Ti-Simone, still happily unmarried to her common-law husband, Max Dominique, once her sister's husband. The elder Simone, frightened that she would lose the millions she had stashed away in various banks, passed her days phoning friends to complain about her finances and watching television by herself in her bedroom. Marie-Denise and her husband, Mario Théard, lived contentedly nearby.

In the U.S. the Bennetts were considerably less happy than the Duvaliers. Ernest Bennett had left his wife, Aurore, to live with a mistress, a Haiti Air stewardess. Bennett's namesake, Ernest, known as Ti-Nes, complained that he was short of money, while his American wife, Mary, confided tearfully to friends that he was unfaithful to her.[31]

In exile the Duvaliers and the Bennetts were as selfish and banal as they had been in Haiti. And with official French and Swiss collaboration, they continued to enjoy the hundreds of millions they had stolen while they were still in power and stripping their devastated homeland of its last resources.

Meanwhile, in the fine modern Police Headquarters building in Port-au-Prince, prisoners were dying and released prisoners told tales of brutality rivaling those of the old Fort Dimanche. Many of the new Haitian "disappeareds" had been incarcerated at Police Headquarters, packed forty or more into tiny cells designed for four, gasping for breath, asphyxiated by lack of oxygen. The food ration was insufficient and unhealthy, and inmates died quickly from diarrhea and dehydration or from malnutrition. Women were often held in common cells with men and sold for money by prisoners to other prisoners. Men too were raped, usually at gunpoint and just before death, by associates of the Detective Bureau.

Then on October 13 lawyer and minor presidential candidate Yves Volel vowed publicly that he would free Jean Raymond Louis, imprisoned for a month without charge or trial. With his lawyer's toga draped over one arm and the Constitution clutched in the other, Volel led a small group to Police Headquarters. He spoke to waiting newsmen, then turned and walked toward the building. In full view of Haitian journalists, plainclothes policemen grabbed him, beat him, then shot him in the head.

The Bar Association boycotted the courthouse for a week. The Provisional Electoral Council urged the government "to condemn most categorically the murder of a candidate in full exercise of his rights and to open up an inquiry regarding his murder, or else face the gravest doubts about the government's real intentions concerning coming elections."

The government remained mute. In this climate of terror and insecurity, Haitian electors waited out the six weeks until the elections.

And yet election preparations proceeded. Over one million out of three million eligible voters registered. The Electoral Council set up provincial bureaus. Over one hundred high-ranking army officers spent a week studying law and security measures "to permit the Electoral Council to do its work entirely independently." Politicians again campaigned in the provinces, abandoned since Athis was murdered.

Then the council had to postpone municipal and senatorial elections because of a dearth of candidates, while the new elected President would confront thirty-four defeated rivals. The Catholic bishops appealed to the presidential contenders: "Is it indispensable for you to be the Chief of State in order to serve your country with dignity and value? Does not the multitude of candidates create confusion which makes the electoral verdict difficult?" An opinion poll revealed that most Haitians had never heard of any of the candidates. Ten percent identified the name of Sylvio Claude, 9 percent knew Louis Déjoie. Only 1 percent recognized any of the others.

By October the council faced the critical issue of the Duvalierist candidates, barred by Article 291 of the Constitution from running. Clovis Désinor and General Claude Raymond began campaigning anyway, explaining that Article 291 did not apply to them.

Tension mounted. The entire point of ousting Jean-Claude Duvalier was at stake. The CNG, under tremendous pressure from its Duvalierist colleagues to allow Duvalierists to run, reacted angrily to American counter-pressure, denouncing it as a challenge to their authority. And they responded with contemptuous silence to repeated requests from Electoral Councilors after Duvalierist goons threatened them and attacked their offices.

Instead, the junta focused on strengthening the army through decentralizing and restructuring. First, Namphy installed himself as its commander in chief, a newly created position with a three-year mandate. He also promoted three colonels to generals, and upped Regala from brigadier to major general. The new army, with its potential for sixteen generals, including one in each geographical department, was designed to ensure army supremacy even after—or if—the upcoming elections transferred power to a civilian President.

The point of no return came on November 2. Even without protection, the council announced its official rejection of twelve Duvalierist candidates. That night Haiti exploded. Armed men sent out by some of those candidates burned down the council's Port-au-Prince offices, destroying files, computers, and motorcycles. The downtown department store co-owned by council member Emmanuel Ambroise was also burned to the ground. Though both buildings were located close to a large police station and the Teleco headquarters where soldiers patrol all night, military spokesmen insisted nobody had heard the assault on the council building's heavy metal doors or smelled the overpoweringly acrid stench as the building's interior was gutted by fire. It was perfectly clear that the army had no intention of defending the council.

The nightly terrorist attacks against electoral bureaus and officials continued in Port-au-Prince and in the provinces. Presidential candidates Sylvio Claude, Marc Bazin, Leslie Manigat, and Grégoire Eugène were also attacked. The printing shop preparing the ballots for the November 29 elections was torched, and all its materials and printing machines were destroyed.

Suddenly, for two weeks, there was a lull in the violence. A new poll reported that four candidates together accounted for 82 percent of electoral support. They were, in order of popularity, Sylvio Claude, Gérard Gourgue, Marc Bazin, and Louis Déjoie. People began speculating as to which of the "Big Four" would win.

The uneasy calm ended abruptly. During the night of November 22 armed men burned down Salomon Market, a sprawling establishment covering several city blocks. Arson and terrorist attacks now took place in broad daylight, on voting bureaus, parked cars, unlucky passers by, private homes, and businesses. Once again, Haitian schools shut their doors to wait out the election violence.

Finally, the army reacted. Impervious to the Electoral Council's pleas for protection, to the growing pile of corpses, to murderers walking unscathed through the streets, the army responded furiously when the people began to defend themselves because they believed "leftists" were organizing the vigilantes.

Two days before the elections Haiti was an armed camp, with grenades, gasoline, and Uzis on one side, and stones, gasoline, and endless manpower on the other. Thousands fled Port-au-Prince to escape the violence, while thousands fled the countryside for the anonymity of Port-au-Prince—to escape the violence.

General Namphy attempted to justify the army's refual to stop it. "We could not intervene, we did not know who was firing on whom. If we had intervened, we would have risked bearing alone the responsibility for the violence and we would have been accused of spoiling the elections."

Through all the chaotic violence the Electoral Council continued to work. Because the army refused any protection, council offices were like military outposts, with locked gates manned by suspicious guards who frisked all visitors before allowing them to pass through a maze of sandbags piled high and thick as bulwarks against assassins' bullets.

In a final cynical gesture of contempt, the government reneged on its promise to lend the council helicopters to distribute equipment and ballots to outlying regions. The council chartered two in Miami. The army refused them permission to fly. Before Election Day the council officially acknowledged that voters in some areas would not be able to vote.

The army, having already decided to sabotage and abort the elections, tolerated this systematic sabotage of preparations for them. But the Haitian people wanted elections, even disorganized, incomplete, imperfect elections. The new watchword was, "It'll be the first step. Next time will be better." In the same country where a ballot could be bought for a *gourde,* other men and women would pay with their lives for the privilege of voting.

Election eve was the worst ever. Volleys of machine guns, pistols, and rifles blasted through the long tropical night, interspersed with the "thoosh" of firebombs and the heavier boom of detonating grenades. And it wasn't stopped, because the government wanted it to continue.

Early on election morning Namphy and his colleagues met in the palace. Five days earlier they had drafted a decree abolishing the Electoral Council. Now they would enforce it. Then they themselves would hold the "right" sort of elections.

Dawn broke mild and clear on Bloody Sunday. The Macoutes, exhilarated by a night-long spree of shooting, burning, and destroying, hurled themselves into the final task. They mowed down thirty-three civilians and a Dominican journalist who begged for his life. They wounded and maimed hundreds, terrorized thousands, and after three exhausting hours stopped Haiti's first free elections in thirty years.

Even in face of death the people had tried to vote. Some who survived attacks simply crossed themselves and stood back in line, determined to cast their votes. Even after the elections were canceled, thousands insisted on voting anyway.

At 9 a.m., after their sad announcement that the elections had failed, the electoral councillors separated and hid. The streets of the nation were as bleak and empty as the national sorrow at the death of hope. The U.S. cut off all but humanitarian aid. Diplomatic phone lines hummed: Is there a gun at Namphy's forehead?

Namphy himself demystified the situation weeks later as he chatted with a foreign diplomat. "Mr. Ambassador, how many voters do you think there are in Haiti?" "About 2.8 million," replied his puzzled visitor. "You are wrong, Mr. Ambassador. Only one. The army. Ha ha," Namphy guffawed.

"The army only did its duty," he told France's *Libération* magazine reporter Christian Lionet. He dismissed the notion that Bloody Sunday had betrayed the people, depriving them of the election for which they had forced Duvalier out. "The politicians let it be believed that the people pushed Duvalier out, but that's not true," he said. Namphy also commented bitterly on the Church, which the army was publicly accusing of turning the people against the military. "I have heard a bishop [Willy Romélus of Jérémie] say what happened [on Bloody Sunday] was a shameful thing. It's that bishop who is a shameful thing. The bishops were named by Duvalier. . . . I'm Catholic, but I no longer respect priests."

The new, government-run elections were scheduled for January 17, in time to allow Namphy to resign on February 7, 1988, in favor of a civilian President. To ensure that they appeared democratic and fairly run, certain candidates had to be eliminated: leftists, rabble-rousers, notorious Duvalierists. A great deal was at stake. The new President had to be eminently respectable, intelligent, moderate, and sensible, palatable to both the army and to critical foreign donor nations.

The government also mobilized some *houngans* and *mambos* to garner popular support, a strategy borrowed directly from Papa Doc's arsenal of tactics. People began to mutter about a new regime called "papadocracy."

Bloody Sunday had not exhausted the bloodletters. Right to the eve of the new elections, armed gangs still roamed, and every morning fly-ridden corpses dotted the streets. Rumors of a 152-name death list circulated. In Carrefour Feuilles houses were attacked with grenades and machine guns, blasting out walls, ripping up tin roofs.

By mid-December, before Haiti's joyless Christmas, the government was ready with its new election law, simple and severe. All public officers would be elected at the same time: President, deputies, senators, and mayors. In Haitian tradition, candidates would furnish their own ballots. At the polls voters would hand their ballots to the precinct president, who would verify them, then deposit the ballots in the voting urns. Soldiers would man each polling station. The Supreme Court would rule on the eligibility of candidates. Citizens who unsuccessfully challenged a candidate's right to stand for office would face fines of up to $200 and twenty-five-day jail terms. Anyone who urged voters to boycott the elections could be fined up to $200 and two years' imprisonment.

Reaction to the new law was swift. The four most popular candidates, Bazin, Gourgues, Claude, and Déjoie, united as the "Group of Four" and vowed they would boycott the elections. The Catholic bishops announced they would not encourage voters to participate. The Americans labeled the elections "rigged," but Richard Holwill, Deputy Assistant Secretary of State for the Caribbean, confided, "You can't, at this point, go to Namphy with a stick. We could go with a stick, and everybody would feel good, but it ain't going to change anything."

Other candidates undermined the Group of Four's appeal to invalidate the elections and registered to run. Grégoire Eugène, Hubert de Ronceray, and Leslie Manigat all argued that the army was a Haitian reality that had to be accommodated, not challenged. Their candidacies were a bitter pill for the boycotting Group of Four but cheered the government because all were moderates, so it was not crucial which of them won.

The government went ahead and ordered the various organizations named by the Constitution to select new electoral councillors. When most refused it simply nominated its own men, civil servants and professionals unknown to the public. Eight formerly disbarred Duvalierist candidates once again registered. Eugène, de Ronceray and Manigat banded together and approached the government with a twofold proposition. They would continue on as candidates only if the Duvalierists were rejected and the army pledged not to interfere in the elections—they intended to fight it out freely among themselves on the electoral front. The deal was struck, and the government's creature, the new council, subsequently banned all eight of the Duvalierists.

No foreign government intervened. The U.S. had already cut aid and would do no more. As the editor of *The Miami Herald* put it with succinct poignancy, "Does anyone care about Haiti? Alas, no."

The Namphy government was elated, and Namphy was not unduly

worried about the aid cuts. Within a few months of new elections, he told people, the U.S. would come begging Haiti to accept foreign aid. Meanwhile, Haiti could survive, though civil servants suffered pay cuts, projects were halted, international loan payments were skipped, and new *gourdes* had to be printed, undermining the currency's stability. What now concerned him above all was his pledge to relinquish office on February 7, 1988.

The day before the elections Haiti shut down in a "Day of Reproach." Nationwide, stores and boutiques remained closed. Even pedestrians were rare, as Haitians wary of another electoral bloodbath braced themselves for the morrow.

The opposition leaders were elated by the success of the Day of Reproach and predicted a massive electoral boycott. General Namphy was depressed, bitter against the Church and against the merchants who had closed their doors. He had committed himself to the success of these elections. He had scraped together money for basic election preparations. He had ordered the army to guarantee the safety of the streets. He had not objected to foreign observers. He had even placed his own former chief of staff, General Claude Raymond, under house arrest so there would be no repeat of Bloody Sunday.

But despite all his efforts to make his elections palatable, Port-au-Prince reproached him by turning into a ghost town. And the Catholic bishops announced that for the first time in two centuries, the Church had canceled Sunday mass. On Election Day faithful Catholics should not leave their homes to pray or to vote.

The night resounded with booming thuds as soldiers rolled fifty-gallon oil drums, sandbags, and upended wooden carts to form roadblocks so no gangs could storm polling stations. By sunrise the country was barricaded against attack. Soldiers guarded all of the nation's polling stations. Tanks and troop carriers patrolled the streets. The day passed without violence, without traffic or church bells. The serenity of January 17 proved conclusively that the army could also have prevented Bloody Sunday. But this election was different. It was not going to elect Gérard Gourgue. The winner this time would be Leslie Manigat.

The week before elections Manigat had struck a bargain with Franck Romain, who, despite his reputation for past cruelty, was a popular candidate for mayor of Port-au-Prince. Romain was also an experienced and successful political organizer, and he agreed that his many supporters be given Manigat's presidential ballots along with those they cast for Romain as mayor.[32] Rumors also spread of an agreement between Manigat and Colonel Williams Regala. If Manigat won, Regala would resign from the army and continue on as Defense Minister. What else the two men arranged was not revealed. Jean-Marie Benoit, a dissident co-founder of Manigat's political party, the National Progressive Democratic Party, who had published a book entitled *A Profile of a Candidate—Manigat: A Thousand Reasons Not to Vote for Him,* must have considered issuing a new edition called *A Thousand and Two Reasons Not to Vote for Him.*

Yet many applauded the probable victory of Manigat. He was a brilliant, determined man, and the candidate most likely to convince the Americans to restore desperately needed foreign aid. He had impressive anti-Duvalierist credentials, having spent two months imprisoned by Papa Doc in 1961, followed by flight to the Argentine Embassy and twenty-three years of exile. Despite that, his willingness to compromise with the army and leading Duvalierists indicated that he would have little trouble staying in power. Manigat also had a unique political asset in his second wife, Mirlande, mother of the youngest of his seven daughters, daughter of a retired colonel, and a senatorial candidate with driving ambitions of her own.

On Election Day, contrary to expectation, the army did not coerce people to vote, and few did. Impartial observers estimated the turnout at under 15 percent. There was considerable fraud. Minors voted. Some polling stations had ballots only for certain candidates, usually Leslie Manigat. Precinct officials sometimes instructed obedient voters whom to vote for. People were transported from poll to poll to vote at each one. Election officials ranged from meticulous to sloppy in their administration, in the matters of identifying voters, disqualifying obvious minors, entering names in a registry book. As the polls closed two major candidates sought out the foreign press and cried foul: "I was naive and allowed General Namphy to deceive me," lamented Grégoire Eugène. "The elections were a masquerade in favor of Leslie Manigat," charged Hubert De Ronceray.

Front-runner Manigat admitted irregularities but denied that they invalidated the elections. "Irregularities are natural in Haiti because this is the first time Haitians have been called upon to participate in the democratic process. You are going to ask a weak, fragile, nascent democracy, an infant democracy, to do what big democracies do? That's not fair to us."

Days after the election the Electoral Council announced the results.

Despite near consensus that no more than 450,000 voters had shown up, the official tally was a Duvalieresque 1,062,016 ballots. Of those a healthy 50.38 percent were reported cast for Leslie Manigat. His electoral victory was announced, and the complications of an acrimonious run-off election were avoided.

In France, Jean-Claude Duvalier gave a rare interview, to the French magazine *Paris Match*. Duvalier said about Haiti's new President only that "I don't know him." He denied that he had ever been a dictator. "I never saw myself as a dictator. I believe I was a well-loved President." He also refuted charges that he had embezzled government money and complained that he had been misjudged because of his father's reputation. His legacy had been a heavy one, sighed Baby Doc. "It's crazy how Baby Doc has to pay for his father Papa Doc's reputation."

At 11:05 a.m. on February 7, 1988, at a ceremony attended by several hundred dignitaries, General Henri Namphy presented Leslie Manigat with the red-and-blue presidential sash, then saluted him and withdrew. Behind Manigat stood four military officers with machine guns. Troops in flak jackets, carrying clubs and automatic rifles, guarded him from the front. Leslie Manigat, Haiti's new President, had just inherited the Duvalier legacy.

14 PASSAGES

HAITI'S FORTIETH PRESIDENT LABORED FOR A MERE nineteen weeks before the legacy that he had inherited overwhelmed him. He had made a Faustian bargain: in his zeal to transform Haiti, he had accepted a negotiated rather than elected presidency. His earnest "Little Chats under the Thatch Roofed Bandstand," televised bi-monthly, failed to build popular support as disillusioned Haitans endured economic paralysis, drought, failing crops, a wave of street crime and murders in the capital, and documented charges of ministerial corruption. At the same time, Manigat's promises and priorities, and his efforts to act autonomously alarmed the military men who had arranged his victory. Never enthusiastic, they became mistrustful of Manigat's unwelcome attempts at reform.

The last straw was his plan to restructure the military. He argued that Haiti needed a police force that was no longer a branch of the army, and he challenged his army commander-in-chief's power. The immediate issue was what to do about Colonel Jean-Claude Paul, recently indicted in a Miami court for conspiring to import cocaine. The U.S. had no extradition treaty with Haiti, whose constitution prohibited extradition of Haitian nationals. On Monday, June 13, 1988, Manigat held discussions with Lieutenant General Henri Namphy. The following day, Namphy promoted Colonel Paul to Brigadier General and transferred him to Army General Headquarters—and out of Dessalines Barracks, home of Paul's one thousand fanatically loyal soldiers. Paul refused the "promotion" and fled back to the barracks. A duty officer barred his entry, so Paul scrambled over the six-meter fence and thereby precipitated the crisis that was, ironically, to unify the army and oust civilian Manigat.

Manigat, miscalculating, fired Namphy and placed his family under house arrest, even cutting his telephone lines.[33] Manigat also transferred or retired Namphy's closest associates. The drama ended on Sunday, June 19. At 8.15 p.m., under cover of a prearranged blackout and a deafening quarter-hour's thundering of cannons, grenades, and machine-gun fire, soldiers freed Namphy, stormed the palace, and captured Manigat at his official residence. At 1 a.m., Haiti's newest president appeared on television. "Haitian people, here is your General," he declared hoarsely in Creole, his haggard face half hidden by a metal battle helmet, his right hand clutching a machine gun. "Here is General Namphy. The army and the people, it's the same thing." He made one reference to Manigat. "President of the Republic, you chose to betray the Constitution of 1987 . . . leading to a dictatorship in its most brutal form." Then, waving his machine gun, he shouted, "This time it's the army that will lead the country the way that it should be led!"

The new military government, nicknamed Namphy 2, dismissed Manigat's cabinet, abolished five ministries, and appointed army officers to head the remaining nine. Colonel Paul was reinstated and forgiven. The Senate and Congress were dissolved. For one day, the airport was shut down, and overseas phone lines were blocked. Ex-president Manigat was flown to the Dominican Republic. His Minister of Information and several senior civil servants stayed behind, in Fort Dimanche. "General Namphy is mentally ill," Manigat declared in his first interview in exile.

The Manigat interlude had halted Haiti's progress to democracy and, by rousting Namphy, set in motion a more repressive, corrupt, and inward-looking regime. Cocaine trafficking continued unchecked, protected and facilitated by corrupt army officers. The deterioration of Haitian society continued. And the coup strengthened the hard-core Duvalierists who had encouraged the movement to get rid of Manigat.

"Behind mountains there are mountains," the Haitians say. The Manigat episode was over, and Namphy, Haiti's thirty-ninth president, became its forty-first as well. He and his soldiers had seized the National Palace—and reclaimed the Duvalier legacy.

General Namphy's second regime began badly and ended worse. The democratic sector deplored the coup, and hope turned to bitter disillusionment. Namphy reneged on his promises and pursued only one political theme—unbridled cronyism. He suspended the constitution he had sworn to uphold, and boasted that he had never bothered to read it.

Political analysts struggled to understand this turn of events in Haiti. How had this ailing and erratic man returned to power? The answer: He had been put there. The force behind the Namphy coup was not the inept general. It was the brilliant Colonel Prosper Avril, that wiliest of advisers to every president since François Duvalier. Avril had known that Manigat, whose political survival depended on weakening the army, had to be overthrown. In Manigat's stand-off with Namphy, the titular chief of the army had to win the day.

Then Namphy dug his own grave. "If I ever return to the palace, then you'll see the real Henri Namphy," he had sworn to family intimates the day Leslie Manigat became President. The real Henri Namphy was a man whom power had taught all the wrong lessons. Tragically, he now had another chance to apply them.

The most important lesson was that a Haitian president should act like a Haitian president—like a Duvalier. Namphy moved into the palace, uninhabited since the Duvaliers cursed their quarters and fled. To curry popular favor, he and Gaby—now his unsmiling First Lady—toured the countryside, and Télé-National broadcast sycophantic programs showing them as they inspected provincial classrooms, clinics, irrigation ditches, and farmlands. The government newspaper, *L'Union*, became a photo album of the First Couple.

Namphy also resorted to Duvalier-era repression and terror. Almost daily, the bodies of murdered men and women were found on city streets, often cuffed with army-issue handcuffs. A few were decapitated. The Macoutes, emboldened, resurfaced and regained control of the streets. On July 10, human rights activist Lafontant Joseph was shot to death. A month later, four members of an anti-government peasant group were killed in Labadee, in the North.

But Namphy focused most of his attention on one visible enemy—Catholic priests, whom he branded leftist activists and blamed for fomenting popular discontent. One victim was Canadian priest René Poirier, who was arrested after boycotting a ceremony welcoming the General/President to his parish, and then flung onto a New York-bound plane with neither money nor luggage.

Namphy's real target was "ce petit prêtre," Salesian priest Father Jean-Bertrand Aristide, still relentlessly denouncing Macoutes and Duvalierists from his pulpit, decrying abuses, urging reform in angry words and powerful images that galvanized the beaten-down people and promised preferential treatment for the poor, and a *lavalas,* a cleansing flood to wash away corruption and oppression. Haitians responded *en masse* to this beacon of hope and took courage from predictions of a priestly new president.[34] After Aristide urged worshippers to attend his September 11 mass wearing white armbands to protest against the suspension of the Constitution, the General acted.

The plan—find and destroy—was orchestrated by Port-au-Prince Mayor Franck Romain. On September 11, at 9:15 a.m., Romain's Macoutes met at Saint Jean Bosco Church, sporting red armbands and brandishing machetes, pointed sticks, and guns. At first they stood outside the church and pelted it with stones. Later, as reinforcements arrived, they stormed inside, chanting, "We will drink their blood." Father Aristide, protected by a group of his followers, escaped, as the Macoutes attacked, shooting, beating, stabbing and slashing parishioners, and grabbing handbags to steal money and jewelry. Over the next two hours, the Macoutes killed thirteen people and wounded at least seventy-seven, including a pregnant woman. Outside, policemen stood by and watched as victims fled screaming from the church that the Macoutes then set on fire.

For the next six days, terror reigned in Port-au-Prince, as armed gangs roamed the streets. They torched two more churches. They also invaded the General Hospital, searching for the wounded pregnant woman mentioned in news reports—they wanted her dead. They ripped off bedcovers and examined bare bellies for evidence of a recent Caesarean. Doctors managed to hide the hunted woman and her premature, lacerated baby. Later, the doctors lamented in a communiqué: "When will respect for life be guaranteed in this country?"

Namphy laughed in their faces, and six of his supporters boasted on radio and television about the massacre. "We were after Father Aristide; what you saw . . . was child's play," said one man. "In whatever parish Father Aristide is accepted, a heap of corpses will attend that mass." Mayor Romain blamed Aristide for the massacre, quoting, "He who sows the wind reaps the tempest." General Namphy posed for photographs with his arms around two of the assassins. The Salesian order, under intense pressure from the regime, expelled Aristide. He took this well, saying, "Jesus Christ, you'll remember, was not a priest."[35]

Saint Jean Bosco also ended Namphy's resuscitated Papadocracy as dissident soldiers turned against him. "We soldiers seized two tanks and gave Namphy five minutes to leave," one of them explained on Radio Soleil. "He didn't want to and began shooting. We shot on him and the Macoutes." Namphy tried to address the soldiers through a microphone. "We told him 'No contact,' and began firing on him again. He dropped the microphone and ran." Soon after, Namphy surrendered.

The soldiers permitted Gaby Namphy to pack a single suitcase, and then pushed her and Henri and their young daughter into a tank and drove them to the airport. At 2:00 a.m., as the Namphys waited to depart for any country that would accept them, Prosper Avril, promoted to Brigadier General after Manigat's ouster, appeared on Télé-National with a small group of soldiers, and announced that he had been named President.

"The soldiers have chosen me because they are revolted by the way the government was being conducted," Avril said. One of the soldiers confirmed this: "General Avril is a serious, competent, earnest man who we know is able to do the people's job." And so Prosper Avril, that most accomplished engineer of Duvalierism's vast financial empire, had finally become chief administrator of the Duvalier legacy.

Haitians awoke to a new president, and reprisals began. At the airport, Namphy's military guards wrested his gold bracelet from his wrist and snatched $16,000 U.S. from Gaby's purse. During the long hours of waiting until the Dominican Republic reluctantly agreed to provide temporary asylum, the guards kicked and shoved the family with such bitterness that Gaby later told relatives she was amazed that she survived.

Back in Port-au-Prince, jeering mobs hunted down and killed a dozen Namphy cronies, most of them Macoutes who were stabbed, stoned, and "necklaced" Père Lebrun-style by jeering mobs. (Père Lebrun was a well-known automobile tire dealer who regaled television audiences by sticking his head through and wearing the tires he was advertising.) Other Namphy opponents looted and smashed houses belonging to Namphy and his associates, including Franck Romain and ex-general Claude Raymond, identified as a leader in 1987's Black Sunday election massacre.

The army rank and file also turned against officers accused of injustice, cruelty, favoritism, Duvalierism, Manigatism, or Namphyism. Soldiers handcuffed their commanders and, as civilian onlookers applauded, deposited them in front of the Army General Headquarters. Avril's high command legitimized the soldiers' actions, retiring fifty-seven officers, including eight generals. But under American pressure, he balked at their choice of Colonel Jean-Claude Paul as the new chief of staff, and instead appointed the widely respected General Hérard Abraham. He also promoted himself to Lieutenant General.

President Avril quickly launched a campaign for resumption of foreign aid. To placate the Americans—and neutralize a potential rival—he persuaded Colonel Jean-Claude Paul to retire in exchange for immunity from extradition to the U.S. (Weeks later, Paul died after eating a poisoned bowl of traditional squash soup. His death, though convenient for Avril, was suspected to be the handiwork of Paul's Miami-based wife, furious at being double-crossed in a cocaine payoff deal.) Ever clever, Avril spoke unctuously about democracy and human rights, assuring foreign reporters, "My vision is to enter history as one who has saved the country from anarchy and dictatorship and who has worked to establish an irreversible democracy."

But where was this democracy? Avril refused to announce an election timetable or re-establish the Constitution. He named one of Michèle Bennett's friends, the disreputable Carmen Christophe, mayor of Port-au-Prince. He gave Franck Romain safe conduct to the Dominican Republic. He stopped disarming Macoutes, and scheduled no Macoute trials. He intensified terror in the streets. He allowed prisoners to be tortured or starved to death before they came to trial.[36] He halted the chase after the Duvaliers' stolen millions.

On February 7, 1989, the third anniversary of the Duvaliers' flight, the Haitian masses mourned. The army was so divided that rival officers only dared move about guarded by armed soldiers, and so feared ambush that even nature's calls to palace toilets involved major security precautions. In April, Avril narrowly survived a coup in which forty soldiers died at the hands of comrades-in-arms.

Less than a year later, Avril combated public protest with arrests, beatings and forced exile of leading opponents, including Dr. Louis Roy, an architect of the Haitian Constitution. On March 5, a soldier killed eleven-year-old schoolgirl Rosaline Vaval as she studied on her porch. Rosaline's death sounded the knell for Avril's regime, just as four years earlier, three Gonaives schoolboys' killings had helped push the Duvaliers out of Haiti. On March 10, Avril abdicated in favor of his incorruptible chief of staff, General Hérard Abraham.

*   *   *

Avril hunkered down in his red-and-white gingerbread-style house despite public outrage at his presence, despite furious mob attacks on his supporters' lives and properties, despite the stench of charred Macoutes fouling the tropical air. Only a 1:30 a.m. visit from American ambassador Alvin Adams convinced the latest ex-president and his family he had no choice but exile—and asylum—in Florida.[37]

On March 13, General Abraham honored his promise to surrender power. "I order the army to return to its barracks and stay there," he declared. "Madame President, the armed forces of Haiti are at your command." The general then saluted the woman just inaugurated as Haiti's forty-third president—Ertha Pascal Trouillot, a scholarly lawyer who had been named by the first Namphy government to the Supreme Court and was the sister of jazz guitarist Alix Pascal, permanently paralyzed in the 1960s when a Macoute shot him in the back during a rehearsal.

True to her mandate, Trouillot oversaw Haiti's first genuinely free elections on December 16, 1990. The winner was the Haitian people through their savior, Jean-Bertrand Aristide, victorious with an overwhelming 67 percent of the vote;[38] his party, the National Front for Change and Democracy, won more votes in the Senate and Chamber of Deputies than other parties but did not command a majority.

Weeks before Aristide's inauguration on February 7, 1991, the Macoutes made a last stand; Roger Lafontant, back from Canadian exile and vocal about stopping Aristide, took Trouillot hostage and declared himself President. Enraged Haitians rushed into the streets. General Abraham ordered the army to end the "mutiny," and the coup was crushed. Lafontant was arrested, later convicted of leading the abortive coup, and sentenced to life imprisonment.[39] Infuriated mobs killed scores of Macoutes, smashed the homes and cars of suspected accomplices, and targeted buildings, including the eighteenth-century cathedral in Bel Air, that were connected, even if only peripherally, to Michèle Bennett's uncle, the unrepentant Duvalierist Archbishop Wolff-Ligondé.

On Aristide's inauguration day, exactly five years after Jean-Claude Duvalier was driven out of Haiti, Port-au-Prince was shining clean, swept, and scrubbed by brigades of joyful *Lavalasiens*. One wealthy family donated thousands of paint cans for murals glorifying Aristide. The National Palace gleamed. Aristide's inaugural speech, delivered in Creole before thousands of cheering supporters, many from the poorest rungs of society, was a powerful outpouring of promises and appeals for justice, transparency, and participation. He denounced the $10,000 monthly presidential salary as scandalous when other people could not eat, and reduced it—and the salary of cabinet ministers—to $4,000. True to his priorities, he vowed to provide the poor with food and education.

Aristide also embraced the Haitian diaspora as the "Tenth Department" (Haiti has nine administrative departments) and invited expatriates to offer their skills to their homeland. Stunningly, he made a pre-emptive strike against the military, thanking six out of its eight generals for their service and then calling on General Abraham to retire them. He promoted Lieutenant General Raoul Cédras, who had remained loyal during Lafontant's failed coup, to army chief of staff.

Privately, on that same day, President Aristide served notice that Ertha Trouillot must make herself available for questioning about the circumstances of Lafontant's abortive coup. On April 4, she was arrested on suspicion of having conspired with Lafontant. She spent one night in jail, and was then released after American officials intervened.

Aristide's warning to the army leadership, courageous and risky, mobilized officers against him. His treatment of Ertha Trouillot confirmed American fears that he was suspicious and thirsty for retribution. His soaring sermons had always terrified the elite. "*Vive la guerre!* So that we will all have bread. *Vive la guerre!* So that we will all have houses. *Vive la guerre!* So that we will all have land."[40] His presidential calls for reconciliation were alarming to all of his opponents: Reparations were essential, he declared, and reconciliation without them would be bitter. His campaign against corruption and smuggling were red flags to the army and the elite who fed on both. His plans to decentralize the economy and restore his agricultural nation's capacities for food production through cooperatives frightened landowners. His proposed reform of the cumbersome and inefficient civil service alienated those it had benefited, often by providing a sinecure.

The experience of then-Port-au-Prince mayor Irene Ridoré, who survived several assassination attempts after her massive reform program laid off hundreds of "employees" who did no work and in many cases had never even visited city hall, illustrates how pervasive corruption was in the public service and how difficult and dangerous to eradicate. "The people who were receiving the biggest checks were almost always zombies [phantom workers]," Ridoré said. A local school supply dealer added, Ridoré "came in and said we have four trucks and fourteen drivers, two typewriters and twenty secretaries. That is Haiti, but that has got to stop."[41] Aristide agreed. He also took on landowners by targeting Haiti's grotesquely lopsided land-tenure system for reform. Of the country's estimated 2,161,000 acres of arable land, about 60 percent was owned by farmers whose holdings were at most three acres, and often much less. The large properties, about one thousand holdings of between 250 to 750 acres, were in the hands of a small number of Haiti's most privileged citizens, who often owned more than one property.

Aristide also tackled the issue of rice, already flooding into Haiti with the consequences he had been warning of for years. "You must understand the 'American Plan,' the plan of Delatour and the rich," he had earlier told American journalist Mark Danner. "First, they want to destroy our agriculture: to destroy our rice and all the crops Haiti produces. Why? So the people will come here [to Port-au-Prince] from the land to work in those American factories for almost nothing."[42]

By 1991 this dramatic prediction no longer sounded like a crazed conspiracy theory. Aristide's government meeting with fifty peasant organizations and unions led to a proposal (ironically, an echo of Papa Doc's economic protectionism), that called for the government to stabilize and control the price by buying up the entire rice harvest; it would also limit imports to the period between local harvests. Aristide's rice plan was doomed by the free market policies of the IMF; the arrival of Erly Industries, one of the world's largest rice companies, into the Haitian market; and the mutual interests of Haitian and U.S. rice importers (and smugglers), who stood to lose huge profits if Aristide protected Haitian-grown rice.

The power of the IMF and the World Bank, its twin sister, also extended into the morass of Haiti's financial and administrative core, part of the Duvalier legacy. The IMF demanded radical reform, and Aristide, who used to refer to it as the International Misery Foundation, sensibly and pragmatically complied. He introduced fiscal austerity, anti-corruption and privatization measures that reassured international lenders and hurt the formerly privileged officials and business people who had benefited from past practices. For a short while, Aristide seemed to be making good progress in chipping away at what Haiti scholar Robert Fatton calls "the utter predatory nature of the Duvalierist inheritance."[43]

But the new president fared less well with what was dearest to his heart—raising the minimum wage from fifteen to twenty-five *gourdes* a day, or from $3.00 to $5.00, plus benefits. "We must end this regime where the donkeys do all the work and the horses prance in the sunshine," he vowed. But the horses and their American handlers, along with the business community, factory owners and USAID lobbied hard to prevent such drastic changes; USAID spent an estimated $26 million on the campaign. One of Haiti's biggest selling points, they argued, was its inexhaustible pool of low-waged, docile and industrious workers too poor to dare protest. The specter of these workers earning the extravagant wage of $5.00—about $.50 an hour—was too distressing to contemplate.

Other Aristide initiatives fared better: another adult literacy program similar to Misyon Alfa, shut down under the CNG government; a restructuring of national health facilities; press freedom; plans to improve agrarian credit and anti-erosion programs; and the appointment of ombudsmen to deal with land disputes, simmering throughout the nation. He ordered Haiti's 562 *chefs de section*, often military men and ex-Macoutes who administered each region, to surrender their arms and accept the authority of civilian authorities, the new community councils (CASEC) created by the 1987 Constitution. This process had mixed results, including the violent settling of old scores and the incineration of some *chefs de section*.

Aristide was trying hard to make good on his promises to the people who had voted him into office. But his tactics in running the country were deeply flawed. When he was a hunted, persecuted priest, Aristide had been willing to engage in politics. But after winning the election, he saw no need to expend much energy on the politicians and their always-splintering political parties. Like so many other charismatic Latin American leaders, as Canadian journalist Paul Knox reminds us, Aristide "believed, mistakenly, that the requirement to engage in politics ended on election night, and that all that was left to do was rule."[44]

In early February, as President-elect, Aristide formed his own political party, the Lavalas Political Organization (OPL), with Gerard Pierre-Charles, a left-wing intellectual, author and anti-Duvalierist activist. ("Alone we are weak, together we are strong, Together, together we are the flood.") This new entity was the populist movement grandly christened, and its loyalty was to Aristide personally; dissenters were enemies. The President surrounded himself with adorers and pliant colleagues, such as René Préval, his prime minister.

Aristide also had a crisis thrust on him—the forced repatriation of upwards of fifty thousand Haitians from the sugarcane fields of the Dominican Republic after international outcries likening their living conditions to slavery drove President Balaguer to expel all of them under sixteen or over sixty. Some were deported, others fled to avoid arrests and beatings. Suddenly, Haiti had to absorb thousands of destitute refugees, some with no links to Haiti except heritage.[45]

Aristide was distracted by this latest crisis, but his enemies remained focused on him. They included Macoutes sworn to kill him; the elite whose world-as-they-knew-it he aimed to upend; American interests including USAID whose policies clashed with his; and alienated political allies and friends Aristide had grown cool toward or dropped.

Aristide the president was no less vengeful than Aristide the activist priest who propped a life-sized cloth doll dressed in the garb of a murdered Macoute atop his filing cabinet, and seemed to enjoy how it unsettled and shocked visitors to his office.

It was in this same reckless spirit that he delivered his celebrated "Père Lebrun" speech in front of the National Palace on September 27, 1991, Préval by his side. It was classic Aristide: The bourgeoisie, whose riches were the fruit of thievery "under an evil regime, an evil system," had had seven months to provide jobs for the people, and their time was up. "Put people to work. You must invest your money any old way, so that more people can find work, for: if you don't do it, I am sorry for you! It's not my fault, you understand!?" Then, to the huge crowd (that included General Raoul Cédras) hanging onto his every word: "Now, whenever you are hungry, turn your eyes in the direction of those people who aren't hungry. Whenever you are out of work, turn your eyes in the direction of those who can put people to work. Ask them why not? What are you waiting for?"

Then Aristide alluded specifically to Roger Lafontant, imprisoned in the National Penitentiary. Wait and watch, Aristide cried out, and if Lafontant or another Macoute should escape, "when you catch one, don't hesitate to give him what he deserves." And what was that? Why, a "Père Lebrun." "What a beautiful tool!" Haiti's president enthused.

> What a beautiful instrument! What a beautiful piece of equipment! It's beautiful, yes it's beautiful, it's cute, it's pretty, it has a good smell, wherever you go you want to inhale it. Since the law of the country says Macoute isn't in the game [barred from politics for ten years], whatever happens to him he deserves, he came looking for trouble.[46]

Aristide's speech was blood-chilling, especially for ex-Macoutes, and aggressively unpresidential. Haiti's elite business class were appalled at the implications for their own safety. Aristide, his own worst public relations enemy, had just handed those already plotting to overthrow him the perfect justification.

Two days later, Aristide fell victim to a coup d'état coordinated by General Raoul Cédras and Police Chief Michel "Sweet Micky" François, and financed by members of the elite. As it began, the President's enraged supporters were inspired to kill Sylvio Claude, an Aristide rival, by neck-lacing. In his penitentiary cell, Roger Lafontant was shot to death. Over at Aristide's house outside Port-au-Prince in Tabarre, soldiers mowed down his loyalist supporters and his household's animals. Finally the French ambassador, Jean-Raphael Dufour, appeared with a convoy of cars to drive Aristide to the palace, where he was handcuffed. Cédras, calm and grinning broadly at his captive, gloated, "I am the President now." After the general decided not to shoot him, Aristide was flown to Caracas on a plane sent by Venezuela's president.

There followed three years of the re-Duvalierization of Haiti, and a slow leak in Aristide's reputation as the Haitian people's great libera-tor. With the troublesome priest exiled first in Venezuela and then in the U.S., the Cédras regime settled down to run the nation. Prudently, the general did not snatch the presidency for himself; that burden fell, con-stitutionally, to Supreme Court Justice Joseph Nérette and, after he re-signed in 1992, to Marc Bazin, who in 1990 had won 14 percent of the vote versus Aristide's 67 percent and who filled his cabinet with Aristide opponents.

Post-coup reprisals against Lavalas and Aristide supporters intensi-fied, and at least three thousand were killed. Large numbers went into hiding. Countless others were tortured, mutilated, beaten and perse-cuted. Men suspected of supporting Aristide were humiliated and their genitalia maimed, leaving many impotent or infertile. Their houses, lands, farm animals, and crops were destroyed or stolen. One peasant activist was stripped naked, tied up with a rope covered with pig dung, and tortured. Other men had their hands chopped off so they could not work. A trumpet player's mouth was so damaged he could no longer play.[47] Women were robbed and raped, stabbed, and burnt in breast and vagina, and, if they were visibly pregnant, beaten until they miscarried. A soldier threatened one expectant mother he was hauling off to prison for participating in a demonstration: "I'll keep on beating you until you have to give birth by the nostrils."[48]

Inside prisons, forgotten men and women languished in horrific conditions. In Les Cayes, sick and starving prisoners were walking skeletons. Mondelus Norelus, a prison guard known as Saddam Hussein, forced a prisoner to hack off and eat part of his own ear. Afterward, Norelus carved his initials into the man's buttocks. In the National Penitentiary in Port-au-Prince, where 85 percent of the inmates were political prisoners, small cells were crammed with prisoners, few with even a scrap of cardboard between them and the filthy concrete floor. A trough along the wall of each cell stank of feces and urine.[49] And under the Cédras regime as under the Duvaliers', few of these wretched inmates had any chance of legal redress, much less the light of day.

But the coup had economic and diplomatic consequences— American and international sanctions on everything except humanitarian goods, that is, food and medicine. Poor Haitians suffered. When smugglers failed to import enough fuel, public transportation slowed to a crawl or stopped. Employees could not get to their jobs; market vendors and their customers could not get to market. In the early days of the embargo, Port-au-Prince's assembly industry was hit hard; of forty-four factories, seven were forced to shut down and thirty-two laid off an estimated 32,000 workers and were fighting for survival. With the pressure on, OAS and other officials drafted the Washington Accord, restoring Aristide to power on certain conditions. Despite hardships, Haiti's government and Supreme Court rejected it. But life in sanctioned Haiti was no life at all, and tens of thousands fled by the boatload.[50] President Bush ordered them repatriated, and by the end of 1992, 29,500 had been returned to Haiti. A mere fifty-four were accepted into the U.S. as refugees.

The embargo was leaky and largely exempted those who had supported the coup. The U.S. did not seize a single one of the stateside houses most wealthy Haitians kept as insurance against "troubles." It froze very little money held in U.S. banks. Three months after the embargo began, President Bush permitted Haitian assembly plants to resume trade with the U.S. on certain conditions, including the requirement that manufactured goods contain American parts or raw materials. A resourceful mango exporter successfully argued that his mango trees had American branches grafted on. Afterward, other planters remembered that their limes and breadfruit were also the produce of dual-nationality trees.

To many Aristide supporters, the question became: What embargo? Antoine Izmery, Aristide's wealthy backer, faxed written evidence of smuggling, including bills of lading and phone numbers, to the Office of Foreign Assets Control (OFAC), the embargo agency, and received no response. The Americans "just fuddled around," recalled Lawrence Pezzullo, former U.S. special envoy to Haiti. "We made fools of ourselves, because we didn't go forward with a commitment we made."[51] No wonder Haiti could get away with refusing to allow Aristide to return.

But on January 20, 1993, Bill Clinton took over the presidency from George H.W. Bush, and restoring Aristide to Haiti took on some urgency. Clinton ended the Bush-era fuddling and began to enforce the embargo, forcing Cédras to pay attention and negotiate. (And teaching the elite how to appreciate their single malt Scotch neat, without the ice that was in as short supply as fuel. And killing one thousand children a month, through malnutrition and illnesses caused by lack of access to food, vaccines, and drugs no longer available because of the embargo.[52]) In July, the Governors Island Agreement took shape. Aristide and Cédras agreed to a political truce that would see Aristide return on October 30, 1993, and guarantee amnesty for Cédras and others involved in the coup. With UN and OAS assistance and supervision, Haiti would establish a new police force and modernize its army. Aristide and Cédras pledged to cooperate fully in the peaceful transition to a stable and lasting democratic society so all Haitians could live in a climate of freedom, justice, security and respect for human rights.

But that climate described a fictional country, not Haiti, where a new paramilitary force was ripening. FRAPH, the Revolutionary Front for Haitian Advancement and Progress, masqueraded as a political group but was a seething, neo-Macoutic fraternity of thugs, including former VSN who terrified, attacked and killed, and were often attached to military units as *attachés*. FRAPH was the brainchild of Emmanuel Constant, aka "Toto," General Gérard Constant's son, who had been based in New York and, since 1992, on the CIA payroll ($700 a month), and Louis Jodel Chamblain, a former army sergeant and Macoute whose wife, seven months pregnant, had been murdered by a pro-Aristide gang enraged by her husband's involvement in Roger Lafontant's failed coup in 1990.

FRAPH knew and hated Antoine Izmery, their enemy Aristide's political and financial backer, and an advocate for a strictly enforced embargo. In May of 1992, they had killed Antoine's brother Georges, probably misidentifying him as Antoine. On September 11, 1993, the month before Aristide's scheduled return, ten Duvalierist thugs invaded the Église Sacré Coeur where Izmery had organized a mass to commemorate the Saint Jean Bosco church massacre. Father Antoine Adrien preached a short sermon, pleading for "a suspension of all killing [and for] tranquility, peace, and justice." Then, recalled Father Hugo Triest, another participant, "We were around the altar and a guy with this weapon came up and said, 'He's the one,' and pointed to Izmery. He came closer and pulled his weapon." The assassins hauled Izmery out into the courtyard and shot him point-blank in the head.[53]

On October 14 FRAPH-style Macoutism had an undeservedly spectacular triumph when the USS *Harlan County* steamed into Port-au-Prince harbour loaded with Americans and Canadians on a mission to prepare for Aristide's return. Cédras already regretted signing the Governors Island Agreement, and gave FRAPH free rein to greet the foreigners. On *Harlan County*, observers noted that the slip large enough to dock their large vessel was occupied. Also, two motorboats manned by machine guns were circling the harbor. On shore, Toto Constant and his FRAPH acolytes, including out-of-uniform soldiers, stormed the pier, shrieking, shooting into the air and threatening. After consultation, and mindful of the nineteen American soldiers recently killed in Somalia, President Clinton ordered the ship home. As the jeering crowd watched, the giant ship turned and chugged away. FRAPH's bullies, whom Constant had had to persuade not to run away, swelled up with pride: they had scared away the foreigners, and now their bravado knew no bounds.[54] "We were astonished," Constant admitted. "That was the day FRAPH was actually born."[55]

What better place to strut their stuff than Cité Soleil, a vast shantytown whose denizens overwhelmingly supported Aristide? On December 27, FRAPH recruits swooped, torching shacks, raping women and killing: Amnesty International estimated forty adults and thirty children died. On April 22, 1994, after several smaller attacks, FRAPH and its military accomplices struck the Raboteau slum of Gonaives. Here, too, they burned, beat and tortured, forcing victims to lie in filthy open sewers, and shot and killed about twenty people.

The issue of boat people continued to loom large, and in 1993, President Clinton reneged on his promise to stop the repatriations and decided that Haitians could only apply for refugee status *within* Haiti.

At that Haiti's president-in-exile forced Clinton's hand by declaring that in six months, the Haiti-U.S. accord authorizing the repatriations would end. Aristide's implied threat—that until he was reinstated, the U.S. would be inundated with boat people—was frightening; anti-immigration sentiment was strong, especially in Florida, where most Haitians landed. (The Haitian military, just as concerned about the prospect of Aristide's return, tried hard but failed to stop people from leaving.) Ultimately, the U.S. saw Haitians as "a mass of humanity to be kept out of the country," and, human rights scholar Kurt Mills concludes, the "perceived security aspects of refugee flows were the main impetus behind intervention. . . ."[56] Aristide, the lone Haitian pleading to go back to Haiti, was going to get his way.

But it wasn't easy for him, and the remaining days of his presidency were trickling away; octogenarian Supreme Court Justice Émile Jonassaint had already pledged to organize elections for a new president to take office on February 7, 1995. On August 26, 1994, under extreme pressure, Aristide accepted the Paris Plan, a digest of Structural Adjustment policies that incorporated the IMF, World Bank and American and French ideologies and economic needs: to privatize state-owned monopolies; to reform and downsize the civil service; to encourage free trade through low tariffs; and to maintain the very low minimum wage. Aristide's back was to the wall. With not even six months until the inauguration of a new elected president, he signed the monstrous agreement.

Two days later, at about 8:00 p.m., as Aristide ally Father Jean-Marie Vincent drove his car up to the gates at the rectory of the Montfortain Fathers on the Rue Baussan, in Port-au-Prince, two vehicles filled with members of the army's dreaded Anti-Gang Unit opened fire and repeatedly shot him. An ambulance was called to transport Vincent, who was bleeding profusely, to the hospital. But to make sure that he did not arrive alive, the army vehicles went ahead of the ambulance, leading and blocking it, and driving at a snail's pace. By the time he was delivered into the hands of doctors, Father Vincent had bled to death.[57] Vincent, who had been savagely attacked in the aftermath of the 1987 massacre at Jean-Rabel, was targeted because he was Aristide's close personal friend and refused to stop his work.[58]

The time to restore Aristide through a military intervention had come again. In an address to the nation on September 15, Clinton was unsparing in condemning Cédras.[59]

Cédras and his armed thugs have conducted a reign of terror. Executing children. Raping women. Killing priests. . . . Slaying Haitian orphans. . . . The dictators are said to suspect the children of harboring sympathy toward President Aristide for no other reason than he ran an orphanage in his days as a parish priest. The children fled the orphanages for the streets. Now they can't even sleep there because they're so afraid.

International observers uncovered a terrifying pattern of soldiers and policemen raping the wives and daughters of suspected political dissidents. Young girls, thirteen years old, sixteen years old. People slain and mutilated with body parts left as warnings to terrify others. Children forced to watch as their mothers' faces are slashed with machetes.

Clinton also spelled out the back story, the never-ending crisis of Haitian refugees attempting to reach the U.S.

Thousands of Haitians have already fled toward the United States, risking their lives to escape the reign of terror. As long as Cédras rules, Haitians will continue to seek sanctuary in our Nation. This year, in less than two months, more than 21,000 Haitians were rescued at sea by our Coast Guard and Navy. Today, more than 14,000 refugees are living at our naval base in Guantanamo. The American people have already expended almost $200 million to support them, to maintain the economic embargo. And the prospect of millions and millions more being spent every month for an indefinite period of time loom ahead unless we act.

Three hundred thousand more Haitians, 5 percent of their entire population, are in hiding in their own country. If we don't act, they could be the next wave of refugees at our door. We will continue to face the threat of a mass exodus of refugees and its constant threat to stability in our region and control of our borders.

In Haiti, Cédras and his tough-minded wife, Yannick, watched and worried, until Cédras asked to talk things over with a high-ranked American. Clinton chose former U.S. president Jimmy Carter, who with General Colin Powell and Senator Sam Nunn, was given the assignment of convincing Cédras to avert an invasion by leaving Haiti. On their first try, the Americans sat for hours in Cédras' office, listening to "the same old horseshit that we had heard six million times," as a U.S. embassy witness recalled.[60] At the same time, and unknown to the Carter mission, the Presidential Guard had risen up under Colonel Michel François and was about to arrest Cédras. General Philippe Biamby forestalled the coup. "Gentlemen, you are rebelling so that there won't be a U.S. invasion," he told them. "If I were in your shoes, I would do the same thing. But President Carter is here and tomorrow we will sign an agreement with him saying that there won't be an invasion." The soldiers decided to return to their barracks.

Carter, unaware that he had inadvertently stopped a coup against the man he was desperate to see gone, decided to tackle Yannick Cédras, reputedly the key to the general's decision-making. He later described his negotiating strategy as he sat in the Cédras's spacious and modern Petionville home, their ten-year-old son on his knee, while the "slim and very attractive . . . impressive, powerful and forceful" Yannick served cookies and vowed that her family would die "before yielding to a foreign invasion." Carter summoned his years of living with his own "strong woman" and, he believed, convinced Yannick that "the highest calling of her husband . . . was not to give his life, or the lives of his wife and children, but to protect the lives of the Haitians whom he was sworn to protect."[61]

Then, remembering the suffering of poor Haitian mothers and babies deprived of food and medicine during the embargo, Carter added that he was ashamed of his country's policies. Perhaps to assure the Haitian general of his sincerity, he invited Cédras to teach a Sunday school class at his church in Georgia.[62] Finally Cédras agreed to a new accord, his glee at its terms showing in his "big shit-eating grin."[63] The intervasion, already well advanced, was halted, and combat swimmers were plucked from the water. (An intervasion is the military term for an intervention accomplished through invasion of a sovereign state whose government has requested help in dealing with hostile elements within its population.)

Violent, often deadly, incidents preceded Aristide's now-imminent return. The Multinational Force (MNF) was up to twenty-one thousand troops, including three hundred from the Caribbean Community (CARICOM). (In September, U.S. Major General Michael J. Byron "ensured that CNN covered the arrival of the CARICOM forces in Puerto Rico to play 'mind games' with Cédras" as he watched his fellow West Indians training for the invasion.)[64] But it was Cédras who played mind games with the Americans by balking at going through with the deal unless they agreed to a payment of about US $1 million to rent his and his mother-in-law's houses. The Americans did so, justifying the transaction as being fair market value,[65] and finally Cédras resigned and on October 13, with his General Chief of Staff Biamby, left for the Dominican Republic.

While Cédras remained in Haiti, writes military historian Lieutenant General Walter E. Kretchik, American troops involved in the intervasion "found themselves trying to restore to office a democratically elected leader, while cooperating with the very government that had ousted him in the first place, a government that Washington had branded as illegitimate."[66] On the one hand negotiations with Cédras continued. On the other, the MNF launched raids on FRAPH headquarters in Les Cayes, Cap Haitien, and Port-au-Prince as Haiti was made ready to receive its president, although the UN decided to end the embargo only after Aristide— and Operation Restore Democracy—were safely installed on Haitian soil.

On October 15, a U.S. government plane flew Aristide to the international airport in Port-au-Prince, and a U.S. helicopter ferried him to the National Palace. There Haiti's president released a white dove into the air and cried, "Never again should one more drop of blood flow. No to violence! No to vengeance! Yes to reconciliation!"[67] At that minute, he likely meant what he said.

During Aristide's exile, cynical Haitian military officers had explained that reinstating Aristide would be like putting eggs back into a chicken. After the president returned, graffiti appeared on walls everywhere, showing hands pushing eggs into chickens.

But Aristide was a changed and changing man. His years of exile in the U.S. had taught him many lessons about the nation that exercised such power over Haiti. He had navigated its convoluted political waters, first under a president who disliked him, and then under Clinton, who strongly supported him. Aristide had monitored and, to the extent that he could, influenced Haitian politics and current events. After several failed attempts at selecting a prime minister, he had settled on wealthy printer and publisher Robert Malval, whose longtime friendship with Raoul Cédras had not stopped him from befriending and supporting Aristide, and publicly condemning Cédras' coup. Malval accepted reluctantly ("I don't have the ambition, experience or the ability") and had

given notice that he would serve for only a few months; he was inaugurated at the Haitian Embassy in Washington so that Aristide could attend.[68]

Exile had been a crash course in international relations and politics, and Aristide had absorbed the political lingo and ideological perspectives of his American allies. Malval, his soon-to-be-estranged prime
minister, remarked that Aristide had "grown a lot" during exile. For one
thing, he had accepted or at least swallowed the neoliberal economic
program he had once denounced so fiercely as ruinous to the fundamental interests of the majority of Haitians. The Lavalas movement was
battered by years of military repression and economic embargo, and the
elite and their American allies had regained control of Haiti. Rather than
fighting them, Aristide extended an olive branch. At a gathering arranged
by Malval at the Ambassador Hotel in Coral Gables, Florida, Aristide
made peace with a delegation of the powerful families who had a stranglehold on Haiti's economy and who had financed the coup against him.

Another transformation had taken place in Aristide's personal life:
he had fallen in love. In 1992, at a reception at City College, he met
Mildred Trouillot, American-born with Haitian parents, and an associate lawyer at the New York firm of Robinson, Silverman, Pearce, Ar-
onsohn & Berman. Two months later, Mildred left her firm to join
Aristide's legal team. When he returned to Haiti in 1994, she moved
there, too. "I saw firsthand President Aristide's tenderness and strength
as he served the people, and I was exposed daily to his intellect, his humility, his compassion, his wit," Mildred recalled. "In time, our hearts
became one."[69]

But Aristide was still a priest, though suspended from active ministry. Early in his exile, he had explored the possibility of joining the Episcopal Church, whose priests are permitted to marry. But he did not
pursue this, repeating often that he was "married to" the Haitian people
and would devote his life to them. The Vatican, however, did not hide its
grave concern that he was both president and priest. John Paul II, the
same pope who had cried out that things had to change in Jean-Claude's
Duvalier regime, was no fan of liberation theology or of priestly presidencies. In November 1994, a month after his reinstallation, Aristide
submitted his resignation to the Haitian Conference of Bishops, and the
Vatican accepted it. Aristide was conflicted about resigning, and told one
friend that it had been his life's saddest moment, akin to "cutting off an
arm without anesthetic."[70] But he was now free to marry, and so it was

only a matter of time before Aristide and Mildred announced their engagement.

Meanwhile, Aristide resumed his presidential duties so slowly that critics and even friends wondered about his lack of progress. One of them asked him about it directly. Aristide gave a thoughtful reply:

> The presidential palace was totally sacked. There was no telephone, no water, no desk or chairs. Nothing. To be able to communicate, to meet with people has been extremely difficult and complex, for both infrastructural and security reasons. I can't create too much tension for the U.S. Army with public appearances or with my movements. It could cause an unwanted incident. U.S. soldiers aren't using to seeing crowds who want to touch and speak with their President. In addition, the FRAPH and the Tontons still have a lot of weapons.[71]

Aristide had reason to worry. His enemies accused him of having invited another American military occupation, and he could visit Forces Armées d'Haiti (FAD'H) troops only with American military protection. Nevertheless, the U.S. denied his request to disarm disloyal soldiers. A few months later, nine years to the day after Duvalier fled, Aristide disbanded the FAD'H. He had many reasons to do so: its Duvalierist structuring as a fundamentally corrupt entity; its links with the Tonton Macoutes, the *chefs de section* and later FRAPH; its cozy relations with the elite, whom it protected and did business with; its anti-democratic willingness to make or break presidents; and its willingness to engage in criminal activities and inflict violence on civilians. President Clinton had condemned General Cédras's army as "armed thugs" (though Carter and other American officials claimed to see nobility in them), and supported its abolition. The military had humiliated and driven Aristide into exile. Its seven thousand members accounted for 40 percent of the national budget. "[I]t served as an army of internal occupation," he said. "It never fought an external enemy. It murdered thousands of our people. Why did we need such an army, rather than a suitably trained police force? So we did what we needed to."

Clinton had agreed to a modified disbandment with a core of at least 1,500 soldiers under international supervision to provide a "vital counterweight" in the transition to democracy. But Aristide's broom swept clean, and on February 7, Haiti no longer had even a token army. But what do you do with thousands of forcibly demobilized soldiers who have lost not just poorly paid jobs, but also the connections and power to make money in the wide range of enterprises previously open to them? How do you manage their fury, resentment and bitterness, and their vindictiveness toward Aristide, his government and his supporters?

USAID had set up an Office of Transition Initiatives (OTI) under its Bureau of Humanitarian Response, and it drew up plans to demobilize and then, through stipends and six months of vocational training, to reintegrate former FAD'H members into society. The Haitian government scrounged up the $8.7-million cost "from foreign donor government balance of payments relief," and the program demobilized 6,260, of whom 5,482, or 88 percent registered. But only a single officer was involved, and of the 4,856 graduates, a mere 304 found jobs.[72] Who or what was to blame? The answer lay in Haiti's poor economy and the stigma of being a former soldier, and the soldiers' own sense of victimization at being dismissed, and their total lack of relief or gratitude that a virtual amnesty protected them from prosecution.

But even though Haiti did not need an army, especially when the U.S. and later the UN kept thousands of better-trained troops on the ground, it did need a police force to replace the now-disbanded one that had been an integral part of the military. The first attempt to assemble, screen and train civilian police began in October of 1994. It was a joint U.S.-Haiti effort focused on former FAD'H soldiers and, because the cursory vetting seldom uncovered human rights violators, these men were accepted and then lumped together with civilians and repatriated boat people to form the first Haitian National Police (HNP). Together these recruits trained at the new police academy, the first class in January of 1995; six months later, the cadets graduated and began their police work.

The new HNP was not a success, and after all but 2,500 American soldiers left Haiti and were replaced by UN forces, CIVIPOL, the UN policing agency, was widely criticized for failing to check abuse within the HNP. Furthermore, the Haitian National Police Academy's multinational staff was floundering in its attempts to train recruits. Internal police rivalries exploded in violence, and "insecurity" became the watchword in most neighborhoods.

In the countryside, the police who replaced the *chefs de section* disdained riding mules or donkeys, so they seldom ventured into rural areas that could not be reached by car. Instead, these policemen spent their days in the towns doing "very, very little policing," according to American anthropologist Timothy Schwartz, who lived in Jean-Rabel and elsewhere in Haiti for over a decade. Rural Haitians soon learned how unreliable the police were—Schwartz mentions the case of the thief whom the police concluded "beat himself to death"—and instead, preferred to take matters into their own machete-equipped hands.[73]

The U.S. had provided millions of dollars to create an anti-drug enforcement unit to pursue the uncontrolled cocaine trafficking that used Haiti as a transit point between Colombia and the U.S., and a Coast Guard to patrol for narcotic smugglers and also boat people. But both the Coast Guard and the Anti-Drug Enforcement unit were disappointing. The drug trade that Aristide, in exile, had estimated at about fifty tons of cocaine worth more than a billion dollars continued to flourish; his colleague, Patrick Elie, described the enormous quantity of "drugs and drug money in Haiti," and added, "I'm just scared of what I see."[74] The principal change was that now that most of the army officers and soldiers who formerly collaborated with and benefited from the drug trade had been dislodged, newly empowered Lavalas officials and police eagerly took their place and reaped the stupendous profits.

Despite many setbacks, Haiti was less turbulent and more hopeful than it had been since 1991, and its president began to re-organize his government. After Malval made good on his notice to resign as prime minister, Aristide vacillated between replacing him with Claudette Werleigh, his foreign affairs minister in his government-in-exile, or his old friend Smarck Michel, a millionaire rice importer and wholesaler who had hidden Aristide from army assassins and contributed to buying his house. Werleigh was Aristide's ideological soulmate; Michel, on the other hand, had resigned as commerce minister in 1991 because he strongly disagreed with Aristide's plan to fix and subsidize the cost of foodstuffs, and argued instead for creating jobs and reducing government intervention in the economy. But after key economists, among them Leslie Delatour, refused to serve under Werleigh and warned that her policies would scare off the Americans and foreign lending agencies, Aristide appointed Michel, who wasted no time urging Haitians to "walk hand in hand with the military authorities, Haitian and foreign."[75]

Michel's contentious appointment was a preview of part II of Aristide's first presidency, and the direct consequence of his decision to swallow the Washington Accord he despised. It was also a sly piece of maneuvering; he used Michel as his scapegoat, the man to blame for reducing trade tariffs to under 10 percent, for laying off civil servants, and for privatizing the state-owned utility (electricity, telephone, water) companies, the flour mill and cement plant, and the (oh-so-lucrative to its employees) port authority that had all been mired in corruption and incompetence but that, reformed, could have contributed large sums of money to the national treasury.

Aristide's ploy was canny. He waited it out and in less than a year, the beleaguered Michel resigned. This time Aristide got his way and appointed Claudette Werleigh as his prime minister. Once-fervent supporters saw through his strategy. "Aristide always has a double-face, a double-game, at every juncture," said peasant leader Olry St. Louis. "He looks at the moment to see how to act so he can use it to his advantage and make political capital from it. . . . The first person who signed the thing [Washington Accord] at the beginning was Aristide. He could have refused, because the people were behind him."[76]

St. Louis almost certainly got the last part wrong. It's doubtful that Aristide could have held out against the wishes of the Americans and, at the same time, convinced them to reinstall him in Haiti and provide military support and financial assistance. But St. Louis was right about Aristide's two-facedness; his habit of espousing and then reversing opinions was no secret. "An idea may be as quickly approved as abandoned, thus giving to his political action a contradictory nature that will continue to prevent him from rising to the level of his incredible destiny," a colleague later marveled.[77]

Aristide's still-enormous popular support and his habit of circumventing politicians and political parties led him to indulge in personal grudges and jealousies even at the cost of alienating his allies. That included Evans Paul, mayor of Port-au-Prince (as his wife, Irene Ridoré's successor) and co-founder of the FNCD, Aristide's electoral party of record that he abandoned for the OPL. (After he left OPL in late 1996 and formed Fanmi Lavalas [FL], the OPL was renamed the Organisation du Peuple en Lutte, the Organization of Struggling People.)

Quite apart from the increasingly acrimonious and divisive political struggles, Aristide's reluctance to accept that the Constitution of 1987 forbid him from extending his presidential term for the years he had spent in exile, and ever louder accusations that he seemed to be abandoning democracy, Aristide faced a nation in exceedingly poor condition. The administrative apparatus had been effectively gutted. For

months after his restoration, the U.S. Army Reserve civil affairs officers
assumed control over almost all of Haiti's ministries. They sifted through
accounts and other documents, catalogued each ministry's property and
even directed activities.[78] Haiti was quickly losing every aspect of its
autonomy.

There was also an occupying army of foreign NGOs and troops
supposedly undertaking relief efforts to assist the millions devastated by
the embargo. Most of the foreigners were American, mutually suspicious
and uncooperative as they competed for funding, strove to seem independent and tried to claim exclusive credit for shared accomplishments.
Most of the estimated 2,000 NGOs were illicit—only 170 had registered
with the Ministry of Planning—and had simply implanted themselves in
Haiti. Those who had operated under the Cédras regime were assumed
to be corrupt. Others worked clandestinely to avoid paying bribes.

According to plan, the U.S. military attempted to liaise with recognized NGOs to relieve the suffering population though, Kretchik writes,
they "lagged in their support of essential U.S. government programs and
policies." These efforts were complicated by orders specifically forbidding American military from assisting in upgrading the country's infrastructure beyond what U.S. military necessity demanded. For example,
the soldiers could build only one bridge for military use over a swollen
stream, though the local population needed and requested two others.
"Lacking support of the necessary civilian agencies, U.S. Army commanders, attempting to help the Haitian people, soon became masters of
creating military justifications for what, in reality, was nation assistance," Kretchik reveals.[79]

By the time they left in 1999, the soldiers, who had arrived with
road-building equipment, had managed to build and repair 134 miles of
roads and bridges, dug sixty-four new wells, and renovated forty-eight
schools.[80] But these nation assisting accomplishments came at high cost
and, writes Alex Dupuy, President Clinton "placed Haiti under the trust-
eeship of the international regulatory and aid organizations."[81] In other
words, at great expense, considerable planning and with good intentions, the U.S. and its allies bypassed and thereby emasculated the Haitian government, stripping it of the power to develop its own vision and
policies.

One policy was food aid, a crucial item in an agricultural nation.
Aristide and his Lavalas colleagues—Father Jean-Marie Vincent in Jean-
Rabel had been among them—had always fiercely opposed food aid. But

now an army of NGOs was delivering, indeed flooding, the rural countryside with food, and destroying the peasant farmer economy. Of course, some hungry people were eating this food, but for every sated belly, there was a ruined farmer. That was because donated corn, wheat, and rice from the U.S. were heavily subsidized—38 percent annually, and grain from France and Germany, 48 percent. How could Haiti's farmers compete? They could not, and the trickle of city-bound farmers swelled into a surging river. Clinton's plan, which decades later he would beg forgiveness for, was working. Haiti's agricultural base was under attack, and the beneficiaries were, as planned, the owners of the assembly industries of Port-au-Prince.

On the ground, most aid workers were deeply troubled by the nefarious effect of food aid. "Everyone was always outraged, but quietly," Timothy Schwartz recalls.[82] CARE and Catholic Relief Services (CRS), for example, were key players in the now-discredited American plan. An American CRS worker explained why food aid was so disturbing:

> CARE and CRS revenue comes from two sources: Donations from organizations and individuals are one. But here in Haiti and in many poor countries the biggest source is food. CARE and CRS and many of the other big charities get paid a fee every time they tranship food for USAID. They also get large gifts from USAID in what is called monetized food aid which means that USAID gives money but . . . in the form of food and the requirement is that food must be sold on the local markets. Without food distribution CRS and CARE would be nothing. . . . And we need income. Twenty-some percent of all revenue that we take in here goes back to headquarters in Baltimore to pay salaries and operating expenses. For CARE it is much more.[83]

Niche Pierre, an assistant director at CARE, provided specific figures. "Five million of CARE Haiti's $15 million annual budget is from monetized food, food that we sell directly to the market. The rest of the money comes in cash from USAID and donations."[84]

Just as surprising and counterintuitive were the results of anthropologist Schwartz's five-year study of Jean-Rabel, where for all but one year, "farmers claim they produce surpluses, big surpluses, surpluses well beyond their nutritional needs." Yet during those years the region re ceived massive food aid, at least half a pound of food per day for every man, woman and child, from the governments of Germany, France, and Holland, and World Vision, Child Care and Compassion International. That food, monetized, financed the aid agencies but crushed the farmers.

One farmer named Dajensen explained what happened. "They deliver it and sell it on the local market when we are selling our own crops . . . even when they intend to feed it to the hungry very little gets here. Most of it is stolen or embezzled and then sold. That crashes the market." Dajensen spelled out the consequences.

> [W]e aren't subsistence farmers. We need cash. And we get cash from farming. And we got no way to store crops. Never once has any one of these foreign organizations tried to help us with storage technology. So when we can't sell our crops for a good price it hurts. We have to buy soap, water vessels, brooms. We have to pay school tuition, we have to buy books . . . pay for medicines when one of our family gets sick. And brother, we get sick.[85]

In the 1990s, a concerned French development agency director measured the impact of food aid during the harvest season from March to June. The first delivery pushed the market price for local maize (corn) down by 50 percent, the second delivery down a further 20 percent and the third another 10 percent. Yet CARE, for example, did not deliver aid *during* the embargo or *during* droughts, but rather *after* the embargo and *during* years of plentiful rain, the best harvest years when it was not needed.

Out in that same countryside, a priest had long pondered the plight of the poorest Haitians. They could organize themselves politically, Father Joseph Philippe knew, but in most other ways they were helpless. If they dreamt of improving their businesses, their only recourse was ruinous money-lenders, because no bank or credit union would give them a loan. The illiterate peasant or *ti machann*—woman street vendor—could not raise the capital for merchandise to expand their business. The coffee cooperative could not get credit to produce and process coffee beans for export. The Haitian with an expatriate family member had trouble finding safe, non-usurious ways to receive money transfers, or to exchange it into *gourdes* at a fair rate. Clearly, Father Joseph concluded, these Haitians needed a bank of their own.

That bank was Fondasyon Kole Zepol—Shoulder-to-Shoulder Foundation—known as Fonkoze. In 1994 thirty-two grassroots leaders drew up the necessary paperwork and in 1995 Fonkoze became an officially recognized foundation. But it needed a director with considerable banking experience, someone like American Anne Hastings, a successful management consultant in Washington who was seeking "to give back rather than take more." The Peace Corps' Director of International Operations told her that he knew a priest in Haiti who was doing "amazing work." Three days after Hastings submitted her resumé, Father Joseph phoned and left her a brief phone message. "We are very pleased you have decided to work with us in Haiti," he said. "You may be Director of our new bank, Fonkoze. Thank you."

Hastings, who remains Fonkoze's C.E.O., went to Haiti. Fifteen minutes into her first conversation with Father Joseph, she knew "he had more vision than all the top executives that had been her clients in D.C. put together." He also wasted no time chatting. He pulled out a rickety typing table, took pencil and pen in hand and said, "Let's get to work." Then Father Joseph introduced the new director to Fonkoze's guiding principles, as profound as they were breathtakingly simple:

- Women constitute the backbone of Haiti's economy.
- You must not give a woman a loan and then leave her to her own resources; instead you must be by her side as she struggles to make her way out of poverty.
- All Haitians deserve a chance to participate in their country's economic development.
- A political democracy cannot survive without economic democracy.
- Nothing in Haiti can be effective if the Haitians in the Diaspora do not endorse and support it, because it is those Haitians who keep Haiti's economy afloat through the remittances they send home.[86]

What a contrast to Structural Adjustment Policies! Structural Adjustment (SAP) was an economic model rooted in neoliberalism and wielded like a hammer on struggling nations with such economic woes and levels of indebtedness that they capitulated—essentially to their stern debtors—and tried desperately to make SAP work. Otherwise, how could they repay those debtors, whether or not their loans had been ethical, productive and made in good faith to credible governments or rulers? Unfortunately, in SAP logic, debt repayment and economic restructuring trump health, education and development, which must be sacrificed despite the terrible price of lowering already-low standards of living.[87]

Fonkoze was not concerned with foreign debt repayment or overarching global economic policy implications. Fonkoze had a Haitian perspective and vision—"to encourage greater economic opportunity, reduce income inequality, and to become an institution itself that had democratic principles and practices infused into the organization."[88] By 1996 Fonkoze stepped out into the sunlight, hired nine employees for its single branch office, lent 110 clients about 348,515 *gourdes*[89] and attracted 193 people who deposited 1,175,801 *gourdes*. A year later, 52 employees in 11 branches loaned 1,542 women about 5,158,185 *gourdes*, while 3,444 depositors contributed 3,273,342 *gourdes*.[90] (In 1996 and 1997, the respective exchange rates were 15 and 17.53 *gourdes* to the U.S. dollar.)

Father Joseph Philippe acted independently of governments, Haitian and foreign. Aristide, however, constrained by promises and *realpolitik*, and driven by mercurial changes of opinion, talked out of both sides of his mouth. One day he called Bill Clinton his twin brother and attempted to explain how the SAP could benefit Haiti, while the next he denounced the SAP this twin had imposed on him.

But Aristide had to swallow his nation's pride. In early November, he traveled under heavy American security to Cap Haitien to work his rhetorical magic after American Marines killed ten Haitians in a shootout. The population had been outraged, a rebellion had broken out, and Lieutenant Colonel Claudel Josephat, commander of the District of the North, had resigned. Only after Josephat's surrender to U.S. forces in Port-au-Prince could Aristide risk the trip to Cap Haitien.

Also in November, Hurricane Gordon pounded Haiti, damaging and destroying buildings and property so badly that a tally was impossible. The deforested mountainsides left the countryside defenseless against the rushing rainwater that soon flooded the lower lands and killed the majority of Gordon's 1,122 victims. Yet this new calamity did not stop the Americans from repatriating more boat people, and Aristide had to agree to accept them.

On January 7, 1995, a U.S. Coast Guard cutter disembarked 289 sombre-looking Haitians who had been held at the U.S. refugee camp in

Guantanamo Bay. Two young men were handcuffed and forcibly removed after they refused to budge and shouted, "President Aristide sent for us. Let him come and get us!" One of them, moaning and weeping, was carried down the gangplank. "I don't want to come back to a country like this and die in the streets," he sobbed. Another Haitian repatriate, Fritzman Delusma, also spoke tearfully as he was escorted past rows of recently arrived Bangladeshi soldiers. "I ran away from a hail of bullets [in Raboteau]. They burned my house down. I have nothing here, that's why I don't want to come back. I'd be better off killing myself."[91] The Red Cross handed all the repatriates a toothbrush and the equivalent of $16.50, and then ferried them to a bus stop to make their way back to their ruined lives.[92]

Aristide also had to deal with and accommodate the elite Haitians such as the Mevs and Brandt families, who controlled the economy and loathed him. He had once threatened them with "Père Lebrun." Now they engaged him in what *Los Angeles Times* reporter Kenneth Freed described as "not a battle of guns, but of electricity, bank accounts, oil tanks and the country's economic future," in a war they waged against Leslie Delatour, Aristide's Central Bank governor. "It is a morality play," a U.S. diplomat said, "with one side, the hard-line, old families, driving to maintain privilege, complete with a whiff of corruption." Delatour put it more starkly: "If they [the Mevses and Brandts] win, everything will go on as before, or worse since they will feel reinforced." Yet in this morality play with Haiti's economic lifeblood at stake, Aristide's support of Delatour was wishy-washy and compromised both by a growing rapprochement between the president and the Great Families, and his fear of them. "Aristide is extremely afraid of the Mevses," an intimate of both Aristide and Delatour said. "The way he has reconstructed the coup has the Mevses' building the coalition for the military, and he is afraid they can do it again. So, he's concerned about not antagonizing them again."[93]

Aristide's honeymoon period, if he had even had one, was over. Rebels launched attacks, and criminals, ever more brazen, kidnapped, robbed, and murdered. On November 7, 1995, Aristide's cousin, Deputy Jean Hubert Feuille, was killed in a daylight ambush that also gravely wounded Deputy Gabriel Fortune, Aristide's bodyguard during his exile. Four days later, at Feuille's funeral at the Cathedral of Our Lady of the Assumption, Aristide raged against UN slackness in finding and seizing illegal arms, and ordered the police to carry out "total, general, capital, legal" disarmament. He also railed against the bullying of U.S. Ambassador William

Swing and U.N. Haiti Chief Lakhdar Brahimi. "The game of hypocrisy is over. We don't have two or three heads of state, we have one," he declared.[94] He then appealed urgently to Haitians to report illegal weapons and urged them to "go to the neighborhoods where there are big houses and heavy weapons" to help the police disarm paramilitary thugs.[95]

Civilians responded enthusiastically, searching cars and houses and finding thousands of arms. A police raid on General Prosper Avril's house turned up a cache of weapons. In Gonaives mobs burned twenty houses, and killed a Duvalierist. In Les Cayes, they killed a former FRAPH leader. The frenzy continued. The raiders surrendered some weapons to the police but kept others for self-defense and, sometimes, to commit crimes. In Cité Soleil, the poorest slum in a desperate city, police fought with armed youths. Newly installed Prime Minister Claudette Werleigh warned against violence that could provide a pretext for another coup d'état.[96]

Incredibly, *The Washington Post* revealed that on October 26 U.S. Secretary of State Warren Christopher had sent Ambassador Swing a cable warning that Prosper Avril and his armed Red Star Organization was "planning a campaign of attacks and assassinations against President Aristide's supporters and the Lavalas party . . . to begin in early December 1995." Yet Swing did not share this information with the Haitian government. And after Aristide ordered the police to arrest Avril, the American Embassy intervened and Avril, tipped off, hunkered down in the Colombian Embassy until, thanks to his excellent relations with powerful Colombian drug lords, he fled Haiti undetected.

Despite the collection of more than fifteen thousand weapons during Aristide's anti-arms campaign, the international force's Operation Street Sweep and cash-for-weapons programs, Haiti remained heavily armed. Knowledgeable officials estimated that two hundred thousand weapons were in circulation, part of the Duvalierist legacy of arming supporters. More murders were committed, reportedly by pro-Aristide assassins. Americans and elite Haitians accused Aristide of calling for extra-judicial retribution. Haiti was once more so volatile that elections had to be postponed for several months.

It didn't help that Aristide's Interior Minister, Brigadier General Mondesir Beaubrun, was apparently plotting to assassinate Aristide's opponents, as American military intelligence informed Aristide's Minister of Justice. One name on Beaubrun's hit list, a jailed accomplice revealed, was Leslie Delatour, Aristide's inconvenient, U.S.-imposed Central Bank director whose plans, including the taxation of the elite, had infuriated the Great Families. Another of Beaubrun's targets was Mireille Durocher-Bertin, a handsome and vivacious young lawyer who had just founded an opposition political party and was the legal advocate for Raoul Cédras, whose government's "integrity" she had defended on American television, and for FRAPH leaders and others accused of drug trafficking.[97]

The day after Major General Fisher wrote him about the assassination plans, Aristide dismissed the information as unfounded, and Beaubrun remained his Interior Minister. (Beaubrun was a notoriously hot-headed and quick-tempered gambler who had recently responded to a protest by opening fire through his office door and killing two guards.)[98] Ambassador Swing was so worried that he cabled the State Department "suggesting calls to Aristide from senior Washington officials to press for an inquiry."[99] Aristide promised that his Justice Minister would warn Madame Durocher-Bertin, but she received no such warning.

On March 28 Durocher-Bertin and her driver, Eugene (Junior) Baillergeau, a private pilot, reputed drug trafficker, and Durocher-Bertin's client and long-time friend, were shot and killed in his white Subaru. It was a targeted hit, the Subaru fiercely attacked, its left front tire shot out, its engine disabled and its occupants hit by a hail of bullets fired by gunmen who leapt out to shoot and then jumped back into their red Mitsubishi jeep and fled. (Their compensation for the hit was a reported five thousand dollars.)

The murder ignited a storm of outrage from the Americans who had attempted to forestall it, and the elite who grieved one of their own and accused Aristide partisans of the killing. Bishops Louis Kebreau and Joseph Lafontant, who would later assist at Aristide's wedding, presided at the funeral and declared that Mireille Bertin had died "crucified like Christ."[100]

Ambassador Swing asked Aristide to request an FBI investigation, and he agreed. The FBI learned that the U.S. military had intercepted radio conversations in which Joseph Medard, then deputy chief of Aristide's bodyguards, and Lieutenant Pierre Lubin, a policeman, discussed following Bertin's car. This awkward situation was compounded by Haitian officials' demanding that the FBI conduct a parallel investigation of twenty murders committed by members of the ousted military regime. Witnesses to Bertin's murder complained that they were being threatened. Meanwhile, others of the Haitian elite and military were assassinated: Michel-Ange Hermann and Max Mayard, former FAD'H officers;

Leslie Grimar, an auto parts dealer; and wealthy airline executive Michel Gonzales, who was shot dead in front of his neighbor Jean-Bertrand Aristide's house.

After six months of stonewalling by Haitian officials, the FBI withdrew from the case, but not before determining that Bertin, Hermann, Mayard and Grimar had all been shot by the same gun. But who held that gun? "Technically, these [FBI] guys are the best in the world," an American official observed. "But unless we find somebody who says, 'I saw the killers, they are these people,' we won't get to the bottom of it."[101]

On June 25, parliamentary elections for two-thirds of the Senate seats, the entire Chamber of Deputies, and seven hundred local and communal boards and councils were marked by a very low turnout (25 to 50 percent) and very serious problems. The California-based printer omitted several candidates' distinctive symbols, a travesty with so many illiterate voters, and omitted other candidates altogether. One and a half million voter registration cards went missing and then mysteriously reappeared. Many polling booths were shuttered. The Kenscoff voting bureau was burned to the ground. In Limbe, Dondon, and Le Borgne, voting was cancelled after armed men attacked them the voting bureaus. A Carrefour (Port-au-Prince) election official was shot. Candidate Jean-Charles Henoc died after being shot in the head in Anse d'Hainault. Elsewhere, other candidates were attacked as well. Aristide's party's overwhelming majority crystallized bitterness against his authoritarian political style that rode roughshod over everyone but his immediate allies. But Aristide declared himself satisfied.

Several countries had paid millions of dollars to sponsor the election, including the U.S. ($10.5 million), the European Union ($2.5 million), Canada ($1.5 million), France ($1.0 million) and Japan ($.5 million). Did these international election patrons get their money's worth? Their answers ranged from qualified yesses to angry nos. "President Aristide badly needs to mend his ways, raising fears that he is taking his country back to one-party rule," *The Washington Post* editorialized. The International Republican Institute (IRI) reported a "nationwide breakdown of the electoral process . . . a total absence of safeguards against fraud, tampering, disappearances, and destruction of election materials." Robert Pastor from the Carter Center denounced the election as the worst of the more than two dozen others he had witnessed worldwide.[102]

But Aristide had gotten what he wanted—a crushing parliamentary majority (made even mightier by fraudulent vote counting) that would obligingly amend the constitutional provision that stood in the way of his remaining in office for another three years, the amount of time he had spent in exile. To encourage this project, his supporters had been distributing Creole pamphlets suggestively asking: "Elections for mayor? Yes. Elections for deputy? Yes. Elections for Senate? Yes. Elections for president? In three years."[103]

Two more elections, on August 16 and September 17, had an even lower turnout—less than 15 percent in many constituencies. Most parties boycotted them, and Aristide's OPL again won most seats. Meanwhile, Aristide was campaigning hard, helicoptering into the provinces and stumping there, and promising millions of *gourdes* for irrigation systems, coffee production, education, and other desperately needed items. But he had an unexpected setback when Parliament, usually tractable, rejected his choice of Lieutenant Colonel Jean-Marie Fourel Celestin as chief of the National Police, and denounced him as corrupt and domineering, an Aristide-henchman who did his boss's bidding. Aristide was, *Haiti Progrès* editorialized in August, revising "a style perfected by dictators Francois Duvalier and Jean-Claude Duvalier during their nearly 30-year rule. . . . Such promises and tours have become another symbol of the rapid degeneration of the once militant priest into a yet another mediocre politician, who now offers retreaded paternalism in the place of mass participation in changing Haitian society."[104]

Aristide's campaign didn't work. Despite high hopes and wily maneuvering, including urging his followers to "go to the neighborhoods where there are big houses and heavy weapons to help the police disarm paramilitary thugs,"[105] Aristide had to step aside and wait another five years before resuming the presidency. Reluctantly and sullenly, he accepted that presidential elections would proceed and he would have to be content with being the *eminence grise* behind his presidential protégé, René Garcia Préval. Even then he waited until December 16, the day before the elections, to proclaim his support for Préval.

Besides being Aristide's staunch supporter and loyal friend, Préval was a fifty-three-year-old agronomist who had been raised abroad after his father fled Haiti as a political refugee. Préval had directed a World Bank-financed project and also operated a bakery fueled by sugar cane ethanol; he met Aristide when he provided bread to the Selavi orphanage. Préval won with 85 percent of the largely boycotted vote, beating out thirteen little-known candidates including Dieuveuil Joseph, who identified himself as the reincarnation of the Virgin Mary.

Aristide, now lame duck president, did not stay on the sidelines. On January 20, in the sprawling garden of his house in Tabarre, at a ceremony presided over by Monseigneur Willy Romelus, with Bishop Joseph Lafontant assisting, he married his sweetheart, Mildred "Minouche" Trouillot. The wedding was so modest that the bride had no bouquet to adorn her coral suit, and no cake to offer hundreds of important guests, including high-ranked American military officers and Anthony Lake, Clinton's National Security adviser.

The marriage hammered home the disappointing (to many) fact that Aristide was no longer a priest. Mildred's very light skin angered others who saw it as a betrayal that yet another dark-skinned Haitian leader had chosen a much lighter wife. But Mildred Aristide was no Michèle Bennett, and criticism of the new First Lady was muted and quickly died away. She was devoted to her husband, and she announced plans to focus on homeless and street children, and the Lafanmi Selavi orphanage Aristide had founded in 1986. Together they also founded the Aristide Foundation, the youth ministry.

On the evening of February 6, Aristide thumbed his nose at the U.S. and announced that Haiti would resume diplomatic relations with Cuba, severed over three decades earlier by Papa Doc Duvalier under American pressure. Inauguration Day arrived. Aristide, in no rush to hand over the presidency, arrived at the palace nearly an hour late. Then the new president, René Préval, took his oath of office. Instead of the traditional (and military-associated) rifle salute, twenty-one doves were released into the air. "After 183 years of history, you're among the first to witness this tremendous event," Préval declared. "Five years ago, an appointed president gave the power to an elected one. Today, an elected one gives it to another elected one. This is all due to the faith, the will of one man . . . who has a vision of a new political vista. . . . Mr. President, [he said to Aristide] you've spread democracy, and it will grow."[106]

Applause was subdued, and few people cheered in the streets. Jobs remained scarce, and insecurity stalked the land. The rich were still rich and the poor were even poorer. Yet one astonishing thing took place that day. For the first time in Haiti's turbulent history, a democratically elected president handed over the reins of power to his democratically elected successor. And five years later, President Préval would stand beside his predecessor and smile as Aristide once again assumed the presidency.

15 TEMPESTS

PRÉVAL'S FIVE YEARS WERE MUCH LOWER KEY THAN ARIStide's, but hardly uneventful. Préval was a much different man, politician and statesman. Calm and reserved where Aristide was excitable and extroverted, Préval focused on his work. He showed no interest in seeking the adulation of large crowds or of undermining his predecessor, although Aristide did not hide his jealousy at relinquishing the presidency to Préval, and made it clear that he was counting the days—365 × 5—until he reclaimed it. While Haitians and foreign diplomats joked that the newlywed Aristides should do Préval a favor by disappearing on a six-month honeymoon cruise, Préval seemed irritated at well-wishers who suggested that Aristide was undermining him. The two had "a very, very, very good relationship," he insisted. "Everyone is talking about divergences. But divergences about what?"[107]

Time would spell out what divergences. Meanwhile, Préval had the unenviable task of taking on all of Aristide's unresolved problems. The list was terrible. The pressure to complete the privatization of state enterprises was relentless, and the elite continued to retain their stranglehold over the deteriorating economy. The soil continued to erode and deforestation to spread. The ex-soldiers and ex-Macoutes were a more menacing presence, and insecurity was endemic. Political parties were fragmented, and politicians fickle. And always, the President was subject to the hectoring of the Americans and other interested foreigners, and the irritation of their "progress report cards" in the form of editorials. Bad or failing grades were costly; as Préval was well aware, the Americans were quick to withhold money when they were dissatisfied.

In Aristide's last few months of office, they had withheld four million dollars.

Just before the election, American journalist Charlayne Hunter-Gault had grilled Aristide about the "rift" between him and the United States. "I mean, is it irreparable?" she had inquired. "Is it as bad as has been portrayed in the media?" Aristide said that it was not, and blamed the new torrent of boat people, whom he called economic refugees, for the withheld four million dollars in promised aid. "You don't think that they should tie their giving aid to progress in economic reform, is that what you're saying?" Hunter-Gault had asked. "We made a lot of progress," Aristide retorted. "I spent one year feeding my people with words, keeping my people in peace, and now . . . we see economic refugees . . . leaving the country. . . . I don't want [that]. They [the Americans] don't want it either."[108] This uneasy (at best) or untenable (at worst) state of affairs would now be Préval's to manage.

Préval also inherited a challenging security infrastructure. Although many people, Aristide included, considered disbanding the FAD'H, his greatest accomplishment, he had been unable to stamp out the powerful influence and connections of former officers and unemployed soldiers, including in his own entourage. The new police force was sadly lacking in efficiency, discipline and honesty, and more and more resembled the military it had replaced. From the minute Préval woke up in the morning to the minute he went to bed, he had to worry about his own safety; even his bodyguards, chosen by and loyal to Aristide, were not necessarily trustworthy. That was made clear on the day that Préval and his wife found her beloved little dog fatally wounded by a machete blow to the spine—in the National Palace.

Everyone knew that Aristide did not want Préval to shine and garner praise, just to hold the fort for five years. Préval accommodated him by working diligently to perform his duties as Aristide's stand-in. Despite his distaste for Structural Adjustment, he set about implementing its policies. In his five years in office, Preval would privatize two of Haiti's smallest state-owned enterprises, the flour mill and the cement plant, in careful deals keeping a 35 percent equity stake for the government but offering foreign and Haitian investors management control. The much larger holdings—electricity, telecommunications, the Port Authority, airport and state banks—remained public.[110] Meanwhile in Tabarre, Aristide acted as if he were still president, undermining Préval's authority and criticizing his efforts to implement the economic program that he himself had committed to in 1994.

Even nature dealt deadly blows. In early November of 1998, Hurricane Georges had killed about 400 people, left 167,332 homeless, destroyed crops and damaged houses and what infrastructure existed. Préval took matters into his own hands. He visited Cuba and accepted Fidel Castro's offer of 500 Cuban doctors to assist with the horrendous health problems in the hurricane's aftermath. "Haiti does not need invasions of soldiers," Castro declared. "It needs an invasion of doctors." An advance delegation of doctors diagnosed Haiti's ailment—"too much chaos," they informed Préval. To end that chaos, they said, the wealth of the country needed to be better distributed. Préval agreed and, at a peasant gathering in the mountains of Kenscoff, he gave a ringing speech that sounded as if Aristide had written it. Haiti needed "social dialogue and a reshuffling of the cards," Préval cried out. "The people who have the wealth of the country in their hands must open their hands. If they don't open their hands, the state will force them to open their hands. That is how to have reconciliation. You can't hold everything in your hands and ask someone to reconcile with you."[111]

This speech articulated the frustrations of a man shackled by too many constraints and too many special interests to accomplish his ambitious goals. Though he managed to resolve Haiti's immediate need for medical care, Haitian doctors who worried that the Cubans would steal their jobs, as well as political opponents who claimed that Haiti would become communist, fought him every step of the way. Everywhere Préval turned, he met with strong resistance. Politically, Lavalas split into rival parties, and the OPL, now hostile, controlled Parliament and blocked Préval at every turn. In January of 1999, after nearly two years of stalemate, Haiti had no budget or functioning government, and foreign aid had been suspended until the Haitian president remedied the situation. On January 11, 1999, an angry and impatient Préval announced on national television that he would rule by decree.

The next day, two gunmen on a motorcycle ambushed Préval's sister, Marie-Claude Calvin, in her car, killing her driver and wounding Calvin in the neck, chest and leg. It was widely assumed that Calvin was scapegoated by her brother's political foes. A somber-faced Aristide was photographed visiting her at the hospital. Calvin survived, and Préval faced a barrage of political attacks. "Préval has staged a coup d'état to establish a dictatorship," declared Mirlande Manigat, former First Lady (and future presidential candidate.) "What is a dictator? He concentrates political power in a single organ of the state. And that is exactly what Préval has done. He does not have an army, but he does have the police."[112] Still Préval did not relent and, for the sake of efficiency and because he shared Aristide's impatience with the complexities of democratic rule, on March 25, he installed a government headed by Jacques-Edouard Alexis and ruled by decree until the elections of May 2000. With so much energy expended on political survival, and a fundamental weakness in its core, Préval's government achieved little other than avoiding collapse.

Haiti was not as lucky. Its economy worsened, and poverty intensified. Strikes and protest demonstrations against Structural Adjustment's austerity measures swept the nation. The Great Families pitted their resources against Préval's meager ones, stymieing his attempts at land reform.[113] Corruption, which Aristide had attempted to reduce, was again the official *modus operandi*. Both petty crimes and felonies became rampant. Kidnappings and political assassinations terrified and embittered many, and some seemed to originate with the Presidential Guard. The sluggish justice system could not respond.

Then before dawn on April 3, 2000, a gunman fired seven shots into the neck and heart of one of Haiti's most famous journalists. Jean Léopold Dominique died on the spot in the courtyard of his station, Radio Inter; the station's caretaker, Jean-Claude Louissaint, shot with a special hollow-point bullet, also died. Dominique, son of a reform-minded mulatto family, had been jailed by Papa Doc after his brother Philippe's execution for his participation in the failed Pasquet invasion in 1958. Later, he was hunted down and exiled under Jean-Claude. In 1986, after the Duvaliers fled to France, Dominique and his wife, Michele Montas, returned to Haiti and rebuilt Radio Inter, which broadcast in Creole and offered international as well as Haitian news. Dominique's reformist passion kept him on the perilous path of naming names and detailing incidents and he took on Haiti's most powerful elements.

Who killed him? Dominique spread his ethical net wide, and there were several suspects. Michèle Montas said that "[he] was especially dangerous . . . because he was going to stop a lot of people making a lot of money." But that did not eliminate very many people. Dominique had sharply criticized the electoral officials preparing the 2000 parliamentary elections. He had railed against the pharmaceutical company Pharval, owned by the Boulos family, as the maker and distributor of Afébril, a contaminated cough syrup that killed about one hundred children in 1996.[114] And he had accused Dany Toussaint, Aristide's close associate, of conducting a smear campaign against Préval's confidant and friend Robert "Bob" Manuel. In a broadcast, Dominique had warned Aristide to beware of Toussaint's ambitions. "I know he has enough money to pay and arm henchmen. . . . If he tries to move against me or the radio station and if I'm still alive, I'll close the station down and go into exile once again with my wife and children," Dominique declared.[115]

Dominique's murder shocked and grieved Préval, who ordered three days of official mourning. Sixteen thousand people, including Préval and Aristide, attended Dominique's funeral, held in Sylvio Cator Stadium in Port-au-Prince. Journalists felt personally threatened. Radio Kiskeya's Liliane Pierre-Paul, a childhood friend of Aristide, warned: "If they murdered him, they can murder any journalist."[116] The investigation into Dominique's murder began but remains unsolved, the subject of bitter controversy, much of it directed against Aristide and FL partisans who continually intimidated journalists critical of them. At the time of this writing, the case against the chief suspect, Dany Toussaint, remains unproven.[117]

On May 21, 2000, a month after Dominique's murder, Préval's non-democratic government presided over relatively peaceful legislative elections with a robust participation rate of 60 percent. (The elections had been scheduled for March but had been postponed when it was discovered that a million voters were not registered.) Aristide's FL commanded a majority of votes, but a growing outcry about how votes were counted (though not about the election itself) paralyzed the electoral process. Aristide and Préval resolved the impasse by manipulating the provisional electoral council to ratify their desired results. They also communicated "unequivocal messages" to the council president, Leon Manus, about "the consequences that would follow if . . . [he] refused to publish the final false results."[118] Fearing for his life, the seventy-six-year-old Manus fled to the Dominican Republic and then to the U.S. The day after his defection, the remaining election councillors' official confirmed Aristide's FL party's overwhelming control of the Senate.

Aristide was not content merely to win. Because he could not tolerate opposition, he needed to crush his opponents. As Robert Fatton explains, "A mere majority is simply insufficient . . . for the establishment of presidential monarchism. This is why fraud became necessary to ensure both the annihilation of the anti-Lavalasian parties and the two-thirds majority for Aristide."[119]

Voting for other offices went ahead in July in elections that international observers denounced as fundamentally flawed, and that most opposition parties charged were rigged in favor of Aristide's candidates. In consequence, they boycotted the presidential elections on November 26. Nonetheless, a substantial percentage of registered voters participated and gave Aristide a 92 percent victory. The opposition, now shakily coalesced as the Convergence Démocratique,[120] refused to accept the verdict. Aristide partisans refused to accept their refusal. On January 9, at a press conference at Saint Jean Bosco, Aristide supporters Father Paul Raymond and René Civil read out the names of eighty opposition leaders, religious figures, journalists and others opposed to Aristide's inauguration, and warned that they had three days to change their position, or face violent reprisals.

Yet beginning in October 2000, the same month that demonstrators heaved chairs and bottles of urine at electoral councillors and members of the Haitian National Police were killing Aristide's opponents, a Haitian court meted out long-overdue justice by judging and convicting the assassins of the Raboteau massacre.

The Raboteau Trial was a landmark case. Thirty-four people testified, including victims, eyewitnesses and local officials. Five international experts analyzed the forensic evidence and contextualized the massacre in terms of the current repression and the military structure. American forensic anthropologist Dr. Karen Burns described how her examination of three exhumed corpses confirmed witnesses' accounts. Canadian geneticist Dr. Michele Harvey-Blankenship explained that DNA from two bodies were a match with their relatives. Ambassador Colin Granderson detailed the larger context of the events, and two military experts from Argentina also testified. The prosecution also introduced documentary evidence. Army archives were especially revealing, and included an account of how the Raboteau massacre was covered up.

There were fifty-eight defendants, some behind bars, though key players like Raoul Cédras, his deputy Philippe Biamby, former police chief Michel François, and FRAPH leader (and self-identified CIA informant) Toto Constant and thirty-four other massacre masterminds, were safe in foreign exile. Because extradition efforts failed, and the exiles were apparently untouchable, they could only be tried *in absentia*. The charges included murder, attempted murder, assault, torture, kidnapping, abuse of authority, theft, arson and destruction of property.

On November 9, sixteen of the defendants were convicted of participating in the massacre. A week later, thirty-seven other more were convicted *in absentia*. Twelve were sentenced to life in prison with hard labor. Others were to be jailed for between four to ten years. All had to pay damages into a victims' fund.[121] General Raoul Cédras, who had led the coup against Aristide; his deputy, Philippe Biamby; Toto Constant and Michel François were all sentenced to life in prison with hard labor, and were fined one billion *gourdes* ($43 million). Though they heard the news on foreign radio and remained free, their convictions still mattered. The Raboteau Trial was the first to try military officers and paramilitary leaders for human rights violations committed during the coup, and it also helped to document the coup. René Préval and Minister of Justice Camille LeBlanc left the new president, Jean-Bertrand Aristide, "a muscular example that showed how those who spoke with guns could be made to answer for their crimes," wrote journalist Michael Deibert.[122]

The countdown to Aristide's second presidency neared its final moments. It couldn't come too soon for Préval, newly diagnosed with prostate cancer that he had treated in Cuba. In December, Aristide succumbed to pressure from President Clinton and promised, in writing, to undertake an eight-point list of political reforms. That did not assuage the still-raging Convergence, which had no intention of respecting the electoral results. On February 6, 2001, the day before Aristide's inauguration, the Convergence named elderly lawyer (and legal tutor to Jean-Claude Duvalier) Gérard Gourgue as Provisional President of their "alternative government." Gourgue also called for the rebirth of the FAD'H, a provocation that Aristide would not forget.

The next day in the parliament building, René Préval, beaming, draped the red-and-blue presidential sash around Aristide's shoulders. It was another first, Haiti's first full-term president joyfully transferring power to his elected successor.

Aristide's inaugural speech described an economic program of "investing in human beings." It would also satisfy SAP requirements, increase the GDP by 4 percent annually, limit inflation to less than 10 percent, reduce unemployment to 45 percent and create half a million stable jobs.[123] How would this happen? Through new free trade zones that would spin off myriad miracles: enough electricity to power the nation; potable water for 70 percent of the rural population; increased food sufficiency; repairs to more than two thousand kilometers of primary roads and three thousand kilometres of secondary roads; and the retrofitting of the international airports in Port-au-Prince and Cap Haitien as well as five other airports. All that was lacking to bring this dream to fruition, Aristide concluded, were private-sector partners.

At first partners did not line up to invest.[124] Haiti's political instability, lurking violence and pervasive criminal activity made physical security so tenuous that it was *sauve qui peut* as wealthy Haitians bought and learned how to fire weapons, hired security guards, often ex-soldiers or Macoutes, and trained Rottweilers and other guard dogs to protect their high-walled homes. Haiti's dilapidated infrastructure—inadequate and unreliable electricity, water, telecommunications and roads—made investment unattractive. Insufficient and poor-quality schools, clinics and housing held the work force hostage. The public-sector deficit was ballooning, and the Central Bank's system of direct deficit financing squeezed out private-sector access to credit. Despite Préval's sporadic attempts to root it out, corruption was pervasive in public-sector finances and in government and public service. When Aristide took office, Transparency International ranked Haiti ranked #92, and during his regime it plummeted to # 131, above only Bangladesh and Nigeria.[125] It also ranked Jean-Claude Duvalier the sixth most corrupt leader of the past two decades. The Duvalier legacy remained a crushing burden.

Haiti also had intractable structural problems. Its legal and regulatory framework was defective, with enervating and bribe-invoking red tape and dysfunctional bureaucracies. Its justice system was fundamentally flawed. As one Haiti expert noted, "It was incomprehensible, hence remote from the citizenry; it was corrupt and insecure; it was not independent; it did not provide access to legal assistance or other mechanisms to defend the rights of citizens; its case inquiry procedures were deficient."[126] And, thanks to the custom of relying on personal relationships with government to conduct business and resolve issues, there were poor prospects for dispute resolution.

Elite Haitians, the traditional beneficiaries of Haiti's closed and corrupt system, remained wary of Aristide and of "investing in human beings." They preferred to negotiate monopolies through government contacts and kickbacks and to focus on imports that they resold at greatly inflated prices; at the same time, they limited risks to warehouse inventories. Foreign business interests balked at anything except light assembly factories. They wanted, in times of coup, embargo or other crises, to simply pack up their portable machinery and leave. "If you have orders to fill," an American expatriate businessman explained, "people don't like to hear that you're in Haiti, because if they're going to make a contract to sell these certain products, they want to make sure you're going to be able to deliver."[127]

Aristide's half-hearted attempt at rapprochement with the elite, briefly conducted through Robert Malval, was now in the hands of his intimate friend, Gladys Lauture, who prior to his restoration in 1991 had decorated and supervised renovations at Artistide's house in Tabarre. Lauture, once a confidant of Michèle Bennett, used her connections with Haiti's patrician families on Aristide's behalf. But they disliked and distrusted him, and he reciprocated with verbal attacks that destroyed any bridges Lauture had built. One egregious example was his widely reported speech in Aux Cayes in which, speaking in Creole, Aristide told his large audience that opposition parties "don't like you. . . . You are peasants; you are poor. You are the same color I am. They don't like you. Your hair is kinky, same as mine. They don't like you. Your children are not children of big shots. They don't like you."[128] And, if *they* hadn't liked Aristide before this blatant evocation of racial hatreds that had long plagued Haiti, afterward *they* also feared him.

Aristide's antipathy toward the Haitian business class did not extend to their Dominican counterparts and, to accommodate U.S. economic demands and threats to withhold economic aid, he pushed Codevi (Compagnie de Developpement Industrial) to develop the Ouanaminthe Industrial Park, the first of fourteen planned free trade zones, through the pliant Lavalas parliament. Ouanaminthe, on Haiti's border, is one kilometer from Dajabon in the Dominican Republic. The Industrial Park, 780 square kilometers, was projected to be a huge operation that would eventually comprise forty factories employing twenty thousand people directly, and creating forty thousand indirect jobs. It required the expropriation of nearly a hundred small farms, and the forced relocation of the sharecropper tenant families that had lived and worked on the land.

In April 2002, Aristide permitted Dominican soldiers to strike a camp in the field of one of the expropriated farms, without bothering to consult or notify the farmer. The next day, Haitian National Police including an anti-riot squad arrived in a convoy of SUVs and buses, while Aristide and his Dominican associates, President Hipólito Mejía, a bishop and several industrialists all arrived in helicopters. The bishop blessed the new enterprise. Then Aristide announced that Codevi was a "bright star" and that he Mejía were "baptizing . . . the first child [of a] marriage" between the two countries that he hoped would produce "many more children."[129] This, observes Canadian business writer Jennifer Wells,

> was a polished and hopeful bit of public relations, especially given that Codevi was actually a way for Grupo M, the largest private-sector employer in the Dominican Republic, to harness Haitian labor to affordable and reliable Dominican electricity. . . . [As] the first of fourteen such zones, [it] would result in the ramp-up of thousands, then tens of thousands, and now hundreds of thousands, of minimum-wage garment assembly jobs for offshore manufacturers wooed by tariff breaks. These "bright stars" were positioned politically as the easiest economic bet for a broken, nay, collapsed, country.[130]

Codevi would allow Dominicans to pay Haitian workers their pitifully low wages to manufacture goods that would then enter the U.S. as part of Haiti's unfilled quota. Codevi's first resident was Grupo M, whose clients, Tommy Hilfiger, Banana Republic, The Gap and Abercrombie & Fitch, happily paid Haitians $1.25 per day to finish—with a button, a hem, a seam—nearly-finished garments that Dominicans paid $13 a day had sewn together. Instead of selling Haitians to labor in Dominican cane fields, as the Duvaliers had done, Aristide sold them to Dominicans who could exploit them within Haiti, with the cooperation of the Haitian government.[131] The priest who had so passionately denounced assembly factory jobs as the death knoll of Haitian independence was no longer recognizable in this secular politician who so confidently inaugurated Codevi.

In other financial dealings, Aristide also took a page from Duvalierism and acquired his money the old-fashioned way, by embezzling it. Learning how was easy. The Duvalier legacy provided precedents and teaching aids, and Aristide was not averse to surrounding himself with Duvalierist advisers.

The story begins with the telephone company and the U.S. International Settlements Policy (ISP) of fixed fees, designed to protect American companies from price competition from foreign companies where there was no competition. For specified countries, one of them Haiti,

U.S. companies had to make the terms of their contracts public so that nobody could undercut anybody else, and American companies could get the best terms. In practice, the policy also resulted in establishing decent prices for poor countries, giving them, as business writer Lucy Komisar describes it, "a break."

In all countries, telecom arrangements work like this: "International phone calls access the routing systems of both the caller's country and the recipient's. The phone company where the call originates routinely pays a per-minute charge or 'termination fee' for accessing the overseas system."[132] Without termination fees, the country receiving calls would not be reimbursed for maintaining its infrastructure.

In Haiti's case, the twenty-three-cent ISP-established termination fee could and should have been a very good deal, because Teleco's long-distance revenues were one of the country's few sources of hard currency. But where did all that money go? Two Teleco-related lawsuits trace how the looting took place. Duplicity was the name of the game, and both Americans and Haitians played it. Stateside, some firms violated their duty to either pay the per-minute rate fixed by the Federal Communications Commission (FCC) or inform the FCC that they had arranged to pay lower rates. But why would poor Haiti agree to less than the U.S.-mandated rate? Because in return for a much lower rate—nine instead of twenty-three cents per minute—the American company Integrated Device Technology (IDT) agreed *not* to pay Teleco but rather to make its deposits to Mont Salem, an account in an offshore Turks and Caicos bank. Who owned this biblically named company? All indications are that it was Aristide's. In a related law case, D. Michael Jewett, in 2003 IDT's associate regional vice-president for the Caribbean, testified that one of his superiors told him that IDT had struck a sweetheart phone deal with Haiti—nine cents rather than the FCC-mandated twenty-three-cents for U.S.-originated calls—in return for three of those nine cents being remitted to Aristide.

Aristide himself negotiated with IDT through an executive who met with him in Haiti in August of 2003, a meeting CEO Howard Jonas later characterized as "highly unusual. . . . In most cases, you're just talking to the head of the telecom. It was unusual that the president himself would be involved with it."[133] Following this unusual presidential meeting, the IDT executive appointed Jewett as the "go-between for all commercial correspondence between Teleco Haiti and Mont Salem," which he referred to as the private bank account of the president of Haiti, Jean-

Bertrand Aristide. The deal was legalized in a contract dated October 22, 2003 and signed by IDT's CFO Norman Rosenberg and, on November 6 by Teleco's Jean René Duperval and Alfonse Inevil. Teleco's accounts were falsified by naming Mont Salem rather than IDT as its telecom carrier. The monies involved were huge. In one six-month period, the three-cent kickback to Aristide's Mont Salem amounted to $302,588.

Nor was IDT the only telecom involved. Among the others was Canada's Skyytel, a Montréal company. Skyytel president Colin Povall concedes that his telecom also agreed to pay Teleco nine cents per minute via Mont Salem, supposedly Teleco's agent. "Mont Salem approached us," Povall said. "We never met anybody in Haiti." He added, however, that his Haitian-Canadian contact "was dealing with some powerful people [in Haiti]." The estimated kickbacks from Skyytel to Mont Salem amounted to $872,371.[134]

Years later, in South Africa, in an interview with Nicolas Rossier, Aristide laughed off the question, "Can you put these accusations [about your personal involvement with the Teleco scandal] to rest?" "First, they are lying," Aristide said. "Second, what can we expect from a mental slave? [Laughs] He will lie for his masters. He is paid to lie for his masters, so I am not surprised by these nonsensical allegations. As I said, they are lying." Rossier persisted: "But it's possible that under you at some level in your government there was some corruption involving Teleco and IDT?" Aristide responded with a robust lie. "I never heard about things like that when I was there and I never knew about it."[135]

It wasn't just Teleco, reports corruption-buster Lucy Komisar:

> Aristide and his associates looted government coffers, wrote checks to front companies for nonexistent purchases, padded invoices to get kickbacks from vendors, secretly owned companies that cheated Haiti of taxes, and laundered the money they stole through shell companies and secret bank accounts set up in the United States and the offshore tax havens of Turks and Caicos and the British Virgin Islands.

"Aristide's corruption is documented by incorporation papers, copies of bank checks, bank transfer documents, invoices, company payment statements, and sworn testimony," Komisar added.[136] She has copies of twelve checks that total $4,662,000, from the years 2001 to

2002. A Haitian Administrative Commission of Enquiry, headed by former Haitian senator Paul Denis, documented $17,489,415 transferred abroad by Aristide and his collaborators.[137] About $2.4 million went to Fanmi Lavalas and to Aristide's Foundation, giving him the means to further his humanitarian works and to fulfill his commitment as champion of the poor.

Duvalieristically, Aristide relatives also figured in the reports. Lesly Lavelanet, husband of Dominique Trouillot, Mildred Trouillot's older sister, had several mentions. The Administrative Inquiry Commission, established after Aristide's 2004 departure and known as the Denis Commission, estimated that from August 2002 to January 2004, Lavelanet's Global Spectrum imported over 20 million kilos of rice without paying customs duties. Customs officials, including Director-General Jean Jacques Valentin, testified that they were obeying direct instructions from either Finance Minister Gustave Faubert or President Aristide's personal secretary, Ginette Céant, to admit Lavelanet's rice into Haiti despite his non-payment of duties. The loss to Haiti's Customs—56,696,363.30 *gourdes* (approximately $1.42 million).[138] Aristide, the man who had so hated the deadly implications of imported rice, was now complicit in ushering it in duty-free.

A white American businessman of pseudonym "Patrick James" observed about doing business in Cédras-era Haiti: "The interconnectedness of the Haitian business community is amazing. . . . The elite are somehow interconnected or related. Basically they have to work together in order to keep their power intact." Clearly, Aristide and his entrepreneurial—and enterprising—in-laws had learned that lesson well.[139] Aristide's wife and brother-in-law, Erickson Trouillot, also earned huge sums as registered lobbyists for the Haitian government—Mildred, a total of $512,634, and Erickson Trouillot, $208,000.

In the five-year period from 1997 to 2002, the government of Haiti paid lobbyists $7.3 million. This included $4,902,459 to the firm of Aristide spokesman Ira Kurzban, and $1,175,522 to lawyer Brian Concannon.[140] Did the government of Haiti get value for its money? Not by the usual measure—American funding to Haiti—which declined during this period. "It was a waste of money," opined Robert Maguire, Haiti specialist at Trinity College in Washington. "Some of it is scandalous." Instead of expensive lobbyists, other Caribbean governments opt for larger embassy and consular staff to address their international needs. For the same five-year period, for example, the next-door Dominican

Republic spent $1.18 million on lobbying. Honduras, with a population of 6.5 million, spent $815,000.[141]

Aristide inherited a Haiti awash in drugs, and Préval had made little headway in reining it in. In 1998, for example, a huge shipment of Colombian cocaine bound for the U.S. landed instead on the Haitian coast near Aquin. Police rushed to the scene, beat the villagers who were parceling it out among themselves, and disappeared with the cocaine. Afterward, HNP Inspector General Eucher Luc Joseph warned that cocaine had become a "gangrene" in Haitian society, and had torn the police force apart. As the result of the incident at Aquin, Haiti's public security chief and Préval's trusted friend, Robert Manuel, sounded the alarm about the international drug cartels and their "macabre plots" to infiltrate Haiti; corrupt its officials, politicians and the HNP; and destabilize the already chaotic nation so that it could not put up any resistance to drug trafficking.

Manuel was no scaremongerer; the U.S. Drug Enforcement Administration also despaired of making progress. "To say Haiti is a black hole is an understatement. It's wide open," one official lamented.[142] General Barry R. McCaffrey, director of the United States anti-drug effort, added, "We've got weak to nonexistent democratic institutions, a police force that is on the verge of collapse from internal corruption and an eroding infrastructure that is creating a path of very little resistance."[143] Many officials, politicians and police officers—the latter earned an average of $313 monthly—found the pay-offs too seductive to resist. They also participated eagerly in drug busts, and then seized and sold the cocaine themselves.

The stakes were astronomical. The U.S. estimated that 10 percent of all the cocaine smuggled into the country—in bulk terms, at least eighty tons—was transhipped through the Caribbean, especially Haiti. (The drugs were easily smuggled in, then either flown directly into the U.S. or first shipped in boats known as *yolas* to Puerto Rico before transhipment to the U.S.) In the three years of Aristide's second presidency, Colombian drug traffickers paid out about $1,500 per pound to Haitian officials, or about $250 million. And this was in a country whose government had a total budget of $300 million. In a single year, while Haiti spent about $30 million on its justice system, including police and courts, drug traffickers were dispensing nearly three times as much—$78 million—on bribes, often to the people involved in that same justice system. "The ability of the noncorrupt Haitian law enforcement and customs authorities to combat this is diminishing rapidly," McCaffrey said. "The political will to support them isn't there."

The business elite were equally complacent. On July 9, 2003, at the farewell luncheon offered for outgoing American ambassador Dean Curran by the Haitian-American Chamber of Commerce, Curran startled his hosts by condemning Haitian society's tolerance for drug trafficking. "The traffickers are well-known. They are supplied by your stores, you sell houses to them or build new ones for them, you take their deposits, you educate their children, you elect them to positions in the Chamber of Commerce."[144]

Haitian officials who looked beyond drug trade's enormous profits and understood how it corrupted and rotted Haiti's government attempted to fight it, a Sisyphean task that was also deeply dangerous. And some Haitians were resentful at criticism of their drug-enforcement efforts. "Given how much cocaine the United States says comes through here, you'd think they'd be as good at catching drug boats as they are with stopping refugee boats, which they excel at," said a high-ranking official. "They say this is a war, but is it?"[145]

In Haiti, drug business was conducted at high levels of government. A small sampling of those indicted for or eventually convicted of Haiti-U.S. drug trafficking and related crimes suggests the extent of its pervasiveness. Four were senior police officers: Rudy Therassan, former head of the HNP Research and Investigation division; Jean Nesly Lucien, former HNP director; Romaine Lestin, former head of the HNP at the international airport (he extorted money from Colombian and Haitian drug smugglers and then cleared their cocaine-filled planes to proceed to the U.S.); Hermione Leonard, former HNP regional commander and Rudy Therassan's wife. Others were Stephanie Ambroise, American Airlines director of airport security, and her husband, Yonel Joassaint; Fourel Celestin, former president of the Haitian Senate; Immacula Bazile and Wilnet Content, former Lavalas members of Parliament; Moise Elnu, a HNP officer; Pascal Garoute, owner of Gold's Gym Shopping Mall in Pétionville (he hired groups of HNP to provide security for incoming drug planes); former army officers, including Guy Philippe, and an assortment of businessmen and others whose vocations are listed as drug trafficking.

Two others were Aristide's intimate friends and associates. Beaudoin "Jacques" Ketant was a cocaine trafficker connected with the Medellin, Cali and Norte de Valle cartels. Ketant operated several airstrips, sometimes improvised by halting traffic on stretches of highways, and through his government connections, could safely import cocaine into Haiti. From there to the U.S., he employed an army of smugglers including "swallowers," drug mules who swallowed baggies of cocaine and excreted it at their American destination. "[Ketant] really trusted Aristide," a diplomat commented. "They were close. They were collaborators."[146] In 2001 Ketant was featured on America's Most Wanted List, thanks to his conviction for drug trafficking in the U.S. in 1997 *in absentia*. Far from shunning his friend, Aristide accepted Ketant's offer to build a Carnival grandstand in front of the National Palace, where Ketant also celebrated the festivities.

Ketant was even godfather to Aristide's youngest daughter, Michaelle, born in September of 1998. His white palatial home in Port-au-Prince's wealthy gated community of Vivi Michel, worth $8 million, was furnished with two hundred rare paintings, including some by Picasso and Monet. Ketant owned mansions and luxury apartments elsewhere, including in Florida, had fleets of cars and millions of dollars in cash.

But in 2003, when his goddaughter Michaelle was only four, Ketant and Aristide had a lethal falling out. It began in February, when masked men (one of whom Ketant swore was Rudy Therassan) killed both Ketant's drug-smuggling younger brother, Hector Ketant, and his bodyguard, Hermann Charles, after abducting them from a busy street in Pétionville. Hector was executed, Ketant later testified in a Miami federal court, over a dispute about Aristide's take on a cocaine shipment. Instead of his usual 30 percent of the profits, Aristide demanded 80 percent of the gross shipment of more than fourteen hundred pounds so he could finance that year's Carnival. Hector refused, pistols were drawn and Hector shot Rudy Therassan in the shoulder. Therassan, Aristide's agent in the transaction, returned fire and killed Hector. Afterward, he retrieved an incriminating list of government officials associated with Ketant's drug business.

In May, after a schoolgirl at the private American-run Union School preferred another boy to Ketant's nephew at a school party, both the nephew and Ketant's son retaliated by beating up and forcing the young rival into the trunk of their car. Courageously, the principal expelled the Ketant boys and refused to reconsider her decision. Enraged, Jacques Ketant and his bodyguards stormed into Union School and threatened her. Parents, including American diplomats, complained at the highest levels that this invasion into Union School was intolerable. By June, Aristide succumbed to American pressure. He invited Ketant to the palace, where Therassan arrested him, drove him to the airport and relinquished him into the custody of American Drug Enforcement Agency agents who escorted him to Miami, and jail.

During his trial, which ended with his conviction, a twenty-seven-year prison sentence and $30 million in fines and forfeitures, Ketant raged against Aristide. "He turned the country into a narco-country. The man is a drug lord. He controlled the drug world in Haiti." He also blamed Aristide for his brother Hector's murder. "It's a one-man show, your honor," Ketant told Judge Federico A. Moreno. "You either pay [Aristide] or you die." [147] His attorney, Ruben Oliva, added: "Certainly the government was the godfather. Everyone in Haiti that was engaged in this activity had to pay the government." "I've been paying him throughout the years," Ketant said. Every month, he said, he personally delivered $500,000 to Aristide's home in a suitcase with a combination lock set to 7-7-7, Aristide's favorite number.[148] "He betrayed me just like Judas betrayed Jesus," Ketant said bitterly.[149] (One of Ketant's five ex-wives was more loyal and, helped by Haitian police officers, emptied his mansion of its treasures before they could be forfeited, as per his sentence.)

Oriel Jean, chief of presidential security, was even closer to Aristide than Ketant and the highest-level official to use his position and authority to traffic drugs and launder money. Though Jean's U.S. visitor's visa was withdrawn along with those of other alleged drug smugglers,[150] Aristide kept him in his trusted position at the palace. Jean was arrested at Toronto's Pearson International Airport—carrying $17,000 cash and a check for $300,000—and extradited to the U.S. In a Miami court, he was convicted of cocaine trafficking. Jean's testimony confirmed Ketant's and added other accomplices, including drug lord Serge Edouard,[151] for whom Aristide authorized a national security ID card granting free access throughout Haiti.

A multitude of drug trials that would follow Aristide's 2004 ouster convicted about twenty Haitians and documented a nation deeply involved in drug trafficking. Evidence showed that one of Aristide's first actions as President was to summon Oriel Jean, Rudy Therassant, two government security advisers and a district commander to his home in Tabarre where they devised a plan to "shake down" Colombian and

Haitian drug smugglers for kickbacks for both Aristide's personal and political activities. A fee schedule was established. Afterward, the bribe money was regularly delivered to Aristide personally, to his FL party, his Aristide Foundation for Democracy and for special events such as Carnival and a nation-wide celebration of his birthday on July 15.

Other testimonies revealed that the traffickers also spent $75,000 buying and shipping an ambulance to the Aristide Foundation. They gave him $200,000 for a helicopter, but he kept the money and instead used government funds to rent one from Miami's Biscayne Helicopters. Some money went to purchase weapons for both the HNP and the street gangs known as Aristide's *chimères*—young, armed, unemployed slum-dwellers easily mobilized to organize violent pro-Aristide demonstrations, control the streets and silence opponents. When the national treasury was empty, Ketant's drug money covered the paychecks of restive civil servants.

This wealth of information convinced American officials that Aristide was a lead player or an accomplice in drug trafficking. As General McCaffrey observed, "It's hard to imagine that Aristide himself isn't taking part in this enormously lucrative form of criminal activity."[152] But American officials lacked evidence, specifically the financial records required by evidentiary legal standards, to lay charges against him.[153]

Aristide's Haiti was looking more and more like Jean-Claude Duvalier's. The national coffers were empty, but the drug trade was thriving. The President and his large entourage enjoyed opulent lifestyles impossible to sustain on their salaries. High in the hills overlooking Port-au-Prince, busy contractors erected mansion after mansion. In the slums below, the people endured in suffering. Safety was so compromised that Aristide (rightly) feared assassination and felt safe only with strapping white American bodyguards contracted from the California-based Steele Foundation at a cost of millions annually. Although the Haitian government provided Haitian security guards, it paid the Steele contract as well.

The drug trade and crooked business dealings seduced officials and made Parliament scarcely functional. Aristide's vision of democracy looked like a melange of corruption, authoritarianism and the (constitutionally forbidden) cult of personality justified by electoral victory. His growing reliance on *chimères* seemed Duvalieresque, except that his *chimères* were not organized hierarchically as the Tontons Macoutes had been. Also unlike the Macoutes, Aristide's *chimères* could—and increasingly did—turn against him. Aristide was still well loved, but by far fewer people.

One who had never loved him was the unsavory Prosper Avril, convicted in a U.S. District Court of systematic and egregious human rights abuses, and held personally liable for $41 million to compensate his victims. Now Avril was back in Haiti, meeting with Convergence politicians at the upscale Villa Creole hotel and attending what he described as "patriotic workshops of constructive debate on the Haitian problems." He was also promoting one of his self-published books, *Haiti: 1995-2001 The Black Book on Insecurity*, which detailed the rash of kidnappings, muggings, robberies and murders he blamed on the HNP. On May 26, as he sat in a Pétionville restaurant signing copies of the book, six black-clad members of a SWAT team barged in, arrested him for plotting to overthrow the government and threw him into the National Penitentiary. "O abominable crime!" Avril lamented, "O public misfortune! O foolish and contemptible act of a so-called democrat!"[154] The Convergence demanded Avril's release. But Aristide had no intention of releasing this treacherous man with a personal vendetta against him.

Street crime and political violence were making Haiti even more chaotic, dangerous and desperate. On June 20, 2001, Aristide lectured new police recruits at HNP headquarters about tackling the *zenglendos*—criminals—who committed street crimes.

> If a *zenglendo* stops a car out in the street, takes the car keys, forces the driver to get out and drives away with the vehicle, then that person is guilty. You do not need to take him to court to answer to the judge, because the car does not belong to him. If a criminal carries out physical violence against somebody out in the street with intent to kill that person, you do not need to wait for that criminal to appear before the judge, you can prevent that murderer from taking action. When it has to do with criminals it is zero tolerance. Period and full stop.[155]

The news spread quickly. Zero tolerance? That meant take the law into your own hands, and administer your own personal or political version of justice with a fist, a machete or a gun. On November 30 at City Hall in Petit-Goâve, which was already reeling from anti-government agitation, Mayor Emmanuel Antoine, his assistants Dumey Bony and Cimeres Bolière, four government officials[156] and Raymond Jean Fleury, coordinator of Aristide gang Dòmi nan Bwa (Sleep in the Woods) held a press conference. These officials, especially Bony, spoke vehemently about the need for "zero tolerance" toward Brignol Lindor, news director of Radio Echo 2000 and an Aristide critic, and four guests on a recent debating show called *Dialogue*.[157]

On December 3, Brignol Lindor and a friend were on their way out of Petit-Goâve in a blue Montero jeep when members of Dòmi nan Bwa ambushed and attacked them. The friend managed to escape. Lindor sought refuge at a nearby house, but its inhabitants turned out to be Dòmi nan Bwa members. They surrendered him to the mob, which stoned and hacked him to death with machetes. Two days later, a riot broke out as police interrupted Lindor's funeral and opened fire as four thousand mourners proceeded toward the cemetery.[158]

Lindor's murder was a milestone in the escalation of political violence and vigilantism, and sparked furious anti-Aristide sentiment. Graffiti artists once content to write "Aba Lavalas!" (down with Lavalas) used red paint to scrawl "Aba Aristide!" as well.[159] Then, in Port-au-Prince, came the notorious attack on the National Palace on December 17.

The "facts" are curious. At about 1:30 to 2:00 a.m., about twenty men dressed in camouflage uniform leapt down from pickup trucks, opened fire and attacked the palace. Some clambered over the northern fence, while others gained access on the west. Presidential Security[160] guards made no attempt to resist, and the attackers walked right into the palace. Their entry was facilitated by two more "facts"—HNP were complicit with the attackers, and that night (an official OAS report later discovered) the main gate to the palace had been left unlocked and unchained.

The attackers then spent several hours, until about 5:30 a.m., in various rooms, looking for documents and ammunition. They took Aristide's laptop and briefcase (which was later recovered on the palace grounds), as well as unspecified material from the Steele Foundation office. They damaged the offices of the President, the First Lady and the President's private secretary, and also the diplomatic lounge. During their leisurely rampage, they used purloined two-way police transistor radios to announce to the more than one hundred personnel on that frequency that they were on a mission from the disbanded army, that Aristide was no longer President and that Guy Philippe was the new

HNP chief. While they did all this inside the palace, they also fired continuously with M-50 machine guns and Uzis.

During the invasion, palace security planned a counterattack during which, they said, they shot and killed former army officer and palace security guard Chavre Milot, whom they identified as co-commander of the attackers. But the injuries on Milot's corpse did not seem consistent with gunfire, and hadn't he vowed, post-1991 coup, that if Aristide returned, he'd commit suicide? Could he have done himself in without Presidential Security to help? Nobody could say for sure, because before the coroner arrived, Milot's corpse was gone.

What happened next was much clearer. After the attackers tried and failed to reach Aristide's home in Tabarre, they proceeded to the Dominican border and crossed over. But in Port-au-Prince and elsewhere, as soon as the news spread, reprisals began against the alleged perpetrators, Aristide's political opponents. Hundreds of his *chimères*, machetes in hand, surrounded the palace and shouted, "We'll never accept another coup d'état!" In response to skeptics who suspected a hoax, palace spokesman Jacques Maurice declared, "This is an attempted coup d'état. This is not a staged event."

Nobody suspected that the reprisals were staged. Aristide partisans burned tires, set up roadblocks and smashed and torched the offices and private residences of Convergence politicians—the Convergence itself, the Konfederazion Inite Demokratic (KID), the Congrès National des Mouvements Démocratiques (KONAKOM), the Mobilisation pour le Developpement National (MDN), the Alliance pour l'Avancement et la Libération d'Haiti (ALAH), and the Parti Democratique Chrétien d'Haïti (PDCH), and of course OPL. Fanmi Lavalas militants pillaged and burned. Even when armed men fired shots, the police watched without intervening. Police Chief Lucien Nesly shrugged off criticism with the comment that the police were not trained for combat. By nightfall, many Convergence members had neither homes nor offices, and the same scenario was repeated in cities and towns across Haiti.

In the aftermath, at least eleven Haitian journalists reporting these events sought asylum in foreign embassies or attempted to flee Haiti. Several had guns pointed at them and were forced to yell, "Long Live Aristide!" Three women's organizations issued a bitter press release.

> The Lavalas government has declared there was an attempted
> coup d'état on the night of 16–17 December and that in order

to protect the government "the population" reacted. Which population? Since when has the Haitian population been armed? How many members of the population are able to drive around in cars and trucks at the very moment of this insecurity? When the population makes demands, civil society organizations are with them. We, the members of the women's organizations that have signed below, cannot explain the pillage and destruction of premises belonging to the opposition, of individual residences, of a social research center, or the threats against the press, culminating in some stations ceasing their news broadcasts.[161]

Aristide, uncharacteristically silent, finally issued a cryptic, clichéd statement: "I say to the Haitian people continue to mobilize peacefully, in all of the country, continue to mobilize peacefully, respect the rights of political parties, respect the rights of journalists, respect the rights of each and every citizen, respect the rights of all people without distinction." Michèle Montas, Jean Dominique's widow, lamented that no one was safe, not journalists, not human rights workers, not even ordinary citizens.

After the coup or supposed coup—Haitian media testifying before a subsequent OAS commission agreed only that "something had taken place at the Palace that day"—and the retaliatory deaths and attacks it triggered, Aristide faced more sustained opposition and what almost amounted to guerrilla warfare. But Guy Philippe, who telephoned journalists to insist that he had nothing to do with the coup, was safe in the Dominican Republic. The Dominicans detained him under house arrest while diplomats sought a country that would accept him, but refused to extradite him to Haiti. In comfortable exile, Philippe plotted to overthrow his enemy Aristide.

Aristide's presidency was in freefall. Comparisons with Duvalierism were more frequent. "A lot of local authorities are behaving exactly like the Tonton Macoutes under Duvalier," said Jean-Claude Bajeux, director of the Haitian Ecumenical Human Rights Center. "What we are seeing now are offshoots of anarchy that go through the local authorities."[162] The Popular Organizations were transforming themselves into fighting cells. Two of their leaders, René Civil (Jeunesse Pouvoir Populaire) and Paul Raymond (coordinator of Ti Kominote Legliz) were accused of (and denied) publicly threatening opposition leaders. And the disapproving international community continued to withhold loans and aid money.

The summer of 2002 saw a new crisis, the widespread failure of banking cooperatives. As elsewhere in the Caribbean, Haiti had informal village co-ops for savings and loans, and formalized banking institutions that catered to a more prosperous clientele and offered annual interest rates of between 2 and 7 percent. In the late 1990s, another kind of venture opened up, cooperatives that offered super-high monthly interest rates—from 10 to 15 percent. Before long, three hundred of these "ten percenters" were competing to attract clients, wooing them with cell phones and CD players. At the height of the movement, investors numbered 185,000. Coeurs Unis (United Hearts), whose director was Lavalas insider David Chéry, aired cheery ads in which a jolly man in peasant garb promised 12 percent interest per month.

How could co-ops offer such high interest rates? Some managers did not seem to know. Many explained that they owed their good fortune to the Aristide government's largesse in allowing them to import rice, sugar and other consumer goods duty-free. In Jacmel, Coeur Unis director Chéry bought taxis and buses, gas stations, schools and property including—for four times its estimated value—the twenty-eight-room Mirage Hotel. The Mirage had forty employees and few guests, but it was conveniently located on "Cocaine Alley," a road near the beach known as the locale for Colombian drug drops.

Financially astute Haitians warned government officials that the ten percenters were either pyramid schemes—("Do new deposits pay interest on old deposits?" mused former planning minister Marc Bazin)[163]—or else money launderers for drug traffickers. This seemed a reasonable suspicion, especially after huge sums invested at commercial banks were transferred to the co-ops right after American legislation came into effect requiring banks—but not co-ops—to notify authorities of deposits exceeding $10,000. To dispel fears about complicity in laundering drug money, and to avoid being cut adrift by its American counterparts, Haiti's largest commercial bank, Sogebank, returned $9 million in deposits to twenty co-ops after they refused to open their books for inspection.[164]

Until they were struck by the panic of impending ruin, Haitians giddily sold homes, property and cars, and borrowed money to invest in the co-ops that President Aristide himself encouraged. Cooperatives, he declared in a speech at Sylvio Cator soccer stadium, were "the people's capitalism," an alternative to the elite's stranglehold monopoly of banks and other core economic sectors that would develop the broken economy.[165]

In the summer of 2002, the co-ops suddenly went bust, bankrupting their mostly working-class investors. (A few desperate policemen threatened managers with guns until they got their money back.) Aristide, widely blamed for the debacle, denied it. "There is no crisis of the cooperative movement," he declared, pledging that "the state will abandon nobody who deposited money in a cooperative and was victimized."[166] By school-opening in October, he promised, the government would reimburse everybody who lost money. But that would have amounted to at least $240 million, 60 percent of the national budget, and the government coffers were empty. Protests roiled throughout Haitian cities, co-op bank managers went into hiding or fled abroad, and a movement of "fleeced investors,"[167] the National Coordination of the Collective Victims of Cooperatives (CONASOVIC), joined the anti-Aristide ranks as the scandal and ruin of scores of trusting Haitians added ballast to Aristide's already sinking ship.

On September 23, the government made a horrible situation worse by arresting Rosemond Jean, director of CONASOVIC, as he was organizing a huge demonstration to demand that Aristide pay out the money he had promised. The arrest was dramatic—Jean's mouth was duct-taped shut and his head was covered by a black plastic bag—and he was taken to the palace, where CIMO agents, policemen trained and equipped like U.S. SWAT teams,[168] beat him. Then, without a warrant, they ransacked and searched his house, and claimed to have found weapons and grenades but failed to produce them. Nonetheless, Jean was imprisoned in the National Penitentiary. And there he stayed, hunger striking and refusing to let up in his struggle for the cooperative victims. In late March of 2003, he was released on bail and promptly held a press conference at which, proving that prisons (like politics) make strange bedfellows, he revealed that a fellow inmate, the now-disgraced and incarcerated Coeurs Unis director David Chéry,[169] had confided to him that government officials routinely extorted funds from the co-ops.[170]

By 2003, Haiti was near collapse. The *gourde* lost half its value in a single year. Haitians complained that the government provided new SUVs for their officials while ordinary Haitians struggled to survive. Palace security staff were bitter about how inferior their salary and perquisites were in comparison to those of Aristide's trusted white Steele

Foundation contractors. Thousands of civil servants had no reliable salary and went unpaid for months. To "Aba Titid," (Down with Little Aristide) graffiti writers added, "Aristide, Thief."

Physical violence also escalated. Aristide's partisans targeted media critics, and the list of assaults and murders continued to grow. Radio stations were forced to close. At least thirty reporters were assaulted for covering protests at which Aristide's resignation was demanded. Leaflets in Port-au-Prince warned of a bloodbath should the President be removed from office. On a radio broadcast, leader Jean-Marie Perrier, a leader of one of the pro-Aristide Organisations Populaires (People's Organizations, or OP) made threats against reporters Wendy Richard, Marie-Lucie Bonhomme, Valéry Numa, Lilianne Pierre-Paul and Sony Bastien for their public comments about Aristide's resignation. Similar threats were made on air by FL parliamentarians who named other reporters. *Chimères* raided and besieged radio stations and threatened to torch them. Policemen with machine guns shut down others. In Cap Haitien, two gunmen shot and wounded radio station director and opposition supporter Jean-Robert Lalanne. Communications Minister Lilas Desquiron demanded that media members adopt a "responsible attitude."

On December 11, in response to threats from Aristide supporters, including the intimidation of reporter Nancy Roc, Radio Métropole, Radio Vision 2000, Radio Caraïbes and Radio Kiskeya stopped broadcasting until the next day. Liliane Pierre-Paul, a childhood friend of Aristide, declared that his officials could not tolerate the media reporting on his deteriorating political fortunes. Throughout Haiti, they were literally shooting at the messengers. In 2003 alone, fifteen journalists fled into exile after attacks or threats. One was Michèle Montas, who had already lost her beloved husband, Jean Dominique. "Lavalas [was] a party Jean worked to put in power," she said in exile in the U.S. "We thought things would change for participation and transparency. In fact, nothing has changed and impunity reigns. In fact, it is reinforced by the apparent inability of the President to control the violence."[171]

And Aristide was quickly losing the students, once so committed to his cause. On December 5, the State University of Haiti, his alma mater, was the site of the most galvanizing event to date. The students had demonstrated before, blaming Aristide for interfering in the university's administration, and Lavalas for ruining Haiti's economy. This time, *chimères* smashed down the walls of the Social Sciences School and beat protesting students inside, while the police shot at students outside.

University rector and executive councillor Pierre-Marie Michel Paquiot, a mathematics and physics professor, rushed to the scene. "I was inside a room with some students. They [*chimères*] got inside the room with guns and started shooting at everybody and asking the students to shout, 'Long Live Aristide.' " One put a gun to Pasquiot's head. Two others pounded his legs with metal bars. Paquiot fell to the ground, both legs broken. "I was hurt, I was a victim, but this is not an isolated case," he said. "They stomped on a girl student lying next to me, kicking her and walking over her body."[172]

At least twenty-five of five hundred student protesters were injured. So were reporters covering the event: Rodson Josselin of Haiti Press Network and Venel Casseus of Radio Kiskeya. So was Wilson Laleau, economics professor and vice-president for academic affairs, who was struck on the head and narrowly escaped being strangled with his own necktie. "All I could do was pray," Laleau recalled.[173] Paquiot underwent surgery on both legs for ruptured tendons and major thigh muscles. On January 12, he arrived in the U.S. in a wheelchair, both legs in casts, for further medical treatment.[174]

Amnesty International condemned the attacks. The Haitian government said a commission would investigate. Paquiot blamed Aristide for the tensions in Haiti: "I am not going to say he is behind everything that has gone on, but he has created such an atmosphere where people can do anything. . . . He has no vision for the country. The university has to be respected, and we [the university council] had addressed a letter to the nation asking Aristide to leave office. This violence is no longer acceptable. The most important thing we intellectuals can do is to denounce what is going on."[175] Government supporters, however, insisted that students could not protest against the government, though they could demonstrate to uphold the autonomy of their university.

If the government was in disarray and decline, with its officials resigning in droves, the opposition was proliferating. "I began to think that every Haitian was a political agglomeration-in-waiting," observed Trinidadian Reginald Dumas, UN Special Adviser to Haiti. "[T]here was no coherence of organization or management. Emotions of the moment were fine—emotion always has its place—but durability had to have a firmer foundation."[176]

The Group of 184, created on January 20, 2003, and led by industrialist Andy Apaid, was sad proof of this. An ungainly civil society movement of 184 business, cultural, social, media, educational and rural community groups and individuals,[177] the Group of 184 had an expressed goal of creating a social contract between Haitian citizens and their state, and between the multitudinous political parties, and thereby end the political paralysis. The reality was that the Group of 184 was united primarily by a mutual loathing of Aristide and a shared mission to push him out of office before his term ended in 2006. Group members were also linked to the U.S. government-funded International Republican Institute (IRI), which in Haiti added overthrowing Aristide to its mission of grassroots democratization.

In a nation whose politicians seemed impervious to the overarching need to merge minor differences into a common cause, the Group of 184 was as much a hopeful sign of alliance as it was a discouraging example of impermanence. Yet despite its growing strength, it could not compete with Lavalas, even as Lavalas eroded and lost its partisans to other groups. One of the Group of 184's most intractable problems was that, in a country accustomed to strong leadership, it had no truly popular leader. Only Aristide could claim that title.

The Group of 184 also resorted to violence so that Haiti often seemed a pitched camp. As disbanded and bitterly anti-Aristide FAD'H members drifted into the Group of 184—one was Dany Toussaint, widely suspected of involvement in killing Jean Dominique—armed and often murderous attacks on Lavalas and government officials rivaled those of Lavalas on the opposition. In the end, political intransigence was as lethal as the non-stop killings. Both destroyed the fabric of society, crushed hope and pushed Haiti closer to the abyss.

The electoral schedule required elections in late 2003, because most legislators' terms of office expired in January. But opposition politicians were so fixated on forcing Aristide's resignation that they rejected his plan to organize elections within six months. Marc Bazin resigned from his thankless job as Minister of Negotiation after he could not engineer a rapprochement between government and opposition. The Group of 184 blamed Aristide for this, because by failing to stop criminal gangs or to arrest those responsible for political violence, he had deprived Haitian citizens of the conditions necessary for exercising their political, social and economic rights, making it "impossible to have elections that are free, transparent and credible."[178] Yet without those elections, how else could Aristide rule except by decree, as Préval had done? The Group's real goal, it was clear, was to put up insurmountable obstacles to elections in the hopes of forcing Aristide to resign. And to punish Aristide, these same obstructionists also made impassioned appeals to foreign governments to withhold promised loans and aid to Haiti.

CARICOM, which had fraternally admitted Haiti as its fifteenth full member on July 2, 2002, was struck by the political impasse. Eugenia Charles, CARICOM's representative to the OAS, tried and failed to make headway. The opposition, she complained, "were not agreeing on anything. They cannot get together to form a plan. No one . . . was talking about what the Haitian people themselves want." [179]

In 2003, Aristide resorted to stopgap measures to deflect the growing malaise. To placate Haiti's millions of vodoun practitioners, he issued a decree recognizing vodoun and permitting its *houngans* to officiate at weddings, baptisms and funerals. He also increased the minimum wage to 70 *gourdes* daily, although the plunging exchange rate between *gourde* and U.S. dollar made this gesture ineffectual. He initiated a two-week Christmas of Solidarity Program which, at a cost of $1.6 million, offered hundreds of poor Haitians bowls of soup, gifts and free concerts, and gave out 20,000 fifty-day jobs. Aristide also sent the French government a bill for $21,685,135,571.48, the equivalent (he calculated) of the 90 million gold *francs* France had exacted in reparations from Haiti after the 1804 Revolution. Radio and television spots declared, "Hand over my dollars so I can celebrate my independence!" [180] France declined to hand over a single cent.

The Haitian people remained restive and unhappy. They did not understand why the government allowed inflation and the devalued *gourde* to jack up prices. They went on strike when the government, under intense financial pressure from international lenders, ended its subsidies to gasoline, causing the price of kerosene and low-octane gasoline to shoot up 96 and 74 percent respectively, and refrigerators to sputter and die from want of fuel. (The fortunate elite were already practised at drinking their single malt Scotch neat.) With their President's *chimèrization* and his opposition's gangsterism also on the rise, Haitians wanted security in the streets. They wanted justice, that most elusive of conditions. They wanted Aristide to resign, or they wanted him to stay and honor the dimmed promises that once shone so brightly.

Instead, they got relentless insecurity, terror and bloodshed. The story of the Amiot Metayer and the Cannibal Army is a sad and ugly glimpse into the innards of Aristide's Haiti in its terminal stages. Amiot Metayer, a former law student and anti-Duvalierist, was an Aristide militant who headed the Cannibal Army, a tough gang of *chimères,* often longshoremen. Amiot and his brother Buteur controlled the patronage at Gonaives' port, where Buteur held the position of assistant director. On one memorable foray, Metayer and his Cannibal Army targeted Pastor Luc Mesadieu, Jean-Claude Duvalier's one-time dentist turned Protestant evangelist, and a member of the anti-Aristide New Christian Movement for a New Haiti. Mesadieu managed to conceal himself, and his assistant, Ramy Daran, refused to give him away. In revenge, the Cannibal Army doused Daran with gasoline and burned him to death, then for good measure torched twenty houses.

Amiot Metayer was in the shadows of countless arsons and assassinations, including the murder of a young reformist deputy, Marc-Andre Durogène, a strong critic of smuggling and corruption at Gonaives' port. Amiot Metayer had become so notorious that arresting and judging him was almost a mantra for Aristide's opposition and the shocked international community. On July 4, 2003, Aristide capitulated to the pressure. But rather than risk a standard arrest, he "invited" his devoted supporter to the palace, where Metayer was overpowered and flown—in Aristide's personal helicopter—to the National Penitentiary.

The Cannibal Army went on the rampage, protesting so violently against Aristide's duplicity that, to defuse their fury, he had Metayer delivered back to Gonaives, albeit to the jailhouse. Buteur Metayer and the Cannibal Gang took it from there. Armed to the teeth and driving a stolen bulldozer, they smashed down the jailhouse wall and liberated Metayer and 158 (of 221) other prisoners, including Jean Tatoune, a FRAPH member jailed for life at hard labor for his role in the 1994 Raboteau massacre. The Army celebrated by torching government buildings and firing guns. The police, outmanned and out-maneuvered, retreated and summoned help from the riot police.

Metayer, cocky in his fiefdom of Raboteau, took to the airwaves of Radio Métropole to retaliate. "Aristide has betrayed the people and I call on the people of Gonaives, of Cité Soleil, of Petit Goâve, to fight. We will fight until the death!" In another broadcast: "Aristide no longer works for the people. Therefore he must go." Added Jean Tatoune, Metayer's former deadliest enemy suddenly become great friend, "We call on the entire population of the country to demonstrate against Aristide."[181]

The situation was tricky. Aristide resolved it by offering mendacious assurances to Metayer that his case would be revisited. Metayer thanked him by calling off the protests. He also set the Cannibal Army on anti-Aristide protesters and on journalists covering demonstrations. But he no longer collaborated with Jean Tatoune, who remained virulently anti-Aristide. "Aristide armed these people and he can no longer control them," Michèle Montas lamented.

Now Aristide faced more pressure, from an alliance of Haitian businessmen and industrialists, and from the OAS, about countenancing Metayer's free passage in Gonaives; Metayer and other Aristide murderers and thugs must be arrested. Metayer and Tatoune, meanwhile, were persecuting journalists and fighting each other, trashing and torching each other's strongholds.

As OAS and CARICOM demands for Metayer's arrest intensified, Aristide bought time by promising to re-arrest him. Instead, a suggestible or intimidated judge legitimized Metayer's escape by dismissing all the charges against him. Earlier, Judge Marcel Jean fled to the U.S. and a deputy prosecutor fled to the Dominican Republic for refusing to do this. "Someone can't kill people, burn their houses, and burn the courthouse and not be brought to justice," Jean said from the safety of Florida. "This country has no future if this is how justice will be treated."[182] Departing Ambassador Dean Curran concurred: "The impunity of criminals is like a stone around the neck of the Haitian economy."[183]

Aristide sent a close associate to Gonaives with an offer for Metayer: voluntarily return to the penitentiary, submit to a trial that would end in acquittal, and pocket $200,000. But Metayer had been fooled once. He declined and sent a message back to the palace. In the event of an attempt to re-arrest him, he would spill the beans about certain nefarious government activities he knew so much about.

Aristide understood Metayer's message. A few days later, a palace emissary, Odonel Paul, invited the unsuspecting Metayer out for an evening he never returned from. His tortured, bullet-riddled body was found with eyes and heart removed. Buteur Metayer and Winter Etienne, the brothers' right-hand man, soon learned about the palace's role in the killing, and declared war. Gonaives was shut down for sixteen days and became a battleground. On one side were government forces; on the other, the Cannibal Army, renamed the Artibonite National Revolutionary Front for the Liberation of Haiti, who were being trained and organized by ex-soldiers. The latter had been sent by Cap Haitien radio owner Robert Lalanne, and were armed with weapons provided by some of the Group of 184. Spokesman Winter Etienne declared on Radio Métropole:

> Aristide killed Amiot Metayer because Metayer knew he was the one who killed Jean Dominique. . . . Aristide killed Amiot because he knew that Amiot clearly said that if they arrested him, he would reveal the truth about the events of 17 December, that he would publicly declare that it was a plot, a coup mounted to kill and destroy the Convergence people. . . . We are not afraid of Aristide. The people of Gonaives are stronger than Aristide and his army. Aristide must leave and he will have to leave. That is our motto.[184]

It was the beginning of the end for Aristide's presidency, with the most ignoble of turncoats fighting furiously against the man who had inspired, mobilized and armed them in his service. Both sides unsheathed shining words, images, battle cries: Betrayal! The people! Freedom Fighters! Vengeance! Dignity! Patriotism! Rebellion! Gonaives, Haiti's heartland! Like other *chimères* and despite its new incarnation as part of the Artibonite Resistance Front, the Cannibal Army ate its own kind. On February 5, with Buteur Metayer at its head, the Army/Front led Gonaives into open rebellion.

In no time anti-Aristide reinforcements appeared: disbanded FAD'H military, former rural *chefs de section*, former FRAPH members, the disgruntled, dispossessed, disillusioned, discouraged. Aristide fought back, urging those of his still-loyal *chimères* to retaliate, attack, shed blood, save his presidency. In early February in Saint Marc, in a rare and brief victory, his forces—the PNH, the Unité de Sécurité de la Garde du Palais National (USGPN), the Haitian unit responsible for Palace Security, and a local gang known as *Bale Wouze* (Clean Sweep) fought and won against rebels in the neighborhood of La Scierie. They beat, raped and killed, including by decapitation, and in two weeks, a Human Rights Watch member confirmed, they committed at least twenty-seven murders. Bale Wouze "don't make arrests, they kill," a shocked local priest reported.[185] But Saint Marc was an exception for Artistide forces. Within two weeks, the rebellion had spread to north and central Haiti, and the government had lost control of over half the country.

And who were these winning warriors? The commander of "rebel" forces was young Guy Philippe,[186] from 1995 to 2000 an HNP officer and chief of police in Port-au-Prince's Delmas region, and an alumnus of Collège St. Louis de Gonzague, Haiti's most prestigious and well-connected high school. (Jean-Claude Duvalier had flunked his way through classes there.) At Philippe's side, under his leadership: Buteur Metayer, Winter Etienne and their Army, FRAPH men Jean Tatoune, Jodel Chamblain,[187] reputedly so ferocious that his colleagues feared him, and other ex-soldiers, such as Sergeant Remissainthe Ravix. Wealthy Haitian businessmen supplied and financed them. Advisers such as Paul Arcelin, a former Canadian professor and Haitian ambassador to the Dominican Republic, guided them. The Convergence and dissident Aristide officials—Senators Louis-Gérald Gilles, Prince Pierre Sonson, Joseph Médard, Dany Toussaint, more than one cabinet minister and palace security members encouraged them.

They moved quickly over Haiti, taking Saint-Michel de l'Attalaye, Hinche and Gonaives, gathering steam and fighters. By the time they captured Cap Haitien on February 22, thousands participated. Two days later, half of Haiti was under rebel control. On February 28, rebel reinforcements arrived by boat and bus, giving Philippe a total of about two thousand men. That same day, in preparing for the grand finale, an attack on Port-au-Prince, he also bought $75,000 worth of ammunition. Philippe visualized himself as Haiti's Hugo Chavez and he appointed himself chief of the (disbanded but now self-resurrecting) underground military. Meetings with Convergence politicians about how to run post-Aristide Haiti fed his illusions. "What had been agreed . . . was that we would establish a government of national consensus with representatives from all sectors of the country, including Lavalas. The president of the *cour de cassation* would be Provisional President, and my men were to be responsible for the country's security, without any foreign intervention," he recalled.[188]

But unknown to Philippe, other more important negotiations were already deciding Haiti's future, and they did not include him. Nor, unsurprisingly, did they include Aristide, whom several parties to the negotiations had already decided to expel. CARICOM was decidedly not one of these. Yet despite the vigorous efforts of fellow West Indians to draft an acceptable power-sharing agreement that included disarming the *chimères*, Aristide alone agreed to it. The opposition refused out of hand, and their U.S. and French associates easily swallowed their position that no compromise with Aristide, "the source of the problem," was acceptable.[189] (Guy Philippe's interesting version is that "the leaders of Haiti's rotten political class and mafioso oligarchy convinced the Americans and the French to get rid of Aristide. . . . Aristide was afraid, very afraid, and he agreed to resign.")[190]

Aristide was trapped. He warned of terrible bloodshed and pleaded for international military intervention "as soon as possible" to quash the rebellion. The UN Security Council, France, Canada and the U.S. declined, although the latter had landed fifty Marines to protect the U.S. Embassy. On February 27, the rebels were less than thirty miles from Port-au-Prince. What to do? Stories about ensuing events vary wildly. Aristide's, astonishingly, is that he had nothing to worry about, South Africa was sending a shipment of weapons, and the rebels stood no chance. The Americans, knowing they had mere hours to act before Aristide's forces mopped up the rebellion, "grabbed their chance while they had it, and bundled us . . . [Aristide, Mildred and several others] onto a plane in the middle of the night." Translation: the Americans kidnapped Aristide. Guy Philippe corroborated this, saying that the opposition politicians who were the most influential with foreigners, if not Haitians,[191] had advised the U.S. Embassy to kidnap Aristide to prevent Philippe from seizing power.

A host of other sources, including U.S. Ambassador Foley and several reporters begged to differ, saying that Aristide had pleaded with them for help and that, at the last minute, they arranged it. They also recalled that Mildred had left Christine and Michaelle in Florida after they all attended a funeral there, which could be seen as evidence that Aristide (or at least Mildred) realized that his days in Haiti were likely numbered. But Reginald Dumas met nobody, at the UN or elsewhere, who believed the U.S. story. "It was generally agreed that Aristide was not a nice person, but was that sufficient reason to arrange his departure?" he mused.[192]

Another Haitian president had been forced into exile. Aristide and Mildred were flown first to Bagui in the Central African Republic, then to Jamaica, where Christine and Michaelle rejoined them, and finally to South Africa. For seven years, the South African government lodged the family in the posh Pretoria suburb of Muckleneuk and provided security guards, office staff, transportation and living expenses at an annual cost of 5 million rand, about $712,990 annually.[193] Both the Aristides were also appointed non-stipendiary research fellows, Jean-Bertrand in the College of Human Sciences and Mildred in the Centre for African Renaissance Studies.[194]

In exile, Aristide learned Zulu, suffered serious eye problems that led to multiple surgeries and yearned to return to Haiti. In as many press conferences as his South African hosts permitted, and in interviews and the occasional article, he expressed no remorse about his corrupt, chaotic and violent regime. In his version of events he had been sinned against but had never sinned; he had been a blameless president with many important accomplishments, albeit one who confessed to not being a good politician. His opponents and critics, he declared, must be in the thrall of white men.

Back in Haiti, Aristide's presidential replacement was Boniface Alexandre, the Supreme Court Justice, as the Constitution specified. On March 5, 2004, a Tripartite Council appointed a seven-member Council of Sages representing the Catholic and Anglican Churches, the Convergence, Fanmi Lavalas, the state university, Signal FM Radio and a women's group.[195] The Sages bucked Haiti's recent experiences of months-long periods with no prime minister and in only a few days agreed on sixty-nine-year-old Gérard Latortue, one of a short list of candidates that included former General Herard Abraham and former prime minister Smarck Michel.

A day later, Latortue flew back to the country he had left fifteen years earlier and was sworn into office. A Paris-educated economics professor, he had fled Papa Doc's Haiti and later worked for the UN's Organization for Industrial Development in Togo, Ivory Coast and Vienna. In 1988 he had returned to Haiti and served as Foreign Minister in Leslie Manigat's four-month presidency. Afterward, he had relocated to South Florida, where he hosted the popular Haitian Television Network of America (HTN) talk shows *Revue de la semaine* and *L'invité*. In 2001, Latortue reported, President Aristide had invited him to join his cabinet, but he had declined and remained in Florida.

Unlike his predecessors, Prime Minister Latortue was expected to act as Haiti's CEO, while Boniface, its unelected President, acted as a figurehead of state. Latortue's task was to govern and prepare the country for elections to produce a new President. In tumultuous post-Aristide Haiti, this process would take two years.

Though the U.S. and the United Nations Stabilization Mission in Haiti (MINUSTAH)[196] rushed to provide military security, Aristide's departure had not halted the advance of the armed insurgents marauding the countryside, attacking and killing Aristide supporters and burning down their houses and businesses. Guy Philippe, in particular, was out of control. He declared in a radio broadcast that Haiti was in his hands, that he would be a candidate in the upcoming presidential elections, and that he intended to arrest Aristide's loyal prime minister, Yvon Neptune, on corruption charges. After his announcement, a mob burned and looted Neptune's house. Neptune himself had to be helicoptered to safety. Philippe's colleague, Louis-Jodel Chamblain, gave himself up to Haitian authorities, saying tearfully, "The Haitian people will see if justice is for real." Philippe, hiding out from the UN forces but not from journalists willing to trek out to visit him, applauded his friend: "I'm sorry, but Chamblain is a hero." One U.S. official was appalled. "Talk about taking one step forward and two steps back," he said.[197]

Latortue's two-year regime was marked by the same divisiveness as Aristide's. Only his cabinet, which included both presidential runners-up and several technocrats, was an exception. Elsewhere, human rights investigators reported that attacks, persecution and murders, most targeting Aristide partisans, had increased in number and severity. (It didn't help that in Gonaives, Latortue had praised the rebels as "freedom fighters.") The number of rape victims also skyrocketed as sexual assault became a political weapon.

The new government, wielding judicial tools, banned Yvon Neptune and thirty-six other Aristide officials from leaving Haiti before corruption charges could be laid against them. On June 27, Neptune surrendered himself to the police and remained in custody for over two years without being charged; finally, he was released on health and humanitarian grounds. Much of his incarceration was spent in solitary confinement, in a $5,000-a-month villa the UN peacekeepers paid for and guarded.

Human rights groups decried Neptune's treatment, as well as other wrongful detentions and abuses. They also had grave concerns about Latortue's security chief, his cousin, Youri Latortue, who was Guy Philippe's good friend and a reputed drug trafficker nicknamed Mister 30 Percent for the amount of kickback he allegedly demanded on government contracts.

CARICOM, too, was concerned, and refused to recognize Latortue's presidency. The Latortue government responded angrily, withdrawing Haiti from CARICOM[198] and announcing that it would extradite Aristide so he could be tried on charges of corruption and human rights abuses. Latortue also ridiculed and dropped Aristide's demand for reparations from France, and granted a tax holiday of up to three years to large (but not small) commercial enterprises that had suffered during the "troubles" preceding Aristide's ouster.

In September of 2004, Haiti was struck by a natural disaster in the form of Jeanne, which began as a tropical storm and then reached its crescendo as a hurricane. Jeanne dumped rain onto the denuded mountains, which funneled it toward the Artibonite Valley and Gonaives. The raging water created mudslides and flooding, washing away crops, cars, houses, and livestock, and drowning nearly three thousand people. Two hundred thousand people lost their homes. Jeanne also severely damaged Port-de-Paix, Gros Morne and Chansolme.

Haiti's preparations for presidential elections slowed to a crawl. On February 7, 2006, after four delays and with substantial assistance from the OAS and the UN, the elections finally took place. Rene Préval ran against thirty-two other contenders, including Guy Philippe,[199] Franck Romain, Dany Toussaint, Leslie Manigat, Marc Bazin, Gerard Gourges and Luc Mesadieu, and he won 48.8 percent of the vote. But the elections were marred by widespread fraud: the most egregious example was that ballots marked for Préval had been discarded; they were later discovered in a garbage dump. Préval's supporters erupted in rage at what they styled electoral theft. Under pressure, the Electoral Council and the Latortue government agreed to forgo the constitutionally mandated new round of elections and do a recalculation of the original tally that gave Préval a majority of 51.1 percent, and victory.[200] In May, after the April 21 second round of elections filled the thirty-seat Senate and ninety-nine-member Chamber of Deputies, Préval was sworn in as President. He replaced Latortue with his old colleague Jacques-Edouard Alexis as Prime Minister. Latortue, who had returned to his home in Boca Raton, watched the inaugural ceremony on television and rejoiced that he was finally free.

Préval and his cabinet inherited a nation still seething with political violence and bitterness, street and organized drug crime, rape and kidnappings that increasingly targeted children, a deteriorating environment and the terrible destruction of Hurricane Jeanne. The treasury was depleted, and civil servants were paid sporadically or not at all. At one point, workers at Port-au-Prince's General Hospital, unpaid for six months, dramatized their strike action by piling the corpses of eleven children higgledy-piggledy onto a gurney and putting them on public display in the hospital courtyard in an effort to force the government's hand.[201]

In addition to Haiti's chronic insolvency, Préval had to deal with the most abusive remnants of Aristide's regime. As a secret cable from U.S. Ambassador Janet Sanderson reported, Préval "either tolerated or was forced to accept gross abuses on the part of close associates of Aristide."[202] Now Préval distanced himself from Aristide, and at his first meeting with Ambassador Sanderson "bitterly" reminded her that visiting American officials had often slighted him by making him "the last stop after Tabarre (where Aristide lived) when visitors came."[203]

With Aristide gone, Préval attempted to smash the heavily armed urban gangs that Aristide had encouraged. "I will not control them, I will eliminate them," he vowed.[204] By the end of 2006, these former *chimères* were lords of Port-au-Prince's Cité Soleil, a slum with warrens of shanties that were dangerous and difficult to access. The police were either frightened of or linked to these criminals, who acted with impunity. They kidnapped, raped, stole and killed. They hijacked vehicles on the nearby airport road and terrorized the port, industrial area and petroleum storage building. They hired themselves out to protect and to assassinate. Their cocky leaders gained notoriety in boastful television interviews, and won popularity by sharing some of their booty with acolytes, and by giving handouts to slum dwellers and paying their children's school fees. Préval's uncompromising "disarm or die" attitude toward these gangs mostly failed. Later, however, his strategy of arranging truces among rival gangs was more successful. As well, a drastic reduction in the number of high-profile kidnappings made the streets safer.

Préval also attempted to crack down on Haiti's seemingly intractable drug trafficking but made little progress. Préval's anger, Ambassador Sanderson realized, was fueled by "a growing frustration with the inflow of drugs into the country's political process and the irritation that his government is unable to address something that could indeed pose a personal threat to his future after the presidency."[205] A case in point was Préval's fury when Guy Philippe, whom the U.S. had indicted for drug trafficking, evaded arrest after a supposedly surprise raid by heavily armed U.S. Drug Enforcement Agency and Haitian anti-drug agents. They swooped down on his yellow, two-story house in the hillside above Les Cayes to find only his wife and maid at home, while Philippe was conveniently absent.

Unlike those Haitian office-holders who saw drug trafficking as a golden goose in a nation of scrawny pullets, Préval understood that it was profoundly corrupting and ruinous to good governance. He argued that the drug trade in Haiti was driven by drug addiction in the U.S., an American problem that the U.S. should try to eradicate. Without a huge demand for illegal narcotics in North America, Haitian drug trafficking would not exist. During a press conference with visiting Canadian Prime Minister Stephen Harper, Préval underscored the urgency of the problem. Drug traffickers, he declared, are "the single biggest destabilizing factor facing weak countries like Haiti."[206]

Poverty and food insecurity were other destabilizing factors. In April of 2008, hungry food rioters challenged Préval's presidency as hungry Haitians echoed world protests against soaring food costs: In just one year, rice, beans and fruit prices in Haiti had risen by 50 percent. The riots turned deadly as four rioters and one Nigerian UN soldier were shot to death. Haitian senators led by Youri Latortue blamed Prime Minister Alexis for the crisis and, in a special session, voted him out of office. With Alexis scapegoated, Préval sought to defuse the situation by reducing the price of a sack of rice from $51 to $43. He then managed, on the third try, to replace Alexis with a new Prime Minister the Senate approved—his old reform-minded comrade Michèle Pierre-Louis.[207] She became Minister of Justice and Public Security as well.

That triumph was drowned out by four hurricanes that pummeled Haiti in quick succession that summer: Fay, Gustav, Hanna and Ike. The skies opened up, and rain pounded eroded hillsides into oozing mud that slithered downward, covering everything in its path, laying waste fields full of crops[208] and smashing houses. The plains flooded and transformed huge chunks of Haiti into mudflats. Nearly eight hundred drowned, and hundreds of thousands lost their homes and livelihoods. Cities became slick, muddy ruins—low-lying Gonaives was inundated by over nine feet of water—and major roads were unusable.

Prime Minister Michèle Pierre-Louis identified the roots of the problem: deforestation and erosion, the primacy of charcoal fuel and poor farming techniques, the planned destruction of Haiti's agriculture and the intense urbanization that followed, and the reckless construction of shanties on fragile slopes and hillsides. "The whole country is facing an ecological disaster," she said. "We cannot keep going on like this. We are going to disappear one day. There will not be four hundred, five hundred or a thousand deaths. There are going to be a million deaths."[209]

In November, UN Secretary-General Ban Ki-moon commissioned the economist Paul Collier, author of *The Bottom Billion: Why the Poor-*

est Countries are Failing and What Can Be Done About It, to report on the economic impact of the hurricanes on Haiti's economy and to propose a strategy for achieving economic security. Collier visited Haiti for four days in December, factored Haiti into the Bottom Billion, and submitted his report in January of 2009.[210]

What Collier saw in Haiti did not dampen his habitual optimism about the possibilities of economic development: "Haiti is classified as a 'fragile state,'" he wrote. "Yet compared to other fragile states its fundamentals are highly propitious. Essentially, if the international community cannot succeed in Haiti then it is hard to see it succeeding elsewhere." Unlike fragile or failed African states, Haiti was in a stable region close to the U.S. market. The Dominican Republic, its immediate neighbor, was "peaceful and prosperous," and offered no "clandestine support for guerrilla groups"—a curious observation, given the Dominican tradition of allowing Haitian dissidents to launch their strikes from Dominican soil. Haiti's status as a narco-state was "merely a matter of international criminality" and ought to prompt North Americans to "invest in achieving decisive change" in their region's weakest link. Collier saw no evidence of "intractable structural socio-political problems," such as ethnic strife, organized paramilitary political groups or an army "with delusions of a political role." Its government was "good by the standards of most post-conflict situations. Both the President and the Prime Minister have integrity, experience and ability, and a deep concern with the maintenance of social peace." (Ironically, Pierre-Louis would be fired ten months later.) Collier did take note of "powerful forces for inertia" but thought they would not "rule out more limited and tightly focused action."

Haiti's greatest potential lay in the assembly industry, Collier wrote, and its "huge and proximate diaspora," which provided the homeland with "a massive flow of remittances, a reservoir of skills, and a powerful political lobby." That lobby, he said, had won Haiti Canada's second largest aid programme and via the U.S. Haitian Hemispheric Opportunity through Partnership Encouragement Act (HOPE II), "the best trade deal on earth, with duty-free, quota-free access and generous rules of origin guaranteed for a decade."[211] Haiti was "now the world's safest production location for garments," and thanks to "its poverty and relatively unregulated labour market," its labor costs were "fully competitive with China, which is the global benchmark." Collier saw promise in Haiti's experienced labor pool of now unemployed garment assemblers, the country's ports, its access to Dominican ports and its proximity to the American market.

Collier also warned that Haiti's "exceptionally rapid population growth" and accelerating "youth tsunami" required immediate attention in the form of jobs. (An unspoken subtext was that this tsunami might otherwise crash down on American shores. In 2009 the U.S. was preparing to repatriate thirty thousand illegal Haitians.) The nation's development was also contingent on the existence of basic services, food security and environmental sustainability.

Collier's report echoed the American vision of Haiti as a low-waged product assembler dotted with Export Processing Zones (EPZ) reinforced by a proper legal framework and essential infrastructure: ports, roads, electricity. But his rosy picture of one hundred thousand newly employed Haitians spinning off a million more jobs did not square with calculations that a minimum of 15,244.48 *gourdes* per month (about $13.88 a day) was needed to support one adult and two children,[212] without any of the discretionary spending that would create new jobs. Nor do tax-exempt factories contribute to social services or have much "value added" in Haiti.[213]

As well, Collier's comment that "the existing industry finds that male and female labour are equally good and employs them in equal proportions so that the social consequences of employment expansion need not be divisive" was puzzling, because the majority of Haitian garment assembly workers are women, which has striking social implications.[214] But if he intended his comment to guide factory owners in their employment practices rather than describe usual practices, that casts it in a different light.

The UN and the U.S. endorsed the Collier Report without reservation. Bill Clinton was named UN envoy to Haiti. Ban Ki-moon, Clinton's traveling companion in Haiti, lauded HOPE II, with its "duty-free, quota-free access to U.S. markets for the next nine years," as Haiti's Big Chance. Ban concluded: "This is a foundation to build on. It is a chance to consolidate the progress Haiti has made in winning a measure of political stability, with the help of the U.N. peacekeeping mission, and move beyond aid to genuine economic development. Given the country's massive unemployment, particularly among youth, that means one thing above all else: jobs."[215]

Like it or not (and reinforcing Clinton's admission that his neoliberal economic policy had purposely destroyed Haiti's agriculture in order to drive people from farmland to urban factories), Haiti's future was in assembly garments. Its needy people, who garbed themselves in "Kennedy," the name for cheaply purchased, secondhand, U.S.-donated clothes, would find salvation in factories established in Export Producing Zones. Ban enthused that they might even aspire to earn, like the tee-shirt assemblers he and Clinton had visited, the munificent sum of $7.00 a day, which would "[vault] them into the Haitian middle class."[216]

Aristide had caved in, and now Préval did, too. His cooperation[217] won his insecure nation essential security in the form of a renewal of the UN's mandate to provide security through MINUSTAH. At the April 2009 Haiti Donors' Conference in Washington, Haiti also obtained pledges totaling $353 million.[218] But Préval faced determined resistance from his own team as Haitian politicians managed to unite and pass a bill that almost tripled the minimum wage from 70 *gourdes* ($1.75) to 200 *gourdes* ($5) daily, not enough (as per Ban's calculations) to vault them into the middle class, but more than enough to alarm elite and foreign employers who would lose $ 0.18 per pair of pants.

Préval was caught between two powerful and conflicting interests. Even if HOPE II was flawed, it had passed only after ferocious battles in Congress. American garment manufacturers with Asian factories argued that granting Haiti such easy access to U.S. markets would hurt their competing products, and they lobbied hard to defeat it. Lobbyists for American manufacturers with Haitian business interests, on the other hand, strongly supported HOPE II (as did manufacturers in Haiti, crippled by the embargo). These manufacturers also insisted that low wages were essential to compensate for the costs associated with Haiti's almost total lack of infrastructure. Préval, with his back to the wall, refused to officially acknowledge the minimum-wage legislation.[219] In the resulting confusion, both manufacturers and workers were unsure of its legality, and it was often flouted.[220]

Préval, navigating one political crisis after another, next lost his able and highly regarded prime minister. In late October of 2009, scrappy senators voted to remove Pierre-Louis for reasons that were unclear. Perplexed political analysts wondered whether (and if so, why) Préval desired her political demise. Was it because of rumors that she was a lesbian and lived with a woman? Or committed same-sex adultery when she was married?[221] The nine-hour debate, which invoked "morality," yet referred only to alleged procedural missteps in the 2008 electoral ratification of the prime minister, was a marathon of shouting and stamping, with raging senators "storming out of the room, accusing each other of carrying weapons and marching up and down the aisle of the narrow chamber as Senate President Kelly Bastien rang a silver bell to call for order."

The about-to-be-fired Prime Minister refused to attend what she knew would be a kangaroo session. In a gracious but biting letter to Bastien, Pierre-Louis explained. "At a time when efforts are under way for Haiti to join the international community and it has possibilities of investment, national and international, to better the lives of the Haitian population . . . my government decides not to participate in this hearing. I leave the senators of the republic to face their responsibility in front of the nation."[222]

Within two weeks, Haiti had its sixth prime minister since 2004, and another new cabinet. New Prime Minister Max Bellerive's government had the same priorities as the old one, he announced: improving infrastructure, attracting investment, building up the garment assembly sector to take advantage of HOPE II, and commitment to Clinton's vision for Haiti. "The only way that we are going to change Haiti is through private investment, through creating jobs in Haiti," Bellerive said, just as Pierre-Louis had.[223]

This latest political crisis was resolved. Préval had achieved a fragile political stability and reduced insecurity in the streets. His prostate cancer had not recurred, and his overall health was good. It was time for the President to make changes in his personal life, and on December 6, 2009, he married his fiancée, Elisabeth Debrosse Delatour, the brilliant, disciplined and polished economic adviser who had nudged out even his beloved sister and close friends as his most trusted confidante.

EPILOGUE

ON THE AFTERNOON OF TUESDAY, JANUARY 13, 2010, the President worked in his office, and outside on the National Palace's broad front stairs, the new First Lady stood conferring with her cultural adviser, renowned artist Philippe Dodard, about how to position schoolchildren on those same stairs during upcoming Carnival celebrations. Just before 4:45 p.m., Dodard walked away to join his eighteen-year-old son, who was waiting in the car. Préval and Elisabeth headed out to attend the 150th anniversary of the Haitian School of Law. At 4:53, a 7.0 magnitude earthquake erupted 8.1 miles beneath the earth's surface and struck Haiti with one of the world's worst natural disasters.

Underneath the National Palace, the earth trembled and shook. In thirty-five seconds captured in slow motion by security video cameras, the imposing structure shuddered and crumbled. White clouds of pulverized plaster and other detritus billowed out and then up into the sky, while crackles, booms and explosive sounds filled the air. The quavering walls sent chunks of ruined material smashing down onto the ground. The magnificent dome collapsed. A security guard dashed outside, arms outstretched and flailing as he struggled to keep upright and to fend off the deadly hail. In the palace's red-carpeted interior corridor, two guards ran frantically up and down, yanking at door knobs to find an exit. Then, as the building blasted its death throes, the men disappeared in a haze of crushed masonry. Soon they reappeared onscreen, still pitching from side to side in their frenzy to escape being buried alive.

The palace was a microcosm of the nation. For thirty-five long seconds the earth under much of Haiti shook, from the epicenter of Léogane, 90 percent destroyed, Gressier and Carrefour, nearly 50 percent,

Jacmel more than 50 percent, Petit-Goâve 15 percent destroyed, to Port-au-Prince, the bursting capital of three million crammed into a city designed for a few hundred thousand, 60 percent now in ruins. And, at 4:54 p.m., a long keening rose as Port-au-Prince's stricken inhabitants vocalized their terror and grief. Hundreds of thousands were injured or dying, and countless were dead.

It was estimated that at least three hundred thousand had perished, as bodies were found interred in collapsed buildings, littering streets and courtyards, and crushed under cement or brick rubble. For weeks after, bodies were pulled or prised out of the ruins; a few survivors were removed, too, some with amputations performed to extricate them.

Families were severed, parents rendered childless, children orphaned. The earthquake decimated the civil service and wreaked havoc on the education system: Five hundred teachers died, along with two hundred other education workers and four thousand students. Victims included rich and poor. Among them were Rudy Bennett, Michèle Bennett Duvalier's younger brother; Carmelle and Cavour Delatour, parents of the well-connected brothers Patrick, Lionel, Mario and Leslie (Elisabeth Préval's deceased husband); Archbishop Joseph Miot of Port-au-Prince; Georges Anglade, writer and Préval adviser, with his wife, Mireille; Micha Gaillard, opposition leader; Hedi Annabi, head of the UN mission to Haiti; and Doug Coates, the Canadian acting UN police commissioner. All of Haiti grieved.

Scores of aftershocks tormented survivors. Three million were affected by the earthquake, and at least one and half million made homeless. Survivors were traumatized. "I imagine that not since the Crimean War have surgeons seen and amputated so many limbs," said an on-site anesthesiologist from Doctors without Borders. "Can you imagine having an amputation with no anesthesia, or a lingering and spreading infection with no antibiotics, or a child in need of an injection with only a large-gauge needle meant for an adult?" asked an American medical relief worker.

But until foreign relief workers struggled through the broken landscape days later, nobody came to the rescue, or so it seemed to increasingly hungry, thirsty and exhausted survivors forced to sleep outside the walls of unsafe buildings, sheltered by bedsheets. The one source for news and survival tips was Signal FM 90.5, the sole surviving radio station, which assumed the role of a community bulletin board. Where was the Haitian government? Why was it missing in action? Because the government administration had fallen as the ministry buildings collapsed onto civil servants and the legislative building onto the lawmakers. Michel Clairie, the vice-president of the Senate, tried and failed to escape, and was rescued five hours later, buried under rubble. Public buildings near the palace were leveled; the ministries of the Interior and of Health, the Tax Office, the Courthouse and the Senate were all leveled, too. Tax receipts, legal records and land and property deeds were obliterated. The police station still stood but was unsafe. The old Casernes Dessalines was a heap of bricks. Sixteen thousand civil servants, more than 20 percent of the total, lay dead in the ruins. (Those inclined to sneak out earlier, Haitians said, were spared the fate of their more dedicated colleagues.) The earthquake demolished 73 of Haiti's 373 hospitals, clinics and training institutes, and killed and injured doctors, nurses and medical personnel. The Hotel Christopher, temporary headquarters of the UN, crashed down and killed 102 UN staff.

Haitians could find neither solace nor sanctuary inside churches, none of which remained standing, not even the great Catholic Cathedral or the famed Episcopalian Église Ste Trinité, with its famous murals. But many people gathered together and prayed outside the remains of these majestic buildings.

Ruins were everywhere as officials tallied the damage: Over 60 percent of Port-au-Prince was destroyed. Two hundred and fifty thousand buildings were smashed, including twenty-five thousand commercial establishments, which brought the private sector to its knees. Overnight, Haiti lost 50 percent of its Gross National Product, an estimated $11 to $14 billion. In every possible way, the earthquake exposed Haiti's gaping fault lines, the catastrophic mismanagement, exploitation, inequities and corruption that were so integral to the Duvalier legacy and so little changed even democratic decades later.

Duvalierism explained why Haiti's earthquake had such terrible consequences compared to one of similar magnitude in Chile just six weeks later. In Chile, a nation with good governance and an infrastructure boasting earthquake-resistant buildings, just five hundred people died. But during the Duvalier era, environmental degradation and deforestation had begun the steady migration of poor farming families into the cities, where the growing population was jam-packed into shoddy housing in slums.

The corruption that permeated the Haitian state extended to the construction industry, where building codes were ignored and inspectors accepted bribes to overlook flaws in structures that would later crumble in the earthquake. In minister of tourism Patrick Delatour's words, "The death toll that we have sustained out of that earthquake is due . . . to the habit that the Haitian people have in building without builders, doing architecture without architects, and planning without planners— meaning in fact using techniques of construction that are totally out of code and out of standard." This habit, he might have added, is directly traceable to the corruption of Duvalierism, and explains as well the collapsed port, destroyed roads and impenetrable congestion that for weeks prevented substantial aid from reaching the ruined heartland.

Within weeks in Port-au-Prince, 1.7 million Haitians were refugees, living in squalid settlements built from bedsheets, tarps and tents. These camps were pitched on any unoccupied patch of land, the lawn outside the National Palace, street meridians, the Pétionville Golf Club, private and government land and in the courtyards of even tiny houses too unsafe to enter. Camps swelled into quasi-permanent settlements, unequal and rivalrous, as foreign NGOs, stretched to the limit of their resources, took responsibility for those they could, while others were bereft of food, drinking water, fuel, sanitation, equipment, tools, communication, lights and medical supplies. Lacking drainage, camps flooded in the rainy season. Women and girls were unsafe there. As insecurity festered along with misery, violence in the form of rape stalked the unlit camps and spared no one, not even children as young as two years old.

But the worse tragedy was the absence—many described it as abdication—of the government. "Pain made me speechless. As a person I was paralyzed," Préval later attempted to explain. "I was much criticized for not having spoken. [But] to say what? To the thousands of parents whose children were dead. To the hundreds of schoolchildren I was hearing scream, 'Come help me!' " He paused and sighed. "I couldn't find the words to say to those people." One consequence of this paralysis was that NGOs bypassed Haitian officials and, in the name of efficiency and transparency, assumed control of these refugee camp fiefdoms. "International donors have often been unwilling to invest in state institutions, perpetuating their weakness," concluded the authors of *Building a More Resilient Haitian State*. "Corruption, political turmoil, and a general lack of capacity encourage international donors to channel funds through NGOs instead. As a result, the Haitian state is significantly

weaker than it could be, and dependence on foreign donors is reinforced."

Yet so much money was available to rebuild! At the Donors' Conference at UN headquarters in New York in March of 2010, over one
hundred and fifty countries and international organizations pledged
$5.3 billion over the next eighteen months. "Thank you," President
Préval responded. "The international community did their part, and
now the Haitian people will do their share." Hillary Clinton insisted on
it. "The leaders of Haiti must take responsibility for their country's reconstruction," she said. "And we in the global community must also do
things differently. It will be tempting to fall back on old habits—to work
around the government rather than to work with them as partners, or to
fund a scattered array of well-meaning projects rather than making the
deeper, long-term investments that Haiti needs now."

But there were other realities. As the cynical or perhaps Pollyanna-
ish saying goes, every crisis contains opportunity, and in Haiti, catastrophic crises suggested colossal opportunity. The NGOs grasped that
opportunity most effectively, the elite and government most rapaciously
and cunningly.

NGOs are instruments of the aid industry, and a substantial part of
foreign aid is funneled through them. Haiti, nicknamed "The Republic
of NGOs," has more NGOs present than anywhere else on the planet.
Before the earthquake, more than three thousand NGOs delivered services that the governments of most sovereign states customarily deliver.
These services included everything from education and medical care
(Partners in Health and the Cuban physicians were the finest) to—
ironically—feeding programs geared to the victims of the agriculture-
destroying policies instituted by the donor governments.

One consequence of the presence of NGOs is that Haiti's governments are circumvented and made weaker and more ineffectual. The
Haitian state becomes dependent on foreign aid, and on the NGOs and
their contractors who control it, reinforcing its inadequate and compromised infrastructure. A culture of vying for foreign assistance encour-
ages the needy to engage in a rhetoric of competing hardships and
atrocities, which their leaders and elite exploit to further their own entirely different interests.

One year after the earthquake, Oxfam would issue a stinging report: *Haiti Still Buried Under the Rubble of Dueling NGOs*. Despite
Hillary Clinton's scolding and Préval's promises, the apocalyptic condi-

tion of post-earthquake Haiti defied all attempts at reform. Though they shared a mandate to tackle Haiti's broken infrastructure, the NGOs also waged war on each other; instead of cooperating and coordinating, they squabbled, double-dealt and struck out for themselves and their own aims.

The catastrophic earthquake might have been the catalyst for a collective moment of truth in the form of a spiritual rebirth on the part of Haiti's government. But though Préval continued his workaholic schedule, his administration seemed mired in inertia, focused on elaborately detailed plans that were never translated into tangible achievements. Official corruption continued unchecked, though in Haiti, as in other poor countries, "corruption levels can mean the difference between life or death when money for hospitals or clean water is at play," as Huguette Labelle, the president of Transparency International, has observed.

After, as before, the earthquake, customs officials at both port and airport were obstructive and corrupt. While Port-au-Prince lay buried under rubble, Port Customs authorities blocked earth-moving equipment. Doctors without Borders, unable to retrieve twenty vehicles from customs, had to spend $126,000 on rental cars. The batteries on two Red Cross/Red Crescent tanker trucks for use in sanitation went dead after weeks at the port. Road-building equipment, ambulances, mattresses and bedding, medical supplies and all manner of urgent aid items were blocked. Port-au-Prince customs chief Jean-Jacques Valentin seemed unconcerned and scolded NGOs for improper paperwork. "A minimum respect for the rules is needed," he said. "Buildings may have collapsed but the law is still there."

The customs office at Port Lafiteau, north of Port-au-Prince, was no better, and kept the Wishmobile, a thirty-six foot-mobile medical unit with examination and triage rooms, with accompanying ambulance and a container of medical supplies, waiting for a tax bill to be paid. "I obey and apply the law, I do not interpret it," declared Eric Charles, Port Customs director. It was not that simple. After the NGO involved refused to pay the initial tax of $65,000, customs agents demanded repeat inspections and then demanded $23,379 to release the vehicles. The executive director of the Granted Wish Foundation, Stefanie R. Colleti, said that customs officials also pressured the NGO to transfer the vehicles' into their names. Meanwhile two emergency room physicians flown into Port-au-Prince were prevented from offering their medical services in the Wishmobile.

The attitude of customs reflected the attitude of the government. Land issues are another excellent illustration, because the difficulty—or impossibility—of conquering the issue of land ownership was at the root of the failure to establish permanent settlements. A glimpse at Haiti's byzantine land laws suggests the immensity of the problem. To buy state land that one is squatting on, for instance, requires legal proof of at least five years' occupancy, or at least proof that such a contract has been applied for. It involves, explains economist Mats Lundahl, "16 different public authorities and 64 administrative steps and requires a total of 749 days. Thereafter the tenant has to pay rent regularly for five years before he or she can initiate the process that leads to a purchase. Altogether 31 public entities have to be involved in 111 administrative steps over a period of 4,112 days. Finally, the price of the plot has to be paid."

How does this affect land in and around Port-au-Prince, home to more than half of Haiti's population? Six years before the earthquake, 263,000 homes had no legal title and were on various kinds of illegally occupied lands. Thirty-eight percent of these were large parcels of agricultural land subdivided by squatters; 24 percent were deteriorated plots near the city core; 6 percent were in Cité Soleil and government-approved; 2 percent were privately owned lands; and 7 percent were lands with government-approved housing projects on them. Pre-earthquake, this situation deprived millions of their real-estate capital, humble or not; these lands were, in Lundahl's words, "dead or sleeping capital." After the earthquake, the most pressing issue became obtaining important swaths of suitable land to use in establishing permanent settlements and rehousing Haiti's internal refugees. The government had the power to legislate solutions. Instead, the land issue confounded it to the point of paralysis.

Private land issues were more blatant. The government had the right to seize private land on the basis of "eminent domain" and compensate owners fairly. But the example of the "model" camp at Corail-Cesseless tells an ugly story of how Haiti's government exercised that right. In the winter of 2010, Préval invoked eminent domain and seized a block of land fifteen miles north of Port-au-Prince to establish a model camp. It was a vast property, one and a quarter times the size of Manhattan, treeless and backed by denuded mountains, a flood plain during the rainy season, when torrents of water knocked down the camp's tents and terrified residents.

Corail-Cesselesse was also distant from food markets and employment opportunities. Aid workers criticized its location and wondered why it was chosen for such ambitious development, and equipped with better infrastructure—security, lighting, latrines and storm-resistant tents—than other camps. U.S. military engineers and UN peacekeepers improved the soil, grading and covering it with gravel. Corail-Cesselesse was also designated as a site for garment assembly factories.

Investigative journalists revealed the mystery behind Corail-Cesselesse. The owner was Nabatec Development, whose president, Gerard-Emily "Aby" Brun, directed the relocation of about five thousand displaced Haitians to the camp. And as compensation for the seizure of its wasteland, Nabatec was eligible for part of the $7 million the Préval government had budgeted for the purpose. Elsewhere, too, landowners demanded astronomical prices for their land when the government approached them.

Before year's end, Haiti entered the age of cholera. The outbreak began in the rice-growing Artibonite region, and then spread throughout the country, killing thousands and sickening hundreds of thousands. Cholera found a perfect host in Haiti because people there were forced to drink the same polluted water they bathed and laundered in. MINUS-TAH's Nepalese soldiers were widely blamed for introducing the disease, a South Asian strain, through waste water from their outhouses on the edge of the Artibonite River. Terrified protesters rioted, demanding that the Nepalese leave. "The epidemic of cholera, a highly contagious disease, is no longer a simple emergency, it's now a matter of national security," Haiti's Health Ministry director, Gabriel Thimote, warned.

By March of 2011, the reported tally was 4,672 dead out of 252,640 cases diagnosed, and medical experts cautioned that these figures underreported the disease, which afflicted so many people in remote areas lacking health care. Without clean water, antibiotics and vaccinations, the otherwise easily curable disease was a killer. A report in the *Lancet* predicted about 779,000 new cases between March and November of 2011. "[It] will last far longer than the initial projections," said Dr. Sanjay Basu, a study author.

By the first anniversary of the earthquake, Haiti looked too much like it had a year earlier. The odious tent cities had millions of inhabitants. One of the very best was located in the former Pétionville Golf Club and was run by American movie actor Sean Penn. *Mother Jones* reporter Mac McLelland visited. She was thirsty but hesitated to buy a drink so she could avoid the communal toilets. "It's only eight o'clock, but it's dark, and plenty of girls before me have been assaulted on that short trip." The toilets stank overpoweringly and spread contagious diseases. The stench inside one "fantastically neat" mud-floored plastic hovel caused McLelland to vomit.

Camp residents included a sick unemployed mother who hadn't eaten in days, amputees who struggled to navigate the muddy paths, and a skinny man in frantic search of MINUSTAH soldiers because thugs were threatening to burn down his tent if he and his family didn't move out; they wanted his spot and his tarp. And this was the best camp, envied by other camp dwellers.

Haitians and foreigners lament the lack of substantial progress—the tent cities and the nine million cubic meters of rubble remaining are its most visible signs—and debate its causes and possible solutions. Donors have not delivered most of the money pledged: As of the end of 2010, only 21 percent of the donations had been disbursed, a fraction of that—$234 million—to the government of Haiti. Many NGOs also spent much less than they raised in pledges. "The money is not there," said Leslie Voltaire, Haiti's liaison with the United Nations. "The Haitian people think the government is stealing the money, and the international community doesn't want to say there is no money, and the government, which doesn't communicate, doesn't want to say there is no money."

Under Préval's leadership, the government not only maintained a defensive silence, but also reinforced foreign perceptions of Haiti as a weak, ineffective and corrupt state. In *Haiti in the Balance: Why Foreign Aid Has Failed and What We Can do About it,* public administration specialist Terry F. Buss points to "political instability and poor governance as the most important drivers of failure, from which all other negative consequences would follow," a view few now disagree with.

Before the earthquake, Préval was making modest progress. After it, he and his government lost their way. NGOs and private citizens have been responsible for most of Haiti's small improvements. NGOs provide an estimated 75 percent of health care, leaving Haiti's hospitals and clinics to founder. NGOs administer camps that offer unaccustomed services—free sanitation, free clean water, and free accommodation—and some people prefer them to the hardscrabble slums. The fears that energetic NGOs might pre-empt the legitimate work of the Haitian state were well founded.

When the earthquake struck, Préval's government was in its final months, but in the chaos and despair of post-earthquake Haiti, legislative and presidential elections scheduled for February 28, 2010, were postponed until November 28. The presidential frontrunners were strikingly unprepossessing: singer Michel "Sweet Mickey" Martelly, a Haitian Kompa singer notorious for mooning his audiences; Mirlande Manigat, law professor and First Lady during her husband Leslie's short presidency; Jude Celestin, a mechanical engineer, Préval's daughter Patricia's friend and Preval's protégé; and Charles Henri Baker, a wealthy garment factory owner. (Haitian-American singer Wyclef Jean's much heralded candidacy had been rejected because he failed the residency requirements. Afterward he reconciled with his one-time rival Martelly and began to campaign for him.) Because of his obsession with avoiding exile, the fate of so many other presidents, Préval did his utmost to ensure Celestin's victory.

The elections generated little enthusiasm. The Fanmi Lavalas was excluded on specious grounds. Haitians were exhausted and beaten down, and millions were in camps. About 27.1 percent of those registered voted and no individual candidate garnered a significant percentage of votes. But Préval had a personal stake in the election, and the Electoral Council he controlled announced that Mirlande Manigat and Jude Celestin led the pack and would face each other in a second round. Martelly's supporters erupted in protests. Foreign observers criticized the results as inconsistent with their findings. Préval stubbornly refused to budge but finally succumbed to international pressure. On February 3, election officials formally announced that Martelly had indeed won more votes than Celestin and, on March 20, would compete with Manigat for the presidency.

Two weeks earlier, on January 17, a former president had stunned Haitians by slipping almost unannounced into the country. Jean-Claude Duvalier came, he said, to help the victims of the earthquake. Jean-Claude was one of millions of Haitians impoverished by the earthquake. Hours before it struck, Switzerland had decided to grant him access to the final $5.9 million in his Swiss bank account. Immediately after the quake, embarrassed Swiss authorities had reversed that decision and announced that the funds would be restored to the battered nation he had plundered. Penniless and ailing, Jean-Claude returned to his homeland, perhaps to die.

On his second day home, the police politely escorted the gaunt and shuffling former dictator to the courthouse, where he was charged with corruption, theft and misappropriation of funds. As crowds waited outside, pro- and anti-Duvalier demonstrators cheered and jeered, and hurled insults at one another.

Four of Duvalier's victims filed suits against him for arbitrary arrest, detention, torture and forced exile. Liliane Pierre-Paul, one of the complainants, wept as she described how Jean-Claude Duvalier's Macoutes tortured her. Michèle Montas declared: "It's mind-boggling that a man like Duvalier thinks he can come back after twenty-five years and nothing will be held against him. I hope that what we did this morning will be the beginning of a succession of people who will file judicial complaints."

In this shattered nation of tent camps and destitution, it would be more satisfying if Duvalier were not penniless and in frail health, and more convenient if Haiti were not in the throes of political crisis and functional paralysis. But in a nation deprived of everything else, true justice demands that Jean-Claude Duvalier be held accountable for perpetuating a regime notorious for torture, arbitrary detention, rape, kidnapping and murder.

Duvalier's reappearance was a grotesque reminder of a terrifying and epic chapter in Haiti's history. Sadly, some Haitians recalled instead that under the Duvaliers you could walk safely through the streets, buy goods at cheaper prices, and in Papa Doc's day, get medical care for free. And in the judgement of young Haitians who had never lived under either Duvalier, but who had grown up in the turmoil of failed presidencies, military interventions, the earthquake and cholera, Jean-Claude might just be "the breath of fresh air" everyone longed for.

This nostalgia for the Duvalierist past was not ubiquitous. The Duvaliers' victims did not forget their torment. A large contingent of Haitians remained committed to Aristide and his dreams for them. Many others were too beaten down to care.

In South Africa, Jean-Bertrand Aristide cared deeply. On March 18, two days before the presidential election, he and his family defied urgent requests from the highest-ranked American officials to delay his return until after the elections. But Préval had agreed to issue him a passport (though not to allocate fifty policemen to guard him), and the South African government provided a private plane to the restore the ousted president to Haiti. Escorting him was American actor Danny Glover, who explained: "People of good conscience cannot be idle while a former dictator is able to return unhindered while a democratic leader who peacefully handed over power to another elected president is restricted from returning to his country by external forces."

Aristide had repeatedly expressed no further interest in politics, just a sincere desire to serve his people as a teacher. But as soon as he landed at the Port-au-Prince airport, he denounced the exclusion of FL from elections. "The exclusion of Fanmi Lavalas is the exclusion of the majority," he declared, "tantamount to cutting the branch on which we sit. The solution to the problem of exclusion is the inclusion of all Haitians because 'Tout moun se moun!'—We are all human beings!"

The rest of his homecoming speech was vintage Aristide. "My sisters and brothers, if you could place your hands on my heart, you would feel how it beats faster for telling you bravo, thank you, bravo, thank you!" he exclaimed. Then, offering visions of Haiti's hidden treasures: "With the little ball of education centered in the court of dignity, we will kick exclusion outside so that the new generation will begin to benefit from the wealth resting deep within Haiti: gold, copper, uranium, bauxite, silver. The calcium carbonate at Miragoane is valued at more than $23 billion. The petroleum reserves are no doubt larger than estimated. But we Haitians, we are the greatest wealth."

Thousands of cheering supporters accompanied the Aristides to Tabarre, where fans leapt over the walls and packed the vast courtyard. Inside their imposing house, repainted and readied for occupancy though still lacking Internet or landlines, the Aristides greeted well-wishers and rested after their long journey.

At dawn two days later, voters lined up and selected yet another President to govern them, confident of succeeding where former presidents had failed, and hopeful for the future in the dawn of the new regime. But the state of the nation was grim, and the presidential legacy heavy. Which of the four presidents—Jean-Claude Duvalier, nursing stomach pains in his borrowed villa high in the breezy mountains above Port-au-Prince; Jean-Bertrand Aristide, contentedly settled into his stately home in suburban Tabarre; René Préval in the National Palace; Michel "Sweet Mickey" Martelly, the President-elect—would not be moved and challenged by this bitter observation:

> Our government never cared about the national inheritance
> and never attempted to stop social grievances. They talked a
> lot about liberty, only to fool the free world instead of using

it fairly as a domestic policy. The Country is split into two groups: the exploiters—restless and foolhardy minority—monopolize the administrative power and paralyze the progress of the masses; the exploited—the great majority—[are] victims of a wrongful and cruel system.[224]

Behind mountains, there are mountains, as the Haitian people know. The man who uttered those words was François "Papa Doc" Duvalier, just after he was first named Haiti's chosen leader.

ILLUSTRATION CREDITS

1. Photo of lithograph, c. 1795, by MPI/Getty Images/Istock. Copyright: Istock.

2. Illustration from Jacques Nicolas Léger, *Haiti, Her History and Her Detractors*. New York: Neale,1907.

3. Copyright: Jean Guery.

4. Haitian National Office of Tourism.

5. Copyright: Jean-Max Benjamin.

6. Copyright: Louise Abbott.

7. Source: National Archives and Records Administration, Public Papers of the Presidents of the United States: Photographic Portfolio 1994, Vol. II, William J. Clinton.

8. Copyright: Grameen Foundation.

9. Copyright: Lucy Komisar.

10. Credit: UN/Sophia Paris.

11. Credit: UN/Evan Schneider. Copyright: UN.

12. Credit: Claudia Dewald for Istock. Copyright: Istock.

13. Credit: UN/Logan Abassi, Jan. 12, 2010. Copyright: UN.

14. Credit: UN/Logan Abassi, 13 January 2010, Copyright: UN

15. Credit: Marcello Casal Jr., Jan. 20, 2010. Source: Wikimedia Commons. Copyright: Agencia Brasil.

16. Credit: US Navy/MC1 Joshua Lee Kelsey, Jan. 19, 2010. Copyright: U.S. Navy.

17. Credit: UN/Marco Dormino (sic),August 12, 2010. Copyright: UN.

18. Credit: Pasquale Gorriz, Feb. 17, 2010. Copyright: UN

SOURCES FOR CHAPTERS 1-13

HAITI IS A CHRONICLE OF A COUNTRY'S DETERIORA-tion during three decades of Duvalierism, and it has been written over the two-year aftermath of that regime. Freedom of speech is still qualified by fear and habit, because Haitians survived by mistrusting their fellows, weighing each word and, for the most part, holding their tongues or dissembling. In the first flush of euphoria after Jean-Claude Duvalier fled in 1986, many spoke openly for the first time, eager to confide experiences and information long concealed. Two years later that frankness is fast fading, as people reconsider the consequences of their revelations.

Haiti deals with material that is still sensitive and dangerous. My system of documenting my information must necessarily reflect my informants' anxiety. "I'll tell you about this incident because it'll provide you with insight into so-and-so, but you mustn't use it. So-and-so would know you heard it from me, since I'm the only one who knows about it," I was told over and over. I respected those confidences in my text, and my reference notes are equally circumspect.

I originally planned to document each chapter, section by section, but discarded this plan after I realized that being too specific blew too many covers, and in any case the sources for some vital material could not be identified. Finally I decided on general reference notes, accompanied by a select bibliography of published works.

Haiti is based on six categories of source material:

1. interviews
2. my personal journals, observations, and private conversations
3. Haitian newspapers and periodicals

4. newspaper clippings from outside Haiti
5. books, articles, reports, and personal reminiscences published in Haiti and elsewhere
6. my reports filed during the period from 1986 to 1988.

INTERVIEWS

From 1986 to 1988 I conducted interviews with over one hundred people, in French, Creole, and English. Many took place over two or more sessions. Many were taped, when the subjects did not object. Others spoke freely but on condition I take notes only by computer or by pen, recording their words and not their voices. Several spoke freely but on condition of anonymity, though I was permitted to take notes. A few spoke only if I took no notes and did not identify them.

The following is a list of those interviewed, with as much identification as possible.

Moyse Ambroise, a small merchant in Mirabalais, who in 1983 ran for magistrate against Madame Nason, Madame Max Adolphe's sister.

Dr. Robert Amelingmeier, American veterinarian in charge of PEPPADEP field operations, until 1988 director of the Interim Swine Repopulation Project.

Joseph Baguidy, François Duvalier's Foreign Minister and a trusted aide. He wrote prolifically and was one of *noirism*'s and Duvalierism's chief exponents. Baguidy also gave me copies of several of his books.

Arlette, Léon, and Eric Baptiste, Haiti's third largest coffee exporters. In self-defense, Eric Baptiste shot and killed Interior Minister Dr. Roger Lafontant's bodyguard. Baptiste was jailed, his family threatened, and the case gained international notoriety. Eric's sister, Arlette, and father, Léon, gave me extensive information about the case.

Max Beauvoir, a Paris-educated chemical engineer who became a *houngan,* and whom Jean-Claude Duvalier consulted in the final weeks of his struggle to keep power.

Elisabeth Bellande, daughter of Marcelle Hakime, who spent a childhood of terror as Macoutes terrorized her family, raped and nearly killed her aunt, while her father escaped to Venezuela and broadcast anti-Duvalier programs, which jeopardized his family's lives.

Marcelle Hakime Bellande, Haiti's first woman dentist, who attended medical school with François Duvalier and whom Duvalier tried to enlist to campaign for him. Her sister, Yvonne Hakime Rimpel, was raped and nearly killed by Macoutes. Duvalier forced Marcelle to divorce her husband, Pierre-Edouard.

Pierre-Edouard Bellande, Marcelle Hakime's ex-husband, journalist arrested by François Duvalier, who later fled to an embassy, then devoted his life in exile to anti-Duvalierist journalism.

Timothy Benford, an American whose public relations firm handled Haiti's touristic public relations in the 1980s.

Lucien Charles, houngan serving Baron Samedi, formerly a rural section chief and rural policeman.

Jean Joseph Charles, painter, sculptor, and intellectual, a Fort Dimanche survivor who lives precariously on the edge of starvation and homelessness.

Anne Denise Hilaire Cius, the mother of Jean-Robert Cius, one of the three students killed on November 28, 1985, in Gonaives, which precipitated the downfall of Jean-Claude Duvalier.

General Gérard Constant, François Duvalier's chief of staff for eight and a half years until Papa Doc abruptly retired him in 1970 and appointed Colonel Claude Raymond as his replacement. General Constant granted me many interviews, lent me books on the regime, and arranged other interviews for me. General Constant served as Haiti's ambassador to the Dominican Republic under the CNG.

Reverend Lucien Coté, charismatic Canadian priest, pastor of St. Hélène's Church in Jérémie.

Harold Courlander, world-renowned ethnomusicologist and longtime Haiti visitor who knew ethnologist François Duvalier.

Dr. Jean-Jacques Delate, French veterinarian responsible for repopulation with Creole pigs.

Dr. Marie-Marcelle Deschamps, specialist in internal medicine and infectious diseases, involved in AIDS research in conjunction with Cornell University.

Clovis Désinor, longtime François Duvalier finance minister and one of the regime's moderates widely expected to succeed Papa Doc. Fired in later 1970, Désinor was active in the ouster of Jean-Claude Duvalier and declared himself a candidate for presidential elections on November 29, 1987, and December 17, 1988. He was disqualified both times for his close ties with Papa Doc.

Jean Divers, prefect of Jérémie in 1986.

Dr. Bruce Dollar, detective with Kroll Associates, the New York-based detective firm hired to trace the money stolen by the Duvaliers and their associates.

Katherine Dunham, American dancer, *mambo,* former lover of President Dumarsais Estimé, and longtime Haiti resident.

Robert Duval, known as "Bobby," imprisoned in Fort Dimanche under Jean-Claude Duvalier's regime, now a political activist and founder of the human-rights organization League of Former Political Prisoners.

Hector Estimé, an agronomist whose brother, Rameau, was François Duvalier's Justice Minister. Hector was imprisoned in Fort Dimanche with Rameau and cousin Wiltern. Both Rameau and Wiltern died there. Hector was a candidate in both the November 29, 1987, and January 17, 1988, presidential elections.

Lionel Estimé, son of President Dumarsais Estimé.

Grégoire Eugène, law professor, Jean-Claude Duvalier's tutor, and later a vocal anti-Duvalierist politician and author. Eugène also provided me with copies of *Fraternité,* the opposition journal he published during Jeanclaudism.

Dr. Jacques Fourcand, U.S.-trained neurosurgeon who was François Duvalier's personal physician and trusted aide.

Dr. Neville Gallimore, Jamaica's Social Affairs Minister, the Seaga government's special emissary who was instrumental in convincing Jean-Claude and Michèle Duvalier that they had to leave.

Dr. Jean-Claude Garcia-Zamor, professor of public administration at

Howard University and specialist in Haitian public-sector management.

Gabriel Guerrier, news director of Radio Cacique, shut down by Jean-Claude Duvalier for its antigovernment opinions.

Father Rosaire Guévin, the Canadian priest who stood next to Jean-Robert Cius when soldiers shot him in the courtyard of Gonaives' Immaculate Conception College.

Commander David Edward Henrickson, U.S. Coast Guard attaché, spokesman for the Haitian Migrant Intervention Operation, catching boat people attempting to enter the U.S. illegally.

Israel, Jean-Pierre, a *houngan* with a reputation in his village of Soissons as a powerful healer who two decades ago sliced off his little toes after the gods instructed him to do so in a dream, and who has since prospered and makes a good living healing, predicting, and farming.

Voltaire Jean, the pseudonym for an elderly mason who knew François Duvalier and Interior Minister Jean Julmé.

Antoine Jean-Charles, former attorney general of Jérémie subsequently persecuted by Macoutes. After Jean-Claude Duvalier's flight, he served briefly as dean of Port-au-Prince's tribunal.

Claudie Jocelyn Jean-Charles, Antoine's wife, who kept a journal for much of the Papa Doc years. Many extracts of her journal were read to me.

Dinois Jeanty, houseman for General Roger St. Albin and then Clélie Ovide, Simone Duvalier's mother.

Ex-Colonel Samuel Jérémie, Jean-Claude Duvalier's chauffeur after the fatal attack on the Duvalier children's chauffeur and bodyguards at Collège Bird in 1963. Jérémie rose to become a powerful officer, in charge of the State Stores and the Anti-Smuggling Brigade. I interviewed him frequently during his 1986 court-martial for murder, torture, and military misconduct.

Colonel Abel Jérome, commandant of Jérémie during the 1964 Vespers of Jérémie. Jerome also gave me documents concerning the vespers, including one from François Duvalier.

Lionece Jocelyn, an unemployed laborer who became a "bot pipple" in 1985, hoping to reach Miami. Jocelyn's younger brother was killed by the captain. The boat went aground near Cuba, and after Jocelyn's repatriation he was imprisoned in Fort Dimanche.

Aubelin Jolicoeur, Graham Greene's "Petit Pierre," Haitian journalist, and tourism official under François Duvalier and briefly tourism director and Information Ministry official in 1986.

Dieudonné Lamothe, Haiti's best marathon runner. I interviewed Lamothe extensively in 1984–85 for a magazine article as well as for this book. On April 26, 1988, Lamothe won the Marathon de La Francophonie in 2 hours, 14 minutes, and 22 seconds.

Maurice Lédy, cousin of Clément Jumelle who was present when François Duvalier's goons stole Jumelle's body from the hearse carrying him to the cemetery.

Jean Bellavoix Léonie, appointed Jérémie attorney general in 1986, who officially investigated the 1964 Vespers of Jérémie.

Orestil Louissaint, a gas-station owner in Lestère who extended François Duvalier $12,600 credit at his gas pumps when Duvalier was campaigning in 1957. Duvalier never repaid the money, instead persecuted Louissaint and jailed him in Fort Dimanche. Jean-Claude Duvalier repaid the money after his father's death.

Ulrick Masson, teacher in Mirabalais, hometown of Madame Max Adolphe, forced to vote for François Duvalier when he was twelve and later imprisoned for anti-Duvalier activities.

Michel Mézile, a Jérémie accountant jailed during the 1964 vespers and one of the few survivors.

Dr. Georges Michel, surgeon, journalist, and historian, severely beaten during Black Friday in 1980. Dr. Michel was director of Radio Nationale until Manigat's government replaced him.

Joseph Namphy, businessman and manager of the El Rancho Hotel, brother of General Henri Namphy.

Reverend Luc Nérée, Baptist pastor and founder of Aid to Children and father of Dr. Bob Nérée, editor of an opposition revue. In 1977 Macoutes attacked and nearly killed Reverend Nérée in an incident that gained international notoriety.

Paul Nixon, American marine salvage operator hired by François Duvalier.

Liénard Numa, brother of Marcel Numa, executed in 1964 with Louis Drouin for his role in the "Young Haiti" invasion. Numa's mother also spoke to me about Marcel and showed me family photograph albums.

Reverend Léona Paul, Protestant pastor and for twenty-two years chaplain of the Laboule Macoutes. Like so many other Macoutes, Paul was never armed, and when Jean-Claude Duvalier fled he simply discarded his uniform and continued to live a normal life in his community.

Dr. Edner Poux, member of the Consultive Council appointed to advise the constituent assembly about the Constitution and later retained to advise the Namphy government.

Father Raymond Reynaud, curé in Jérémie, active in the Youth Council, which helped organize resistance to Jean-Claude Duvalier.

Lucien Rigaud, businessman who lobbied for Haiti in the 1970s and was subsequently imprisoned by Jean-Claude Duvalier. Rigaud's testimony helped convict U.S. Congressman Daniel Flood of influence peddling.

Jed Ringel, lawyer with New York-based Stroock & Stroock & Lavan, hired by the Haitian government to prepare the legal case to repatriate hundreds of millions of dollars stolen by Jean-Claude Duvalier, his family, and associates.

Esther Rocourt, American-born nurse and widow of the Reverend Robert Rocourt, for decades a missionary in the Jérémie area, who nursed Sanette Balmir when the Macoute leader was dying of advanced diabetes.

Selden Rodman, American expert on Haitian art, who invited François Duvalier to his Port-au-Prince home in 1954 after a friend assured him Duvalier would be Haiti's next President.

Albert Salas, a "medic" who belonged to the MOP, the workers' organization Duvalier once worked for. Salas saw the massacre at Bel-Air when Duvalier had people buried alive and cemented under a cross.

Georges Salomon, former Duvalier ambassador and minister, who as Foreign Affairs Minister helped coordinate the ouster of Jean-Claude Duvalier.

Max Sam, son of Demosthènes Sam, who built the Hotel Oloffson. Sam, whose cousin President Vilbrun Sam was hacked to death in 1915, remembers the Americans billeting his home for use as the Marine Hospital, forcing his family to move.

Pierre Sam, briefly Jean-Claude Duvalier's reformist Minister of Planning, Haiti's ambassador to the U.S. and the OAS during the two-year Namphy government's regime.

Suzanne Seitz, for fifteen years director of the Hotel Oloffson.

Yvonne and Joel Trimble, American missionaries with Haiti for Christ Ministries, longtime Haiti residents.

INTERVIEWS ON CONDITION OF ANONYMITY

There are several categories of people who spoke, usually with great candor, on condition of anonymity. Some had been friends of the Duvaliers or the Bennetts. A few were afraid of the men and women they talked about, but more often they simply feared being publicly linked with them.

Several members of the Haitian commercial and industrial establishment agreed to be interviewed if their names were not mentioned. Some had heavy ties to the regime, others had none. The kind of information and explanations they provided, often accompanied by documentation, were vital to a study of Haiti's kleptocratic society and government.

Military men seldom talk on record, but several soldiers and officers in the Presidential Guard and the Corps of Léopards provided me with much valuable information.

The description of the functioning of Michèle Bennett's Bon Repos Hospital also owes much to anonymous informants who gave me access to files and reports and account books.

Several relatives of prominent Duvalierists and Macoutes volunteered information and documents. They wanted the truth known, without revealing their role in the expose to the relatives in question. I was even given one of the ugly but made-to-order Swiss watches with a tiny photo of Jean-Claude and Michèle on the face that the First Couple distributed as Christmas presents in 1981.

OTHER INTERVIEWS

Several incidents in *Haiti* are based on multiple short interviews it would be fruitless to describe individually. Before writing about the Vespers of Jérémie I twice visited Jérémie, retraced the site of the incidents, and interviewed many townspeople who reminisced about them.

I based my description of the 1985 Belloc Massacre on testimony presented during the eighteen-day trial of Samuel Jérémie. I visited Jérémie's "uprooted" properties and interviewed neighbors and went to Belloc, where I interviewed many eyewitnesses to the massacre. During the trial I also spent many lunchtimes in the Police General Headquarters cafeteria discussing the case with the prosecution and defense lawyers.

The descriptions of both the Pierre Denis "disappearance" and the imprisonment and death of Jean-Jacques Dessalines Ambroise and his wife, Lucette Lafontant, were based on testimony given during the respective trials of Edouard C. Paul and Luc Désyr as well as additional interviews I was granted.

My account of the late nineteenth-century domino game and vodoun *cérémonie* in Grande-Rivière-du-Nord in which somber predictions were made to Tiresias and Vilbrun Sam were vividly described to me by my centenarian grandmother-in-law, Sé-Rose, who heard about them from the Sams.

My references to vodoun are based on written studies but also on personal experiences at *cérémonies* in Port-au-Prince and the provinces. For articles and for this book I have interviewed many *houngans* and *mambos,* including several adepts of the secret and dangerous Bizango rites. These latter, introduced to me by a former Tonton Macoute, spoke reluctantly and reacted with extreme hostility when they realized that I was familiar with some of their special *loas.*

I spoke to former Macoutes, including one man in hiding for his life. An insistent relative convinced him to see me, but only on my fifth visit to his shack in a dusty warren in a city slum did he appear, and he made it clear that this would be our only interview. He was very intelligent, weighed his every word, spoke openly only about Astrel Benjamin, his former Macoute commandant who is dead, and lied defiantly about his own inglorious career.

I personally knew Madeleine Pierre-Louis, the madwoman who howled at night because her pigs were dead. She was one of my first Haitian experiences, part of the cool mountain nights pierced by her shrieks, the conch and drums from a nearby *houmfor,* and the occasional blasts of rifles as Macoutes let the neighborhood know they were patrolling.

I witnessed the band of Macoutes described in the Prologue as they passed yards away from my house and I watched as they marched over to Argentine Bellegarde School and back again. I found the body of the old man they left behind on the Avenue Martin Luther King. I visited the school afterward. I went into the morgue to verify the body count for my reports.

I went twice to Jean-Rabel to write about the July 1987 massacres. I interviewed dozens of people in Jean-Rabel and La Coma, talked to survivors from both Non-Group and Tet Ansamn, and in Port-au-Prince interviewed Father Jean-Marie Vincent. I also talked to the military investigators who formed part of the team that later produced the official government report.

To describe the attack on the priests near St. Marc I interviewed Father Jean-Bertrand Aristide and Brothers Emile Beldor and Joseph Burg.

I have a special interest in the General Hospital and have written several articles about it. I have also accumulated considerable information about AIDS in Haiti.

I have interviewed many experts in reforestation and ecological problems, climbed up mountains to plant saplings, experienced the horrendous storms I wrote about.

MY PERSONAL JOURNALS, OBSERVATIONS, AND CONVERSATIONS

I twice kept journals, once when I first arrived in Haiti and during the events preceding the flight of Jean-Claude Duvalier. Both were quite detailed and I drew on them for parts of Chapters 11 and 12.

My life as a reporter and my husband's as a hotel manager, first at the Hotel Villa St. Louis, then at the El Rancho Hotel, have introduced me to literally thousands of people.

In 1984 and 1985 I often ran into Ernest Bennett, who was always at the airport.

I met Marie-Denise Duvalier Théard at a party.

One summer I scolded my son's new friend, visiting from St. Louis, Missouri, for crying whenever he had to go to see his grandmother, who he said was boring, spoke no English, had no cable TV, and served "gross" food. I later discovered that the lady in question was Madame Max Adolphe, at that time commander of the Tonton Macoutes.

I have met most members of the CNG's government, but have always kept my distance, preferring formal interviews uncomplicated by personal ties when I am researching articles.

I first met Haitian President Leslie Manigat at a dinner party soon after his return to Haiti. He had already announced his intentions to run for the presidency and was considered the most brilliant candidate, but hampered by a reputation as a socialist. He drove me home that night, talking all the way about reforestation and his program. Afterward he and Grégoire Eugène were my first choices for President, although I thought then neither could win because they lacked campaign funds and popular bases.

Dr. Charles P. Romain, the university nominee to the first ill-fated CEP, is dean of the Institute of African Research and Studies at the university, where I taught a course in comparative slavery. Dr. Romain and I remained in touch throughout the CNG-CEP conflict, both hoping for a reconciliation that never came.

I first met Dr. Jean Price-Mars's daughter Marie-Madeleine Price-Mars as a reporter, when she had been severely injured by a mob wanting her land.

HAITIAN NEWSPAPERS AND PERIODICALS

The relative dearth of literature on the Duvalier regime, especially for the Jean-Claude years, make newspapers and periodicals essential literature. I consulted the dailies *Le Nouvelliste, Le Matin, Panorama,* and *Le Nouveau Monde.* I found the weekly *Le Petit Samedi Soir* very helpful, often providing details and color lacking in the more staid, conservative, and self-censored dailies. I also read various issues of the Jeanclaudist periodicals *Le Bulletin d'Information, Le Sceau,* and *L'Assault.* Opposition revues are *Fraternité,* the New York-based weekly newspaper *Haiti Observateur,* and odd issues of an assortment of the revues that pop up and fail so regularly in Haiti, such as *Regard.*

Most of my clippings from outside Haiti, apart from the Haitian-written *Haiti Observateur,* are from the period of the 1980s and most date from 1985. Most heavily represented are *The Christian Science Monitor, The Miami Herald, The Miami News, The New York Times, Newsweek, Time* magazine, *La Presse,* and *Le Devoir. The Washington Times,* March 28, 1984, contains one of Jean-Claude Duvalier's rare interviews. I have files of all the reports filed during January and February 1986 by Phil Davison of Reuters and by William Johnson for Toronto's *Globe and Mail.* I have copies of the wire service reports filed during the 1984 hunger riots at Gonaives and Cap Haitien and during the trial in Puerto Rico that convicted Frantz Bennett of cocaine trafficking.

SELECT BIBLIOGRAPHY

BOOKS

America Watch Committee (U.S.), National Coalition for Haitian Refugees, Caribbean Rights (Organization), *The More Things Change: Human rights in Haiti*. Np: Americas Watch Committee, 1989.

Anglade, Georges. *L'Espace Haitien*. Québec: Les Presses de l'Université du Québec, 1974.

Aristide, Jean-Bertrand, with Christopher Wargny. *Aristide: An Autobiography*. Maryknoll, NY: Orbis Books, 1993.

Aristide, Jean-Bertrand, (tr. Carrol F. Coates). *Dignity*. Charlottesville: University of Virginia Press, 1996.

Auguste, Maurepas. *Genèse d'une République Héréditaire*. Port-au-Prince: Fardin, 1986.

Avril, Prosper. *Justice Versus Politics in Haiti (2001-2004)*. Boca Raton: Universal Publishers, 2007.

Baguidy, Joseph. *Esquisse de Sociologie Haitienne*. Port-au-Prince: n.d.

Balch, Emily Greene. *Occupied Haiti*. New York: Negro Universities Press, 1969.

Ballard, John R. *Upholding democracy: the United States military campaign in Haiti, 1994-1997*. Santa Barbara, Ca: Praeger Publishers, 1998.

Benoit, Max. *Cahier de Folklore et des Traditions Orales d'Haiti*. Port-au-Prince: Imprimerie des Antilles, 1980.

Black, David. *The Plague Years: A Chronicle of AIDS, the Epidemic of Our Times.* New York: Simon and Schuster, 1986.

Brinkerhoff, Derick W., and Jean-Claude Garcia-Zamor. *Politics, Projects, and People: Institutional Development in Haiti.* New York: Praeger, 1986.

Buss, Terry F. *Haiti in the Balance: Why Foreign Aid Has Failed And What We Can Do About It.* Washington, D.C.: Brookings Institution Press, 2009.

Clark, Vèvè A. Fieldhands to Stagehands in Haiti: *The Measure of Tradition in Haitian Popular Theatre.* Ph.D. thesis, University of California, Berkeley, 1983.

Cave, Hugh B. *Haiti: Highroad to Adventure.* New York: Henry Holt, 1952.

Corvington, Georges. *Port-au-Prince au Cours des Ans: La Capitale d'Haiti sous l'Occupation 1915–1922.* Port-au-Prince: Henri Deschamps, 1984.

Courlander, Harold. *The Drum and the Hoe: Life and Lore of the Haitian People.* Berkeley: University of California, 1960.

Courlander, Harold. *Haiti Singing.* New York: Cooper Square Publishers, 1973.

Crane, Keith, James Dobbins, Laurel E. Miller, Charles P. Ries, Christopher S. Chivvis, Marla C. Haims, Marco Overhaus, Heather L. Schwartz, and Elizabeth Wilke. *Building a More Resilient Haitian State.* Santa Monica, Ca.: Rand Corporation, 2010. http://www.rand.org/pubs/monographs/MG1039

Daumec, Gérard. *Guides des'Oeuvres Essentielles' du François Duvalier.* Port-au-Prince: Henri Deschamps, 1967.

Davis, Wade. *The Serpent and the Rainbow: A Harvard Scientist's Astonishing Journey into the Secret Society of Haitian Voodoo, Zombis and Magic.* New York: Simon and Schuster, 1985.

Deibert, Michael. *Notes from the Last Testament.* New York: Seven Stories, 2005.

Deibert, Michael. *Notes from the Last Testament.* New York: Seven Stories, 2005.

Deren, Maya. *Divine Horsemen: Voodoo Gods of Haiti.* New York: Chelsea House, 1970.

Diederich, Bernard, and Al Burt. *Papa Doc and the Tonton Macoutes: The Truth About Haiti Today.* New York: McGraw Hill, 1969.

Dorsainvil, J. C. *Histoire d'Haiti.* Port-au-Prince: Henri Deschamps, n.d.

Dumas, Reginald. *An Encounter with Haiti: Notes of a Special Adviser.* Port-of-Spain: Medianet Limited, 2008.

Dunham, Katherine. *Island Possessed.* New York: Doubleday, 1969.

Dupuy, Alex. *The Prophet and Power: Jean-Bertrand Aristide, the International Community, and Haiti.* Lanham, Md: Rowman & Littlefield, 2007.

Fatton, Robert. *Haiti's Predatory Republic.* Boulder: Lynne Riemner, 2002.

Fatton, Robert. *The Roots of Haitian Despotism.* Boulder: Lynne Riemner, 2007.

Ferguson, James. *Papa Doc Baby Doc: Haiti and the Duvaliers.* London: Basil Blackwell, 1987.

Fisman, Raymond and Edward Miguel. *Economic Gangsters: Corruption, Violence, and the Poverty of Nations.* New Haven: Princeton Univ. Press, 2010.

Fombrun, Odette Roy. *Histoire du Drapeau Haitien.* Port-au-Prince: Henri Deschamps, 1986.

Fouchard, Jean. *The Haitian Maroons: Liberty or Death.* New York: E. Blyden Press, 1981.

Fowler, Carolyn. *A Knot in the Thread.* Washington, D.C.: Howard University Press, 1980.

Gaillard, Roger. *Charlemagne Péralte, le Coco.* Port-au-Prince: Le Natal, 1982.

Gaillard, Roger. *Premier Ecrasement du Cacoisme: Les Blancs Débarquent, 1915.* Port-au-Prince: Le Natal, 1981.

Genovese, Eugene. *In Red and Black*. New York: 1972.

Genovese, Eugene. *From Rebellion to Revolution: Afro-American Slave Revolts in the Making of the New World*. New York: Random House, 1981.

George, Susan. *A Fate Worse than Debt*. New York: Grove Press, 1990.

Gingras, Jean-Pierre O. *Duvalier, Caribbean cyclone; the history of Haiti and its present government*. Hicksville, NY: Exposition Press, 1967.

Greene, Graham. *The Comedians*. Aylesbury: Penguin Books, 1984. (First published by The Bodley Head, 1966.)

Hallward, Peter. *Damming the Flood: Haiti, Aristide, and the Politics of Containment*. London: Verso, 2007.

Harvey, William Woodis. *Sketches of Hayti: From the Expulsion of the French to the Death of Christophe*. London: Frank Cass, (1827) 1971.

Healey, David F. *Gunboat Diplomacy in the Wilson Era: The U.S. Navy in Haiti, 1915–1916*. Madison: University of Wisconsin Press, 1976.

Heinl, Robert D., and Nancy G. *Written in Blood: The Story of the Haitian People 1492–1971*. Boston: Houghton Mifflin, 1978.

Herskovits, Melville J. *Life in a Haitian Valley*. New York: Octagon Books, 1975.

Hoffman, Léon-François. *Essays on Haitian Literature*. Washington, D.C.: Three Continents Press, 1984.

Huxley, Francis. *The Invisibles: Voodoo Gods in Haiti*. New York: McGraw-Hill, 1966.

Erica Cappel James. *Democratic Insecurities: Violence, Trauma, and Intervention in Haiti*. Berkeley, Los Angeles, London: University of California Press, 2010.

James, C. L. R. *The Black Jacobins: Toussaint Louverture and the San Domingo Revolution*. New York: Vintage Books, 1963.

Jerome, Yves J. *Toussaint Louverture*. New York: Vintage Books, 1978.

Kennedy, Ellen Conroy, ed. *The Negritude Poets*. New York: Viking, 1975.

Knight, Franklin W. *The Caribbean*. New York: Oxford University Press, 1978.

Korngold, Ralph. *Citizen Toussaint*. New York: Hill and Wang, 1944.

Koski-Karell, Daniel A. *The Boucaneers of Hispaniola*. Washington, D.C.: 1976.

Laguerre, Michel S. *American Odyssey: Haitians in New York City*. New York: Cornell University Press, 1984.

Laguerre, Michel S. *The military and society in Haiti*. Knoxville: University of Tennessee Press, 1993.

Laguerre, Michel S. *Urban Life in the Caribbean: A Study of a Haitian Urban Community*. Cambridge, Mass.: Schenkman Publishing, 1982.

Langley, Lester D. *The United States and the Caribbean, 1900–1970*. Athens: University of Georgia Press, 1980.

Lemoine, Maurice. *Bitter Sugar*. London: Zed Press, 1985.

Leyburn, James. G. *The Haitian People*. New Haven: Yale University Press, 1941.

Logan, Rayford W. *Haiti and the Dominican Republic*. New York: Oxford University Press, 1968.

Lundahl, Mats. *Peasants and Poverty: A Study of Haiti*. New York: St. Martin's Press, 1979.

Mangones, Albert. *Les Monuments du Roi Christophe: La Citadelle, Le Palais Sans Souci, Le Site des Ramiers*. Port-au-Prince: Le Natal, 1980.

Maximilien, Louis. *Le Vodoun Haitien: Rite Radas—Canzo*. Port-au-Prince: Henri Deschamps, 1985.

Métraux, Alfred. *Le Vaudou Haitien*. Paris: Gallimard, 1984.

Mills, James. *The Underground Empire: Where Crime and Governments Embrace*. New York: Dell, 1986.

Moreau de Saint-Méry. *Description Topographique, Physique, Civile, Politique, et Historique de la Partie Française de l'Isle de Saint Dominique.* Paris: Librairie Larose, 1958.

Nadal-Gardère, Marie-José, and Gérald Bloncourt. *Haitian Arts.* Paris: Edition Nathan, 1986.

Nérée, Bob. *Duvalier: Le Pouvoir sur les Autres, de Père en Fils.* Port-au-Prince: Editions Henri Deschamps, 1988.

Nicholls, David. *From Dessalines to Duvalier: Race, Colour and National Independence in Haiti.* Cambridge: Cambridge University Press, 1979.

Nicholls, David. *Haiti in the Caribbean Context.* Basingstoke, England: Macmillan, 1985.

Ott, Thomas O. *The Haitian Revolution, 1789–1804.* Knoxville: The University of Tennessee Press, 1973.

Palmer, Ransford W. *Caribbean Dependence on the United States Economy.* New York: Praeger, 1979.

Parkinson, Wenda. *"This Gilded African": Toussaint L'Ouverture.* London: Quartet Books, 1978.

Patterson, Orlando. *Slavery and Social Death: A Comparative Study.* Cambridge: Harvard University Press, 1982.

Ralph Pezzuloo. *Plunging into Haiti: Clinton, Aristide, and the defeat of diplomacy.* Jackson: University of Mississippi Press, 2010.

Pierre-Charles, Gérard. *Radiographie d'une Dictature: Haiti et Duvalier.* Montréal: Nouvelle Optique, 1973.

Piquion, René. *Manuel de Négritude.* Port-au-Prince: Henri Deschamps.

Price-Mars, Jean. *Ainsi Parla l'Oncle.* Ottawa: Lemeac, 1973.

Price-Mars, Jean. *Vilbrun Guillaume Sam: Ce Méconnu.* Port-au-Prince: 1961.

Prince, Rod. *Haiti: Family Business.* London: Latin American Bureau, 1985.

Rodman, Selden. *Haiti: The Black Republic.* New York: Devin-Adair, 1976.

Rodman, Selden. *The Miracle of Haitian Art*. New York: Doubleday, 1974.

Rodman, Selden. *Where Art is Joy*. New York: Ruggles de Latour, 1988.

Romain, Charles P. *Le Protestantisme Haitien*. Port-au-Prince: Deschamps, 1987.

Romain, J. B. *Développement Rural en Haiti et dans la Caraibe*. Port-au-Prince: Imprimerie M. Rodriguez, 1980.

Rotberg, Robert. *Haiti: The Politics of Squalor*. Boston: Houghton Mifflin, 1971.

Roumain, Jacques. *Masters of the Dew*. London: Heinemann, 1982.

Salgado, Antoine. *Le Phénomène des Zombis dans la Culture Haitienne*. Port-au-Prince: Imprimerie Des Antilles, 1982.

Schmidt, Hans. *The United States Occupation of Haiti, 1915–1934*. New York: Rutgers University Press, 1971.

Schwartz, Timothy T., *Travesty in Haiti: A true account of Christian missions, orphanages, fraud, food aid and drug trafficking*. Charlston: BookSurge Publishing, 2008.

Schwartz, Timothy T. *Fewer Men, More Babies: Sex, Family, and Fertility in Haiti*. Lanham, Md.: Lexington Books, 2009.

Seabrook, William B. *The Magic Island*. New York: Literary Guild of America, 1929.

Shamsie, Yasmine and Andrew S. Thompson (eds.) *Haiti: Hope for a Fragile State*. Waterloo: Wilfrid Laurier University Press, 2006.

Smith, Dudley. *Cane Sugar World*. New York: Palmer Publications, 1978.

Soukar, Michel. *Seize Ans de Lutte pour un Pays Normal*. Port-au-Prince: Impressions Magiques, 1987.

Stebich, Ute. *Haitian Art*. New York: Brooklyn Museum, 1978.

Szulc, Tad. *Fidel: A Critical Portrait*. New York: Avon, 1987.

Tata, Robert J. *Haiti: Land of Poverty*. Washington, D.C.: University Press of America, 1982.

Trouillot, Michel-Rolph. *Les Racines Historiques de l'Etat Duvalierien.* Port-au-Prince: Deschamps, 1986.

Weinstein, Brian, and Aaron Segal. *Haiti: Political Failures, Cultural Successes.* New York: Praeger, 1984.

U.S. Government, Department of Agriculture. *Animal Health: Yearbook of Agricultural Livestock and Pets.* Washington: U.S. Government Printing Office, 1984.

Williams, Eric. *From Columbus to Castro: The History of the Caribbean 1492–1969.* London: André Deutsch, 1983.

Wolkstein, Diane. *The Magic Orange Tree and Other Haitian Folktales.* New York: Knopf, 1978.

ARTICLES, MONOGRAPHS

Abbott, Elizabeth. "The Impact of the Haitian Revolution on the Development of North America." Unpublished paper presented at the closing ceremonies of Cap Haitien's private Université Henri Christophe, June 1983.

Amnesty International on Haiti. "Perpetrators of Past Abuses Threaten Human rights and the Reestablishment of the Rule of Law," 3 March 2004. Online at http://www.nathanielturner.com/amnestyinterna tionalonhaiti.htm.

"An inside look at Haiti's business elite."*Multinational Monitor,* Jan. 1, 1995. An interview with "Patrick James," alias for an American businessman who used to live and work in Haiti. Online at http:// www.allbusiness.com/specialty-businesses/492556-1.html.

Aristide, Mildred. "Forced into exile: Madame Mildred Aristide, wife of former Haitian president Jean Bertrand Aristide, recalls the nightmare of being driven from her country." *Essence Magazine,* Oct. 2005. Online at http://www.aristide.org/articles/MildredAristide .htm.

Ban, Ki-moon. "Haiti's Big Chance." *New York Times,* 30 March 2009. Online at http://www.un.org/sg/articleFull.asp?TID=99& Type=Op-Ed.

Beauvoir, Max. "The Vodun Tradition in Haiti." 1981.

Benton, Leslie A. and Glenn T. Ware. *Haiti: A Case Study of the International Response and the Efficacy of Nongovernmental Organizations in the Crisis.*

Brenner, Marie. "Mythomania: Michèle Duvalier's Riviera Exile." *Vanity Fair,* December 1986.

Carey, Henry F. "Electoral Observation and Democratization in Haiti," in Kevin J. Middlebrook, ed., *Electoral Observation and Democratic Transitions in Latin America* (San Diego: Center for U.S.-Mexican Studies, 1998), pp.141-166. Online at http://www.haitipolicy.org/archives/Archives/1998/carey.htm#N_21_.

Charles, Eugenia. "Haiti Report." 27 Feb 2002. Online at http://www.uscis.gov/portal/site/uscis/menuitem.5af9bb95919f35e66f6141765 43f6d1a/?vgnextoid=4007361cfb98d010VgnVCM10000048f3d6a 1RCRD&vgnextchannel=d2d1e89390b5d010VgnVCM10000048f 3d6a1RCRD.

Chassagne, Albert. *Bain de Sang en Haiti, Les Macoutes Opérant à Jérémie en 1964.* Brooklyn, N.Y.: Imprimerie Parti National Haitien, 1986.

Christian Peacemaker Teams, CPTNET Nov. 16, 1995 Haiti Events Summary. Online at http://www.williambowles.info/haiti-news/archives/cpt_191195.html.

Collier, Paul. "Haiti: From Natural Catastrophe to Economic Security, A Report for the Secretary-General of the United Nations." January 2009 Online at http://www.focal.ca/pdf/haiticollier.pdf.

Coughlin, Dan. "The case of Capt. Lawrence P. Rockwood." *Haiti Progres,* Vol. 12, no. 51, 20 March 1995. Online at http://www.hartford-hwp.com/archives/43a/044.html.

Danner, Mark. "The Struggle For a Democratic Haiti." *The New York Times Magazine,* June 24, 1987.

De Braux, Diane. "Haiti: Incomprise," *Vogue* Promotion, n.d. Photos by Dominique Silberstein and interview with Jean-Claude and Michèle B. Duvalier.

Denis, Paul. "CEA Inquiry into Millions Found Diverted to Aristide Offshore Accounts—Text." *Commission d'Enquete Administrative de*

Paul Denis, 2005-10-24. *Haiti Democracy Project*. Online at http:// www.haitipolicy.org.

Domond, Natalie, Fonkoze Director of Social Impact, in an interview with Oscar. "Haiti, the Fonkoze Model of Social Evolution, Part 2." Online at http://www.nextbillion.net/blog/2011/01/26/in-haiti-the-fonkoze-model-of-social-evolution-part-2.

Duren, Marty. "Interview with 'Travesty in Haiti' author, Dr. Tim Schwartz–Part 1." Online at http://www.martyduren.com/2010/02/23/ interview-with-travesty-in-haiti-author-dr-tim-schwartz-part-1/.

Eugène, Grégoire. *Le Miracle Haitien Est Possible: Un Plaidoyer pour le Développement*. Port-au-Prince: Fardin, 1985.

Eugène, Grégoire. *Spectre de Guerre Civile*. Port-au-Prince: Imprimerie l'Immaculée, 1986.

Eugène, Grégoire. *Le Procès de Luc Désyr: Une Parodie de la Justice*. Port-au-Prince: L'Imprimerie l'Immaculée, 1986.

Fonkoze website. http://www.fonkoze.org/aboutfonkoze/whoweare/ ourhistory.html.

Gorostiaga, Xabier. "Haiti: Geoculture: The Key to Understanding Haiti?" *Revisto Envio*, No. 162, Jan. 1995. Online at http://www .envio.org.ni/articulo/1826.

Haiti Equality Collective. 2011. *The Haiti Gender Shadow Report. Ensuring Haitian Women's Participation and Leadership in all Stages of National Relief and Reconstruction* 2010. Online at http://www .genderaction.org/publications/2010/gsr.pdf.

Haiti: Government of Haiti's Lobbying Activities Top Firms and Individuals 1991 to 2004. Online at www.haitipolicy.org/Lobbying3.xls

Hallward, Peter. "Insurgency and Betrayal." March 27, 2007, interview with Guy Philippe. Online at http://www.zcommunications.org/ insurgency-and-betrayal-by-peter-hallward.

Hunter-Gault, Charlayne, interview with J.-B. Aristide, Dec. 5, 1995. Transcript. Online at http://www.pbs.org/newshour/bb/latin_ america/haiti_12-5.htm.

"International Donors' Conference Towards a New Future for Haiti." March 31, 2010. Online at http://www.haiticonference.org/story.html.

James, Clara. "Aristide's 'different' capitalism is the same old story," *Dollars and Sense: The Magazine of Economic Justice*, 2002-12-20. Online at http://www.haitipolicy.org/content/454.htm?PHPSESSID =6321cf5e7fe78.

Kelley, Martha. "Assessing the Investment Climate in Haiti: Policy Challenges." Workshop on Foreign Direct Investment in the Caribbean Basin and Latin America 5-6 April 2001, Curacao Centre for Co-operation with Non-Members Directorate for Financial, Fiscal and Enterprise Affairs. Online at http://www.oeConvergence.org/ dataoeConvergence/4/42/1897610.pdf.

Knox, Paul. "Haiti's Fallible Hero:Conferring sainthood on Aristide does not confront the country's deepest problems." *Literary Review of Canada,* Jan/Feb. 2009.

Komisar, Lucy. "Haiti Telecom Kickbacks Tarnish Aristide." Special to *CorpWatch*, December 29th, 2005. Online at http://thekomis arscoop.com/. 5066688387.html?mod=googlenews_wsj.

Komisar, Lucy. "Follow Aristide's Money Offshore: How Haiti was looted with the help of tax haven shell companies & secret bank accounts and U.S. citizens & corporations." Haiti Democracy Project, Nov 10, 2005. *The Komisar Scoop,* online at http://thekomisarscoop .com/2005/11/follow-aristides-money-offshore-how-haiti-was-looted-with-the-help-of-tax-haven-shell-companies-secret-bank-accounts-and-us-citizens-corporations/.

Komisar, Lucy. "Lingering Problem for IDT: Former employee alleges bribe payment to Haiti's Aristide; company denies allegation." Barron's, Sept. 10, 2010. Online at http://online.barrons.com/article/SB 60001424052970204878604575491793087489302.html.

Kretchik, Walter E. "Planning for 'Intervasion' (sic); The Strategic and Operation Setting for Uphold Democracy." Command and General Staff College. Online at http://www.cgsc.edu/carl/resources/csi/kre tchik/chapter2.asp.

Kretchik, Walter E. "Uphold Democracy, A Comparative Summary and Conclusion." Online at http://www.globalsecurity.org/military/ library/report/1998/kretchik-chapter5.htm.

Leibman, Dena (ed.) "Unequal Equation: The Labor Code and Worker Rights in Haiti," AFL-CIO. American Center for International Labor Solidarity, Washington, D.C, July 2003. Online at http://www .solidaritycenter.org/files/UnequalEquation.pdf.

Lionet, Christian. "Le Contra—Attacque du Général Namphy." *Libération,* December 1987, reprinted in *Le Matin,* December, 18, 1987.

Lundahl, Mats. "Sources of Growth in the Haitian Economy." Inter-American Development Bank, June 2004. Online at http://www.iadb .org/regions/re2/HASourceOfGrowth.pdf.

Maguire, Robert. "Haiti After the Donors' Conference: A Way Forward." United States Institute of Peace *Special Report.* Online at http://www.usip.org/files/resources/haiti_after_donors_conference .pd.

McLelland, Mac. "Haiti Dispatch: Inside Sean Penn's Tent City." *Mother Jones,* Oct. 20, 2010. Online at http://motherjones.com/print/82961.

Mills, Kurt. "Refugees as an Impetus for Intervention: The Case of Haiti." *Refuge,* Vol. 15, No. 3 (June 1996). Online at http://pi .library.yorku.ca/ojs/index.php/refuge/article/viewFile/21192/ 19863.

National Human Rights Defense Network. "Report on the Assassination of Journalist Brignol Lindor in Petit Goâve, 3 December 2001." 3 April 2003. Online at http://www.rnddh.org/article.php3?id_ article=168.

Pina, Kevin. "Documents reçus." 31 Aug. 2009. Online at http://fjmv .org/029/HTML/infoscom.html.

Rawls, Wendell. "Baby Doc's Haitian Terror." *The New York Times Magazine,* May 14, 1978.

Reporters Without Borders. "Who Killed Jean Dominique? *'If they murdered him, they can murder any journalist'* An investigation in Haiti." 19-25 March 2001. Online at http://en.rsf.org/haiti-who-killed-jean-dominique-25-03-2001,03223.html.

Roc, Nancy. "Haiti: the bitter grapes of corruption." *FRIDE,* March 2009. Online at http://www.google.ca/search?q=nancy+roc+the+bitt

er+grapes&ie=utf-8&oe=utf-8&aq=t&rls=org.mozilla:en-US: official&client=firefox-a.

Sanderson, Jane. "Comprehensive assessment of President Préval's decision-making process and leadership style." US Embassy cable dated March 7, 2007. Online at http://www.haitian-truth.org/ wikileaks-a-look-at-Prévals-private-side-Prévals-entire-policy-seemed-to-be-encapsulated-in-the-formulation-disarm-or-die/.

Schuller, Mark. "Haiti needs new development approaches, not more of the same." *Haiti Analysis,* June 18, 2009. Online at http://www .haitianalysis.com/2009/6/18/haiti-needs-new-development-approaches-not-more-of-the-same.

"The Seizure of Haiti by the United States." New York Foreign Policy Association, April 1922.

Shamsie, Yasmine. "Time for a 'High-Road' Approach to EPZ Development in Haiti." Paper prepared for the Conflict Prevention and Peace Forum (CPPF) S.S.R.C. Jan. 24, 2010. Online at http://webarchive. ssrc.org/pdfs/Yasmine_Shamsie_Economic_Processing_Zones_ CPPF_Briefing_Paper_on_Haiti_Jan_2011_f.pdf.

Stumbo, Bella. "Haiti's 'Baby Doc' Governs in Isolation." *Los Angeles Times,* December 17, 1985.

Urraca, Claude. "Haiti: Le Prix du Sang," *Le Point,* January 17, 1988.

United States v Larence P. Rockwood, II, U.S. Court of Appeals for the Armed Forces, Argued February 26, 1999, Decided September 30, 1999. Online at http://www.armfor.uscourts.gov/opinions/ 1999Term/98-0488.htm

U.S. Congress Committee on International Relations. "Haiti: human rights and police issues." One Hundred Fourth Congress, second session, Jan.4, 1996. Online at http://www.archive.org/stream/haiti humanrights00unit/haitihumanrights00unit_djvu.txt.

U.S. Congressional Record, Proceedings and Debates of the 106th Congress, Second Session, V. 146, Pt. 10, July 10, 2000 to July 17, 2000. Online http://books.google.com/books?id=8yu8YymmxMEC&pg= PA14080&lpg=PA14080&dq=U.S.+Congressional+Record,+July+ 13,+2000.+V.+146,+Pt.+10,+July+10,+2000+to+July+17,+2000&s

ource=bl&ots=-7_5HeSHH7&sig=wM_tb7_yuiWnngXOMzOQD
uJ5WdA&hl=en&ei=fjmWTbmQEcKBtgf1saz3Cw&sa=X&oi=
book_result&ct=result&resnum=1&ved=0CBcQ6AEwAA#v=onep
age&q=haiti&f=false.

REPORTS

Americas Watch. *Haiti: Duvalierism Since Duvalier.* New York: 1986.

Foreign Areas Studies, The American University. *Haiti: A Country Study.* Washington, D.C.: U.S. Government Printing Office, 1985.

Haiti Government, Ministère du Commerce et de l'Industrie. *Haiti: A Guide for Investors.* Port-au-Prince: 1985.

Haiti, Government. Office National du Tourisme et des Relations Publiques. *Inventaire Général des Ressources Touristiques Haiti:* Tome 1: *Port-au-Prince.* Port-au-Prince: Le Natal, 1983.

U.S. Government. *The Trial Record of Denmark Vesey.* (With an introduction by John Oliver Killens.) Boston: Beacon Press, (1822) 1970.

U.S.A.I.D. *Haiti: Country Environmental Profile, a Field Study.* 1985.

RECORDS

Bontemps, Saint-Ange. "Entrevue de Mr. St. Ange Bontemps," *Jeunesse Culture de Jérémie,* August 1986.

Charles, Clémard Joseph. *Le Jour dans la Nuit.* Geneva: Imprimerie Victor Chevalier, 1985.

Craige, John Houston. "Haitian Vignettes," *The National Geographic Magazine,* Vol. LXVI, #4, October 1934.

Douglass, William. *A Black Diplomat in Haiti.* Salisbury, N.C.: Documentary Publications, 1977.

Duvalier, François. Oeuvres Essentielles. Tome 1: *Eléments d'une Doctrine;* Tome 2: *La Marche à la Présidence;* Tome 3: *La Révolution au Pouvoir;* Tome 4: *La Révolution au Pouvoir.* Port-au-Prince: Presses Nationales d'Haiti, 1966–67.

Duvalier, François. *Mémoires d'un Leader du Tiers Monde.* Paris: Hachette, 1969.

Duvalier, François. *Studies on the Problem of Classes Across Haitian History.* (The book is also reproduced in Hebrew.) Port-au-Prince: (1948) 1967.

Duvalier, François. (First published under pseudonym Abderrahman.) *Médaillons.* Port-au-Prince: 1968.

Duvalier, François. *Hommage au Matron Inconnu.* Port-au-Prince: 1968.

Duvalier, Jean-Claude. *Discours et Messages 1981–1982.* Port-au-Prince: Deschamps, 1985.

Duvalier, Jean-Claude. *Message du President à Vie de la République à l'Occasion du 22 Avril 1985.* Port-au-Prince: Deschamps, 1985.

Greene, Graham. *Ways of Escape: An Autobiography.* New York: Simon and Schuster, 1980.

Mathon, Alix. *Témoignage sur les Evènements de 1957.* Port-au-Prince: Fardin, 1980.

Paquin, Lyonel. *The Haitians: Class and Color Politics.* Brooklyn, N.Y.: Multi—type, 1983.

Soukar, Michel. *Un General Parle: Entretien avec un Chef d'état—major sous François Duvalier.* Port-au-Prince: Le Natal, 1987.

Sylvain, Franck. *Les 56 Jours de Franck Sylvain.* Port-au-Prince: Deschamps, 1980.

TV DOCUMENTARIES

Bradley, Ed. *60 Minutes.* CBS. Documentary on post-Duvalierist Haiti, April 1986.

Enderlin, François, "Continents Sans Visa," Swiss television, 1968.

Mury, Gérald, "Continents Sans Visa," Swiss television, 1981.

Walters, Barbara. *20/20.* ABC. Interviewing Jean-Claude and Michèle B. Duvalier, June 1986.

My Own Wire Reports

I reported on a near-daily basis during all but the final weeks of the period covered in Chapter 13, and my files are an important source for reconstructing and interpreting those events. I also wrote features for British and Canadian newspapers and magazines, on the plight of the Haitian sugarcane cutters, the pigs of Haiti, the ecological catastrophe, as well as political analyses.

NOTES

1 In 1991, this article won a National Magazine Award for Environmental Writing.
2 Transparency International estimates are quoted in a report by the Stolen Assets Recovery Initiative, a joint venture of the World Bank and the United Nations Office of Drugs and Crime. *Associated Press,* 4 Feb. 2007.
3 Comparisons with recent earthquakes in China and Italy, for example, underscore the man-made consequences of Haiti's. In China, one in every 595 people affected died; in Italy that number was one in every 190; in Haiti, it was one in every 15.
4 Reuters, Port-au-Prince, 11 April 1987, "Another Blow for Haiti: A Sugar Mill Closes," *New York Times,* 12 April 1987. Online at http://www .nytimes.com/1987/04/12/world/another-blow-for-haiti-a-sugar-mill-closes .html.
5 *Ibid.*
6 In my last four years in Haiti, local rice production held fairly steady but faced increasingly stiff competition from US imports, which increased from 7,337 tons in 1985 to 54,465 in 1988. By 1989, Haiti rice production declined sharply while US imports rose until in 1992, they were far greater than Haiti's. See Josiane Georges, "Trade and the Disappearance of Haitian Rice," *Ted Case Studies* #725 June 2004. Online at http://www1.american .edu/TED/haitirice.htm (TED is the acronym for The Trade & Environment Database.)
7 Artibonite rice farmers grow swamp rice, often an indigenous variety. Elsewhere, they grow mountain rice mainly for their own consumption.
8 Bill Clinton speaks to Amy Goodman, *Democracy Now!,* online at http:// www.democracynow.org/2010/4/1/clinton_rice.
9 Papa Doc was protectionist and kept Haiti's markets as closed as he could.
10 Haiti is now the US's third largest rice importer.
11 For years street vendors hawked CareBears made from mismatched pieces

stolen from the factory, with red arms, blue legs and a yellow body, for example.

12 David Gutnik, CBC Report, online at http://www.cbc.ca/world/story/2010/02/03/f-haiti-notebook.html.

13 Richard Coles quoted in Simon Denyer, "Special Report: Is aid doing Haiti more harm than good?" *Reuter*, Oct. 25, 2010. Online at ahttp://www.re uters.com/article/2010/10/25/us-haiti-idUSTRE69O2T320101025 http://www.reuters.com/article/2010/10/25/us-haiti-idUSTRE69O2T 320101025.

14 Michel Laguerre, *The Military and Society in Haiti,* p. 155.

15 *The New York Times* obituary, Dec. 31, 1997, referred to her as "The 'Mama Doc' of Haiti."

16 The broadcast was in Sept. 2007. Online at http://www.nytimes.com/2008/03/23/world/americas/23haiti.html.

17 http://www.haitian-truth.org/interview-de-jean-claude-duvalier-par-deborah-ball-pour-le-wall-street-journal-2/.

18 See Laguerre, *The Military and Society in Haiti,* pp. 116-117.

19 Alex Dupuy provides interesting details about how the Duvalierist financial system operated. See *The Prophet and Power*, pp. 32, 36-40, 42-3.

20 See also Robert Fatton, *Haiti's Predatory Republic*, p. 57.

21 Speaking about "Jean-Claude Duvalier's hesitant, contradictory, and ultimately ill-fated process of liberalization," Fatton observes that "In spite of its failure, it brought about the birth of what was to become an increasingly assertive civil society," p. 57.

22 See Elizabeth Abbott, *Sugar: A Bittersweet History,* pp. 387-393 for a more comprehensive description of Haitian cane workers in the Dominican Republic.

23 Dupuy, *The Prophet and Power,* p. 51, itemizes Haiti's disastrous condition.

24 Dissident soldiers - Mouvman Solda Dayiti - Haiti's Soldiers' Movement-appealed for Duvalier's arrest. Fatton, *Haiti's Predatory Republic,* p. 62.

25 Two months after I moved to Haiti in June, 1983, Lafontant became Minister of the Interior, which made my husband's warnings about him all the more frightening. And my *permet de séjour,* Haiti's equivalent of a Green Card, was signed by Lafontant.

26 Henri Namphy had entered military college during Magloire's presidency and had a deep respect for him.

27 In *Krik? Krak!*, Edwidge Danticat writes about a peasant woman, Défilé, who languishes in a Port-au-Prince prison, accused of killing a child by sorcery. Because her guards believe their emaciated and ailing prisoner takes her skin off at night and puts it back on in the morning, they beat Défilé to death: "Her skin, it was too loose. They said prison could not cure her," fellow inmates tell her daughter.

28 In *Travesty in Haiti,* anthropologist Timothy T. Schwartz describes how in one pig repopulation center, members of *Tet Kole Ti Peyizan,* Haiti's most powerful peasant organization, "attacked a center and slit the throats of the

imported pigs." A standing joke was that the whites had killed the small, black Haitian pigs so they could replace it with big fat white pigs. p 73.

29 *The Inter-American Commission on Human Rights*, 1986-7, contains an account of the Charlot Jacquelin case that points overwhelmingly to military/police involvement in Jacquelin's disappearance and probable execution. Online at http://pdf.usaid.gov/pdf_docs/PCAAA408.pdf.

30 The CNG denounced Misyon Alfa as encouraging communists, and pressured the Church to shut it down. In Nov. 1987, the bishops suspended the program.

31 In 1998, back in Haiti, Bennett was sentenced to and served two years in prison for illicit enrichment.

32 Details of this arrangement are reported in Americas Watch Committtee, *The More Things Change—Human Rights in Haiti, February, 1989*, p. 20. Youth were paid one or two dollars to vote, at some polling stations, more than once, but only for Manigat. They complained that it was hard to remove the indelible ink between votes.

33 Namphy's family members were also threatened.

34 In July 1988, on the way home after fetching my young son from school, my husband's driver detoured and took Ivan to a house in Port-au-Prince where a group of people were sitting and chatting, and introduced him to Father Aristide as "Haiti's next president." Aristide shook Ivan's hand and smiled.

35 Cited by Deborah Sontag, "Populist priest captures hearts of Haitians," *Miami Herald,* 26 Nov. 1990, in Dupuy, *The Prophet and Power,* p. 78. In his autobiography, he added, "Let there be no doubt: my expulsion from the Salesians has not changed my Christian conscience, blunted my fidelity to the dispossessed, nor cooled the burning questions I addressed to the Catholic hierarchy."

36 America Watch Committee, *The More things change—human rights in Haiti.* Feb. 1989. Between April to early July, 1988, 11 prisoners died of torture and 7 of starvation at Port-au-Prince's *Recherches Criminelles* or Criminal Investigations, renamed the Anti-Gang Investigation Unit. This report lists them by name and manner of death. pp. 65-66.

37 Haitians refer to this visit as a "phone call" that means the American heel coming down onto a dissident leader. See Dupuy, *The Prophet and Power,* footnote 4, p. 99.

38 Marc Bazin, favoured and financed by the Americans, came in second with only 14 percent.

39 In 1991, Lafontant was murdered in prison. In 1994, his widow, Gladys, charged Aristide with ordering her husband's murder. http://www.jstor.org/pss/2203724.

40 Cited by Mark Danner, "The Struggle For a Democratic Haiti," *The New York Times Magazine,* June 24, 1987.

41 Howard French, "A Haitian Mayor's Credo: No Work, No Pay," *New York Times,* Oct. 7, 1990.

42 Cited by Danner.

43 Fatton, *Haiti's Predatory Republic*, p. 80.

44 *Paul Knox,* "Haiti's Fallible Hero: Conferring sainthood on Aristide does not confront the country's deepest problems," *Literary Review of Canada,* Jan/Feb. 2009.

45 Aristide's ouster reversed the tide, and tens of thousands of Haitians streamed into the D.R., including about two-thirds of the expelled/fled cane workers. Some people accused the Dominicans of interfering in Haitian politics by creating a crisis for Aristide when he was already fighting for political survival.

46 Père Lebrun speech online at http://www.hartford-hwp.com/archives/43a/009.html.

47 These examples are from Erica Cappel James, *Democratic Insecurities: Violence, Trauma, and Intervention in Haiti,* p. 68-9.

48 *Ibid.* p. 70.

49 These conditions were documented by Captain Lawrence P. Rockwood, a military counter-intelligence officer with the US Army's 10th Mountain Division, after he was deployed to Haiti on Sept. 19, 1994, in preparation for Aristide's return in Oct. Rockwood reported these atrocities and then, because he saw no response, charged his immediate commanders with criminal negligence for allowing gross human rights violation, including murder, to continue. Rockwood was forced to undergo and passed psychiatric evaluation. He was then court-martialled, convicted on several charges, including conduct unbecoming an officer, and dismissed from the Army.

50 In the decade between 1981 and 1990, 24,000 boat people had been interdicted but only six had been allowed to claim refugee status in the U.S.

51 Quoted by Sydney P. Freedberg and Rachel L. Swarns, "Poorly Enforced Sanctions Botch U.S. Embargo of Haiti," *The Seattle Times,* Nov. 3, 1994.

52 Reuters. " U.N. Embargo on Haiti Is Killing 1,000 Children a Month, Study Says," *Los Angeles Times,* Nov. 9, 1993.

53 Prominent Backer of Aristide Is Slain After Mass," *New York Times,* Sept. 12, 1993.

54 This was, said Admiral Paul David Miller, USN, then commander in chief of US forces in the region, "one of the dismal days of recent naval history." John R. Ballard, *Upholding democracy: the United States military campaign in Haiti, 1994–1997.* Footnote 46, p. 56.

55 Cited by Ian Martin, "Haiti: Mangled Multilateralism," *Foreign Policy,* No. 95, Summer, 1994, pp. 72-73, cited in Fatton, *Haiti's Predatory Republic,* ft. 65, p. 104.

56 Kurt Mills, "Refugees as an Impetus for Intervention: The Case of Haiti." *Refuge,* Vol. 15, No. 3 (June 1996).

57 Kevin Pina, "Documents reçus," 31 Aug. 2009, Online at http://fjmv.org/029/HTML/infoscom.html.

58 For over a decade before Jean-Claude fled Haiti, Father Vincent had worked in the arid hinterland of Jean-Rabel, organizing Tet Ansam to pur-

sue land redistribution and even more importantly, winning farmers the right "to identify and claim their right to state land." Vincent was also a fierce opponent of food donations. "They lead to corruption, and to dependence on others. That's what the Americans want, to make us dependent on them."

59 William J. Clinton, Address to the Nation on Haiti, Sept. 15, 1994, Online at http://www.presidency.ucsb.edu/ws/index.php?pid=49093.

60 Ralph Pezzuloo, *Plunging into Haiti: Clinton, Aristide, and the defeat of diplomacy,* p. 265.

61 *Ibid.* p. 266.

62 Tom F. Driver, Sheffield, Mass., July 22, 1995, "Letter to the Editor," *New York Times,* 28 July 1995. Driver is a member of Witness for Peace's Haitian task force.

63 Pezzuloo, p.269.

64 Walter E. Kretchik, "Planning for 'Intervasion': The Strategic and Operation Setting for Uphold Democracy," Command and General Staff College, Online at http://www.cgsc.edu/carl/resources/csi/kretchik/chapter2.asp.

65 The negotiations with Cédras were extremely complex and took several sessions. For a fascinating and detailed account, see Ballard, *Upholding democracy: the United States military campaign in Haiti, 1994-1997.*

66 Walter E. Kretchik, "Uphold Democracy, A Comparative Summary and Conclusion." Online at http://www.globalsecurity.org/military/library/report/1998/kretchik-chapter5.htm.

67 Cited in Michael Deibert, *Notes from the Last Testament,* p. 43.

68 Greg Miller, "Haiti Prime Minister Installed as First Step to Democracy, *"Los Angeles Times,* Aug. 31, 1993.

69 Mildred Aristide, "Forced into exile: Madame Mildred Aristide, wife of former Haitian president Jean Bertrand Aristide, recalls the nightmare of being driven from her country. *Essence Magazine,* Oct. 2005. Online at http://www.aristide.org/articles/MildredAristide.htm.

70 Xabier Gorostiaga, "Haiti: Geoculture: The Key to Understanding Haiti?" *Revisto Envio,* No. 162, Jan. 1995.

71 *Ibid.*

72 James, *Democratic Insecurities,* pp. 123-4.

73 Schwartz, *Travesty in Haiti,* p. 35.

74 Quoted by John Kifner, "Haiti Murder Investigation: Avenues with Few Answers," *New York Times,* 11 April, 1995.

75 Quoted by *Los Angeles Times,* 9 Nov., 1994.

76 Cited by Deibert, *Notes from the Last Testament,* p. 47.

77 Cited by Fatton, *Haiti's Predatory Republic,* p. 85. In 1992, when Aristide was in exile, he appointed business leader Malval as prime minister. Malval remained in this post until Aristide returned to Haiti.

78 Leslie A. Benton, Glenn T. Ware, *Haiti: A Case Study of the International Response and the Efficacy of Nongovernmental Organizations in the Crisis,* p. 27.

79 Kretchik, "Uphold Democrary."

80 Deibert, *Notes from the Last Testament,* p. 95.

81 Alex Dupuy, cited by Robert Fatton, *The Roots of Haitian Despotism,* p. 203.

82 http://www.martyduren.com/2010/02/23/interview-with-travesty-in-haiti-author-dr-tim-schwartz-part-1/.

83 Schwartz, *Travesty in Haiti,* p. 94.

84 *Ibid,* p. 95.

85 *Ibid,* p. 101.

86 Fonkoze's website has a wealth of information about its history and guiding principles. http://www.fonkoze.org/.

87 Among many other excellent works on this subject, see Susan George's seminal *A Fate Worse than Debt.*

88 Natalie Domond, Fonkoze Director of Social Impact, in an interview with Oscar "Haiti, the Fonkoze Model of Social Evolution, Part 2" online at http://www.nextbillion.net/blog/2011/01/26/in-haiti-the-fonkoze-model-of-social-evolution-part-2.

89 This is the amount of loans outstanding in 1996. It does not include portions already repaid.

90 This is the amount of loans outstanding in 1997. It does not include portions already repaid.

91 Associated Press, "U.S. Unloads 289 at pier in 2nd Haiti repatriation," *Deseret News,* 8 Jan., 1995. Online at http://www.deseretnews.com/article/397572/US-UNLOADS-289-AT-PIER-IN-2ND-HAITI-REPATRIATION.html.

92 *Ibid.* "Fifty-four involuntary returnees arrived on Friday. Beginning Monday, about 400 will be returned each day until all 3,500 remaining in Guantanamo Bay are repatriated, U.S. Embassy spokesman Stan Schrager said.

93 Kenneth Freed, "National Agenda: Rich vs. Poor: Haiti's Elite Tests Aristide," *Los Angeles Times,* 31 Jan. 1995.

94 Aristide quoted in *Haiti Progrès,* 15 Nov., 1995, cited by Kim Ives, "Review of a Review: Answering recent distortions." http://www.iacenter.org/haiti/revofrev.htm.

95 Larry Rohter, "Tensions Build Again in Haiti, Imperiling Peace," *New York Times,* 30 Nov., 1995.

96 Christian Peacemaker Teams, CPTNET Nov. 16, 1995 Haiti Events Summary. Online at http://www.williambowles.info/haiti-news/archives/cpt_191195.html.

97 "Full report online at Haiti : human rights and police issues,"hearing before the Committee on International Relations, House of Representatives, One Hundred Fourth Congress, second session, January 4, 1996http://www.archive.org/stream/haitihumanrights00unit/haitihumanrights00unit_djvu.txt.

98 "He was very nasty, unnecessarily so," said Raymond W. Kelly, the former New York City Police Commissioner, who tried to mediate the dispute, said

of the Minister. Quoted by John Kifner, "Haiti Murder Investigation: Avenues with Few Answers," *New York Times,* April 11, 1995.

99 "Haiti: human rights and police issues."

100 John Kifner, "Haiti Murder Investigation: Avenues with Few Answers," *New York Times,* April 11, 1995.

101 *Ibid.*

102 Cited by *Haiti Progres,* "This Week in Haiti" August 2–8, 1995 Vol. 13, No. 19, online at http://www.williambowles.info/haiti-news/archives/hp_080895.html; Pastor's comments reported by Henry F. Carey, "Electoral Observation and Democratization in Haiti," in Kevin J. Middlebrook, ed., *Electoral Observation and Democratic Transitions in Latin America* (San Diego: Center for U.S.-Mexican Studies, 1998), pp.141-166. Online at http://www.haitipolicy.org/archives/Archives/1998/carey.htm#N_21_.

103 *Ibid.*

104 *Ibid.*

105 Larry Rohter, "Tensions Build Again in Haiti, Imperiling Peace," *New York Times,* 30 Nov., 1995.

106 Mark Fineman, "New Haiti Leader Assumes Power," *Los Angeles Times*, 8 Feb., 1996.

107 Larry Rohter, "Preval Is Haiti's President, but Thoughts Focus on Aristide's Future," *New York Times,* 9 Feb. 1996.

108 Charlayne Hunter-Gault interview with J.-B. Aristide, Dec. 5, 1995. Newsmaker interview with president Aristide. *Transcript.* In Haiti, presidential elections are set for December 17, 1995. Charlayne Hunter-Gault interviews outgoing president, Jean-Bertrand Aristide about his commitment to hold free elections and his turbulent years in office. Online at http://www.pbs.org/newshour/bb/latin_america/haiti_12-5.html.

110 Martha N. Kelley, "Assessing the Investment Climate in Haiti: Policy Challenges," Workshop on Foreign Direct Investment in the Caribbean Basin and Latin America 5-6 April 2001, Curacao Centre for Co-operation with Non-Members Directorate for Financial, Fiscal and Enterprise Affairs Online at http://www.oeConvergence.org/dataoeConvergence/4/42/1897610.pdf.

111 *Haiti Progres,* Vol. 16, no. 38, 9-15 December 1998, online at http://www.hartford-hwp.com/archives/43a/145.html.

112 Quoted by Michael Norton, "Critics Say Coup Successful, Haitian Democracy in the Balance, *Topeka Capital-Journal,* 14 Jan. 1999. Online at http://findarticles.com/p/articles/mi_qn4179/is_19990114/ai_n11717229/.

113 A thousand landowners had large holdings of 250 to 750 acres each. Most Haitian farmers owned less than three acres, rented land or sharecropped.

114 The children died of acute kidney failure after glycerine from China, contaminated with diethylene glycol, was shipped to Haiti where it was made up into cough syrup.

115 Reporters Without Borders, "Who Killed Jean Dominique? *'If they mur-dered him, they can murder any journalist'* An investigation in Haiti," 19-25 March 2001. Online at http://en.rsf.org/haiti-who-killed-jean-dom inique-25-03-2001,03223.html.

116 *Ibid.* Sen. Rudolph Boulos responded to insinuations about his family's involvement: "I can tell you that hundreds of journalists, government ministers, and the president of Haiti himself also expressed themselves on the Pharval issue at the time. These repeated interventions did not result in the murder of any of them. The radio broadcasts of Mr. Dominique would not constitute a motive for an act as odious as his murder."

117 Reporters Without Borders, "Who Killed Jean Dominique?"

118 Congressional Record, July 13, 2000. V. 146, Pt. 10, July 10, 2000 to July 17, 2000.

119 Fatton, *Haiti's Predatory Republic*, p. 120.

120 The Convergence was created on May 22, 2000 to unite those opposed to Aristide.

121 Amnesty International on Haiti, "Perpetrators of Past Abuses Threaten Human rights and the Reestablishment of the Rule of Law," 3 March 2004. Online at http://www.nathanielturner.com/amnestyinternationalonhaiti .htm.

122 Michael Deibert, *Notes from the Last Testament*, p. 122.

123 Fatton, *Haiti's Predatory Republic*, p. 201. These jobs would come from both private and public sectors.

124 Martha N. Kelley, a resident American economic counsellor, summarized these reasons in"Assessing the Investment Climate in Haiti: Policy Challenge."

125 This was in 2003.

126 Reginald Dumas, *An Encounter with Haiti*, p. 67.

127 "An inside look at Haiti's business elite."*Multinational Monitor*, Jan. 1, 1995. An interview with "Patrick James," alias for an American businessman who used to live and work in Haiti. Online at http://www .allbusiness.com/specialty-businesses/492556-1.html.

128 David Gonzalez, "Aristide of Haiti: Pragmatist or Demagogue?" *New York Times*, Dec. 13, 2002.

129 Clara James, "Aristide's "different" capitalism is the same old story," *Dollars and Sense: The Magazine of Economic Justice*, 2002-12-20. Online at http://www.haitipolicy.org/content/454.htm?PHPSESSID=6321cf5e 7fe78.

130 Jennifer Wells, "Haiti's garment industry hanging by a thread," *Toronto Star*, 15 Oct. 2010.

131 In "Aristide's "different" capitalism is the same old story," Clara James provides an excellent analysis of the free trade zone politics and economics in terms of neoliberalism and the economic program Aristide had committed himself to in return for American military support to return him to Haiti.

132 Lucy Komisar, CorpWatch, "Haiti Telecom Kickbacks Tarnish Aristide," 29 Dec. 2005, *The Komisar Scoop*. Online at http://thekomisarscoop. com/2005/12/haiti-telecom-kickbacks-tarnish-aristide/.

133 Quoted in "Lingering Problem for IDT," Barron's, Sept. 10, 2010. Online at http://online.barrons.com/article/SB60001424052970204878604575491 793087489302.html.

134 Lucy Komisar, "Haiti Telecom Kickbacks Tarnish Aristide."

135 Nicolas Rossier, "An Exclusive Interview with Former Haitian President Jean-Bertrand Aristide," *Huffington Post,* Nov. 15, 2010, Online at http:// www.huffingtonpost.com/nicolas-rossier/post_1263_b_783706.html.

136 Lucy Komisar, "Follow Aristide's Money Offshore: How Haiti was looted with the help of tax haven shell companies & secret bank accounts and U.S. citizens & corporations," Haiti Democracy Project, Nov 10, 2005. *The Komisar Scoop,* online at http://thekomisarscoop.com/2005/11/ follow-aristides-money-offshore-how-haiti-was-looted-with-the-help-of-tax-haven-shell-companies-secret-bank-accounts-and-us-citizens-corporations/

137 The report, "CEA Inquiry into Millions Found Diverted to Aristide Offshore Accounts—Text," *Commission d'Enquete Administrative de Paul Denis*, 2005-10-24. *Haiti Democracy Project*, is available online at http:// www.haitipolicy.org.

138 Lavelanet, who lives in Coral Gables, Florida, controlled several companies including Digitek SA and Global Spectrum SA. The Denis Commission reported suspicious financial transactions in both companies.

139 "An inside look at Haiti's business elite."Multinational Monitor, 1 Jan. 1995. An interview with "Patrick James."

140 Haiti: Government of Haiti's Lobbying Activities Top Firms and Individuals 1991 to 2004. Online at www.haitipolicy.org/Lobbying3.xls.

141 Steve Miller, "Haitian government spent millions on lobbying U.S., *Washington Times,* March 5, 2004. Online at http://goliath.ecnext.com/ coms2/gi_0199-755182/Haitian-government-spent-millions-on.html.

142 Quoted by Mark Fineman, *Los Angeles Times,* 30 Oct. 1998.

143 Quoted by David Gonzales, "Drug Runners are Finding the Going Easy in Haiti, *New York Times,* 30 July, 2000. Online at http://query.nytimes.com/ gst/fullpage.html?res=9B07E0D8153DF933A05754C0A9669C8B63& pagewanted=2.

144 Cited by Deibert, *Notes from the Last Testament,* p. 345.

145 Quoted by David Gonzalez, "Drug Runners Are Finding the Going Easy in Haiti," *New York Times,* 30 July 2000.

146 Steven Dudley, "Drug allegation gave US leverage on Aristide," *Boston Globe,* March 1, 2004.

147 Catherine Wilson, "At Sentencing Haitian Druglord says Aristide Controls Haiti Drugs," Associated Press, Feb. 25, 2004. Online at http://www .webster.edu/~corbetre/haiti-archive-new/msg19191.html.

148 Jay Weaver and Jacqueline Charles, "Drug Probe Targets Aristide," Part 1,

Miami Herald, July 2, 2006. This money also enabled Therassan to use Route 9 as a landing strip for drug-laden airplanes. Police would barricade it off and reserve it for his exclusive use whenever he requested.

149 Catherine Wilson, "At Sentencing Haitian Druglord says Aristide Controls Haiti Drugs."

150 Another was director of the National Palace motor pool, Anthony Nazaire.

151 Edouard was convicted on drug charges in a U.S. court and is serving a life sentence.

152 Andrea Mitchell, "U.S.: Officials allow use of country as stopover from Colombia," NBC News, Feb. 23, 2004. http://www.webster.edu/~corbetre/ haiti-archive-new/msg19031.html.

153 Jay Weaver and Jacqueline Charles, "Drug Probe Targets Aristide," Part 1, *Miami Herald,* July 2, 2006.

154 Prosper Avril, *Justice Versus Politics in Haiti (2001-2004),* pp. Viii-ix.

155 Quoted by Deibert, *Notes from the Last Testament,* p. 144.

156 Jean Wilio Manéus (TELECO director), Robenson Desrosiers (Customs director), Fritznel Poussin (Social Services director).

157 Déus Jean François, Roger Panoski, Frantz Fontenelle and Frantz Sagaille.

158 For a detailed report see "Report on the Assassination of Journalist Brignol Lindor in Petit Goâve, 3 December 2001", *National Human Rights Defense Network,* posted 3 April 2003. Online at http://www.rnddh.org/ article.php3?id_article=168. See also Michael Deibert, "Brignol Lindor: Cinq Ans Après," Nov. 30, 2006. Online at http://michaeldeibert .blogspot.com/2006/11/brignol-lindor-cinq-ans-aprs.html. Deibert attended Lindor's funeral.

159 Jacqueline Charles, "Violence eroding Aristide's Rule," *Miami Herald,* December 13, 2001.

160 The Presidential Security consisted of the USGPN and the USP. The USGPN, General Security Unit of the National Palace, is a specialized unit within the HNP. Since 1997, the USGPN has been mandated to ensure security at the National Palace, specifically the safety and security of National Palace buildings, the private residences of the current and former Haitian presidents, and to escort the presidential convoy when the President travels in a vehicle. The USP, Security Unit of the Presidential Guard, is responsible for protecting the president.

161 The 12/19 press release was issued by Myriam Merlet of Enfofanm, Yolette Jeanty of Kay Famn and Eveline Larrieux of SOFA. Online at http://w3 .uchastings.edu/boswell_01/Text/haiti_report.htm.

162 Quoted by Jacqueline Charles, "Violence eroding Aristide's rule," *Miami Herald,* Dec. 13, 2001.

163 Quoted by Michael Norton, "Cooperative banks go burst, losing life savings for thousands and adding to despair in Haiti, Associated Press, July 16, 2002. Online at http://www.wehaitians.com/july%202002%20 news%20briefing%20and%20analysis.html.

164 The commercial banks held deposits totalled an estimated 25 billion

gourdes ($1 billion), the cooperative banks about 2-3.75 billion *gourdes* ($80-150 million).

165 David Gonzalez, "A Get-Rich Scheme Collapses, Leaving Haiti Even Poorer," *New York Times*, July 26, 2002.

166 Michael Norton, "Cooperative banks go burst, losing life savings for thousands and adding to despair in Haiti, Associated Press, 16 July 2002.

167 "This Week in Haiti," Haiti Progres, *Vol.20 no.19, 24–30 July 2002.*

168 Companie d'Intervention et de Maintien de l'Ordre, or the Company for Intervention and Maintaining Order, CIMO units "emerged as particularly abusive elements within the HNP. . . . The units [have] violated Haitian police law by carrying heavy weapons. Rather than defuse crises, the units' aggressive practices, which [have] included gratuitous destruction of property and beating and kicking passersby, [have] often worsened tense situations." Human Rights Watch, December 1998. Online at http://www.unhcr.org/refworld/country,,USCIS,,HTI,4562d94e2,3ae6a6b5b,0.html.

169 He had been caught at the Dominican border town of Dajabon with his mother, brother and maid, arrested and flown to the National Penitentiary in Aristide's handy helicopter.

170 "Rosemond Jean persiste et signe. La lutte continue en faveur des sociétaires bafoués Mercredi, 2 avril 2003, 09:28. Radio Métropole, http://www.metropolehaiti.com/metropole/full_poli_fr.php?id=6313.

171 Quoted by David Gonzales, "A Haitian Survivor Mourns, and Keeps Fighting," *New York Times,* 29 March 2003.

172 Jacqueline Charles, "Haitian Exiles Aid University President Beaten by Aristiders," *Miami Herald,* 10 Jan. 2004.

173 *Ibid.*

174 Paquiot, 55, traveled to New Orleans where a Weston-based Haitian group arranged rehabilitation and follow-up medical treatment on both his legs at Touro Hospital.

175 Jacqueline Charles, "Haitian Exiles Aid University President Beaten by Aristiders," *Miami Herald,* Jan. 10, 2004.

176 Dumas, *An Encounter with Haiti,* p. 67.

177 As new members joined the numbers rose to about 300, but the name remained 184.

178 Quoted by Associated Press, 20 Jan. 2003. Online at http://www.uscis.gov/portal/site/uscis/menuitem.5af9bb95919f35e66f614176543f6d1a/?vgnextoid=4007361cfb98d010VgnVCM10000048f3d6a1RCRD&vgnextchannel=d2d1e89390b5d010VgnVCM10000048f3d6a1RCRD.

179 Eugenia Charles, "HAITI REPORT" 27 Feb 2002. Online at http://www.uscis.gov/portal/site/uscis/menuitem.5af9bb95919f35e66f614176543f6d1a/?vgnextoid=4007361cfb98d010VgnVCM10000048f3d6a1RCRD&vgnextchannel=d2d1e89390b5d010VgnVCM10000048f3d6a1RCRD.

180 Jacqueline Charles, "Aristide pushes for restitution from France," *Miami Herald,* Dec. 18, 2003. Online at http://www.latinamericanstudies.org/haiti/haiti-restitution.htm.

181 Quoted by Deibert, *Notes from the Last Testament,* pp. 233, 236.

182 Lynch, Marika. *Miami Herald.* "Haitian Escapes Charges," 16 May 2003.

183 Quoted by Deibert, *Notes from the last Testament,* p. 344.

184 Quoted by BBC Monitoring, 3 October 2003. Online at http://www.haiti-news.com/?Cannibal-Army-spokesman-denounces.

185 Michael Deibert, "Haiti's Aristide should be greeted with prosecution, not praise," Feb. 17, 2011. Online at http://deiberthaiti.blogspot.com/2011/02/haitis-aristide-should-be-greeted-with.html. See also Joanne Mariner, "Partial Justice in Haiti," 12 April 2004. Online at http://writ.news.findlaw.com/mariner/20040412.html.

186 In "Insurgency and Betrayal," March 27, 2007, Peter Hallward conducted an extensive emailed interview with Guy Philippe, in French, and reproduced it in its entirety, as per Philippe's instructions. Online at http://www.zcommunications.org/insurgency-and-betrayal-by-peter-hallward.

187 Louis Jodel Chamblain was deputy leader of FRAPH. He was convicted for involvement in 1994 Raboteau massacre and 1993 murder of Antoine Izméry. He was sentenced in both trials to forced labor for life.

188 Quoted in "Insurgency and Betrayal," March 27, 2007. Online at http://www.zcommunications.org/insurgency-and-betrayal-by-peter-hallward.

189 Quoted by Dumas, *An Encounter with Haiti,* p. 33.

190 Quoted in "Insurgency and Betrayal," March 27, 2007. Online at http://www.zcommunications.org/insurgency-and-betrayal-by-peter-hallward.

191 Philippe listed Andy Apaid, Reginald Boulos, Serge Gilles and Evans Paul among others.

192 Dumas, *An Encounter with Haiti,* p. 54.

193 These expenses were about the same as a South African cabinet minister's.

194 These appointments were controversial and prompted questions in parliament. Education minister Naledi Pandor responded that the Aristides would receive salaries only if their research appeared in "accredited publications" and explained that they were not employed by the university. The African Christian Democratic Party complained that Aristide was bankrolling the Haitian conflict." See Sheena Adams, "No Unisa salaries for Aristide and wife," *IOL News,* November 9 2004. Online at http://www.iol.co.za/news/politics/no-unisa-salaries-for-aristide-and-wife-1.226475.

195 The National and International Center for Documentation and Information on Women in Haiti (ENFOFAMN).

196 MINUSTAH took over from the Multinational Interim Force on 1 June 2004. See online at http://www.un.org/en/peacekeeping/missions/minustah/background.shtml.

197 Cited by *Miami Herald,* April 30, 2004, online at http://www.historycommons.org/context.jsp?item=the_2004_removal_of_jean-bertrand_aristide_551&scale=5.

198 He also pleaded for readmission to CARICOM, but two years elapsed before it ended Haiti's suspension and welcomed it as a fully participating member.

199 Guy Philippe won only 1.92 percent of the votes.
200 The recalculation involved discarding blank ballots, increasing the percentage Preval had won.
201 Stevenson Jacobs, "long unpaid striking workers display corpses of infants in protest," Associated Press, Dec. 14, 2006. Accompanying photos show the children, a wounded prisoner chained to a bed and other patients lying untended. Online at http://www.wehaitians.com/december%202006%20news%20and%20analysis%20this%20month.html.
202 "Comprehensive assessment of President Préval's decision-making process and leadership style," US Embassy cable dated March 7, 2007, Online at http://www.haitian-truth.org/wikileaks-a-look-at-Prévals-private-side-Prévals-entire-policy-seemed-to-be-encapsulated-in-the-formulation-disarm-or-die/.
203 *Ibid.*
204 Claire Marshall, "Challenging future for Haitians," BBC News, 6 Feb. 2006. Online at http://news.bbc.co.uk/2/hi/americas/4684256.stm.
205 "Comprehensive assessment of President Préval's decision-making process and leadership style," US Embassy cable dated March 7, 2007.
206 Quoted in Stevenson Jacobs, "Haiti, U.S. to continue joint offensives," *U.S.A Today,* 20 July 2007. Online at http://www.usatoday.com/news/topstories/2007-07-20-326122731_x.htm.
207 Pierre-Louis had established the George Soros-supported Fondasyon Konesans Ak Libète (Knowledge and Freedom Foundation or FOKAL,) which established a network of over fifty community libraries, a cultural centre, a youth debating program and a running water initiative. She was also a co-founder of Preval's bakery and a long-time reform ally.
208 Sixty percent of the harvest was lost.
209 Rory Carroll, "We are going to disappear one day," *The Guardian,* 8 Nov. 2008. Online at http://www.guardian.co.uk/world/2008/nov/08/haiti-hurricanes.
210 Paul Collier, "Haiti: From Natural Catastrophe to Economic Security, A Report for the Secretary-General of the United Nations," January 2009 Online at http://www.focal.ca/pdf/haiticollier.pdf.
211 HOPE II was a modification of HOPE I, passed in Dec. 2006. See http://fpc.state.gov/documents/organization/145132.pdf.
212 These calculations were made in a 2008 study by the Washington-based Worker Rights Consortium, which calculated caloric needs, rent, school fees and uniforms, fuel, food and necessities.
213 Mark Schuller, "Haiti needs new development approaches, not more of the same," *Haiti Analysis,* 18 June 2009. Online at http://www.haitianalysis.com/2009/6/18/haiti-needs-new-development-approaches-not-more-of-the-same.
214 Yasmine Shamsie, "Time for a "High-Road" Approach to EPZ Development in Haiti," Paper prepared for the Conflict Prevention and Peace Forum (CPPF) Social Science Research Council January 24, 2010; also Haiti

Equality Collective. *The Haiti Gender Shadow Report. Ensuring Haitian Women's Participation and Leadership in all Stages of National Relief and Reconstruction* 2010 Online at http://www.genderaction.org/publications/2010/gsr.pdf.

215 Ban Ki-moon, "Haiti's Big Chance," *New York Times,* 30 March 2009 Online at http://www.un.org/sg/articleFull.asp?TID=99&Type=Op-Ed.

216 *Ibid.*

217 The American Ambassador believed Preval was a neoliberal by persuasion.

218 See Robert Maguire, "Haiti After the Donors' Conference: A Way Forward," United States Institute of Peace *Special Report*, Online at http://www.usip.org/files/resources/haiti_after_donors_conference.pdf.

219 He refused to publish the legislation, though it had sailed through parliament.

220 Prime Minister Pierre-Louis later explained that "the 200 gourdes passed. The only sector where it's being negotiated is the workers starting in the export industry. . . . the beginners, because it takes time for the entrepreneur to train that person and the wage at that level are subsidized." Quoted by "Haitian Prime Minister Michele Pierre-Louis fired by the Senate," October 30, 2009. Online at http://www.medihacker.org/2009/10/haitian-prime-minister-michele-pierre-louis-fired/.

221 For a gallery of media speculation about how Pierre-Louis' sexual orientation might have affected her political career, see http://globalvoicesonline.org/2008/08/09/michele-pierre-louis-haitis-new-prime-minister/.

222 Jonathan Katz, "Haitian Prime Minister Fired by Senate, *Associated Press,* 31 Oct. 2009. Online at http://www.thegrio.com/politics/haitian-prime-minister-fired-by-senate.php.

223 Quoted by Jonathan Katz, "New Haitian Prime Minister Vows To Attract Investment, Create Jobs," *Associated Press,* 12 Nov. 2009. Online at http://www.daytondailynews.com/news/nation-world-news/new-haiti-pm-promises-to-focus-on-investment-396916.html.

224 Quoted by Jean-Pierre Gingras, *Duvalier, Caribbean Cyclone*, pp. 105-6.

INDEX